Micro House PC Hardware Library Volume III: Motherboards

by

Micro House International, Inc.

Scott Mueller

A Division of Macmillan Computer Publishing
201 West 103rd Street,
Indianapolis, Indiana 46290

Micro House PC Hardware Library Volume III: Motherboards

Copyright© 1998 by Que®

All rights reserved. No part of this book shall be reproduced, stored in a retrieval system, or transmitted by any means, electronic, mechanical, photocopying, recording, or otherwise, without written permission from the publisher. No patent liability is assumed with respect to the use of the information contained herein. Although every precaution has been taken in the preparation of this book, the publisher and author assume no responsibility for errors or omissions. Neither is any liability assumed for damages resulting from the use of the information contained herein.

International Standard Book Number: 0-7897-1665-8

Library of Congress Catalog Card Number: 98-84620

Printed in the United States of America

First Printing: June 1998

00 99 98   4 3 2 1

Trademarks

All terms mentioned in this book that are known to be trademarks or service marks have been appropriately capitalized. Que cannot attest to the accuracy of this information. Use of a term in this book should not be regarded as affecting the validity of any trademark or service mark.

Credits

Executive Editor:	Jim Minatel
Managing Editors	Thomas Hayes
	Patrick Kanouse
Senior Editor	Elizabeth A. Bruns
Copy Editor	Patricia Kinyon
Indexers	Christine Nelsen
	Ginny Bess
Production	Mandie Rowell

Contents at a Glance

CHAPTER 1 MOTHERBOARDS 1

CHAPTER 2 MOTHERBOARD SETTINGS AND SPECIFICATIONS . 49

APPENDIX A MANUFACTURER CONTACT INFORMATION 387

    Manufacturer Index 435

    Index 439

Table of Contents

CHAPTER 1 MOTHERBOARDS 1
Replacement Motherboards 1
Knowing What to Look For (Selection Criteria) 1
    Documentation 5
    ROM BIOS Compatibility 5
    Using Correct Speed-Rated Parts 11
Motherboard Form Factors 12
    Backplane Systems 12
    Full-Size AT 13
    Baby-AT 13
    ATX 15
    NLX 17
Memory 20
    Memory Speeds and Types 21
    SIMMs and DIMMs 24
    Memory Banks 29
Processor Specifications 30
    Processor Memory Addressing Limits 31
    Processor Speed Ratings 32
    Processor Sockets 35
Motherboard Interface Connectors 39
Motherboard CMOS RAM Addresses 43

CHAPTER 2 MOTHERBOARD SETTINGS AND SPECIFICATIONS . 49
Interface Connections 49
Default Jumper Settings 49
Undocumented Jumpers 50
Board Element Naming Conventions 50
Motherboard Settings 50
ABIT COMPUTER CORPORATION 51
ADVANCED INTEGRATION RESEARCH, INC. 54
AMERICAN MEGATRENDS, INC. 60

AST RESEARCH, INC. 91
ASUS COMPUTER INTERNATIONAL 99
COMPAQ COMPUTER CORPORATION 120
DELL COMPUTER CORPORATION 139
DIGITAL EQUIPMENT CORPORATION 177
FIRST INTERNATIONAL COMPUTER, INC. 192
GEMLIGHT COMPUTER, LTD. 196
GIGA-BYTE TECHNOLOGY CO., LTD. 199
HEWLETT-PACKARD COMPANY 216
IBM CORPORATION 222
INTEL CORPORATION 269
IPC CORPORATION, LTD. 310
MICRONICS COMPUTERS, INC. 313
MICRO-STAR INTERNATIONAL CO., LTD. 346
PACKARD BELL 350
SHUTTLE COMPUTER INTERNATIONAL, INC. 356
SIEMENS NIXDORF INFORMATIONSSYSTEME AG 359
SILICON STAR INTERNATIONAL, INC. 361
SOYO COMPUTER CO., LTD. 365
SUPER MICRO 372
TYAN COMPUTER CORPORATION 375
ZEOS INTERNATIONAL, LTD. 382

APPENDIX A MANUFACTURER CONTACT INFORMATION 387

Manufacturer Index 435

Index 439

About the Authors

Micro House International, Inc.

Micro House International, a privately held company headquartered in Boulder, Colorado, is the leading provider of PC hardware technical information libraries and hard drive setup and configuration software. Micro House information products and utilities are used by network administrators, help desk and IT professionals, resellers, and system integrators throughout the world for installation, maintenance, and upgrades of multivendor PCs and networks. Among the company's key information products and utilities are SupportSource, Support On Site for Hardware, the Micro House® Technical Library, DrivePro®, and EZ-Drive®. For more information about any Micro House products, please see the Micro House web site at http://www.microhouse.com.

Scott Mueller

Scott Mueller is the Series Editor for the **Scott Mueller Library** series of technical PC books all published by QUE. Scott is president of Mueller Technical Research, an international personal computer research and corporate training firm. Since 1982, MTR has specialized in the industry's longest running, most in-depth, accurate and effective corporate technical training seminars, maintaining a client list that includes Fortune 500 companies, the U.S. and foreign governments, major software and hardware corporations, as well as PC enthusiasts and entrepreneurs. His seminars have been presented to thousands of PC professionals throughout the world.

Scott Mueller has developed and presented personal computer training courses in all areas of PC hardware and software. He is an expert in PC hardware, operating systems, data-recovery techniques, and local area networks. MTR seminars are available on an on-site contract basis or publicly through the American Research Group (ARG). For more information about a custom computer training seminar for your organization, contact:

> Mueller Technical Research
>
> 21718 Mayfield Lane
>
> Barrington, IL 60010-9733
>
> (847) 726-0709
>
> (847) 726-0710 Fax
>
> Internet: 73145.1566@compuserve.com

For more information about attending a public seminar, contact:

> American Research Group
>
> 114 Edinburgh South, Suite 200
>
> Cary, NC 27512
>
> (919)461-8600
>
> (919)461-8846 Fax

http://www.arg.com

email: questions@arg.com

Scott has many popular books, articles, and course materials to his credit, including *Upgrading and Repairing PCs*, which has sold more than 1 million copies, making it by far the most popular PC hardware book on the market today. His 2 hour video titled "*Your PC-The Inside Story*" *is available through* LearnKey, Inc. For ordering information, contact:

LearnKey, Inc.

1845 West Sunset Boulevard

St. George, UT 84770

(800) 937-3279

(801) 674-9733

(801) 674-9734 Fax

When he is not working on PC related books or teaching seminars, Scott can usually be found in the garage working on his LT4 powered '94 Impala SS, LT4 powered '95 Caprice 9C1 (police package), or Buick Turbo V6 powered '89 Trans Am, as well as various other performance car related projects. He can also be found testing the vehicles at the local drag strip, or showing them off at car shows or the local cruise/drive-in scene.

We'd Like to Hear from You!

Que Corporation has a long-standing reputation for high-quality books and products. To ensure your continued satisfaction, we also understand the importance of customer service and support.

Tech Support If you need assistance with the information in this book or you have feedback for us about the book, please contact Macmillan Technical Support by phone at 317-581-3833 or via email at support@mcp.com.

Orders, Catalogs, and Customer Service To order other Que or Macmillan Computer Publishing books, catalogs, or products, please contact our Customer Service Department

Phone: 1-800-428-5331

Fax: 1-800-835-3202

International Fax: 1-317-228-4400

Or visit our online bookstore at http://www.mcp.com/.

Introduction

The purpose of this text is to be a practical and easy reference for today's most popular motherboards used in desktop computers. While PC technicians and support staff will get the most use from this book in their daily dealings with PC motherboards, PC hobbyists and enthusiasts will also find it a valuable reference to keep handy whenever they need to work on a PC. The settings and connectors on your motherboard affect most of the other sub-systems so a detailed knowledge of motherboards and reference to the specifications is essential.

The **Micro House PC Hardware Library Volume III: Motherboards** contains detailed diagrams and tables listing the connectors, jumpers, specifications, settings, and defaults for over 100 common motherboards. It focuses on Pentium, Pentium Pro, and Pentium II systems in a variety of form factors (ATX, baby AT, NLX, and others).

The CD-ROM included with the **Micro House PC Hardware Library** contains the content of the tables from the book in fully searchable electronic format.

About This Book

This book is arranged into two chapters.

Chapter One covers basic motherboard components and concepts common to many systems. Included in this are detailed discussions of memory speeds, types, and banks and processor capabilities and sockets. Understanding memory configuration and ensuring proper motherboard support for your processor are two of the most important parts of configuring or troubleshooting a motherboard.

Chapter Two is a listing of many popular motherboards. This chapter includes a diagram for each card listed showing jumper and connector locations and tables of the relevant connections, pins, jumper defaults, and jumper uses. For most of the motherboards listed, the specifications also include processor speed settings, possible memory bank configurations, and processor socket voltage settings where applicable.

Appendix A lists manufacturer contact information for most major motherboard vendors. You will also find vendors for items such as BIOSs, BIOS upgrades, system vendors, video chips, and other motherboard components.

Chapter 1

Motherboards

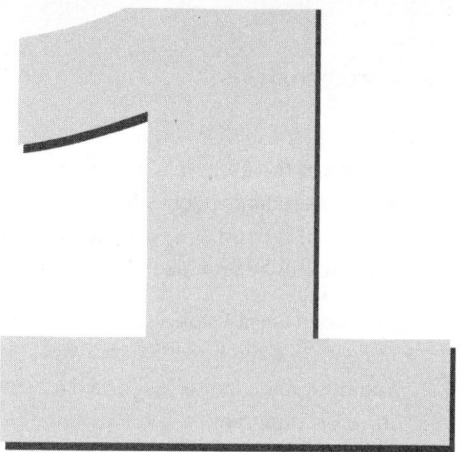

Easily the most important component in a PC system is the *main board* or *motherboard*. Some companies, such as IBM, refer to the motherboard as a *system board* or *planar*. All of these terms are interchangeable. In this chapter we will examine the different types of motherboards available, as well as those components usually contained on the motherboard and motherboard interface connectors.

Replacement Motherboards

Some manufacturers go out of their way to make their systems as physically incompatible as possible with any other system. Replacement parts, repairs, and upgrades are virtually impossible to find—except, of course, from the original system manufacturer, at a significantly higher price than the equivalent part would cost to fit a standard PC-compatible system.

For example, if the motherboard in your current AT-chassis system (or any system using a Baby-AT motherboard and case) dies, you can find any number of replacement boards that will bolt directly in, with your choice of processors and clock speeds, at very good prices. If the motherboard dies in a newer IBM, Compaq, Hewlett-Packard, Packard Bell, Gateway, AST, or other proprietary-shaped system, you'll pay for a replacement available only from the original manufacturer, and you have little or no opportunity to select a board with a faster or better processor than the one that failed. In other words, upgrading or repairing one of these systems via a motherboard replacement is difficult and usually not cost-effective.

Knowing What to Look For (Selection Criteria)

As a consultant, I am often asked to make recommendations for purchases. Making these types of recommendations is one of the most frequent tasks a consultant performs. Many consultants charge a large fee for this advice. Without guidance, many individuals don't have any rhyme or reason to their selections, and instead base their choices solely on magazine reviews or, even worse, on some personal bias. To help eliminate this haphazard selection process, I have developed a simple checklist that will help you select a system. This list takes into consideration several important system aspects that are overlooked by most checklists. The goal is to ensure that the selected system truly is compatible and has a long life of service and upgrades ahead.

2 Motherboards

It helps to think like an engineer when you make your selection. Consider every aspect and detail of the motherboards in question. For instance, you should consider any future uses and upgrades. Technical support at a professional level (as opposed to a user level) is extremely important. What support will be provided? Is there documentation, and does it cover everything else?

In short, a checklist is a good idea. Here is one for you to use in evaluating any PC-compatible system. You might not have to meet every one of these criteria to consider a particular system, but if you miss more than a few, consider staying away from that system. The items at the top of the list are the most important, and the items at the bottom are perhaps of lesser importance (although I think each item is important). The rest of this chapter discusses in detail the criteria in this checklist:

- *Processor*. At minimum, a Pentium motherboard should use the second-generation 3.3v Pentium processor, which has a 296-pin Socket 5 or Socket 7 configuration that differs physically from the 273-pin Socket 4 first-generation design. Pentium motherboards with the Socket 7 configuration also support newer processors with MMX technology, including AMD's K6. All second-generation Pentiums (75MHz and up) are fully SL Enhanced. Newer Pentium Pro and Pentium II processors have their own unique motherboard configurations, and are not compatible with other Pentium-based motherboards.

- *Processor Sockets*. A Pentium motherboard should have at least one ZIF socket that follows the Intel Socket 7 (321-pin) specification. The Socket 7 with an adjacent VRM (Voltage Regulator Module) socket will allow the best selection of future Pentium processors that will be available at higher speeds. Although Socket 5 is similar to Socket 7, many of the newer and faster Pentiums—including the MMX-equipped processors—require Socket 7. Pentium Pro (P6) motherboards use Socket 8, and many are set up for multiple processors. Before going to the expense of buying a multi-processor board, ensure that your operating system is able to handle it. For instance, while Windows 95 cannot really benefit from more than one CPU, Windows NT, OS/2, and some others may run considerably faster.

- *Motherboard Speed*. A Pentium or Pentium Pro motherboard should run at 60 or 66MHz and be speed-switchable between these speeds. Notice that all the Pentium and Pentium Pro processors sold today run at a multiple of the motherboard speed. For example, Pentium 75 runs at a motherboard speed of 50MHz; Pentium 60, 90, 120, 150, and 180MHz chips run at a 60MHz base motherboard speed; and the Pentium 66, 100, 133, 166, 200, and 233 run at a 66MHz motherboard speed setting. The Pentium Pro 150, 180, and 200 run at 50, 60, and 66MHz speeds, respectively. All components on the motherboard (especially cache memory) should be rated to run at the maximum allowable motherboard speed. Pentium II motherboards currently run at 66MHz, although the next generation of Pentium IIs will use a 100MHz motherboard. If you are looking for a new Pentium II motherboard and performance is critical, this boost in motherboard speed will have a dramatic overall performance benefit.

- *Cache Memory*. All Pentium motherboards should have 256KB to 512KB of Level 2 cache on-board. Most Pentium Pro processors have a built-in 256KB or 512KB Level 2 cache (some newer versions have 1MB), but may also have more Level 2 cache on the motherboard for even better performance. Pentium II processors also have a built-in L2 cache in the Slot 1 S.E.C. cartridge. The Level 2 Cache should be of a Write-Back design, and must be populated with chips that are fast enough to support the maximum motherboard speed, which should be 15ns or faster for 66MHz maximum motherboard speeds. For Pentium boards, the cache should be a Synchronous SRAM (Static RAM) type, which is also called *Pipelined Burst SRAM*.

- *SIMM Memory*. All Pentium and Pentium Pro motherboards should use either 72-pin SIMMs or 168-pin DIMMs (Dual In-line Memory Modules). Due to the 64-bit design of these boards, the 72-pin SIMMs must be installed in matched pairs, while DIMMs are installed one at a time (one per 64-bit bank). Carefully consider the total amount of memory that the board supports. While 16MB is regarded as a bare minimum for today's memory hungry applications, you may actually require much more. Pentium motherboards should support at least 128MB, and many current Pentium II boards support more than 1GB! A motherboard should contain at least four memory sockets (72-pin, 168-pin, or a combination), and the more the better. For maximum performance, look for systems that support SDRAM (Synchronous DRAM) or EDO (Extended Data Out) type SIMMs/DIMMs. The SIMMs should be rated at 70ns or faster.

Mission-critical systems ideally should use Parity SIMMs and ensure that the motherboard fully supports parity checking or even ECC (Error Correcting Code) as well. Note that the popular Intel Triton Pentium chipset (82430FX) does not support parity-checked memory at all, but their other Pentium chipsets, such as the older Neptune (82430NX) and newer Triton II (82430HX), do offer parity support. Triton II even offers ECC capability using standard parity SIMMs. All the current Pentium Pro chipsets also support parity memory, and are ideal for file servers and other mission-critical uses when equipped with parity SIMMs or DIMMs.

- *Bus Type*. Pentium, Pentium Pro, and Pentium II motherboards should have three or four ISA bus slots and three or four PCI local bus slots. Take a look at the layout of the slots to ensure that cards inserted into them will not block access to memory sockets, or be blocked by other components in the case. An AGP bus for newer video cards is also desirable.

- *BIOS*. The motherboard should use an industry-standard BIOS, such as those from AMI, Phoenix, Microid Research, or Award. The BIOS should be of a Flash ROM or EEPROM (Electrically Erasable Programmable Read-Only Memory) design for easy updating. The BIOS should support the Plug and Play (PnP) specification, Enhanced IDE or Fast ATA, and 2.88MB floppy drives. APM (Advanced Power Management) support should be built into the BIOS as well.

- *Form Factor*. For maximum flexibility, the Baby-AT form factor is still a safe bet. It can be installed in the widest variety of case designs and is retrofittable in most systems. For the greatest performance and future flexibility, many newer motherboards and systems incorporate the new ATX form factor, which has distinct performance and functional advantages over Baby-AT. Additionally, the new NLX form factor has been developed by Intel as an improvement on the ATX. Although it is new, the NLX specification is supported by a number of manufacturers, so it could prove to be a popular board in the coming years.

- *Built-in interfaces*. Ideally, a motherboard should contain as many built-in standard controllers and interfaces as possible (except video). A motherboard should have a built-in floppy controller that supports 2.88MB drives, built-in primary and secondary local bus (PCI or VL-Bus), Enhanced IDE (also called Fast ATA) connectors, two built-in high-speed serial ports (must use 16550A type buffered UARTs), and a built-in high-speed parallel port (must be EPP/ECP-compliant). A built-in PS/2 type mouse port should be included, although one of the serial ports can be used for a mouse as well.

Some newer systems, particularly those with ATX and NLX form factors, should include a built-in USB (Universal Serial Bus) port. USB ports will become a "must-have" item on multimedia systems in the near future. A built-in SCSI port is a bonus as long as it conforms to ASPI (Advanced SCSI Programming Interface) standards. Built-in network adapters are acceptable, but usually an ISA slot card network adapter is more easily supported via standard drivers and is more easily upgraded as well. Built-in video adapters are also a bonus in some situations, but because there are many different video chipset and adapter designs to choose from, generally there are better choices in external local bus video adapters. The same goes for built-in sound cards; they usually offer basic Sound Blaster compatibility and function, but often do not include other desirable features found on most plug-in sound cards, such as wavetable support.

- *Plug and Play (PnP)*. The motherboard should fully support the Intel PnP specification. This will allow automatic configuration of PCI adapters as well as PnP ISA adapters.

> **Tip**
>
> Even if a motherboard doesn't list that it's PnP-compatible, it may be. PCI motherboards are required to be PnP-compatible because it is a part of the PCI standard.

- *Power Management*. The motherboard should fully support SL Enhanced processors with APM (Advanced Power Management) and SMM (System Management Mode) protocols that allow for powering down various system components to different levels of readiness and power consumption.
- *Motherboard Chipset*. Pentium and Pentium MMX motherboards should use a high-performance chipset—preferably one that allows parity checking, such as the Intel Triton II (430HX). The popular original Intel Triton (430FX) chipset, along with the newer 430TX and 430VX chipsets, does not support parity-checked memory. For critical applications using Pentium motherboards where accuracy and data integrity are important, I recommend you use a board based on the Triton II (430HX) chipset or any others like it that support ECC memory using true parity memory modules. As a bonus, the 430HX chipset supports USB and dual CPUs, making it truly versatile.

Pentium Pro and Pentium II motherboards currently have the high-end Orion (450KX and 450GX) chipsets, as well as the less expensive Natoma (440FX) chipset. All three chipsets support parity memory, USB, and multiple CPUs, and are suitable for critical application use.

Another new Pentium II chipset is the Intel 440LX AGPset. The 440LX chipset is Intel's first to support the Accelerated Graphics Port (AGP), using the 8243LX PCI AGP Controller (PAC). Intended for 3D graphics and multimedia applications, the chipset employs a technique called Quad Port Acceleration, which uses separate buffers and arbiters for the main processor bus, the PCI bus, the graphics port, and SDRAM. The chipset also supports the power management functions defined in Intel's Advanced Configuration and Power Interface (ACPI) specification, and the Quantum Ultra DMA protocol, which increases the transfer rate of the ATA/IDE interface to 33 megabytes per second.

You may notice that these selection criteria seem fairly strict and may disqualify many motherboards on the market, including what you already have in your system! These criteria will guarantee you the highest-quality motherboard, however, offering the latest in PC technology that will be upgradable and expandable, and that will provide good service for many years.

Documentation

As mentioned, extensive documentation is an important factor to consider when you're planning to purchase a motherboard. Most motherboard manufacturers design their boards around a particular chipset, which actually counts as the bulk of the motherboard circuitry. There are a number of manufacturers offering chipsets, such as Intel, Opti, VIA, SiS, and others. I recommend obtaining the data book or other technical documentation on the chipset directly from the chipset manufacturer. Many of these vendors are listed with their contact information in Appendix A.

One of the more common questions I hear about a system relates to the BIOS Setup program. People want to know what the "Advanced Chipset Setup" features mean and what will be the effects of changing them. Often they go to the BIOS manufacturer thinking that the BIOS documentation will offer help. Usually, however, people find that the BIOS documentation has no real coverage of the chipset setup features. You will find this information in the data book provided by the chipset manufacturer. Although these books are meant to be read by the engineers who design the boards, they contain all the detailed information about the chipset's features, especially those that might be adjustable. With the chipset data book, you will have an explanation of all the controls in the Advanced Chipset Setup section of the BIOS Setup program.

Besides the main chipset data books, I also recommend collecting any data books on the other major chips in the system. This would include any floppy or IDE controller chips, Super I/O chips, and of course the main processor. You will find an incredible amount of information on these components in the data books.

> **Caution**
>
> Most chipset manufacturers only make a particular chip for a short time, rapidly superseding it with an improved or changed version. The data books are only available during the time the chip is being manufactured, so if you wait too long, you will find that such documents may no longer be available. The time to collect documentation on your motherboard is *now*!

ROM BIOS Compatibility

The issue of ROM BIOS compatibility is important. If the BIOS is not compatible, any number of problems can result. Several reputable companies that produce PC-compatibles have developed their own proprietary ROM BIOS that works just like IBM's. Also, many of the PC-compatibles' OEMs

6 Motherboards

have designed ROMs that work specifically with additional features in their systems while effectively masking the effects of these improvements from any software that would "balk" at the differences.

OEMs Many OEMs (Original Equipment Manufacturers) have developed their own compatible ROMs independently. Companies such as Compaq and AT&T have developed their own BIOS products that are comparable to those offered by AMI, Phoenix, and others. These companies also offer upgrades to newer versions that often can offer more features and improvements or fix problems with the older versions. If you use a system with a proprietary ROM, make sure that it is from a larger company with a track record and one that will provide updates and fixes as necessary. Ideally, upgrades should be available for download from the Internet.

Several companies have specialized in the development of a compatible ROM BIOS product. The three major companies that come to mind in discussing ROM BIOS software are American Megatrends, Inc. (AMI), Award Software, and Phoenix Software. Each company licenses its ROM BIOS to a motherboard manufacturer so that the manufacturer can worry about the hardware rather than the software. To obtain one of these ROMs for a motherboard, the OEM must answer many questions about the design of the system so that the proper BIOS can be either developed or selected from those already designed. Combining a ROM BIOS and a motherboard is not a haphazard task. No single generic, compatible ROM exists, either. AMI, Award, Microid Research, and Phoenix ship variations of their BIOS code to different manufacturers, each one custom-tailored to that specific system, much like DOS can be.

AMI Although AMI customizes the ROM code for a particular system, it does not sell the ROM source code to the OEM. An OEM must obtain each new release as it becomes available. Because many OEMs don't need or want every new version developed, they might skip several version changes before licensing a new one. The AMI BIOS is currently the most popular BIOS in PC systems today. Newer versions of the AMI BIOS are called *Hi-Flex* due to the high flexibility found in the BIOS configuration program. The AMI Hi-Flex BIOS is used in Intel, AMI, and many other manufacturers' motherboards. One special AMI feature is that it is the only third-party BIOS manufacturer to make its own motherboard.

During powerup, the BIOS ID string is displayed on the lower-left corner of the screen. This string tells you valuable information about which BIOS version you have, as well as certain settings that are determined by the built-in setup program.

> **Tip**
>
> A good trick to help you view the BIOS ID string is to shut down and either unplug your keyboard or hold down a key as you power back on. This will cause a keyboard error, and the string will remain displayed.

The primary BIOS Identification string (ID String 1) is displayed by any AMI BIOS during the POST (Power On Self-Test) at the bottom-left corner of the screen, below the copyright message. Two additional BIOS ID strings (ID String 2 and 3) can be displayed by the AMI Hi-Flex BIOS by pressing the Insert key during POST. These additional ID strings display the options that are installed in the BIOS.

The general BIOS ID String 1 format for older AMI BIOS versions is shown in Table 1.1.

Table 1.1 ABBB-NNNN-mmddyy-KK.

Position	Description
A	BIOS Options: 　　D = Diagnostics built-in 　　S = Setup built-in 　　E = Extended Setup built-in
BBB	Chipset or Motherboard Identifier: 　　C&T = Chips & Technologies chipset 　　NET = C&T NEAT 286 chipset 　　286 = Standard 286 motherboard 　　SUN = Suntac chipset 　　PAQ = Compaq motherboard 　　INT = Intel motherboard 　　AMI = AMI motherboard 　　G23 = G2 chipset 386 motherboard
NNNN	The manufacturer license code reference number
mmddyy	The BIOS release date, mm/dd/yy
KK	The AMI keyboard BIOS version number

The BIOS ID String 1 format for AMI Hi-Flex BIOS versions is shown in Table 1.2.

Table 1.2 AB-CCcc-DDDDDD-EFGHIJKL-mmddyy-MMMMMMMM-N.

Position	Description
A	Processor Type: 　　0 = 8086 or 8088 　　2 = 286 　　3 = 386 　　4 = 486 　　5 = Pentium 　　6 = Pentium Pro
B	Size of BIOS: 　　0 = 64KB BIOS 　　1 = 128KB BIOS
CCcc	Major and Minor BIOS version number
DDDDDD	Manufacturer license code reference number 　　0036xx = AMI 386 motherboard, xx = Series # 　　0046xx = AMI 486 motherboard, xx = Series # 　　0056xx = AMI Pentium motherboard, xx = Series # 　　0066xx = AMI Pentium Pro motherboard, xx = Series #
E	1 = Halt on Post Error

Table 1.2 AB-CCcc-DDDDDD-EFGHIJKL-mmddyy-MMMMMMMM-N (continued).

Position	Description
F	1 = Initialize CMOS every boot
G	1 = Block pins 22 and 23 of the keyboard controller
H	1 = Mouse support in BIOS/keyboard controller
I	1 = Wait for F1 key on POST errors
J	1 = Display floppy error during POST
K	1 = Display video error during POST
L	1 = Display keyboard error during POST
mmddyy	BIOS Date, mm/dd/yy
MMMMMMMM	Chipset identifier or BIOS name
N	Keyboard controller version number

AMI Hi-Flex BIOS ID String 2 is shown in Table 1.3

Table 1.3 AAB-C-DDDD-EE-FF-GGGG-HH-II-JJJ.

Position	Description
AA	Keyboard controller pin number for clock switching

B	Keyboard controller clock switching pin function:
	    H = High signal switches clock to high speed
	    L = High signal switches clock to low speed

C	Clock switching through chip set registers:
	    0 = Disable
	    1 = Enable

DDDD	Port address to switch clock high
EE	Data value to switch clock high
FF	Mask value to switch clock high
GGGG	Port Address to switch clock low
HH	Data value to switch clock low
II	Mask value to switch clock low
JJJ	Pin number for Turbo Switch Input

AMI Hi-Flex BIOS ID String 3 is shown in Table 1.4.

Table 1.4 AAB-C-DDD-EE-FF-GGGG-HH-II-JJ-K-L.

Position	Description
AA	Keyboard controller pin number for cache control

B	Keyboard controller cache control pin function:
	    H = High signal enables the cache
	    L = High signal disables the cache

Table 1.4 AAB-C-DDD-EE-FF-GGGG-HH-II-JJ-K-L (continued).

Position	Description
C	1 = High signal is used on the keyboard controller pin
DDD	Cache control through Chipset registers: 0 = Cache control off 1 = Cache control on
EE	Port address to enable cache
FF	Data value to enable cache
GGGG	Mask value to enable cache
HH	Port address to disable cache
II	Data value to disable cache
JJ	Mask value to disable cache
K	Pin number for resetting the 82335 memory controller
L	BIOS Modification Flag: 0 = The BIOS has not been modified 1[nd]9, A[nd]Z = Number of times the BIOS has been modified

The AMI BIOS has many features, including a built-in setup program activated by pressing the Delete or Esc key in the first few seconds of booting up your computer. The BIOS will prompt you briefly for which key to press and when to press it. The AMI BIOS offers user-definable hard disk types, essential for optimal use of many IDE or ESDI drives. The newer BIOS versions also support Enhanced IDE drives and will auto-configure the drive parameters.

A unique AMI BIOS feature is that, in addition to the setup, it has a built-in, menu-driven diagnostics package, essentially a very limited version of the stand-alone AMIDIAG product. The internal diagnostics are not a replacement for more comprehensive disk-based programs (the menu-driven diagnostics do not do extensive memory testing, for example, and the hard disk low-level formatter works only at the BIOS level rather than at the controller register level) , but they can help in a pinch. The diagnostic package's limitations often have prevented it from being capable of formatting severely damaged disks.

The AMI BIOS is sold through distributors, a list of which is available at
http://www.ami.com/distributor.html.

Award Award is unique among BIOS manufacturers because it sells its BIOS code to the OEM and allows the OEM to customize the BIOS. Of course, this BIOS is no longer Award BIOS, but rather a highly customized version. AST uses this approach on its systems, as do other manufacturers, to maintain total control over the BIOS code without having to write it from scratch. Although AMI and Phoenix customize the ROM code for a particular system, they do not sell the ROM's source code to the OEM. Some OEMs that seem to have developed their own ROM code started with a base of source code licensed to them by Award or some other company.

The Award BIOS has all the normal features you expect, including a built-in setup program activated by pressing Ctrl+Alt+Esc. This setup offers user-definable drive types, required in order to fully use IDE or ESDI hard disks. The POST is good, and Award runs technical support on its Web site at **http://www.award.com**.

In all, the Award BIOS is high quality, has minimal compatibility problems, and offers a high level of support.

Phoenix For many years, the Phoenix BIOS has been a standard of compatibility by which others are judged. Phoenix was one of the first third-party companies to legally reverse-engineer the IBM BIOS, using a "clean room" approach. In this approach, a group of engineers studied the IBM BIOS and wrote a specification for how that BIOS should work and which features should be incorporated. This information then was passed to a second group of engineers who had never seen the IBM BIOS. They could then legally write a new BIOS to the specifications set forth by the first group. This work would be unique and not a copy of IBM's BIOS; however, it would function the same way. This code has been refined over the years and has very few compatibility problems compared to some of the other BIOS vendors.

The Phoenix BIOS excels in two areas that put it high on my list of recommendations. One is that the POST is excellent. The BIOS outputs an extensive set of beep codes that can be used to diagnose severe motherboard problems that would prevent normal operation of the system. In fact, this POST can isolate memory failures in Bank 0 right down to the individual chip with beep codes alone. The Phoenix BIOS also has an excellent setup program that's free from unnecessary frills but still offers all the features one would expect, such as user-definable drive types. The built-in setup is activated by pressing either Ctrl+Alt+S or Ctrl+Alt+Esc, depending on the version of BIOS you have.

Micronics motherboards have always used the Phoenix BIOS, and these motherboards are used in many of the popular name-brand-compatible systems. Phoenix has been one of the largest OEMs of Microsoft MS-DOS. If you have MS-DOS, you also have the Phoenix OEM version. Phoenix licenses its DOS to other computer manufacturers, as long as they use the Phoenix BIOS. Because of its close relationship with Microsoft, it has had access to the DOS source code, which helps in eliminating compatibility problems.

Although Phoenix does not operate a technical support service by itself, their largest nationwide distributor, Micro Firmware, Inc., does. Online information is available at **http://www.firmware.com**. Micro Firmware offers upgrades to many systems with a Phoenix BIOS, including Packard Bell, Gateway 2000 (with Micronics motherboards), Micron Technologies, and other systems.

Unless the ROM BIOS is a truly compatible custom OEM version such as Compaq's, you might want to install in the system the ROM BIOS from one of the known quantities, such as AMI, Award, or Phoenix. These companies' products are established as ROM BIOS standards in the industry, and frequent updates and improvements ensure that a system containing these ROMs will have a long life of upgrades and service.

Using Correct Speed-Rated Parts

Some PC-compatible vendors use substandard parts in their systems to save money. Because the CPU is one of the most expensive components on the motherboard, and many motherboards are sold to system assemblers without the CPU installed, it is tempting for the assembler to install a CPU rated for less than the actual operating speed. A system could be sold as a 100MHz system, for example, but when you look "under the hood," you may find a CPU rated for only 90MHz. The system does appear to work correctly, but for how long? If the company that manufactures the CPU chip installed in this system had tested the chip to run reliably at 100MHz, it would have labeled the part accordingly. After all, the company could sell the chip for more money if it worked at the higher clock speed.

When a chip is run at a speed higher than it is rated for, it will run hotter than it would normally. This may cause the chip to overheat occasionally, which would appear as random, frustrating lockups and glitches. I highly recommend that you avoid any system whose operation speed exceeds the design of its respective parts.

This practice is easy to fall into because the faster-rated chips cost more money, and Intel and other chip manufacturers usually rate their chips very conservatively. I have taken several 25MHz 486 processors and run them at 33MHz, and they seemed to work fine. The Pentium 90 chips I have tested seem to run fine at 100MHz. Although I might purchase a Pentium 90 system and make a decision to run it at 100MHz, if I were to experience lockups or glitches in operation, I would immediately return it to 90MHz and retest. If I purchase a 100MHz system from a vendor, I fully expect it to have 100MHz parts, not 90MHz parts running past their rated speed! These days, many chips will have some form of heat sink, which helps to prevent overheating but can also sometimes cover up for a "pushed" chip. If the price is too good to be true, ask before you buy: "Are the parts really manufacturer-rated for the system speed?"

To determine the rated speed of a CPU chip, look at the writing on the chip. Most of the time, the part number will end in a suffix of *[nd]xxx*, where the *xxx* is a number indicating the maximum speed. For example, [nd]100 indicates that the chip is rated for 100MHz operation.

> **Caution**
>
> Be careful when running software to detect processor speed. Such programs can only tell you what speed the chip is currently running at, not what the true rating is. Also ignore the speed indicator lights on the front of some cases. These digital displays can literally be set via jumpers to read any speed you desire! They have no true relation to actual system speed.

Motherboard Form Factors

There are several compatible form factors used for motherboards. The form factor refers to the physical dimensions and size of the board, and dictates what type of case the board will fit into. The types of motherboard form factors generally available are the following:

- Backplane Systems
- Full-size AT
- Baby-AT
- LPX
- ATX
- NLX

Backplane Systems

Not all systems have a motherboard in the true sense of the word. In some systems, the components normally found on a motherboard are located instead on an expansion adapter card plugged into a slot. The board with the slots is called a *backplane*, and systems using this type of construction are called *backplane systems*.

Backplane systems come in two main types: *passive* and *active*. A passive backplane means the main backplane board does not contain any circuitry at all, except for the bus connectors and maybe some buffer and driver circuits. All the circuitry found on a conventional motherboard is contained on one or more expansion cards installed in slots on the backplane. Some backplane systems use a passive design that incorporates the entire system circuitry into a single *mothercard*. The mothercard is essentially a complete motherboard that is designed to plug into a slot in the passive backplane. The passive backplane/mothercard concept allows the entire system to be easily upgraded by changing one or more cards. Because of the expense of the high-function mothercard, this type of system design is rarely found in PC systems. The passive backplane design does enjoy popularity in industrial systems, which are often rack-mounted. Some high-end file servers also feature this design.

An active backplane means the main backplane board contains bus control and usually other circuitry as well. Most active backplane systems contain all the circuitry found on a typical motherboard, except for the processor complex. The *processor complex* is the name of the circuit board that contains the main system processor and any other circuitry directly related to it, such as clock control, cache, and so forth. The processor complex design allows the user to easily upgrade the system later to a new processor type by changing one card. In effect, it amounts to a modular motherboard with a replaceable processor section. Most modern PC systems that use a backplane design use an active backplane/processor complex. Both IBM and Compaq have used this type of design in some of their high-end (server class) systems, for example. This allows an easier and generally more affordable upgrade than the passive backplane/mothercard design because the processor complex board is usually much cheaper than a mothercard. Unfortunately, because there are no standards for the processor complex interface to the system, these boards are proprietary and can only be purchased from the system manufacturer. This limited market and availability causes the prices of these boards to be higher than most complete motherboards from other manufacturers.

The motherboard system design and the backplane system design have both advantages and disadvantages. Most original personal computers were designed as backplanes in the late 1970s. Apple and IBM shifted the market to the now-traditional motherboard with a slot-type design because this type of system generally is cheaper to mass-produce than one with the backplane design. The theoretical advantage of a backplane system, however, is that you can upgrade it easily to a new processor and a new level of performance by changing a single card. For example, you can upgrade a system's processor just by changing the card. In a motherboard-design system, you often must change the motherboard itself, a seemingly more formidable task. Unfortunately, the reality of the situation is that a backplane design is often much more expensive to upgrade, and the bus remains fixed on the backplane, which precludes more comprehensive upgrades that involve adding local bus slots, for example.

Another nail in the coffin of backplane designs is the upgradable processor. Intel has designed all 486, Pentium, Pentium MMX, and Pentium Pro processors to be upgradable to faster processors (sometimes called *OverDrive processors*) in the future by simply swapping (or adding) the new processor chip. Changing only the processor chip for a faster one is the easiest and generally most cost-effective way to upgrade without changing the entire motherboard.

Because of the limited availability of the processor complex boards or mothercards, they usually end up being more expensive than a completely new motherboard that uses an industry-standard form factor. Intel recently announced the new NLX form factor for the Pentium II, and it shares some traits with traditional backplane systems. The NLX has been promised considerable industry support, so we may well see affordable backplane systems in the near future.

Full-Size AT

The *full-size AT motherboard* is so named because it matches the original IBM AT motherboard design. This allows for a very large board of up to 12 inches wide by 13.8 inches deep. The keyboard connector and slot connectors must conform to specific placement requirements to fit the holes in the case. This type of board will fit into full-size AT or Tower cases only. Because these motherboards will not fit into the popular Baby-AT or Mini-Tower cases, and because of advances in component miniaturization, they are no longer being produced by most motherboard manufacturers.

Baby-AT

The Baby-AT form factor is essentially the same as the original IBM XT motherboard, with modifications in screw hole positions to fit into an AT-style case (see Figure 1.1). These motherboards also have specific placement of the keyboard connector and slot connectors to match the holes in the case. Note that virtually all full-size AT and Baby-AT motherboards use the standard 5-pin DIN type connector for the keyboard. Baby-AT motherboards will fit into every type of case except the Low Profile or Slimline cases. Because of their flexibility, this is now the most popular motherboard form factor. Figure 1.1 shows the dimensions and layout of a Baby-AT motherboard.

The LPX boards are characterized by several distinctive features. The most noticeable is that the expansion slots are mounted on a bus riser card that plugs into the motherboard. Expansion cards must plug sideways into the riser card. This sideways placement allows for the low-profile case design. Slots will be located on one or both sides of the riser card depending on the system and case design.

Another distinguishing feature of the LPX design is the standard placement of connectors on the back of the board. An LPX board will have a row of connectors for video (VGA 15-pin), parallel (25-pin), two serial ports (9-pin each), and mini-DIN PS/2-style mouse and keyboard connectors. All of these connectors are mounted across the rear of the motherboard and protrude through a slot in the case. Some LPX motherboards may have additional connectors for other internal ports, such as Network or SCSI adapters. Figure 1.2 shows the standard form factors for the LPX and Mini-LPX motherboards used in many systems today.

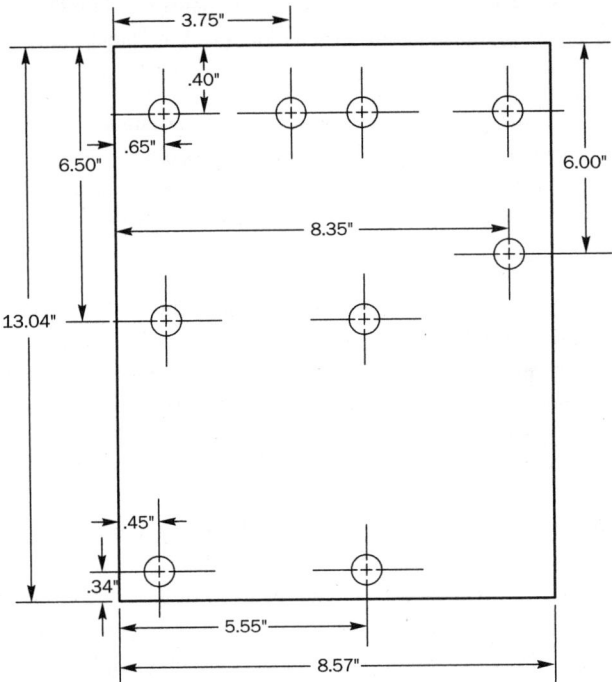

FIG. 1.1 Baby-AT motherboard form factor.

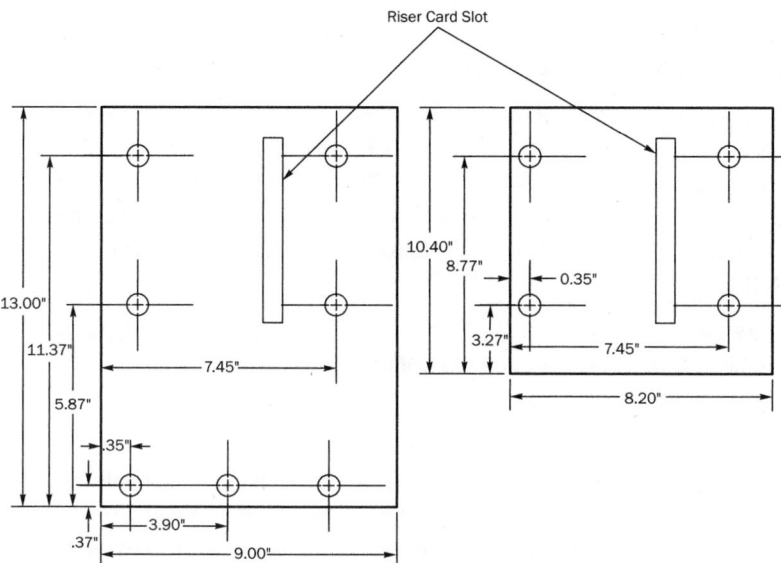

FIG. 1.2 LPX and Mini-LPX motherboard form factors.

ATX

The ATX form factor is a recent evolution in motherboard form factors. ATX is a combination of the best features of the Baby-AT and LPX motherboard designs, with many new enhancements and features thrown in. The ATX form factor is essentially a Baby-AT motherboard turned sideways in the chassis, along with a modified power supply location and connector. The most important thing to know about the ATX form factor is that it is physically incompatible with the previous Baby-AT and LPX designs. In other words, a different case and power supply are required to match the ATX motherboard. These new case and power supply designs have become common, and can be found in many new systems.

The official ATX specification was released by Intel in July 1995, and has been written as an open specification for the industry. The latest revision of the specification is Version 2.01, published in February 1997. Intel has published detailed specifications so other manufacturers can use the ATX design in their systems.

ATX improves on the Baby-AT and LPX motherboard designs in several major areas:

- ■ *Built-in double high external I/O connector panel.* The rear portion of the motherboard includes a stacked I/O connector area that is 6.25 inches wide by 1.75 inches tall. This allows external connectors to be located directly on the board and negates the need for cables running from internal connectors to the back of the case, as with Baby-AT designs.

- ■ *Single keyed internal power supply connector.* This is a boon for the average end user, who always had to worry about interchanging the Baby-AT power supply connectors and subsequently blowing the motherboard! The ATX specification includes a single keyed and shrouded power connector that is easy to plug in, and that cannot be installed incorrectly. This connector also features pins for supplying 3.3v to the motherboard, which means that ATX motherboards will not require built-in voltage regulators that are susceptible to failure.

- *Relocated CPU and memory*. The CPU and memory modules are relocated so they cannot interfere with any bus expansion cards, and they can easily be accessed for upgrade without removing any of the installed bus adapters. The CPU and memory are relocated next to the power supply so they have a single fan blowing air across them, thus eliminating the need for inefficient and failure-prone CPU cooling fans. There is room for a large passive heat sink above the CPU as well.

- *Relocated internal I/O connectors*. The internal I/O connectors for the floppy and hard disk drives are relocated to be near the drive bays and out from under the expansion board slot and drive bay areas. This means that internal cables to the drives can be much shorter, and accessing the connectors will not require card or drive removal.

- *Improved cooling*. The CPU and main memory are cooled directly by the power supply fan, eliminating the need for separate case and CPU cooling fans. Also, the ATX power supply fan blows *into* the system chassis, thus pressurizing it, which greatly minimizes dust and dirt intrusion into the system. If desired, an air filter can be easily added to the air intake vents on the power supply, creating a system that is even more immune to dirt or dust in the environment.

- *Lower cost to manufacture*. The ATX specifications eliminate the need for the rat's nest of cables to external port connectors found on Baby-AT motherboards, additional CPU or chassis cooling fans, and on-board 3.3v voltage regulators. Also, it uses a single power supply connector and allows for shorter internal drive cables. These factors greatly reduce not only the cost of the motherboard, but also the cost of a complete system, including the case and power supply.

Figure 1.3 shows the new ATX system layout and chassis features. Notice how virtually the entire motherboard is clear of the drive bays, and how the devices like CPU, memory, and internal drive connectors are easy to access and do not interfere with the bus slots. Also notice the power supply orientation and the single power supply fan that blows into the case directly over the heat-generating items like the CPU and memory.

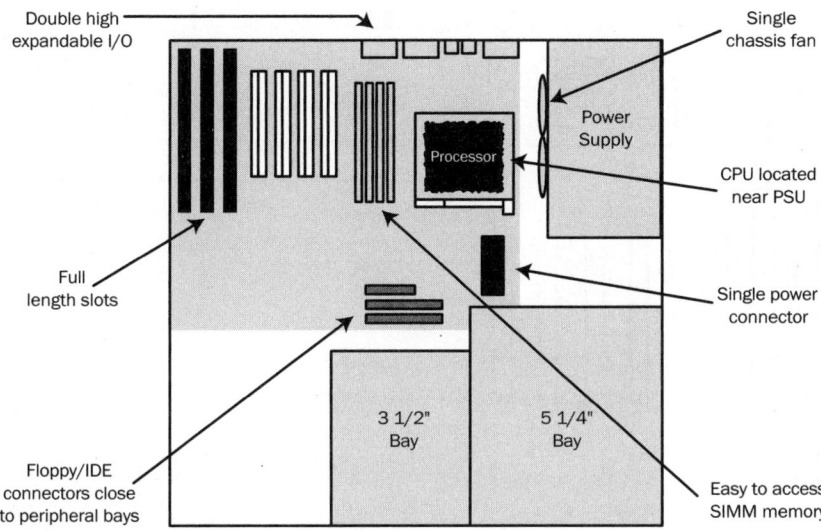
FIG. 1.3 ATX system chassis layout and features.

The ATX motherboard is basically a Baby-AT design rotated sideways. The expansion slots are now parallel to the shorter side and do not interfere with the CPU, memory, or I/O connector sockets. In addition to a full-sized ATX layout, Intel also has specified a mini-ATX design that will fit into the same case. Although the case holes are similar to the Baby-AT case, cases for the two formats are generally not compatible. The power supplies would require a connector adapter to be interchangeable, but the basic ATX power supply design is similar to the standard Slimline power supply. The ATX and mini-ATX motherboard dimensions are shown in Figure 1.4.

Clearly, the advantages of the ATX form factor make it a good choice for high-end systems. For backward-compatibility, Baby-AT is still hard to beat, and there are still more Baby-AT motherboards, cases, and power supplies on the market than the ATX versions. With the coming of NLX motherboards and the support that form factor is receiving from the industry, it seems unlikely that ATX will be the all-encompassing wave of the future.

NLX

NLX is the latest development in desktop motherboard technology, and may prove to be the form factor of choice in the near future. It is a low-profile form factor similar in appearance to LPX, but with a number of improvements designed to allow full integration of the latest technologies. Whereas the primary limitation of LPX boards includes an inability to handle the physical size of newer processors, as well as their higher thermal characteristics, the NLX form factor has been designed specifically to address these problems.

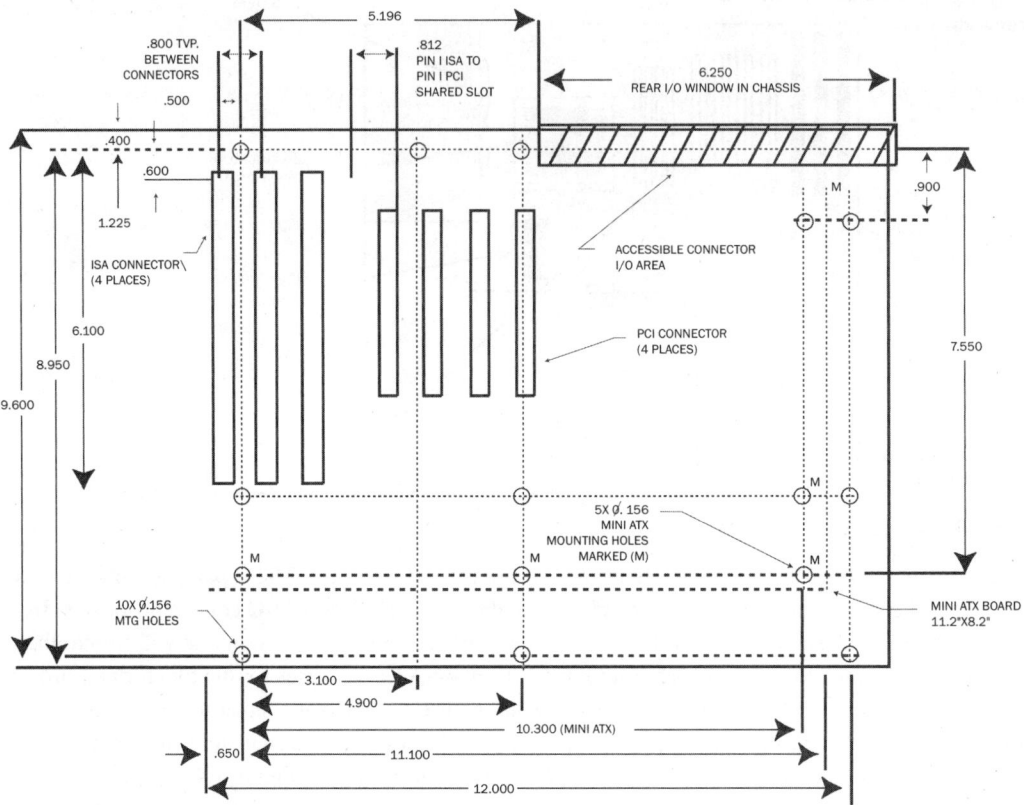

FIG. 1.4 ATX and Mini-ATX motherboard form factors.

Specific advantages of the NLX form factor include:

- *Support for current processor technologies.* This is especially important in Pentium II systems, because the size of the Single Edge Contact cartridge this processor uses can limit its use on existing Baby-AT and LPX motherboards. Although a few motherboard manufacturers currently offer ATX-based Pentium II systems, they generally only have room for two 72-pin SIMM sockets!

- *Flexibility in the face of rapidly changing processor technologies.* Backplane-like flexibility has been built into the form by allowing a new motherboard to be easily and quickly installed without tearing your entire system to pieces. But unlike traditional backplane systems, many industry leaders are putting their support behind NLX, including AST, Digital, Gateway, Hewlett-Packard, IBM, Micron, NEC, and others.

- *Support for other emerging technologies.* This includes Accelerated Graphics Port (AGP) high-performance graphic solutions, Universal Serial Bus (USB), and tall memory modules and DIMM technology. Furthermore, with the emerging importance of multimedia applications, connectivity support for such things as video playback, enhanced graphics, and extended audio has been built into the motherboard. This should represent a good cost savings over expensive daughterboard arrangements that have been necessary for many advanced multimedia uses in the past.

Figure 1.5 shows the basic NLX system layout, and the NLX motherboard dimensions are shown in Figure 1.6. Notice that, like ATX, the system is clear of the drive bays and other chassis-mounted components. Also, the motherboard and I/O cards (which, like the LPX form factor, are mounted parallel to the motherboard) easily can be slid in and out of the side of the chassis, leaving the riser card and other cards in place. The processor itself can be easily accessed and enjoys greater cooling than in a more closed-in layout.

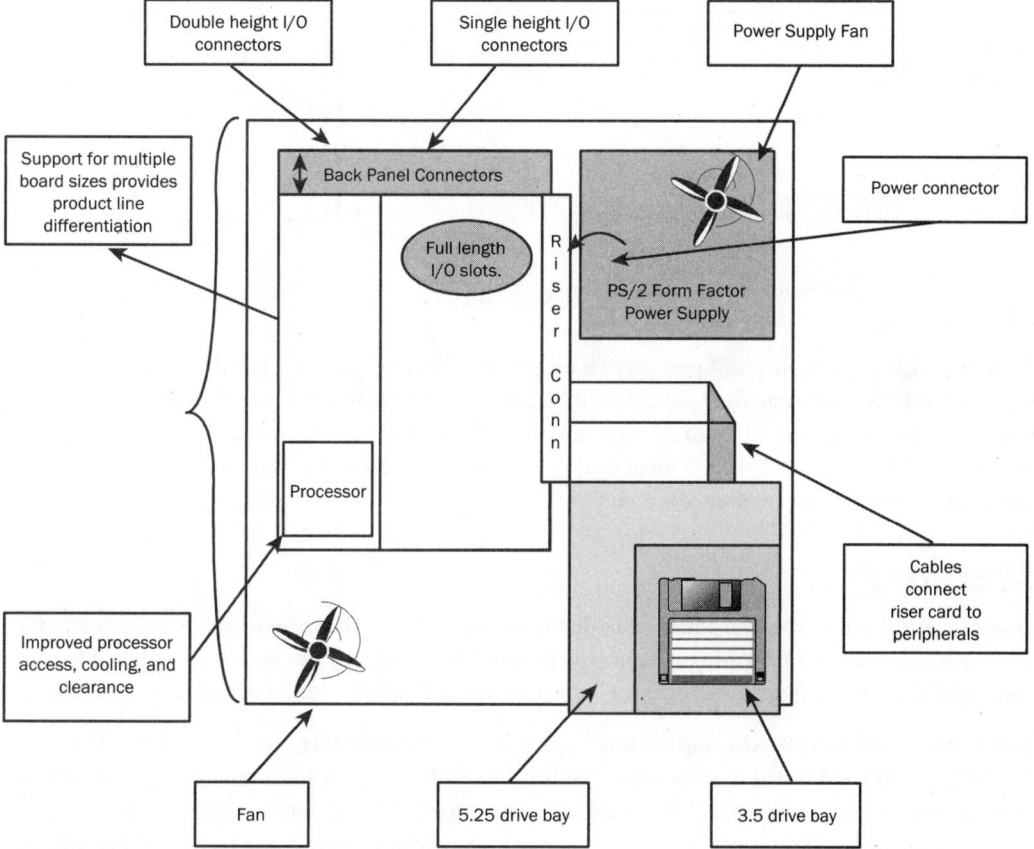

FIG. 1.5 NLX system chassis layout and features.

As you can see, the NLX form factor has been designed for maximum flexibility and space efficiency. Even extremely long I/O cards will fit easily without fouling on other system components, as has been such a problem with Baby-AT form factor systems.

20 Motherboards

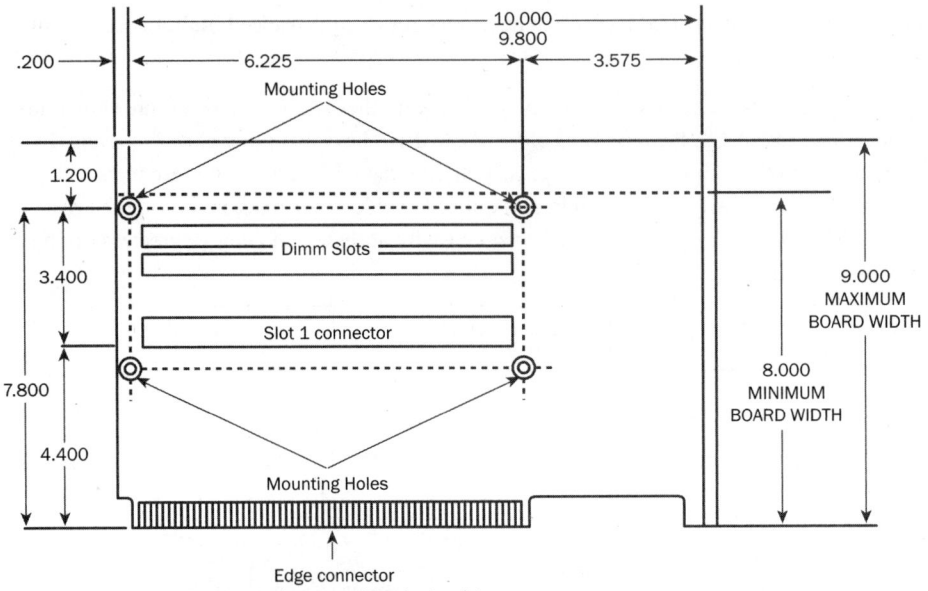

FIG. 1.6 NLX motherboard dimensions.

ATX and NLX form factors will probably be used in most future systems. I usually do not recommend LPX style systems if upgradability is a factor because it is not only difficult to locate a new motherboard that will fit, but LPX systems are also limited in expansion slots and drive bays as well. Baby-AT systems still offer a great deal of flexibility at present, but for future systems, ATX and NLX configurations are the way to go.

Memory

Dynamic RAM is the type of memory chip that is used for most of the main memory in a modern PC. The main advantages of DRAM are that it is very dense, meaning you can pack a lot of bits into a very small chip, and it is very inexpensive, which makes it affordable for large amounts of memory.

The memory cells in a DRAM chip are tiny capacitors that retain a charge to indicate a bit. The problem with DRAM is that it is dynamic, and because of the design it must be constantly *refreshed* or the electrical charges in the individual memory capacitors will drain and the data will be lost. Refresh occurs when the system memory controller takes a tiny break and accesses all of the rows of data in the memory chips, refreshing the contents of each row. Most systems have a memory controller (normally built into the motherboard chipset), which is set for an industry-standard refresh rate of 16us (microseconds). This means that every 16us, all the rows in the memory are read to refresh the data.

Refreshing the memory unfortunately takes processor time away from other tasks because each refresh cycle takes several CPU cycles to complete. In older systems, the refresh cycling could take 10% or more of the total CPU time. With modern systems running in the hundreds of megahertz, refresh overhead is now on the order of 1percent or less of the total CPU time. Some systems allow you to alter the refresh timing parameters via the CMOS setup, but be aware that decreasing the time between refresh cycles can allow some of the memory cells to begin draining, which can cause random soft memory errors to appear. (A *soft error* is a data error that is not caused by a defective chip.) It is safer to stick with the recommended or default refresh timing in most cases. Because refresh consumes less than 1% of modern system overall bandwidth, altering the refresh rate has little effect on performance.

DRAMs use only one transistor and capacitor pair per bit, which makes them very dense. They offer a lot more memory capacity per chip than other types of memory. There are currently DRAM chips available with densities of up to 256M-bits or more. This means that there are DRAM chips with 256 million or more transistors! Compare this to a Pentium II, which has 7.5 million transistors, and it makes the processor look wimpy by comparison. The difference is that in a memory chip, the transistors and capacitors are all consistently arranged in a (normally square) grid of very simple repetitive structures, unlike the processor, which is a much more complex circuit of different structures and elements interconnected in a highly irregular fashion.

The transistor for each DRAM bit cell is used to read the charge state of the adjacent capacitor. If the capacitor is charged, the cell is read to contain a 1, and no charge indicates a 0. The charge in the tiny capacitors is constantly draining, which is why the memory must be refreshed constantly. Even a momentary power interruption, or anything that interferes with the refresh cycles, will cause a DRAM memory cell to lose the charge and therefore the data.

DRAM is used in PC systems because it is inexpensive and the chips can be densely packed, meaning a lot of memory capacity can fit into a small space. Unfortunately DRAM is also slow, normally much slower than the processor. For this reason, there have been many different types of DRAM architectures developed in order to improve performance.

Memory Speeds and Types

The speed and performance issue with memory is confusing to some people because memory speed is usually expressed in nanoseconds (ns), while processor speed is expressed in megahertz (MHz).

A *nanosecond* is one-billionth of a second, a very short time indeed. To put it in perspective, note that the speed of light is 186,282 miles (299,792 kilometers) per second in a vacuum. In one-billionth of a second, a beam of light would travel a mere 11.80 inches or 29.98 centimeters, less than the length of a typical ruler!

Chip and system speed has been expressed in *megahertz*, which is millions of cycles per second. There are systems today with processors running 500 MHz or faster, and we should see speeds expressed in GHz (*gigahertz*, or billions of cycles per second) within a few years.

Because it is confusing to speak in all these different terms for speeds, I thought it would be interesting to see how they compare. Table 1.5 shows the relationship between nanoseconds and megahertz for the speeds associated with PCs today.

Table 1.5—The relationship between clock speeds in megahertz (MHz) to cycle times in nanoseconds (ns).

Clock Speed	Cycle Time	Clock Speed	Cycle Time
6 MHz	166 ns	120 MHz	8.3 ns
8 MHz	125 ns	133 MHz	7.5 ns
10 MHz	100 ns	150 MHz	6.6 ns
12 MHz	83 ns	166 MHz	6.0 ns
16 MHz	62 ns	180 MHz	5.5 ns
20 MHz	50 ns	200 MHz	5.0 ns
25 MHz	40 ns	233 MHz	4.2 ns
33 MHz	30 ns	250 MHz	4.0 ns
40 MHz	25 ns	300 MHz	3.3 ns
50 MHz	20 ns	333 MHz	3.0 ns
60 MHz	16 ns	350 MHz	2.8 ns
66 MHz	15 ns	400 MHz	2.5 ns
75 MHz	13 ns	450 MHz	2.2 ns
80 MHz	12 ns	500 MHz	2.0 ns
100 MHz	10 ns	550 MHz	1.8 ns

As you can see, as clock speeds increase, cycle time decreases. If you examine this table, you can clearly see that the DRAM memory that is used in the typical PC is totally inadequate when compared to processor speeds of 400MHz and higher. Note that until recently, most DRAM memory used in PCs has been rated at an access time of 60ns, which works out to be only about 16.7MHz! When you consider that this super-slow memory has been installed in systems running up to 300MHz or faster, you can see what a mismatch there is between processor and memory performance.

System memory timing is a little more involved than converting ns to MHz. All memory accesses involve first selecting a row address, then a column address, and then transferring the data. The initial setup for a memory transfer where the row and column addresses are selected is a necessary overhead normally referred to as *latency*. The access time for memory is the cycle time plus latency for selecting the row and column addresses. For example, memory rated at 60ns normally has a latency of about 25ns (to select the row and column address) and a cycle time of about 35ns to actually transfer the data. Thus, the true memory clock rate in a system with 60ns memory would be on the order of 28.5MHz (35ns = 28.5MHz). Even so, a single memory transfer will still require a full 60ns, so consecutive transfers will happen at a rate of only 16.7MHz (60ns) because of the added latency.

Fast Page Mode (FPM) DRAM Standard DRAM is accessed via a technique called *paging*. Normal memory access requires that a row and column address be selected, which takes time. Paging allows for faster access to all the data within a given row of memory by keeping the row address the same and only changing the column. Memory that uses this technique is called *page mode* or *fast page mode* memory. Other variations on page mode were called *static column* or *nibble mode* memory.

To improve further on memory access speeds, systems have evolved to allow for faster access to DRAM. One of the more significant changes was the implementation of *burst mode* access in the 486 and later processors. Burst mode cycling takes advantage of the fact that most memory accesses are consecutive in nature. After setting up the row and column addresses for a given access, you can use burst mode to access the next three adjacent addresses with no additional latency. A burst access is normally limited to four total accesses. To describe this, we often refer to the timing in the number of cycles for each access. A typical burst mode access of standard DRAM would be expressed as x-y-y-y, where the x is the time for the first access (latency plus cycle time) and y represents the number of cycles required for each consecutive access.

Standard 60ns DRAM normally runs 5-3-3-3 burst mode timing. This means the first access takes a total of five cycles (on a 66MHz system bus, this would be about 75ns total or 5x15ns cycles), while the consecutive cycles take three cycles each (3x15ns = 45ns). As you can see, the actual system timing is somewhat less than the memory is technically rated for. Note that without the bursting technique, memory access would be 5-5-5-5 because the full latency would be needed for each memory transfer.

DRAM memory that supports paging as well as this bursting technique is called *Fast Page Mode (FPM)* memory. The term comes from the fact that memory accesses to data on the same page can be done with less latency. Most 486 and newer systems use FPM memory, while older systems use conventional DRAM.

EDO RAM Starting in 1995, a new type of memory called *Extended Data Out (EDO) RAM* became available for Pentium systems. EDO, also referred to as *Hyper Page Mode,* is a modified form of FPM memory and was invented and patented by Micron Technology, who have licensed production to numerous other memory manufacturers. EDO memory consists of specially manufactured chips that allow for a timing overlap between successive accesses. The name *Extended Data Out* refers specifically to the fact that, unlike FPM, the data output drivers on the chip are not turned off when the memory controller removes the column address to begin the next cycle. This allows the next cycle to overlap the previous one, saving approximately 10ns per cycle.

EDO improves cycle times by allowing the memory controller to begin a new column address instruction while it is reading data at the current address. This is almost identical to what was achieved in older systems by interleaving banks of memory, but unlike interleaving, you don't need to install two identical banks of memory in the system at a time.

EDO RAM allows for burst mode cycling of 5-2-2-2, as compared to the 5-3-3-3 of standard Fast Page Mode memory. This means that to do four memory transfers, EDO would require 11 total system cycles, as compared to 14 total cycles for FPM. This is a 22% improvement in overall cycling time, but in actual testing EDO normally increases overall system benchmark speed by about 5%. Even though the overall system improvement may seem small, the important thing about EDO is that it uses the same basic DRAM chip design as FPM, meaning there is virtually no additional cost over FPM. As such, EDO costs about the same as FPM and offers higher performance.

To actually utilize EDO memory, your motherboard chipset must support it. Most motherboard chipsets since the Intel 430FX (Triton), which debuted in 1995, have offered support for EDO.

Because EDO memory chips cost the same to manufacture as standard chips, combined with the fact that Intel began to support EDO in all their chipsets, the PC market jumped on the EDO bandwagon full force.

EDO RAM is ideal for systems with bus speeds of up to 66MHz, which fit perfectly with the PC market up through 1997. However, for 1998 and beyond, the market for EDO will rapidly decline as the newer and faster SDRAM (Synchronous DRAM) architecture becomes the standard for new PC system memory.

Burst EDO A variation of EDO is *Burst Extended-Data-Out Dynamic Random Access Memory (BEDO DRAM)*. BEDO is basically EDO memory with special burst features for even speedier data transfers. Unfortunately, only one chipset (Intel 440FX Natoma) supported it and it was quickly overshadowed by SDRAM, which seemed to be favored among PC system chipset and system designers. You won't see BEDO being used in systems today, and it is no longer in production.

SDRAM *SDRAM* stands for *Synchronous DRAM*, a type of DRAM that runs in synchronization with the memory bus. SDRAM delivers information in very fast bursts using a high-speed, clocked interface. SDRAM removes most of the latency involved in asynchronous DRAM because the signals are already in synchronization with the motherboard clock.

Like EDO RAM, your chipset must support this type of memory for it to be usable in your system. Starting in 1997 with the 430VX and 430TX, all of Intel's subsequent chipsets fully support SDRAM, making it the most popular type of memory for new systems. SDRAM is especially suited to the Pentium II architecture and the new high performance motherboards that run it.

The performance of SDRAM is a dramatic improvement over FPM or EDO RAM. Because SDRAM is still a type of DRAM, the initial latency is the same, but overall cycle times are much faster than with FPM or EDO. SDRAM timing for a burst access would be 5-1-1-1, meaning that four memory reads would complete in only eight system bus cycles, as compared to 11 cycles for EDO and 14 cycles for FPM.

Besides the fact that SDRAM can work in fewer cycles, it is also capable of supporting 100MHz (10ns) or faster system bus cycling, which has become the new standard for system speed as of 1998. Virtually all new PC systems sold in 1998, and probably for two years thereafter, will include SDRAM memory.

It is anticipated that this figure will be pushed to 200MHz in order to keep up with faster systems in the near future. SDRAM is sold in DIMM form, and is often rated by MHz speed rather than ns cycling time. You will see SDRAM sold as 66MHz or 15ns, 83MHz or 12ns, or 100MHz or 10ns. Although SDRAM is significantly faster than previous types of memory, prices are not appreciably higher, which has made the acceptance of SDRAM even more rapid.

SIMMs and DIMMs

For memory storage, most modern systems have adopted the single in-line memory module (SIMM) or dual in-line memory module (DIMM) as alternatives to individual memory chips. These small boards plug into special connectors on a motherboard or memory card. The individual memory chips are soldered to the SIMM/DIMM, so removing and replacing individual memory chips is impossible.

Instead, you must replace the entire module if any part of it fails. The SIMM/DIMM is treated as though it were one large memory chip.

PC systems have two main physical types of SIMMs—30-pin (8 bits plus optional parity) and 72-pin (32 bits plus optional parity bits)—with various capacities and other specifications. The 30-pin SIMMs are smaller than the 72-pin versions, and may have chips on either one or both sides. 30-pin SIMMs are basically obsolete, and they are being followed rapidly by the 72-pin versions. This is true primarily because 64-bit systems—which would require eight 30-pin SIMMs or two 72-pin SIMMs per bank—are now the industry standard. DIMMs, which have become popular on Pentium-MMX and Pentium Pro-based systems, are 168-pin units with 64-bit (non-parity) or 72-bit (parity or ECC) data paths.

Figures 1.7, 1.8, and 1.9 show typical 30-pin (8-bit) and 72-pin (32-bit) SIMMs, as well as a 168-pin (64-bit) DIMM. The pins are numbered from left to right and are connected through to both sides of the module on the SIMMs. The pins on the DIMM are different on each side. Note that all dimensions are in both inches and millimeters (in parentheses).

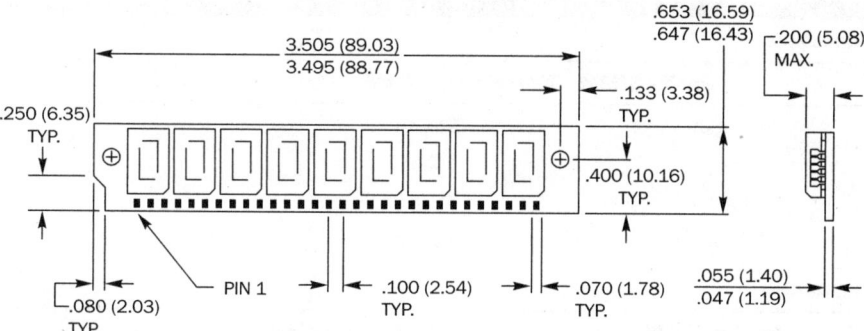

FIG. 1.7 A typical 30-pin (8-bit) SIMM.

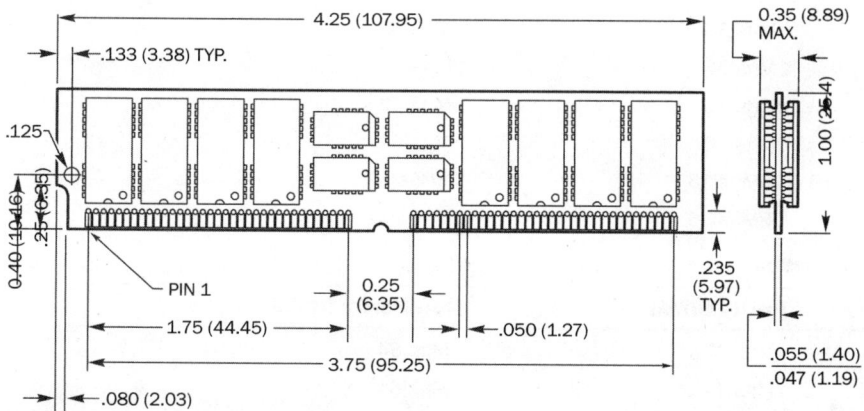

FIG. 1.8 A typical 72-pin (32-bit) SIMM.

26 Motherboards

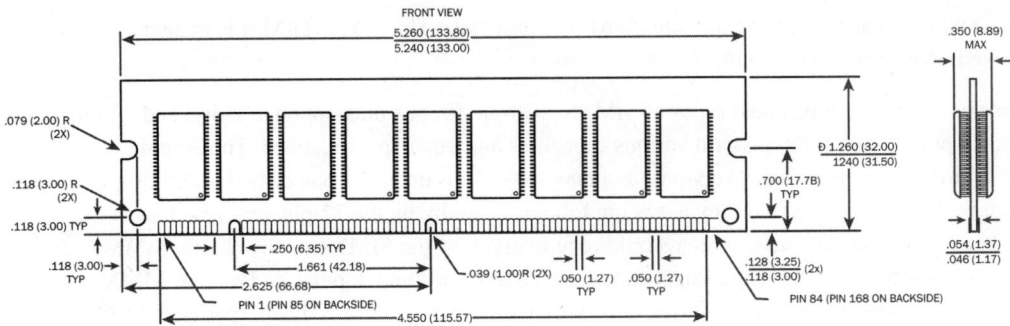

FIG. 1.9 A typical 168-pin (64-bit) DIMM.

These memory modules are extremely compact, considering the amount of memory they hold. SIMMs and DIMMs are available in several capacities and speeds. Table 1.6 lists the different capacities available for both the 30-pin and 72-pin SIMMs, as well as 168-pin DIMMs.

Table 1.6 SIMM and DIMM capacities.

30-Pin SIMM Capacities

Capacity	Parity SIMM	Non-Parity SIMM
256K	256K[ts]9	256K[ts]8
1M	1M[ts]9	1M[ts]8
4M	4M[ts]9	4M[ts]8
16M	16M[ts]9	16M[ts]8

72-Pin SIMM Capacities

Capacity	Parity SIMM	Non-Parity SIMM
1M	256K[ts]36	256K[ts]32
2M	512K[ts]36	512K[ts]32
4M	1M[ts]36	1M[ts]32
8M	2M[ts]36	2M[ts]32
16M	4M[ts]36	4M[ts]32
32M	8M[ts]36	8M[ts]32
64M	16M[ts]36	16M[ts]32
128M	32M[ts]36	32M[ts]32

168-Pin DIMM Capacities

Capacity	Parity DIMM	Non-Parity DIMM
8M	1M[ts]72	1M[ts]64
16M	2M[ts]72	2M[ts]64
32M	4M[ts]72	4M[ts]64

Capacity	Parity DIMM	Non-Parity DIMM (continued)
64M	8M[ts]72	8M[ts]64
128M	16M[ts]72	16M[ts]64
256M	32M[ts]72	32M[ts]64

Dynamic RAM (DRAM) SIMMs and DIMMs of each type and capacity are available in different speed ratings. SIMMs have been available in many different speed ratings, ranging from 120ns for some of the slowest to 50ns for some of the fastest. DIMMs are available in speeds from 60ns to 10ns or faster. Many of the first systems to use SIMMs used versions rated at 120ns. These were quickly replaced in the market by 100ns and even faster versions. Today, you generally purchase EDO SIMMs rated at 60ns and SDRAM DIMMs rated at 10ns. Both faster and slower ones are available, but they are not frequently required and are difficult to obtain.

If a system requires a specific speed, you can almost always substitute faster speeds if the one specified is not available. There are no problems in mixing SIMM speeds, as long as you use SIMMs equal to or faster than the system requires. Because often there's very little price difference between the different speeds, I usually buy faster SIMMs than are needed for a particular application. This may make them more usable in a future system that may require the faster speed.

Note

Most DIMMs are Synchronous DRAM (SDRAM) memory, which means they deliver data in very high-speed bursts using a clocked interface. SDRAM supports bus speeds of up to 100MHz, with data transfer rates of up to 200MHz possible in the future.

Several variations on the 30-pin SIMMs can affect how they work (if at all) in a particular system. First, there are actually two variations on the pinout configurations. Most systems use a *generic* type of SIMM, which has an industry-standard pin configuration. Many older IBM systems used a slightly modified 30-pin SIMM, starting with the XT-286, introduced in 1986, through the PS/2 Model 25, 30, 50, and 60. These systems require a SIMM with different signals on five of the pins. These are known as *IBM-style* 30-pin SIMMs. You can modify a generic 30-pin SIMM to work in the IBM systems and vice versa, but purchasing a SIMM with the correct pinouts is much easier. Be sure you tell the SIMM vendor if you need the specific IBM-style versions.

Another issue concerning the 30-pin SIMM is the chip count. The SIMM itself acts as if it were a single chip, eight bits wide (with optional parity), and it really does not matter how this total is derived. Older SIMMs were constructed with eight or nine individual one-bit-wide chips to make up the module, whereas many newer SIMMs use two four-bit-wide chips and, optionally, one one-bit-wide chip for parity, making a total of two or three chips on the SIMM. Accessing the two or three-chip SIMMs can require adjustments to the refresh timing circuits on the motherboard, and many older 386 and 486 motherboards could not cope. Most newer motherboards automatically handle the slightly different refresh timing of both the 2/3-chip or 8/9-chip SIMMs, and in this case the 2/3-chip versions are more reliable, use less power, and generally cost less as well. If you have an older system, most likely it will also work with the 2/3-chip SIMMs, but some do not. Unfortunately, the only way to know is to try them. To prevent the additional time required to change them for 8/9-chip versions if the 2/3-chip versions don't work in an older system, it seems wise to stick with the 8/9-chip variety in any older systems.

The 72-pin SIMMs do not have different pinouts and are differentiated only by capacity and speed. These SIMMs are not affected by the number of chips on them. The 72-pin SIMMs are ideal for 32-bit systems like 486 machines because they comprise an entire bank of memory (32 data bits plus four parity bits). When you configure a 32-bit (486) system that uses 72-pin SIMMs, you can usually add or remove memory as single SIMM modules (except on systems that use interleaved memory schemes to reduce wait states). This is because a 32-bit chip like a 486 reads and writes banks of memory 32 bits wide, and a 72-pin SIMM is exactly 32 bits wide (36 bits with optional parity).

In 64-bit systems—which includes any Pentium or newer processor—72-pin SIMMs must be used in pairs to fill a single bank. A few motherboard manufacturers offer so-called "SIMM-saver" motherboards that are designed for newer Pentium processors, but have both 72- and 30-pin SIMM sockets. Although this is not the most desirable arrangement, it allows users on a budget to reuse their old 30-pin SIMMs. In this situation, eight 30-pin SIMMs can be used at a time to fill one bank. Alternatively, you could pair four 30-pin SIMMs with one 72-pin SIMM to create one bank. This really is not a very efficient setup because it consumes large amounts of space on the motherboard.

Other available options are SIMM stackers and converters. These items allow you to use 30-pin SIMMs in 72-pin sockets, thereby saving you the expense of scrapping all those old 30-pin SIMMs you have lying around. Again, such adapters can cause problems—especially if overhead clearance is tight—so investigate carefully before you buy. With the falling prices of SIMMs today, you are probably better off staying with 72-pin SIMMs and 168-pin DIMMs.

Remember that some older, high-performance 486 systems use interleaved memory to reduce wait states. This requires a multiple of two 72-pin (36-bit or 32-bit) SIMMs because interleaved memory access is alternated between the SIMMs to improve performance. Thus, a 32-bit processor ends up using two 32-bit banks together in an alternating fashion.

> **Note**
>
> A *bank* is the smallest amount of memory that can be addressed by the processor at one time, and usually corresponds to the data bus width of the processor. If the memory is interleaved, a virtual bank may be twice the absolute data bus width of the processor.

You cannot always replace a SIMM with a greater-capacity unit and expect it to work. Systems may have specific design limitations as to the maximum capacity of SIMM they will take. A larger-capacity SIMM works only if the motherboard is designed to accept it in the first place. Consult your system documentation to determine the correct capacity and speed to use.

SIMMs were designed to eliminate *chip creep*, which occurs when a chip works its way out of its socket. Chip creep is caused by the normal thermal expansion and contraction from powering a system on and off. Eventually, chip creep leads to poor contact between the chip leads and the socket, and memory errors and problems begin.

The original solution for chip creep was to solder all the memory chips to the printed circuit board. This approach was impractical, however. Memory chips fail more frequently than most other types of chips, and soldering chips to the board made the units difficult to service.

The SIMM/DIMM is the best compromise between socketed and soldered chips. The chips are soldered to the module, but you can replace the socketed module easily. In addition, the SIMM/DIMM is held tight to the motherboard by a locking mechanism that does not work loose due to contraction and expansion, but is easy for you to loosen manually. This solution is a good one, but it can increase repair costs. You must replace what amounts to, in some cases, an entire bank rather than one defective chip.

All systems on the market today use SIMMs, and many use DIMMs. Even Apple Macintosh systems use SIMMs and DIMMs. The SIMM/DIMM is not a proprietary memory system but rather an industry-standard device. As mentioned, some SIMMs have slightly different pinouts and specifications other than speed and capacity, so be sure that you obtain the correct SIMMs for your system.

Memory Banks

Memory chips are organized in banks on motherboards and memory cards. You should know the memory bank layout and position on the motherboard and memory cards when you're adding memory to the system. In addition, memory diagnostics report error locations by byte and bit addresses, and you must use these numbers to locate which bank in your system contains the problem.

The banks usually correspond to the data bus capacity of the system's microprocessor. Table 1.7 shows the widths of individual banks based on the type of PC.

Table 1.7 Memory bank widths on different systems.

Processor	Data Bus	Memory Bank Size (No Parity)	Memory Bank Size (Parity)	30-pin SIMMS per Bank	72-pin SIMMs Per Bank	168-pin DIMMs per Bank
8088	8-bit	8-bits	9-bits	1	N/A	N/A
8086	16-bit	16-bits	18-bits	2	N/A	N/A
286	16-bit	16-bits	18-bits	2	N/A	N/A
386SX, SL, SLC	16-bit	16-bits	18-bits	2	N/A	N/A
386DX	32-bit	32-bits	36-bits	4	1	N/A
486SLC, SLC2	16-bit	16-bits	18-bits	2	N/A	N/A
486SX, DX,DX2,DX4	32-bit	32-bits	36-bits	4	1	N/A
Pentium	64-bit	64-bits	72-bits	8	2	1
Pentium Pro, PII	64-bit	64-bits	72-bits	8	2	1

The number of bits for each bank can be made up of single chips, SIMMs, or DIMMs. For example, in a 486 system that would use a 32-bit bank, you could make up a bank of 32 individual one-bit-wide chips, or you could use eight individual four-bit-wide chips to make up the data bits. If the system uses parity, four extra bits are required (36 bits total), so you would see one more four-bit-wide or four individual one-bit-wide chips added to the bank for the parity bits.

All the SIMMs in a single bank must be the same size and type. As you can see, the 30-pin SIMMs are less than ideal for 64-bit systems such as Pentiums because you must use them in increments of eight per bank! Because these SIMMs are available in 1MB, 4MB, and 16MB capacities today, a single bank has to be 8MB, 32MB, or 128MB of memory, with no in-between amounts. Using 30-pin SIMMs in 32- and 64-bit systems artificially constrains memory configurations, and such systems are not recommended. If a 32-bit system (such as any PC with a 486 processor) uses 72-pin SIMMs, each SIMM represents a separate bank, and the SIMMs can be added or removed on an individual basis rather than in groups of four, as would be required with 30-pin SIMMs. This makes memory configuration much easier and more flexible. In modern 64-bit systems that use SIMMs, two 72-pin SIMMs are required per bank.

The physical orientation used on a motherboard or memory card is arbitrary and determined by the board's designers. Documentation covering your system or card comes in very handy. You can determine the layout of a motherboard or adapter card through testing, but this takes time and may be difficult, particularly after you have a problem with a system.

Processor Specifications

Many confusing specifications are quoted in discussions of processors. Processors can be identified by two main parameters: how *wide* they are and how *fast* they are. The speed of a processor is a fairly simple concept. Speed is counted in MHz, or megahertz, which means millions of cycles per second. Faster is better! The width of a processor is a little more complicated to discuss because there are three main specifications in a processor that are expressed in width. They are:

- Data input and output bus
- Internal registers
- Memory address bus

Table 1.8 lists the primary specifications for the Intel family of processors used in IBM and compatible PCs.

Table 1.8 Intel processor specifications.

Processor	CPU Clock	Voltage	Internal Register Size	Data Bus Width	Address Bus Width	Max. Memory	Integral (L1) Cache	L1 Cache Type	Integral FPU	No. of Transis
8088	1x	5v	16-bit	8-bit	20-bit	1MB	No	-	No	29,000
8086	1x	5v	16-bit	16-bit	20-bit	1MB	No	-	No	29,000
286	1x	5v	16-bit	16-bit	24-bit	16MB	No	-	No	134,000
386SX	1x	5v	32-bit	16-bit	24-bit	16MB	No	-	No	275,000
386SL	1x	3.3v	32-bit	16-bit	24-bit	16MB	0KB*	WT	No	855,000
386DX	1x	5v	32-bit	32-bit	32-bit	4GB	No	-	No	275,000
486SX	1x	5v	32-bit	32-bit	32-bit	4GB	8KB	WT	No	1,185,00
486SX2	2x	5v	32-bit	32-bit	32-bit	4GB	8KB	WT	No	1,185,00

Table 1.8 Intel processor specifications (continued).

Processor	CPU Clock	Voltage	Internal Register Size	Data Bus Width	Address Bus Width	Max. Memory	Integral (L1) Cache	L1 Cache Type	Integral FPU	No. of Transistors
487SX	1x	5v	32-bit	32-bit	32-bit	4GB	8KB	WT	Yes	1,200,000
486DX	1x	5v	32-bit	32-bit	32-bit	4GB	8KB	WT	Yes	1,200,000
486SL**	1x	3.3v	32-bit	32-bit	32-bit	4GB	8KB	WT	Opt.	1,400,000
486DX2	2x	5v	32-bit	32-bit	32-bit	4GB	8KB	WT	Yes	1,100,000
486DX4	2-3x	3.3v	32-bit	32-bit	32-bit	4GB	16KB	WT	Yes	1,600,000
486Pentium OD	2.5x	5v	32-bit	32-bit	32-bit	4GB	2x16KB	WB	Yes	3,100,000
Pentium 60/66	1x	5v	32-bit	64-bit	32-bit	4GB	2x8KB	WB	Yes	3,100,000
Pentium 75-200	1.5-3x	3.3v***	32-bit	64-bit	32-bit	4GB	2x8KB	WB	Yes	3,300,000
Pentium MMX	1.5-3x	2.5-2.8v	32-bit	64-bit	32-bit	4GB	2x16KB	WB	Yes	4,100,000
Pentium Pro	2-3x	3.3v	32-bit	64-bit	36-bit	64GB	2x8KB	WB	Yes	5,500,000
Pentium II MMX	3.5-5x	2.8v	32-bit	64-bit	36-bit	64GB	2x16KB	WB	Yes	7,500,000

```
FPU = Floating-point unit (internal math coprocessor)
WT = Write-through cache (caches reads only)
WB = Write-back cache (caches both reads and writes)
Note that the Pentium Pro processor includes 256KB, 512KB, or
1MB of full core speed L2 cache in a separate die within the
chip.
Note that the Pentium II processor includes 512KB of 1/2 core
speed L2 cache on the processor card.
The transistor count figures do not include the optional 256KB
or 512KB Level 2 cache that's built into the Pentium Pro and
Pentium II CPU packages. The L2 cache contains an additional
15.5 (256KB), 31 (512KB), or 62 million (1MB) transistors!
* The 386SL contains an integral-cache controller, but the
cache memory must be provided outside the chip.
** Intel later marketed SL Enhanced versions of the SX, DX,
and DX2 processors. These processors were available in both 5v
and 3.3v versions and included power-management capabilities.
*** There are several different voltage variations of Pentium
processors, including what Intel calls VRE (3.5v), STD (3.3v),
and newer 3.1v, 2.8v, 2.5v, 2.1v, and 1.8v versions.
```

Processor Memory Addressing Limits

In addition to evolving to higher speeds, newer processors can address much more memory than older processors. Computers use the binary (base 2) numbering system, so a two-digit number provides only four unique addresses (00, 01, 10, and 11) calculated as 2 to the power of 2; and a three-digit number provides only eight addresses (000 to 111), which is 2 to the 3rd power. For example, the 8086 and 8088 processors use a 20-bit address bus that calculates as a maximum of 2 to the 20th power or 1,048,576 bytes (1MB) of address locations. Table 1.9 describes the memory-addressing capabilities of Intel processors.

32 Motherboards

Table 1.9 Intel processor memory-addressing capabilities.

Processor Family	Address Bus	Bytes	Kilobytes	Megabytes	Gigabytes
8088/8086	20-bit	1,048,576	1,024	1	-
286/386SX	24-bit	16,777,216	16,384	16	-
386DX/486/Pentium	32-bit	4,294,967,296	4,194,304	4,096	4
Pentium Pro/II	36-bit	68,719,476,736	67,108,864	65,536	64

Processor Speed Ratings

A common source of misunderstanding about processors is their different speed ratings. This section covers processor speed in general and then provides more specific information about Intel processors.

A single cycle is the smallest element of time for the processor. Every action requires at least one cycle, and usually more. To transfer data to and from memory, for example, a modern processor such as the Pentium II needs a minimum of three cycles to set up the first memory transfer, and then only a single cycle per transfer for the next three to six consecutive transfers. The extra cycles on the first transfer are normally called wait states. A *wait state* is a clock tick in which nothing happens, to ensure that the processor isn't getting ahead of the rest of the computer.

The time required to execute instructions also varies. The original 8086 and 8088 processors take an average of 12 cycles to execute a single instruction. The 286 and 386 processors improve this rate to about 4.5 cycles per instruction. The 486 drops the rate further to two cycles per instruction, or one instruction every cycle in clock multiplied versions (DX2, DX4). The Pentium includes twin instruction pipelines and other improvements that provide for operation at two instructions per cycle, while the Pentium Pro and Pentium II can execute as many as three or more instructions per cycle.

Different instruction execution times (in cycles) make it difficult to compare systems based purely on clock speed, or number of cycles per second. A 400MHz Pentium II is about equal to a 600MHz Pentium, which is about equal to a 1200MHz 486, which is about equal to a 2400MHz 386 or 286, which is about equal to a 4800MHz 8088! Considering that the original PC's 8088 ran at only 4.77MHz, we have systems today that are more than 1,000 times faster. As you can see, you have to be careful in comparing systems based on pure MHz alone; many other factors affect system performance.

How can two processors that run at the same clock rate perform differently, with one running "faster" than the other? The answer is simple: efficiency.

Intel has devised a specific series of benchmarks, called the iCOMP 2.0 (Intel Comparative Microprocessor Performance) index, that can be run against Intel chips to produce a relative gauge of performance. It has recently been updated to reflect performance on 32-bit systems. Table 1.10 shows the relative power, or iCOMP 2.0 index, for several processors.

Table 1.10 Intel iCOMP 2.0 index ratings.

Processor	iCOMP 2.0 Index
Pentium 75	67
Pentium 100	90

Table 1.10 Intel iCOMP 2.0 index ratings (continued).

Processor	iCOMP 2.0 Index
Pentium 120	100
Pentium 133	111
Pentium 150	114
Pentium 166	127
Pentium 200	142
Pentium-MMX 166	160
Pentium-MMX 200	182
Pentium-MMX 233	203
Pentium Pro 180	197
Pentium Pro 200	220
Pentium II 233	267
Pentium II 266	303
Pentium II 300	332
Pentium II 333	366

The iCOMP 2.0 index is derived from several independent benchmarks and is a stable indication of relative processor performance. The benchmarks balance integer with floating point and multimedia performance.

Modern systems use a variable frequency synthesizer circuit, usually found in the main motherboard chipset, to control the motherboard speed and CPU speed. Most Pentium motherboards will have three or four speed settings. The processors used today are available in a variety of versions that run at different frequencies based on a given motherboard speed. For example, most of the Pentium chips run at a speed that is some multiple of the true motherboard speed, as shown in Table 1.11.

Table 1.11 Intel processor and motherboard speeds.

CPU Type/Speed	CPU Clock	Motherboard Speed
Pentium 60	1x	60
Pentium 66	1x	66
Pentium 75	1.5x	50
Pentium 90	1.5x	60
Pentium 100	1.5x	66
Pentium 120	2x	60
Pentium 133	2x	66
Pentium 150	2.5x	60
Pentium/Pentium Pro/MMX 166	2.5x	66

Table 1.11 Intel processor and motherboard speeds (continued).

CPU Type/Speed	CPU Clock	Motherboard Speed
Pentium/Pentium Pro 180	3x	60
Pentium/Pentium Pro/MMX 200	3x	66
Pentium-MMX/Pentium II 233	3.5x	66
Pentium II 266	4x	66
Pentium II 300	4.5x	66
Pentium II 333	5x	66
Pentium II 350	3.5x	100
Pentium II 400	4x	100
Pentium II 450	4.5x	100

If all other variables are equal—including the type of processor, the number of wait states (empty cycles) added to different types of memory accesses, and the width of the data bus—you can compare two systems by their respective clock rates. However, the construction and design of the memory subsystem can have an enormous effect on a system's final execution speed.

When building a processor, a manufacturer tests it at different speeds, temperatures, and pressures. After the processor is tested, it receives a stamp indicating the maximum safe speed at which it will operate under the wide variation of temperatures and pressures encountered in normal operation. The rating system is usually simple. For example, the top of the processor in one of my systems is marked like this:

   A80486DX2-66

The *A* is Intel's indicator that this chip has a Ceramic Pin Grid Array form factor, or an indication of the physical packaging of the chip. The *80486DX2* is the part number, which identifies this processor as a clock-doubled 486DX processor. The *-66* at the end indicates that this chip is rated to run at a maximum speed of 66MHz. Because of the clock doubling, the maximum motherboard speed is 33MHz. This chip would be acceptable for any application in which the chip runs at 66MHz or slower. For example, you could use this processor in a system with a 25MHz motherboard, in which case the processor would happily run at 50MHz.

Most 486 motherboards also have a 40MHz setting, so the DX2 would run at 80MHz internally. Because this is 14MHz beyond its rated speed, many motherboards would not work; or if they worked at all, it would only be for a short time. On the other hand, I have found that most of the newer chips marked with -66 ratings seem to run fine (albeit somewhat hotter!) at the 40/80MHz settings. This is called *overclocking*, and can end up being a simple, cost-effective way to speed up your system. However, I would not recommend this for mission-critical applications where the system reliability is of the utmost importance, because a system pushed beyond specification like this can often exhibit erratic behavior under stress.

Sometimes, however, the markings don't seem to indicate the speed directly. In the older 8086, for example, *-3* translates to 6MHz operation. This marking scheme is more common in some of the older chips that were manufactured before some of the marking standards used today were standardized.

A more modern example would be the Cyrix/IBM 6x86 processors, which use a *PR (Performance Rating)* scale that is not equal to the true clock speed in MHz. For example, the Cyrix/IBM 6x86MX-PR200 actually runs at 166MHz (2.5 x 66MHz)! This is a little misleading because you must set up the motherboard as if a 166MHz processor were being installed, not the 200MHz you might think by virtue of the product markings.

A manufacturer sometimes places the CPU under a *heat sink* (a metal device that draws heat away from an electronic device), which can prevent you from reading the rating printed on the chip. Fortunately, most CPU manufacturers are placing marks on both the top and bottom of the processor. If the heat sink is difficult to remove from the chip, you can take the heat sink and chip out of the socket together and read the markings on the bottom of the processor to determine what you have. Most processors running at 50MHz and higher should have a heat sink installed to prevent the processor from overheating.

Processor Sockets

Intel has created a set of socket designs, named Socket 1 through Socket 8, used for their chips from the 486 through the Pentium Pro. Each socket is designed to support a different range of original and upgrade processors. Table 1.12 shows the specifications of these sockets.

Table 1.12 Intel 486/Pentium CPU socket types and specifications.

Socket #	# of Pins	Pin Layout	Voltage	Supported Processors
Socket 1	169	17x17 PGA	5v	SX/SX2, DX/DX2*, DX4 OverDrive
Socket 2	238	19x19 PGA	5v	SX/SX2, DX/DX2*, DX4 OverDrive, 486 Pentium OverDrive
Socket 3	237	19x19 PGA	5v/3.3v	SX/SX2, DX/DX2, DX4, 486 Pentium OverDrive
Socket 4	273	21x21 PGA	5v	Pentium 60/66, Pentium 60/66 OverDrive
Socket 5	320	37x37 SPGA	3.3v	Pentium 75-133, Pentium 75+ OverDrive
Socket 6**	235	19x19 PGA	3.3v	DX4, 486 Pentium OverDrive
Socket 7	321	37x37 SPGA	VRM	Pentium 75-233, Pentium 75+ OverDrive
Socket 8	387	dual pattern SPGA	VRM	Pentium Pro

*DX4 also can be supported with the addition of an aftermarket 3.3v voltage-regulator adapter.
**Socket 6 was a paper standard only and was never actually implemented in any systems.
PGA = Pin Grid Array
SPGA = Staggered Pin Grid Array
VRM = Voltage Regulator Module

36 Motherboards

Sockets 1, 2, 3, and 6 are 486 processor sockets, and are shown together in Figure 1.10 so you can see the overall size comparisons and pin arrangements between these sockets. Sockets 4, 5, 7, and 8 are Pentium and Pentium Pro processor sockets, and are also shown together in Figure 1.11 so you can see the overall size comparisons and the pin arrangements between these sockets.

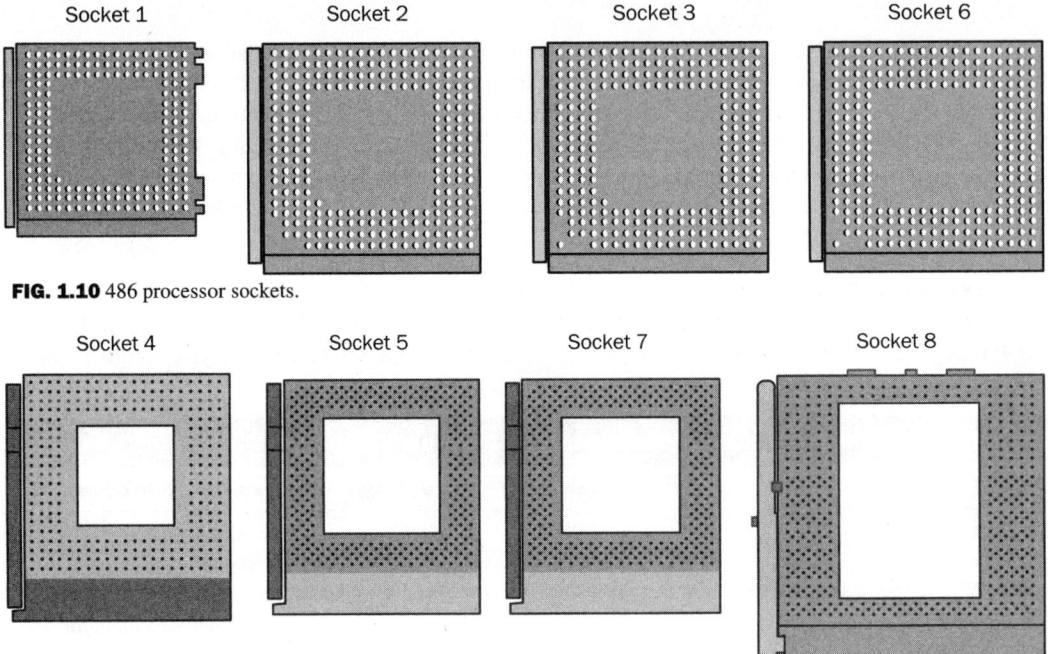

FIG. 1.10 486 processor sockets.

FIG. 1.11 Pentium and Pentium Pro processor sockets.

The original OverDrive socket, now officially called Socket 1, is a 169-pin PGA socket. Motherboards that have this socket can support any of the 486SX, DX, and DX2 processors, as well as the DX2/OverDrive versions. This type of socket is found on most 486 systems that originally were designed for OverDrive upgrades.

Intel's Pentium OverDrive Processors for 486-based machines plug into a processor sockets with the Socket 2 or Socket 3 design. These sockets will hold any 486 SX, DX, or DX2 processor, as well as the Pentium OverDrive. Intel released the design of Socket 2 a little prematurely and found that the chip ran too hot for many systems. The company solved this problem by adding a special active heat sink to the Pentium OverDrive processor. This active heat sink is a standard heat sink with a built-in electric fan. Unlike the aftermarket glue-on or clip-on fans for processors that you may have seen, this one actually draws 5v power directly from the socket. No external connection to disk drive cables or the power supply is required. The fan/heat sink assembly clips and plugs directly into the processor, providing for easy replacement if the fan ever fails.

Another requirement of the active heat sink is additional clearance—no obstructions for an area about 1.4 inches off the base of the existing socket. In systems that were not designed with this feature, the Pentium OverDrive upgrade will be difficult or impossible.

Another problem with this particular upgrade is power consumption. The 5v Pentium OverDrive processor will draw up to 2.5 amps at 5v (including the fan), or 12.5 watts, which is more than double the 1.2 amps (6 watts) drawn by the DX2 66 processor. Intel did not provide this information when it established the socket design, so the company set up a testing facility to certify systems for thermal and mechanical compatibility with the Pentium OverDrive upgrade. For the greatest peace of mind, ensure that your system is certified compatible before you attempt this upgrade.

Because of problems with the original Socket 2 specification and the enormous amount of heat the 5v version of the Pentium OverDrive processor generates, Intel came up with an improved design. The new processor is the same as the previous Pentium OverDrive processor, except that it runs on 3.3v and draws a maximum 3.0 amps of 3.3v (9.9 watts) and 0.2 amp of 5v (1 watt) to run the fan, for a total of 10.9 watts. This configuration provides a slight improvement over the 5v version of this processor. The fan will be easy to remove from the OverDrive processor for replacement, if it ever fails.

To support both the DX4 processor, which runs on 3.3v, and the 3.3v Pentium OverDrive processor, Intel had to create a new socket. In addition to the new 3.3v chips, this new socket supports the older 5v SX, DX, DX2, and even the 5v Pentium OverDrive chip. The design, called Socket 3, is the most flexible upgradable 486 design.

Socket 3 has one additional pin and several others plugged compared with Socket 2. Socket 3 provides for better keying, which prevents an end user from accidentally installing the processor in an improper orientation. One serious problem exists, however: This socket cannot automatically determine the type of voltage that will be provided to it. A jumper is likely to be added on the motherboard near the socket to enable the user to select 5v or 3.3v operation.

> **Caution**
>
> Because this jumper must be manually set, however, a user could install a 3.3v processor in this socket when it is configured for 5v operation. This installation will instantly destroy a very expensive chip when the system is powered on. It will be up to the end user to make sure that this socket is properly configured for voltage, depending on which type of processor is installed. If the jumper is set in 3.3v configuration and a 5v processor is installed, no harm will occur, but the system will not operate properly unless the jumper is reset for 5v.

The original Pentium processor 60MHz and 66MHz versions had 273 pins and would plug into a 273-pin Pentium processor socket—a 5v-only socket, because all the original Pentium processors run on 5v. This socket (Socket 4) will accept the original Pentium 60MHz or 66MHz processor, as well as the OverDrive processor.

Although both processors will run on 5v, the original Pentium processor was created with a circuit size of 0.8 micron, making that processor much more power-hungry than the newer 0.6-micron circuits used in the OverDrive and the other Pentium processors. Shrinking the circuit size is one of the best ways to decrease power consumption. Although the OverDrive processor for Pentium-based systems indeed will draw less power than the original processor, additional clearance may have to be allowed for the active heat sink (fan) assembly that is mounted on top. As in other OverDrive processors with built-in fans, the power to run the fan will be drawn directly from the chip socket, so no separate power-supply connection is required. Also, the fan will be easy to replace if it ever fails.

When Intel redesigned the Pentium processor to run at 75, 90, and 100MHz, the company went to a 0.6-micron manufacturing process as well as 3.3v operation. This change resulted in lower power

38 Motherboards

consumption: only 3.25 amps at 3.3v (10.725 watts). Therefore, the 100MHz Pentium processor can use far less power than even the original 60MHz version. The newest 120MHz and higher Pentium, Pentium Pro, and Pentium II chips use an even smaller die 0.35-micron process. This results in even lower power consumption and allows extremely high clock rates without overheating.

The Pentium 75 and higher processors actually have 296 pins, although they plug into the official Intel Socket 5 design, which calls for a total 320 pins. The additional pins are used by the Pentium OverDrive for Pentium Processors. This socket has the 320 pins configured in a Staggered Pin Grid Array, in which the individual pins are staggered for tighter clearance.

Several OverDrive processors for existing Pentiums are currently available. If you have a first-generation Pentium 60 or 66 with a Socket 4, you can purchase a standard Pentium OverDrive chip that effectively doubles the speed of your old processor. For second-generation 75MHz, 90MHz, and 100MHz Pentiums using Socket 5 or Socket 7, an OverDrive chip with MMX technology is available. Processor speeds after the upgrade are 125MHz for the Pentium 75, 150MHz for the Pentium 90, and 166MHz for the Pentium 100.

The Pentium OverDrive for Pentium Processors has an active heat sink assembly that draws power directly from the chip socket. The chip requires a maximum of 4.33 amps at 3.3v to run the chip (14.289 watts) and 0.2 amp at 5v to run the fan (1 watt), which adds up to a total power consumption of 15.289 watts. This is less power than the original 66MHz Pentium processor requires, yet it runs a chip that is as much as four times faster!

The last 486 socket was created especially for the DX4 and the 486 Pentium OverDrive processor. Socket 6 is a slightly redesigned version of Socket 3, with an additional two pins plugged for proper chip keying. Socket 6 has 235 pins and will accept only 3.3v 486 or OverDrive processors. This means that Socket 6 will accept only the DX4 and the 486 Pentium OverDrive processor. Because this socket provides only 3.3v, and because the only processors that plug into it are designed to operate on 3.3v, there's no chance that potentially damaging problems will occur, like those with the Socket 3 design. Socket 6 has seen very limited use.

Socket 7 is essentially the same as Socket 5, with one additional key pin in the opposite inside corner of the existing key pin. Socket 7 therefore has 321 pins total in a 21x21 SPGA (Staggered Pin Grid Array) arrangement. The real difference with Socket 7 is not the socket itself, but the companion *VRM (Voltage Regulator Module)* that must accompany it.

The VRM is a small circuit board that contains all the voltage regulation circuitry used to drop the 5v power supply signal to the correct voltage for the processor. The VRM was implemented for several good reasons. One is that voltage regulators tend to run hot and are very failure-prone. If these circuits are soldered onto the motherboard, as has been done with the Pentium Socket 5 design, it's very likely that a failure of the regulator will require a complete motherboard replacement. Although technically the regulator could be replaced, many of them are surface-mount-soldered, which would make the whole procedure very time-consuming and expensive. Besides, in this day and age, when the top-of-the-line motherboards are only worth $250 (less the processor and any memory), it's not cost-effective to service them. Having a replaceable VRM plugged into a socket will make it easy to replace the regulators if they ever fail.

Although replaceability is nice, the main reason behind the VRM design is that Intel is building new Pentium processors to run at a variety of voltages. Intel has several different versions of the Pentium,

Pentium-MMX, Pentium Pro, and Pentium II processors that run at 3.3v (called *VR*) and 3.465v (called *VRE*), as well as 3.1v, 2.8v, and 2.45v.

In other words, if you want to purchase a Pentium board that can be upgraded to the next generation of even higher-speed processors—and that is easily repairable if the voltage regulators fail—look for a system with a Socket 7 and VRM.

SEC Abandoning the chip-in-a-socket approach used by virtually all processors up until this point, the Pentium II chip is characterized by its *Single Edge Contact (SEC)* cartridge design. The processor, along with several L2 cache chips, is mounted on a small circuit board (much like an oversized memory SIMM), which is then sealed in a metal-and-plastic cartridge. The cartridge is then plugged into the motherboard through an edge connector called Slot 1, which looks very much like an adapter card slot.

Slot 1 is the connection to the motherboard, and has 242 pins. The SEC cartridge processor is plugged into slot 1 and secured with a *processor retention mechanism*, which is just a fancy name for a bracket to hold it in place. There may also be a retention mechanism or support for the processor heat sink as well.

The main reason for going to this package was to be able to move the L2 cache memory off the motherboard and onto the processor in an economical and scaleable way. Using the SEC design, Intel can easily offer Pentium II processors with more or less cache and a faster or slower cache as well.

Motherboard Interface Connectors

There are a variety of different connectors on a modern motherboard. Tables 1.13 through 1.22 contain the pinouts of most of the different interface and I/O connectors you will find.

Table 1.13 ATX motherboard power connector.

Pin	Signal Name
1	+3.3 V
2	+3.3 V
3	Ground
4	+5 V
5	Ground
6	+5 V
7	Ground
8	PWRGD (Power Good)
9	+5 VSB (Standby)
10	+12 V
11	+3.3 V
12	-12 V
13	Ground

Table 1.13 ATX motherboard power connector (continued).

Pin	Signal Name
14	PS-ON# (Power Supply Remote On/Off Control)
15	Ground
16	Ground
17	Ground
18	-5 V
19	+5 V
20	+5 V

Table 1.14 Baby-AT motherboard power connectors.

Pin	Name
1	PWRGD (Power Good)
2	+5 V
3	+12 V
4	-12 V
5	Ground
6	Ground
7	Ground
8	Ground
9	-5 V
10	+5 V
11	+5 V
12	+5 V

Table 1.15 Serial port pin-header connectors.

Pin	Signal Name
1	DCD
2	DSR
3	Serial In—(SIN)
4	RTS
5	Serial Out—(SOUT)
6	CTS
7	DTR
8	RI
9	GND
10	Not Connected

Table 1.16 Parallel port pin-header connector.

Signal Name	Pin	Pin	Signal Name
STROBE-	1	2	AUTO FEED-
Data Bit 0	3	4	ERROR-
Data Bit 1	5	6	INIT-
Data Bit 2	7	8	SLCT IN-
Data Bit 3	9	10	Ground
Data Bit 4	11	12	Ground
Data Bit 5	13	14	Ground
Data Bit 6	15	16	Ground
Data Bit 7	17	18	Ground
ACJ-	19	20	Ground
BUSY	21	22	Ground
PE (Paper End)	23	24	Ground
SLCT	25	26	N/C

Table 1.17 Motherboard mouse pin-header connector.

Pin	Signal
1	Gnd
2	Data
3	N/C
4	Vcc
5	CLK
6	KEY
7	KEY
8	N/C

Table 1.18 Infrared Data (IrDA) pin-header connector.

Pin	Signal Name
1	+5 V
2	Key
3	IrRX
4	Ground
5	IrTX
6	CONIR (Consumer IR)

Table 1.19 Battery connector.

Pin	Signal
1	Gnd
2	Unused
3	KEY
4	+6v

Table 1.20 LED and keylock connector.

Pin	Signal
1	LED Power (+5v)
2	KEY
3	Gnd
4	Keyboard Inhibit
5	Gnd

Table 1.21 Speaker connector.

Pin	Signal
1	Ground
2	KEY
3	Board-Mounted Speaker
4	Speaker Output

Table 1.22 Microprocessor fan power connector.

Pin	Signal Name
1	Ground
2	+12V
3	Sense tachometer

Caution

Do not place a jumper on this connector; serious board damage will result if the 12v is shorted to ground.

Note that some boards have a board-mounted piezo speaker. It is enabled by placing a jumper over pins 3 and 4, which routes the speaker output to the board-mounted speaker. Removing the jumper allows a conventional speaker to be plugged in.

Motherboard CMOS RAM Addresses

Table 1.23 shows the information maintained in the 64-byte standard CMOS RAM module. This information controls the configuration of the system and is read and written by the system Setup program.

In the original AT system, a Motorola 146818 chip was used. Modern systems incorporate the CMOS into the chipset or Super I/O chip, or use a special battery and *NVRAM (Non-Volatile RAM)* module from companies like Dallas or Benchmarq. The standard format of the information stored in the CMOS RAM is shown in Table 1.23.

Table 1.23 AT CMOS RAM addresses.

Offset Hex	Offset Dec	Field Size	Function
00h	0	1 byte	Current second in binary coded decimal (BCD)
01h	1	1 byte	Alarm second in BCD
02h	2	1 byte	Current minute in BCD
03h	3	1 byte	Alarm minute in BCD
04h	4	1 byte	Current hour in BCD
05h	5	1 byte	Alarm hour in BCD
06h	6	1 byte	Current day of week in BCD
07h	7	1 byte	Current day in BCD
08h	8	1 byte	Current month in BCD
09h	9	1 byte	Current year in BCD

0Ah	10	1 byte	Status register A
			  Bit 7 = Update in progress
			    0 = Date and time can be read
			    1 = Time update in progress
			  Bits 6[nd]4 = Time frequency divider
			    010 = 32.768KHz
			  Bits 3[nd]0 = Rate selection frequency
			    0110 = 1.024KHz square wave frequency

0Bh	11	1 byte	Status register B
			  Bit 7 = Clock update cycle
			    0 = Update normally
			    1 = Abort update in progress
			  Bit 6 = Periodic interrupt
			    0 = Disable interrupt (default)
			    1 = Enable interrupt
			  Bit 5 = Alarm interrupt
			    0 = Disable interrupt (default)
			    0 = Disable interrupt (default)
			    1 = Enable interrupt

44 Motherboards

Table 1.23 AT CMOS RAM addresses (continued).

Offset Hex	Offset Dec	Field Size	Function

			Bit 4 = Update-ended interrupt
			    0 = Disable interrupt (default)
			    1 = Enable interrupt
			Bit 3 = Status register A square wave frequency
			    0 = Disable square wave (default)
			    1 = Enable square wave
			Bit 2 = Date format
			    0 = Calendar in BCD format (default)
			    1 = Calendar in binary format
			Bit 1 = 24-hour clock
			    0 = 24-hour mode (default)
			    1 = 12-hour mode
			Bit 0 = Daylight Savings Time
			    0 = Disable Daylight Savings (default)
			    1 = Enable Daylight Savings

0Ch	12	1 byte	Status register C Bit 7 = IRQF flag Bit 6 = PF flag Bit 5 = AF flag Bit 4 = UF flag Bits 3-0 = Reserved

0Dh	13	1 byte	Status register D
			Bit 7 = Valid CMOS RAM bit
			    0 = CMOS battery dead
			    1 = CMOS battery power good
			Bits 6[nd]0 = Reserved

0Eh	14	1 byte	Diagnostic status
			Bit 7 = Real-time clock power status
			    0 = CMOS *has not* lost power
			    1 = CMOS *has* lost power
			Bit 6 = CMOS checksum status
			    0 = Checksum is good
			    1 = Checksum is bad
			Bit 5 = POST configuration information status
			    0 = Configuration information is valid
			    1 = Configuration information is invalid

Table 1.23 AT CMOS RAM addresses (continued).

Offset Hex	Offset Dec	Field Size	Function

			Bit 4 = Memory size compare during POST
			    0 = POST memory equals configuration
			    1 = POST memory *not equal* to configuration
			Bit 3 = Fixed disk/adapter initialization
			    0 = Initialization good
			    1 = Initialization failed
			Bit 2 = CMOS time status indicator
			    0 = Time is valid
			    1 = Time is Invalid
			Bits 1-0 = Reserved

0Fh	15	1 byte	Shutdown code
			    00h = Power on or soft reset
			    01h = Memory size pass
			    02h = Memory test pass
			    03h = Memory test fail
			    04h = POST end; boot system
			    05h = JMP double word pointer with EOI
			    06h = Protected mode tests pass
			    07h = Protected mode tests fail
			    07h = Protected mode tests fail
			    08h = Memory size fail
			    09h = Int 15h block move
			    0Ah = JMP double word pointer without EOI
			    0Bh = used by 80386

10h	16	1 byte	Floppy disk drive types
			    Bits 7-4 = Drive 0 type
			    Bits 3-0 = Drive 1 type
			        0000 = None
			        0001 = 360K
			        0010 = 1.2M
			        0011 = 720K
			        0100 = 1.44M

11h	17	1 byte	Reserved

12h	18	1 byte	Hard disk types
			    Bits 7[nd]4 = Hard disk 0 type (0[nd]15)
			    Bits 3[nd]0 = Hard disk 1 type (0[nd]15)

13h	19	1 byte	Reserved
14h	20	1 byte	Installed equipment

46 Motherboards

Table 1.23 AT CMOS RAM addresses (continued).

Offset Hex	Offset Dec	Field Size	Function
			Bits 7[nd]6 = Number of floppy disk drives
			00 = 1 floppy disk drive
			01 = 2 floppy disk drives
			Bits 5[nd]4 = Primary display
			00 = Use display adapter BIOS
			01 = CGA 40-column
			10 = CGA 80-column
			11 = Monochrome Display Adapter
			Bits 3[nd]2 = Reserved
			Bit 1 = Math coprocessor present
			Bit 0 = Floppy disk drive present
15h	21	1 byte	Base memory low-order byte
16h	22	1 byte	Base memory high-order byte
17h	23	1 byte	Extended memory low-order byte
18h	24	1 byte	Extended memory high-order byte
19h	25	1 byte	Hard Disk 0 Extended Type (0[nd]255)
1Ah	26	1 byte	Hard Disk 1 Extended Type (0[nd]255)
1Bh	27	9 bytes	Reserved
2Eh	46	1 byte	CMOS checksum high-order byte
2Fh	47	1 byte	CMOS checksum low-order byte
30h	48	1 byte	Actual extended memory low-order byte
31h	49	1 byte	Actual extended memory high-order byte
32h	50	1 byte	Date century in BCD
33h	51	1 byte	POST information flag
			Bit 7 = Top 128KB base memory status
			0 = Top 128KB base memory not installed
			1 = Top 128KB base memory installed
			Bit 6 = Setup program flag
			0 = Normal (default)
			1 = Put out first user message
			Bits 5[nd]0 = Reserved
34h	52	2 bytes	Reserved

Table 1.24 shows the values that may be stored by your system BIOS in a special CMOS byte called the *diagnostics status byte*. By examining this location with a diagnostics program, you can determine whether your system has set *trouble codes*, which indicate that a problem has occurred previously.

Table 1.24 CMOS RAM (AT and PS/2) diagnostic status byte codes.

Bit Number 7 6 5 4 3 2 1 0	Hex	Function
1	80	Real-time clock (RTC) chip lost power
. 1	40	CMOS RAM checksum is bad
. . 1	20	Invalid configuration information found at POST
. . . 1	10	Memory size compare error at POST
. . . . 1 . . .	08	Fixed disk or adapter failed initialization
. . . . . 1 . .	04	Real-time clock (RTC) time found invalid
. . . . . . 1 .	02	Adapters do not match configuration
. . . . 1	01	Time-out reading an adapter ID
. . . .	00	No errors found (Normal)

If the Diagnostic status byte is any value other than zero, you will normally get a CMOS configuration error on bootup. These types of errors can be cleared by rerunning the Setup program.

Chapter 2
Motherboard Settings and Specifications

Interface Connections

While the interface connections are indentified in the following figures and tables, pinouts for industry standard interface connections are not listed in these tables. Tables of pins for the following common connectors can all be found in "Motherboard Interface Connectors" in Chapter One:

- power connectors
- serial ports
- parallel ports
- mouse port
- infrared
- battery
- LED and keylock
- Speaker
- Processor fan

IDE and SCSI connector pinouts can be found in Chapter Two "Hard Disk Interfaces" of *Micro House PC Hardware Library Volume I: Hard Drives*.

Default Jumper Settings

The default or most common jumpers positions are denoted by the ⇨ symbol. Pin 1, Jumper 1, and Switch 1 are indicated by a white pin or switch where possible as shown in figure 2-1. Pin 1 or other pin numbers used for reference may be indicated by number on the motherboard diagram as well.

50 Motherboard Settings and Specifications

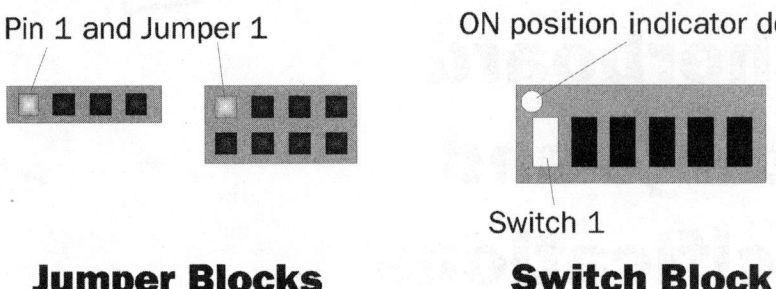

Jumper Blocks   **Switch Block**

Figure 2-1: Jumper and Switch Block Conventions

The switch's ON position is indicated by the white dot. Always verify the ON position by examining the switch on the actual hardware. When the ON position is not known to us there will be no white dot.

Undocumented Jumpers

Some jumper settings are specified as "unidentified," "factory configured – do not alter," or may have a dash. Information was not available on these jumpers or settings and their configuration should not be altered.

Board Element Naming Conventions

Whenever possible, diagrams contained in this chapter use the same jumper and switch labels as the manufacturer. If the labeling information provided by the manufacturer is unclear or not available, an alternate label standard is used. Under the alternate standard, all jumpers are labeled with the prefix "JP," while all connectors are labeled with the prefix "CN." Slots are labeled with the prefix "SL." In most cases, the jumper *numbers* remain the same as the manufacturer's labels. In the cases where the jumper numbers in this book differ from those silk-screened on the board, the settings listed are consistent with this book's diagrams. Where a whole set of jumpers are labeled with one number, we label them with that same number followed by a letter.

Motherboard Settings

The remainder of this chapter contains information on specific hardware settings for selected motherboards.

ABIT COMPUTER CORPORATION
PP6 (REV. 0.2)

Processor	Pentium Pro
Processor Speed	150/166/180/200MHz
Chip Set	Intel
Video Chip Set	None
Maximum Onboard Memory	512MB
Maximum Video Memory	None
Cache	256/512KB (located on Pentium Pro CPU)
BIOS	Award
Dimensions	330mm x 218mm
I/O Options	32-bit PCI slots (4), floppy drive interface, green PC connector, IDE interfaces (2), parallel port, PS/2 mouse port, serial ports (2), IR connector, VRM connector, USB connector
NPU Options	None

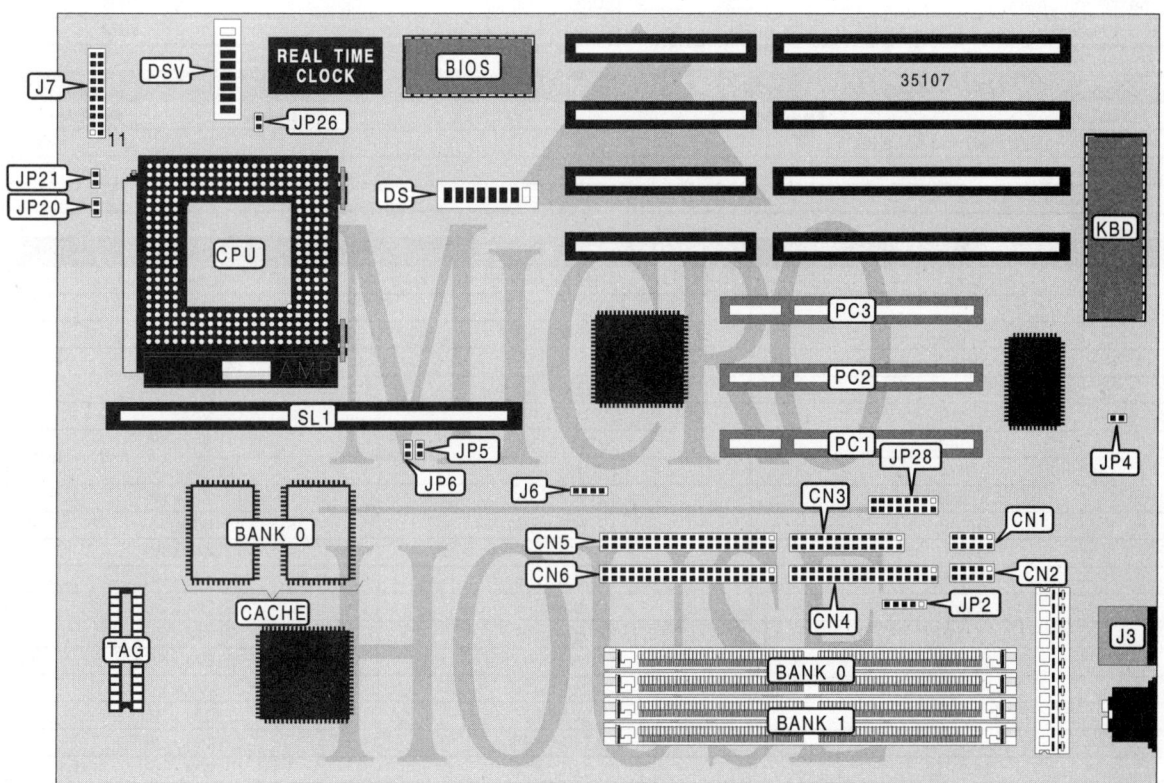

Continued on next page...

ABIT COMPUTER CORPORATION
PP6 (REV. 0.2)

...continued from previous page

CONNECTIONS

Purpose	Location	Purpose	Location
Serial port 1	CN1	Reset switch	J9 pins 1 & 2
Serial port 2	CN2	Green PC connector	J9 pins 7 & 8
Parallel port	CN3	IDE interface LED	J9 pins 9 & 10
IDE interface 1	CN4	Speaker	J9 pins 11 - 14
IDE interface 2	CN5	Power LED & keylock	J9 pins 16 - 20
Floppy drive interface	CN6	PS/2 mouse port	MS1
Chassis fan power	FAN1	32-bit PCI slots	PC1 – PC4
Chassis fan power	FAN2	USB connector	USB
IR connector	IR1	VRM connector	VRM

USER CONFIGURABLE SETTINGS

	Function	Label	Position
⇨	Factory configured - do not alter	JP5	Unidentified
⇨	CMOS memory normal operation	JP11	Open
	CMOS memory clear	JP11	Closed

DRAM CONFIGURATION

Size	Bank 0	Bank 1
8MB	(2) 1M x 36	None
16MB	(2) 2M x 36	None
16MB	(2) 1M x 36	(2) 1M x 36
24MB	(2) 2M x 36	(2) 1M x 36
32MB	(2) 4M x 36	None
32MB	(2) 2M x 36	(2) 2M x 36
40MB	(2) 4M x 36	(2) 1M x 36
48MB	(2) 4M x 36	(2) 2M x 36
64MB	(2) 8M x 36	None
64MB	(2) 4M x 36	(2) 4M x 36
72MB	(2) 8M x 36	(2) 1M x 36
80MB	(2) 8M x 36	(2) 2M x 36
96MB	(2) 8M x 36	(2) 4M x 36
128MB	(2) 8M x 36	(2) 8M x 36
128MB	(2) 16M x 36	None
136MB	(2) 16M x 36	(2) 1M x 36
144MB	(2) 16M x 36	(2) 2M x 36
160MB	(2) 16M x 36	(2) 4M x 36
192MB	(2) 16M x 36	(2) 8M x 36
256MB	(2) 16M x 36	(2) 16M x 36
256MB	(2) 32M x 36	None
512MB	(2) 32M x 36	(2) 32M x 36

Note: Board accepts EDO memory. Board also accepts x 32 SIMMs

Continued on next page...

ABIT COMPUTER CORPORATION
PP6 (REV. 0.2)

. . . continued from previous page

CACHE CONFIGURATION
Note: 256KB/512KB cache is located on the Pentium Pro CPU.

CPU SPEED SELECTION							
CPU speed	Clock speed	Multiplier	SW1/1	SW1/2	SW1/3	SW1/4
150MHz	60MHz	2.5x	Off	On	On	On
166MHz	66MHz	2.5x	Off	On	On	On
180MHz	60MHz	3x	On	Off	On	On
200MHz	66MHz	3x	On	Off	On	On

CPU SPEED SELECTION (CON'T)							
CPU speed	Clock speed	Multiplier	SW1/5	SW1/6	SW1/7	SW1/8
150MHz	60MHz	2.5x	On	Off	Off	On
166MHz	66MHz	2.5x	Off	On	On	Off
180MHz	60MHz	3x	On	Off	Off	On
200MHz	66MHz	3x	Off	On	On	Off

CPU VOLTAGE SELECTION				
Voltage	JP6/pins 1 & 2	JP6/pins 3 & 4	JP6/pins 5 & 6	JP6/pins 7 & 8
⇨ 2.0v	Open	Open	Open	Open
2.1v	Closed	Open	Open	Open
2.2v	Open	Closed	Open	Open
2.3v	Closed	Closed	Open	Open
2.4v	Open	Open	Closed	Open
2.5v	Closed	Open	Closed	Open
2.6v	Open	Closed	Closed	Open
2.7v	Closed	Closed	Closed	Open
2.8v	Open	Open	Open	Closed
2.9v	Closed	Open	Open	Closed
3.0v	Open	Closed	Open	Closed
3.1v	Closed	Closed	Open	Closed
3.2v	Open	Open	Closed	Closed
3.3v	Closed	Open	Closed	Closed
3.4v	Open	Closed	Closed	Closed
3.5v	Closed	Closed	Closed	Closed

ADVANCED INTEGRATION RESEARCH, INC.
P6KDI

Processor	Pentium II
Processor Speed	180/200/233/266MHz
Chip Set	Intel
Video Chip Set	None
Maximum Onboard Memory	1GB (EDO supported)
Maximum Video Memory	None
Cache	256/512/1024KB (located on Pentium II CPU)
BIOS	AMI
Dimensions	305mm x 244mm
I/O Options	32-bit PCI slots (4), floppy drive interface, green PC connector, IDE interfaces (2), SCSI interface, Ultra-Wide SCSI interface, parallel port, PS/2 mouse port, serial ports (2), IR connector, USB connector, ATX power connector, RAID slot, CPU Slot 1 (2)
NPU Options	None

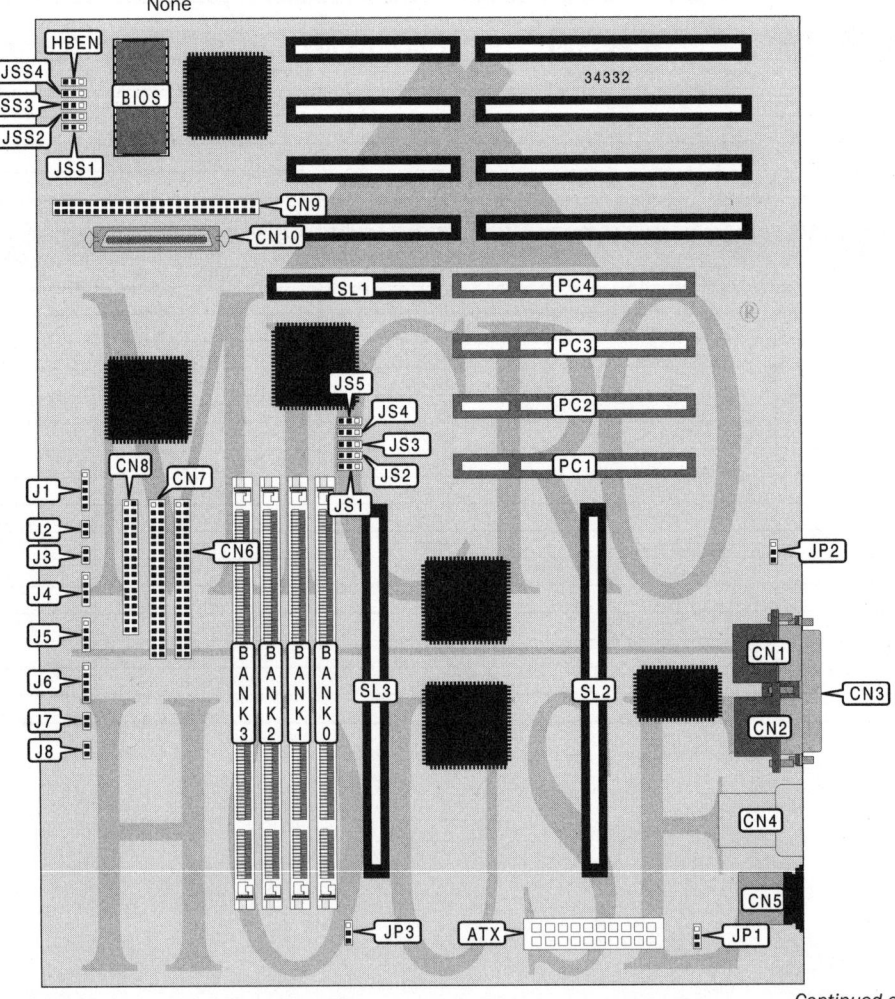

Continued on next page...

ADVANCED INTEGRATION RESEARCH, INC.
P6KDI

...continued from previous page

CONNECTIONS

Purpose	Location	Purpose	Location
ATX power connector	ATX	Reset switch	J3
Serial port 2	CN1	Speaker	J4
Serial port 1	CN2	IDE interface LED	J5
Parallel port	CN3	Power LED & keylock	J6
USB connector	CN4	Turbo LED	J7
PS/2 mouse port	CN5	Soft off power supply	J8
IDE interface 1	CN6	Chassis fan power	JP1
IDE interface 2	CN7	Chassis fan power	JP2
Floppy drive interface	CN8	Chassis fan power	JP3
SCSI interface	CN9	32-bit PCI slots	PC1 – PC4
Ultra-Wide SCSI interface	CN10	RAID slot	SL1
IR connector	J1	CPU Slot 1	SL2
Green PC connector	J2	CPU Slot 1	SL3

USER CONFIGURABLE SETTINGS

Function	Label	Position
◇ SCSI low byte enabled	HBEN	Pins 2 & 3 closed
SCSI high byte enabled	HBEN	Pins 1 & 2 closed

DIMM CONFIGURATION

Size	Bank 0	Bank 1	Bank 2	Bank 3
8MB	(1) 1M x 64	None	None	None
16MB	(1) 1M x 64	(1) 1M x 64	None	None
16MB	(1) 2M x 64	None	None	None
24MB	(1) 1M x 64	(1) 1M x 64	(1) 1M x 64	None
32MB	(1) 1M x 64	(1) 1M x 64	(1) 1M x 64	(1) 1M x 64
32MB	(1) 2M x 64	(1) 2M x 64	None	None
32MB	(1) 4M x 64	None	None	None
48MB	(1) 2M x 64	(1) 2M x 64	(1) 2M x 64	None
64MB	(1) 2M x 64	(1) 2M x 64	(1) 2M x 64	(1) 2M x 64
64MB	(1) 4M x 64	(1) 4M x 64	None	None
64MB	(1) 8M x 64	None	None	None
96MB	(1) 4M x 64	(1) 4M x 64	(1) 4M x 64	None
128MB	(1) 4M x 64	(1) 4M x 64	(1) 4M x 64	(1) 4M x 64
128MB	(1) 8M x 64	(1) 8M x 64	None	None
128MB	(1) 16M x 64	None	None	None
192MB	(1) 8M x 64	(1) 8M x 64	(1) 8M x 64	None
256MB	(1) 8M x 64	(1) 8M x 64	(1) 8M x 64	(1) 8M x 64
256MB	(1) 16M x 64	(1) 16M x 64	None	None
256MB	(1) 32M x 64	None	None	None

Continued on next page...

ADVANCED INTEGRATION RESEARCH, INC.
P6KDI

...continued from previous page

DIMM CONFIGURATION (CON'T)				
Size	Bank 0	Bank 1	Bank 2	Bank 3
384MB	(1) 16M x 64	(1) 16M x 64	(1) 16M x 64	None
512MB	(1) 16M x 64	(1) 16M x 64	(1) 16M x 64	(1) 16M x 64
512MB	(1) 32M x 64	(1) 32M x 64	None	None
768MB	(1) 32M x 64	(1) 32M x 64	(1) 32M x 64	None
1GB	(1) 32M x 64	(1) 32M x 64	(1) 32M x 64	(1) 32M x 64

Note: Board accepts EDO memory. Board also accepts x 72 SIMMs.

CACHE CONFIGURATION
Note: 256KB/512KB cache is located on the Pentium II CPU.

CPU SPEED SELECTION					
CPU speed	JS1	JS2	JS3	JS4	JS5
180MHz	1 & 2	1 & 2	1 & 2	1 & 2	1 & 2
200MHz	2 & 3	2 & 3	2 & 3	2 & 3	1 & 2
233MHz	2 & 3	2 & 3	2 & 3	2 & 3	1 & 2
266MHz	2 & 3	2 & 3	2 & 3	2 & 3	1 & 2

Note: Pins designated should be in the closed position.

CPU SPEED SELECTION (CON'T)				
CPU speed	JSS1	JSS2	JSS3	JSS4
180MHz	1 & 2	2 & 3	1 & 2	1 & 2
200MHz	1 & 2	2 & 3	1 & 2	1 & 2
233MHz	2 & 3	2 & 3	1 & 2	1 & 2
266MHz	1 & 2	1 & 2	2 & 3	1 & 2

Note: Pins designated should be in the closed position.

ADVANCED INTEGRATION RESEARCH, INC.
P6KPI

Processor	Pentium II
Processor Speed	180/200/233/266/300MHz
Chip Set	Intel
Video Chip Set	None
Maximum Onboard Memory	1GB (EDO supported)
Maximum Video Memory	None
Cache	256/512KB (located on Pentium II CPU)
BIOS	AMI
Dimensions	305mm x 244mm
I/O Options	32-bit PCI slots (4), floppy drive interface, green PC connector, IDE interfaces (2), SCSI interface, Ultra-Wide SCSI interface, parallel port, PS/2 mouse port, serial ports (2), IR connector, USB connector, ATX power connector, RAID slot, CPU Slot 1
NPU Options	None

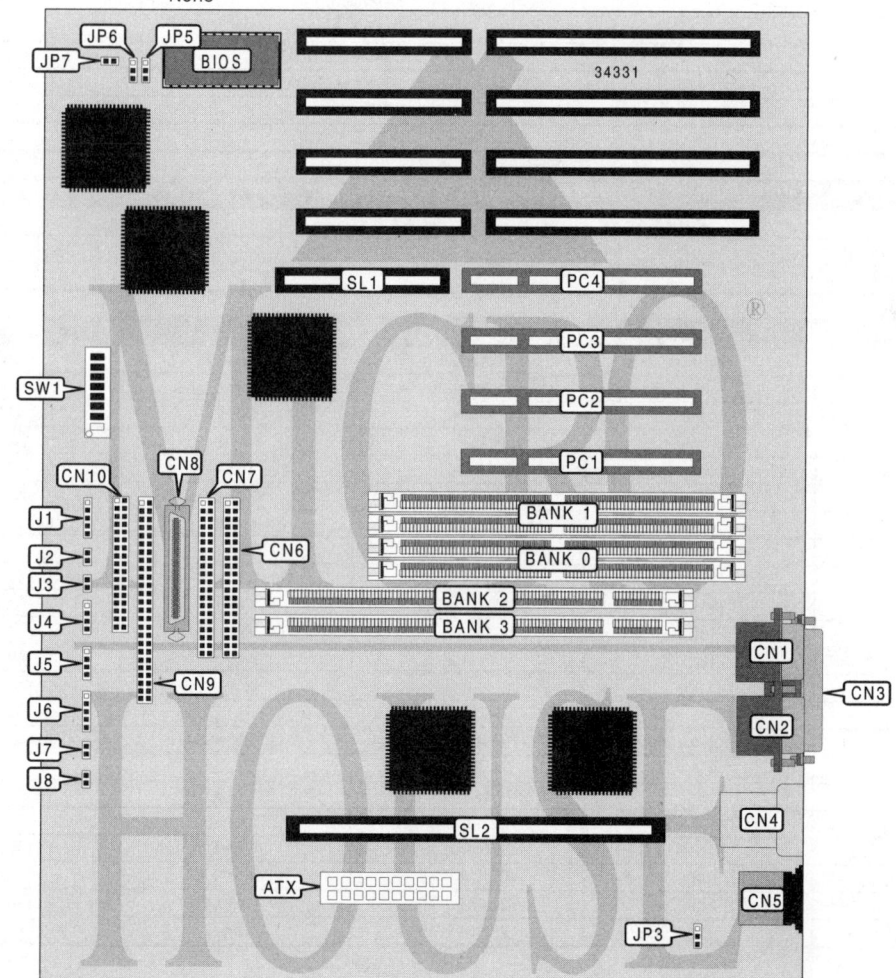

Continued on next page...

ADVANCED INTEGRATION RESEARCH, INC.
P6KPI

. . . continued from previous page

CONNECTIONS			
Purpose	**Location**	**Purpose**	**Location**
ATX power connector	ATX	Reset switch	J3
Serial port 2	CN1	Speaker	J4
Serial port 1	CN2	IDE interface LED	J5
Parallel port	CN3	Power LED & keylock	J6
USB connector	CN4	Turbo LED	J7
PS/2 mouse port	CN5	Soft off power supply	J8
IDE interface 1	CN6	Chassis fan power	JP3
IDE interface 2	CN7	Case fan power	JP5
Ultra-Wide SCSI interface	CN8	Case fan power	JP6
SCSI interface	CN9	Case sensor	JP7
Floppy drive interface	CN10	32-bit PCI slots	PC1 – PC4
IR connector	J1	RAID slot	SL1
Green PC connector	J2	CPU Slot 1	SL2

USER CONFIGURABLE SETTINGS			
Function		**Label**	**Position**
⇨ SCSI low byte enabled		SW1/8	On
SCSI high byte enabled		SW1/8	Off

DIMM/DRAM CONFIGURATION				
Size	**Bank 0**	**Bank 1**	**Bank 2**	**Bank 3**
8MB	(2) 1M x 36	None	None	None
8MB	None	None	None	(1) 1M x 64
16MB	(2) 1M x 36	(2) 1M x 36	None	None
16MB	None	None	(1) 1M x 64	(1) 1M x 64
16MB	(2) 2M x 36	None	None	None
16MB	None	None	None	(1) 2M x 64
24MB	(2) 1M x 36	(2) 1M x 36	(1) 1M x 64	None
32MB	(2) 1M x 36	(2) 1M x 36	(1) 1M x 64	(1) 1M x 64
32MB	(2) 2M x 36	(2) 2M x 36	None	None
32MB	None	None	(1) 2M x 64	(1) 2M x 64
32MB	(2) 4M x 36	None	None	None
32MB	None	None	None	(1) 4M x 64
48MB	(2) 2M x 36	(2) 2M x 36	(1) 2M x 64	None
64MB	(2) 2M x 36	(2) 2M x 36	(1) 2M x 64	(1) 2M x 64
64MB	(2) 4M x 36	(2) 4M x 36	None	None
64MB	None	None	(1) 4M x 64	(1) 4M x 64
64MB	(2) 8M x 36	None	None	None
64MB	None	None	None	(1) 8M x 64
96MB	(2) 4M x 36	(2) 4M x 36	(1) 4M x 64	None
128MB	(2) 4M x 36	(2) 4M x 36	(1) 4M x 64	(1) 4M x 64
128MB	(2) 8M x 36	(2) 8M x 36	None	None

Continued on next page. . .

ADVANCED INTEGRATION RESEARCH, INC.
P6KPI

...continued from previous page

DIMM/DRAM CONFIGURATION (CON'T)				
Size	Bank 0	Bank 1	Bank 2	Bank 3
128MB	None	None	(1) 8M x 64	(1) 8M x 64
128MB	(2) 16M x 36	None	None	None
128MB	None	None	None	(1) 16M x 64
192MB	(2) 8M x 36	(2) 8M x 36	(1) 8M x 64	None
256MB	(2) 8M x 36	(2) 8M x 36	(1) 8M x 64	(1) 8M x 64
256MB	(2) 16M x 36	(2) 16M x 36	None	None
256MB	None	None	(1) 16M x 64	(1) 16M x 64
256MB	(2) 32M x 36	None	None	None
384MB	(2) 16M x 36	(2) 16M x 36	(1) 16M x 64	None
512MB	(2) 16M x 36	(2) 16M x 36	(1) 16M x 64	(1) 16M x 64
512MB	(2) 32M x 36	(2) 32M x 36	None	None
768MB	(2) 32M x 36	(2) 32M x 36	(1) 32M x 64	None
1GB	(2) 32M x 36	(2) 32M x 36	(1) 32M x 64	(1) 32M x 64

Note: Board accepts EDO memory. Board also accepts non-parity SIMMs & DIMMs.

CACHE CONFIGURATION
Note: 256KB/512KB cache is located on the Pentium II CPU.

CPU SPEED SELECTION							
Speed	SW1/1	SW1/2	SW1/3	SW1/4	SW1/5	SW1/6	SW1/7
180MHz	Off	Off	Off	On	Off	On	On
200MHz	On	On	Off	On	Off	On	On
233MHz	On	On	Off	Off	Off	On	On
266MHz	On	On	Off	On	On	Off	On
300MHz	On	On	Off	Off	On	Off	On

AMERICAN MEGATRENDS, INC.
APOLLO III

Processor	Pentium
Processor Speed	75/90/100/120/133/150/166/180/200MHz
Chip Set	Intel
Video Chip Set	None
Maximum Onboard Memory	256MB (EDO supported)
Maximum Video Memory	None
Cache	256/512KB
BIOS	AMI
Dimensions	254mm x 218mm
I/O Options	32-bit PCI slots (4), floppy drive interface, green PC connector, IDE interfaces (2), parallel port, PS/2 mouse interface, serial ports (2), IR connector, USB connectors (2)
NPU Options	None

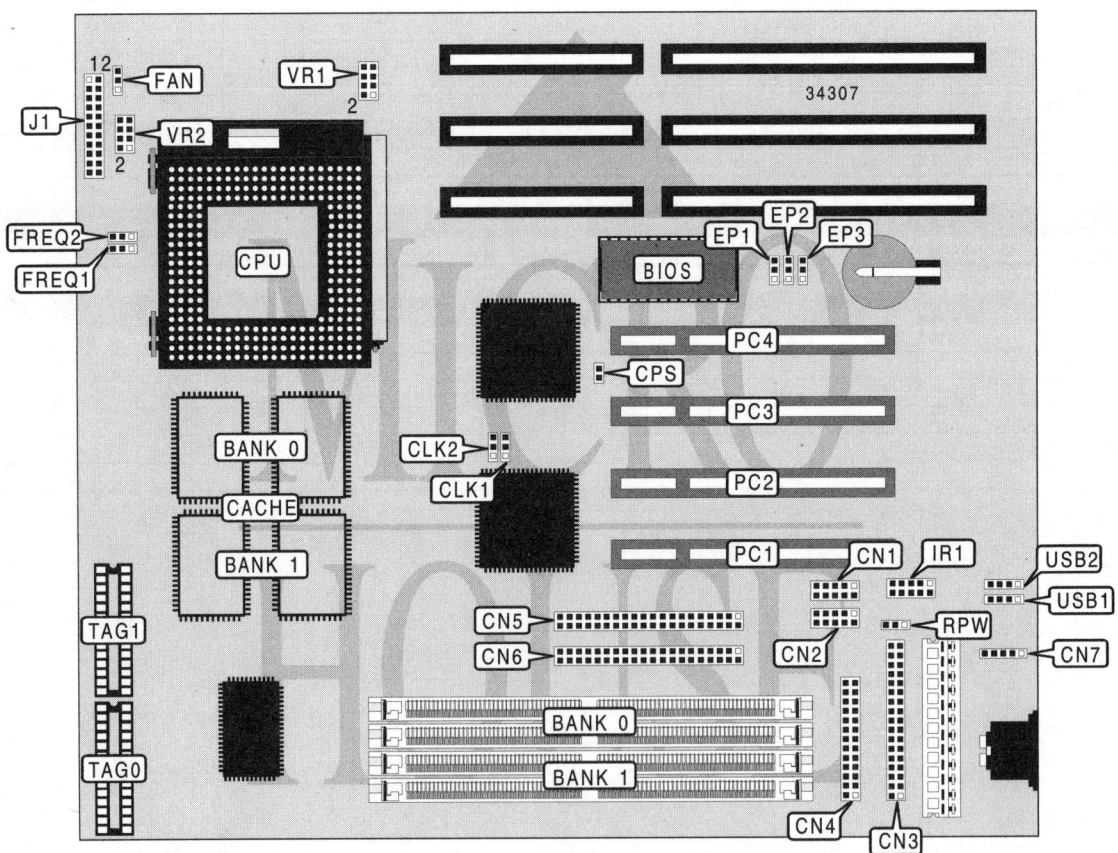

Continued on next page...

AMERICAN MEGATRENDS, INC.
APOLLO III

...continued from previous page

CONNECTIONS			
Purpose	**Location**	**Purpose**	**Location**
Serial port 2	CN1	Green PC connector	J1/pins 8 & 9
Serial port 1	CN2	Green PC LED	J1/pins 10 & 11
Floppy drive interface	CN3	Speaker	J1/pins 12 - 15
Parallel port	CN4	IDE interface LED	J1/pins 16 & 17
IDE interface 2	CN5	Remote power	J1/pins 18 & 19
IDE interface 1	CN6	Reset switch	J1/pins 20 & 21
PS/2 mouse interface	CN7	32-bit PCI slots	PC1 – PC4
Chassis fan power	FAN	Soft off power supply	RPW
IR connector	IR1	USB connector 1	USB1
Power LED & keylock	J1/pins 1 - 5	USB connector 2	USB2
Turbo LED	J1/pins 6 & 7		

USER CONFIGURABLE SETTINGS		
Function	**Label**	**Position**
⇨ CMOS memory normal operation	CPS	Open
CMOS memory clear	CPS	Closed

DRAM CONFIGURATION		
Size	**Bank 0**	**Bank 1**
8MB	(2) 1M x 36	None
16MB	(2) 2M x 36	None
24MB	(2) 2M x 36	(2) 1M x 36
32MB	(2) 2M x 36	(2) 2M x 36
40MB	(2) 4M x 36	(2) 1M x 36
48MB	(2) 4M x 36	(2) 2M x 36
64MB	(2) 8M x 36	None
64MB	(2) 4M x 36	(2) 4M x 36
72MB	(2) 8M x 36	(2) 1M x 36
80MB	(2) 8M x 36	(2) 2M x 36
96MB	(2) 8M x 36	(2) 4M x 36
128MB	(2) 8M x 36	(2) 8M x 36
128MB	(2) 16M x 36	None
136MB	(2) 16M x 36	(2) 1M x 36
144MB	(2) 16M x 36	(2) 2M x 36
160MB	(2) 16M x 36	(2) 4M x 36
192MB	(2) 16M x 36	(2) 8M x 36
256MB	(2) 16M x 36	(2) 16M x 36
Note: Board accepts EDO memory.		

CACHE CONFIGURATION				
Size	**Bank 0**	**Bank 1**	**TAG 0**	**TAG 1**
256KB	(2) 32K x 32	None	(1) 8K x 8	None
512KB	(2) 32K x 32	(2) 32K x 32	(1) 16K x 8	(1) 16K x 8

Continued on next page...

AMERICAN MEGATRENDS, INC.
APOLLO III

...continued from previous page

CPU SPEED SELECTION						
CPU speed	Clock speed	Multiplier	CLK1	CLK2	FREQ1	FREQ2
75MHz	50MHz	1.5x	2 & 3	2 & 3	1 & 2	1 & 2
90MHz	60MHz	1.5x	2 & 3	1 & 2	1 & 2	1 & 2
100MHz	66MHz	1.5x	1 & 2	2 & 3	1 & 2	1 & 2
120MHz	60MHz	2x	2 & 3	1 & 2	2 & 3	1 & 2
133MHz	66MHz	2x	1 & 2	2 & 3	2 & 3	1 & 2
150MHz	60MHz	2.5x	2 & 3	1 & 2	2 & 3	2 & 3
166MHz	66MHz	2.5x	1 & 2	2 & 3	2 & 3	2 & 3
180MHz	60MHz	3x	2 & 3	1 & 2	1 & 2	2 & 3
200MHz	66MHz	3x	1 & 2	2 & 3	1 & 2	2 & 3

Note: Pins designated should be in the closed position.

CPU VOLTAGE SELECTION (SINGLE)		
Voltage	VR1	VR2
3.3v	Pins 3 & 4 closed	Pins 1 & 2, 3 & 4 closed
✧ 3.49v	Pins 1 & 2 closed	Pins 1 & 2, 3 & 4 closed

CPU VOLTAGE SELECTION (DUAL)		
Voltage	VR1	VR2
2.8v	Pins 5 & 6 closed	Pins 5 & 6, 7 & 8 closed
3.3v	Pins 5 & 6 closed	Pins 5 & 6, 7 & 8 closed

FLASH BIOS SELECTION			
Type	EP1	EP2	EP3
AMD 28F020	Open	Pins 1 & 2 closed	Pins 2 & 3 closed
Intel 28F001BX-T	Pins 1 & 2 closed	Pins 1 & 2 closed	Open
Intel 28F010	Pins 1 & 2 closed	Pins 2 & 3 closed	Open
✧ SST 29EE010	Pins 2 & 3 closed	Pins 2 & 3 closed	Open
SST 29EE020	Open	Pins 2 & 3 closed	Pins 2 & 3 closed

AMERICAN MEGATRENDS, INC.
GOLIATH QUAD

Processor	Pentium Pro
Processor Speed	133/150/180/200/233/240/283/300/325MHz
Chip Set	Intel
Video Chip Set	None
Maximum Onboard Memory	1GB (EDO supported)
Maximum Video Memory	None
Cache	256/512KB (located on Pentium Pro CPU)
BIOS	AMI
Dimensions	333mm x 305mm
I/O Options	External memory card slot, 32-bit PCI slots (6), floppy drive interface, IDE interface, parallel port, PS/2 mouse interface, serial ports (2), VRM connectors (4), CPU slots (2)
NPU Options	None

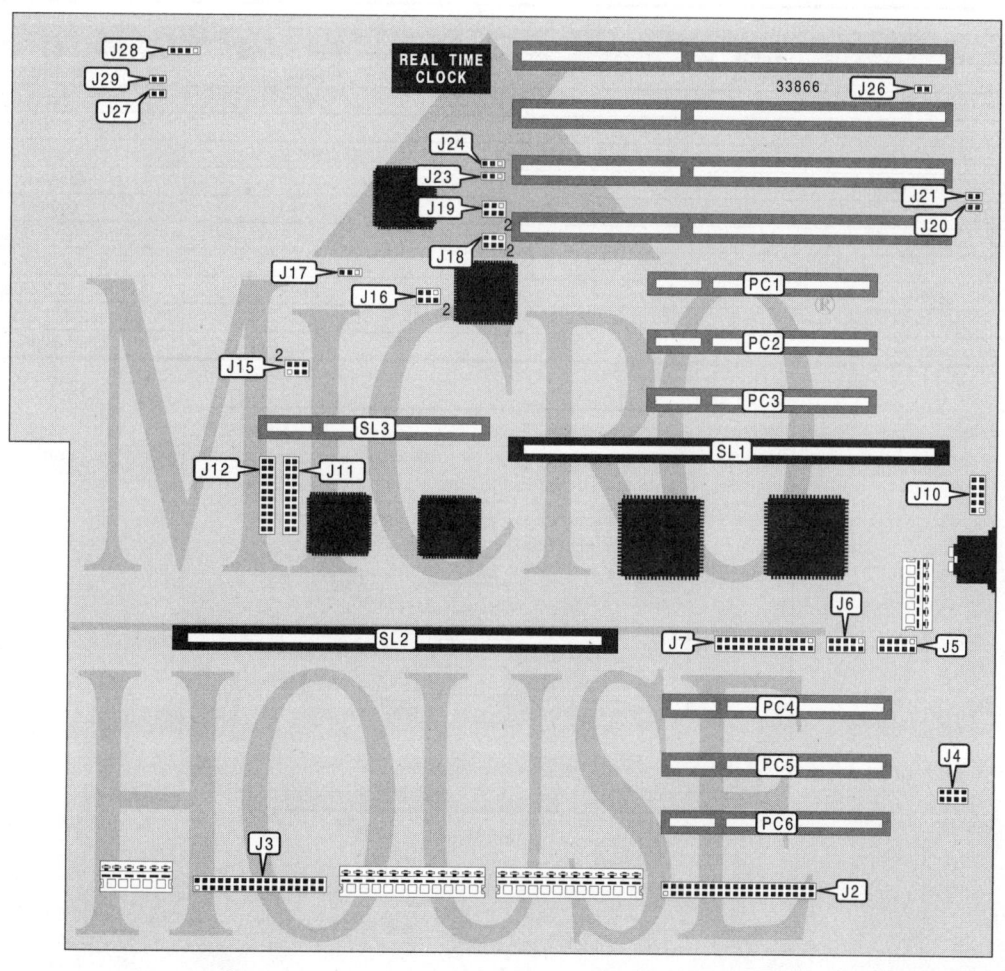

Continued on next page...

64 Motherboard Settings and Specifications

AMERICAN MEGATRENDS, INC.
GOLIATH QUAD

...continued from previous page

CONNECTIONS

Purpose	Location	Purpose	Location
IDE interface	J2	Reset switch	J27
Floppy drive interface	J3	Speaker	J28
Serial port 1	J5	IDE interface LED	J29
Serial port 2	J6	CPU slot	SL1
Parallel port	J7	CPU slot	SL2
PS/2 mouse interface	J10	External memory card	SL3
Power LED & keylock	J22	32-bit PCI slots	PC1 - PC6
Note: The location of J22 is unidentified.			

USER CONFIGURABLE SETTINGS

	Function	Label	Position
⇨	Factory configured - do not alter	J4	Open
⇨	Factory configured - do not alter	J17	Pins 2 & 3 closed
⇨	Factory configured - do not alter	J20	Open
	IDE DREQ enabled	J21	Closed
	IDE DREQ disabled	J21	Open
⇨	Parallel port IRQ select IRQ7	J23	Pins 1 & 2 closed
	Parallel port IRQ select IRQ5	J23	Pins 2 & 3 closed
⇨	PS/2 mouse IRQ12 enabled	J24	Pins 1 & 2 closed
	PS/2 mouse IRQ12 disabled	J24	Pins 2 & 3 closed
⇨	Factory configured - do not alter	J26	Unidentified

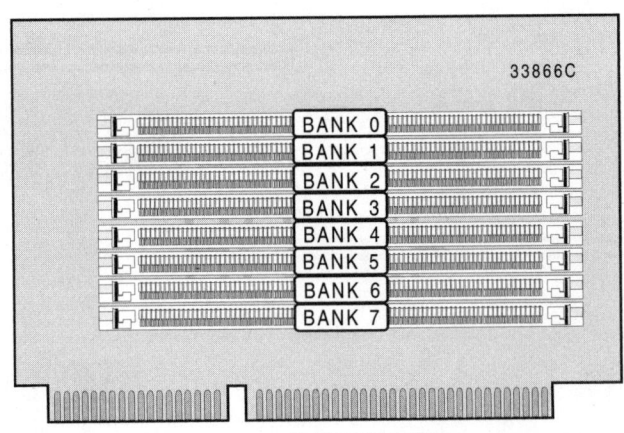

MEMORY CARD

Continued on next page...

AMERICAN MEGATRENDS, INC.
GOLIATH QUAD

. . . continued from previous page

DIMM CONFIGURATION				
Size	Bank 0	Bank 1	Bank 2	Bank 3
16MB	(1) 2M x 72	None	None	None
32MB	(1) 2M x 72	(1) 2M x 72	None	None
64MB	(1) 2M x 72	(1) 2M x 72	(1) 2M x 72	(1) 2M x 72
32MB	(1) 2M x 72	None	None	None
64MB	(1) 2M x 72	(1) 2M x 72	None	None
128MB	(1) 2M x 72	(1) 2M x 72	(1) 2M x 72	(1) 2M x 72
8MB	(1) 1M x 72	None	None	None
32MB	(1) 1M x 72	(1) 1M x 72	(1) 1M x 72	(1) 1M x 72
64MB	(1) 1M x 72	(1) 1M x 72	(1) 1M x 72	(1) 1M x 72
32MB	(1) 4M x 72	None	None	None
128MB	(1) 4M x 72	(1) 4M x 72	(1) 4M x 72	(1) 4M x 72
256MB	(1) 4M x 72	(1) 4M x 72	(1) 4M x 72	(1) 4M x 72
128MB	(1) 16M x 72	None	None	None
512MB	(1) 16M x 72	(1) 16M x 72	(1) 16M x 72	(1) 16M x 72
1GB	(1) 16M x 72	(1) 16M x 72	(1) 16M x 72	(1) 16M x 72

Note: Board accepts EDO memory. Board also accepts 8M x 72 DIMMs.

DIMM CONFIGURATION (CON'T)				
Size	Bank 4	Bank 5	Bank 6	Bank 7
16MB	None	None	None	None
32MB	None	None	None	None
64MB	None	None	None	None
32MB	(1) 2M x 72	None	None	None
64MB	(1) 2M x 72	(1) 2M x 72	None	None
128MB	(1) 2M x 72	(1) 2M x 72	(1) 2M x 72	(1) 2M x 72
8MB	None	None	None	None
32MB	None	None	None	None
64MB	(1) 1M x 72	(1) 1M x 72	(1) 1M x 72	(1) 1M x 72
32MB	None	None	None	None
128MB	None	None	None	None
256MB	(1) 4M x 72	(1) 4M x 72	(1) 4M x 72	(1) 4M x 72
128MB	None	None	None	None
512MB	None	None	None	None
1GB	(1) 16M x 72	(1) 16M x 72	(1) 16M x 72	(1) 16M x 72

Note: Board accepts EDO memory.

DIMM VOLTAGE CONFIGURATION		
Voltage	J11	J12
3.3v	1 & 2, 3 & 4, 5 & 6, 7 & 8, 9 & 10, 11 & 12, 13 & 14, 15 & 16, 17 & 18, 19 & 20	Open

CACHE CONFIGURATION
Note: 256KB/512KB cache is located on the Pentium Pro CPU.

Continued on next page. . .

AMERICAN MEGATRENDS, INC.
GOLIATH QUAD

. . . continued from previous page

CPU SPEED SELECTION			
CPU speed	**Clock speed**	**J15**	**J190**
133MHz	66MHz	1 & 2, 3 & 4, 5 & 6, 7 & 8	1 & 2, 3 & 4, 5 & 6, 7 & 8
150MHz	60MHz	1 & 2, 3 & 4, 7 & 8	1 & 2, 3 & 4, 7 & 8
180MHz	60MHz	1 & 2, 3 & 4, 5 & 6	1 & 2, 3 & 4, 5 & 6
200MHz	66MHz	1 & 2, 3 & 4, 5 & 6	1 & 2, 3 & 4, 5 & 6
233MHz	66MHz	1 & 2, 3 & 4	1 & 2, 3 & 4
240MHz	60MHz	3 & 4, 5 & 6, 7 & 8	3 & 4, 5 & 6, 7 & 8
283MHz	66MHz	3 & 4, 7 & 8	3 & 4, 7 & 8
300MHz	60MHz	3 & 4, 5 & 6	3 & 4, 5 & 6
325MHz	60MHz	3 & 4	3 & 4

Note: Pins designated should be in the closed position. The location of J190 is unidentified. J15 sets CPU card 1 and J190 sets CPU card 2.

PCI SPEED SELECTION			
CPU speed	**External**	**Internal**	**J16**
150MHz	60MHz	30MHz	Pins 1 & 2, 5 & 6 closed
180MHz	60MHz	30MHz	Pins 1 & 2, 5 & 6 closed
200MHz	66MHz	33MHz	Pins 3 & 4 closed

DMA CHANNEL SELECTION		
Channel	**J18**	**J19**
⇨ None	Open	Open
0	Pins 1 & 2 closed	Pins 1 & 2 closed
1	Pins 3 & 4 closed	Pins 3 & 4 closed
3	Pins 5 & 6 closed	Pins 5 & 6 closed

Continued on next page. . .

AMERICAN MEGATRENDS, INC.
GOLIATH QUAD

...continued from previous page

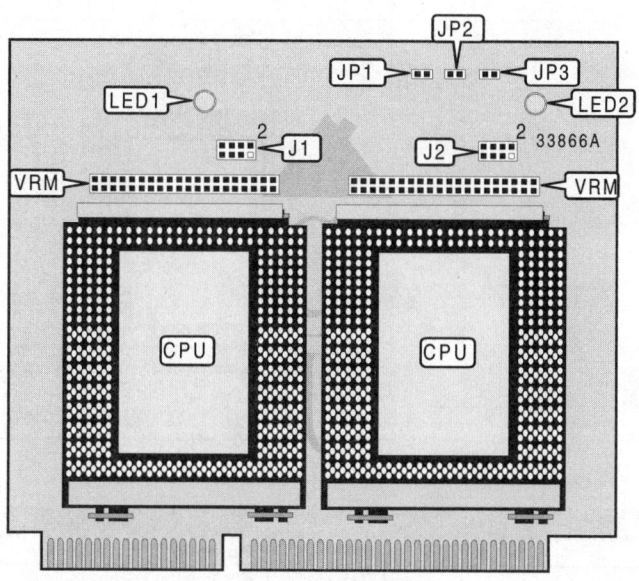

CPU CARD 1

CONNECTIONS			
Purpose	**Location**	**Purpose**	**Location**
Overheat LED	LED1	Chassis fan power	JP2
Overheat LED	LED2	VRM connectors	VRM
Chassis fan power	JP1		

USER CONFIGURABLE SETTINGS		
Function	**Label**	**Position**
⋄ Factory configured - do not alter	JP3	Closed

CPU VOLTAGE SELECTION		
Voltage	**J1**	**J2**
3.3v	Pins 1 & 2, 5 & 6, 7 & 8 closed	Pins 1 & 2, 5 & 6, 7 & 8 closed

Continued on next page...

AMERICAN MEGATRENDS, INC.
GOLIATH QUAD

... continued from previous page

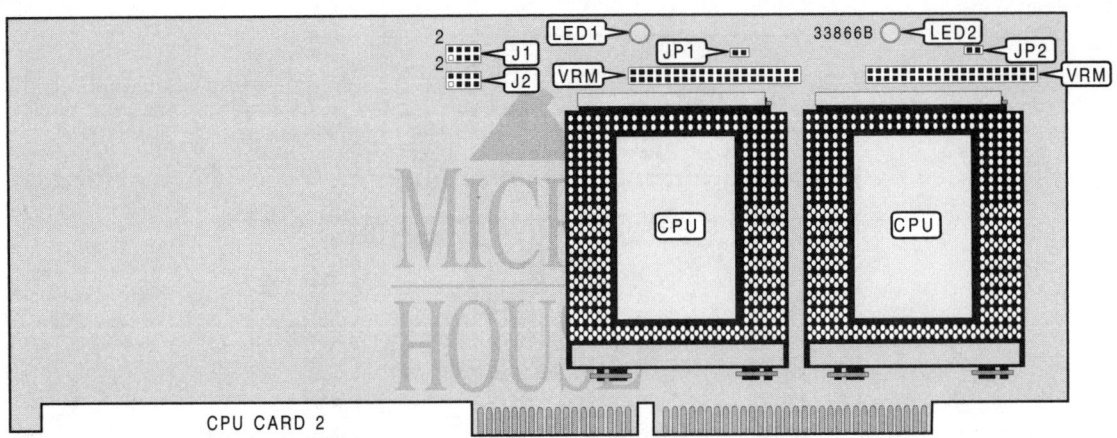

CPU CARD 2

CONNECTIONS			
Purpose	**Location**	**Purpose**	**Location**
Overheat LED	LED1	Chassis fan power	JP2
Overheat LED	LED2	VRM connectors	VRM
Chassis fan power	JP1		

CPU VOLTAGE SELECTION		
Voltage	**J1**	**J2**
3.3v	Pins 1 & 2, 5 & 6, 7 & 8 closed	Pins 1 & 2, 5 & 6, 7 & 8 closed

MISCELLANEOUS TECHNICAL NOTES.
Note: The LEDs on CPU Card 1 and CPU Card2 are 'overheat' indicators. If any of these LEDs come on on either card, turn computer off as soon as possible to prevent damage.
Note: If installing CPU card 1 only, insert the terminator card in CPU socket 2. Do not use CPU card 2 only

AMERICAN MEGATRENDS, INC.
MEGAPRO

Processor	Pentium Pro
Processor Speed	133/150/166/180/200MHz
Chip Set	Unidentified
Video Chip Set	None
Maximum Onboard Memory	512MB (EDO supported)
Maximum Video Memory	None
Cache	256/512KB (located on Pentium Pro CPU)
BIOS	AMI
Dimensions	355mm x 304mm
I/O Options	32-bit PCI slots (4), floppy drive interface, green PC connector, IDE interfaces (2), parallel port, PS/2 mouse interface, serial ports (2), VGA interface, IR connector, VRM connectors (2), USB connectors (2)
NPU Options	None

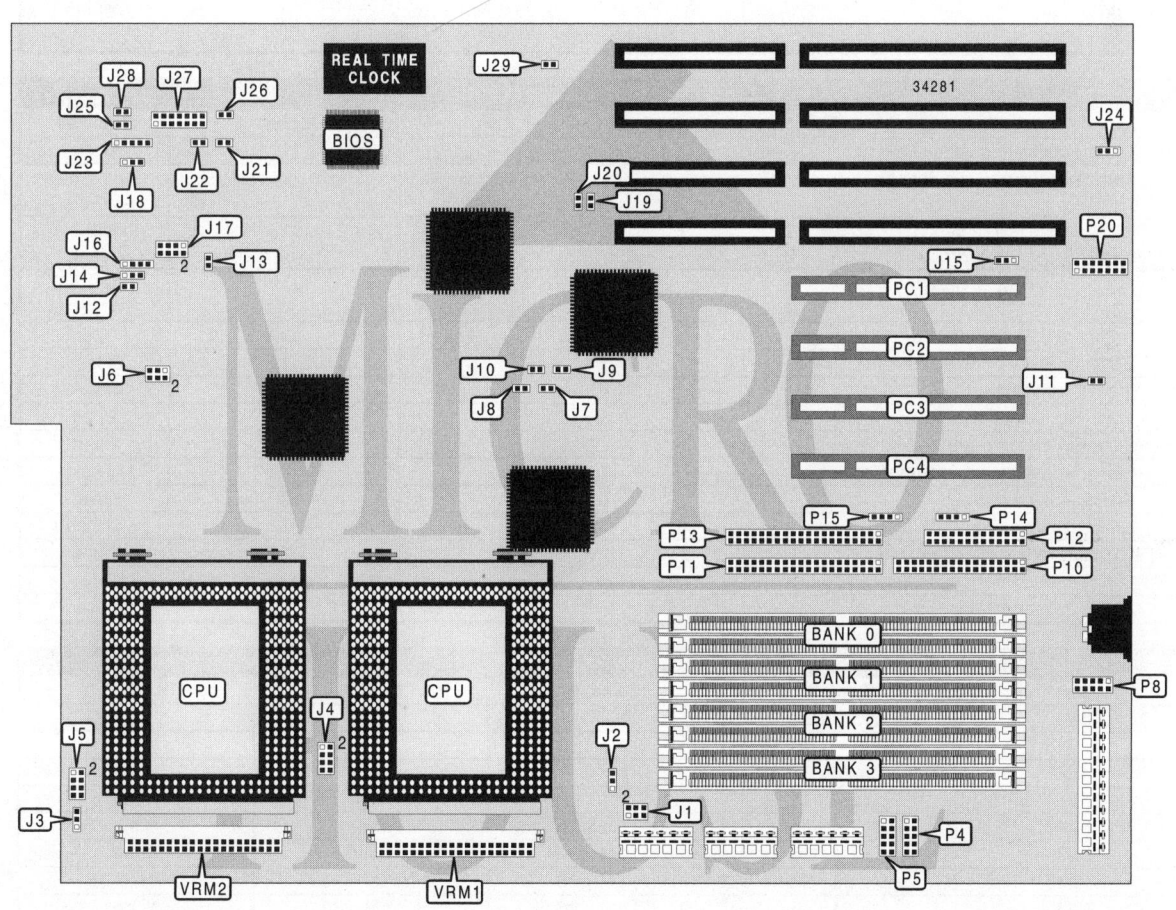

Continued on next page...

AMERICAN MEGATRENDS, INC.
MEGAPRO

...continued from previous page

CONNECTIONS			
Purpose	**Location**	**Purpose**	**Location**
CPU fan	J2	PS/2 mouse interface	P8
CPU fan	J3	Floppy drive interface	P10
Chassis door connector	J12	IDE interface 1	P11
IDE interface LED	J13	Parallel port	P12
Speaker	J16	IDE interface 2	P13
Chassis fan power	J18	USB connector 1	P14
Green PC connector	J21	USB connector 2	P15
Power LED & keylock	J23	VGA connector	P20
Turbo LED	J26	32-bit PCI slots	PC1 – PC4
Reset switch	J28	VRM connector 1	VRM1
Serial port 1	P4	VRM connector 2	VRM2
Serial port 2	P5		

USER CONFIGURABLE SETTINGS		
Function	**Label**	**Position**
✧ Factory configured - do not alter	J11	Open
✧ Factory configured - do not alter	J14	Pins 1 & 2 closed
PS/2 mouse IRQ12 enabled	J15	Pins 2 & 3 closed
PS/2 mouse IRQ12 disabled	J15	Pins 1 & 2 closed
✧ On board PCI VGA enabled	J19	Open
On board PCI VGA disabled	J19	Closed
✧ PCI IRQ disabled	J20	Closed
PCI IRQ enabled	J20	Open
✧ Server management SMI disabled	J22	Open
Server management SMI enabled	J22	Closed
✧ External SMI disabled	J25	Open
External SMI enabled	J25	Closed
✧ Factory configured - do not alter	J27	Open
✧ CMOS memory normal operation	J29	Open
CMOS memory clear	J29	Closed

DRAM CONFIGURATION				
Size	**Bank 0**	**Bank 1**	**Bank 2**	**Bank 3**
8MB	(2) 1M x 36	None	None	None
16MB	(2) 1M x 36	(2) 1M x 36	None	None
16MB	(2) 2M x 36	None	None	None
24MB	(2) 1M x 36	(2) 1M x 36	(2) 1M x 36	None
24MB	(2) 1M x 36	(2) 2M x 36	None	None
24MB	(2) 2M x 36	(2) 1M x 36	None	None
32MB	(2) 1M x 36	(2) 1M x 36	(2) 1M x 36	(2) 1M x 36
32MB	(2) 2M x 36	(2) 1M x 36	(2) 1M x 36	None
32MB	(2) 2M x 36	(2) 2M x 36	None	None

Continued on next page...

AMERICAN MEGATRENDS, INC.
MEGAPRO

...continued from previous page

DRAM CONFIGURATION (CON'T)				
Size	**Bank 0**	**Bank 1**	**Bank 2**	**Bank 3**
32MB	(2) 4M x 36	None	None	None
40MB	(2) 1M x 36	(2) 2M x 36	(2) 2M x 36	None
40MB	(2) 1M x 36	(2) 4M x 36	None	None
40MB	(2) 2M x 36	(2) 1M x 36	(2) 1M x 36	(2) 1M x 36
40MB	(2) 4M x 36	(2) 1M x 36	None	None
48MB	(2) 2M x 36	(2) 2M x 36	(2) 2M x 36	None
48MB	(2) 2M x 36	(2) 4M x 36	None	None
48MB	(2) 4M x 36	(2) 1M x 36	(2) 1M x 36	None
56MB	(2) 2M x 36	(2) 2M x 36	(2) 2M x 36	(2) 1M x 36
56MB	(2) 4M x 36	(2) 1M x 36	(2) 1M x 36	(2) 1M x 36
64MB	(2) 4M x 36	(2) 2M x 36	(2) 2M x 36	None
64MB	(2) 4M x 36	(2) 4M x 36	None	None
64MB	(2) 8M x 36	None	None	None
72MB	(2) 4M x 36	(2) 4M x 36	(2) 1M x 36	None
72MB	(2) 8M x 36	(2) 1M x 36	None	None
80MB	(2) 2M x 36	(2) 8M x 36	None	None
80MB	(2) 4M x 36	(2) 2M x 36	(2) 2M x 36	(2) 2M x 36
80MB	(2) 8M x 36	(2) 1M x 36	(2) 1M x 36	None
88MB	(2) 8M x 36	(2) 1M x 36	(2) 1M x 36	(2) 1M x 36
96MB	(2) 4M x 36	(2) 4M x 36	(2) 4M x 36	None
96MB	(2) 4M x 36	(2) 8M x 36	None	None
96MB	(2) 8M x 36	(2) 2M x 36	(2) 2M x 36	None
112MB	(2) 4M x 36	(2) 4M x 36	(2) 4M x 36	(2) 2M x 36
112MB	(2) 8M x 36	(2) 2M x 36	(2) 2M x 36	(2) 2M x 36
128MB	(2) 4M x 36	(2) 4M x 36	(2) 4M x 36	(2) 4M x 36
128MB	(2) 8M x 36	(2) 4M x 36	(2) 4M x 36	None
128MB	(2) 8M x 36	(2) 8M x 36	None	None
128MB	(2) 16M x 36	None	None	None
136MB	(2) 16M x 36	(2) 1M x 36	None	None
144MB	(2) 16M x 36	(2) 2M x 36	None	None
144MB	(2) 16M x 36	(2) 1M x 36	(2) 1M x 36	None
152MB	(2) 16M x 36	(2) 1M x 36	(2) 1M x 36	(2) 1M x 36
160MB	(2) 16M x 36	(2) 4M x 36	None	None
160MB	(2) 8M x 36	(2) 4M x 36	(2) 4M x 36	(2) 4M x 36
160MB	(2) 16M x 36	(2) 2M x 36	(2) 2M x 36	None
176MB	(2) 16M x 36	(2) 2M x 36	(2) 2M x 36	(2) 2M x 36
192MB	(2) 8M x 36	(2) 8M x 36	(2) 8M x 36	None
192MB	(2) 16M x 36	(2) 4M x 36	(2) 4M x 36	None
192MB	(2) 16M x 36	(2) 8M x 36	None	None
200MB	(2) 8M x 36	(2) 8M x 36	(2) 8M x 36	(2) 1M x 36

Continued on next page...

AMERICAN MEGATRENDS, INC.
MEGAPRO

...continued from previous page

DRAM CONFIGURATION (CON'T)

Size	Bank 0	Bank 1	Bank 2	Bank 3
208MB	(2) 8M x 36	(2) 8M x 36	(2) 8M x 36	(2) 2M x 36
224MB	(2) 8M x 36	(2) 8M x 36	(2) 8M x 36	(2) 4M x 36
224MB	(2) 16M x 36	(2) 4M x 36	(2) 4M x 36	(2) 4M x 36
256MB	(2) 8M x 36	(2) 8M x 36	(2) 8M x 36	(2) 8M x 36
256MB	(2) 16M x 36	(2) 8M x 36	(2) 8M x 36	None
256MB	(2) 16M x 36	(2) 16M x 36	None	None
264MB	(2) 16M x 36	(2) 16M x 36	(2) 1M x 36	None
288MB	(2) 16M x 36	(2) 16M x 36	(2) 4M x 36	None
320MB	(2) 16M x 36	(2) 16M x 36	(2) 8M x 36	None
320MB	(2) 16M x 36	(2) 8M x 36	(2) 8M x 36	(2) 8M x 36
384MB	(2) 16M x 36	(2) 16M x 36	(2) 16M x 36	None
400MB	(2) 16M x 36	(2) 16M x 36	(2) 16M x 36	(2) 2M x 36
416MB	(2) 16M x 36	(2) 16M x 36	(2) 16M x 36	(2) 4M x 36
512MB	(2) 16M x 36	(2) 16M x 36	(2) 16M x 36	(2) 16M x 36

Note: Board accepts EDO memory.

CACHE CONFIGURATION

Note: 256KB/512KB cache is located on the Pentium Pro CPU.

CPU SPEED SELECTION

CPU speed	Clock speed	Multiplier	J7	J8	J9
133MHz	66MHz	2x	Open	Closed	Open
150MHz	60MHz	2.5x	Closed	Open	Closed
166MHz	66MHz	2.5x	Open	Closed	Open
180MHz	60MHz	3x	Closed	Open	Closed
200MHz	66MHz	3x	Open	Closed	Open

CPU SPEED SELECTION

CPU speed	Clock speed	Multiplier	J10	J17	J24
133MHz	66MHz	2x	Closed	1 & 2, 3 & 4, 5 & 6, 7 & 8	1 & 2
150MHz	60MHz	2.5x	Open	3 & 4, 5 & 6, 7 & 8	1 & 2
166MHz	66MHz	2.5x	Closed	3 & 4, 5 & 6, 7 & 8	1 & 2
180MHz	60MHz	3x	Open	1 & 2, 5 & 6, 7 & 8	1 & 2
200MHz	66MHz	3x	Closed	1 & 2, 5 & 6, 7 & 8	1 & 2

Note: Pins designated should be in the closed position.

Continued on next page...

AMERICAN MEGATRENDS, INC.
MEGAPRO

...continued from previous page

CPU VOLTAGE SELECTION		
Voltage	**J4**	**J5**
None	Open	Open
2.1v	7 & 8	7 & 8
2.2v	5 & 6	5 & 6
2.3v	5 & 6, 7 & 8	5 & 6, 7 & 8
2.4v	3 & 4	3 & 4
2.5v	3 & 4, 7 & 8	3 & 4, 7 & 8
2.6v	3 & 4, 5 & 6	3 & 4, 5 & 6
2.7v	3 & 4, 5 & 6, 7 & 8	3 & 4, 5 & 6, 7 & 8
2.8v	1 & 2	1 & 2
2.9v	1 & 2, 7 & 8	1 & 2, 7 & 8
3.0v	1 & 2, 5 & 6	1 & 2, 5 & 6
3.1v	1 & 2, 5 & 6, 7 & 8	1 & 2, 5 & 6, 7 & 8
3.2v	1 & 2, 3 & 4	1 & 2, 3 & 4
⇨ 3.3v	1 & 2, 3 & 4, 7 & 8	1 & 2, 3 & 4, 7 & 8
3.4v	1 & 2, 3 & 4, 5 & 6	1 & 2, 3 & 4, 5 & 6
3.5v	1 & 2, 3 & 4, 5 & 6, 7 & 8	1 & 2, 3 & 4, 5 & 6, 7 & 8
Note: Pins designated should be in the closed position.		

3.3V POWER SELECTION		
Setting	**J1**	**J6**
From voltage regulator	Open	1 & 2, 3 & 4, 5 & 6
From power supply	1 & 2, 3 & 4, 5 & 6	Open
Note: Pins designated should be in the closed position.		

AMERICAN MEGATRENDS, INC.
MEGARUM

Processor	Pentium II
Processor Speed	120/133/150/166/180/200/210/233/240/266MHz
Chip Set	Unidentified
Video Chip Set	ATI
Maximum Onboard Memory	1GB (EDO supported)
Maximum Video Memory	2MB
Cache	256/512KB (located on Pentium II CPU)
BIOS	AMI
Dimensions	330mm x 218mm
I/O Options	32-bit PCI slots (6), floppy drive interface, green PC connector, IDE interfaces (2), SCSI interfaces (2), Wide SCSI interfaces (2), parallel port, PS/2 mouse interface, serial ports (2), VGA interface, VRM connectors (2), USB connectors (2), CPU Slot 1s (2)
NPU Options	None

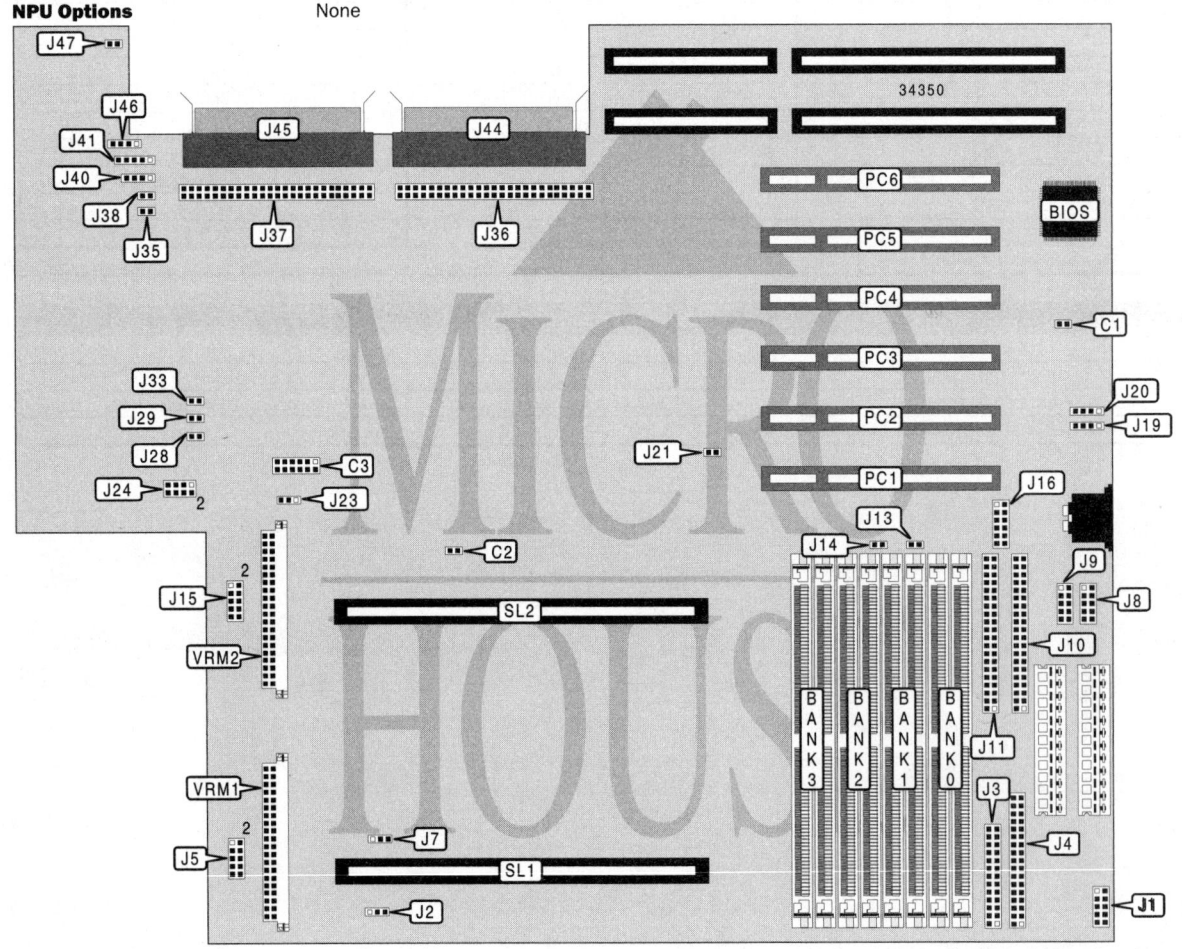

Continued on next page...

AMERICAN MEGATRENDS, INC.
MEGARUM

. . . continued from previous page

CONNECTIONS

Purpose	Location	Purpose	Location
PS/2 mouse interface	J1	Turbo LED	J33
CPU fan power 1	J2	SCSI interface 1	J36
Parallel port	J3	SCSI interface 2	J37
Floppy drive interface	J4	IDE interface LED	J38
CPU fan power 2	J7	SCSI interface LED	J40
Serial port 2	J8	Power LED & keylock	J41
Serial port 1	J9	Wide SCSI interface 1	J44
IDE interface	J10	Wide SCSI interface 2	J45
IDE interface	J11	Speaker	J46
VGA interface	J16	System override connector	J47
Green PC connector	J18	32-bit PCI slots	PC1 – PC6
USB connector 1	J19	CPU Slot 1	SL1
USB connector 2	J20	CPU Slot 2	SL2
Chassis fan power	J23	VRM connector 1	VRM1
Reset switch	J28	VRM connector 2	VRM2
Chassis intrusion connector	J29		
Note: The location of J18 is unidentified.			

USER CONFIGURABLE SETTINGS

Function	Label	Position
◇ Factory configured - do not alter	C1	Unidentified
◇ Factory configured - do not alter	C2	Unidentified
◇ Factory configured - do not alter	C3	Unidentified
◇ PCI IRQ disabled for onboard PCI VGA	J13	Closed
PCI IRQ enabled for onboard PCI VGA	J13	Open
◇ On board video enabled	J14	Open
On board video disabled	J14	Closed
◇ CMOS memory normal operation	J35	Open
CMOS memory clear	J35	Closed

DRAM CONFIGURATION

Size	Bank 0	Bank 1	Bank 2	Bank 3
8MB	(2) 1M x 36	None	None	None
16MB	(2) 1M x 36	(2) 1M x 36	None	None
16MB	(2) 2M x 36	None	None	None
24MB	(2) 1M x 36	(2) 1M x 36	(2) 1M x 36	None
32MB	(2) 1M x 36	(2) 1M x 36	(2) 1M x 36	(2) 1M x 36
32MB	(2) 2M x 36	(2) 2M x 36	None	None
32MB	(2) 4M x 36	None	None	None
48MB	(2) 2M x 36	(2) 2M x 36	(2) 2M x 36	None
64MB	(2) 2M x 36	(2) 2M x 36	(2) 2M x 36	(2) 2M x 36
64MB	(2) 4M x 36	(2) 4M x 36	None	None

Continued on next page. . .

AMERICAN MEGATRENDS, INC.
MEGARUM

...continued from previous page

DRAM CONFIGURATION (CON'T)				
Size	**Bank 0**	**Bank 1**	**Bank 2**	**Bank 3**
64MB	(2) 8M x 36	None	None	None
96MB	(2) 4M x 36	(2) 4M x 36	(2) 4M x 36	None
128MB	(2) 4M x 36	(2) 4M x 36	(2) 4M x 36	(2) 4M x 36
128MB	(2) 8M x 36	(2) 8M x 36	None	None
128MB	(2) 16M x 36	None	None	None
192MB	(2) 8M x 36	(2) 8M x 36	(2) 8M x 36	None
256MB	(2) 8M x 36	(2) 8M x 36	(2) 8M x 36	(2) 8M x 36
256MB	(2) 16M x 36	(2) 16M x 36	None	None
256MB	(2) 32M x 36	None	None	None
384MB	(2) 16M x 36	(2) 16M x 36	(2) 16M x 36	None
512MB	(2) 16M x 36	(2) 16M x 36	(2) 16M x 36	(2) 16M x 36
512MB	(2) 32M x 36	(2) 32M x 36	None	None
768MB	(2) 32M x 36	(2) 32M x 36	(2) 32M x 36	None
1GB	(2) 32M x 36	(2) 32M x 36	(2) 32M x 36	(2) 32M x 36

Note: Board accepts EDO memory. Do not use 16M x 36 SIMMs that have more than 36 chips per SIMM.

CACHE CONFIGURATION
Note: 256KB/512KB cache is located on the Pentium II CPU.

CPU SPEED SELECTION		
Speed	**J21**	**J24**
120MHz	Open	Pins 1 & 2, 3 & 4, 5 & 6, 7 & 8 closed
133MHz	Closed	Pins 1 & 2, 3 & 4, 5 & 6, 7 & 8 closed
150MHz	Open	Pins 3 & 4, 5 & 6, 7 & 8 closed
166MHz	Closed	Pins 3 & 4, 5 & 6, 7 & 8 closed
180MHz	Open	Pins 1 & 2, 5 & 6, 7 & 8 closed
200MHz	Closed	Pins 1 & 2, 5 & 6, 7 & 8 closed
210MHz	Open	Pins 5 & 6, 7 & 8 closed
233MHz	Closed	Pins 5 & 6, 7 & 8 closed
240MHz	Open	Pins 1 & 2, 3 & 4, 7 & 8 closed
266MHz	Closed	Pins 1 & 2, 3 & 4, 7 & 8 closed

Continued on next page...

AMERICAN MEGATRENDS, INC.
MEGARUM

. . . continued from previous page

CPU VOLTAGE SELECTION		
Voltage	**J5**	**J15**
1.8v	1 & 2, 3 & 4, 7 & 8	1 & 2, 3 & 4, 7 & 8
1.85v	1 & 2, 3 & 4, 7 & 8, 9 & 10	1 & 2, 3 & 4, 7 & 8, 9 & 10
1.9v	1 & 2, 3 & 4, 5 & 6	1 & 2, 3 & 4, 5 & 6
1.95v	1 & 2, 3 & 4, 5 & 6, 9 & 10	1 & 2, 3 & 4, 5 & 6, 9 & 10
2.0v	1 & 2, 3 & 4, 5 & 6, 7 & 8	1 & 2, 3 & 4, 5 & 6, 7 & 8
2.05v	1 & 2, 3 & 4, 5 & 6, 7 & 8, 9 & 10	1 & 2, 3 & 4, 5 & 6, 7 & 8, 9 & 10
2.1v	9 & 10	9 & 10
2.2v	7 & 8	7 & 8
2.3v	7 & 8, 9 & 10	7 & 8, 9 & 10
2.4v	5 & 6	5 & 6
2.5v	5 & 6, 9 & 10	5 & 6, 9 & 10
2.6v	5 & 6, 7 & 8	5 & 6, 7 & 8
2.7v	5 & 6, 7 & 8, 9 & 10	5 & 6, 7 & 8, 9 & 10
2.8v	3 & 4	3 & 4
2.9v	3 & 4, 9 & 10	3 & 4, 9 & 10
3.0v	3 & 4, 7 & 8	3 & 4, 7 & 8
3.1v	3 & 4, 7 & 8, 9 & 10	3 & 4, 7 & 8, 9 & 10
3.2v	3 & 4, 5 & 6	3 & 4, 5 & 6
➪ 3.3v	3 & 4, 5 & 6, 9 & 10	3 & 4, 5 & 6, 9 & 10
3.4v	3 & 4, 5 & 6, 7 & 8	3 & 4, 5 & 6, 7 & 8
3.5v	3 & 4, 5 & 6, 7 & 8, 9 & 10	3 & 4, 5 & 6, 7 & 8, 9 & 10

Note: Pins designated should be in the closed position. J5 controls Slot 1 & J15 controls Slot 2.

78 Motherboard Settings and Specifications

AMERICAN MEGATRENDS, INC.
MERLIN PCI

Processor	Pentium Pro
Processor Speed	150/166/180/200MHz
Chip Set	Natoma
Video Chip Set	None
Maximum Onboard Memory	512MB (EDO supported)
Maximum Video Memory	None
Cache	256/512KB (located on Pentium Pro CPU)
BIOS	AMI
Dimensions	330mm x 218mm
I/O Options	32-bit PCI slots (4), floppy drive interface, green PC connector, IDE interfaces (2), parallel port, PS/2 mouse interface, serial ports (2), VRM connector, USB connectors (2), VRM connector
NPU Options	None

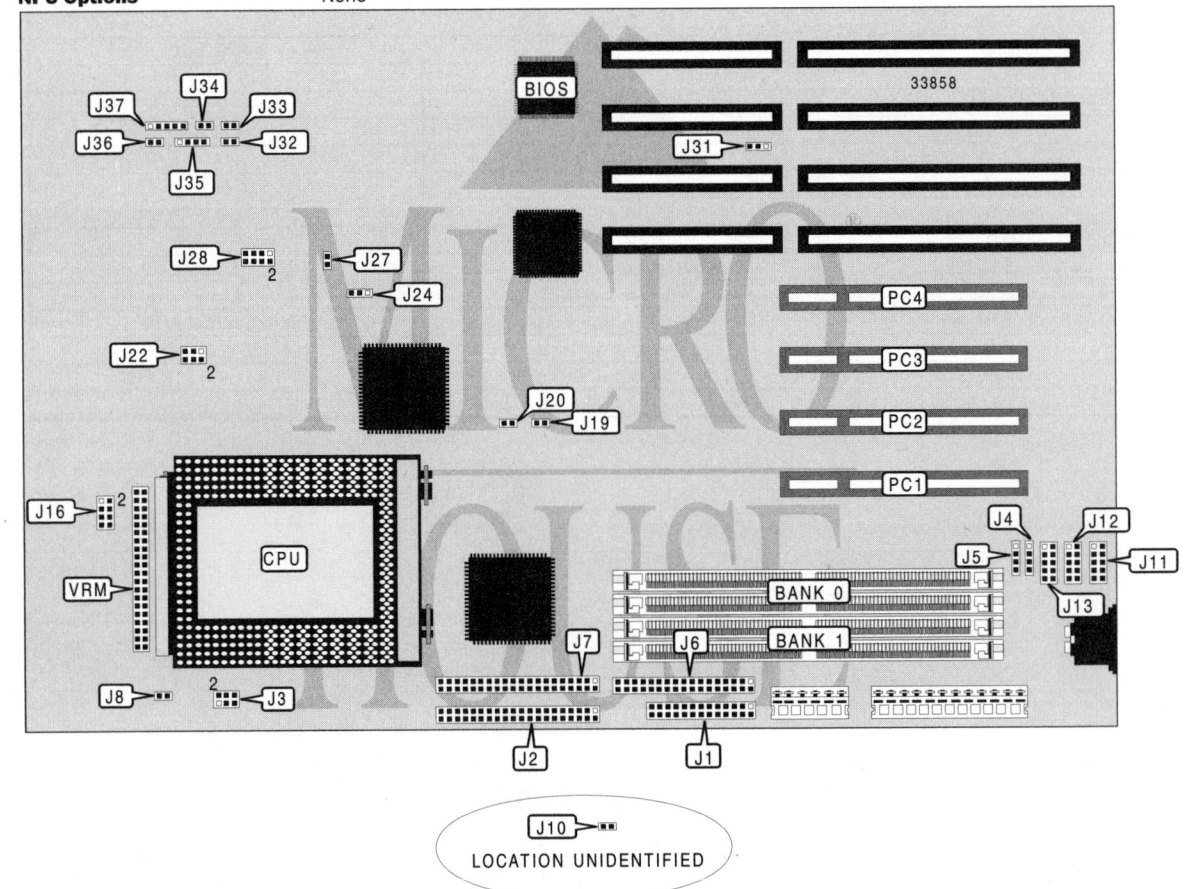

Continued on next page...

AMERICAN MEGATRENDS, INC.
MERLIN PCI

... continued from previous page

CONNECTIONS			
Purpose	**Location**	**Purpose**	**Location**
Parallel port	J1	Serial port 2	J12
IDE interface 1	J2	Serial port 1	J13
USB connector 2	J4	Reset switch	J32
USB connector 1	J5	Turbo switch	J34
Floppy drive interface	J6	Speaker	J35
IDE interface 2	J7	IDE interface LED	J36
Chassis fan power	J8	Power LED & keylock	J37
Green PC connector	J10	32-bit PCI slots	PC1 - PC4
PS/2 mouse interface	J11	VRM connector	VRM

USER CONFIGURABLE SETTINGS		
Function	**Label**	**Position**
◊ Factory configured - do not alter	J24	Unidentified
◊ Factory configured - do not alter	J27	Unidentified
PS/2 mouse IRQ12 enabled	J31	Pins 1 & 2 closed
PS/2 mouse IRQ12 disabled	J31	Pins 2 & 3 closed
◊ Factory configured - do not alter	J33	Unidentified

DRAM CONFIGURATION		
Size	**Bank 0**	**Bank 1**
8MB	(2) 1M x 36	None
16MB	(2) 2M x 36	None
16MB	(2) 1M x 36	(2) 1M x 36
24MB	(2) 2M x 36	(2) 1M x 36
32MB	(2) 4M x 36	None
32MB	(2) 2M x 36	(2) 2M x 36
40MB	(2) 4M x 36	(2) 1M x 36
48MB	(2) 2M x 36	(2) 4M x 36
64MB	(2) 8M x 36	None
64MB	(2) 4M x 36	(2) 4M x 36
72MB	(2) 8M x 36	(2) 1M x 36
80MB	(2) 2M x 36	(2) 8M x 36
96MB	(2) 8M x 36	(2) 4M x 36
128MB	(2) 16M x 36	None
128MB	(2) 8M x 36	(2) 8M x 36
136MB	(2) 16M x 36	(2) 1M x 36
144MB	(2) 16M x 36	(2) 2M x 36
160MB	(2) 16M x 36	(2) 4M x 36
192MB	(2) 16M x 36	(2) 8M x 36
256MB	(2) 32M x 36	None
256MB	(2) 16M x 36	(2) 16M x 36

Continued on next page...

AMERICAN MEGATRENDS, INC.
MERLIN PCI

. . . continued from previous page

DRAM CONFIGURATION (CON'T)		
Size	**Bank 0**	**Bank 1**
264MB	(2) 32M x 36	(2) 1M x 36
272MB	(2) 32M x 36	(2) 2M x 36
288MB	(2) 32M x 36	(2) 4M x 36
320MB	(2) 32M x 36	(2) 8M x 36
384MB	(2) 32M x 36	(2) 16M x 36
512MB	(2) 32M x 36	(2) 32M x 36

Note: Board accepts EDO memory. Board also accepts x 32 SIMMs. Banks are interchangeable.

CACHE CONFIGURATION
Note: 256KB/512KB cache is located on the Pentium Pro CPU.

CPU SPEED SELECTION					
CPU speed	**Clock speed**	**Multiplier**	**J19**	**J20**	**J28**
150MHz	60MHz	2.5x	Open	Closed	3 & 4, 5 & 6, 7 & 8
166MHz	66MHz	2.5x	Closed	Open	3 & 4, 5 & 6, 7 & 8
180MHz	60MHz	3x	Open	Closed	1 & 2, 5 & 6, 7 & 8
200MHz	66MHz	3x	Closed	Open	1 & 2, 5 & 6, 7 & 8

Note: Pins designated should be in the closed position.

CPU VOLTAGE SELECTION	
Voltage	**J16**
None	Open
2.1v	Pins 7 & 8 closed
2.2v	Pins 5 & 6 closed
2.3v	Pins 5 & 6, 7 & 8 closed
2.4v	Pins 3 & 4 closed
2.5v	Pins 3 & 4, 5 & 6 closed
2.6v	Pins 3 & 4, 5 & 6 closed
2.7v	Pins 3 & 4, 5 & 6, 7 & 8 closed
2.8v	Pins 1 & 2 closed
2.9v	Pins 1 & 2, 7 & 8 closed
3.0v	Pins 1 & 2, 5 & 6 closed
3.1v	Pins 1 & 2, 5 & 6, 7 & 8 closed
3.2v	Pins 1 & 2, 3 & 4 closed
3.3v	Pins 1 & 2, 3 & 4, 7 & 8 closed
3.4v	Pins 1 & 2, 3 & 4, 5 & 6 closed
3.5v	Pins 1 & 2, 3 & 4, 5 & 6, 7 & 8 closed

VOLTAGE SELECTION		
Setting	**J3**	**J22**
From regulator	Open	Pins 1 & 2, 3 & 4, 5 & 6 closed
From 3.3v power supply	Pins 1 & 2, 3 & 4, 5 & 6 closed	Open

AMERICAN MEGATRENDS, INC.
PEGASUS

Processor	Pentium II
Processor Speed	200/233/266/300MHz
Chip Set	Unidentified
Video Chip Set	None
Maximum Onboard Memory	768MB (EDO supported)
Maximum Video Memory	None
Cache	256/512KB (located on Pentium II CPU)
BIOS	AMI
Dimensions	330mm x 218mm
I/O Options	32-bit PCI slots (4), floppy drive interface, green PC connector, IDE interfaces (2), parallel port, PS/2 mouse interface, serial ports (2), IR connector, VRM connector, USB connectors (2), CPU Slot 1
NPU Options	None

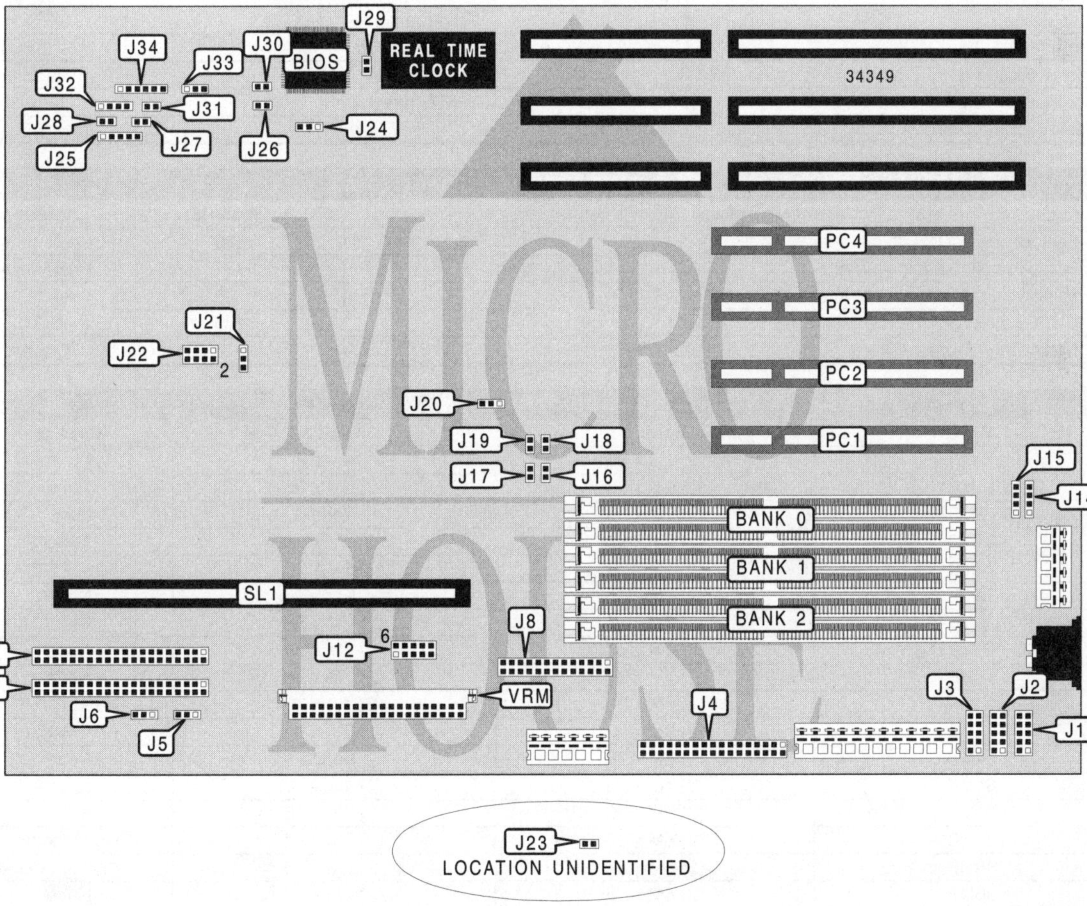

Continued on next page...

AMERICAN MEGATRENDS, INC.
PEGASUS

...continued from previous page

CONNECTIONS			
Purpose	**Location**	**Purpose**	**Location**
PS/2 mouse interface	J1	Power LED & keylock	J25
Serial port 2	J2	Reset switch	J27
Serial port 1	J3	Turbo LED	J28
Floppy drive interface	J4	Green PC connector	J30
Chassis fan power	J5	IDE interface LED	J31
CPU fan power	J6	Speaker	J32
Parallel port	J8	Chassis fan power	J33
IDE interface 2	J9	IR connector	J34
IDE interface 1	J11	32-bit PCI slots	PC1 – PC4
USB connector 2	J14	CPU Slot 1	SL1
USB connector 1	J15	VRM connector	VRM
Chassis door intrusion connector	J23		

USER CONFIGURABLE SETTINGS		
Function	**Label**	**Position**
✧ Factory configured - do not alter	J20	Unidentified
✧ Factory configured - do not alter	J24	Unidentified
✧ Factory configured - do not alter	J26	Unidentified
✧ CMOS memory normal operation	J29	Open
CMOS memory clear	J29	Closed

DRAM CONFIGURATION			
Size	**Bank 0**	**Bank 1**	**Bank 2**
8MB	(2) 1M x 36	None	None
16MB	(2) 1M x 36	(2) 1M x 36	None
16MB	(2) 2M x 36	None	None
24MB	(2) 2M x 36	(2) 1M x 36	None
24MB	(2) 1M x 36	(2) 1M x 36	(2) 1M x 36
32MB	(2) 4M x 36	None	None
32MB	(2) 2M x 36	(2) 2M x 36	None
40MB	(2) 4M x 36	(2) 1M x 36	None
48MB	(2) 4M x 36	(2) 2M x 36	None
48MB	(2) 4M x 36	(2) 1M x 36	(2) 1M x 36
56MB	(2) 4M x 36	(2) 2M x 36	(2) 1M x 36
64MB	(2) 8M x 36	None	None
64MB	(2) 4M x 36	(2) 4M x 36	None
80MB	(2) 8M x 36	(2) 2M x 36	None
80MB	(2) 8M x 36	(2) 1M x 36	(2) 1M x 36
88MB	(2) 8M x 36	(2) 2M x 36	(2) 1M x 36
96MB	(2) 8M x 36	(2) 4M x 36	None
96MB	(2) 4M x 36	(2) 4M x 36	(2) 4M x 36
96MB	(2) 8M x 36	(2) 2M x 36	(2) 2M x 36

Continued on next page...

AMERICAN MEGATRENDS, INC.
PEGASUS

. . . continued from previous page

DRAM CONFIGURATION (CON'T)

Size	Bank 0	Bank 1	Bank 2
104MB	(2) 8M x 36	(2) 4M x 36	(2) 1M x 36
112MB	(2) 8M x 36	(2) 4M x 36	(2) 2M x 36
128MB	(2) 8M x 36	(2) 4M x 36	(2) 4M x 36
128MB	(2) 16M x 36	None	None
128MB	(2) 8M x 36	(2) 8M x 36	None
136MB	(2) 8M x 36	(2) 8M x 36	(2) 1M x 36
136MB	(2) 16M x 36	(2) 1M x 36	None
144MB	(2) 16M x 36	(2) 2M x 36	None
144MB	(2) 16M x 36	(2) 1M x 36	(2) 1M x 36
160MB	(2) 16M x 36	(2) 4M x 36	None
160MB	(2) 16M x 36	(2) 2M x 36	(2) 2M x 36
168MB	(2) 16M x 36	(2) 4M x 36	(2) 1M x 36
176MB	(2) 16M x 36	(2) 4M x 36	(2) 2M x 36
192MB	(2) 16M x 36	(2) 8M x 36	None
192MB	(2) 16M x 36	(2) 4M x 36	(2) 4M x 36
200MB	(2) 16M x 36	(2) 8M x 36	(2) 1M x 36
208MB	(2) 16M x 36	(2) 8M x 36	(2) 2M x 36
224MB	(2) 16M x 36	(2) 8M x 36	(2) 4M x 36
256MB	(2) 16M x 36	(2) 16M x 36	None
256MB	(2) 16M x 36	(2) 8M x 36	(2) 8M x 36
256MB	(2) 32M x 36	None	None
264MB	(2) 16M x 36	(2) 16M x 36	(2) 1M x 36
272MB	(2) 16M x 36	(2) 16M x 36	(2) 2M x 36
288MB	(2) 16M x 36	(2) 16M x 36	(2) 4M x 36
320MB	(2) 16M x 36	(2) 16M x 36	(2) 8M x 36
384MB	(2) 16M x 36	(2) 16M x 36	(2) 16M x 36
512MB	(2) 32M x 36	(2) 32M x 36	None
520MB	(2) 32M x 36	(2) 32M x 36	(2) 1M x 36
528MB	(2) 32M x 36	(2) 32M x 36	(2) 2M x 36
544MB	(2) 32M x 36	(2) 32M x 36	(2) 4M x 36
576MB	(2) 32M x 36	(2) 32M x 36	(2) 8M x 36
640MB	(2) 32M x 36	(2) 32M x 36	(2) 16M x 36
768MB	(2) 32M x 36	(2) 32M x 36	(2) 32M x 36

Note: Board accepts EDO memory. Board also accepts x 32 SIMMs. Do not use 16M x 36 SIMMs that have more than 36 chips per SIMM.

CACHE CONFIGURATION

Note: 256KB/512KB cache is located on the Pentium II CPU.

Continued on next page. . .

AMERICAN MEGATRENDS, INC.
PEGASUS

. . . continued from previous page

CPU SPEED SELECTION					
CPU speed	**Clock speed**	**Multiplier**	**J16**	**J17**	**J18**
200MHz	66MHz	3x	Closed	Open	Closed
233MHz	66MHz	3.5x	Closed	Open	Closed
266MHz	66MHz	4x	Closed	Open	Closed
300MHz	66MHz	4.5x	Closed	Open	Closed

CPU SPEED SELECTION (CON'T)					
CPU speed	**Clock speed**	**Multiplier**	**J19**	**J21**	**J22**
200MHz	66MHz	3x	Open	1 & 2	1 & 2, 5 & 6, 7 & 8
233MHz	66MHz	3.5x	Open	1 & 2	5 & 6, 7 & 8
266MHz	66MHz	4x	Open	1 & 2	1 & 2, 3 & 4, 7 & 8
300MHz	66MHz	4.5x	Open	1 & 2	3 & 4, 7 & 8

Note: Pins designated should be in the closed position.

CPU VOLTAGE SELECTION	
Voltage	**J12**
1.8v	Pins 1 & 6, 2 & 7, 4 & 9 closed
1.85v	Pins 1 & 6, 2 & 7, 4 & 9, 5 & 10 closed
1.9v	Pins 1 & 6, 2 & 7, 3 & 8 closed
1.95v	Pins 1 & 6, 2 & 7, 3 & 8, 5 & 10 closed
2.0v	Pins 1 & 6, 2 & 7, 3 & 8, 4 & 9 closed
2.05v	Pins 1 & 6, 2 & 7, 3 & 8, 4 & 9, 5 & 10 closed
2.1v	Pins 5 & 10 closed
2.2v	Pins 4 & 9 closed
2.3v	Pins 4 & 9, 5 & 10 closed
2.4v	Pins 3 & 8 closed
2.5v	Pins 3 & 8, 5 & 10 closed
2.6v	Pins 3 & 8, 4 & 9 closed
2.7v	Pins 3 & 8, 4 & 9, 5 & 10 closed
⇨ 2.8v	Pins 2 & 7 closed
2.9v	Pins 2 & 7, 5 & 10 closed
3.0v	Pins 2 & 7, 4 & 9 closed
3.1v	Pins 2 & 7, 4 & 9, 5 & 10 closed
3.2v	Pins 2 & 7, 3 & 8 closed
3.3v	Pins 2 & 7, 3 & 8, 5 & 10 closed
3.4v	Pins 2 & 7, 3 & 8, 4 & 9 closed
3.5v	Pins 2 & 7, 3 & 8, 4 & 9, 5 & 10 closed

AMERICAN MEGATRENDS, INC.
TITAN II PCI

Processor	Pentium
Processor Speed	75/90/100MHz
Chip Set	Unidentified
Video Chip Set	None
Maximum Onboard Memory	512MB
Maximum Video Memory	None
Cache	256/512KB
BIOS	AMI
Dimensions	351mm x 307mm
I/O Options	32-bit PCI slots (4), floppy drive interface, green PC connector, IDE interfaces (2), parallel port, PS/2 mouse interface, serial ports (2), green VGA interface
NPU Options	None

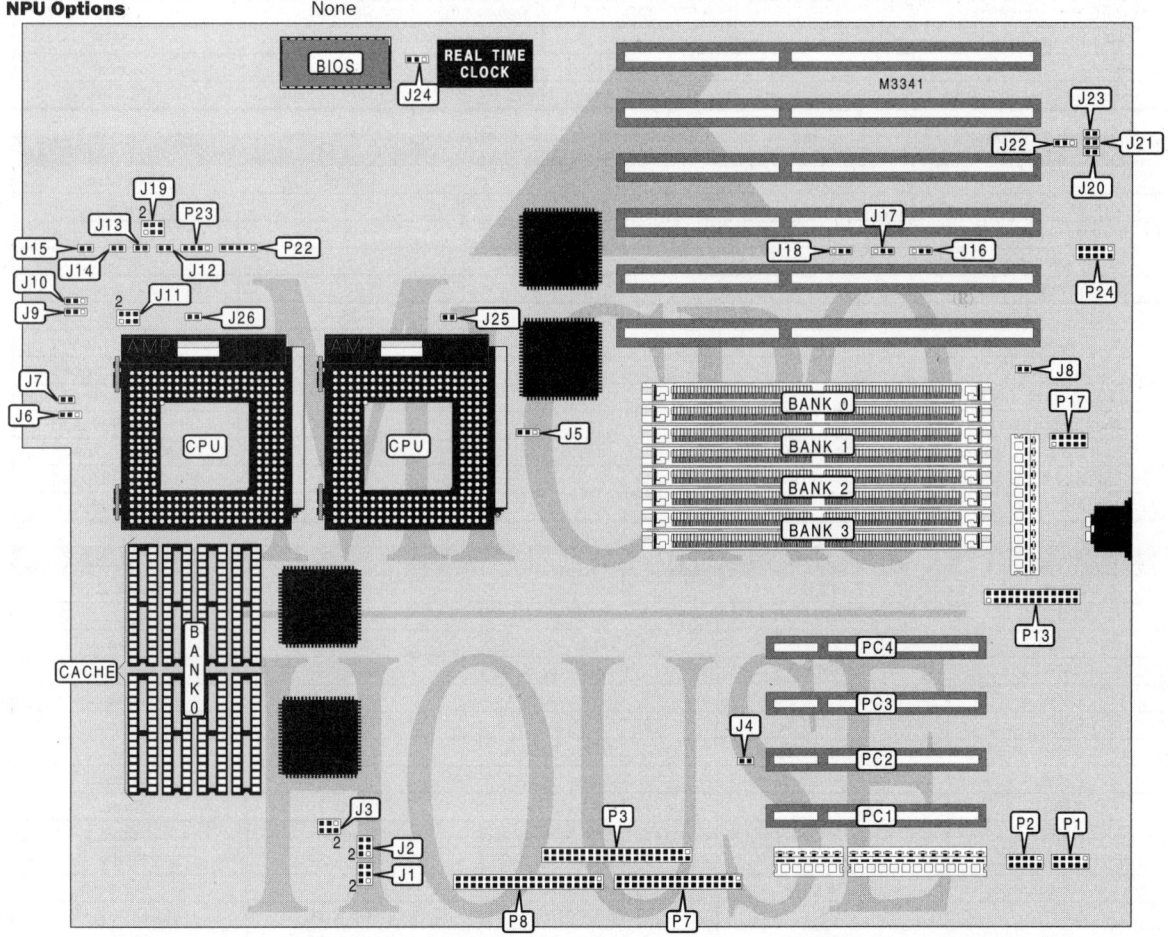

Continued on next page...

AMERICAN MEGATRENDS, INC.
TITAN II PCI

...continued from previous page

CONNECTIONS

Purpose	Location	Purpose	Location
Reset switch	J12	Serial port 2	P2
Turbo LED	J13	IDE interface 1	P3
IDE interface LED	J14	Floppy drive interface	P7
Diagnostic LED	J15	IDE interface 2	P8
Green PC connector	J20	Parallel port	P13
Password LED	J21	PS/2 mouse interface	P17
Green PC connector	J23	Power LED & keylock	P22
Chassis fan power	J25	Speaker	P23
Chassis fan power	J26	Green VGA interface	P24
Serial port 1	P1	32-bit PCI slots	PC1 - PC4

USER CONFIGURABLE SETTINGS

Function	Label	Position
Jumper information unavailable	J4	N/A
⇨ Factory configured - do not alter CPU type select	J5	Pins 2 & 3 closed
Single processor installed	J6	Pins 2 & 3 closed
Dual processors installed	J6	Pins 1 & 2 closed
Jumper information unavailable	J8	N/A
PLL normal operation	J10	Pins 2 & 3 closed
PLL test mode	J10	Pins 1 & 2 closed
⇨ Parallel port IRQ select IRQ7	J18	Pins 1 & 2 closed
Parallel port IRQ select IRQ5	J18	Pins 2 & 3 closed
Password LED select power LED through password LED	J22	Pins 1 & 2 closed
Password LED select separate LED through J21.	J22	Pins 2 & 3 closed
⇨ Flash BIOS voltage select 12v	J24	Pins 2 & 3 closed

DRAM CONFIGURATION

Size	Bank 0	Bank 1	Bank 2	Bank 3
2MB	(2) 256K x 36	None	None	None
4MB	(2) 512K x 36	None	None	None
4MB	(2) 256K x 36	(2) 256K x 36	None	None
6MB	(2) 512K x 36	(2) 256K x 36	None	None
6MB	(2) 256K x 36	(2) 256K x 36	(2) 256K x 36	None
6MB	(2) 256K x 36	(2) 512K x 36	None	None
8MB	(2) 1M x 36	None	None	None
8MB	(2) 512K x 36	(2) 256K x 36	(2) 256K x 36	None
8MB	(2) 512K x 36	(2) 512K x 36	None	None
8MB	(2) 256K x 36	(2) 256K x 36	(2) 256K x 36	(2) 256K x 36
10MB	(2) 1M x 36	(2) 256K x 36	None	None
10MB	(2) 512K x 36	(2) 256K x 36	(2) 256K x 36	(2) 256K x 36
10MB	(2) 256K x 36	(2) 512K x 36	(2) 512K x 36	None
10MB	(2) 256K x 36	(2) 1M x 36	None	None
12MB	(2) 1M x 36	(2) 256K x 36	(2) 256K x 36	None

Continued on next page...

AMERICAN MEGATRENDS, INC.
TITAN II PCI

. . . continued from previous page

Size	Bank 0	Bank 1	Bank 2	Bank 3
\multicolumn{5}{c}{**DRAM CONFIGURATION (CON'T)**}				
12MB	(2) 1M x 36	(2) 512K x 36	None	None
12MB	(2) 512K x 36	(2) 512K x 36	(2) 512K x 36	None
12MB	(2) 512K x 36	(2) 1M x 36	None	None
14MB	(2) 1M x 36	(2) 256K x 36	(2) 256K x 36	(2) 256K x 36
14MB	(2) 256K x 36	(2) 512K x 36	(2) 512K x 36	(2) 512K x 36
16MB	(2) 2M x 36	None	None	None
16MB	(2) 1M x 36	(2) 512K x 36	(2) 512K x 36	None
16MB	(2) 1M x 36	(2) 1M x 36	None	None
16MB	(2) 512K x 36	(2) 512K x 36	(2) 512K x 36	(2) 512K x 36
18MB	(2) 2M x 36	(2) 256K x 36	None	None
18MB	(2) 256K x 36	(2) 1M x 36	(2) 1M x 36	None
18MB	(2) 256K x 36	(2) 2M x 36	None	None
20MB	(2) 2M x 36	(2) 256K x 36	(2) 256K x 36	None
20MB	(2) 2M x 36	(2) 512K x 36	None	None
20MB	(2) 1M x 36	(2) 512K x 36	(2) 512K x 36	(2) 512K x 36
20MB	(2) 512K x 36	(2) 1M x 36	(2) 1M x 36	None
20MB	(2) 512K x 36	(2) 2M x 36	None	None
22MB	(2) 2M x 36	(2) 256K x 36	(2) 256K x 36	(2) 256K x 36
24MB	(2) 2M x 36	(2) 512K x 36	(2) 512K x 36	None
24MB	(2) 2M x 36	(2) 1M x 36	None	None
24MB	(2) 1M x 36	(2) 1M x 36	(2) 1M x 36	None
24MB	(2) 1M x 36	(2) 2M x 36	None	None
26MB	(2) 256K x 36	(2) 1M x 36	(2) 1M x 36	(2) 1M x 36
28MB	(2) 2M x 36	(2) 512K x 36	(2) 512K x 36	(2) 512K x 36
28MB	(2) 512K x 36	(2) 1M x 36	(2) 1M x 36	(2) 1M x 36
32MB	(2) 4M x 36	None	None	None
32MB	(2) 2M x 36	(2) 1M x 36	(2) 1M x 36	None
32MB	(2) 2M x 36	(2) 2M x 36	None	None
32MB	(2) 1M x 36	(2) 1M x 36	(2) 1M x 36	(2) 1M x 36
34MB	(2) 4M x 36	(2) 256K x 36	None	None
34MB	(2) 256K x 36	(2) 2M x 36	(2) 2M x 36	None
34MB	(2) 256K x 36	(2) 4M x 36	None	None
36MB	(2) 4M x 36	(2) 256K x 36	(2) 256K x 36	None
36MB	(2) 4M x 36	(2) 512K x 36	None	None
36MB	(2) 512K x 36	(2) 2M x 36	(2) 2M x 36	None
36MB	(2) 512K x 36	(2) 4M x 36	None	None
38MB	(2) 4M x 36	(2) 256K x 36	(2) 256K x 36	(2) 256K x 36
40MB	(2) 4M x 36	(2) 512K x 36	(2) 512K x 36	None
40MB	(2) 4M x 36	(2) 1M x 36	None	None
40MB	(2) 2M x 36	(2) 1M x 36	(2) 1M x 36	(2) 1M x 36
40MB	(2) 1M x 36	(2) 2M x 36	(2) 2M x 36	None
40MB	(2) 1M x 36	(2) 4M x 36	None	None

Continued on next page. . .

AMERICAN MEGATRENDS, INC.
TITAN II PCI

. . . continued from previous page

Size	Bank 0	Bank 1	Bank 2	Bank 3
\multicolumn{5}{c}{DRAM CONFIGURATION (CON'T)}				
44MB	(2) 4M x 36	(2) 512K x 36	(2) 512K x 36	(2) 512K x 36
48MB	(2) 4M x 36	(2) 1M x 36	(2) 1M x 36	None
48MB	(2) 4M x 36	(2) 2M x 36	None	None
48MB	(2) 2M x 36	(2) 2M x 36	(2) 2M x 36	None
48MB	(2) 2M x 36	(2) 4M x 36	None	None
50MB	(2) 256K x 36	(2) 2M x 36	(2) 2M x 36	(2) 2M x 36
52MB	(2) 512K x 36	(2) 2M x 36	(2) 2M x 36	(2) 2M x 36
56MB	(2) 4M x 36	(2) 1M x 36	(2) 1M x 36	(2) 1M x 36
56MB	(2) 1M x 36	(2) 2M x 36	(2) 2M x 36	(2) 2M x 36
64MB	(2) 8M x 36	None	None	None
64MB	(2) 4M x 36	(2) 2M x 36	(2) 2M x 36	None
64MB	(2) 4M x 36	(2) 4M x 36	None	None
64MB	(2) 2M x 36	(2) 2M x 36	(2) 2M x 36	(2) 2M x 36
66MB	(2) 8M x 36	(2) 256K x 36	None	None
66MB	(2) 256K x 36	(2) 4M x 36	(2) 4M x 36	None
66MB	(2) 256K x 36	(2) 8M x 36	None	None
68MB	(2) 8M x 36	(2) 256K x 36	(2) 256K x 36	None
68MB	(2) 8M x 36	(2) 512K x 36	None	None
68MB	(2) 512K x 36	(2) 4M x 36	(2) 4M x 36	None
68MB	(2) 512K x 36	(2) 8M x 36	None	None
70MB	(2) 8M x 36	(2) 256K x 36	(2) 256K x 36	(2) 256K x 36
72MB	(2) 8M x 36	(2) 512K x 36	(2) 512K x 36	None
72MB	(2) 8M x 36	(2) 1M x 36	None	None
72MB	(2) 1M x 36	(2) 4M x 36	(2) 4M x 36	None
72MB	(2) 1M x 36	(2) 8M x 36	None	None
76MB	(2) 8M x 36	(2) 512K x 36	(2) 512K x 36	(2) 512K x 36
80MB	(2) 8M x 36	(2) 1M x 36	(2) 1M x 36	None
80MB	(2) 8M x 36	(2) 2M x 36	None	None
80MB	(2) 4M x 36	(2) 2M x 36	(2) 2M x 36	(2) 2M x 36
80MB	(2) 2M x 36	(2) 4M x 36	(2) 4M x 36	None
80MB	(2) 2M x 36	(2) 8M x 36	None	None
88MB	(2) 8M x 36	(2) 1M x 36	(2) 1M x 36	(2) 1M x 36
96MB	(2) 8M x 36	(2) 2M x 36	(2) 2M x 36	None
96MB	(2) 8M x 36	(2) 4M x 36	None	None
96MB	(2) 4M x 36	(2) 4M x 36	(2) 4M x 36	None
96MB	(2) 4M x 36	(2) 8M x 36	None	None
98MB	(2) 256K x 36	(2) 4M x 36	(2) 4M x 36	(2) 4M x 36
100MB	(2) 512K x 36	(2) 4M x 36	(2) 4M x 36	(2) 4M x 36
104MB	(2) 1M x 36	(2) 4M x 36	(2) 4M x 36	(2) 4M x 36
112MB	(2) 8M x 36	(2) 2M x 36	(2) 2M x 36	(2) 2M x 36
112MB	(2) 2M x 36	(2) 4M x 36	(2) 4M x 36	(2) 4M x 36
128MB	(2) 8M x 36	(2) 4M x 36	(2) 4M x 36	None

Continued on next page. . .

AMERICAN MEGATRENDS, INC.
TITAN II PCI

...continued from previous page

DRAM CONFIGURATION (CON'T)				
Size	Bank 0	Bank 1	Bank 2	Bank 3
128MB	(2) 8M x 36	(2) 8M x 36	None	None
128MB	(2) 4M x 36	(2) 4M x 36	(2) 4M x 36	(2) 4M x 36
128MB	(2) 16M x 36	None	None	None
130MB	(2) 256K x 36	(2) 8M x 36	(2) 8M x 36	None
130MB	(2) 16M x 36	(2) 256K x 36	None	None
132MB	(2) 512K x 36	(2) 8M x 36	(2) 8M x 36	None
132MB	(2) 16M x 36	(2) 256K x 36	(2) 256K x 36	None
134MB	(2) 16M x 36	(2) 256K x 36	(2) 256K x 36	(2) 256K x 36
136MB	(2) 1M x 36	(2) 8M x 36	(2) 8M x 36	None
136MB	(2) 16M x 36	(2) 1M x 36	None	None
144MB	(2) 2M x 36	(2) 8M x 36	(2) 8M x 36	None
144MB	(2) 16M x 36	(2) 1M x 36	(2) 1M x 36	None
152MB	(2) 16M x 36	(2) 1M x 36	(2) 1M x 36	(2) 1M x 36
160MB	(2) 8M x 36	(2) 4M x 36	(2) 4M x 36	(2) 4M x 36
160MB	(2) 4M x 36	(2) 8M x 36	(2) 8M x 36	None
192MB	(2) 8M x 36	(2) 8M x 36	(2) 8M x 36	None
194MB	(2) 256K x 36	(2) 8M x 36	(2) 8M x 36	(2) 8M x 36
196MB	(2) 512K x 36	(2) 8M x 36	(2) 8M x 36	(2) 8M x 36
200MB	(2) 1M x 36	(2) 8M x 36	(2) 8M x 36	(2) 8M x 36
208MB	(2) 2M x 36	(2) 8M x 36	(2) 8M x 36	(2) 8M x 36
224MB	(2) 4M x 36	(2) 8M x 36	(2) 8M x 36	(2) 8M x 36
256MB	(2) 8M x 36	(2) 8M x 36	(2) 8M x 36	(2) 8M x 36
256MB	(2) 16M x 36	(2) 16M x 36	None	None
384MB	(2) 16M x 36	(2) 16M x 36	(2) 16M x 36	None
512MB	(2) 16M x 36	(2) 16M x 36	(2) 16M x 36	(2) 16M x 36

CACHE CONFIGURATION	
Size	Bank 0
256KB	(8) 32K x 8
512KB	(8) 64K x 8

CACHE JUMPER CONFIGURATION	
Size	J9
256KB	Pins 1 & 2 closed
512KB	Pins 2 & 3 closed

CPU SPEED SELECTION		
CPU speed	Clock speed	J7
75MHz	50MHz	Open
90MHz	60MHz	Open
100MHz	50MHz	Closed
100MHz	66MHz	Open

Continued on next page...

AMERICAN MEGATRENDS, INC.
TITAN II PCI

. . . continued from previous page

DMA CHANNEL SELECTION		
Channel	J16	J17
⇨ Disabled	Open	Open
1	Pins 1 & 2 closed	Pins 1 & 2 closed
3	Pins 2 & 3 closed	Pins 2 & 3 closed

3.3V POWER SUPPLY SELECTION					
Setting	J1	J2	J3	J11	J19
Internal	Open	Open	1&2, 3&4, 5&6	Open	1&2, 3&4, 5&6
External	1&2, 3&4, 5&6	1&2, 3&4, 5&6	Open	1&2, 3&4, 5&6	Open

Note: Pins designated should be in the closed position. If external setting is selected, connect power cables to P5 and P6.

AST RESEARCH, INC.
MANHATTAN G PENTIUM (202671-102, 103)

Processor	Pentium
Processor Speed	75/90/100MHz
Chip Set	Unidentified
Max. Onboard DRAM	128MB
Cache	256KB
BIOS	Unidentified
Dimensions	330mm x 218mm
I/O Options	Floppy drive interface, IDE interface, parallel port, PS/2 mouse port, serial ports (2), 8514 video pass through connector, VGA port, riser slot
NPU Options	None

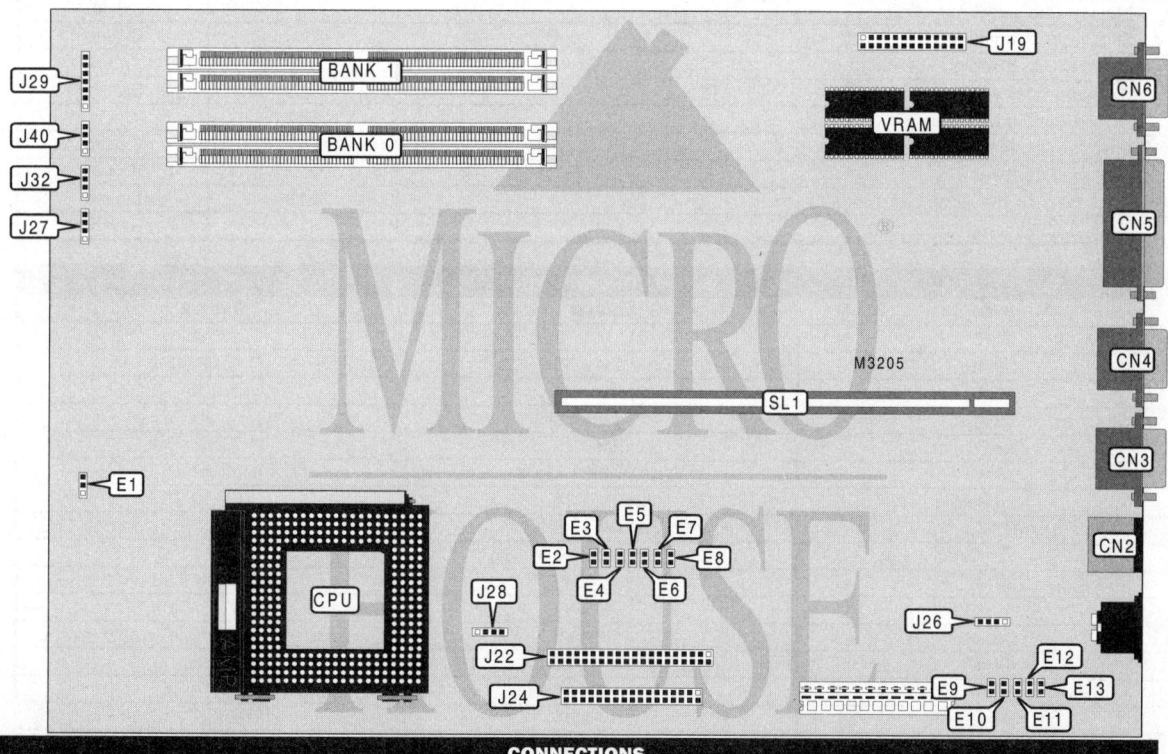

CONNECTIONS			
Purpose	Location	Purpose	Location
PS/2 mouse port	CN2	External battery	J26
Serial port	CN3	Speaker	J27
Serial port	CN4	Chassis fan power	J28
Parallel port	CN5	Front panel connector	J29
VGA port	CN6	Chassis fan power	J32
8514 video pass through connector	J19	IDE interface LED	J40
IDE interface	J22	Riser slot	SL1
Floppy drive interface	J24		

Continued on next page...

AST RESEARCH, INC.
MANHATTAN G PENTIUM (202671-102, 103)

...continued from previous page

USER CONFIGURABLE SETTINGS

Function	Jumper	Position
◊ Factory configured - do not alter	E4	Open
◊ Factory configured - do not alter (model extension # -301)	E5	Open
◊ Factory configured - do not alter (model extension # -302)	E5	Closed
◊ Factory configured - do not alter	E6	Open
◊ Factory configured - do not alter	E8	Open
◊ Monitor type select color	E9	Closed
Monitor type select monochrome	E9	Open
◊ Setup access enabled	E10	Closed
Setup access disabled	E10	Open
◊ On board video enabled	E11	Closed
On board video disabled	E11	Open
◊ Password enabled	E12	Closed
Password disabled	E12	Open
◊ Flash BIOS normal operation	E13	Closed
Flash BIOS force update at boot	E13	Open

DRAM CONFIGURATION

Size	Bank 0	Bank 1
8MB	(2) 1M x 36	NONE
10MB	(2) 1M x 36	(2) 256K x 36
16MB	(2) 2M x 36	NONE
16MB	(2) 1M x 36	(2) 1M x 36
18MB	(2) 2M x 36	(2) 256K x 36
18MB	(2) 256K x 36	(2) 2M x 36
24MB	(2) 2M x 36	(2) 1M x 36
32MB	(2) 4M x 36	NONE
32MB	(2) 2M x 36	(2) 2M x 36
34MB	(2) 4M x 36	(2) 256K x 36
40MB	(2) 4M x 36	(2) 1M x 36
48MB	(2) 4M x 36	(2) 2M x 36
64MB	(2) 8M x 36	NONE
64MB	(2) 4M x 36	(2) 4M x 36
66MB	(2) 8M x 36	(2) 256K x 36
68MB	(2) 8M x 36	(2) 512K x 36
72MB	(2) 8M x 36	(2) 1M x 36
80MB	(2) 8M x 36	(2) 2M x 36
96MB	(2) 8M x 36	(2) 4M x 36
128MB	(2) 8M x 36	(2) 8M x 36

CACHE CONFIGURATION

Note: 256KB cache is factory installed and is not configurable. The location is unidentified.

Continued on next page...

AST RESEARCH, INC.
MANHATTAN G PENTIUM (202671-102, 103)

...continued from previous page

CPU SPEED CONFIGURATION (IMI415)					
Speed	**E1**	**E2**	**E3**	**E7**
75MHz	pins 2 & 3 closed	Open	Closed	Closed
90MHz	pins 2 & 3 closed	Open	Closed	Open
100MHz	pins 2 & 3 closed	Closed	Closed	Open

CPU SPEED CONFIGURATION (IMI470)					
Speed	**E1**	**E2**	**E3**	**E7**
75MHz	pins 2 & 3 closed	Open	Closed	Open
90MHz	pins 2 & 3 closed	Open	Closed	Closed
100MHz	pins 2 & 3 closed	Closed	Closed	Closed

VIDEO MEMORY CONFIGURATION	
Note:	512KB is factory installed and is not configurable.

94 Motherboard Settings and Specifications

AST RESEARCH, INC.
MANHATTAN V PENTIUM
(202620-001, 002, 011, 012)

Processor	Pentium
Processor Speed	90/100/133MHz
Chip Set	Unidentified
Max. Onboard DRAM	256MB
Cache	256KB
BIOS	Unidentified
Dimensions	330mm x 218mm
I/O Options	32-bit PCI slots (3), CPU slot, floppy drive interface, SCSI interfaces (2), parallel port, PS/2 mouse port, serial ports (2), 8514 video pass through connector, VGA port
NPU Options	None

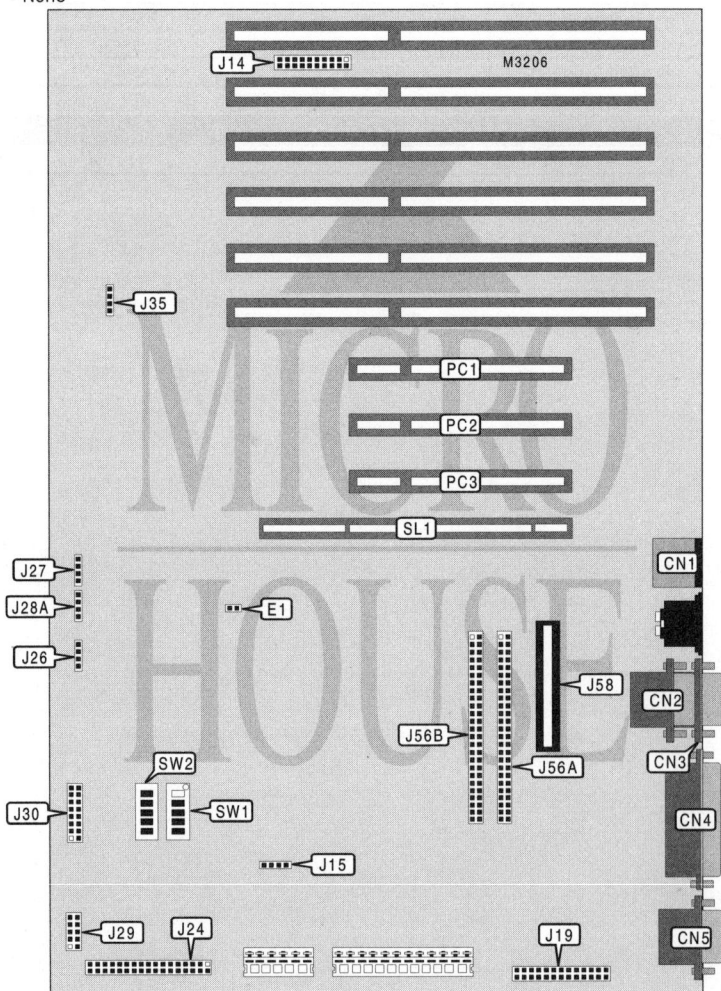

Continued on next page...

AST RESEARCH, INC.
MANHATTAN V PENTIUM (202620-001, 002, 011, 012)

...continued from previous page

CONNECTIONS			
Purpose	**Location**	**Purpose**	**Location**
PS/2 mouse port	CN1	Speaker	J27
Serial port	CN2	Chassis fan power	J28A
Serial port	CN3	Front panel console LED	J29
Parallel port	CN4	SCSI interface LED	J35
VGA port	CN5	Internal SCSI interface	J56A
System management interface	J14	External SCSI interface	J56B
Remote power connector	J15	XP interface board connector	J58
8514 video pass through connector	J19	32-bit PCI slots	PC1 - PC3
Floppy drive interface	J24	CPU slot	SL1
External battery	J26		

USER CONFIGURABLE SETTINGS		
Function	**Jumper/Switch**	**Position**
⇨ CMOS memory normal operation	E1	Open
CMOS memory clear	E1	Closed
⇨ Factory configured - do not alter	J30	N/A
⇨ Flash BIOS normal operation	SW1/1	Off
Flash BIOS force update at boot	SW1/1	On
⇨ Password enabled	SW1/2	Off
Password disabled	SW1/2	On
⇨ Monitor type select color	SW1/3	Off
Monitor type select monochrome	SW1/3	On
⇨ EISA CMOS memory normal operation	SW1/4	Off
EISA CMOS memory clear	SW1/4	On
⇨ Setup access enabled	SW1/5	Off
Setup access disabled	SW1/5	On
⇨ Factory configured - do not alter	SW2	N/A

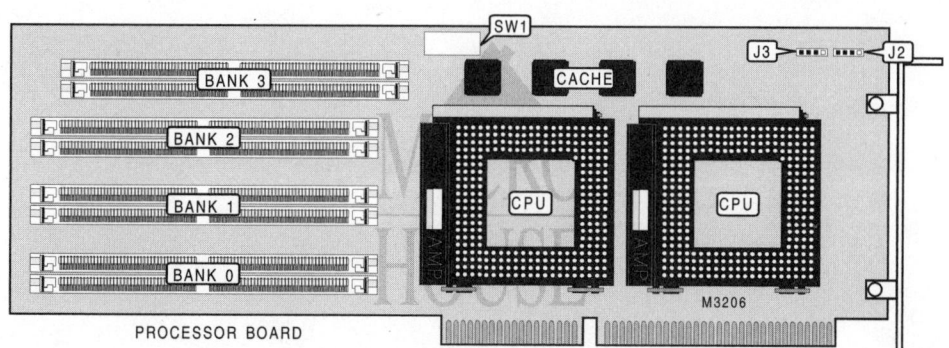

PROCESSOR BOARD

Continued on next page...

AST RESEARCH, INC.
MANHATTAN V PENTIUM
(202620-001, 002, 011, 012)

...continued from previous page

CONNECTIONS			
Purpose	**Location**	**Purpose**	**Location**
Chassis fan power	J2	Chassis fan power	J3

USER CONFIGURABLE SETTINGS		
Function	**Switch**	**Position**
⇨ Factory configured - do not alter	SW1	N/A

DRAM CONFIGURATION				
Size	**Bank 0**	**Bank 1**	**Bank 2**	**Bank 3**
16MB	(2) 2M x 36	NONE	NONE	NONE
32MB	(2) 2M x 36	(2) 2M x 36	NONE	NONE
32MB	(2) 4M x 36	NONE	NONE	NONE
48MB	(2) 4M x 36	(2) 2M x 36	NONE	NONE
64MB	(2) 2M x 36	(2) 2M x 36	(2) 4M x 36	NONE
64MB	(2) 8M x 36	NONE	NONE	NONE
80MB	(2) 2M x 36	(2) 4M x 36	(2) 4M x 36	NONE
80MB	(2) 8M x 36	(2) 2M x 36	NONE	NONE
80MB	(2) 4M x 36	(2) 2M x 36	(2) 4M x 36	NONE
96MB	(2) 2M x 36	(2) 2M x 36	(2) 4M x 36	(2) 4M x 36
96MB	(2) 2M x 36	(2) 2M x 36	(2) 8M x 36	NONE
96MB	(2) 4M x 36	(2) 4M x 36	(2) 4M x 36	NONE
112MB	(2) 2M x 36	(2) 4M x 36	(2) 4M x 36	(2) 4M x 36
112MB	(2) 2M x 36	(2) 4M x 36	(2) 8M x 36	NONE
112MB	(2) 2M x 36	(2) 8M x 36	(2) 4M x 36	NONE
112MB	(2) 8M x 36	(2) 2M x 36	(2) 4M x 36	NONE
112MB	(2) 4M x 36	(2) 2M x 36	(2) 4M x 36	(2) 4M x 36

Continued on next page...

AST RESEARCH, INC.
MANHATTAN V PENTIUM
(202620-001, 002, 011, 012)

...continued from previous page

Size	Bank 0	Bank 1	Bank 2	Bank 3
112MB	(2) 4M x 36	(2) 2M x 36	(2) 8M x 36	NONE
128MB	(2) 2M x 36	(2) 2M x 36	(2) 4M x 36	(2) 8M x 36
128MB	(2) 2M x 36	(2) 2M x 36	(2) 8M x 36	(2) 4M x 36
128MB	(2) 8M x 36	(2) 4M x 36	(2) 4M x 36	NONE
128MB	(2) 4M x 36	(2) 4M x 36	(2) 4M x 36	(2) 4M x 36
128MB	(2) 4M x 36	(2) 4M x 36	(2) 8M x 36	NONE
128MB	(2) 4M x 36	(2) 8M x 36	(2) 4M x 36	NONE
144MB	(2) 2M x 36	(2) 4M x 36	(2) 4M x 36	(2) 8M x 36
144MB	(2) 2M x 36	(2) 4M x 36	(2) 8M x 36	(2) 4M x 36
144MB	(2) 2M x 36	(2) 8M x 36	(2) 4M x 36	(2) 4M x 36
144MB	(2) 2M x 36	(2) 8M x 36	(2) 8M x 36	NONE
144MB	(2) 8M x 36	(2) 2M x 36	(2) 4M x 36	(2) 4M x 36
144MB	(2) 8M x 36	(2) 2M x 36	(2) 8M x 36	NONE
144MB	(2) 4M x 36	(2) 4M x 36	(2) 4M x 36	(2) 8M x 36
144MB	(2) 4M x 36	(2) 4M x 36	(2) 8M x 36	(2) 4M x 36
160MB	(2) 2M x 36	(2) 2M x 36	(2) 8M x 36	(2) 8M x 36
160MB	(2) 8M x 36	(2) 4M x 36	(2) 4M x 36	(2) 4M x 36
160MB	(2) 8M x 36	(2) 4M x 36	(2) 8M x 36	NONE
160MB	(2) 8M x 36	(2) 8M x 36	(2) 4M x 36	NONE
160MB	(2) 4M x 36	(2) 4M x 36	(2) 4M x 36	(2) 8M x 36
160MB	(2) 4M x 36	(2) 4M x 36	(2) 8M x 36	(2) 4M x 36
160MB	(2) 4M x 36	(2) 8M x 36	(2) 4M x 36	(2) 4M x 36
160MB	(2) 4M x 36	(2) 8M x 36	(2) 8M x 36	NONE
176MB	(2) 2M x 36	(2) 4M x 36	(2) 8M x 36	(2) 8M x 36
176MB	(2) 2M x 36	(2) 8M x 36	(2) 4M x 36	(2) 8M x 36
176MB	(2) 2M x 36	(2) 8M x 36	(2) 8M x 36	(2) 4M x 36
176MB	(2) 8M x 36	(2) 2M x 36	(2) 4M x 36	(2) 8M x 36
176MB	(2) 8M x 36	(2) 2M x 36	(2) 8M x 36	(2) 4M x 36
176MB	(2) 4M x 36	(2) 2M x 36	(2) 8M x 36	(2) 8M x 36
192MB	(2) 8M x 36	(2) 4M x 36	(2) 4M x 36	(2) 8M x 36
192MB	(2) 8M x 36	(2) 4M x 36	(2) 8M x 36	(2) 4M x 36
192MB	(2) 8M x 36	(2) 8M x 36	(2) 4M x 36	(2) 4M x 36
192MB	(2) 8M x 36	(2) 8M x 36	(2) 8M x 36	NONE
192MB	(2) 4M x 36	(2) 4M x 36	(2) 8M x 36	(2) 8M x 36
192MB	(2) 4M x 36	(2) 8M x 36	(2) 4M x 36	(2) 8M x 36
192MB	(2) 4M x 36	(2) 8M x 36	(2) 8M x 36	(2) 4M x 36
208MB	(2) 2M x 36	(2) 8M x 36	(2) 8M x 36	(2) 8M x 36
208MB	(2) 8M x 36	(2) 2M x 36	(2) 8M x 36	(2) 8M x 36
224MB	(2) 8M x 36	(2) 4M x 36	(2) 8M x 36	(2) 8M x 36
224MB	(2) 8M x 36	(2) 8M x 36	(2) 4M x 36	(2) 8M x 36
224MB	(2) 8M x 36	(2) 8M x 36	(2) 8M x 36	(2) 4M x 36
224MB	(2) 4M x 36	(2) 8M x 36	(2) 8M x 36	(2) 8M x 36
256MB	(2) 8M x 36	(2) 8M x 36	(2) 8M x 36	(2) 8M x 36

Continued on next page...

AST RESEARCH, INC.
MANHATTAN V PENTIUM
(202620-001, 002, 011, 012)

. . . continued from previous page

CACHE CONFIGURATION

Note: 256KB cache is factory installed and is not configurable.

ASUS COMPUTER INTERNATIONAL
KN97-X

Processor	Pentium II
Processor Speed	233/266MHz
Chip Set	Intel
Video Chip Set	None
Maximum Onboard Memory	384MB (EDO supported)
Maximum Video Memory	None
Cache	256/512KB (located on Pentium II CPU)
BIOS	Unidentified
Dimensions	305mm x 244mm
I/O Options	32-bit PCI slots (5), CD-ROM audio in (3), floppy drive interface, green PC connector, IDE interfaces (2), parallel port, PS/2 mouse port, serial ports (2), IR connector, USB connectors (2), ATX power connector. game/MIDI port, microphone in, line in, line out, CPU Slot 1
NPU Options	None

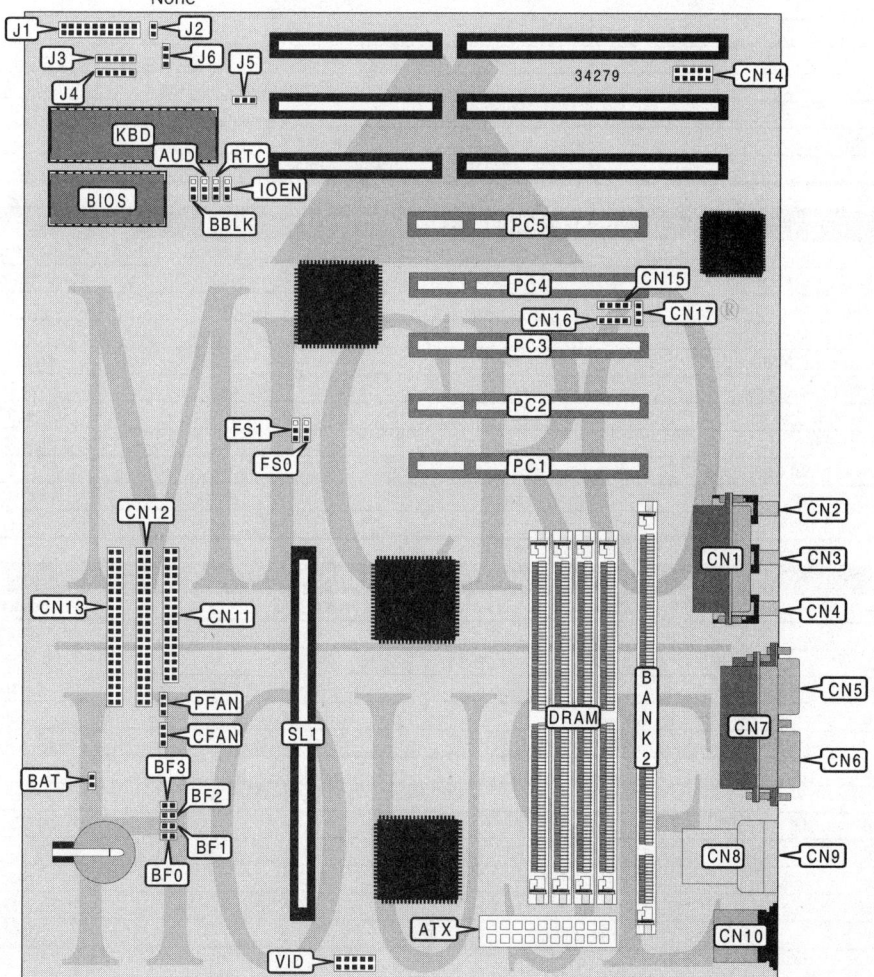

Continued on next page...

ASUS COMPUTER INTERNATIONAL
KN97-X

...continued from previous page

CONNECTIONS			
Purpose	**Location**	**Purpose**	**Location**
ATX power connector	ATX	IDE interface 1	CN13
CPU fan	CFAN	Modem connector	CN14
Game/MIDI port	CN1	Mitsumi CD-ROM audio in	CN15
Microphone in	CN2	Sony CD-ROM audio in	CN16
Line in	CN3	Panasonic CD-ROM audio in	CN17
Line out	CN4	Front panel connector	J1
Serial port 2	CN5	IDE interface LED	J2
Serial port 1	CN6	IR connector	J3
Parallel port	CN7	Volume control connector	J4
USB connector 1	CN8	Chassis alarm	J5
USB connector 2	CN9	Chassis fan power	J6
PS/2 mouse port	CN10	Power fan	PFAN
Floppy drive interface	CN11	32-bit PCI slots	PC1 – PC5
IDE interface 2	CN12	CPU Slot 1	SL1

USER CONFIGURABLE SETTINGS		
Function	**Label**	**Position**
◊ Factory configured - do not alter	AUD	Unidentified
◊ Battery test normal operation	BAT	Closed
Battery test test mode	BAT	Open
◊ Flash BIOS write protect disabled	BBLK	Pins 1 & 2 closed
Flash BIOS write protect enabled	BBLK	Pins 2 & 3 closed
◊ On board I/O enabled	IOEN	Pins 1 & 2 closed
On board I/O disabled	IOEN	Pins 2 & 3 closed
◊ CMOS memory normal operation	RTC	Pins 2 & 3 closed
CMOS memory clear	RTC	Pins 1 & 2 closed
◊ Factory configured - do not alter	VID	Unidentified

DIMM/DRAM CONFIGURATION			
Size	**Bank 0**	**Bank 1**	**Bank 2**
8MB	(2) 1M x 36	None	None
8MB	None	None	(1) 1M x 64
16MB	(2) 2M x 36	None	None
16MB	(2) 1M x 36	(2) 1M x 36	None
16MB	None	None	(1) 2M x 64
16MB	(2) 1M x 36	None	(1) 1M x 64
24MB	(2) 2M x 36	(2) 1M x 36	None
24MB	(2) 1M x 36	None	(1) 2M x 64
24MB	(2) 2M x 36	None	(1) 1M x 64
32MB	(2) 4M x 36	None	None
32MB	(2) 2M x 36	(2) 2M x 36	None
32MB	None	None	(1) 4M x 64

Continued on next page...

ASUS COMPUTER INTERNATIONAL
KN97-X

...continued from previous page

Size	Bank 0	Bank 1	Bank 2
\multicolumn{4}{c}{DIMM/DRAM CONFIGURATION (CON'T)}			
32MB	(2) 2M x 36	None	(1) 2M x 64
40MB	(2) 4M x 36	(2) 1M x 36	None
40MB	(2) 1M x 36	None	(1) 4M x 64
40MB	(2) 4M x 36	None	(1) 1M x 64
48MB	(2) 4M x 36	(2) 2M x 36	None
48MB	(2) 2M x 36	None	(1) 4M x 64
48MB	(2) 4M x 36	None	(1) 2M x 64
64MB	(2) 8M x 36	None	None
64MB	(2) 4M x 36	(2) 4M x 36	None
64MB	None	None	(1) 8M x 64
64MB	(2) 4M x 36	None	(1) 4M x 64
72MB	(2) 8M x 36	(2) 1M x 36	None
72MB	(2) 1M x 36	None	(1) 8M x 64
72MB	(2) 8M x 36	None	(1) 1M x 64
80MB	(2) 8M x 36	(2) 2M x 36	None
80MB	(2) 2M x 36	None	(1) 8M x 64
80MB	(2) 8M x 36	None	(1) 2M x 64
96MB	(2) 8M x 36	(2) 4M x 36	None
96MB	(2) 4M x 36	None	(1) 8M x 64
96MB	(2) 8M x 36	None	(1) 4M x 64
128MB	(2) 16M x 36	None	None
128MB	(2) 8M x 36	(2) 8M x 36	None
128MB	(2) 8M x 36	None	(1) 8M x 64
136MB	(2) 16M x 36	None	(1) 1M x 64
144MB	(2) 16M x 36	None	(1) 2M x 64
144MB	(2) 16M x 36	(2) 2M x 36	None
160MB	(2) 16M x 36	None	(1) 4M x 64
160MB	(2) 16M x 36	(2) 4M x 36	None
192MB	(2) 16M x 36	None	(1) 8M x 64
192MB	(2) 16M x 36	(2) 8M x 36	None
256MB	(2) 16M x 36	(2) 16M x 36	None
384MB	(2) 16M x 36	(2) 16M x 36	(1) 16M x 64

Note: Board accepts EDO memory. The location of banks 0 & 1 is unidentified.

CACHE CONFIGURATION
Note: 256KB/512KB cache is located on the Pentium II CPU.

CPU SPEED SELECTION

CPU speed	Clock speed	Multiplier	FS0	FS1	BF0
233MHz	66MHz	3.5x	2 & 3	1 & 2	Open
266MHz	66MHz	4x	2 & 3	1 & 2	Closed

Continued on next page...

ASUS COMPUTER INTERNATIONAL
KN97-X

...continued from previous page

CPU SPEED SELECTION (CON'T)					
CPU speed	**Clock speed**	**Multiplier**	**BF1**	**BF2**	**BF3**
233MHz	66MHz	3.5x	Open	Closed	Closed
266MHz	66MHz	4x	Closed	Open	Closed

ASUS COMPUTER INTERNATIONAL
P/I-P65UP5

Processor	Pentium/Pentium Pro (located on CPU card)
Processor Speed	75/90/100/120/133/150/166/180/200MHz
Chip Set	Intel
Video Chip Set	None
Maximum Onboard Memory	512MB (EDO supported)
Maximum Video Memory	None
Cache	256/512KB (located on CPU card)
BIOS	Unidentified
Dimensions	330mm x 218mm
I/O Options	32-bit PCI slots (5), floppy drive interface, green PC connector, IDE interfaces (2), parallel port, serial ports (2), CPU slot, IR connector, USB connector, MediaBus slot
NPU Options	None

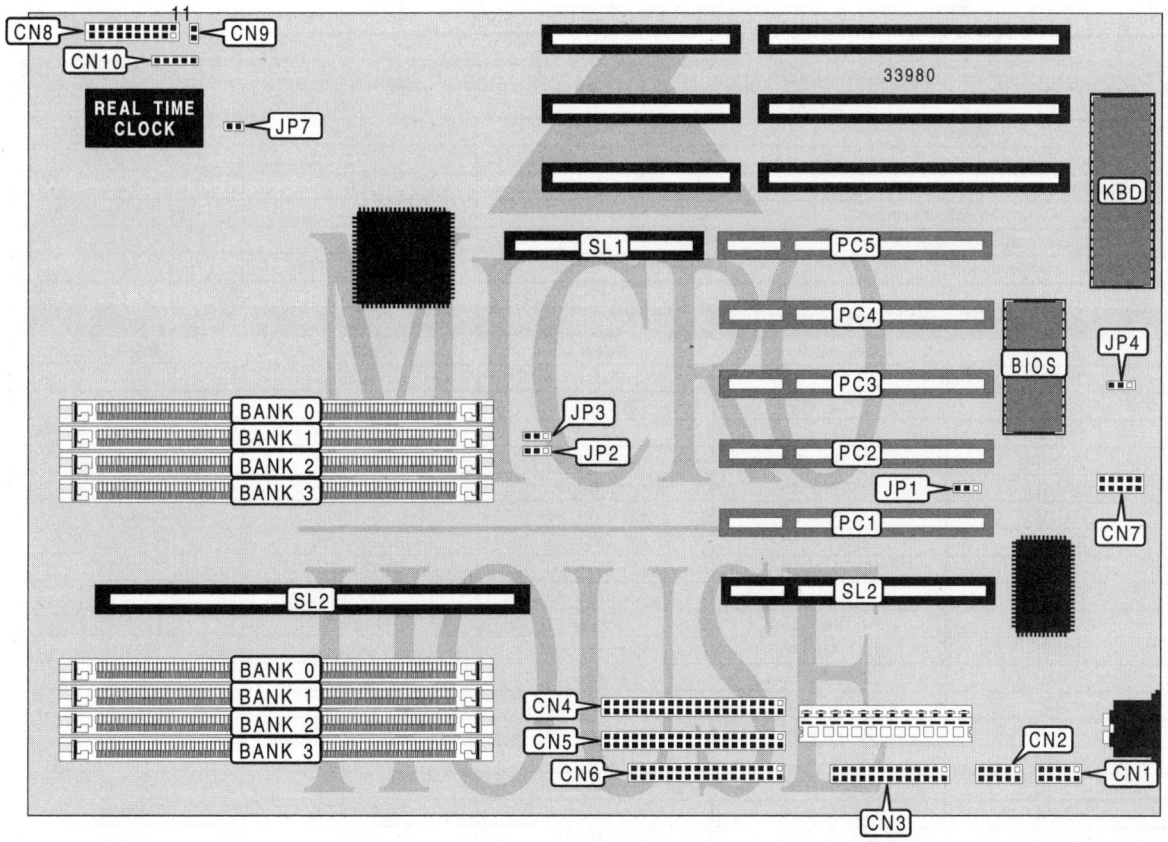

Continued on next page...

ASUS COMPUTER INTERNATIONAL
P/I-P65UP5

. . . continued from previous page

CONNECTIONS			
Purpose	**Location**	**Purpose**	**Location**
Serial port 1	CN1	Power LED	CN8 pins 12 & 13
Serial port 2	CN2	Green PC connector	CN8 pins 14 & 15
Parallel port	CN3	ATX power switch	CN8 pins 16 & 17
IDE interface 1	CN4	Reset switch	CN8 pins 19 & 20
IDE interface 2	CN5	IDE interface LED	CN9
Floppy drive interface	CN6	IR connector	CN10
USB connector	CN7	32-bit PCI slots	PC1 – PC5
Power LED & keylock	CN8 pins 1 - 5	MediaBus slot	SL1
Speaker	CN8 pins 7 - 10	CPU slot	SL2

USER CONFIGURABLE SETTINGS		
Function	**Label**	**Position**
† On board I/O enabled	JP1	Pins 1 & 2 closed
On board I/O disabled	JP1	Pins 2 & 3 closed
† Flash BIOS write protect disabled	JP4	Pins 1 & 2 closed
Flash BIOS write protect enabled	JP4	Pins 2 & 3 closed
† CMOS memory normal operation	JP7	Open
CMOS memory clear	JP7	Closed

DRAM CONFIGURATION				
Size	**Bank 0**	**Bank 1**	**Bank 2**	**Bank 3**
8MB	(2) 1M x 36	None	None	None
16MB	(2) 1M x 36	(2) 1M x 36	None	None
16MB	(2) 2M x 36	None	None	None
24MB	(2) 1M x 36	(2) 1M x 36	(2) 1M x 36	None
24MB	(2) 1M x 36	(2) 2M x 36	None	None
24MB	(2) 2M x 36	(2) 1M x 36	None	None
32MB	(2) 1M x 36	(2) 1M x 36	(2) 1M x 36	(2) 1M x 36
32MB	(2) 2M x 36	(2) 1M x 36	(2) 1M x 36	None
32MB	(2) 2M x 36	(2) 2M x 36	None	None
32MB	(2) 4M x 36	None	None	None
40MB	(2) 1M x 36	(2) 2M x 36	(2) 2M x 36	None
40MB	(2) 1M x 36	(2) 4M x 36	None	None
40MB	(2) 2M x 36	(2) 1M x 36	(2) 1M x 36	(2) 1M x 36
40MB	(2) 4M x 36	(2) 1M x 36	None	None
48MB	(2) 2M x 36	(2) 2M x 36	(2) 2M x 36	None
48MB	(2) 2M x 36	(2) 4M x 36	None	None
48MB	(2) 4M x 36	(2) 1M x 36	(2) 1M x 36	None
48MB	(2) 4M x 36	(2) 2M x 36	None	None
56MB	(2) 1M x 36	(2) 2M x 36	(2) 2M x 36	(2) 2M x 36
56MB	(2) 4M x 36	(2) 1M x 36	(2) 1M x 36	(2) 1M x 36

Continued on next page. . .

ASUS COMPUTER INTERNATIONAL
P/I-P65UP5

. . . continued from previous page

DRAM CONFIGURATION (CON'T)				
Size	**Bank 0**	**Bank 1**	**Bank 2**	**Bank 3**
64MB	(2) 2M x 36	(2) 2M x 36	(2) 2M x 36	(2) 2M x 36
64MB	(2) 4M x 36	(2) 2M x 36	(2) 2M x 36	None
64MB	(2) 4M x 36	(2) 4M x 36	None	None
64MB	(2) 8M x 36	None	None	None
72MB	(2) 1M x 36	(2) 4M x 36	(2) 4M x 36	None
72MB	(2) 1M x 36	(2) 8M x 36	None	None
72MB	(2) 8M x 36	(2) 1M x 36	None	None
80MB	(2) 2M x 36	(2) 4M x 36	(2) 4M x 36	None
80MB	(2) 2M x 36	(2) 8M x 36	None	None
80MB	(2) 4M x 36	(2) 2M x 36	(2) 2M x 36	(2) 2M x 36
80MB	(2) 8M x 36	(2) 1M x 36	(2) 1M x 36	None
80MB	(2) 8M x 36	(2) 2M x 36	None	None
88MB	(2) 8M x 36	(2) 1M x 36	(2) 1M x 36	(2) 1M x 36
96MB	(2) 4M x 36	(2) 4M x 36	(2) 4M x 36	None
96MB	(2) 4M x 36	(2) 8M x 36	None	None
96MB	(2) 8M x 36	(2) 2M x 36	(2) 2M x 36	None
96MB	(2) 8M x 36	(2) 4M x 36	None	None
104MB	(2) 1M x 36	(2) 4M x 36	(2) 4M x 36	(2) 4M x 36
112MB	(2) 2M x 36	(2) 4M x 36	(2) 4M x 36	(2) 4M x 36
112MB	(2) 8M x 36	(2) 2M x 36	(2) 2M x 36	(2) 2M x 36
128MB	(2) 4M x 36	(2) 4M x 36	(2) 4M x 36	(2) 4M x 36
128MB	(2) 8M x 36	(2) 4M x 36	(2) 4M x 36	None
128MB	(2) 8M x 36	(2) 8M x 36	None	None
128MB	(2) 16M x 36	None	None	None
136MB	(2) 1M x 36	(2) 8M x 36	(2) 8M x 36	None
136MB	(2) 16M x 36	(2) 1M x 36	None	None
144MB	(2) 2M x 36	(2) 8M x 36	(2) 8M x 36	None
144MB	(2) 16M x 36	(2) 1M x 36	(2) 1M x 36	None
144MB	(2) 16M x 36	(2) 2M x 36	None	None
152MB	(2) 16M x 36	(2) 1M x 36	(2) 1M x 36	(2) 1M x 36
160MB	(2) 4M x 36	(2) 8M x 36	(2) 8M x 36	None
160MB	(2) 8M x 36	(2) 4M x 36	(2) 4M x 36	(2) 4M x 36
160MB	(2) 16M x 36	(2) 2M x 36	(2) 2M x 36	None
160MB	(2) 16M x 36	(2) 4M x 36	None	None
176MB	(2) 16M x 36	(2) 2M x 36	(2) 2M x 36	(2) 2M x 36
192MB	(2) 8M x 36	(2) 8M x 36	(2) 8M x 36	None
192MB	(2) 16M x 36	(2) 4M x 36	(2) 4M x 36	None
192MB	(2) 16M x 36	(2) 8M x 36	None	None
200MB	(2) 1M x 36	(2) 8M x 36	(2) 8M x 36	(2) 8M x 36
208MB	(2) 2M x 36	(2) 8M x 36	(2) 8M x 36	(2) 8M x 36

Continued on next page. . .

106 Motherboard Settings and Specifications

ASUS COMPUTER INTERNATIONAL
P/I-P65UP5

. . . continued from previous page

DRAM CONFIGURATION (CON'T)				
Size	Bank 0	Bank 1	Bank 2	Bank 3
224MB	(2) 4M x 36	(2) 8M x 36	(2) 8M x 36	(2) 8M x 36
224MB	(2) 16M x 36	(2) 4M x 36	(2) 4M x 36	(2) 4M x 36
256MB	(2) 8M x 36	(2) 8M x 36	(2) 8M x 36	(2) 8M x 36
256MB	(2) 16M x 36	(2) 8M x 36	(2) 8M x 36	None
256MB	(2) 16M x 36	(2) 16M x 36	None	None
Note: Board accepts EDO memory. Board also accepts x 32 SIMMs. Banks are interchangeable.				

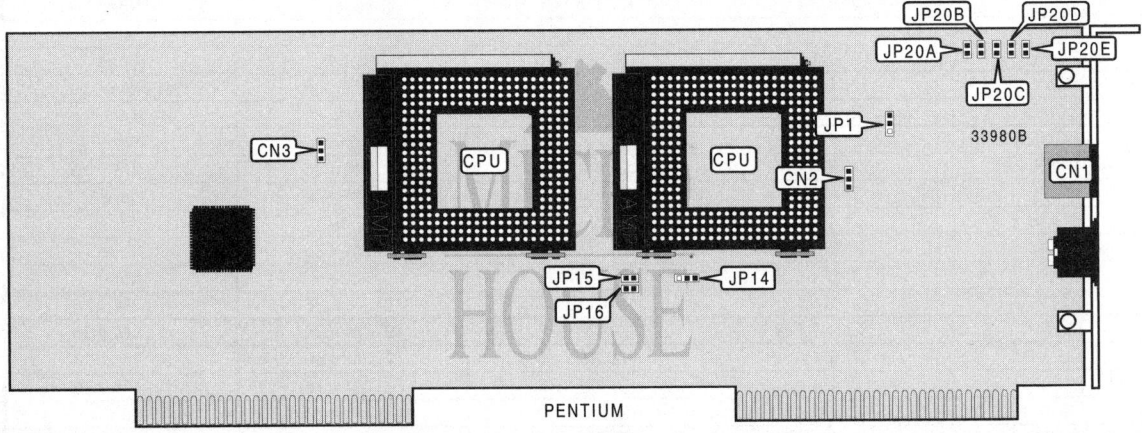

CONNECTIONS			
Purpose	Location	Purpose	Location
PS/2 mouse port	CN1	Chassis fan power	CN3
Chassis fan power	CN2		

CACHE CONFIGURATION
Note: Board is factory installed with 512KB cache.

CPU SPEED SELECTION				
CPU speed	Clock speed	Multiplier	JP15	JP16
75MHz	50MHz	1.5x	Open	Open
90MHz	60MHz	1.5x	Open	Open
100MHz	66MHz	1.5x	Open	Open
120MHz	60MHz	2x	Open	Closed
133MHz	66MHz	2x	Open	Closed
150MHz	60MHz	2.5x	Closed	Closed
166MHz	66MHz	2.5x	Closed	Closed
200MHz	66MHz	3x	Closed	Open

Continued on next page. . .

ASUS COMPUTER INTERNATIONAL
P/I-P65UP5

. . . continued from previous page

| CPU TYPE SELECTION ||
Type	JP14
Single CPU	Pins 2 & 3 closed
⇨ Dual CPUs	Pins 1 & 2 closed

| CPU TYPE SELECTION ||
Type	JP1
STD/VR	Pins 1 & 2 closed
VRE	Pins 2 & 3 closed

| CPU VOLTAGE SELECTION |||||||
Voltage	JP20A	JP20B	JP20C	JP20D	JP20E
2.5v	Closed	Open	Open	Open	Open
2.7v	Open	Closed	Open	Open	Open
2.8v	Open	Open	Closed	Open	Open
2.9v	Open	Open	Open	Closed	Open
Reserved	Open	Open	Open	Open	Closed

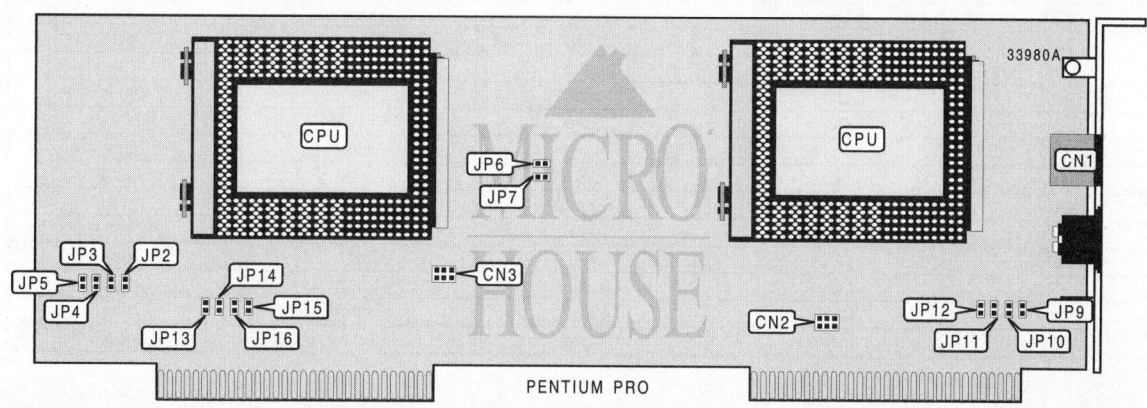

| CONNECTIONS ||||
Purpose	Location	Purpose	Location
Chassis fan power	CN1	PS/2 mouse port	CN3
Chassis fan power	CN2		

CACHE CONFIGURATION
Note: 256KB/512KB cache is located on the Pentium Pro CPU.

Continued on next page...

ASUS COMPUTER INTERNATIONAL
P/I-P65UP5

...continued from previous page

CPU SPEED SELECTION						
CPU speed	**Clock speed**	**Multiplier**	**JP2**	**JP3**	**JP6**	**JP7**
150MHz	60MHz	2.5x	1 & 2	2 & 3	Open	Closed
166MHz	66MHz	2.5x	2 & 3	1 & 2	Closed	Open
180MHz	60MHz	3x	1 & 2	2 & 3	Open	Closed
200MHz	66MHz	3x	2 & 3	1 & 2	Closed	Open

Note: Pins designated should be in the closed position.

CPU SPEED SELECTION (CON'T)						
CPU speed	**Clock speed**	**Multiplier**	**JP13**	**JP14**	**JP15**	**JP16**
150MHz	60MHz	2.5x	Closed	Open	Closed	Closed
166MHz	66MHz	2.5x	Closed	Open	Closed	Closed
180MHz	60MHz	3x	Closed	Closed	Open	Closed
200MHz	66MHz	3x	Closed	Closed	Open	Closed

CPU VOLTAGE SELECTION (CPU 1)				
Voltage	**JP2**	**JP3**	**JP4**	**JP5**
2.1v	Open	Open	Open	Closed
2.2v	Open	Open	Closed	Open
2.3v	Open	Open	Closed	Closed
2.4v	Open	Closed	Open	Open
2.5v	Open	Closed	Open	Closed
2.6v	Open	Closed	Closed	Open
2.7v	Open	Closed	Closed	Closed
2.8v	Closed	Open	Open	Open
2.9v	Closed	Open	Open	Closed
3.0v	Closed	Open	Closed	Open
3.1v	Closed	Open	Closed	Closed
3.2v	Closed	Closed	Open	Open
3.3v	Closed	Closed	Open	Closed
3.4v	Closed	Closed	Closed	Open
3.5v	Closed	Closed	Closed	Closed

Continued on next page...

ASUS COMPUTER INTERNATIONAL
P/I-P65UP5

...continued from previous page

CPU VOLTAGE SELECTION (CPU 2)				
Voltage	**JP9**	**JP10**	**JP11**	**JP12**
2.1v	Closed	Open	Open	Open
2.2v	Open	Closed	Open	Open
2.3v	Closed	Closed	Open	Open
2.4v	Open	Open	Closed	Open
2.5v	Closed	Open	Closed	Open
2.6v	Open	Closed	Closed	Open
2.7v	Closed	Closed	Closed	Open
2.8v	Open	Open	Open	Closed
2.9v	Closed	Open	Open	Closed
3.0v	Open	Closed	Open	Closed
3.1v	Closed	Closed	Open	Closed
3.2v	Open	Open	Closed	Closed
3.3v	Closed	Open	Closed	Closed
3.4v	Open	Closed	Closed	Closed
3.5v	Closed	Closed	Closed	Closed

110 Motherboard Settings and Specifications

ASUS COMPUTER INTERNATIONAL
P/I-P6RP4

Processor	Pentium Pro
Processor Speed	150/166MHz
Chip Set	Intel
Video Chip Set	None
Maximum Onboard Memory	512MB
Maximum Video Memory	None
Cache	256/512KB (on Pentium Pro CPU)
BIOS	AMI
Dimensions	330mm x 218mm
I/O Options	32-bit PCI slots (4), floppy drive interface, green PC connector, IDE interfaces (2), parallel port, PS/2 mouse interface, serial ports (2), IR connector, MediaBus connector, VRM connector
NPU Options	None

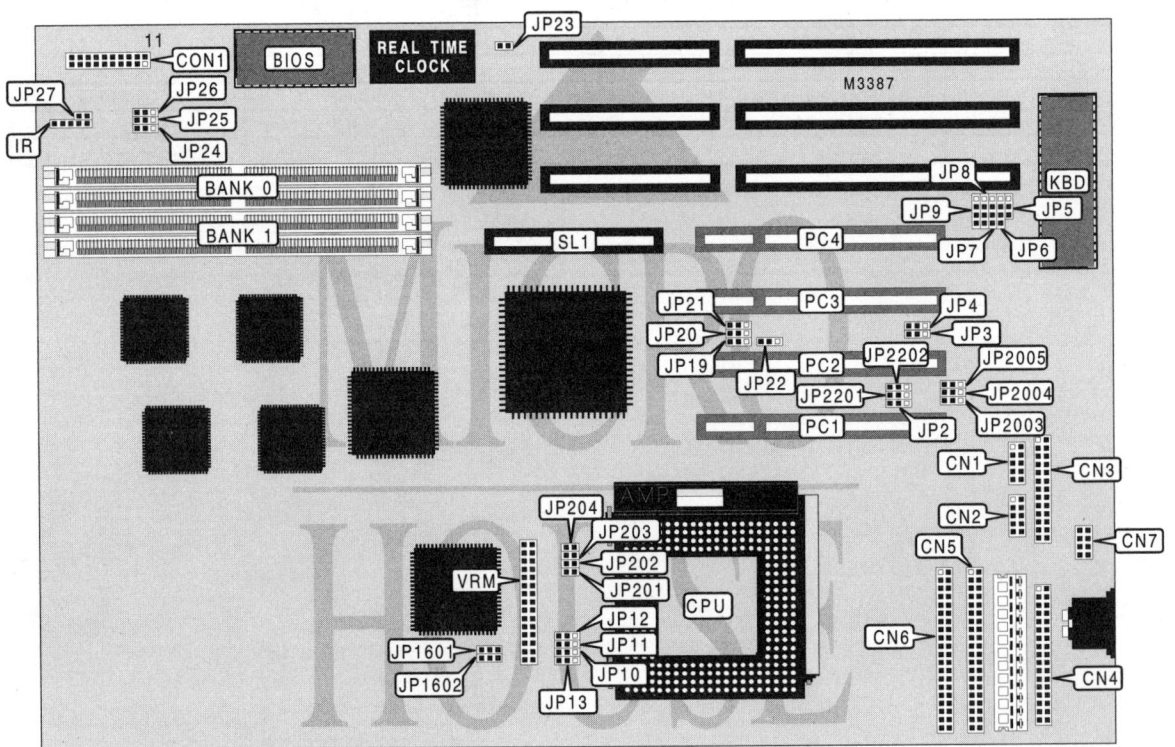

Continued on next page...

ASUS COMPUTER INTERNATIONAL
P/I-P6RP4

. . . continued from previous page

CONNECTIONS			
Purpose	**Location**	**Purpose**	**Location**
Serial port 1	CN1	Green PC connector	CON1 pins 14 & 15
Serial port 2	CN2	Reset switch	CON1 pins 19 & 20
Parallel port	CN3	IDE interface LED	JP27
Floppy drive interface	CN4	Chassis fan power	JP1601
IDE interface 2	CN5	Chassis fan power	JP1602
IDE interface 1	CN6	IR connector	IR
PS/2 mouse interface	CN7	32-bit PCI slots	PC1 - PC4
Power LED & keylock	CON1 pins 1 - 5	MediaBus slot	SL1
Speaker	CON1 pins 7 - 10	VRM connector	VRM
Turbo LED	CON1 pins 12 & 13		

USER CONFIGURABLE SETTINGS		
Function	**Label**	**Position**
◇ IDE interface enabled	JP2	Pins 1 & 2 closed
IDE interface disabled	JP2	Pins 2 & 3 closed
◇ PS/2 mouse IRQ enabled	JP5	Pins 1 & 2 closed
PS/2 mouse IRQ disabled	JP5	Pins 2 & 3 closed
◇ CMOS memory normal operation	JP23	Open
CMOS memory clear	JP23	Closed
◇ Flash BIOS voltage select 5v	JP24	Pins 1 & 2 closed
Flash BIOS voltage select 12v	JP24	Pins 2 & 3 closed
◇ Flash BIOS write protect enabled	JP25	Pins 1 & 2 closed
Flash BIOS write protect disabled	JP25	Pins 2 & 3 closed
◇ Flash BIOS boot block write disabled	JP26	Pins 1 & 2 closed
Flash BIOS boot block write enabled	JP26	Pins 2 & 3 closed
◇ On board I/O enabled	JP2005	Pins 1 & 2 closed
On board I/O disabled	JP2005	Pins 2 & 3 closed

DRAM CONFIGURATION		
Size	**Bank 0**	**Bank 1**
8MB	(2) 1M x 36	None
16MB	(2) 2M x 36	None
16MB	(2) 1M x 36	(2) 1M x 36
32MB	(2) 4M x 36	None
32MB	(2) 2M x 36	(2) 2M x 36
64MB	(2) 8M x 36	None
64MB	(2) 4M x 36	(2) 4M x 36
128MB	(2) 8M x 36	(2) 8M x 36
128MB	(2) 16M x 36	None
256MB	(2) 16M x 36	(2) 16M x 36
256MB	(2) 32M x 36	None
512MB	(2) 32M x 36	(2) 32M x 36

Continued on next page. . .

ASUS COMPUTER INTERNATIONAL
P/I-P6RP4

. . . continued from previous page

CACHE CONFIGURATION

Note: 256KB/512KB cache is located on the Pentium Pro CPU.

CPU BUS CORE SELECTION

Bus:core	Bus	CPU core	JP19	JP20	JP21	JP22
1/2	60MHz/66MHz	120MHz/133MHz	2 & 3	2 & 3	2 & 3	2 & 3
1/3	60MHz/66MHz	180MHz/200MHz	2 & 3	2 & 3	2 & 3	1 & 2
1/4	N/A	N/A	2 & 3	1 & 2	2 & 3	2 & 3
1/5	N/A	N/A	2 & 3	1 & 2	2 & 3	1 & 2
⇨ 2/5	60MHz/66MHz	150MHz/166MHz	1 & 2	2 & 3	2 & 3	2 & 3
2/7	N/A	N/A	1 & 2	2 & 3	2 & 3	1 & 2

Note: Pins designated should be in the closed position.

CPU VOLTAGE SELECTION

Voltage	JP10	JP11	JP12	JP13
VID	Pins 1 & 2 closed	Pins 1 & 2 closed	Pins 1 & 2 closed	Pins 1 & 2 closed
2.1v	Open	Open	Open	Pins 2 & 3 closed
2.2v	Open	Open	Pins 2 & 3 closed	Open
2.3v	Open	Open	Pins 2 & 3 closed	Pins 2 & 3 closed
2.4v	Open	Pins 2 & 3 closed	Open	Open
2.5v	Open	Pins 2 & 3 closed	Open	Pins 2 & 3 closed
2.6v	Open	Pins 2 & 3 closed	Pins 2 & 3 closed	Open
2.7v	Open	Pins 2 & 3 closed	Pins 2 & 3 closed	Pins 2 & 3 closed
2.8v	Pins 2 & 3 closed	Open	Open	Open
2.9v	Pins 2 & 3 closed	Open	Open	Pins 2 & 3 closed
3.0v	Pins 2 & 3 closed	Open	Pins 2 & 3 closed	Open
3.1v	Pins 2 & 3 closed	Open	Pins 2 & 3 closed	Pins 2 & 3 closed
3.2v	Pins 2 & 3 closed	Pins 2 & 3 closed	Open	Open
3.3v	Pins 2 & 3 closed	Pins 2 & 3 closed	Open	Pins 2 & 3 closed
3.4v	Pins 2 & 3 closed	Pins 2 & 3 closed	Pins 2 & 3 closed	Open
3.5v	Pins 2 & 3 closed	Pins 2 & 3 closed	Pins 2 & 3 closed	Pins 2 & 3 closed

CPU VOLTAGE INDENTIFICATION SELECTION

Setting	JP201	JP202	JP203	JP204
⇨ Pull high disabled	Open	Open	Open	Open
Pull high enabled	Closed	Closed	Closed	Closed

DMA CHANNEL SELECTION

Channel	JP3	JP4
1	Pins 1 & 2 closed	Pins 1 & 2 closed
3	Pins 2 & 3 closed	Pins 2 & 3 closed

Continued on next page. . .

ASUS COMPUTER INTERNATIONAL
P/I-P6RP4

. . . continued from previous page

PCI MASTER/SLAVE SELECTION			
Master	**Slave**	**JP2201**	**JP2202**
PCI IDE	PCI slot 1	Pins 1 & 2 closed	Pins 1 & 2 closed
PCI slot 1	PCI IDE	Pins 2 & 3 closed	Pins 2 & 3 closed

PCI IRQ SELECTION					
Setting	**IRQ**	**JP6**	**JP7**	**JP8**	**JP9**
PCI 1	IRQ14	1 & 2	N/A	N/A	N/A
PCI 1	IRQ15	N/A	1 & 2	N/A	N/A
PCI 2	IRQ14	3 & 4	N/A	N/A	N/A
PCI 2	IRQ15	N/A	3 & 4	N/A	N/A
PCI 3	IRQ14	N/A	N/A	1 & 2	N/A
PCI 3	IRQ15	N/A	N/A	N/A	1 & 2
PCI 4	IRQ14	N/A	N/A	3 & 4	N/A
PCI 4	IRQ15	N/A	N/A	N/A	3 & 4
IRQ routing by chipset	IRQ14	2 & 3	N/A	2 & 3	N/A
⇨ IRQ routing by chipset	IRQ15	N/A	2 & 3	N/A	2 & 3
Note: Pins designated should be in the closed position.					

SERIAL PORT 2 SELECTION		
Setting	**JP2003**	**JP2004**
⇨ Used as COM2	Pins 1 & 2 closed	Pins 1 & 2 closed
Used as IR connector	Pins 2 & 3 closed	Pins 2 & 3 closed

ASUS COMPUTER INTERNATIONAL
P/I-XP6NP5

Processor	Pentium Pro
Processor Speed	150/166/180/200MHz
Chip Set	Intel
Video Chip Set	None
Maximum Onboard Memory	256MB (EDO supported)
Maximum Video Memory	None
Cache	256/512KB (located on Pentium Pro CPU)
BIOS	Unidentified
Dimensions	330mm x 218mm
I/O Options	32-bit PCI slots (5), floppy drive interface, green PC connector, IDE interfaces (2), parallel port, PS/2 mouse port, serial ports (2), IR connector, USB connector, ATX power connector, MediaBus slot
NPU Options	None

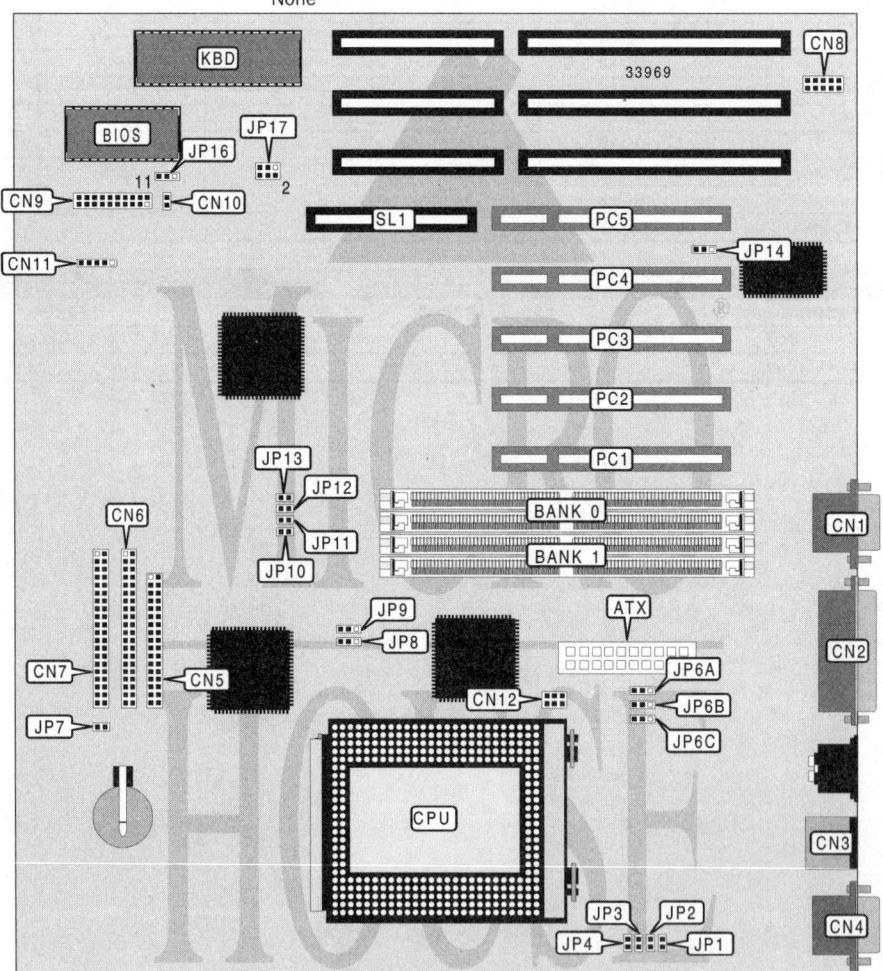

Continued on next page...

ASUS COMPUTER INTERNATIONAL
P/I-XP6NP5

. . . continued from previous page

CONNECTIONS			
Purpose	**Location**	**Purpose**	**Location**
ATX power connector	ATX	Speaker	CN9 pins 7 - 10
Serial port 2	CN1	System power LED	CN9 pins 12 & 13
Parallel port	CN2	Green PC connector	CN9 pins 14 & 15
PS/2 mouse port	CN3	ATX power switch	CN9 pins 16 & 17
Serial port 1	CN4	Reset switch	CN9 pins 19 & 20
Floppy drive interface	CN5	IDE interface LED	CN10
IDE interface 2	CN6	IR connector	CN11
IDE interface 1	CN7	Chassis fan power	CN12
USB connector	CN8	32-bit PCI slots	PC1 – PC5
Power LED & keylock	CN9 pins 1 - 5	MediaBus slot	SL1

USER CONFIGURABLE SETTINGS		
Function	**Label**	**Position**
Battery test lead normal operation	JP7	Closed
Battery test lead test mode	JP7	Open
† On board I/O enabled	JP14	Pins 1 & 2 closed
On board I/O disabled	JP14	Pins 2 & 3 closed
† CMOS memory normal operation	JP16	Pins 2 & 3 closed
CMOS memory clear	JP16	Pins 1 & 2 closed
† Flash BIOS normal operation	JP17	Pins 1 & 2 closed
Flash BIOS boot block enabled	JP17	Pins 2 & 3 closed

DRAM CONFIGURATION		
Size	**Bank 0**	**Bank 1**
8MB	(2) 1M x 36	None
16MB	(2) 2M x 36	None
16MB	(2) 1M x 36	(2) 1M x 36
24MB	(2) 2M x 36	(2) 1M x 36
32MB	(2) 4M x 36	None
32MB	(2) 2M x 36	(2) 2M x 36
40MB	(2) 4M x 36	(2) 1M x 36
48MB	(2) 4M x 36	(2) 2M x 36
64MB	(2) 8M x 36	None
64MB	(2) 4M x 36	(2) 4M x 36
72MB	(2) 8M x 36	(2) 1M x 36
80MB	(2) 8M x 36	(2) 2M x 36
96MB	(2) 8M x 36	(2) 4M x 36
128MB	(2) 8M x 36	(2) 8M x 36
128MB	(2) 16M x 36	None

Continued on next page. . .

ASUS COMPUTER INTERNATIONAL
P/I-XP6NP5

. . . continued from previous page

DRAM CONFIGURATION (CON'T)

Size	Bank 0	Bank 1
136MB	(2) 16M x 36	(2) 1M x 36
144MB	(2) 16M x 36	(2) 2M x 36
160MB	(2) 16M x 36	(2) 4M x 36
192MB	(2) 16M x 36	(2) 8M x 36
256MB	(2) 16M x 36	(2) 16M x 36

Note: Board accepts EDO memory. Banks are interchangeable.

CACHE CONFIGURATION

Note: 256KB/512KB cache is located on the Pentium Pro CPU.

CPU SPEED SELECTION

CPU speed	Clock speed	Multiplier	JP8	JP9	JP10	JP11	JP12	JP13
150MHz	60MHz	2.5x	2 & 3	1 & 2	Closed	Closed	Closed	Open
166MHz	66MHz	2.5x	1 & 2	2 & 3	Closed	Closed	Closed	Open
180MHz	60MHz	3x	2 & 3	1 & 2	Closed	Closed	Open	Closed
200MHz	66MHz	3x	1 & 2	2 & 3	Closed	Closed	Open	Closed

Note: Pins designated should be in the closed position.

CPU VOLTAGE SELECTION

Voltage	JP1	JP2	JP3	JP4
2.1v	Open	Open	Open	Closed
2.2v	Open	Open	Closed	Open
2.3v	Open	Open	Closed	Closed
2.4v	Open	Closed	Open	Open
2.5v	Open	Closed	Open	Closed
2.6v	Open	Closed	Closed	Open
2.7v	Open	Closed	Closed	Closed
2.8v	Closed	Open	Open	Open
2.9v	Closed	Open	Open	Closed
3.0v	Closed	Open	Closed	Open
3.1v	Closed	Open	Closed	Closed
3.2v	Closed	Closed	Open	Open
3.3v	Closed	Closed	Open	Closed
3.4v	Closed	Closed	Closed	Open
3.5v	Closed	Closed	Closed	Closed

3.3V POWER SOURCE SELECTION

Source	JP6A	JP6B	JP6C
⇨ATX power supply	Pins 2 & 3 closed	Pins 2 & 3 closed	Pins 2 & 3 closed
Onboard regulator	Pins 1 & 2 closed	Pins 1 & 2 closed	Pins 1 & 2 closed

ASUS COMPUTER INTERNATIONAL
PCI/I-P54TP4

Processor	Pentium
Processor Speed	75/90/100MHz
Chip Set	Unidentified
Max. Onboard DRAM	128MB
Cache	256/512KB
BIOS	Award
Dimensions	330mm x 218mm
I/O Options	32-bit PCI slots (4), floppy drive interface, green PC connector, IDE interfaces (2), parallel port, PS/2 mouse interface, serial ports (2)
NPU Options	None

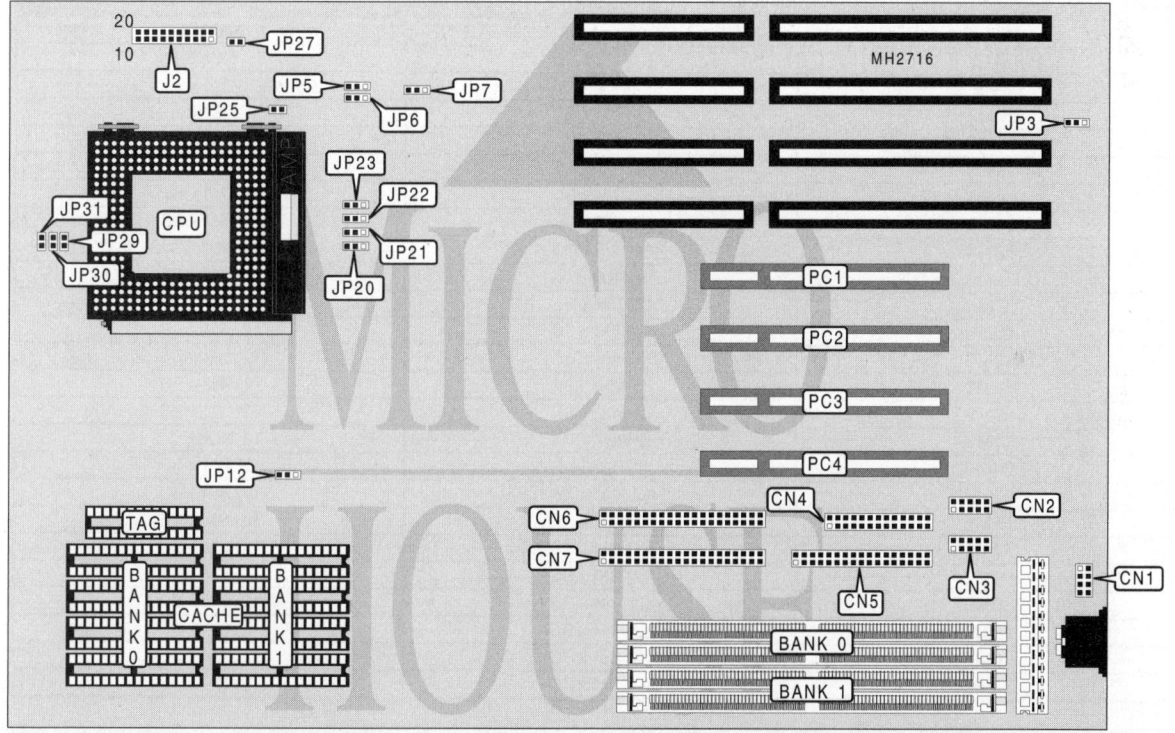

CONNECTIONS			
Purpose	**Location**	**Purpose**	**Location**
PS/2 mouse interface	CN1	Power LED & keylock	J2 pins 1 - 5
Serial port 1	CN2	Speaker	J2 pins 7 - 10
Serial port 2	CN3	Turbo LED	J2 pins 12 - 13
Parallel port	CN4	Green PC connector	J2 pins 14 - 15
Floppy drive interface	CN5	Reset switch	J2 pins 19 - 20
IDE interface (primary)	CN6	IDE interface LED	JP27
IDE interface (secondary)	CN7	32-bit PCI slots	PC1 - PC4

Continued on next page...

ASUS COMPUTER INTERNATIONAL
PCI/I-P54TP4

...continued from previous page

USER CONFIGURABLE SETTINGS		
Function	**Jumper**	**Position**
◇ On board I/O enabled	JP3	pins 1 & 2 closed
On board I/O disabled	JP3	pins 2 & 3 closed
◇ PS/2 mouse enabled	JP7	pins 1 & 2 closed
PS/2 mouse disabled	JP7	pins 2 & 3 closed
◇ CPU external clock speed select 1.5x	JP25	Open
CPU external clock speed select 2x	JP25	Closed

DRAM CONFIGURATION		
Size	**Bank 0**	**Bank 1**
8MB	(2) 1M x 36	NONE
8MB	NONE	(2) 1M x 36
16MB	(2) 2M x 36	NONE
16MB	NONE	(2) 2M x 36
16MB	(2) 1M x 36	(2) 1M x 36
24MB	(2) 1M x 36	(2) 2M x 36
24MB	(2) 2M x 36	(2) 1M x 36
32MB	(2) 4M x 36	NONE
32MB	NONE	(2) 4M x 36
32MB	(2) 2M x 36	(2) 2M x 36
40MB	(2) 1M x 36	(2) 4M x 36
40MB	(2) 4M x 36	(2) 1M x 36
48MB	(2) 2M x 36	(2) 4M x 36
48MB	(2) 4M x 36	(2) 2M x 36
64MB	(2) 8M x 36	NONE
64MB	NONE	(2) 8M x 36
64MB	(2) 4M x 36	(2) 4M x 36
72MB	(2) 1M x 36	(2) 8M x 36
72MB	(2) 8M x 36	(2) 1M x 36
80MB	(2) 2M x 36	(2) 8M x 36
80MB	(2) 8M x 36	(2) 2M x 36
96MB	(2) 4M x 36	(2) 8M x 36
96MB	(2) 8M x 36	(2) 4M x 36
128MB	(2) 8M x 36	(2) 8M x 36

CACHE CONFIGURATION			
Size	**Bank 0**	**Bank 1**	**TAG**
256KB	(4) 32K x 8	(4) 32K x 8	(1) 8K x 8 or (1) 32K x 8
512KB	(4) 64K x 8	(4) 64K x 8	(1) 32K x 8

CACHE JUMPER CONFIGURATION	
Size	**JP12**
256KB	pins 2 & 3 closed
512KB	pins 1 & 2 closed

Continued on next page...

ASUS COMPUTER INTERNATIONAL
PCI/I-P54TP4

. . . continued from previous page

		CPU SPEED CONFIGURATION		
Speed	**JP20**	**JP21**	**JP22**	**JP23**
75MHz	pins 1 & 2 closed	pins 1 & 2 closed	pins 1 & 2 closed	pins 2 & 3 closed
90MHz	pins 2 & 3 closed	pins 1 & 2 closed	pins 2 & 3 closed	pins 1 & 2 closed
100MHz	pins 2 & 3 closed	pins 2 & 3 closed	pins 1 & 2 closed	pins 2 & 3 closed

	CPU VOLTAGE CONFIGURATION		
Voltage	**JP29**	**JP30**	**JP31**
3.4v	Closed	Open	Open
3.5v	Open	Closed	Open
3.6v	Open	Open	Closed

	BIOS CONFIGURATION	
Setting	**JP5**	**JP6**
Flash BIOS programming disabled	pins 1 & 2 closed	pins 2 & 3 closed
Flash BIOS programming enabled	pins 2 & 3 closed	pins 2 & 3 closed

COMPAQ COMPUTER CORPORATION
DESKPRO 4000/6000 (PENTIUM PRO)

Processor	Pentium Pro
Processor Speed	180/200MHz
Chip Set	Unidentified
Video Chip Set	Cirrus Logic
Maximum Onboard Memory	256MB
Maximum Video Memory	2MB
Cache	256/512KB (located on Pentium Pro CPU)
BIOS	Unidentified
Dimensions	330mm x 218mm
I/O Options	Unidentified
NPU Options	None

CONNECTIONS

Note: The location and types of all I/O options are unidentified.

USER CONFIGURABLE SETTINGS

Function	Label	Position
⇨ Factory configured - do not alter	E2	Unidentified
⇨ Power on password enabled	SW1/1	Off
Power on password disabled	SW1/1	On

DRAM CONFIGURATION

Size	Bank 0	Bank 1	Bank 2	Bank 3
16MB	(2) 2M x 36	None	None	None
32MB	(2) 2M x 36	(2) 2M x 36	None	None
32MB	(2) 4M x 36	None	None	None
48MB	(2) 2M x 36	(2) 2M x 36	(2) 2M x 36	None
64MB	(2) 2M x 36	(2) 2M x 36	(2) 2M x 36	(2) 2M x 36
64MB	(2) 4M x 36	(2) 4M x 36	None	None
64MB	(2) 8M x 36	None	None	None
96MB	(2) 4M x 36	(2) 4M x 36	(2) 4M x 36	None
128MB	(2) 4M x 36	(2) 4M x 36	(2) 4M x 36	(2) 4M x 36
128MB	(2) 8M x 36	(2) 8M x 36	None	None
192MB	(2) 8M x 36	(2) 8M x 36	(2) 8M x 36	None
256MB	(2) 8M x 36	(2) 8M x 36	(2) 8M x 36	(2) 8M x 36
256MB	(2) 16M x 36	(2) 16M x 36	None	None

CACHE CONFIGURATION

Note: 256KB/512KB cache is located on the Pentium Pro CPU.

VIDEO MEMORY CONFIGURATION

Note: The location of the video memory is unidentified.

CPU SPEED SELECTION

CPU speed	Clock speed	Multiplier	SW1/2	SW1/3	SW1/4	SW1/5	SW1/6
180MHz	66MHz	2.5x	Off	On	On	Off	On
200MHz	66MHz	3x	On	On	On	Off	On

Continued on next page...

COMPAQ COMPUTER CORPORATION
DESKPRO 4000/6000 (PENTIUM PRO)

...continued from previous page

Setting	SW2/1	SW2/2	SW2/3	SW2/4
NETWORK SELECTION				
10MB	On	On	On	On
100MB	Off	Off	Off	Off

TECHNICAL NOTE

Note: Diagram not available.

COMPAQ COMPUTER CORPORATION
DESKPRO 5120/5133/5150/5166

Processor	Pentium
Processor Speed	75/90/100/120/125/133/150/166MHz
Chip Set	Unidentified
Video Chip Set	Unidentified
Maximum Onboard Memory	192MB (EDO supported)
Maximum Video Memory	2MB
Cache	256KB
BIOS	Unidentified
Dimensions	330mm x 218mm
I/O Options	Unidentified
NPU Options	None

CONNECTIONS

Purpose	Location
External battery	P3

Note: The location and types of all other I/O options are unidentified.

USER CONFIGURABLE SETTINGS

Function	Label	Position
Battery type select internal	E5	Pins 1 & 2 closed
Battery type select external	E5	Pins 2 & 3 closed
Password enabled	E6	Pins 1 & 2 closed
Password disabled	E6	Pins 2 & 3 closed

DRAM CONFIGURATION

Size	Bank 0	Bank 1	Bank 2
8MB	(2) 1M x 36	None	None
16MB	(2) 1M x 36	(2) 1M x 36	None
16MB	(2) 2M x 36	None	None
24MB	(2) 2M x 36	(2) 1M x 36	None
24MB	(2) 1M x 36	(2) 1M x 36	(2) 1M x 36
32MB	(2) 4M x 36	None	None
32MB	(2) 2M x 36	(2) 2M x 36	None
40MB	(2) 4M x 36	(2) 1M x 36	None
48MB	(2) 4M x 36	(2) 2M x 36	None
48MB	(2) 4M x 36	(2) 1M x 36	(2) 1M x 36
64MB	(2) 8M x 36	None	None
64MB	(2) 4M x 36	(2) 4M x 36	None
80MB	(2) 8M x 36	(2) 2M x 36	None
96MB	(2) 8M x 36	(2) 4M x 36	None
96MB	(2) 4M x 36	(2) 4M x 36	(2) 4M x 36
128MB	(2) 8M x 36	(2) 8M x 36	None
192MB	(2) 8M x 36	(2) 8M x 36	(2) 8M x 36

Note: Board accepts EDO memory.

CACHE CONFIGURATION

Note: The location of the cache is unidentified.

Continued on next page...

COMPAQ COMPUTER CORPORATION
DESKPRO 5120/5133/5150/5166

... continued from previous page

VIDEO MEMORY CONFIGURATION

Note: The location of the video memory is unidentified.

CPU SPEED SELECTION

CPU speed	Clock speed	Multiplier	S1/1	S1/2	S1/3	S1/4
75MHz	50MHz	1.5x	On	Off	Off	Off
90MHz	60MHz	1.5x	Off	Off	Off	Off
100MHz	66MHz	1.5x	Off	Off	On	Off
100MHz	50MHz	2x	On	On	Off	Off
120MHz	60MHz	2x	Off	On	Off	Off
125MHz	50MHz	2.5x	On	On	Off	On
133MHz	66MHz	2x	Off	On	On	Off
150MHz	60MHz	2.5x	Off	On	Off	On
166MHz	66MHz	2.5x	Off	On	On	On

TECHNICAL NOTE

Note: Diagram not available.

COMPAQ COMPUTER CORPORATION
PRESARIO 7100 SERIES (PENTIUM SYSTEM)

Processor	Pentium
Processor Speed	75/90/100MHz
Chip Set	UMC
Video Chip Set	Trio
Maximum Onboard Memory	128MB
Maximum Video Memory	2MB
Cache	256KB
BIOS	Unidentified
Dimensions	330mm x 218mm
I/O Options	Floppy drive interface, IDE interfaces (2), parallel port, PS/2 mouse port, serial port, VGA VESA feature connector, VGA port, riser slot, speaker/headphone out connector, line in connector, audio line in connector, game/MIDI connector, CD-ROM audio in connector, modem connector, microphone connector
NPU Options	None

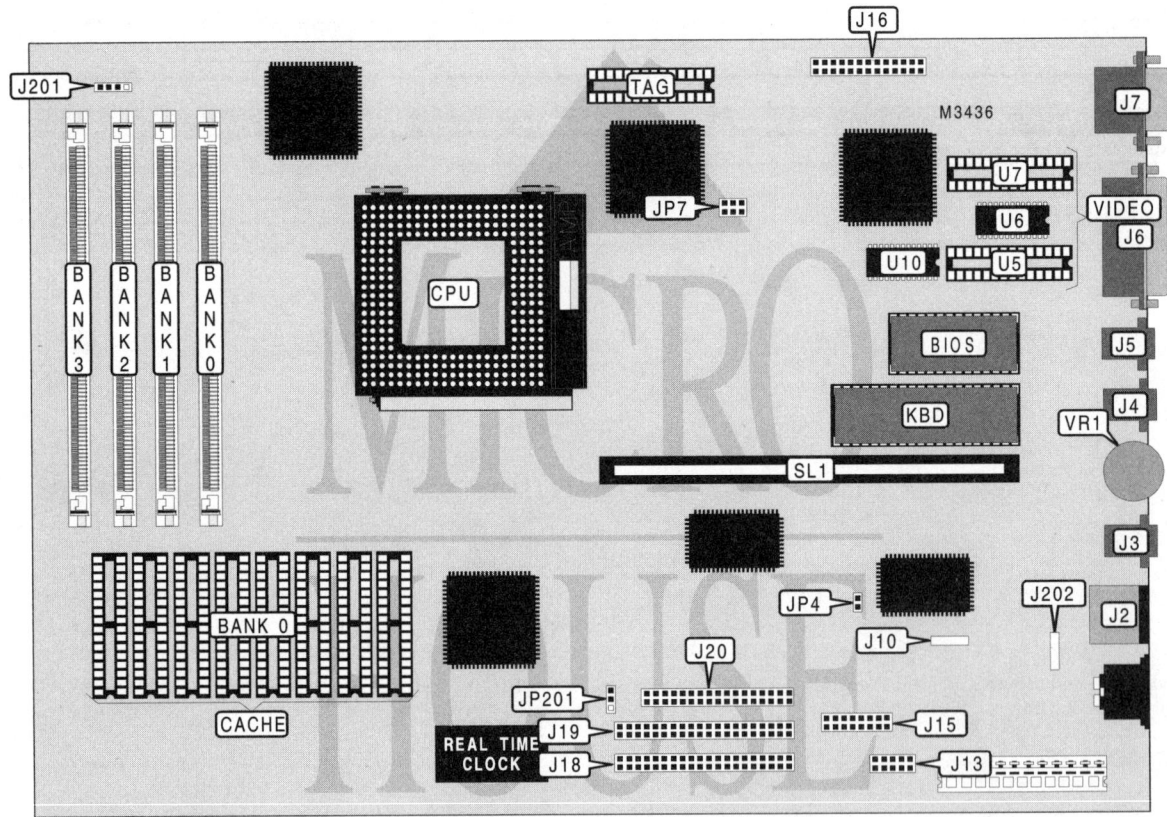

Continued on next page...

COMPAQ COMPUTER CORPORATION
PRESARIO 7100 SERIES (PENTIUM SYSTEM)

. . . continued from previous page

CONNECTIONS			
Purpose	**Location**	**Purpose**	**Location**
PS/2 mouse port	J2	VGA VESA feature connector	J16
Speaker/headphone out connector	J3	IDE interface 2	J18
Audio line in connector	J4	IDE interface 1	J19
Microphone in connector	J5	Floppy drive interface	J20
Parallel port	J6	IDE interface LED	J201
VGA port	J7	Modem connector	J202
CD-ROM audio in connector	J10	Riser slot	SL1
Serial port	J13	Volume control	VR1
Game/MIDI interface	J15		

USER CONFIGURABLE SETTINGS		
Function	**Label**	**Position**
⇨ ESS1688 sound subsystem enabled	JP4	Open
ESS1688 sound subsystem disabled	JP4	Closed
⇨ CMOS memory normal operation	JP201	Pins 2 & 3 closed
CMOS memory clear	JP201	Pins 1 & 2 closed

DRAM CONFIGURATION				
Size	**Bank 0**	**Bank 1**	**Bank 2**	**Bank 3**
2MB	(1) 256K x 36	(1) 256K x 36	None	None
4MB	(1) 512K x 36	(1) 512K x 36	None	None
4MB	(1) 256K x 36	(1) 256K x 36	(1) 256K x 36	(1) 256K x 36
8MB	(1) 1M x 36	(1) 1M x 36	None	None
8MB	(1) 512K x 36	(1) 512K x 36	(1) 512K x 36	(1) 512K x 36
16MB	(1) 1M x 36	(1) 1M x 36	(1) 1M x 36	(1) 1M x 36
16MB	(1) 2M x 36	(1) 2M x 36	None	None
32MB	(1) 4M x 36	(1) 4M x 36	None	None
32MB	(1) 2M x 36	(1) 2M x 36	(1) 2M x 36	(1) 2M x 36
48MB	(1) 2M x 36	(1) 2M x 36	(1) 4M x 36	(1) 4M x 36
48MB	(1) 4M x 36	(1) 4M x 36	(1) 2M x 36	(1) 2M x 36
64MB	(1) 8M x 36	(1) 8M x 36	None	None
64MB	(1) 4M x 36	(1) 4M x 36	(1) 4M x 36	(1) 4M x 36
128MB	(1) 8M x 36	(1) 8M x 36	(1) 8M x 36	(1) 8M x 36

CACHE CONFIGURATION		
Size	**Bank 0**	**TAG**
256KB	(8) 32K x 8	(1) 32K x 8

Continued on next page. . .

COMPAQ COMPUTER CORPORATION
PRESARIO 7100 SERIES (PENTIUM SYSTEM)

...continued from previous page

VIDEO MEMORY CONFIGURATION				
Size	U5	U6	U7	U10
1MB	None	512KB	None	512KB
2MB	512KB	512KB	512KB	512KB
Note: The size of the chips is unidentified.				

CPU SPEED SELECTION		
CPU speed	Clock speed	JP7
75MHz	50MHz	Pins 1 & 2 closed
90MHz	60MHz	Pins 3 & 4 closed
100MHz	66MHz	Pins 1 & 2, 5 & 6 closed

COMPAQ COMPUTER CORPORATION
PRESARIO 9200/9600

Processor	Pentium
Processor Speed	100/120/133/150/166/200MHz
Chip Set	Unidentified
Video Chip Set	Unidentified
Maximum Onboard Memory	136MB
Maximum Video Memory	2MB
Cache	Unidentified
BIOS	Unidentified
Dimensions	330mm x 218mm
I/O Options	Unidentified
NPU Options	None

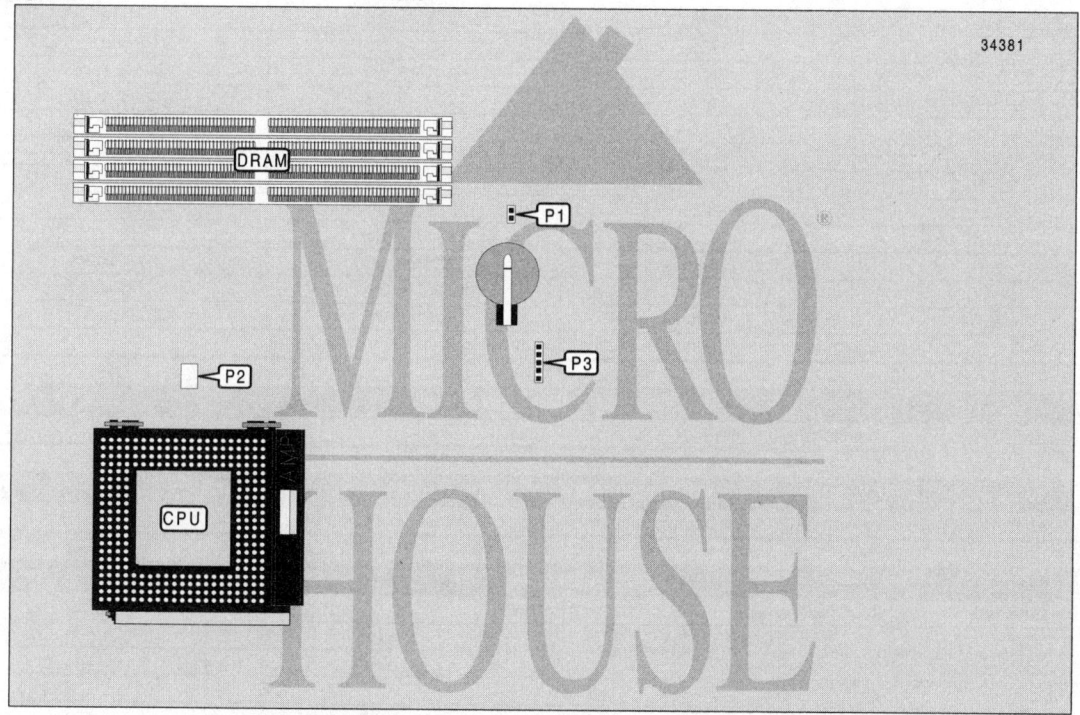

THE LOCATION OF MOST JUMPERS, SWITCHES AND I/O CONNECTORS ARE UNIDENTIFIED

CONNECTIONS
Note: The location and types of all other I/O options are unidentified.

Continued on next page...

COMPAQ COMPUTER CORPORATION
PRESARIO 9200/9600

. . . continued from previous page

USER CONFIGURABLE SETTINGS		
Function	**Label**	**Position**
⇨ CMOS memory normal operation	P1	Closed
CMOS memory clear	P1	Open

DRAM CONFIGURATION			
Size	**Bank 0**	**Bank 1**	**Bank 2**
8MB	8MB	None	None
16MB	8MB	(2) 1M x 36	None
24MB	8MB	(2) 2M x 36	None
24MB	8MB	(2) 1M x 36	(2) 1M x 36
32MB	8MB	(2) 2M x 36	(2) 1M x 36
40MB	8MB	(2) 4M x 36	None
40MB	8MB	(2) 2M x 36	(2) 2M x 36
48MB	8MB	(2) 4M x 36	(2) 1M x 36
56MB	8MB	(2) 4M x 36	(2) 2M x 36
72MB	8MB	(2) 8M x 36	None
72MB	8MB	(2) 4M x 36	(2) 4M x 36
104MB	8MB	(2) 8M x 36	None
136MB	8MB	(2) 8M x 36	(2) 8M x 36

Note: Bank 0 is factory installed and is not configurable. The location of banks 1 & 2 are unidentified.

CACHE CONFIGURATION
Note: The size & location of the cache is unidentified.

VIDEO MEMORY CONFIGURATION
Note: Board is factory installed with 1MB. A 1MB upgrade is available. The location is unidentified.

CPU SPEED SELECTION				
CPU speed	**Clock speed**	**Multiplier**	**P2**	**P3**
100MHz	66MHz	1.5x	A1 & A2, B1 & B2	4 & 5
120MHz	60MHz	2x	A2 & A3, B1 & B2	3 & 4
133MHz	60MHz	2x	A2 & A3, B1 & B2	3 & 4
133MHz	66MHz	2x	A2 & A3, B1 & B2	4 & 5
150MHz	60MHz	2.5x	A2 & A3, B2 & B3	3 & 4
166MHz	66MHz	2.5x	A2 & A3, B2 & B3	4 & 5
200MHz	66MHz	3x	A1 & A2, B2 & B3	4 & 5

Note: Pins designated should be in the closed position.

COMPAQ COMPUTER CORPORATION
PRESARIO CDS 774/972/974/982/992
PRESARIO CDTV 978

Processor	Pentium
Processor Speed	75/90/100MHz
Chip Set	Unidentified
Max. Onboard DRAM	136MB
Cache	256KB
BIOS	Unidentified
Dimensions	330mm x 218mm
I/O Options	Parallel port, PS/2 mouse port, serial ports (2), VGA feature connector, VGA port, modem port, CD-ROM audio connector, modem audio connector, video memory interface
NPU Options	None

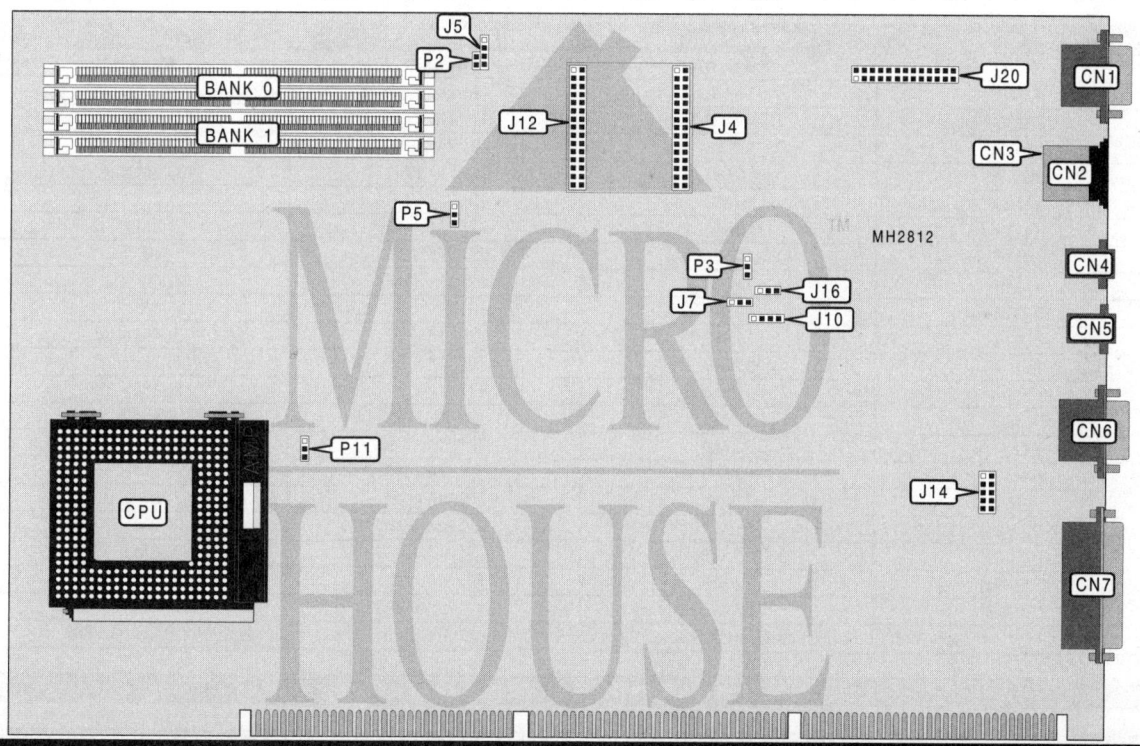

CONNECTIONS

Purpose	Location	Purpose	Location
VGA port	CN1	Video memory connector	J4, J12
PS/2 mouse port	CN2	External battery	J5
Keyboard port	CN3	Modem audio connector	J7
Modem port	CN4	CD-ROM audio connector	J10
Modem port	CN5	Serial port 2	J14
Serial port 1	CN6	VGA feature connector	J20
Parallel port	CN7		

Continued on next page...

COMPAQ COMPUTER CORPORATION
PRESARIO CDS 774/972/974/982/992
PRESARIO CDTV 978

. . . continued from previous page

USER CONFIGURABLE SETTINGS		
Function	**Jumper**	**Position**
◊ Factory configured - do not alter	J16	N/A
◊ CMOS memory normal operation	P2	Closed
CMOS memory clear	P2	Open
◊ Password enabled	P3	pins 1 & 2 closed
Password disabled	P3	pins 2 & 3 closed
◊ CPU core to bus ratio speed select 1.5x	P11	pins 1 & 2 closed
CPU core to bus ratio speed select 2x	P11	pins 2 & 3 closed

DRAM CONFIGURATION (75MHZ CPU ONLY)			
Size	**Bank 0A**	**Bank 0**	**Bank 1**
20MB	12MB	(2) 1M x 36	NONE
28MB	12MB	(2) 1M x 36	(2) 1M x 36
28MB	12MB	(2) 2M x 36	NONE
36MB	12MB	(2) 1M x 36	(2) 2M x 36
36MB	12MB	(2) 2M x 36	(2) 1M x 36
44MB	12MB	(2) 2M x 36	(2) 2M x 36
44MB	12MB	(2) 4M x 36	NONE
52MB	12MB	(2) 1M x 36	(2) 4M x 36
52MB	12MB	(2) 4M x 36	(2) 1M x 36
60MB	12MB	(2) 2M x 36	(2) 4M x 36
60MB	12MB	(2) 4M x 36	(2) 2M x 36
76MB	12MB	(2) 4M x 36	(2) 4M x 36
76MB	12MB	(2) 8M x 36	NONE
84MB	12MB	(2) 1M x 36	(2) 8M x 36
84MB	12MB	(2) 8M x 36	(2) 1M x 36
92MB	12MB	(2) 2M x 36	(2) 8M x 36
92MB	12MB	(2) 8M x 36	(2) 2M x 36
108MB	12MB	(2) 4M x 36	(2) 8M x 36
108MB	12MB	(2) 8M x 36	(2) 4M x 36
136MB	12MB	(2) 8M x 36	(2) 8M x 36

Note: Bank 0A is factory installed and is not configurable. Only 8MB of the onboard memory is used when 136MB is installed.

DRAM CONFIGURATION (75MHZ & 90MHZ CPU ONLY)			
Size	**Bank 0A**	**Bank 0**	**Bank 1**
16MB	8MB	(2) 1M x 36	NONE
24MB	8MB	(2) 1M x 36	(2) 1M x 36
24MB	8MB	(2) 2M x 36	NONE
32MB	8MB	(2) 1M x 36	(2) 2M x 36
32MB	8MB	(2) 2M x 36	(2) 1M x 36
40MB	8MB	(2) 2M x 36	(2) 2M x 36
40MB	8MB	(2) 4M x 36	NONE
48MB	8MB	(2) 1M x 36	(2) 4M x 36
48MB	8MB	(2) 4M x 36	(2) 1M x 36

Continued on next page. . .

COMPAQ COMPUTER CORPORATION
PRESARIO CDS 774/972/974/982/992
PRESARIO CDTV 978

...continued from previous page

DRAM CONFIGURATION (75MHZ & 90MHZ CPU ONLY CON'T)			
Size	Bank 0A	Bank 0	Bank 1
56MB	8MB	(2) 2M x 36	(2) 4M x 36
56MB	8MB	(2) 4M x 36	(2) 2M x 36
72MB	8MB	(2) 4M x 36	(2) 4M x 36
72MB	8MB	(2) 8M x 36	NONE
80MB	8MB	(2) 1M x 36	(2) 8M x 36
80MB	8MB	(2) 8M x 36	(2) 1M x 36
88MB	8MB	(2) 2M x 36	(2) 8M x 36
88MB	8MB	(2) 8M x 36	(2) 2M x 36
104MB	8MB	(2) 4M x 36	(2) 8M x 36
104MB	8MB	(2) 8M x 36	(2) 4M x 36
136MB	8MB	(2) 8M x 36	(2) 8M x 36

Note: Bank 0A is factory installed and is not configurable.

DRAM CONFIGURATION (100MHZ CPU ONLY)			
Size	Bank 0A	Bank 0	Bank 1
24MB	16MB	(2) 1M x 36	NONE
32MB	16MB	(2) 1M x 36	(2) 1M x 36
32MB	16MB	(2) 2M x 36	NONE
40MB	16MB	(2) 1M x 36	(2) 2M x 36
40MB	16MB	(2) 2M x 36	(2) 1M x 36
48MB	16MB	(2) 2M x 36	(2) 2M x 36
48MB	16MB	(2) 4M x 36	NONE
56MB	16MB	(2) 1M x 36	(2) 4M x 36
56MB	16MB	(2) 4M x 36	(2) 1M x 36
64MB	16MB	(2) 2M x 36	(2) 4M x 36
64MB	16MB	(2) 4M x 36	(2) 2M x 36
80MB	16MB	(2) 4M x 36	(2) 4M x 36
80MB	16MB	(2) 8M x 36	NONE
88MB	16MB	(2) 1M x 36	(2) 8M x 36
88MB	16MB	(2) 8M x 36	(2) 1M x 36
96MB	16MB	(2) 2M x 36	(2) 8M x 36
96MB	16MB	(2) 8M x 36	(2) 2M x 36
112MB	16MB	(2) 4M x 36	(2) 8M x 36
112MB	16MB	(2) 8M x 36	(2) 4M x 36
136MB	16MB	(2) 8M x 36	(2) 8M x 36

Note: Bank 0A is factory installed and is not configurable. Only 8MB of the onboard memory is used when 136MB is installed.

CACHE CONFIGURATION
Note: This board is factory installed with 256KB. It is not configurable.

CPU BUS SPEED CONFIGURATION	
Speed	P5
50MHz	pins 2 & 3 closed
60MHz	pins 1 & 2 closed

Continued on next page...

COMPAQ COMPUTER CORPORATION
PRESARIO CDS 774/972/974/982/992
PRESARIO CDTV 978

. . . continued from previous page

VIDEO MEMORY CONFIGURATION

Note: To upgrade video memory, install video module on jumpers J4 & J12.

COMPAQ COMPUTER CORPORATION
PRESARIO SERIES

Processor	Pentium
Processor Speed	60MHz
Chip Set	Unidentified
Max. Onboard DRAM	136MB
Cache	256KB
BIOS	Unidentified
Dimensions	330mm x 218mm
I/O Options	Parallel port, PS/2 mouse port, serial ports (2), VGA feature connector, VGA port, modem port, CD-ROM audio connector, modem audio connector, video memory interface
NPU Options	None

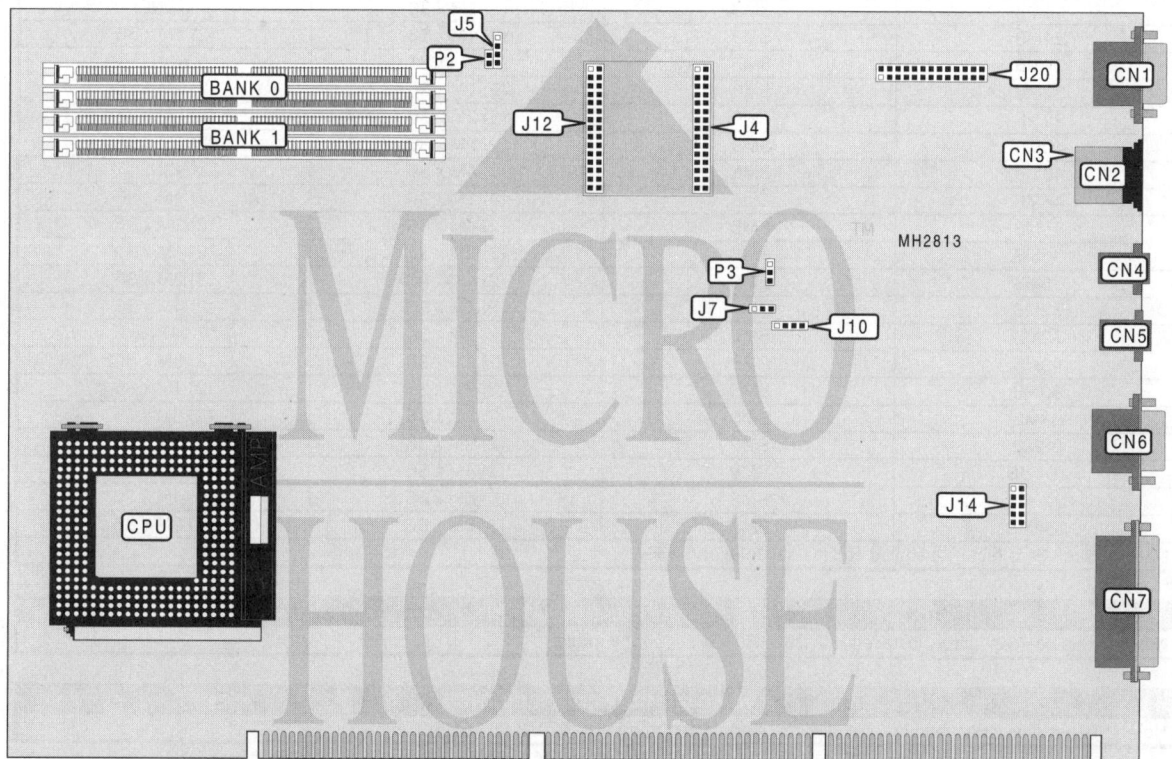

CONNECTIONS			
Purpose	**Location**	**Purpose**	**Location**
VGA port	CN1	Video memory connector	J4, J12
PS/2 mouse port	CN2	External battery	J5
Keyboard port	CN3	Modem audio connector	J7
Modem port	CN4	CD-ROM audio connector	J10
Modem port	CN5	Serial port 2	J14
Serial port 1	CN6	VGA feature connector	J20
Parallel port	CN7		

Continued on next page...

COMPAQ COMPUTER CORPORATION
PRESARIO SERIES

...continued from previous page

USER CONFIGURABLE SETTINGS		
Function	**Jumper**	**Position**
⇨ CMOS memory normal operation	P2	Closed
CMOS memory clear	P2	Open
⇨ Password enabled	P3	pins 1 & 2 closed
Password disabled	P3	pins 2 & 3 closed

DRAM CONFIGURATION			
Size	**Bank 0A**	**Bank 0**	**Bank 1**
16MB	8MB	(2) 1M x 36	NONE
24MB	8MB	(2) 1M x 36	(2) 1M x 36
24MB	8MB	(2) 2M x 36	NONE
32MB	8MB	(2) 1M x 36	(2) 2M x 36
32MB	8MB	(2) 2M x 36	(2) 1M x 36
40MB	8MB	(2) 2M x 36	(2) 2M x 36
40MB	8MB	(2) 4M x 36	NONE
48MB	8MB	(2) 1M x 36	(2) 4M x 36
48MB	8MB	(2) 4M x 36	(2) 1M x 36
56MB	8MB	(2) 2M x 36	(2) 4M x 36
56MB	8MB	(2) 4M x 36	(2) 2M x 36
72MB	8MB	(2) 4M x 36	(2) 4M x 36
72MB	8MB	(2) 8M x 36	NONE
80MB	8MB	(2) 1M x 36	(2) 8M x 36
80MB	8MB	(2) 8M x 36	(2) 1M x 36
88MB	8MB	(2) 2M x 36	(2) 8M x 36
88MB	8MB	(2) 8M x 36	(2) 2M x 36
104MB	8MB	(2) 4M x 36	(2) 8M x 36
104MB	8MB	(2) 8M x 36	(2) 4M x 36
136MB	8MB	(2) 8M x 36	(2) 8M x 36

Note: Bank 0A is factory installed and is not configurable.

CACHE CONFIGURATION
Note: This board is factory installed with 256KB. It is not configurable.

VIDEO MEMORY CONFIGURATION
Note: To upgrade video memory, install video module on jumpers J4 & J12.

COMPAQ COMPUTER CORPORATION
PROLIANT 5000R

Processor	Pentium Pro
Processor Speed	166/200MHz
Chip Set	Unidentified
Video Chip Set	Unidentified
Maximum Onboard Memory	4GB
Maximum Video Memory	Unidentified
Cache	256/512KB (located on Pentium Pro CPU)
BIOS	Unidentified
Dimensions	Unidentified
I/O Options	Fast SCSI-2 interface, parallel port, PS/2 mouse port, serial ports (2), RJ-45 connector, VGA port
NPU Options	None

CONNECTIONS
Note: The location of the connectors is unidentified.

USER CONFIGURABLE SETTINGS

	Function	Label	Position
⇨	On board video enabled	S1/1	Off
	On board video disabled	S1/1	On
⇨	Chassis configuration lock enabled	S1/2	Off
	Chassis configuration lock disabled	S1/2	On
⇨	System installed in a tower chassis	S1/3	Off
	System installed in a rack chassis	S1/3	On
⇨	System boot from floppy controlled through configuration settings	S1/4	Off
	System boot from floppy drive regardless of configuration settings	S1/4	On
⇨	Password enabled	S1/5	Off
	Password disabled	S1/5	On
⇨	CMOS memory normal operation	S1/6	Off
	CMOS memory clear	S1/6	On

DIMM CONFIGURATION
Note: The configuration of the 4GB memory is unidentified.

CACHE CONFIGURATION
Note: 256KB/512KB cache is located on the Pentium Pro CPU.

VIDEO MEMORY CONFIGURATION
Note: The size of the video memory is unidentified.

DRIVE SELECTION

SCSI ID	ID0	ID1	ID2
5	On	Off	On
6	Off	On	On

Continued on next page...

COMPAQ COMPUTER CORPORATION
PROLIANT 5000R

...continued from previous page

MONITOR SELECTION NOTE
Note: The Proliant 5000R is capable of controlling up to 8 servers, each with their own monitor. To select a monitor type for a specific server, first consult either the 4 or 8 Port Monitor Control Selection Table to determine which switches are used for the configuration.. Then refer to the Server Monitor Selection table to determine the individual switch settings.

4 PORT MONITOR CONTROL SELECTION		
Switch	Controlling switches	Server controlled
S1	SW1/1 - 4	1
S1	SW1/5 - 8	2
S2	SW2/1 - 4	3
S2	SW2/5 - 8	4

8 PORT MONITOR CONTROL SELECTION		
Switch	Controlling switches	Server controlled
S1	SW1/1 - 4	1
S1	SW1/5 - 8	2
S2	SW2/1 - 4	3
S2	SW2/5 - 8	4
S3	SW3/1 - 4	5
S3	SW3/5 - 8	6
S4	SW3/1 - 4	7
S4	SW3/5 - 8	8

SERVER MONITOR SELECTION				
Type	SW1/1 orSW1/5	SW1/2 orSW1/6	SW1/3 orSW1/7	SW1/4 orSW1/8
VGA	Off	Off	On	Off
Monochrome	Off	Off	On	Off
VGA	Off	On	Off	Off
SVGA	Off	On	Off	Off
SVGA- Compaq 430	On	On	Off	On
XVGA – IBM8512	Off	On	Off	Off
XVGA – IBM8513	Off	On	Off	Off
XVGA – IBM8514	On	On	Off	Off
XVGA – IBM8515	On	Off	Off	Off
Note: Each bank of switches must reflect the type of monitor configured on the server.				

MISCELLANEOUS TECHNICAL NOTE
Note: Diagram not available.

COMPAQ COMPUTER CORPORATION
PROLINEA 5120/5133/5150/5166

Processor	Pentium
Processor Speed	75/90/100/120/125/133/150/166MHz
Chip Set	Unidentified
Video Chip Set	Unidentified
Maximum Onboard Memory	192MB (EDO supported)
Maximum Video Memory	6MB
Cache	256KB
BIOS	Unidentified
Dimensions	330mm x 218mm
I/O Options	Unidentified
NPU Options	None

CONNECTIONS

Purpose	Location
External battery	P3

Note: The location and types of I/O options are unidentified.

USER CONFIGURABLE SETTINGS

Function	Label	Position
Battery type select internal	E5	Pins 1 & 2 closed
Battery type select external	E5	Pins 2 & 3 closed
Password enabled	E6	Pins 1 & 2 closed
Password disabled	E6	Pins 2 & 3 closed

DRAM CONFIGURATION

Size	Bank 0	Bank 1	Bank 2
8MB	(2) 1M x 36	None	None
16MB	(2) 1M x 36	(2) 1M x 36	None
16MB	(2) 2M x 36	None	None
24MB	(2) 2M x 36	(2) 1M x 36	None
24MB	(2) 1M x 36	(2) 1M x 36	(2) 1M x 36
32MB	(2) 4M x 36	None	None
32MB	(2) 2M x 36	(2) 2M x 36	None
40MB	(2) 4M x 36	(2) 1M x 36	None
48MB	(2) 4M x 36	(2) 2M x 36	None
48MB	(2) 4M x 36	(2) 1M x 36	(2) 1M x 36
64MB	(2) 8M x 36	None	None
64MB	(2) 4M x 36	(2) 4M x 36	None
80MB	(2) 8M x 36	(2) 2M x 36	None
96MB	(2) 8M x 36	(2) 4M x 36	None
96MB	(2) 4M x 36	(2) 4M x 36	(2) 4M x 36
128MB	(2) 8M x 36	(2) 8M x 36	None
192MB	(2) 8M x 36	(2) 8M x 36	(2) 8M x 36

Note: Board accepts EDO memory.

CACHE CONFIGURATION

Note: The location of the cache is unidentified.

Continued on next page...

COMPAQ COMPUTER CORPORATION
PROLINEA 5120/5133/5150/5166

...continued from previous page

VIDEO MEMORY CONFIGURATION
Note: The location of the video memory is unidentified.

CPU SPEED SELECTION

CPU speed	Clock speed	Multiplier	S1/1	S1/2	S1/3	S1/4
75MHz	50MHz	1.5x	On	Off	Off	Off
90MHz	60MHz	1.5x	Off	Off	Off	Off
100MHz	66MHz	1.5x	Off	Off	On	Off
100MHz	50MHz	2x	On	On	Off	Off
120MHz	60MHz	2x	Off	On	Off	Off
125MHz	50MHz	2.5x	On	On	Off	On
133MHz	66MHz	2x	Off	On	On	Off
150MHz	60MHz	2.5x	Off	On	Off	On
166MHz	66MHz	2.5x	Off	On	On	On

TECHNICAL NOTE
Diagram not available.

DELL COMPUTER CORPORATION
DIMENSION XPS HXXX

Processor	Pentium II
Processor Speed	233/266MHz
Chip Set	Intel
Video Chip Set	None
Maximum Onboard Memory	128MB (EDO supported)
Maximum Video Memory	None
Cache	512KB (located on Pentium II CPU)
BIOS	Unidentified
Dimensions	305mm x 244mm
I/O Options	32-bit PCI slots (4), floppy drive interface, IDE interfaces (2), parallel port, PS/2 mouse port, serial ports (2), USB connectors (2), ATX power connector, line in, line out, microphone in, game/MIDI port, CPU Slot 1, CD-ROM audio in
NPU Options	None

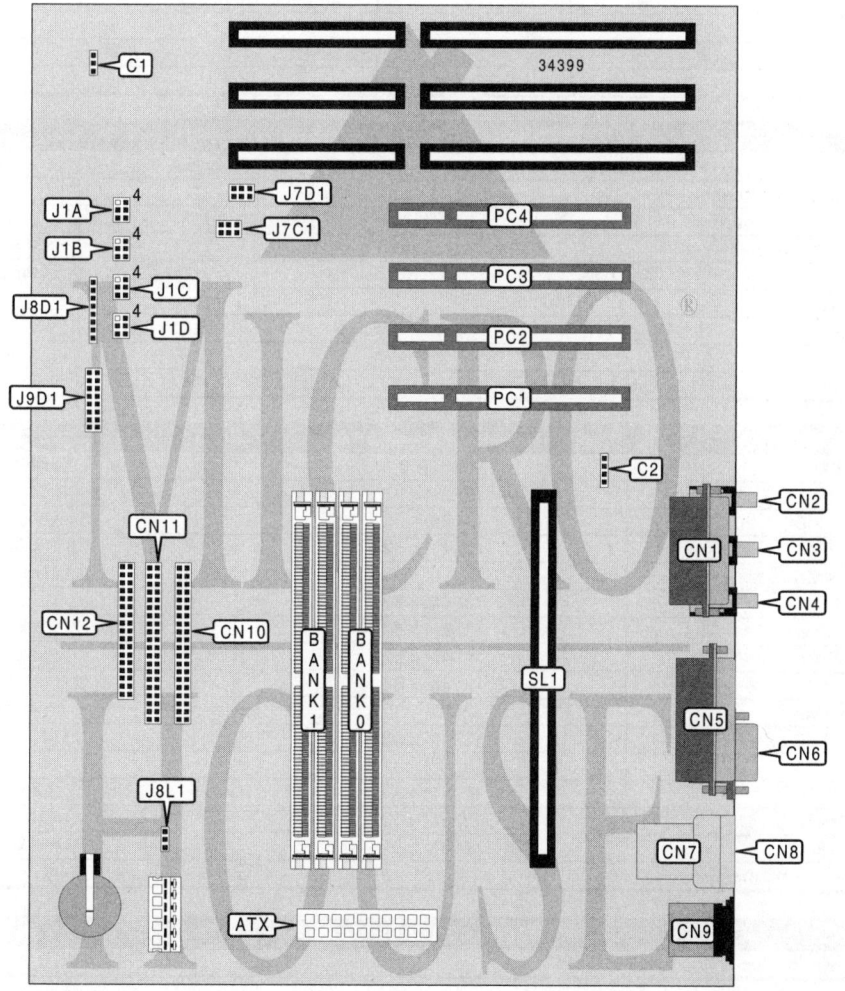

Continued on next page...

DELL COMPUTER CORPORATION
DIMENSION XPS HXXX

. . . continued from previous page

CONNECTIONS			
Purpose	**Location**	**Purpose**	**Location**
ATX power connector	ATX	IDE interface 2	CN10
CD-ROM audio in	C2	IDE interface 1	CN11
Game/MIDI port	CN1	Floppy drive interface	CN12
Microphone in	CN2	Wavetable connector	J7C1
Line in	CN3	Wavetable connector	J7D1
Line out	CN4	SCSI interface LED	J8D1
Serial port	CN5	Chassis fan power	J8L1
Parallel port	CN6	Front panel connector	J9D1
USB connector	CN7	32-bit PCI slots	PC1 – PC4
USB connector	CN8	CPU Slot 1	SL1
PS/2 mouse port	CN9		

USER CONFIGURABLE SETTINGS		
Function	**Label**	**Position**
✧ Factory configured - do not alter	C1	Unidentified
✧ Factory configured - do not alter	J1A	Pins 5 & 6 closed
✧ CMOS memory normal operation	J1C	Pins 5 & 6 closed
CMOS memory clear	J1C	Pins 4 & 5 closed
✧ Password enabled	J1D	Pins 2 & 3 closed
Password disabled	J1D	Pins 1 & 2 closed
✧ Setup access enabled	J1D	Pins 5 & 6 closed
Setup access disabled	J1D	Pins 4 & 5 closed

DRAM CONFIGURATION		
Size	**Bank 0**	**Bank 1**
8MB	(2) 1M x 32	None
16MB	(2) 2M x 32	None
16MB	(2) 1M x 32	(2) 1M x 32
24MB	(2) 2M x 32	(2) 1M x 32
32MB	(2) 4M x 32	None
32MB	(2) 2M x 32	(2) 2M x 32
40MB	(2) 4M x 32	(2) 1M x 32
48MB	(2) 4M x 32	(2) 2M x 32
64MB	(2) 8M x 32	None
64MB	(2) 4M x 32	(2) 4M x 32
72MB	(2) 8M x 32	(2) 1M x 32
80MB	(2) 8M x 32	(2) 2M x 32
96MB	(2) 8M x 32	(2) 4M x 32
128MB	(2) 8M x 32	(2) 8M x 32
Note: Board accepts EDO memory.		

CACHE CONFIGURATION
Note: 512KB cache is located on the Pentium II CPU.

Continued on next page. . .

DELL COMPUTER CORPORATION
DIMENSION XPS HXXX

...continued from previous page

CPU SPEED SELECTION			
CPU speed	**J1A**	**J1B**	**J1C**
233MHz	Pins 2 & 3 closed	Pins 2 & 3, 5 & 6 closed	Pins 2 & 3 closed
266MHz	Pins 1 & 2 closed	Pins 2 & 3, 5 & 6 closed	Pins 2 & 3 closed

142 Motherboard Settings & Specifications

DELL COMPUTER CORPORATION
DIMENSION XPS PROXXX

Processor	Pentium Pro
Processor Speed	150/200MHz
Chip Set	Intel
Video Chip Set	None
Maximum Onboard Memory	128MB
Maximum Video Memory	None
Cache	256KB (on Pentium Pro CPU)
BIOS	Unidentified
Dimensions	330mm x 218mm
I/O Options	32-bit PCI slots (4), floppy drive interface, green PC connector, IDE interfaces (2), parallel port, PS/2 mouse port, serial ports (2)
NPU Options	None

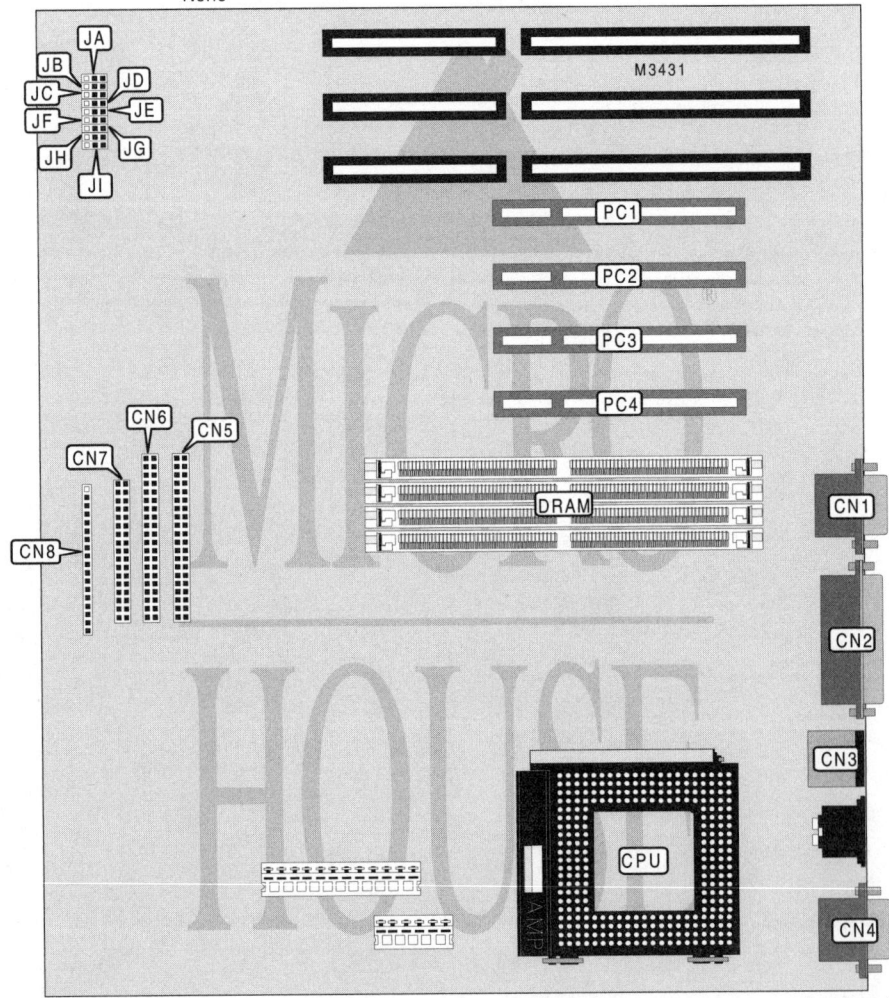

Continued on next page...

DELL COMPUTER CORPORATION
DIMENSION XPS PROXXX

...continued from previous page

CONNECTIONS

Purpose	Location	Purpose	Location
Serial port 2	CN1	IDE interface	CN6
Parallel port	CN2	Floppy drive interface	CN7
PS/2 mouse port	CN3	Front panel connector	CN8
Serial port 1	CN4	32-bit PCI slots	PC1 - PC4
IDE interface	CN5		

USER CONFIGURABLE SETTINGS

Function	Label	Position
On board speaker enabled	CN8	Pins 2 & 3 closed
On board speaker disabled	CN8	Pins 2 & 3 open
⇨ Password normal operation	JE	Pins 2 & 3 closed
Password clear	JE	Pins 1 & 2 closed
⇨ CMOS memory normal operation	JF	Pins 2 & 3 closed
CMOS memory clear	JF	Pins 1 & 2 closed
Setup access enabled	JG	Pins 2 & 3 closed
Setup access disabled	JG	Pins 1 & 2 closed
⇨ Factory configured - do not alter	JH	Pins 2 & 3 closed
⇨ Factory configured - do not alter	JI	Pins 2 & 3 closed

DRAM CONFIGURATION

Size	Bank 0	Bank 1
16MB	(2) 2M x 32	None
18MB	(2) 2M x 32	(2) 256K x 32
32MB	(2) 4M x 32	None
32MB	(2) 2M x 32	(2) 2M x 32
48MB	(2) 4M x 32	(2) 2M x 32
48MB	(2) 2M x 32	(2) 4M x 32
64MB	(2) 8M x 32	None
64MB	(2) 4M x 32	(2) 4M x 32
80MB	(2) 8M x 32	(2) 2M x 32
80MB	(2) 2M x 32	(2) 8M x 32
96MB	(2) 8M x 32	(2) 4M x 32
96MB	(2) 4M x 32	(2) 8M x 32
128MB	(2) 8M x 32	(2) 8M x 32

Note: The location of banks 0 & 1 are unidentified.

CACHE CONFIGURATION

Note: 256KB cache is located on the Pentium Pro CPU.

CPU SPEED SELECTION

Speed	JA	JB	JC	JD
150MHz	Pins 1 & 2 closed	Pins 1 & 2 closed	Pins 1 & 2 closed	Pins 2 & 3 closed
200MHz	Pins 2 & 3 closed	Pins 2 & 3 closed	Pins 2 & 3 closed	Pins 1 & 2 closed

DELL COMPUTER CORPORATION
OPTIPLEX GXL/GXM

Processor	Pentium
Processor Speed	90/100/120/133/150/166/200MHz
Chip Set	Intel
Video Chip Set	S3
Maximum Onboard Memory	128MB (EDO supported)
Maximum Video Memory	2MB
Cache	256/512KB
BIOS	Unidentified
Dimensions	330mm x 218mm
I/O Options	Audio in-CD-ROM, Ethernet 10BaseT connector, floppy drive interface, IDE interfaces (2), parallel port, PS/2 mouse port, serial ports (2), VESA feature connector, VGA port, riser slot, cache slot, ATX power connector, line in, line out, microphone in
NPU Options	None

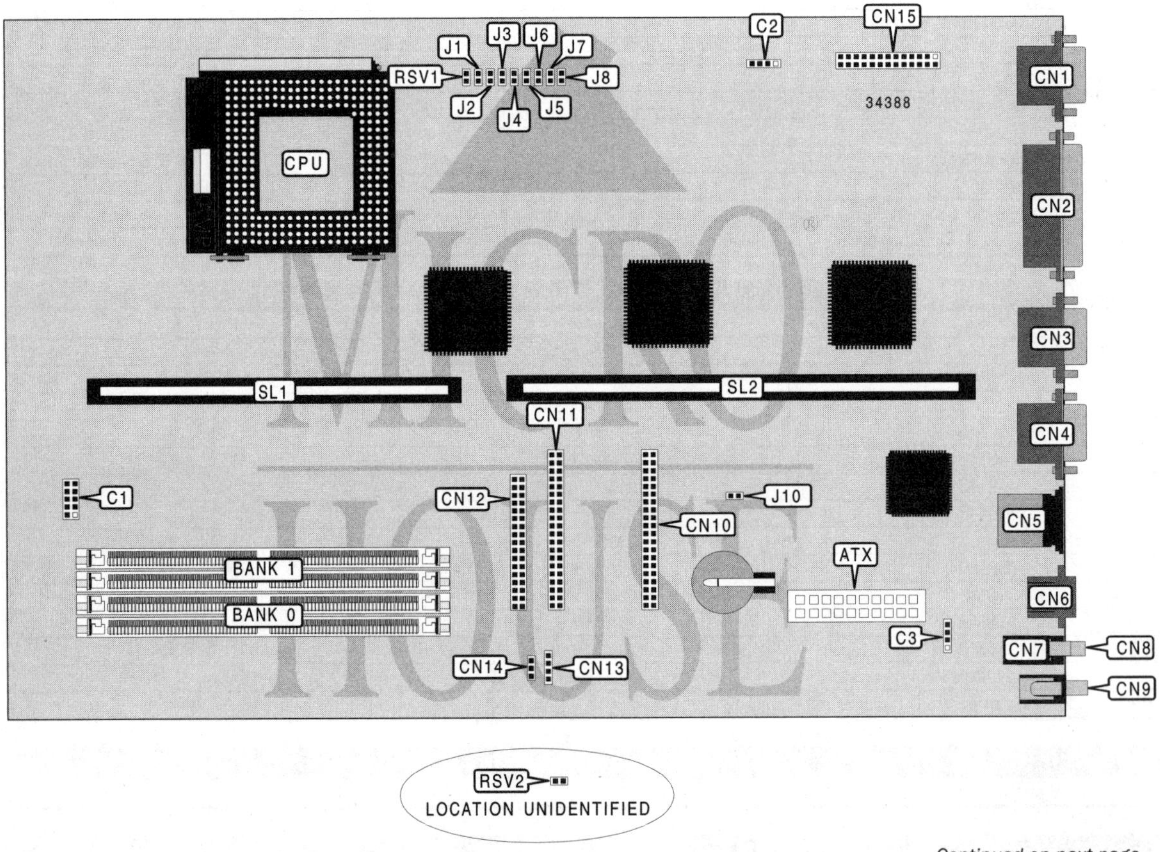

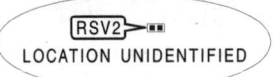

Continued on next page...

DELL COMPUTER CORPORATION
OPTIPLEX GXL/GXM

. . . continued from previous page

CONNECTIONS

Purpose	Location	Purpose	Location
ATX power connector	ATX	Microphone in	CN8
Front panel connector	C1	Line out	CN9
IDE interface LED 1	C2	IDE interface 1	CN10
IDE interface LED 2	C3	IDE interface 2	CN11
VGA port	CN1	Floppy drive interface	CN12
Parallel port	CN2	Audio in-CD-ROM	CN13
Serial port 2	CN3	Chassis fan power	CN14
Serial port 1	CN4	VESA feature connector	CN15
PS/2 mouse port	CN5	Cache slot	SL1
Ethernet 10BaseT connector	CN6	Riser slot	SL2
Line in	CN7		

USER CONFIGURABLE SETTINGS

Function	Label	Position
⇨ Factory configured - do not alter	J1	Open
⇨ Password enabled	J2	Closed
Password disabled	J2	Open
⇨ Factory configured - do not alter	J8	Open
⇨ EPROM normal operation	J10	Open
EPROM clear	J10	Closed

DRAM CONFIGURATION

Size	Bank 0	Bank 1
8MB	(2) 1M x 32	None
16MB	(2) 2M x 32	None
16MB	(2) 1M x 32	(2) 1M x 32
24MB	(2) 2M x 32	(2) 1M x 32
32MB	(2) 4M x 32	None
32MB	(2) 2M x 32	(2) 2M x 32
40MB	(2) 4M x 32	(2) 1M x 32
48MB	(2) 4M x 32	(2) 2M x 32
64MB	(2) 8M x 32	None
64MB	(2) 4M x 32	(2) 4M x 32
72MB	(2) 8M x 32	(2) 1M x 32
80MB	(2) 8M x 32	(2) 2M x 32
96MB	(2) 8M x 32	(2) 4M x 32
128MB	(2) 8M x 32	(2) 8M x 32

CACHE CONFIGURATION

Size	SL1
256KB	256KB module installed
512KB	512KB module installed

Continued on next page. . .

DELL COMPUTER CORPORATION
OPTIPLEX GXL/GXM

. . . continued from previous page

VIDEO MEMORY CONFIGURATION
Note: Board accepts 2MB of video memory. The location and configuration is unidentified.

CPU SPEED SELECTION					
CPU speed	**Clock speed**	**Multiplier**	**J3**	**J4**	**J5**
90MHz	60MHz	1.5x	Open	Open	Open
100MHz	66MHz	1.5x	Open	Open	Open
120MHz	60MHz	2x	Open	Open	Closed
133MHz	66MHz	2x	Open	Closed	Open
150MHz	60MHz	2.5x	Closed	Open	Open
166MHz	66MHz	2.5x	Open	Open	Open
200MHz	66MHz	3x	Open	Open	Open

CPU SPEED SELECTION (CON'T)					
CPU speed	**Clock speed**	**Multiplier**	**J6**	**J7**	**RSV1**	**RSV2**
90MHz	60MHz	1.5x	Open	Closed	Open	Open
100MHz	66MHz	1.5x	Closed	Open	Open	Open
120MHz	60MHz	2x	Open	Open	Open	Open
133MHz	66MHz	2x	Open	Open	Open	Open
150MHz	60MHz	2.5x	Open	Open	Open	Open
166MHz	66MHz	2.5x	Open	Open	Closed	Open
200MHz	66MHz	3x	Open	Open	Open	Closed

DELL COMPUTER CORPORATION
OPTIPLEX DGX

Processor	Pentium
Processor Speed	90/100/120/133/150/166MHz
Chip Set	Unidentified
Video Chip Set	ATI
Maximum Onboard Memory	512MB
Maximum Video Memory	2MB
Cache	256/512KB
BIOS	Unidentified
Dimensions	330mm x 218mm
I/O Options	Floppy drive interface, IDE interface, parallel port, PS/2 mouse port, serial ports (2), feature connector, VGA port, riser slot, cache slot
NPU Options	None

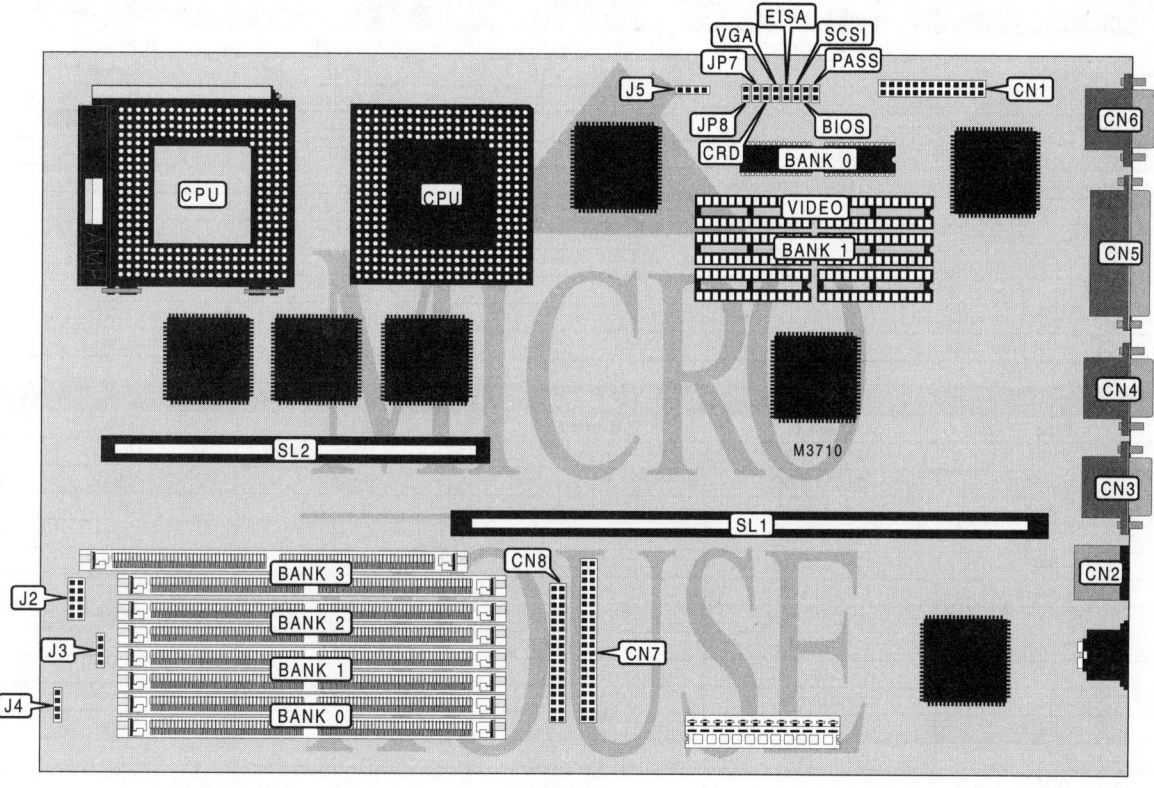

Continued on next page...

DELL COMPUTER CORPORATION
OPTIPLEX DGX

. . . continued from previous page

CONNECTIONS

Purpose	Location	Purpose	Location
Feature connector	CN1	Floppy drive interface	CN8
PS/2 mouse port	CN2	Front panel connector	J2
Serial port 2	CN3	Speaker	J3
Serial port 1	CN4	External battery	J4
Parallel port	CN5	IDE interface LED	J5
VGA port	CN6	Riser slot	SL1
IDE interface	CN7	Cache slot	SL2

USER CONFIGURABLE SETTINGS

Function	Label	Position
✧ Flash BIOS update enabled	BIOS	Closed
Flash BIOS update disabled	BIOS	Open
✧ Factory configured - do not alter	CRD	Unidentified
✧ EISA configuration settings cleared at boot	EISA	Open
EISA configuration settings not cleared at boot	EISA	Closed
✧ Password enabled	PASS	Closed
Password disabled	PASS	Open
✧ SCSI host adapter is terminated	SCSI	Closed
SCSI host adapter is not terminated	SCSI	Open
✧ On board video enabled	VGA	Closed
On board video disabled	VGA	Open

DRAM CONFIGURATION

Size	Bank 0	Bank 1	Bank 2	Bank 3
8MB	(2) 1M x 36	None	None	None
16MB	(2) 2M x 36	None	None	None
16MB	(2) 1M x 36	(2) 1M x 36	None	None
24MB	(2) 2M x 36	(2) 1M x 36	None	None
24MB	(2) 1M x 36	(2) 1M x 36	(2) 1M x 36	None
32MB	(2) 4M x 36	None	None	None
32MB	(2) 2M x 36	(2) 2M x 36	None	None
32MB	(2) 2M x 36	(2) 1M x 36	(2) 1M x 36	None
32MB	(2) 1M x 36	(2) 1M x 36	(2) 1M x 36	(2) 1M x 36
40MB	(2) 4M x 36	(2) 1M x 36	None	None
40MB	(2) 2M x 36	(2) 2M x 36	(2) 1M x 36	None
40MB	(2) 2M x 36	(2) 1M x 36	(2) 1M x 36	(2) 1M x 36
48MB	(2) 4M x 36	(2) 2M x 36	None	None
48MB	(2) 4M x 36	(2) 1M x 36	(2) 1M x 36	None
48MB	(2) 2M x 36	(2) 2M x 36	(2) 2M x 36	None
48MB	(2) 2M x 36	(2) 2M x 36	(2) 1M x 36	(2) 1M x 36
56MB	(2) 4M x 36	(2) 2M x 36	(2) 1M x 36	None
56MB	(2) 4M x 36	(2) 1M x 36	(2) 1M x 36	(2) 1M x 36
56MB	(2) 2M x 36	(2) 2M x 36	(2) 2M x 36	(2) 1M x 36

Continued on next page. . .

DELL COMPUTER CORPORATION
OPTIPLEX DGX

...continued from previous page

Size	Bank 0	Bank 1	Bank 2	Bank 3
\multicolumn{5}{c}{**DRAM CONFIGURATION (CON'T)**}				
64MB	(2) 8M x 36	None	None	None
64MB	(2) 4M x 36	(2) 4M x 36	None	None
64MB	(2) 4M x 36	(2) 2M x 36	(2) 2M x 36	None
64MB	(2) 4M x 36	(2) 2M x 36	(2) 1M x 36	(2) 1M x 36
64MB	(2) 2M x 36	(2) 2M x 36	(2) 2M x 36	(2) 2M x 36
72MB	(2) 8M x 36	(2) 1M x 36	None	None
72MB	(2) 4M x 36	(2) 4M x 36	(2) 1M x 36	None
72MB	(2) 4M x 36	(2) 2M x 36	(2) 2M x 36	(2) 1M x 36
80MB	(2) 8M x 36	(2) 2M x 36	None	None
80MB	(2) 8M x 36	(2) 1M x 36	(2) 1M x 36	None
80MB	(2) 4M x 36	(2) 4M x 36	(2) 2M x 36	None
80MB	(2) 4M x 36	(2) 4M x 36	(2) 1M x 36	(2) 1M x 36
80MB	(2) 4M x 36	(2) 2M x 36	(2) 2M x 36	(2) 2M x 36
88MB	(2) 8M x 36	(2) 2M x 36	(2) 1M x 36	None
88MB	(2) 8M x 36	(2) 1M x 36	(2) 1M x 36	(2) 1M x 36
88MB	(2) 4M x 36	(2) 4M x 36	(2) 2M x 36	(2) 1M x 36
96MB	(2) 8M x 36	(2) 4M x 36	None	None
96MB	(2) 8M x 36	(2) 2M x 36	(2) 2M x 36	None
96MB	(2) 8M x 36	(2) 2M x 36	(2) 1M x 36	(2) 1M x 36
96MB	(2) 4M x 36	(2) 4M x 36	(2) 4M x 36	None
96MB	(2) 4M x 36	(2) 4M x 36	(2) 2M x 36	(2) 2M x 36
104MB	(2) 8M x 36	(2) 4M x 36	(2) 1M x 36	None
104MB	(2) 8M x 36	(2) 2M x 36	(2) 2M x 36	(2) 1M x 36
104MB	(2) 4M x 36	(2) 4M x 36	(2) 4M x 36	(2) 1M x 36
112MB	(2) 8M x 36	(2) 4M x 36	(2) 2M x 36	None
112MB	(2) 8M x 36	(2) 4M x 36	(2) 1M x 36	(2) 1M x 36
112MB	(2) 8M x 36	(2) 2M x 36	(2) 2M x 36	(2) 2M x 36
112MB	(2) 4M x 36	(2) 4M x 36	(2) 4M x 36	(2) 2M x 36
120MB	(2) 8M x 36	(2) 4M x 36	(2) 2M x 36	(2) 1M x 36
128MB	(2) 16M x 36	None	None	None
128MB	(2) 8M x 36	(2) 8M x 36	None	None
128MB	(2) 8M x 36	(2) 4M x 36	(2) 4M x 36	None
128MB	(2) 8M x 36	(2) 4M x 36	(2) 2M x 36	(2) 2M x 36
128MB	(2) 4M x 36	(2) 4M x 36	(2) 4M x 36	(2) 4M x 36
136MB	(2) 16M x 36	(2) 1M x 36	None	None
136MB	(2) 8M x 36	(2) 8M x 36	(2) 1M x 36	None
136MB	(2) 8M x 36	(2) 4M x 36	(2) 4M x 36	(2) 1M x 36
144MB	(2) 16M x 36	(2) 2M x 36	None	None
144MB	(2) 16M x 36	(2) 1M x 36	(2) 1M x 36	None
144MB	(2) 8M x 36	(2) 8M x 36	(2) 2M x 36	None
144MB	(2) 8M x 36	(2) 8M x 36	(2) 1M x 36	(2) 1M x 36
144MB	(2) 8M x 36	(2) 4M x 36	(2) 4M x 36	(2) 2M x 36

Continued on next page...

DELL COMPUTER CORPORATION
OPTIPLEX DGX

. . . continued from previous page

Size	Bank 0	Bank 1	Bank 2	Bank 3
\multicolumn{5}{c}{**DRAM CONFIGURATION (CON'T)**}				
152MB	(2) 16M x 36	(2) 2M x 36	(2) 1M x 36	None
152MB	(2) 16M x 36	(2) 1M x 36	(2) 1M x 36	(2) 1M x 36
152MB	(2) 8M x 36	(2) 8M x 36	(2) 2M x 36	(2) 1M x 36
160MB	(2) 16M x 36	(2) 4M x 36	None	None
160MB	(2) 16M x 36	(2) 2M x 36	(2) 2M x 36	None
160MB	(2) 16M x 36	(2) 2M x 36	(2) 1M x 36	(2) 1M x 36
160MB	(2) 8M x 36	(2) 8M x 36	(2) 4M x 36	None
160MB	(2) 8M x 36	(2) 8M x 36	(2) 2M x 36	(2) 2M x 36
160MB	(2) 8M x 36	(2) 4M x 36	(2) 4M x 36	(2) 4M x 36
168MB	(2) 16M x 36	(2) 4M x 36	(2) 1M x 36	None
168MB	(2) 16M x 36	(2) 2M x 36	(2) 2M x 36	(2) 1M x 36
168MB	(2) 8M x 36	(2) 8M x 36	(2) 4M x 36	(2) 1M x 36
176MB	(2) 16M x 36	(2) 4M x 36	(2) 2M x 36	None
176MB	(2) 16M x 36	(2) 4M x 36	(2) 1M x 36	(2) 1M x 36
176MB	(2) 16M x 36	(2) 2M x 36	(2) 2M x 36	(2) 2M x 36
176MB	(2) 8M x 36	(2) 8M x 36	(2) 4M x 36	(2) 2M x 36
184MB	(2) 16M x 36	(2) 4M x 36	(2) 2M x 36	(2) 1M x 36
192MB	(2) 16M x 36	(2) 8M x 36	None	None
192MB	(2) 16M x 36	(2) 4M x 36	(2) 4M x 36	None
192MB	(2) 16M x 36	(2) 4M x 36	(2) 2M x 36	(2) 2M x 36
192MB	(2) 8M x 36	(2) 8M x 36	(2) 8M x 36	None
192MB	(2) 8M x 36	(2) 8M x 36	(2) 4M x 36	(2) 4M x 36
200MB	(2) 16M x 36	(2) 8M x 36	(2) 1M x 36	None
200MB	(2) 16M x 36	(2) 4M x 36	(2) 4M x 36	(2) 1M x 36
200MB	(2) 8M x 36	(2) 8M x 36	(2) 8M x 36	(2) 1M x 36
208MB	(2) 16M x 36	(2) 8M x 36	(2) 2M x 36	None
208MB	(2) 16M x 36	(2) 8M x 36	(2) 1M x 36	(2) 1M x 36
208MB	(2) 16M x 36	(2) 4M x 36	(2) 4M x 36	(2) 2M x 36
208MB	(2) 8M x 36	(2) 8M x 36	(2) 8M x 36	(2) 2M x 36
216MB	(2) 16M x 36	(2) 8M x 36	(2) 2M x 36	(2) 1M x 36
224MB	(2) 16M x 36	(2) 8M x 36	(2) 4M x 36	None
224MB	(2) 16M x 36	(2) 8M x 36	(2) 2M x 36	(2) 2M x 36
224MB	(2) 16M x 36	(2) 4M x 36	(2) 4M x 36	(2) 4M x 36
224MB	(2) 8M x 36	(2) 8M x 36	(2) 8M x 36	(2) 4M x 36
232MB	(2) 16M x 36	(2) 8M x 36	(2) 8M x 36	(2) 1M x 36
240MB	(2) 16M x 36	(2) 8M x 36	(2) 4M x 36	(2) 2M x 36
256MB	(2) 16M x 36	(2) 16M x 36	None	None
256MB	(2) 16M x 36	(2) 8M x 36	(2) 8M x 36	None
256MB	(2) 16M x 36	(2) 8M x 36	(2) 4M x 36	(2) 4M x 36
256MB	(2) 8M x 36	(2) 8M x 36	(2) 8M x 36	(2) 8M x 36
264MB	(2) 16M x 36	(2) 16M x 36	(2) 1M x 36	None
264MB	(2) 16M x 36	(2) 8M x 36	(2) 8M x 36	(2) 1M x 36

Continued on next page. . .

DELL COMPUTER CORPORATION
OPTIPLEX DGX

. . . continued from previous page

	DRAM CONFIGURATION (CON'T)			
Size	**Bank 0**	**Bank 1**	**Bank 2**	**Bank 3**
272MB	(2) 16M x 36	(2) 16M x 36	(2) 2M x 36	None
272MB	(2) 16M x 36	(2) 16M x 36	(2) 1M x 36	(2) 1M x 36
272MB	(2) 16M x 36	(2) 8M x 36	(2) 8M x 36	(2) 2M x 36
280MB	(2) 16M x 36	(2) 16M x 36	(2) 2M x 36	(2) 1M x 36
288MB	(2) 16M x 36	(2) 16M x 36	(2) 4M x 36	None
288MB	(2) 16M x 36	(2) 16M x 36	(2) 2M x 36	(2) 2M x 36
288MB	(2) 16M x 36	(2) 8M x 36	(2) 8M x 36	(2) 4M x 36
296MB	(2) 16M x 36	(2) 16M x 36	(2) 4M x 36	(2) 1M x 36
304MB	(2) 16M x 36	(2) 16M x 36	(2) 4M x 36	(2) 2M x 36
320MB	(2) 16M x 36	(2) 16M x 36	(2) 8M x 36	None
320MB	(2) 16M x 36	(2) 16M x 36	(2) 4M x 36	(2) 4M x 36
320MB	(2) 16M x 36	(2) 8M x 36	(2) 8M x 36	(2) 8M x 36
328MB	(2) 16M x 36	(2) 16M x 36	(2) 8M x 36	(2) 1M x 36
336MB	(2) 16M x 36	(2) 16M x 36	(2) 8M x 36	(2) 2M x 36
352MB	(2) 16M x 36	(2) 16M x 36	(2) 8M x 36	(2) 4M x 36
384MB	(2) 16M x 36	(2) 16M x 36	(2) 16M x 36	None
384MB	(2) 16M x 36	(2) 16M x 36	(2) 8M x 36	(2) 8M x 36
392MB	(2) 16M x 36	(2) 16M x 36	(2) 16M x 36	(2) 1M x 36
400MB	(2) 16M x 36	(2) 16M x 36	(2) 16M x 36	(2) 2M x 36
416MB	(2) 16M x 36	(2) 16M x 36	(2) 16M x 36	(2) 4M x 36
448MB	(2) 16M x 36	(2) 16M x 36	(2) 16M x 36	(2) 8M x 36
512MB	(2) 16M x 36	(2) 16M x 36	(2) 16M x 36	(2) 16M x 36

CACHE CONFIGURATION	
Size	**SL1**
256KB	256KB module installed
512KB	512KB module installed

VIDEO MEMORY CONFIGURATION		
Size	**Bank 0**	**Bank 1**
512KB	512KB	None
2MB	512KB	(6) 256K x 8
Note: Bank 0 is factory installed and is not configurable.		

CPU SPEED SELECTION		
Speed	**JP7**	**JP8**
90MHz	Closed	Open
100MHz	Open	Closed
120MHz	Closed	Open
133MHz	Open	Closed
166MHz	Open	Closed

DELL COMPUTER CORPORATION
OPTIPLEX GM/GM+

Processor	Pentium
Processor Speed	75/90/100/120/133/150/166MHz
Chip Set	Intel
Video Chip Set	S3
Maximum Onboard Memory	128MB (EDO supported)
Maximum Video Memory	2MB
Cache	256KB
BIOS	Unidentified
Dimensions	330mm x 218mm
I/O Options	Ethernet 10BaseT connector, floppy drive interface, IDE interfaces (2), parallel port, PS/2 mouse port, serial ports (2), VESA feature connector, VGA port, riser slot, cache slot, ATX power connector
NPU Options	None

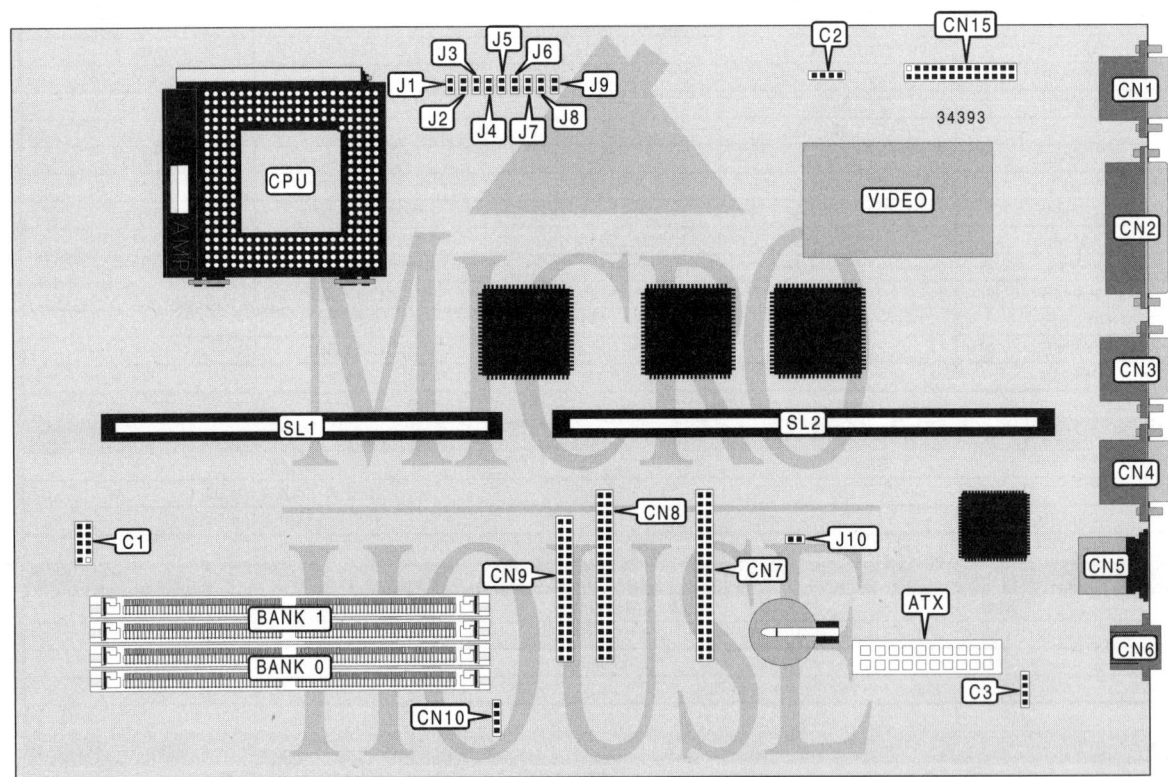

Continued on next page...

DELL COMPUTER CORPORATION
OPTIPLEX GM/GM+

. . . continued from previous page

CONNECTIONS			
Purpose	**Location**	**Purpose**	**Location**
ATX power connector	ATX	Ethernet 10BaseT connector	CN6
Front panel connector	C1	IDE interface 1	CN7
IDE interface LED	C2	IDE interface 2	CN8
IDE interface LED	C3	Floppy drive interface	CN9
VGA port	CN1	Chassis fan power	CN10
Parallel port	CN2	VESA feature connector	CN15
Serial port 2	CN3	Cache slot	SL1
Serial port 1	CN4	Riser slot	SL2
PS/2 mouse port	CN5		

USER CONFIGURABLE SETTINGS		
Function	**Label**	**Position**
◇ Factory configured - do not alter	J2	Open
◇ Password enabled	J3	Closed
Password disabled	J3	Open
◇ NIC setting normal operation	J10	Open
NIC setting clear	J10	Closed

DRAM CONFIGURATION		
Size	**Bank 0**	**Bank 1**
8MB	(2) 1M x 32	None
16MB	(2) 2M x 32	None
16MB	(2) 1M x 32	(2) 1M x 32
24MB	(2) 2M x 32	(2) 1M x 32
32MB	(2) 4M x 32	None
32MB	(2) 2M x 32	(2) 2M x 32
40MB	(2) 4M x 32	(2) 1M x 32
48MB	(2) 4M x 32	(2) 2M x 32
64MB	(2) 8M x 32	None
64MB	(2) 4M x 32	(2) 4M x 32
72MB	(2) 8M x 32	(2) 1M x 32
80MB	(2) 8M x 32	(2) 2M x 32
96MB	(2) 8M x 32	(2) 4M x 32
128MB	(2) 8M x 32	(2) 8M x 32

Note: Board accepts EDO memory.

CACHE CONFIGURATION	
Size	**SL1**
256KB	256KB module installed

VIDEO MEMORY CONFIGURATION
Note: The location of the banks and the chip size is unidentified.

Continued on next page. . .

DELL COMPUTER CORPORATION
OPTIPLEX GM/GM+

...continued from previous page

CPU SPEED SELECTION					
CPU speed	**Clock speed**	**Multiplier**	**J1**	**J4**	**J5**
75MHz	50MHz	1.5x	Open	Open	Open
90MHz	60MHz	1.5x	Open	Open	Open
100MHz	66MHz	1.5x	Open	Open	Open
120MHz	60MHz	2x	Open	Open	Open
133MHz	66MHz	2x	Open	Open	Closed
150MHz	60MHz	2.5x	Open	Closed	Open
166MHz	66MHz	2.5x	Closed	Open	Open

CPU SPEED SELECTION (CON'T)						
CPU speed	**Clock speed**	**Multiplier**	**J6**	**J7**	**J8**	**J9**
75MHz	50MHz	1.5x	Open	Open	Open	Closed
90MHz	60MHz	1.5x	Open	Open	Closed	Open
100MHz	66MHz	1.5x	Open	Closed	Open	Open
120MHz	60MHz	2x	Closed	Open	Open	Open
133MHz	66MHz	2x	Open	Open	Open	Open
150MHz	60MHz	2.5x	Open	Open	Open	Open
166MHz	66MHz	2.5x	Open	Open	Open	Open

DELL COMPUTER CORPORATION
OPTIPLEX GS

Processor	Pentium
Processor Speed	133/166/200MHz
Chip Set	Intel
Video Chip Set	S3
Maximum Onboard Memory	128MB (EDO supported)
Maximum Video Memory	2MB
Cache	256KB
BIOS	Unidentified
Dimensions	305mm x 244mm
I/O Options	Floppy drive interface, IDE interfaces (2), parallel port, PS/2 mouse port, serial ports (2), VGA port, riser slot, ATX power connector
NPU Options	None

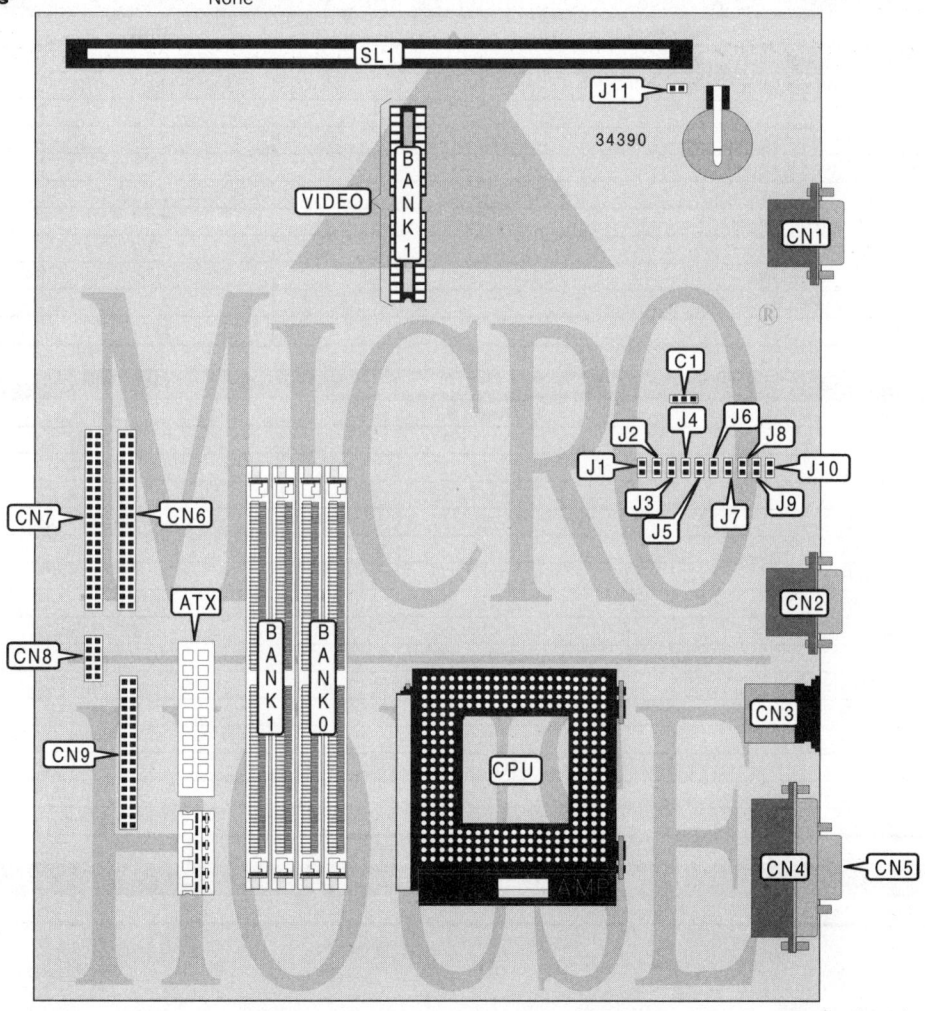

Continued on next page...

DELL COMPUTER CORPORATION
OPTIPLEX GS

...continued from previous page

CONNECTIONS			
Purpose	**Location**	**Purpose**	**Location**
ATX power connector	ATX	IDE interface 1	CN6
VGA port	CN1	IDE interface 2	CN7
Serial port 2	CN2	Front panel connector	CN8
PS/2 mouse port	CN3	Floppy drive interface	CN9
Parallel port	CN4	Riser slot	SL1
Serial port 1	CN5		

USER CONFIGURABLE SETTINGS		
Function	**Label**	**Position**
◇ Factory configured - do not alter	C1	Open
◇ Factory configured - do not alter	J1	Open
Password enabled	J2	Closed
Password disabled	J2	Open
◇ Factory configured - do not alter	J6	Open
◇ Factory configured - do not alter	J7	Open
◇ Factory configured - do not alter	J8	Open
◇ Factory configured - do not alter	J9	Unidentified
◇ Factory configured - do not alter	J10	Unidentified
NIC setting normal operation	J11	Open
NIC setting clear	J11	Closed

DRAM CONFIGURATION		
Size	**Bank 0**	**Bank 1**
8MB	(2) 1M x 32	None
16MB	(2) 2M x 32	None
16MB	(2) 1M x 32	(2) 1M x 32
24MB	(2) 2M x 32	(2) 1M x 32
32MB	(2) 4M x 32	None
32MB	(2) 2M x 32	(2) 2M x 32
40MB	(2) 4M x 32	(2) 1M x 32
48MB	(2) 4M x 32	(2) 2M x 32
64MB	(2) 8M x 32	None
64MB	(2) 4M x 32	(2) 4M x 32
72MB	(2) 8M x 32	(2) 1M x 32
80MB	(2) 8M x 32	(2) 2M x 32
96MB	(2) 8M x 32	(2) 4M x 32
128MB	(2) 8M x 32	(2) 8M x 32

Note: Board accepts EDO memory.

CACHE CONFIGURATION
Note: The location of the cache is unidentified.

Continued on next page...

DELL COMPUTER CORPORATION
OPTIPLEX GS

...continued from previous page

VIDEO MEMORY CONFIGURATION		
Size	Bank 0	Bank 1
1MB	1MB	None
2MB	1MB	(2) 256K x 8

Note: Bank 0 is factory installed and is not configurable. The location is unidentified.

CPU SPEED SELECTION					
CPU speed	Clock speed	Multiplier	J3	J4	J5
133MHz	66MHz	2x	Open	Open	Closed
166MHz	66MHz	2.5x	Open	Closed	Open
200MHz	66MHz	3x	Closed	Open	Open

158 Motherboard Settings & Specifications

DELL COMPUTER CORPORATION
OPTIPLEX GS+

Processor	Pentium
Processor Speed	133/166/200MHz
Chip Set	Intel
Video Chip Set	S3
Maximum Onboard Memory	128MB (EDO supported)
Maximum Video Memory	2MB
Cache	256KB
BIOS	Unidentified
Dimensions	305mm x 244mm
I/O Options	Ethernet 10Base T connector, floppy drive interface, IDE interfaces (2), parallel port, PS/2 mouse port, serial ports (2), VGA port, riser slot, ATX power connector
NPU Options	None

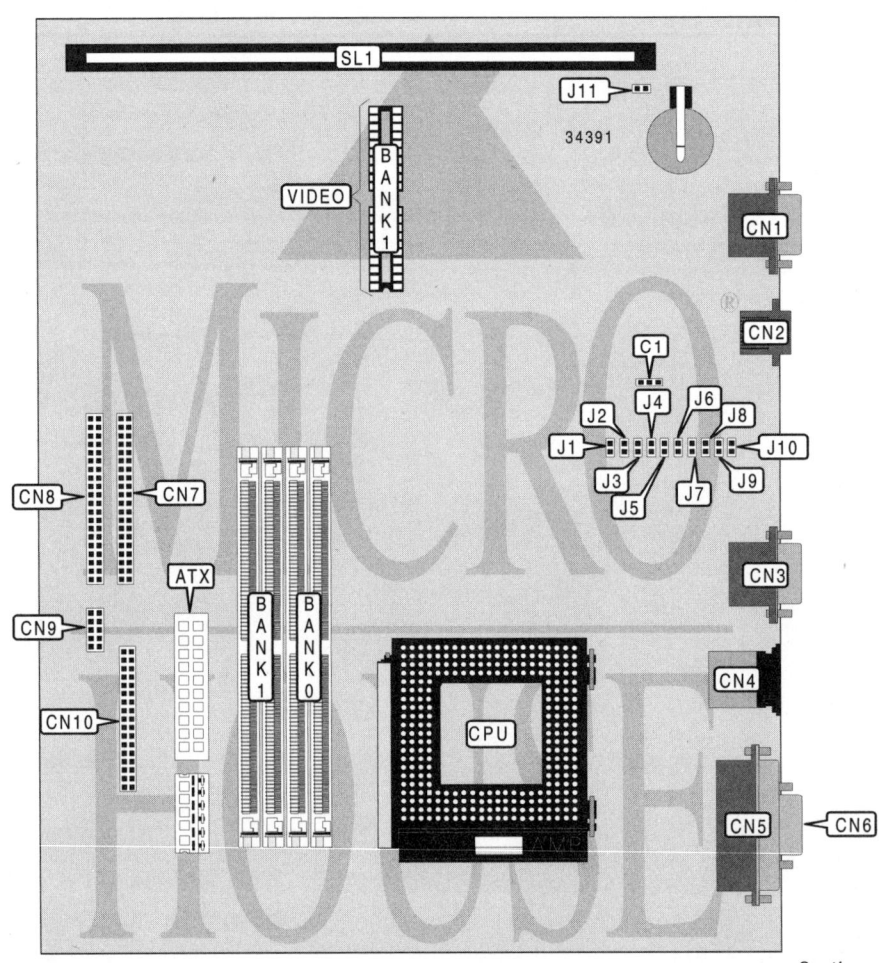

Continued on next page...

DELL COMPUTER CORPORATION
OPTIPLEX GS+

... continued from previous page

CONNECTIONS

Purpose	Location	Purpose	Location
ATX power connector	ATX	Serial port 1	CN6
VGA port	CN1	IDE interface 1	CN7
Ethernet 10Base T connector	CN2	IDE interface 2	CN8
Serial port 2	CN3	Front panel connector	CN9
PS/2 mouse port	CN4	Floppy drive interface	CN10
Parallel port	CN5	Riser slot	SL1

USER CONFIGURABLE SETTINGS

Function	Label	Position
◇ Factory configured - do not alter	C1	Open
◇ Factory configured - do not alter	J1	Open
Password enabled	J2	Closed
Password disabled	J2	Open
◇ Factory configured - do not alter	J6	Open
◇ Factory configured - do not alter	J7	Open
◇ Factory configured - do not alter	J8	Open
◇ Factory configured - do not alter	J9	Unidentified
◇ Factory configured - do not alter	J10	Unidentified
NIC setting normal operation	J11	Open
NIC setting clear	J11	Closed

DRAM CONFIGURATION

Size	Bank 0	Bank 1
8MB	(2) 1M x 32	None
16MB	(2) 2M x 32	None
16MB	(2) 1M x 32	(2) 1M x 32
24MB	(2) 2M x 32	(2) 1M x 32
32MB	(2) 4M x 32	None
32MB	(2) 2M x 32	(2) 2M x 32
40MB	(2) 4M x 32	(2) 1M x 32
48MB	(2) 4M x 32	(2) 2M x 32
64MB	(2) 8M x 32	None
64MB	(2) 4M x 32	(2) 4M x 32
72MB	(2) 8M x 32	(2) 1M x 32
80MB	(2) 8M x 32	(2) 2M x 32
96MB	(2) 8M x 32	(2) 4M x 32
128MB	(2) 8M x 32	(2) 8M x 32

Note: Board accepts EDO memory.

CACHE CONFIGURATION

Note: The location of the cache is unidentified.

Continued on next page...

DELL COMPUTER CORPORATION
OPTIPLEX GS+

. . . continued from previous page

VIDEO MEMORY CONFIGURATION		
Size	Bank 0	Bank 1
1MB	1MB	None
2MB	1MB	(2) 256K x 8

Note: Bank 0 is factory installed and is not configurable. The location is unidentified.

CPU SPEED SELECTION					
CPU speed	Clock speed	Multiplier	J3	J4	J5
133MHz	66MHz	2x	Open	Open	Closed
166MHz	66MHz	2.5x	Open	Closed	Open
200MHz	66MHz	3x	Closed	Open	Open

DELL COMPUTER CORPORATION
OPTIPLEX GX PRO

Processor	Pentium Pro
Processor Speed	180/200MHz
Chip Set	Intel
Video Chip Set	None
Maximum Onboard Memory	512MB
Maximum Video Memory	None
Cache	256/512KB (located on Pentium Pro CPU)
BIOS	Unidentified
Dimensions	305mm x 244mm
I/O Options	Ethernet 10BaseT connector, floppy drive interface, IDE interfaces (2), parallel port, PS/2 mouse port, serial ports (2), riser slot, CPU slot, USB connector, ATX power connector, line in, speaker out, microphone in, audio in-CD-ROM
NPU Options	None

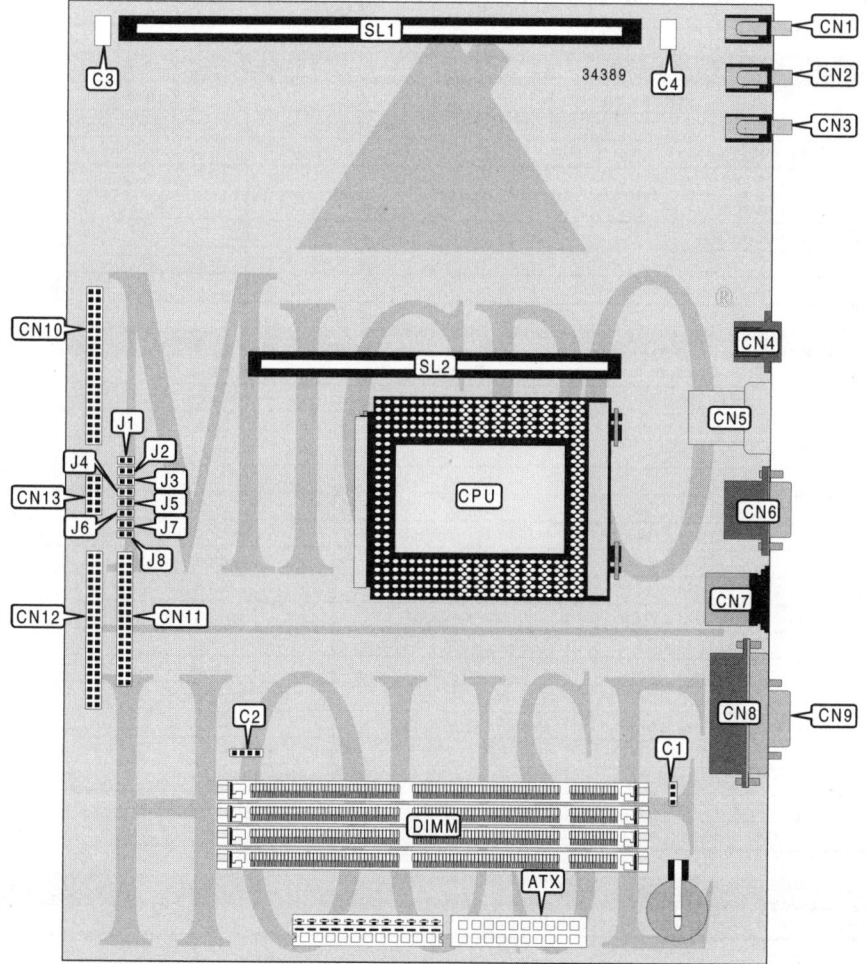

Continued on next page...

DELL COMPUTER CORPORATION
OPTIPLEX GX PRO

...continued from previous page

CONNECTIONS			
Purpose	**Location**	**Purpose**	**Location**
ATX power connector	ATX	Serial port 2	CN6
Chassis fan power	C1	PS/2 mouse port	CN7
Audio in-CD-ROM	C2	Parallel port	CN8
Riser board power connector	C3	Serial port 1	CN9
Riser board power connector	C4	IDE interface 1	CN10
Line in	CN1	Floppy drive interface	CN11
Speaker out	CN2	IDE interface 2	CN12
Microphone in	CN3	Front panel connector	CN13
Ethernet 10BaseT connector	CN4	Riser slot	SL1
USB connector	CN5	CPU slot	SL2

USER CONFIGURABLE SETTINGS		
Function	**Label**	**Position**
✧ Factory configured - do not alter	J3	Open
✧ Factory configured - do not alter	J4	Open
✧ Factory configured - do not alter	J5	Open
✧ Factory configured - do not alter	J6	Open
✧ Factory configured - do not alter	J7	Open
✧ Password enabled	J8	Closed
Password disabled	J8	Open

DIMM CONFIGURATION				
Size	**Bank 0**	**Bank 1**	**Bank 2**	**Bank 3**
16MB	(1) 2M x 64	None	None	None
32MB	(1) 2M x 64	(1) 2M x 64	None	None
32MB	(1) 4M x 64	None	None	None
48MB	(1) 2M x 64	(1) 2M x 64	(1) 2M x 64	None
64MB	(1) 2M x 64	(1) 2M x 64	(1) 2M x 64	(1) 2M x 64
64MB	(1) 4M x 64	(1) 4M x 64	None	None
64MB	(1) 8M x 64	None	None	None
96MB	(1) 4M x 64	(1) 4M x 64	(1) 4M x 64	None
128MB	(1) 4M x 64	(1) 4M x 64	(1) 4M x 64	(1) 4M x 64
128MB	(1) 8M x 64	(1) 8M x 64	None	None
128MB	(1) 16M x 64	None	None	None
192MB	(1) 8M x 64	(1) 8M x 64	(1) 8M x 64	None
256MB	(1) 8M x 64	(1) 8M x 64	(1) 8M x 64	(1) 8M x 64
256MB	(1) 16M x 64	(1) 16M x 64	None	None
384MB	(1) 16M x 64	(1) 16M x 64	(1) 16M x 64	None
512MB	(1) 16M x 64	(1) 16M x 64	(1) 16M x 64	(1) 16M x 64

Note: The location of the banks is unidentified. Board accepts EDO memory.

CACHE CONFIGURATION
Note: 256KB/512KB cache is located on the Pentium Pro CPU.

Continued on next page...

DELL COMPUTER CORPORATION
OPTIPLEX GX PRO

. . . continued from previous page

CPU SPEED SELECTION				
CPU speed	**Clock speed**	**Multiplier**	**J1**	**J2**
180MHz	60MHz	3x	Closed	Open
200MHz	66MHz	3x	Open	Closed

DELL COMPUTER CORPORATION
OPTIPLEX GXI

Processor	Pentium
Processor Speed	133/166/200/233MHz
Chip Set	Intel
Video Chip Set	S3
Maximum Onboard Memory	512MB (EDO supported)
Maximum Video Memory	2MB
Cache	256/512KB
BIOS	Unidentified
Dimensions	305mm x 244mm
I/O Options	Audio in-CD-ROM, floppy drive interface, IDE interfaces (2), parallel port, PS/2 mouse port, serial port, VGA port, riser slot, cache slot, USB connectors (2), ATX power connector, line in, line out, microphone in, NIC daughterboard slot
NPU Options	None

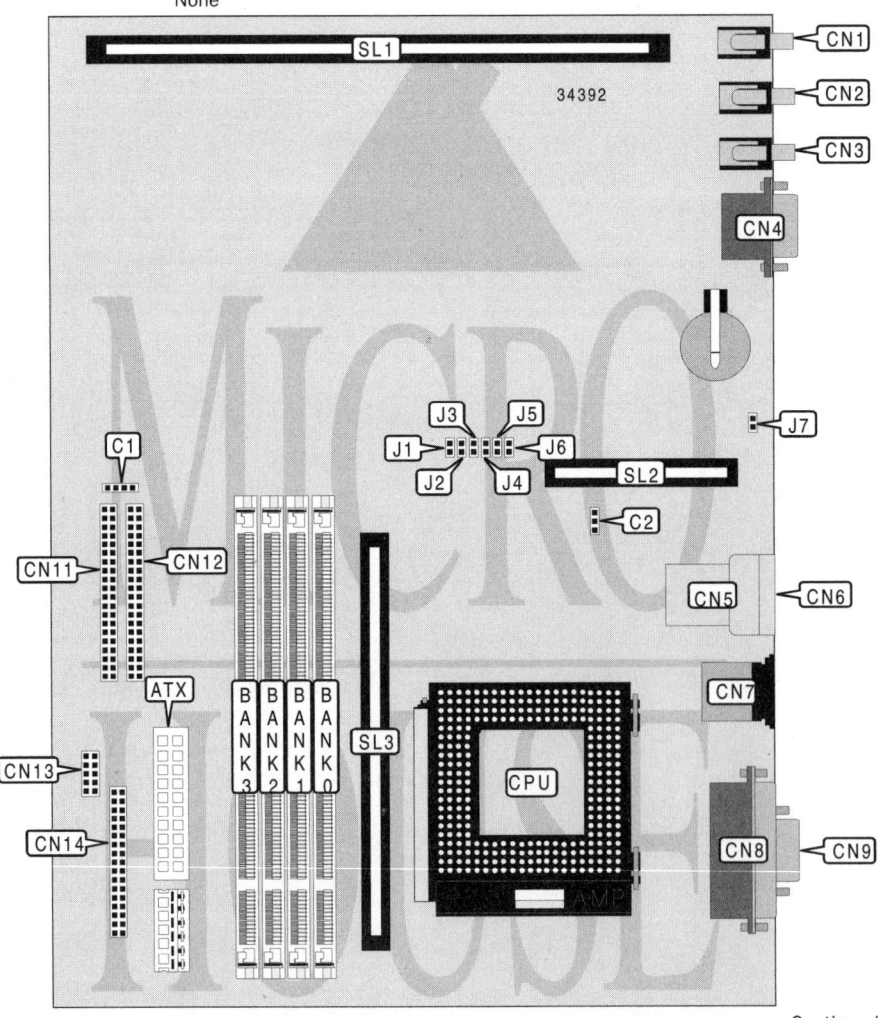

Continued on next page...

DELL COMPUTER CORPORATION
OPTIPLEX GXI

...continued from previous page

CONNECTIONS			
Purpose	**Location**	**Purpose**	**Location**
ATX power connector	ATX	Parallel port	CN8
Audio in-CD-ROM	C1	Serial port	CN9
Chassis fan power	C2	IDE interface 2	CN11
Line in	CN1	IDE interface 1	CN12
Line out	CN2	Front panel connector	CN13
Microphone in	CN3	Floppy drive interface	CN14
VGA port	CN4	Riser slot	SL1
USB connector	CN5	NIC daughterboard slot	SL2
USB connector	CN6	Cache slot	SL3
PS/2 mouse port	CN7		

USER CONFIGURABLE SETTINGS		
Function	**Label**	**Position**
▹ Factory configured - do not alter	J1	Open
Password enabled	J2	Closed
Password disabled	J2	Open
▹ Factory configured - do not alter (Configuration B only)	J6	Open
NIC setting normal operation	J7	Open
NIC setting clear	J7	Closed

Note: For Configuration B, see CPU speed table.

DIMM CONFIGURATION				
Size	**Bank 0**	**Bank 1**	**Bank 2**	**Bank 3**
16MB	(1) 2M x 64	None	None	None
32MB	(1) 2M x 64	(1) 2M x 64	None	None
32MB	(1) 4M x 64	None	None	None
48MB	(1) 2M x 64	(1) 2M x 64	(1) 2M x 64	None
64MB	(1) 2M x 64	(1) 2M x 64	(1) 2M x 64	(1) 2M x 64
64MB	(1) 4M x 64	(1) 4M x 64	None	None
64MB	(1) 8M x 64	None	None	None
96MB	(1) 4M x 64	(1) 4M x 64	(1) 4M x 64	None
128MB	(1) 4M x 64	(1) 4M x 64	(1) 4M x 64	(1) 4M x 64
128MB	(1) 8M x 64	(1) 8M x 64	None	None
128MB	(1) 16M x 64	None	None	None
192MB	(1) 8M x 64	(1) 8M x 64	(1) 8M x 64	None
256MB	(1) 8M x 64	(1) 8M x 64	(1) 8M x 64	(1) 8M x 64
256MB	(1) 16M x 64	(1) 16M x 64	None	None
384MB	(1) 16M x 64	(1) 16M x 64	(1) 16M x 64	None
512MB	(1) 16M x 64	(1) 16M x 64	(1) 16M x 64	(1) 16M x 64

Note: Board accepts EDO memory. Largest size DIMM must be installed in Bank 0 with decreasing sizes in Banks 1 - 3.

Continued on next page...

DELL COMPUTER CORPORATION
OPTIPLEX GXI

. . . continued from previous page

CACHE CONFIGURATION	
Size	TAG
256KB	256KB module installed
512KB	512KB module installed

VIDEO MEMORY CONFIGURATION
Note: The location of the video memory is unidentified.

CPU SPEED SELECTION (CONFIGURATION A)					
CPU speed	Clock speed	Multiplier	J3	J4	J5	J6
133MHz	66MHz	2x	Open	Open	Open	Closed
166MHz	66MHz	2.5x	Open	Open	Closed	Open
200MHz	66MHz	3x	Open	Closed	Open	Open
233MHz	66MHz	3.5x	Closed	Open	Open	Open

CPU SPEED SELECTION (CONFIGURATION B)				
CPU speed	Clock speed	Multiplier	J3	J4	J5
133MHz	66MHz	2x	Open	Open	Closed
166MHz	66MHz	2.5x	Open	Closed	Open
200MHz	66MHz	3x	Closed	Open	Open

DELL COMPUTER CORPORATION
OPTIPLEX XL 575, 590, 5100, 5120, 5133
OPTIPLEX XM 575, 590, 5100, 5120, 5133
OPTIPLEX XMT 575, 590, 5100, 5120, 5133
POWEREDGE EL, POWEREDGE WEBSERVER

Processor	Pentium
Processor Speed	75/90/100/120/133MHz
Chip Set	Intel
Video Chip Set	S3
Maximum Onboard Memory	256MB
Maximum Video Memory	2MB
Cache	256/512KB
BIOS	Unidentified
Dimensions	330mm x 218mm
I/O Options	Floppy drive interface, IDE interfaces (2), parallel port, PS/2 mouse port, serial ports (2), feature connector, VGA port, riser slots (2)
NPU Options	None

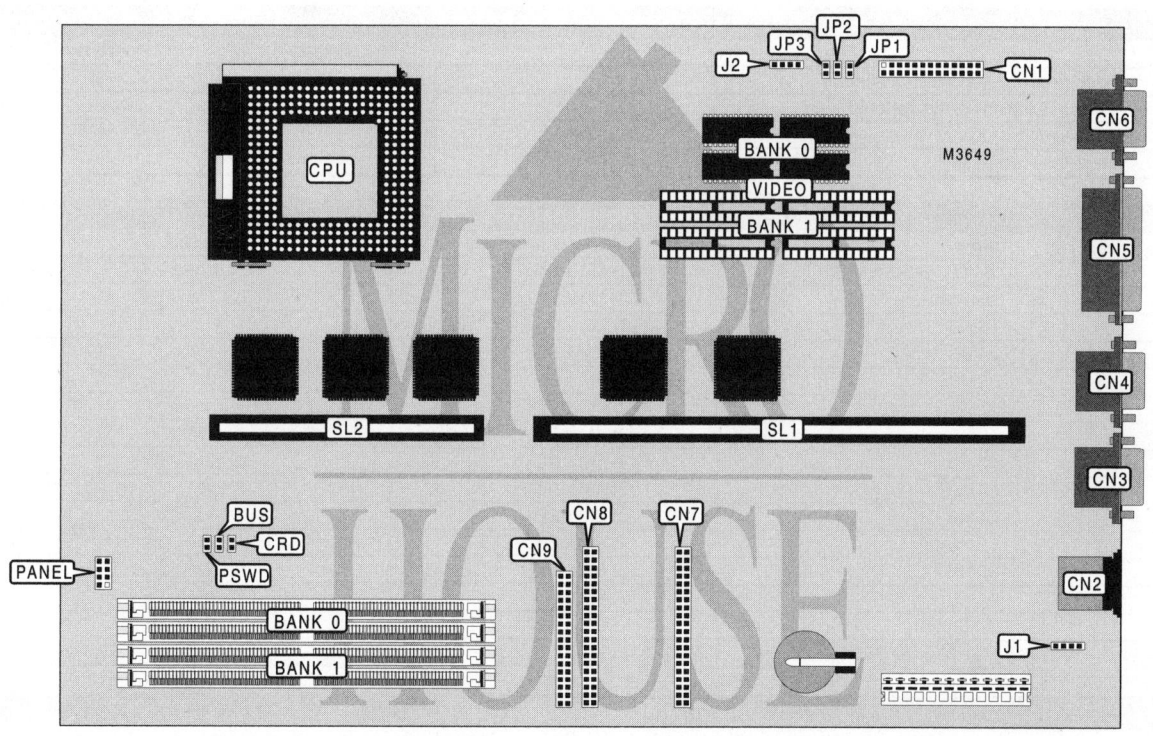

Continued on next page...

DELL COMPUTER CORPORATION
OPTIPLEX XL 575, 590, 5100, 5120, 5133
OPTIPLEX XM 575, 590, 5100, 5120, 5133
OPTIPLEX MMT 575, 590, 5100, 5120, 5133
POWEREDGE EL, POWEREDGE WEBSERVER

...continued from previous page

CONNECTIONS

Purpose	Location	Purpose	Location
Feature connector	CN1	IDE interface 2	CN8
PS/2 mouse port	CN2	Floppy drive interface	CN9
Serial port 1	CN3	IDE interface LED 2	J1
Serial port 2	CN4	IDE interface LED 1	J2
Parallel port	CN5	Front panel connector	PANEL
VGA port	CN6	Riser slot	SL1
IDE interface 1	CN7	Riser slot	SL2

USER CONFIGURABLE SETTINGS

Function	Label	Position
⇨ Factory configured - do not alter	BUS	Open
⇨ Factory configured - do not alter	CRD	Open
⇨ Password enabled	PSWD	Closed
Password disabled	PSWD	Open

DRAM CONFIGURATION

Size	Bank 0	Bank 1
8MB	(2) 1M x 36	None
16MB	(2) 1M x 36	(2) 1M x 36
16MB	(2) 2M x 36	None
24MB	(2) 2M x 36	(2) 1M x 36
32MB	(2) 2M x 36	(2) 2M x 36
32MB	(2) 4M x 36	None
40MB	(2) 4M x 36	(2) 1M x 36
48MB	(2) 4M x 36	(2) 2M x 36
64MB	(2) 4M x 36	(2) 4M x 36
64MB	(2) 8M x 36	None
72MB	(2) 8M x 36	(2) 1M x 36
80MB	(2) 8M x 36	(2) 2M x 36
96MB	(2) 8M x 36	(2) 4M x 36
128MB	(2) 8M x 36	(2) 8M x 36

Note: Board also accepts x 32 SIMMs.

CACHE CONFIGURATION

Note: Board accepts 256KB or 512KB cache. The location is unidentified. The size of the cache chips are unidentified.

Continued on next page...

DELL COMPUTER CORPORATION
OPTIPLEX XL 575, 590, 5100, 5120, 5133
OPTIPLEX XM 575, 590, 5100, 5120, 5133
OPTIPLEX XMT 575, 590, 5100, 5120, 5133
POWEREDGE EL, POWEREDGE WEBSERVER

...continued from previous page

VIDEO MEMORY CONFIGURATION		
Size	Bank 0	Bank 1
1MB	1MB	None
2MB	1MB	1MB

Note: The size of the video memory chips are unidentified.

CPU SPEED SELECTION				
CPU speed	Clock speed	JP1	JP2	JP3
75MHz	50MHz	Closed	Open	Open
90MHz	60MHz	Open	Closed	Open
100MHz	66MHz	Open	Open	Closed
120MHz	60MHz	Open	Closed	Open
133MHz	66MHz	Open	Open	Closed

170 Motherboard Settings & Specifications

DELL COMPUTER CORPORATION
POWEREDGE 4100, 6100

Processor	Pentium Pro
Processor Speed	200MHz
Chip Set	Intel
Video Chip Set	Cirrus Logic
Maximum Onboard Memory	2GB (EDO supported)
Maximum Video Memory	1MB
Cache	512KB (located on Pentium Pro CPU)
BIOS	AMI
Dimensions	355mm x 304mm
I/O Options	External memory card, 32-bit PCI slots (6), floppy drive interface, IDE interface, Ultra-Wide SCSI ports (2), parallel port, PS/2 mouse port, serial ports (2), VGA feature connector, VGA port, CPU slots (2), Server Management connector
NPU Options	None

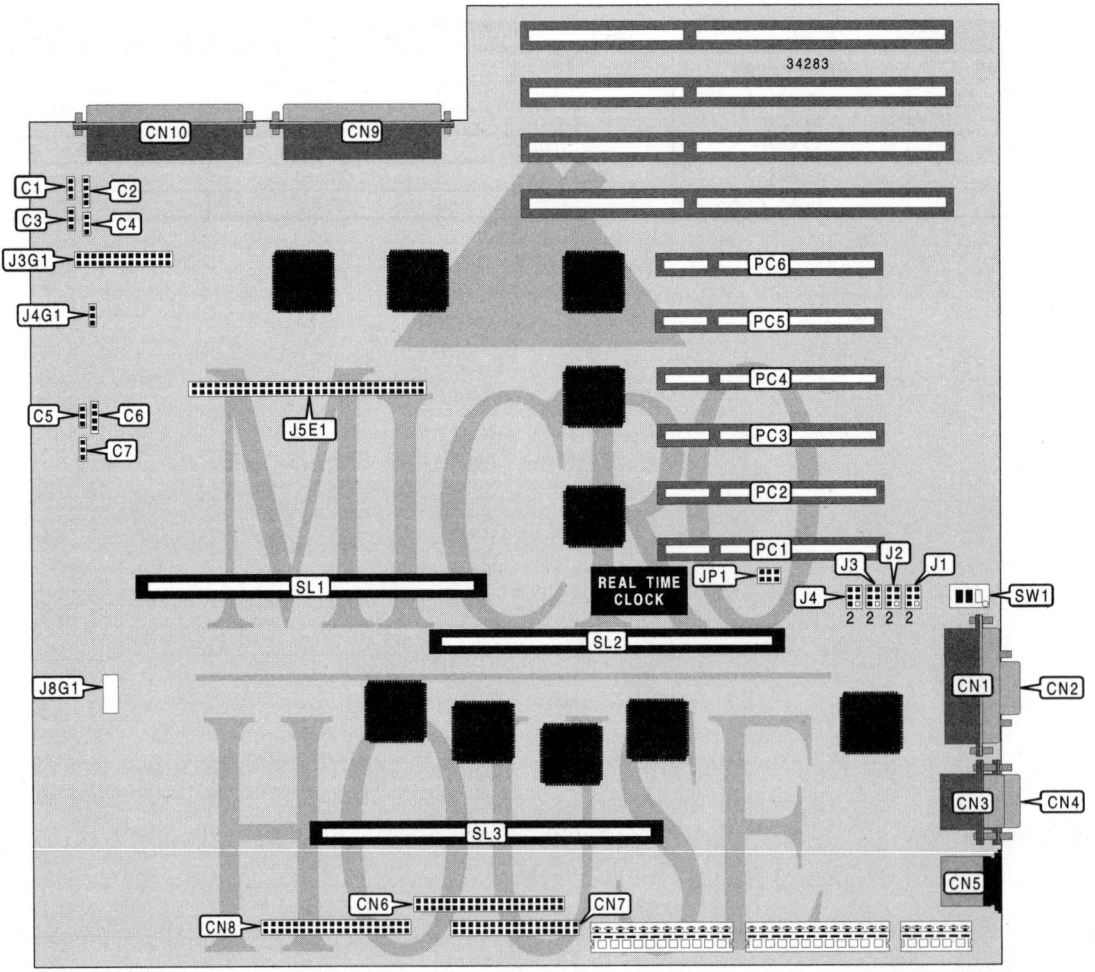

Continued on next page...

DELL COMPUTER CORPORATION
POWEREDGE 4100, 6100

...continued from previous page

CONNECTIONS

Purpose	Location	Purpose	Location
Chassis fan power 4	C1	PS/2 mouse port	CN5
IDE interface LED 2	C2	IDE interface	CN6
Chassis fan power 3	C3	Floppy drive interface	CN7
I2C connector	C4	Front panel connector	CN8
Chassis fan power 2	C5	Ultra-Wide SCSI port 2	CN9
IDE interface LED 1	C6	Ultra-Wide SCSI port 1	CN10
Chassis fan power 1	C7	Server Management connector	J3G1
Parallel port	CN1	32-bit PCI slots	PC1 – PC6
VGA port	CN2	CPU slot 1	SL1
Serial port	CN3	CPU slot 2	SL2
Serial port	CN4	External memory card	SL3

USER CONFIGURABLE SETTINGS

	Function	Label	Position
◇	Flash BIOS normal operation	J1	Pins 1 & 3 closed
	Flash BIOS recovery mode	J1	Pins 3 & 5 closed
◇	Factory configured - do not alter	J1	Pins 2 & 4 closed
◇	Flash BIOS write protect disabled	J2	Pins 3 & 5 closed
	Flash BIOS write protect enabled	J2	Pins 1 & 3 closed
	Floppy drive 0 enabled	J2	Pins 2 & 4 closed
	Floppy drive 0 disabled	J2	Pins 4 & 6 closed
	Floppy drive 1 enabled	J3	Pins 1 & 3 closed
	Floppy drive 1 disabled	J3	Pins 3 & 5 closed
◇	Video sleep register select 03C3H	J3	Pins 2 & 4 closed
	Video sleep register select 46E8H	J3	Pins 4 & 6 closed
◇	RTC power supply enabled	J4	Pins 1 & 3 closed
	RTC power supply disabled	J4	Pins 3 & 5 closed
◇	Factory configured - do not alter	J4	Pins 2, 4, 6 open
◇	Factory configured - do not alter	J4G1	Unidentified
◇	Factory configured - do not alter	J5E1	Unidentified
◇	Factory configured - do not alter	J8G1	Unidentified
◇	Factory configured - do not alter	JP1	Unidentified
◇	CMOS memory normal operation	SW1/1	Off
	CMOS memory clear	SW1/1	On
◇	Password normal operation	SW1/2	Off
	Password clear	SW1/2	On
◇	Factory configured - do not alter	SW1/3	Off

CACHE CONFIGURATION
Note: 512KB cache is located on the Pentium Pro CPU.

VIDEO MEMORY CONFIGURATION
Note: Board is factory installed with 1MB video memory and is not configurable.

Continued on next page...

DELL COMPUTER CORPORATION
POWEREDGE 4100, 6100

. . . continued from previous page

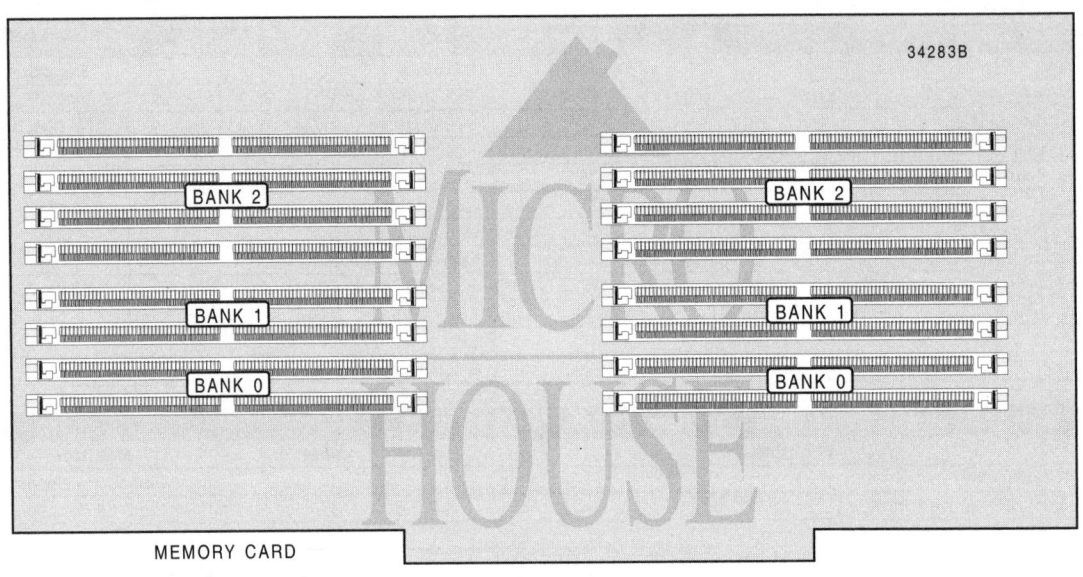

MEMORY CARD

		DRAM CONFIGURATION		
Size	Bank 0	Bank 1	Bank 2	Bank 3
64MB	(4) 4M x 36	None	None	None
128MB	(4) 8M x 36	None	None	None
128MB	(4) 4M x 36	(4) 4M x 36	None	None
256MB	(4) 16M x 36	None	None	None
256MB	(4) 8M x 36	(4) 8M x 36	None	None
256MB	(4) 4M x 36	(4) 4M x 36	(4) 4M x 36	(4) 4M x 36
384MB	(4) 8M x 36	(4) 8M x 36	(4) 4M x 36	(4) 4M x 36
512MB	(4) 32M x 36	None	None	None
512MB	(4) 16M x 36	(4) 16M x 36	None	None
512MB	(4) 8M x 36	(4) 8M x 36	(4) 8M x 36	(4) 8M x 36
640MB	(4) 16M x 36	(4) 16M x 36	(4) 4M x 36	(4) 4M x 36
768MB	(4) 16M x 36	(4) 16M x 36	(4) 8M x 36	(4) 8M x 36
1024MB	(4) 32M x 36	(4) 32M x 36	None	None
1024MB	(4) 16M x 36	(4) 16M x 36	(4) 16M x 36	(4) 16M x 36
1152MB	(4) 32M x 36	(4) 32M x 36	(4) 4M x 36	(4) 4M x 36
1280MB	(4) 32M x 36	(4) 32M x 36	(4) 8M x 36	(4) 8M x 36
1536MB	(4) 32M x 36	(4) 32M x 36	(4) 16M x 36	(4) 16M x 36
2048MB	(4) 32M x 36	(4) 32M x 36	(4) 32M x 36	(4) 32M x 36

Continued on next page. . .

DELL COMPUTER CORPORATION
POWEREDGE 4100, 6100

. . . continued from previous page

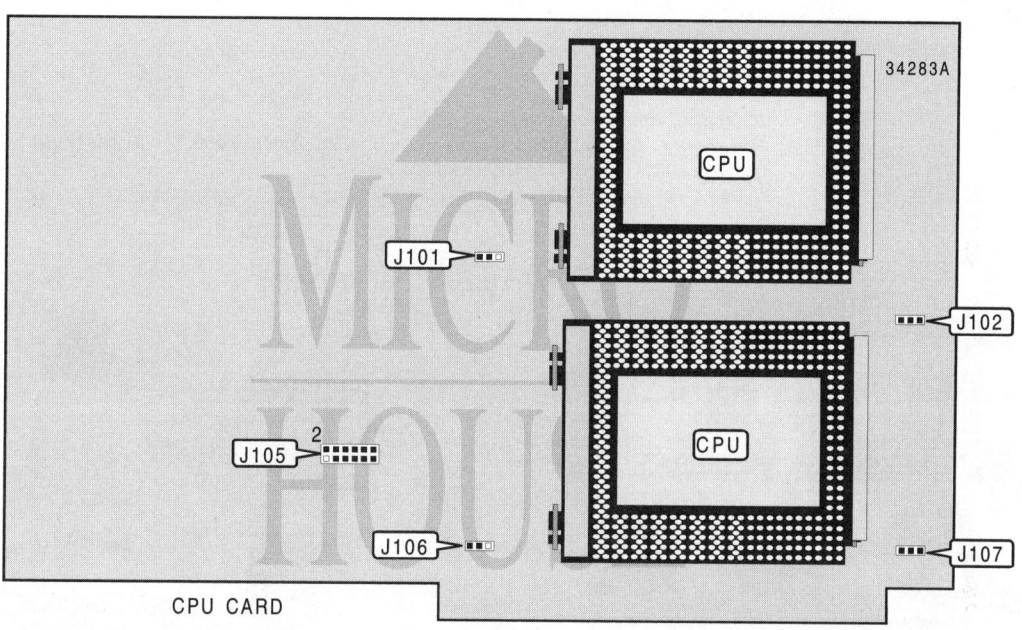

CPU CARD

| USER CONFIGURABLE SETTINGS ||||
Function		Label	Position
	CPU installed in top socket	J101	Pins 2 & 3 closed
	CPU not installed in top socket	J101	Pins 1 & 2 closed
▷	Factory configured - do not alter	J102	Unidentified
	CPU installed in bottom socket	J106	Pins 2 & 3 closed
	CPU not installed in bottom socket	J106	Pins 1 & 2 closed
▷	Factory configured - do not alter	J107	Unidentified

| CPU SPEED SELECTION ||||
CPU speed	Clock speed	Multiplier	J105
200MHz	66MHz	3x	Pins 1 & 2, 5 & 6, 7 & 8 closed

174 Motherboard Settings & Specifications

DELL COMPUTER CORPORATION
POWEREDGE XE 51XX-2 (VER. 1)

Processor	Pentium
Processor Speed	75MHz
Chip Set	Unidentified
Video Chip Set	ATI
Maximum Onboard Memory	512MB
Maximum Video Memory	2MB
Cache	256/512KB
BIOS	Unidentified
Dimensions	330mm x 218mm
I/O Options	Floppy drive interface, IDE interface, parallel port, PS/2 mouse port, serial ports (2), VESA feature connector, VGA port, riser slot, cache slot
NPU Options	None

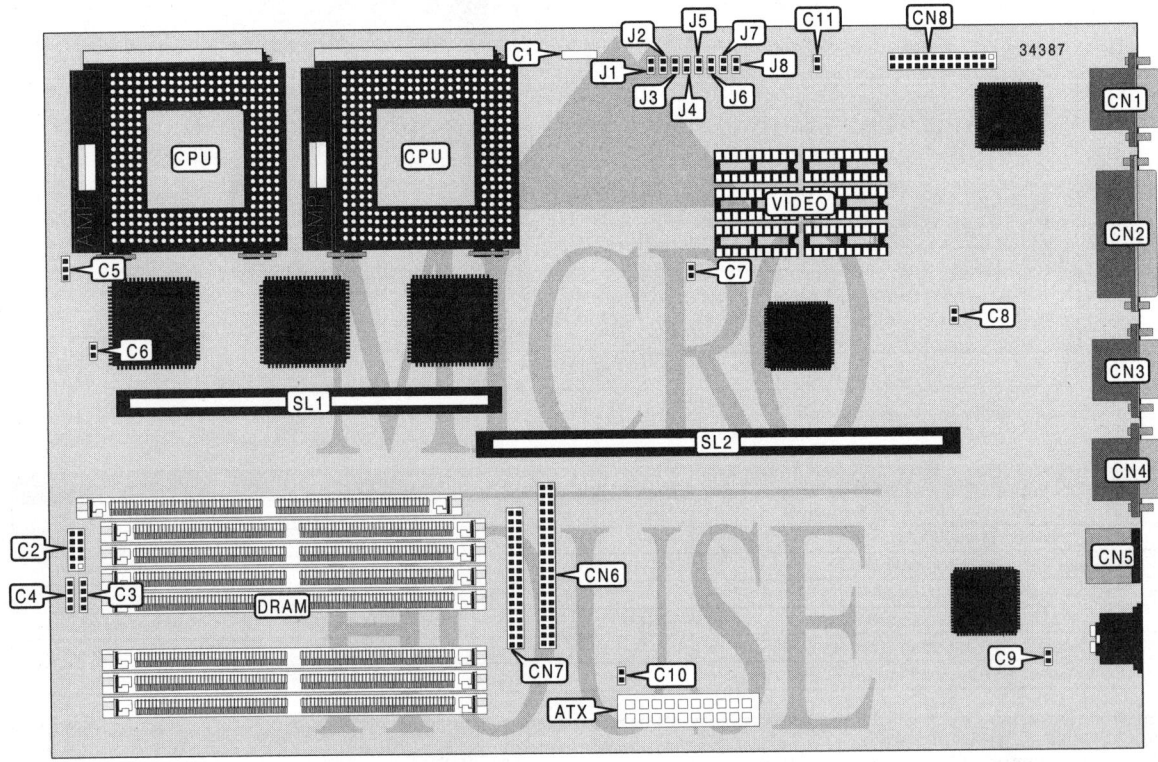

Continued on next page...

DELL COMPUTER CORPORATION
POWEREDGE XE 51XX-2 (VER. 1)

. . . continued from previous page

CONNECTIONS			
Purpose	**Location**	**Purpose**	**Location**
ATX power connector	ATX	Serial port 2	CN3
IDE interface LED	C1	Serial port 1	CN4
Front panel connector	C2	PS/2 mouse port	CN5
Speaker	C3	IDE interface	CN6
External battery	C4	Floppy drive interface	CN7
Chassis fan power	C5	VESA feature connector	CN8
VGA port	CN1	Cache slot	SL1
Parallel port	CN2	Riser slot	SL2

USER CONFIGURABLE SETTINGS		
Function	**Label**	**Position**
✧ Factory configured - do not alter	C6	Unidentified
✧ Factory configured - do not alter	C7	Unidentified
✧ Factory configured - do not alter	C8	Unidentified
✧ Factory configured - do not alter	C9	Unidentified
✧ Factory configured - do not alter	C10	Unidentified
✧ Factory configured - do not alter	J1	Unidentified
✧ Factory configured - do not alter	J2	Unidentified
✧ Factory configured - do not alter	J3	Unidentified
✧ On board video enabled	J4	Closed
On board video disabled	J4	Open
✧ Factory configured - do not alter	J5	Closed
✧ Factory configured - do not alter	J6	Closed
✧ Flash BIOS update enabled	J7	Closed
Flash BIOS update disabled	J7	Open
✧ Password enabled	J8	Closed
Password disabled	J8	Open

DRAM CONFIGURATION				
Size	**Bank 0**	**Bank 1**	**Bank 2**	**Bank 3**
8MB	(2) 1M x 36	None	None	None
16MB	(2) 1M x 36	(2) 1M x 36	None	None
16MB	(2) 2M x 36	None	None	None
24MB	(2) 1M x 36	(2) 1M x 36	(2) 1M x 36	None
32MB	(2) 1M x 36	(2) 1M x 36	(2) 1M x 36	(2) 1M x 36
32MB	(2) 2M x 36	(2) 2M x 36	None	None
32MB	(2) 4M x 36	None	None	None
48MB	(2) 2M x 36	(2) 2M x 36	(2) 2M x 36	None
64MB	(2) 2M x 36	(2) 2M x 36	(2) 2M x 36	(2) 2M x 36
64MB	(2) 4M x 36	(2) 4M x 36	None	None
64MB	(2) 8M x 36	None	None	None

Continued on next page. . .

DELL COMPUTER CORPORATION
POWEREDGE XE 51XX-2 (VER. 1)

. . . continued from previous page

DRAM CONFIGURATION (CON'T)				
Size	Bank 0	Bank 1	Bank 2	Bank 3
96MB	(2) 4M x 36	(2) 4M x 36	(2) 4M x 36	None
128MB	(2) 4M x 36	(2) 4M x 36	(2) 4M x 36	(2) 4M x 36
128MB	(2) 8M x 36	(2) 8M x 36	None	None
128MB	(2) 16M x 36	None	None	None
192MB	(2) 8M x 36	(2) 8M x 36	(2) 8M x 36	None
256MB	(2) 8M x 36	(2) 8M x 36	(2) 8M x 36	(2) 8M x 36
256MB	(2) 16M x 36	(2) 16M x 36	None	None
384MB	(2) 16M x 36	(2) 16M x 36	(2) 16M x 36	None
512MB	(2) 16M x 36	(2) 16M x 36	(2) 16M x 36	(2) 16M x 36

Note: The location of the banks is unidentified.

CACHE CONFIGURATION	
Size	SL1
256KB	256KB module installed
512KB	512KB module installed

VIDEO MEMORY CONFIGURATION			
Size	Bank 0	Bank 1	Bank 2
512KB	512KB	None	None
1MB	512KB	(2) 256K x 8	None
2MB	512KB	(2) 256K x 8	(2) 256K x 8

Note: The location of the banks is unidentified.

DIGITAL EQUIPMENT CORPORATION
CELEBRIS GL (VER. 2), VENTURIS GL (VER. 2)

Processor	Pentium Pro
Processor Speed	150/166/180/200/210/233/240/266MHz
Chip Set	Intel
Video Chip Set	Matrox
Maximum Onboard Memory	192MB
Maximum Video Memory	1MB
Cache	256/512KB (located on Pentium Pro CPU)
BIOS	Unidentified
Dimensions	330mm x 218mm
I/O Options (Backplane)	Parallel port, PS/2 mouse port, serial ports (2), USB connectors (2), VGA port, feature connector, VRM connector
I/O Options (CPU)	32-bit PCI slots (2), IDE interfaces (2), game/MIDI port, floppy drive interface
NPU Options	None

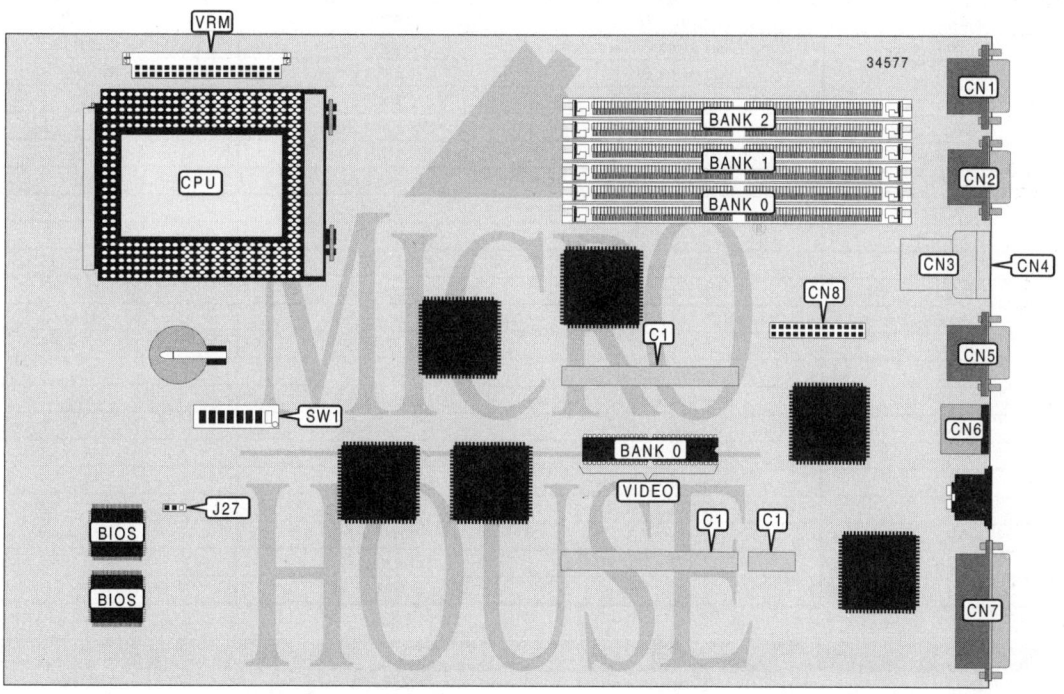

CONNECTIONS			
Purpose	**Location**	**Purpose**	**Location**
Serial port	CN1	PS/2 mouse port	CN6
Serial port	CN2	Parallel port	CN7
USB connector	CN3	VGA feature connector	CN8
USB connector	CN4	VRM connector	VRM
VGA port	CN5		

Continued on next page...

DIGITAL EQUIPMENT CORPORATION
CELEBRIS GL (VER. 2), VENTURIS GL (VER. 2)

...continued from previous page

USER CONFIGURABLE SETTINGS		
Function	**Label**	**Position**
◇ Boot block update disabled	J27	Pins 1 & 2 closed
Boot block update enabled	J27	Pins 2 & 3 closed
◇ Password normal operation	SW1/5	Off
Password clear	SW1/5	On
◇ Recovery mode disabled	SW1/6	Off
Recovery mode enabled	SW1/6	On
◇ CMOS memory normal operation	SW1/7	Off
CMOS memory clear	SW1/7	On
◇ Factory configured - do not alter	SW1/8	Off

SIMM CONFIGURATION			
Size	**Bank 0**	**Bank 1**	**Bank 2**
8MB	(2) 1M x 36	None	None
16MB	(2) 1M x 36	(2) 1M x 36	None
16MB	(2) 2M x 36	None	None
24MB	(2) 1M x 36	(2) 1M x 36	(2) 1M x 36
32MB	(2) 1M x 36	(2) 1M x 36	(2) 2M x 36
32MB	(2) 2M x 36	(2) 2M x 36	None
32MB	(2) 4M x 36	None	None
40MB	(2) 1M x 36	(2) 2M x 36	(2) 2M x 36
48MB	(2) 2M x 36	(2) 2M x 36	(2) 2M x 36
48MB	(2) 1M x 36	(2) 1M x 36	(2) 4M x 36
56MB	(2) 1M x 36	(2) 2M x 36	(2) 4M x 36
64MB	(2) 2M x 36	(2) 2M x 36	(2) 4M x 36
64MB	(2) 8M x 36	None	None
64MB	(2) 4M x 36	(2) 4M x 36	None
72MB	(2) 1M x 36	(2) 4M x 36	(2) 4M x 36
80MB	(2) 2M x 36	(2) 4M x 36	(2) 4M x 36
88MB	(2) 1M x 36	(2) 2M x 36	(2) 8M x 36
96MB	(2) 2M x 36	(2) 2M x 36	(2) 8M x 36
96MB	(2) 4M x 36	(2) 4M x 36	(2) 4M x 36
104MB	(2) 1M x 36	(2) 4M x 36	(2) 8M x 36
136MB	(2) 1M x 36	(2) 8M x 36	(2) 8M x 36

SIMM CONFIGURATION (CON'T)			
Size	**Bank 0**	**Bank 1**	**Bank 2**
112MB	(2) 2M x 36	(2) 4M x 36	(2) 8M x 36
128MB	(2) 4M x 36	(2) 4M x 36	(2) 8M x 36
128MB	(2) 8M x 36	(2) 8M x 36	None
160MB	(2) 4M x 36	(2) 8M x 36	(2) 8M x 36
192MB	(2) 8M x 36	(2) 8M x 36	(2) 8M x 36

CACHE CONFIGURATION
Note: 256KB/512KB cache is located on the Pentium Pro CPU.

Continued on next page...

DIGITAL EQUIPMENT CORPORATION
CELEBRIS GL (VER. 2), VENTURIS GL (VER. 2)

...continued from previous page

VIDEO MEMORY CONFIGURATION			
Note:	The size and configuration of the video memory is unidentified. To install memory upgrade, install module in C1.		

CPU SPEED SELECTION			
CPU speed	**SW1/2**	**SW1/3**	**SW1/4**
150MHz	Off	On	On
166MHz	Off	On	On
180MHz	On	Off	On
200MHz	On	Off	On
210MHz	Off	Off	On
233MHz	Off	Off	On
240MHz	On	On	Off
266MHz	On	On	Off

CPU BUS SPEED SELECTION	
Type	**SW1/1**
60MHz	Off
66MHz	On

Continued on next page...

DIGITAL EQUIPMENT CORPORATION
CELEBRIS GL (VER. 2), VENTURIS GL (VER. 2)

...continued from previous page

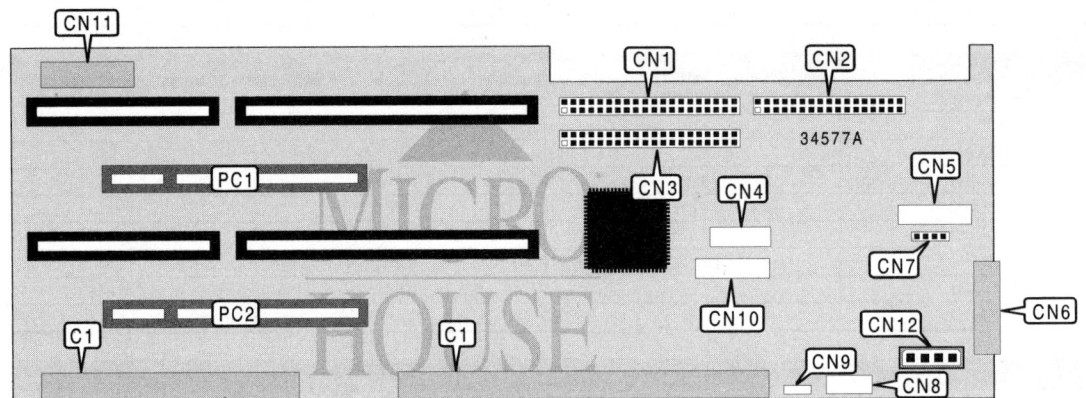

CELEBRIS GL LOW PROFILE BACKPLANE (FRONT VIEW)

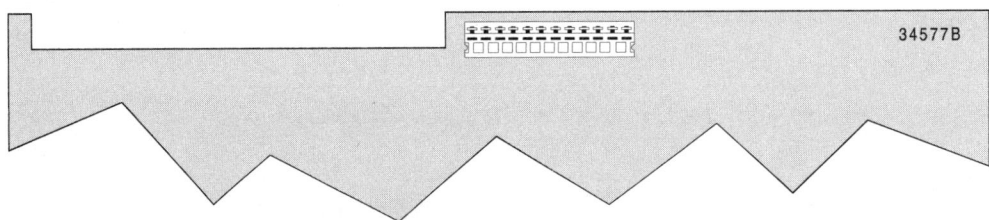

CELEBRIS GL LOW PROFILE BACKPLANE (BACK VIEW)

CONNECTIONS			
Purpose	**Location**	**Purpose**	**Location**
Main Logic Board connectors	C1	Fax/modem connector	CN7
IDE interface 1	CN1	Game/MIDI port	CN8
Floppy drive interface	CN2	SCSI interface LED	CN9
IDE interface 2	CN3	100Base T connector	CN10
10Base T/10Base-2 connector	CN4	Video in connector	CN11
Audio connector	CN5	Audio in - CD-ROM	CN12
Control panel	CN6	32-bit PCI slots	PC1 & PC2

Continued on next page...

DIGITAL EQUIPMENT CORPORATION
CELEBRIS GL (VER. 2), VENTURIS GL (VER. 2)

...continued from previous page

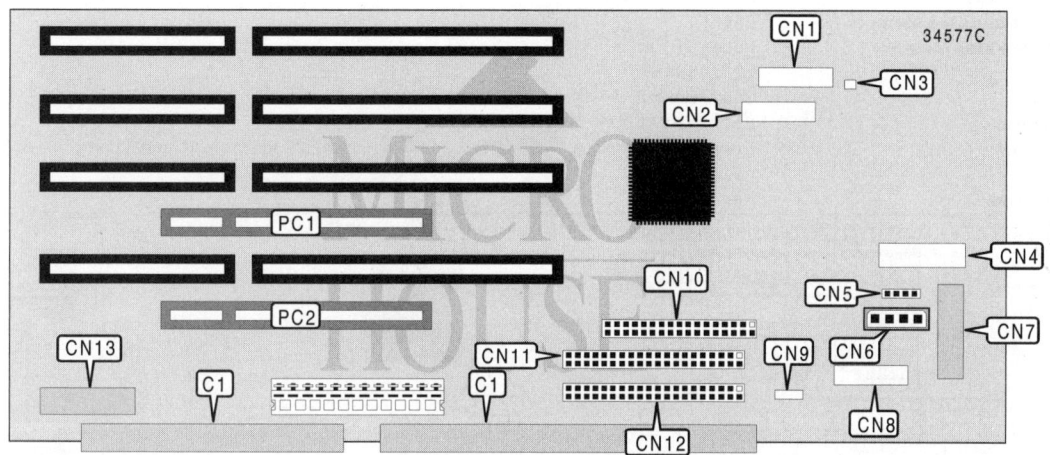

CELEBRIS SHORT TOWER BACKPLANE

CONNECTIONS			
Purpose	**Location**	**Purpose**	**Location**
Main Logic Board connectors	C1	Game/MIDI port	CN8
10Base-T/10Base-2 connector	CN1	SCSI interface LED	CN9
100Base T connector	CN2	Floppy drive interface	CN10
Chassis fan power	CN3	IDE interface 2	CN11
Audio connector	CN4	IDE interface 1	CN12
Fax/modem connector	CN5	Video in connector	CN13
Audio in - CD-ROM	CN6	32-bit PCI slots	PC1 & PC2
Control panel	CN7		

182 Motherboard Settings & Specifications

DIGITAL EQUIPMENT CORPORATION
DECPC LPV, DECPC LPV+

Processor	80486SX/80486DX/80486DX2
Processor Speed	25/33/40/50(internal)/50/66(internal)MHz
Chip Set	Unidentified
Video Chip Set	None
Maximum Onboard Memory	64MB
Maximum Video Memory	None
Cache	128/256KB
BIOS	Unidentified
Dimensions	254mm x 218mm
I/O Options	Floppy drive interface, IDE interface, parallel port, PS/2 mouse port, serial ports (2), VGA port, riser slot
NPU Options	None

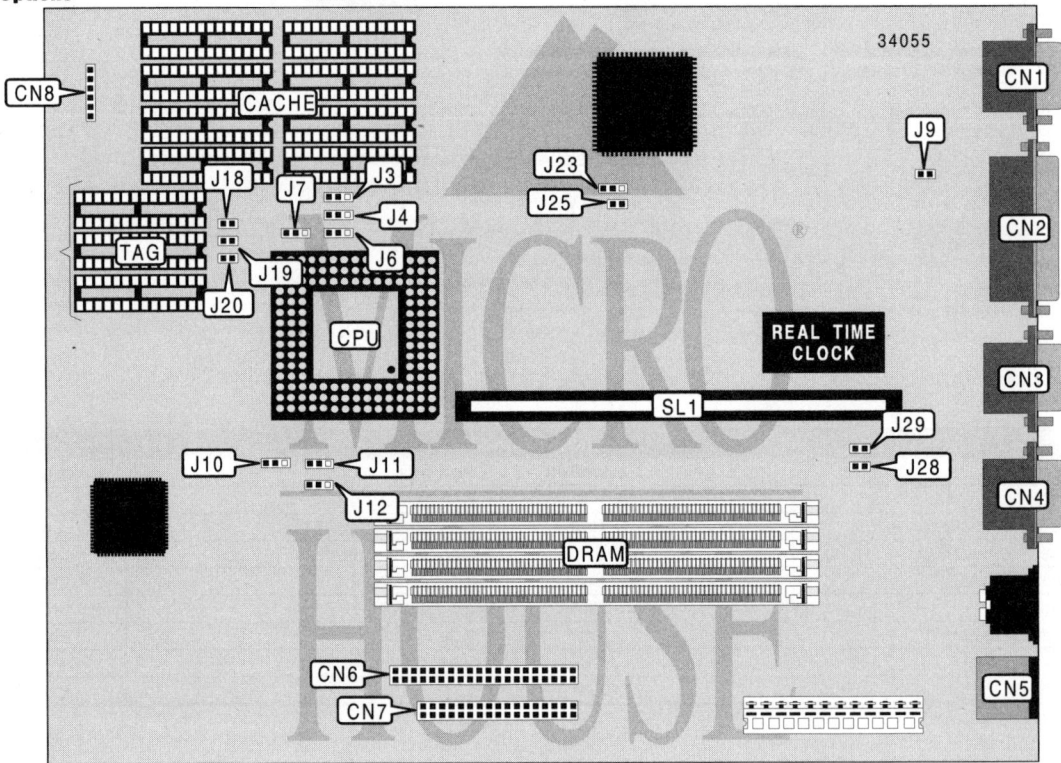

Continued on next page...

DIGITAL EQUIPMENT CORPORATION
DECPC LPV, DECPC LPV+

...continued from previous page

CONNECTIONS			
Purpose	**Location**	**Purpose**	**Location**
VGA port	CN1	IDE interface	CN6
Parallel port	CN2	Floppy drive interface	CN7
Serial port	CN3	Front panel connector	CN8
Serial port	CN4	Cache slot	SL1
PS/2 mouse port	CN5		

USER CONFIGURABLE SETTINGS		
Function	**Label**	**Position**
◇ Reset switch enabled	J9	Closed
Reset switch disabled	J9	Open
◇ RDY signal select VLRDY >CPURDY (connects through CPU bus)	J10	Pins 1 & 2 closed
RDY signal select VLRDY >CPURDY (synchronized through chipset)	J10	Pins 2 & 3 closed
◇ On board video enabled	J23	Pins 1 & 2 closed
On board video disabled	J23	Pins 2 & 3 closed
◇ VGA IRQ9 disabled	J25	Open
VGA IRQ9 enabled	J25	Closed
◇ Flash BIOS normal operation	J27	Open
Flash BIOS recovery mode	J27	Closed
◇ Factory configured - do not alter	J28	Open
◇ Monitor type select monochrome	J29	Open
Monitor type select color	J29	Closed

DRAM CONFIGURATION				
Size	**Bank 0**	**Bank 1**	**Bank 2**	**Bank 3**
4MB	(1) 1M x 36	None	None	None
8MB	(1) 1M x 36	(1) 1M x 36	None	None
12MB	(1) 1M x 36	(1) 1M x 36	(1) 1M x 36	None
16MB	(1) 1M x 36	(1) 1M x 36	(1) 1M x 36	(1) 1M x 36
16MB	(1) 4M x 36	None	None	None
20MB	(1) 1M x 36	(1) 4M x 36	None	None
24MB	(1) 1M x 36	(1) 1M x 36	(1) 4M x 36	None
32MB	(1) 4M x 36	(1) 4M x 36	None	None
40MB	(1) 1M x 36	(1) 1M x 36	(1) 4M x 36	(1) 4M x 36
48MB	(1) 4M x 36	(1) 4M x 36	(1) 4M x 36	None
64MB	(1) 4M x 36	(1) 4M x 36	(1) 4M x 36	(1) 4M x 36

CACHE CONFIGURATION			
Size	**Bank 0**	**Bank 1**	**TAG**
128KB	(4) 32K x 8	None	Unidentified
256KB	(4) 32K x 8	(4) 32K x 8	Unidentified

Continued on next page...

DIGITAL EQUIPMENT CORPORATION
DECPC LPV, DECPC LPV+

... continued from previous page

CACHE JUMPER CONFIGURATION				
Size	**J3**	**J4**	**J6**	**J7**
None	Open	Open	Open	Open
128KB	Pins 1 & 2 closed	Pins 1 & 2 closed	Pins 1 & 2 closed	Pins 1 & 2 closed
256KB	Pins 2 & 3 closed	Pins 2 & 3 closed	Pins 2 & 3 closed	Pins 2 & 3 closed

CPU SPEED SELECTION			
Speed	**J18**	**J19**	**J20**
25MHz	Open	Closed	Closed
33MHz	Closed	Open	Closed
40MHz	Closed	Open	Open
50iMHz	Open	Closed	Closed
50MHz	Open	Open	Open
66iMHz	Closed	Open	Closed

CPU TYPE SELECTION		
Type	**J11**	**J12**
80486SX	Pins 2 & 3 closed	Pins 2 & 3 closed
80486DX	Pins 1 & 2 closed	Pins 1 & 2 closed
80486DX2	Pins 1 & 2 closed	Pins 1 & 2 closed

DIGITAL EQUIPMENT CORPORATION
DECPC LPX

Processor	80486SX/80486DX/80486DX2
Processor Speed	25/33/40/50(internal)/50/66(internal)MHz
Chip Set	Unidentified
Video Chip Set	None
Maximum Onboard Memory	64MB
Maximum Video Memory	None
Cache	128/256KB
BIOS	Unidentified
Dimensions	254mm x 218mm
I/O Options	32-bit VESA local bus slots (2), floppy drive interface, IDE interface, parallel port, PS/2 mouse port, serial ports (2)
NPU Options	None

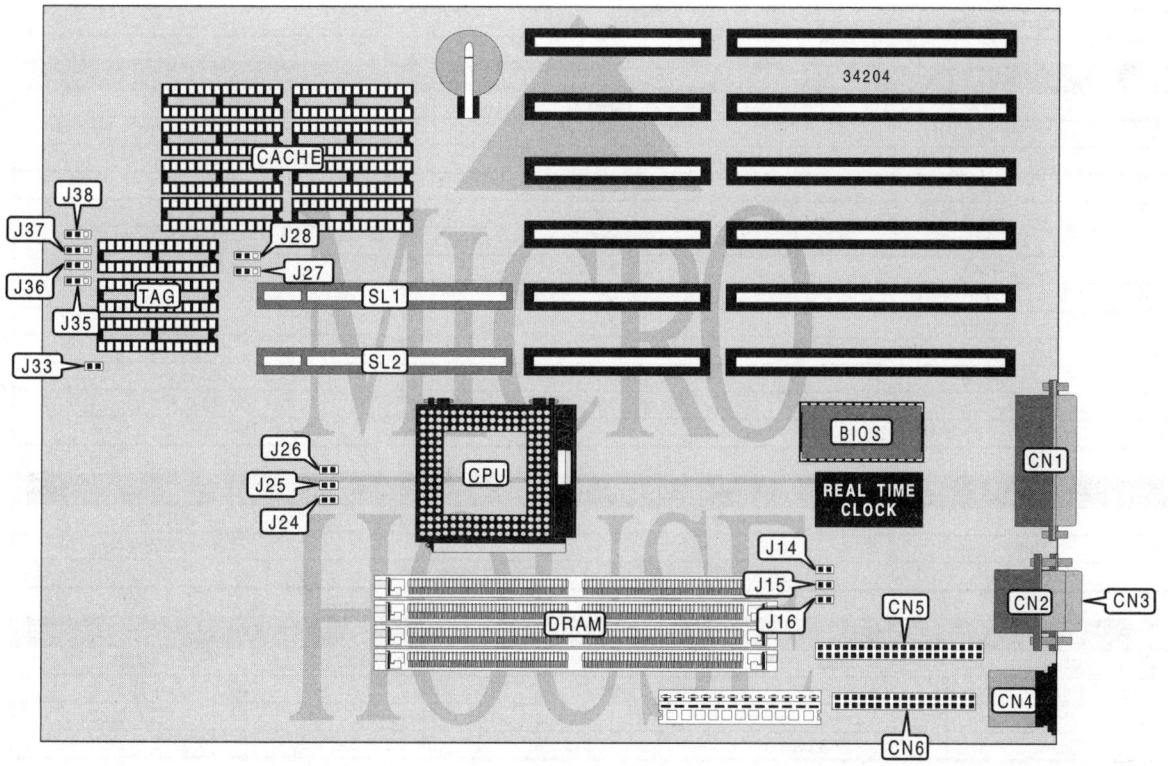

CONNECTIONS

Purpose	Location	Purpose	Location
Parallel port	CN1	IDE interface	CN5
Serial port	CN2	Floppy drive interface	CN6
Serial port	CN3	32-bit VESA local bus slots	SL1 & SL2
PS/2 mouse port	CN4		

Continued on next page...

DIGITAL EQUIPMENT CORPORATION
DECPC LPX

...continued from previous page

USER CONFIGURABLE SETTINGS		
Function	**Label**	**Position**
Flash BIOS normal operation	J14	Open
Flash BIOS recovery mode	J14	Closed
Monitor type select monochrome	J15	Open
Monitor type select color	J15	Closed
Factory configured – do not alter	J16	Open
VLRDY >CPURDY connects to CPU bus ready	J28	Pins 1 & 2 closed
VLRDY >LRDY synchronized through chipset	J28	Pins 2 & 3 closed
Reset switch enabled	J33	Closed
Reset switch disabled	J33	Open

DRAM CONFIGURATION		
Size	**Bank 0**	**Bank 1**
4MB	(2) 256K x 36	(2) 256K x 36
4MB	(2) 512K x 36	None
8MB	(2) 1M x 36	None
16MB	(2) 2M x 36	None
16MB	(2) 1M x 36	(2) 1M x 36
24MB	(2) 2M x 36	(2) 1M x 36
32MB	(2) 4M x 36	None
32MB	(2) 2M x 36	(2) 2M x 36
40MB	(2) 4M x 36	(2) 1M x 36
48MB	(2) 4M x 36	(2) 2M x 36
64MB	(2) 4M x 36	(2) 4M x 36

Note: The location of banks 0 & 1 are unidentified.

CACHE CONFIGURATION			
Size	**Bank 0**	**Bank 1**	**TAG**
128KB	(4) 32K x 8	None	(3) 16K x 4
256KB	(4) 32K x 8	(4) 32K x 8	(3) 16K x 4

CACHE JUMPER CONFIGURATION				
Size	**J35**	**J36**	**J37**	**J38**
None	Open	Open	Open	Open
128KB	Pins 1 & 2 closed	Pins 1 & 2 closed	Pins 1 & 2 closed	Pins 1 & 2 closed
256KB	Pins 2 & 3 closed	Pins 2 & 3 closed	Pins 2 & 3 closed	Pins 2 & 3 closed

Continued on next page...

DIGITAL EQUIPMENT CORPORATION
DECPC LPX

... continued from previous page

CPU SPEED SELECTION			
Speed	**J24**	**J25**	**J26**
25MHz	Closed	Closed	Open
33MHz	Closed	Open	Closed
40MHz	Open	Open	Closed
50iMHz	Closed	Closed	Open
50MHz	Open	Open	Open
66iMHz	Closed	Open	Closed

VL BUS WAIT STATE SELECTION	
Setting	**J27**
⇨ 0	Pins 1 & 2 closed
1	Pins 2 & 3 closed

DIGITAL EQUIPMENT CORPORATION
PRIORIS MX 6200

Processor	Pentium Pro
Processor Speed	200MHz
Chip Set	Unidentified
Video Chip Set	Unidentified
Maximum Onboard Memory	1GB (EDO supported)
Maximum Video Memory	Unidentified
Cache	256/512KB (located on Pentium Pro CPU)
BIOS	Unidentified
Dimensions	355mm x 304mm
I/O Options (Backplane)	32-bit PCI slots (3), floppy drive interface, SCSI interface, Ultra Wide SCSI interface, parallel port, PS/2 mouse port, serial ports (2), VGA port, CPU card slot, Ethernet connector
I/O Options (CPU)	VRM connectors (2)
NPU Options	None

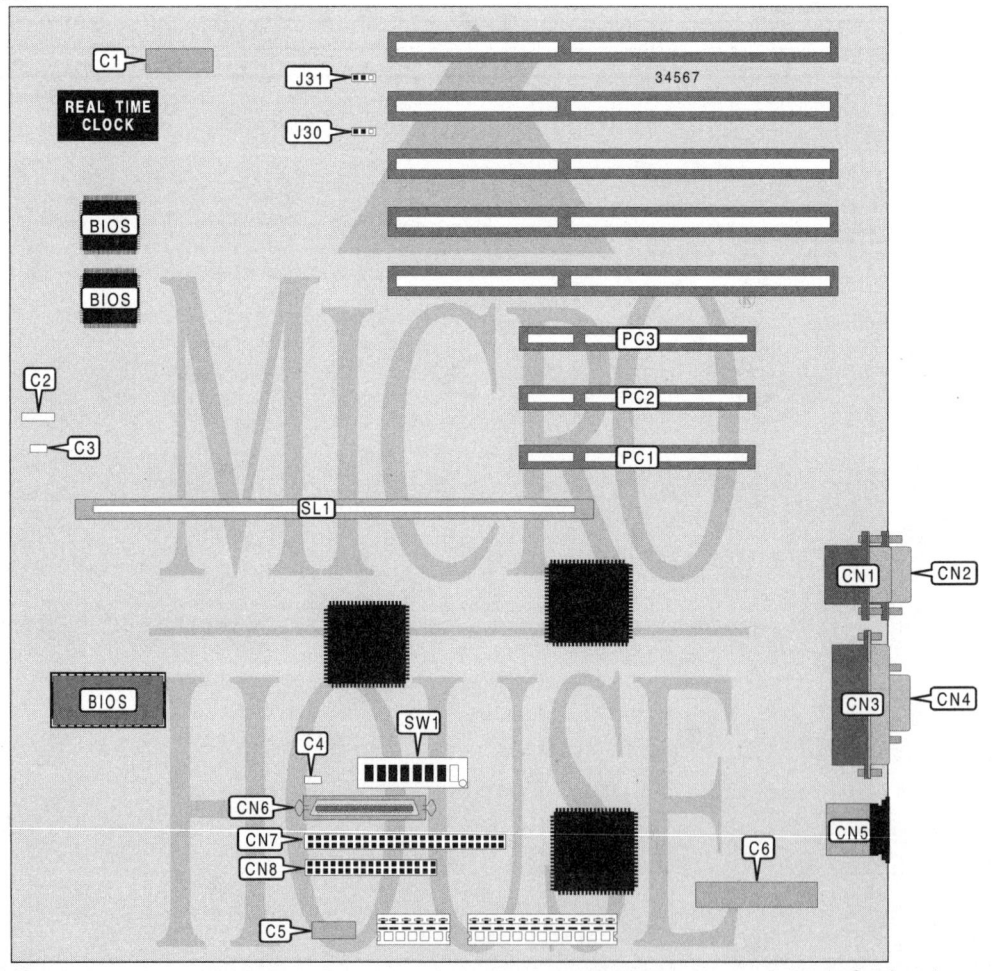

Continued on next page...

DIGITAL EQUIPMENT CORPORATION
PRIORIS MX 6200

. . . continued from previous page

CONNECTIONS			
Purpose	**Location**	**Purpose**	**Location**
Serial port	CN1	RSM connector	C1
Serial port	CN2	Speaker	C2
Parallel port	CN3	Chassis fan power	C3
VGA port	CN4	Chassis fan power	C4
PS/2 mouse port	CN5	Front panel connector	C5
Ultra Wide SCSI interface	CN6	Ethernet connector	C6
SCSI interface	CN7	32-bit PCI slots	PC1 – PC3
Floppy drive interface	CN8	CPU slot	SL1

USER CONFIGURABLE SETTINGS		
Function	**Label**	**Position**
◇ EISA slot 4 master delay select normal	J30	Pins 1 & 2 closed
EISA slot 4 master delay select delay 1 clock cycle	J30	Pins 2 & 3 closed
◇ EISA slot 5 master delay select normal	J31	Pins 1 & 2 closed
EISA slot 5 master delay select delay 1 clock cycle	J31	Pins 2 & 3 closed
◇ BIOS upgrade disabled	SW1/1	Off
BIOS upgrade enabled	SW1/1	On
◇ Flash BIOS normal operation	SW1/2	Off
Flash BIOS recovery mode	SW1/2	On
◇ Boot block disabled	SW1/3	Off
Boot block enabled	SW1/3	On
◇ Password normal operation	SW1/4	Off
Password clear	SW1/4	On
◇ RSM not installed	SW1/5	On
RSM installed	SW1/5	Off
◇ NVRAM memory normal operation	SW1/6	Off
NVRAM memory clear	SW1/6	On
◇ Factory configured - do not alter	SW1/7	Off
◇ Factory configured - do not alter	SW1/8	Off

VIDEO MEMORY CONFIGURATION
Note: The location and size of the video memory is unidentified.

Continued on next page. . .

DIGITAL EQUIPMENT CORPORATION
PRIORIS MX 6200

...continued from previous page

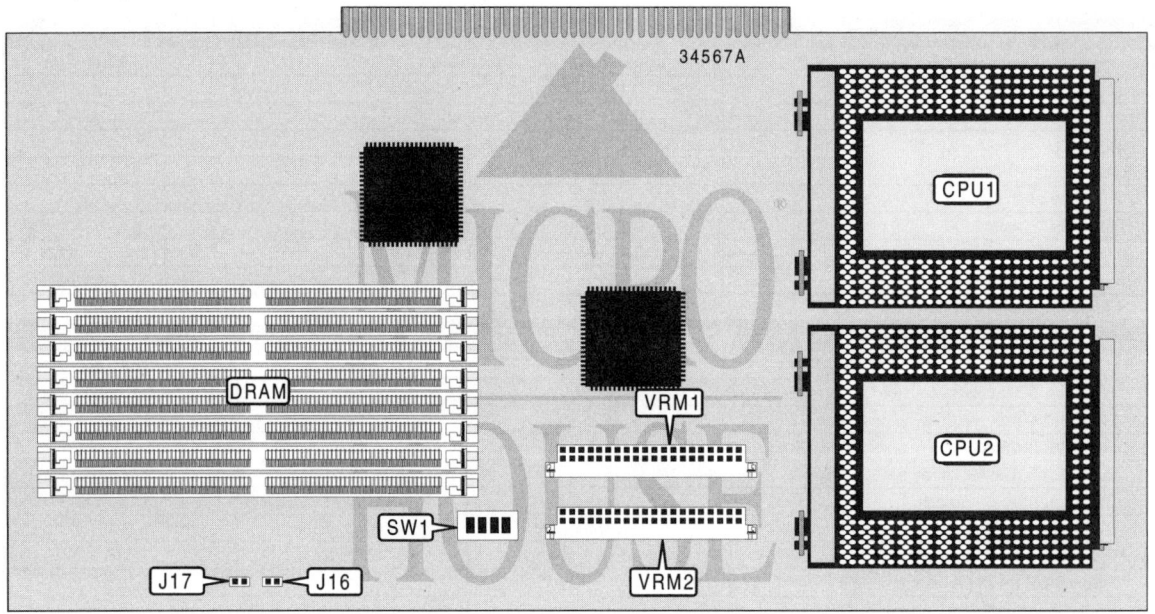

CPU CARD

CONNECTIONS			
Purpose	**Location**	**Purpose**	**Location**
VRM connector	VRM1	VRM connector	VRM2

USER CONFIGURABLE SETTINGS		
Function	**Label**	**Position**
⇨ Factory configured - do not alter	J16	Open
⇨ Factory configured - do not alter	J17	Open

SIMM CONFIGURATION				
Size	**Bank 0**	**Bank 1**	**Bank 2**	**Bank 3**
32MB	(2) 4M x 36	None	None	None
64MB	(2) 4M x 36	(2) 4M x 36	None	None
64MB	(2) 8M x 36	None	None	None
96MB	(2) 4M x 36	(2) 4M x 36	(2) 4M x 36	None
128MB	(2) 4M x 36	(2) 4M x 36	(2) 4M x 36	(2) 4M x 36

Continued on next page...

DIGITAL EQUIPMENT CORPORATION
PRIORIS MX 6200

...continued from previous page

		SIMM CONFIGURATION (CON'T)			
Size	**Bank 0**	**Bank 1**	**Bank 2**	**Bank 3**	
128MB	(2) 8M x 36	(2) 8M x 36	None	None	
128MB	(2) 16M x 36	None	None	None	
192MB	(2) 8M x 36	(2) 8M x 36	(2) 8M x 36	None	
256MB	(2) 8M x 36	(2) 8M x 36	(2) 8M x 36	(2) 8M x 36	
256MB	(2) 16M x 36	(2) 16M x 36	None	None	
256MB	(2) 32M x 36	None	None	None	
384MB	(2) 16M x 36	(2) 16M x 36	(2) 16M x 36	None	
512MB	(2) 16M x 36	(2) 16M x 36	(2) 16M x 36	(2) 16M x 36	
512MB	(2) 32M x 36	(2) 32M x 36	None	None	
768MB	(2) 32M x 36	(2) 32M x 36	(2) 32M x 36	None	
1GB	(2) 32M x 36	(2) 32M x 36	(2) 32M x 36	(2) 32M x 36	

Note: Board accepts EDO memory.

CACHE CONFIGURATION

Note: 256KB/512KB cache is located on the Pentium Pro CPU.

CPU SPEED SELECTION

CPU speed	Clock speed	Multiplier	SW1/1	SW1/2	SW1/3	SW1/4
200MHz	66MHz	3x	On	On	Off	On

FIRST INTERNATIONAL COMPUTER, INC.
KN-6000

Processor	Pentium II
Processor Speed	233/266/300/333MHz
Chip Set	Intel
Video Chip Set	None
Maximum Onboard Memory	768MB (EDO supported)
Maximum Video Memory	None
Cache	256/512KB (located on Pentium II CPU)
BIOS	Award
Dimensions	330mm x 218mm
I/O Options	32-bit PCI slots (5), floppy drive interface, green PC connector, IDE interfaces (2), parallel port, PS/2 mouse interface, serial ports (2), IR connector, USB connectors (2), CPU Slot 1
NPU Options	None

Continued on next page...

FIRST INTERNATIONAL COMPUTER, INC.
KN-6000

...continued from previous page

CONNECTIONS			
Purpose	**Location**	**Purpose**	**Location**
Serial port 1	CN1	Reset switch	FP/pins 12 & 13
Serial port 2	CN2	Turbo LED	FP/pins 15 & 16
Parallel port	CN3	Turbo switch	FP/pins 18 & 19
Floppy drive interface	CN4	IDE interface LED	FP/pins 21 & 22
IDE interface 1	CN5	IR connector	IR1
IDE interface 2	CN6	32-bit PCI slots	PC1 – PC5
PS/2 mouse interface	CN7	Remote power connector	RPW
CPU fan power	FAN1	CPU Slot 1	SL1
Chassis fan power	FAN2	USB connector 1	USB1
Power LED & keylock	FP/pins 1 - 5	USB connector 2	USB2
Speaker	FP/pins 7 - 10		

USER CONFIGURABLE SETTINGS		
Function	**Label**	**Position**
⇨ Password normal operation	CPS	Open
Password clear	CPS	Closed

DRAM CONFIGURATION			
Size	**Bank 0**	**Bank 1**	**Bank 2**
8MB	(2) 1M x 36	None	None
16MB	(2) 1M x 36	(2) 1M x 36	None
16MB	(2) 2M x 36	None	None
24MB	(2) 2M x 36	(2) 1M x 36	None
24MB	(2) 1M x 36	(2) 1M x 36	(2) 1M x 36
32MB	(2) 4M x 36	None	None
32MB	(2) 2M x 36	(2) 2M x 36	None
40MB	(2) 4M x 36	(2) 1M x 36	None
48MB	(2) 4M x 36	(2) 2M x 36	None
48MB	(2) 4M x 36	(2) 1M x 36	(2) 1M x 36
64MB	(2) 8M x 36	None	None
64MB	(2) 4M x 36	(2) 4M x 36	None
80MB	(2) 8M x 36	(2) 2M x 36	None
80MB	(2) 8M x 36	(2) 1M x 36	(2) 1M x 36
96MB	(2) 8M x 36	(2) 4M x 36	None
96MB	(2) 4M x 36	(2) 4M x 36	(2) 4M x 36
96MB	(2) 8M x 36	(2) 2M x 36	(2) 2M x 36
128MB	(2) 8M x 36	(2) 4M x 36	(2) 4M x 36
128MB	(2) 16M x 36	None	None
128MB	(2) 8M x 36	(2) 8M x 36	None
136MB	(2) 8M x 36	(2) 8M x 36	(2) 1M x 36
136MB	(2) 16M x 36	(2) 1M x 36	None
144MB	(2) 16M x 36	(2) 2M x 36	None
144MB	(2) 16M x 36	(2) 1M x 36	(2) 1M x 36

Continued on next page...

FIRST INTERNATIONAL COMPUTER, INC.
KN-6000

...continued from previous page

	DRAM CONFIGURATION (CON'T)		
Size	**Bank 0**	**Bank 1**	**Bank 2**
152MB	(2) 16M x 36	(2) 2M x 36	(2) 1M x 36
160MB	(2) 16M x 36	(2) 4M x 36	None
160MB	(2) 16M x 36	(2) 2M x 36	(2) 2M x 36
168MB	(2) 16M x 36	(2) 4M x 36	(2) 1M x 36
176MB	(2) 16M x 36	(2) 4M x 36	(2) 2M x 36
192MB	(2) 16M x 36	(2) 8M x 36	None
192MB	(2) 16M x 36	(2) 4M x 36	(2) 4M x 36
208MB	(2) 16M x 36	(2) 8M x 36	(2) 2M x 36
224MB	(2) 16M x 36	(2) 8M x 36	(2) 4M x 36
256MB	(2) 16M x 36	(2) 16M x 36	None
256MB	(2) 16M x 36	(2) 8M x 36	(2) 8M x 36
264MB	(2) 16M x 36	(2) 16M x 36	(2) 1M x 36
272MB	(2) 16M x 36	(2) 16M x 36	(2) 2M x 36
288MB	(2) 16M x 36	(2) 16M x 36	(2) 4M x 36
320MB	(2) 16M x 36	(2) 16M x 36	(2) 8M x 36
384MB	(2) 16M x 36	(2) 16M x 36	(2) 16M x 36
256MB	(2) 32M x 36	None	None
264MB	(2) 32M x 36	(2) 1M x 36	None
272MB	(2) 32M x 36	(2) 2M x 36	None
288MB	(2) 32M x 36	(2) 4M x 36	None
320MB	(2) 32M x 36	(2) 8M x 36	None
384MB	(2) 32M x 36	(2) 16M x 36	None
512MB	(2) 32M x 36	(2) 32M x 36	None
520MB	(2) 32M x 36	(2) 32M x 36	(2) 1M x 36
528MB	(2) 32M x 36	(2) 32M x 36	(2) 2M x 36
544MB	(2) 32M x 36	(2) 32M x 36	(2) 4M x 36
576MB	(2) 32M x 36	(2) 32M x 36	(2) 8M x 36
640MB	(2) 32M x 36	(2) 32M x 36	(2) 16M x 36
768MB	(2) 32M x 36	(2) 32M x 36	(2) 32M x 36

Note: Board accepts EDO memory.

CACHE CONFIGURATION
Note: 256KB/512KB cache is located on the Pentium II CPU.

CPU SPEED SELECTION								
CPU speed	**Clock speed**	**Multiplier**	**CLK1**	**CLK2**	**FREQ1**	**FREQ2**	**FREQ3**	**FREQ4**
233MHz	66MHz	3.5x	1 & 2	2 & 3	Open	Open	Closed	Closed
266MHz	66MHz	4x	1 & 2	2 & 3	Closed	Closed	Open	Closed
300MHz	66MHz	4.5x	1 & 2	2 & 3	Open	Closed	Open	Closed
333MHz	66MHz	5x	1 & 2	2 & 3	Closed	Open	Open	Closed

Note: Pins designated should be in the closed position.

Continued on next page...

FIRST INTERNATIONAL COMPUTER, INC.
KN-6000

... continued from previous page

1MB FLASH BIOS SELECTION		
Type	**EP1**	**EP2**
Intel	Open	Pins 2 & 3 closed
SST 29EE010	Open	Open

2MB FLASH BIOS SELECTION		
Type	**EP1**	**EP2**
AMD AM29F002T	Pins 1 & 2 closed	Pins 1 & 2 closed
ATMEL AT29C020	Pins 1 & 2 closed	Open
MXIC MX28F2000P	Pins 1 & 2 closed	Pins 2 & 3 closed
SST 29EE020	Pins 1 & 2 closed	Open

GEMLIGHT COMPUTER, LTD.
GMB-P6IAK (VER. 1.01)

Processor	Pentium II
Processor Speed	233/266/300MHz
Chip Set	Intel
Video Chip Set	None
Maximum Onboard Memory	512MB (EDO supported)
Maximum Video Memory	None
Cache	256/512KB (located on Pentium II CPU)
BIOS	AMI
Dimensions	305mm x 244mm
I/O Options	32-bit PCI slots (5), floppy drive interface, green PC connector, IDE interfaces (2), parallel port, PS/2 mouse port, serial ports (2), IR connector, USB connectors (2), ATX power connector, CPU Slot 1
NPU Options	None

Continued on next page...

GEMLIGHT COMPUTER, LTD.
GMB-P6IAK (VER. 1.01)

...continued from previous page

CONNECTIONS			
Purpose	**Location**	**Purpose**	**Location**
ATX power connector	ATX	IDE interface LED	J1/pins 15 - 18
Parallel port	CN1	Green PC connector	J1/pins 20 & 21
Serial port 2	CN2	Soft off power supply	J1/pins 22 & 23
Serial port 1	CN3	Turbo LED	J1/pins 25 & 26
USB connector	CN4	IR connector	J2
USB connector	CN5	Floppy drive interface	J3
PS/2 mouse port	CN6	IDE interface 1	J7
Speaker	J1/pins 1 - 4	IDE interface 2	J8
Reset switch	J1/pins 6 & 7	32-bit PCI slots	PC1 - PC5
Power LED & keylock	J1/pins 9 - 13	CPU Slot 1	SL1

USER CONFIGURABLE SETTINGS		
Function	**Label**	**Position**
Flash BIOS voltage select 12v	JP1	Pins 2 & 3 closed
Flash BIOS voltage select 5v	JP1	Pins 1 & 2 closed
⇨ CMOS memory normal operation	JP3	Pins 2 & 3 closed
CMOS memory clear	JP3	Pins 1 & 2 closed

SIMM CONFIGURATION				
Size	**Bank 0**	**Bank 1**	**Bank 2**	**Bank 3**
8MB	(2) 1M x 36	None	None	None
16MB	(2) 1M x 36	(2) 1M x 36	None	None
16MB	(2) 2M x 36	None	None	None
24MB	(2) 1M x 36	(2) 1M x 36	(2) 1M x 36	None
32MB	(2) 1M x 36	(2) 1M x 36	(2) 1M x 36	(2) 1M x 36
32MB	(2) 2M x 36	(2) 2M x 36	None	None
32MB	(2) 4M x 36	None	None	None
48MB	(2) 2M x 36	(2) 2M x 36	(2) 2M x 36	None
64MB	(2) 2M x 36	(2) 2M x 36	(2) 2M x 36	(2) 2M x 36
64MB	(2) 4M x 36	(2) 4M x 36	None	None
64MB	(2) 8M x 36	None	None	None
96MB	(2) 4M x 36	(2) 4M x 36	(2) 4M x 36	None
128MB	(2) 4M x 36	(2) 4M x 36	(2) 4M x 36	(2) 4M x 36
128MB	(2) 8M x 36	(2) 8M x 36	None	None
128MB	(2) 16M x 36	None	None	None
192MB	(2) 8M x 36	(2) 8M x 36	(2) 8M x 36	None
256MB	(2) 8M x 36	(2) 8M x 36	(2) 8M x 36	(2) 8M x 36
256MB	(2) 16M x 36	(2) 16M x 36	None	None
384MB	(2) 16M x 36	(2) 16M x 36	(2) 16M x 36	None
512MB	(2) 16M x 36	(2) 16M x 36	(2) 16M x 36	(2) 16M x 36

Note: Board accepts EDO memory. Board also accepts x 32 SIMMs.

Continued on next page...

GEMLIGHT COMPUTER, LTD.
GMB-P6IAK (VER. 1.01)

... continued from previous page

CACHE CONFIGURATION
Note: 256KB/512KB cache is located on the Pentium II CPU.

CPU SPEED SELECTION				
CPU speed	**Clock speed**	**Multiplier**	**JP5**	**JP6**
233MHz	50MHz	1.5x	1 & 2, 3 & 4	1 & 2
266MHz	60MHz	1.5x	1 & 2, 5 & 6, 7 & 8	1 & 2
300MHz	66MHz	1.5x	1 & 2, 5 & 6	1 & 2
Note: Pins designated should be in the closed position.				

GIGA-BYTE TECHNOLOGY CO., LTD.
GA-586AM

Processor	CXM1/Pentium
Processor Speed	75/90/100/120/133/150MHz
Chip Set	UMC
Max. Onboard DRAM	128MB
Cache	256/512/1024KB
BIOS	Award
Dimensions	280mm x 220mm
I/O Options	32-bit PCI slots (4), floppy drive interface, green PC connector, IDE interfaces (2), parallel port, serial ports (2)
NPU Options	None

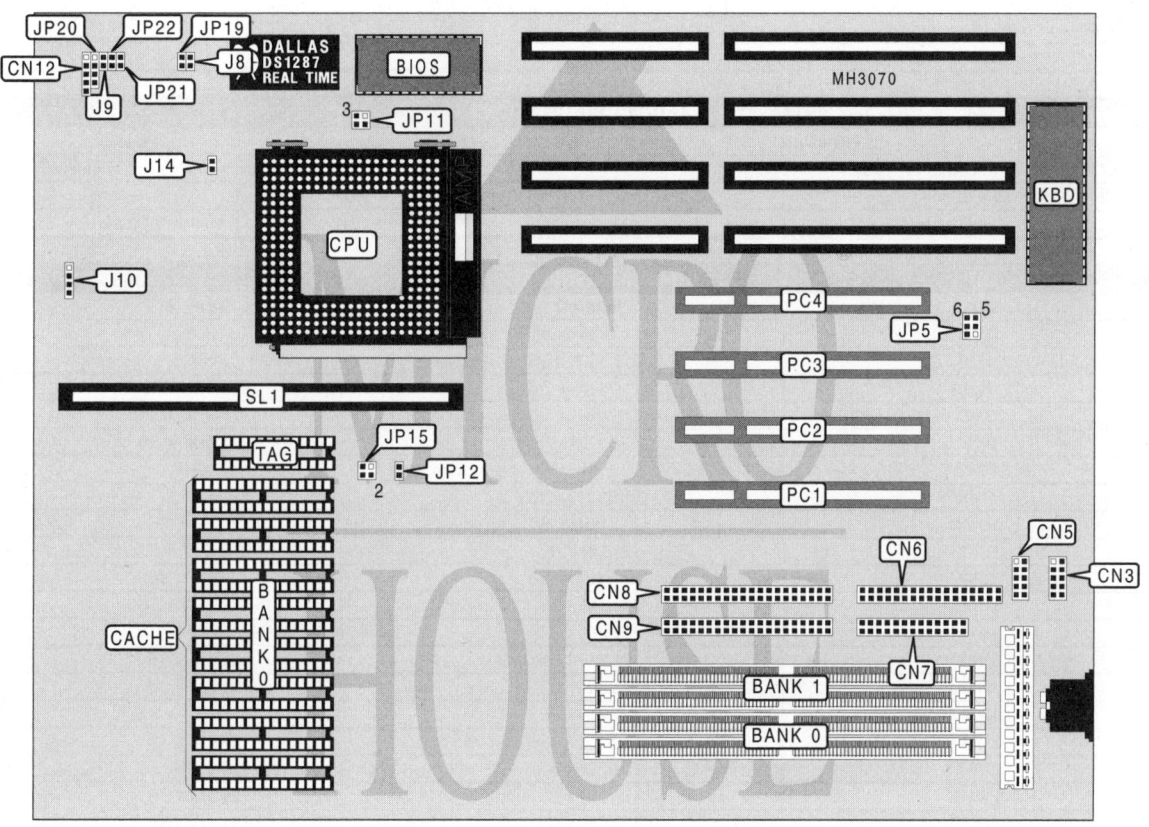

Continued on next page...

GIGA-BYTE TECHNOLOGY CO., LTD.
GA-586AM

. . . continued from previous page

CONNECTIONS			
Purpose	**Location**	**Purpose**	**Location**
Serial port 1	CN3	External battery	J10
Serial port 2	CN5	Chassis fan power	J14
Floppy drive interface	CN6	Green PC connector	JP19
Parallel port	CN7	Speaker	JP20
IDE interface 2	CN8	Reset switch	JP21
IDE interface 1	CN9	Turbo switch	JP22
Power LED & keylock	CN12	32-bit PCI slots	PC1 - PC4
IDE interface LED	J8	Cache slot	SL1
Green PC/turbo LED	J9		

Note: The location of pin 1 on CN6 - CN9 is unidentified.

USER CONFIGURABLE SETTINGS		
Function	**Jumper**	**Position**
⇨ CMOS memory normal operation	J10	pins 2 & 3 closed
CMOS memory clear	J10	Open
Battery type select external	J10	Closed

DRAM CONFIGURATION		
Size	**Bank 0**	**Bank 1**
2MB	(2) 256K x 36	NONE
4MB	(2) 512K x 36	NONE
4MB	(2) 256K x 36	(2) 256K x 36
6MB	(2) 256K x 36	(2) 512K x 36
6MB	(2) 512K x 36	(2) 256K x 36
8MB	(2) 1M x 36	NONE
8MB	(2) 512K x 36	(2) 512K x 36
10MB	(2) 256K x 36	(2) 1M x 36
10MB	(2) 1M x 36	(2) 256K x 36
12MB	(2) 512K x 36	(2) 1M x 36
12MB	(2) 1M x 36	(2) 512K x 36
16MB	(2) 2M x 36	NONE
16MB	(2) 1M x 36	(2) 1M x 36
18MB	(2) 256K x 36	(2) 2M x 36
18MB	(2) 2M x 36	(2) 256K x 36
20MB	(2) 512K x 36	(2) 2M x 36
20MB	(2) 2M x 36	(2) 512K x 36
24MB	(2) 1M x 36	(2) 2M x 36
24MB	(2) 2M x 36	(2) 1M x 36
32MB	(2) 4M x 36	NONE
32MB	(2) 2M x 36	(2) 2M x 36
34MB	(2) 256K x 36	(2) 4M x 36
34MB	(2) 4M x 36	(2) 256K x 36

Continued on next page. . .

GIGA-BYTE TECHNOLOGY CO., LTD.
GA-586AM

...continued from previous page

DRAM CONFIGURATION (CON'T)		
Size	**Bank 0**	**Bank 1**
36MB	(2) 512K x 36	(2) 4M x 36
36MB	(2) 4M x 36	(2) 512K x 36
40MB	(2) 1M x 36	(2) 4M x 36
40MB	(2) 4M x 36	(2) 1M x 36
48MB	(2) 2M x 36	(2) 4M x 36
48MB	(2) 4M x 36	(2) 2M x 36
64MB	(2) 8M x 36	NONE
64MB	(2) 4M x 36	(2) 4M x 36
66MB	(2) 256K x 36	(2) 8M x 36
66MB	(2) 8M x 36	(2) 256K x 36
68MB	(2) 512K x 36	(2) 8M x 36
68MB	(2) 8M x 36	(2) 512K x 36
72MB	(2) 1M x 36	(2) 8M x 36
72MB	(2) 8M x 36	(2) 1M x 36
80MB	(2) 2M x 36	(2) 8M x 36
80MB	(2) 8M x 36	(2) 2M x 36
96MB	(2) 4M x 36	(2) 8M x 36
96MB	(2) 8M x 36	(2) 4M x 36
128MB	(2) 8M x 36	(2) 8M x 36

CACHE CONFIGURATION			
Size	**Bank 0**	**TAG**	**SL1**
256KB (A)	(8) 32K x 8	(1) 8K or (1) 32K x 8	Not installed
256KB (B)	NONE	(1) 8K or (1) 32K x 8	Installed
512KB (A)	(8) 64K x 8	(1) 16K or (1) 32K x 8	Not installed
512KB (B)	NONE	(1) 16K or (1) 32K x 8	Installed
1MB	(8) 128K x 8	(1) 32K x 8	Not installed

CACHE JUMPER CONFIGURATION	
Size	**JP15**
256KB (A)	Open
256KB (B)	Open
512KB (A)	pins 3 & 4 closed
512KB (B)	pins 3 & 4 closed
1MB	pins 1 & 2, 3 & 4 closed

CPU TYPE CONFIGURATION	
Type	**JP12**
CXM1	Closed
Pentium	Open

Continued on next page...

GIGA-BYTE TECHNOLOGY CO., LTD.
GA-586AM

. . . continued from previous page

\multicolumn{3}{c}{CPU SPEED CONFIGURATION}		
Speed	**JP5**	**JP11**
75MHz	pins 1 & 2 closed	Open
90MHz	pins 3 & 4 closed	Open
100MHz	pins 1 & 2, 5 & 6 closed	Open
120MHz	pins 3 & 4 closed	pins 1 & 2 closed
133MHz	pins 1 & 2, 5 & 6 closed	pins 1 & 2, 3 & 4 closed
150MHz	pins 3 & 4 closed	pins 1 & 2 closed

GIGA-BYTE TECHNOLOGY CO., LTD.
GA-586IS

Processor	Pentium
Processor Speed	60/66MHz
Chip Set	Intel
Max. Onboard DRAM	192MB
Cache	256/512KB
BIOS	Award
Dimensions	330mm x 218mm
I/O Options	32-bit PCI bus slots (4)
NPU Options	None

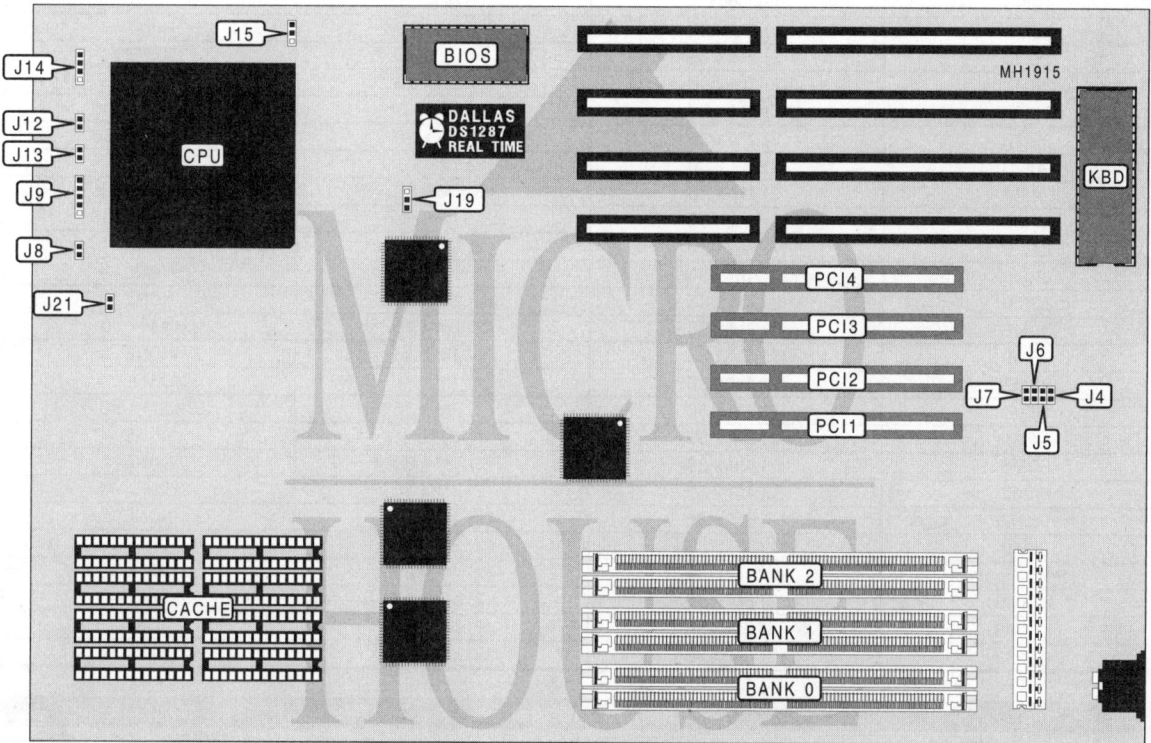

CONNECTIONS			
Purpose	Location	Purpose	Location
Reset switch	J8	CPU cooling fan	J21
Power LED & keylock	J9	32-bit PCI bus slot	PCI1
Turbo switch	J12	32-bit PCI bus slot	PCI2
Turbo LED	J13	32-bit PCI bus slot	PCI3
Speaker	J14	32-bit PCI bus slot	PCI4

Continued next page...

GIGA-BYTE TECHNOLOGY CO., LTD.
GA-5861S

...continued from previous page

DRAM CONFIGURATION

Size	Bank 0	Bank 1	Bank 2
2MB	(2) 256K x 36	NONE	NONE
4MB	(2) 256K x 36	(2) 256K x 36	NONE
4MB	(2) 512K x 36	NONE	NONE
6MB	(2) 256K x 36	(2) 256K x 36	(2) 256K x 36
8MB	(2) 512K x 36	(2) 512K x 36	NONE
8MB	(2) 1M x 36	NONE	NONE
12MB	(2) 512K x 36	(2) 512K x 36	(2) 512K x 36
12MB	(2) 1M x 36	(2) 512K x 36	NONE
16MB	(2) 2M x 36	NONE	NONE
16MB	(2) 1M x 36	(2) 1M x 36	NONE
16MB	(2) 1M x 36	(2) 512K x 36	(2) 512K x 36
20MB	(2) 1M x 36	(2) 1M x 36	(2) 512K x 36
20MB	(2) 2M x 36	(2) 512K x 36	NONE
24MB	(2) 1M x 36	(2) 1M x 36	(2) 1M x 36
24MB	(2) 2M x 36	(2) 512K x 36	(2) 512K x 36
24MB	(2) 2M x 36	(2) 1M x 36	NONE
32MB	(2) 4M x 36	NONE	NONE
32MB	(2) 2M x 36	(2) 2M x 36	NONE
32MB	(2) 2M x 36	(2) 1M x 36	(2) 1M x 36
48MB	(2) 4M x 36	(2) 2M x 36	NONE
48MB	(2) 4M x 36	(2) 1M x 36	(2) 1M x 36
48MB	(2) 2M x 36	(2) 2M x 36	(2) 2M x 36
64MB	(2) 8M x 36	NONE	NONE
64MB	(2) 4M x 36	(2) 4M x 36	NONE
64MB	(2) 4M x 36	(2) 2M x 36	(2) 2M x 36
96MB	(2) 8M x 36	(2) 4M x 36	NONE
96MB	(2) 8M x 36	(2) 2M x 36	(2) 2M x 36
96MB	(2) 4M x 36	(2) 4M x 36	(2) 4M x 36
128MB	(2) 8M x 36	(2) 4M x 36	(2) 4M x 36
128MB	(2) 8M x 36	(2) 8M x 36	NONE
192MB	(2) 8M x 36	(2) 8M x 36	(2) 8M x 36

CACHE CONFIGURATION

Size	Cache	J15
256KB	(8) 32K x 8	pins 1 & 2 closed
512KB	(8) 64K x 8 or (8) 128K x 8	pins 2 & 3 closed

CPU SPEED CONFIGURATION

Type	J19
60MHz	pins 2 & 3 closed
66MHz	pins 1 & 2 closed

Continued next page...

GIGA-BYTE TECHNOLOGY CO., LTD.
GA-586IS

. . . continued from previous page

PCI IRQ SELECT				
IRQ	J4	J5	J6	J7
9	Open	Open	Open	Closed
10	Open	Open	Closed	Open
11	Open	Closed	Open	Open
14	Closed	Open	Open	Open

GIGA-BYTE TECHNOLOGY CO., LTD.
GA-686DX

Processor	Pentium Pro
Processor Speed	150/166/180/200/233/266MHz
Chip Set	Intel
Video Chip Set	None
Maximum Onboard Memory	512MB (EDO supported)
Maximum Video Memory	None
Cache	256/512KB (located on Pentium Pro CPU)
BIOS	Award
Dimensions	305mm x 244mm
I/O Options	32-bit PCI slots (5), floppy drive interface, green PC connector, IDE interfaces (2), parallel port, PS/2 mouse port, serial ports (2), IR connector, USB connector, ATX power connector
NPU Options	None

Continued on next page...

GIGA-BYTE TECHNOLOGY CO., LTD.
GA-686DX

. . . continued from previous page

CONNECTIONS			
Purpose	**Location**	**Purpose**	**Location**
ATX power connector	ATX	Reset switch	J2
Serial port 1	CN1	Power LED	J3
Parallel port	CN2	IDE interface LED	J4
Serial port 2	CN3	IR connector	J5
PS/2 mouse port	CN4	Green PC connector	J6
USB connector (optional)	CN5	Soft on power supply	J7
IDE interface 1	CN6	Green PC LED	J8
IDE interface 2	CN7	Chassis fan power	JP2
Floppy drive interface	CN8	Chassis fan power	JP4
Speaker	J1	32-bit PCI slots	PC1 – PC5

DRAM CONFIGURATION			
Size	**Bank 0**	**Bank 1**	**Bank 2**
8MB	(2) 1M x 36	None	None
16MB	(2) 1M x 36	(2) 1M x 36	None
16MB	(2) 2M x 36	None	None
24MB	(2) 2M x 36	(2) 1M x 36	None
24MB	(2) 1M x 36	(2) 1M x 36	(2) 1M x 36
32MB	(2) 4M x 36	None	None
32MB	(2) 2M x 36	(2) 2M x 36	None
40MB	(2) 4M x 36	(2) 1M x 36	None
48MB	(2) 4M x 36	(2) 2M x 36	None
48MB	(2) 4M x 36	(2) 1M x 36	(2) 1M x 36
56MB	(2) 4M x 36	(2) 2M x 36	(2) 1M x 36
64MB	(2) 8M x 36	None	None
64MB	(2) 4M x 36	(2) 4M x 36	None
80MB	(2) 8M x 36	(2) 2M x 36	None
80MB	(2) 8M x 36	(2) 1M x 36	(2) 1M x 36
88MB	(2) 8M x 36	(2) 2M x 36	(2) 1M x 36
96MB	(2) 8M x 36	(2) 4M x 36	None
96MB	(2) 4M x 36	(2) 4M x 36	(2) 4M x 36
96MB	(2) 8M x 36	(2) 2M x 36	(2) 2M x 36
104MB	(2) 8M x 36	(2) 4M x 36	(2) 1M x 36
112MB	(2) 8M x 36	(2) 4M x 36	(2) 2M x 36
128MB	(2) 8M x 36	(2) 4M x 36	(2) 4M x 36
128MB	(2) 16M x 36	None	None
128MB	(2) 8M x 36	(2) 8M x 36	None
136MB	(2) 8M x 36	(2) 8M x 36	(2) 1M x 36
136MB	(2) 16M x 36	(2) 1M x 36	None
144MB	(2) 16M x 36	(2) 2M x 36	None
144MB	(2) 16M x 36	(2) 1M x 36	(2) 1M x 36
152MB	(2) 16M x 36	(2) 2M x 36	(2) 1M x 36

Continued on next page. . .

GIGA-BYTE TECHNOLOGY CO., LTD.
GA-686DX

...continued from previous page

DRAM CONFIGURATION (CON'T)			
Size	Bank 0	Bank 1	Bank 2
160MB	(2) 16M x 36	(2) 4M x 36	None
160MB	(2) 16M x 36	(2) 2M x 36	(2) 2M x 36
168MB	(2) 16M x 36	(2) 4M x 36	(2) 1M x 36
176MB	(2) 16M x 36	(2) 4M x 36	(2) 2M x 36
192MB	(2) 16M x 36	(2) 8M x 36	None
192MB	(2) 16M x 36	(2) 4M x 36	(2) 4M x 36
200MB	(2) 16M x 36	(2) 8M x 36	(2) 1M x 36
208MB	(2) 16M x 36	(2) 8M x 36	(2) 2M x 36
224MB	(2) 16M x 36	(2) 8M x 36	(2) 4M x 36
256MB	(2) 16M x 36	(2) 16M x 36	None
256MB	(2) 16M x 36	(2) 8M x 36	(2) 8M x 36
256MB	(2) 32M x 36	None	None
264MB	(2) 16M x 36	(2) 16M x 36	(2) 1M x 36
264MB	(2) 32M x 36	(2) 1M x 36	None
272MB	(2) 16M x 36	(2) 16M x 36	(2) 2M x 36
272MB	(2) 32M x 36	(2) 2M x 36	None
288MB	(2) 16M x 36	(2) 16M x 36	(2) 4M x 36
288MB	(2) 32M x 36	(2) 4M x 36	None
320MB	(2) 16M x 36	(2) 16M x 36	(2) 8M x 36
320MB	(2) 32M x 36	(2) 8M x 36	None
384MB	(2) 16M x 36	(2) 16M x 36	(2) 16M x 36
384MB	(2) 32M x 36	(2) 16M x 36	None
512MB	(2) 32M x 36	(2) 32M x 36	None

Note: Board accepts EDO memory.

CACHE CONFIGURATION
Note: 256KB/512KB cache is located on the Pentium Pro CPU.

CPU SPEED SELECTION				
Speed	S1/1	S1/2	S1/3	S1/4
150MHz	On	On	Off	Off
166MHz	Off	On	Off	Off
180MHz	On	Off	On	Off
200MHz	Off	Off	On	Off
233MHz	Off	On	On	Off
266MHz	Off	Off	Off	On

GIGA-BYTE TECHNOLOGY CO., LTD.
GA-686FX

Processor	Pentium Pro
Processor Speed	150/166/180/200MHz
Chip Set	Unidentified
Video Chip Set	None
Maximum Onboard Memory	512MB
Maximum Video Memory	None
Cache	256/512KB (located on Pentium Pro CPU)
BIOS	Award
Dimensions	330mm x 218mm
I/O Options	32-bit PCI slots (4), floppy drive interface, green PC connector, IDE interfaces (2), parallel port, PS/2 mouse interface, serial ports (2), IR connector, USB connectors (2), ATX power connector
NPU Options	None

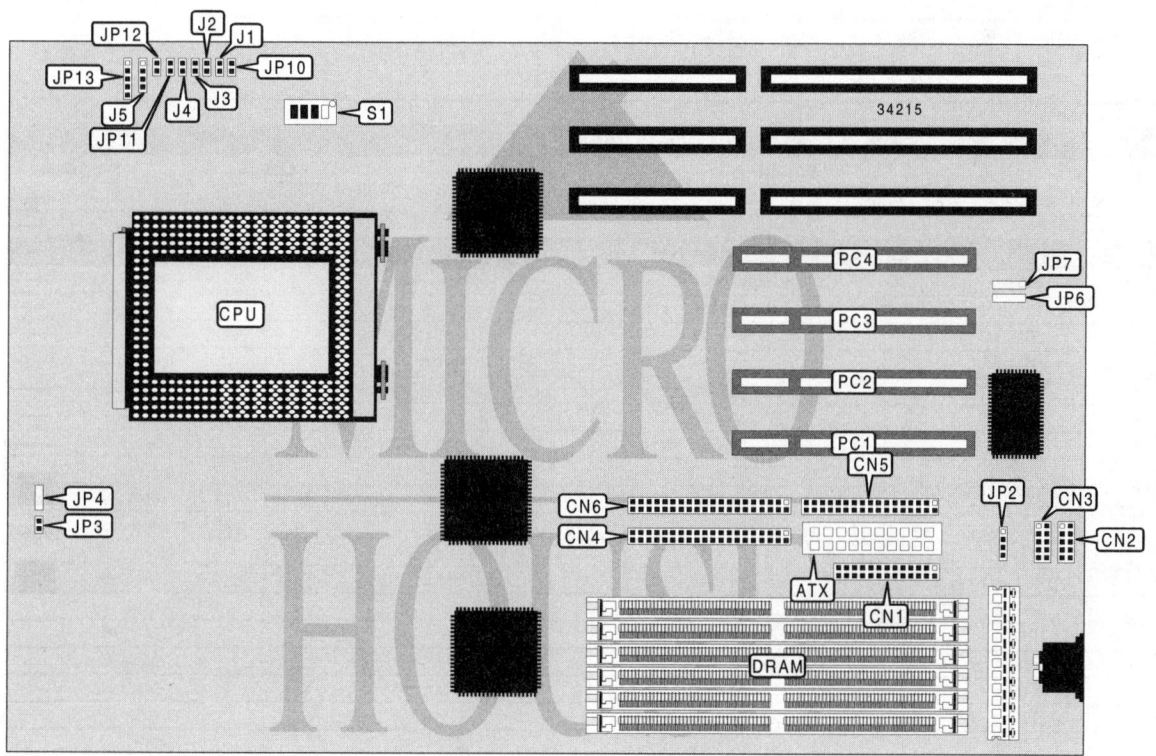

Continued on next page...

GIGA-BYTE TECHNOLOGY CO., LTD.
GA-686FX

...continued from previous page

CONNECTIONS			
Purpose	**Location**	**Purpose**	**Location**
ATX power connector	ATX	Speaker	J5
Parallel port	CN1	PS/2 mouse interface	JP2
Serial port 2	CN2	Chassis fan power	JP3
Serial port 1	CN3	USB connector	JP6
IDE interface 1	CN4	USB connector	JP7
Floppy drive interface	CN5	Soft off power supply	JP10
IDE interface 2	CN6	Turbo switch	JP11
IDE interface LED	J1	Turbo LED	JP12
Green PC connector	J2	Power LED & keylock	JP13
Green PC LED	J3	32-bit PCI slots	PC1 – PC4
Reset switch	J4		

USER CONFIGURABLE SETTINGS		
Function	**Label**	**Position**
◇ Factory configured - do not alter	JP4	Unidentified

DRAM CONFIGURATION			
Size	**Bank 0**	**Bank 1**	**Bank 2**
8MB	(2) 1M x 36	None	None
16MB	(2) 1M x 36	(2) 1M x 36	None
16MB	(2) 2M x 36	None	None
24MB	(2) 1M x 36	(2) 1M x 36	(2) 1M x 36
24MB	(2) 2M x 36	(2) 1M x 36	None
32MB	(2) 1M x 36	(2) 1M x 36	(2) 2M x 36
32MB	(2) 2M x 36	(2) 2M x 36	None
32MB	(2) 4M x 36	None	None
40MB	(2) 2M x 36	(2) 2M x 36	(2) 1M x 36
40MB	(2) 4M x 36	(2) 1M x 36	None
48MB	(2) 2M x 36	(2) 2M x 36	(2) 2M x 36
48MB	(2) 4M x 36	(2) 2M x 36	None
56MB	(2) 4M x 36	(2) 2M x 36	(2) 1M x 36
64MB	(2) 4M x 36	(2) 2M x 36	(2) 2M x 36
64MB	(2) 4M x 36	(2) 4M x 36	None
64MB	(2) 8M x 36	None	None
72MB	(2) 8M x 36	(2) 1M x 36	None
72MB	(2) 4M x 36	(2) 4M x 36	(2) 1M x 36
80MB	(2) 8M x 36	(2) 2M x 36	None
80MB	(2) 4M x 36	(2) 4M x 36	(2) 2M x 36
80MB	(2) 8M x 36	(2) 1M x 36	(2) 1M x 36
88MB	(2) 8M x 36	(2) 2M x 36	(2) 1M x 36
96MB	(2) 8M x 36	(2) 2M x 36	(2) 2M x 36

Continued on next page...

GIGA-BYTE TECHNOLOGY CO., LTD.
GA-686FX

. . . continued from previous page

Size	Bank 0	Bank 1	Bank 2
96MB	(2) 8M x 36	(2) 4M x 36	None
96MB	(2) 4M x 36	(2) 4M x 36	(2) 4M x 36
104MB	(2) 8M x 36	(2) 4M x 36	(2) 1M x 36
112MB	(2) 8M x 36	(2) 4M x 36	(2) 2M x 36
128MB	(2) 16M x 36	None	None
128MB	(2) 8M x 36	(2) 8M x 36	None
128MB	(2) 8M x 36	(2) 4M x 36	(2) 4M x 36
136MB	(2) 16M x 36	(2) 1M x 36	None
136MB	(2) 8M x 36	(2) 8M x 36	(2) 1M x 36
144MB	(2) 16M x 36	(2) 1M x 36	(2) 1M x 36
144MB	(2) 16M x 36	(2) 2M x 36	None
144MB	(2) 8M x 36	(2) 8M x 36	(2) 2M x 36
152MB	(2) 16M x 36	(2) 2M x 36	(2) 1M x 36
160MB	(2) 16M x 36	(2) 2M x 36	(2) 2M x 36
160MB	(2) 16M x 36	(2) 4M x 36	None
168MB	(2) 16M x 36	(2) 4M x 36	(2) 1M x 36
176MB	(2) 16M x 36	(2) 4M x 36	(2) 2M x 36
192MB	(2) 16M x 36	(2) 4M x 36	(2) 4M x 36
192MB	(2) 16M x 36	(2) 8M x 36	None
200MB	(2) 16M x 36	(2) 8M x 36	(2) 1M x 36
208MB	(2) 16M x 36	(2) 8M x 36	(2) 2M x 36
224MB	(2) 16M x 36	(2) 8M x 36	(2) 4M x 36
256MB	(2) 16M x 36	(2) 8M x 36	(2) 8M x 36
256MB	(2) 16M x 36	(2) 16M x 36	None
256MB	(2) 32M x 36	None	None
264MB	(2) 16M x 36	(2) 16M x 36	(2) 1M x 36
264MB	(2) 32M x 36	(2) 1M x 36	None
272MB	(2) 16M x 36	(2) 16M x 36	(2) 2M x 36
272MB	(2) 32M x 36	(2) 2M x 36	None
280MB	(2) 32M x 36	(2) 2M x 36	(2) 1M x 36
288MB	(2) 32M x 36	(2) 2M x 36	(2) 2M x 36
288MB	(2) 32M x 36	(2) 4M x 36	None
296MB	(2) 32M x 36	(2) 4M x 36	(2) 1M x 36
304MB	(2) 32M x 36	(2) 4M x 36	(2) 2M x 36
320MB	(2) 32M x 36	(2) 4M x 36	(2) 4M x 36
320MB	(2) 32M x 36	(2) 8M x 36	None
328MB	(2) 32M x 36	(2) 8M x 36	(2) 1M x 36
336MB	(2) 32M x 36	(2) 8M x 36	(2) 2M x 36
352MB	(2) 32M x 36	(2) 8M x 36	(2) 4M x 36
384MB	(2) 32M x 36	(2) 8M x 36	(2) 8M x 36

Continued on next page. . .

GIGA-BYTE TECHNOLOGY CO., LTD.
GA-686FX

...continued from previous page

DRAM CONFIGURATION (CON'T)			
Size	**Bank 0**	**Bank 1**	**Bank 2**
384MB	(2) 32M x 36	(2) 16M x 36	None
392MB	(2) 32M x 36	(2) 16M x 36	(2) 1M x 36
400MB	(2) 32M x 36	(2) 16M x 36	(2) 2M x 36
416MB	(2) 32M x 36	(2) 16M x 36	(2) 4M x 36
448MB	(2) 32M x 36	(2) 16M x 36	(2) 8M x 36
512MB	(2) 32M x 36	(2) 16M x 36	(2) 16M x 36
512MB	(2) 32M x 36	(2) 32M x 36	None

CACHE CONFIGURATION

Note: 256KB/512KB cache is located on the Pentium Pro CPU.

CPU SPEED SELECTION				
CPU speed	**S1/1**	**S1/2**	**S1/3**	**S1/4**
150MHz	On	On	Off	Off
166MHz	Off	On	Off	Off
180MHz	On	Off	On	Off
200MHz	Off	Off	On	Off

GIGA-BYTE TECHNOLOGY CO., LTD.
GA-686NX

Processor	Pentium Pro
Processor Speed	150/166/180/200/233/266MHz
Chip Set	Intel
Video Chip Set	None
Maximum Onboard Memory	512MB (EDO supported)
Maximum Video Memory	None
Cache	256/512KB (located on Pentium Pro CPU)
BIOS	Award
Dimensions	305mm x 244mm
I/O Options	32-bit PCI slots (4), floppy drive interface, green PC connector, IDE interfaces (2), parallel port, PS/2 mouse port, serial ports (2), IR connector, VRM connector, USB connector, ATX power connector
NPU Options	None

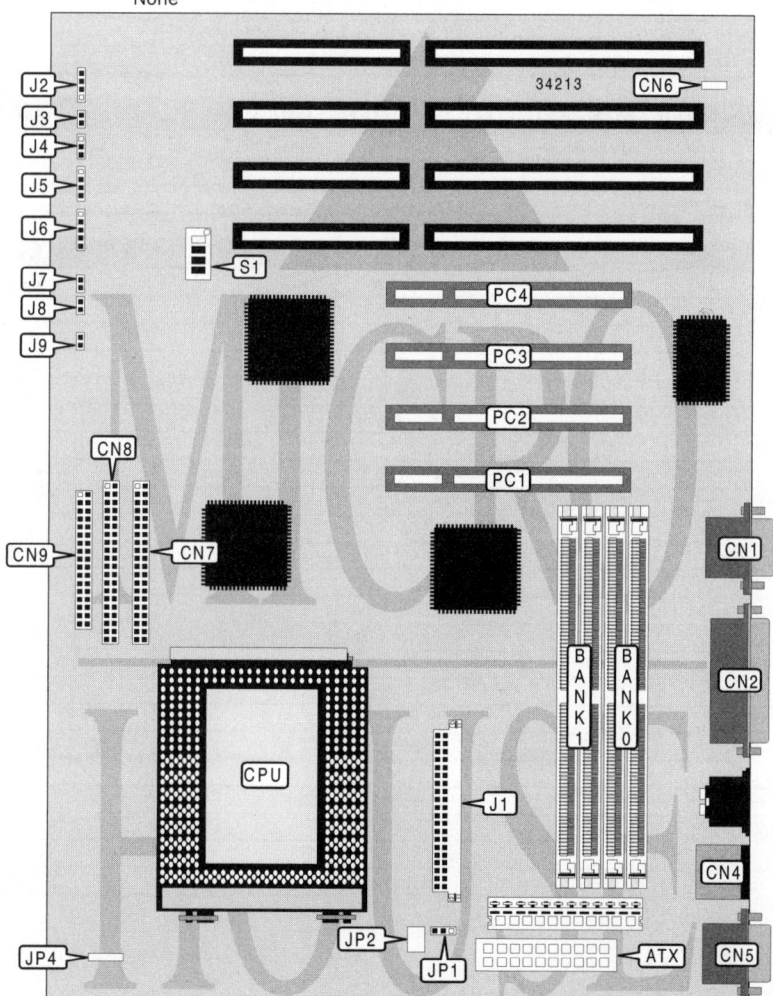

Continued on next page...

GIGA-BYTE TECHNOLOGY CO., LTD.
GA-686NX

...continued from previous page

CONNECTIONS			
Purpose	**Location**	**Purpose**	**Location**
ATX power supply	ATX	Speaker	J2
Serial port 2	CN1	Reset switch	J3
Parallel port	CN2	Power LED	J4
PS/2 mouse port	CN4	IDE interface LED	J5
Serial port 1	CN5	IR connector	J6
USB connector	CN6	Green PC connector	J7
IDE interface 2	CN7	Soft on power supply	J8
IDE interface 1	CN8	Green PC LED	J9
Floppy drive interface	CN9	Chassis fan power	JP1
VRM connector	J1	32-bit PCI slots	PC1 – PC4

USER CONFIGURABLE SETTINGS		
Function	**Label**	**Position**
⇨ Factory configured - do not alter	JP2	Unidentified
⇨ Factory configured - do not alter	JP4	Unidentified

DRAM CONFIGURATION		
Size	**Bank 0**	**Bank 1**
8MB	(2) 1M x 36	None
16MB	(2) 2M x 36	None
16MB	(2) 1M x 36	(2) 1M x 36
24MB	(2) 2M x 36	(2) 1M x 36
32MB	(2) 4M x 36	None
32MB	(2) 2M x 36	(2) 2M x 36
40MB	(2) 4M x 36	(2) 1M x 36
48MB	(2) 4M x 36	(2) 2M x 36
64MB	(2) 8M x 36	None
64MB	(2) 4M x 36	(2) 4M x 36
72MB	(2) 8M x 36	(2) 1M x 36
80MB	(2) 8M x 36	(2) 2M x 36
96MB	(2) 8M x 36	(2) 4M x 36
128MB	(2) 8M x 36	(2) 8M x 36
128MB	(2) 16M x 36	None
136MB	(2) 16M x 36	(2) 1M x 36
144MB	(2) 16M x 36	(2) 2M x 36
160MB	(2) 16M x 36	(2) 4M x 36
192MB	(2) 16M x 36	(2) 8M x 36
256MB	(2) 16M x 36	(2) 16M x 36
256MB	(2) 32M x 36	None
264MB	(2) 32M x 36	(2) 1M x 36

Continued on next page...

GIGA-BYTE TECHNOLOGY CO., LTD.
GA-686NX

...continued from previous page

Size	Bank 0	Bank 1
DRAM CONFIGURATION (CON'T)		
272MB	(2) 32M x 36	(2) 2M x 36
288MB	(2) 32M x 36	(2) 4M x 36
320MB	(2) 32M x 36	(2) 8M x 36
384MB	(2) 32M x 36	(2) 16M x 36
512MB	(2) 32M x 36	(2) 32M x 36

Note: Board accepts EDO memory.

CACHE CONFIGURATION

Note: 256KB/512KB cache is located on the Pentium Pro CPU.

Speed	S1/1	S1/2	S1/3	S1/4
CPU SPEED SELECTION				
150MHz	On	On	Off	Off
166MHz	Off	On	Off	Off
180MHz	On	Off	On	Off
200MHz	Off	Off	On	Off
233MHz	Off	On	On	Off
266MHz	Off	Off	Off	On

216 Motherboard Settings & Specifications

HEWLETT-PACKARD COMPANY
HP NETSERVER LE

Processor	80487SX/80486DX/ODP486SX/80486DX2/Pentium Overdrive
Processor Speed	33/66(internal)MHz
Chip Set	Hewlett Packard
Max. Onboard DRAM	128MB
Cache	None
BIOS	Phoenix
Dimensions	330mm x 218mm
I/O Options	Floppy drive interface, IDE interface, parallel port, SCSI interface, SCSI port, serial ports (2), PS/2 mouse port, VGA port
NPU Options	None

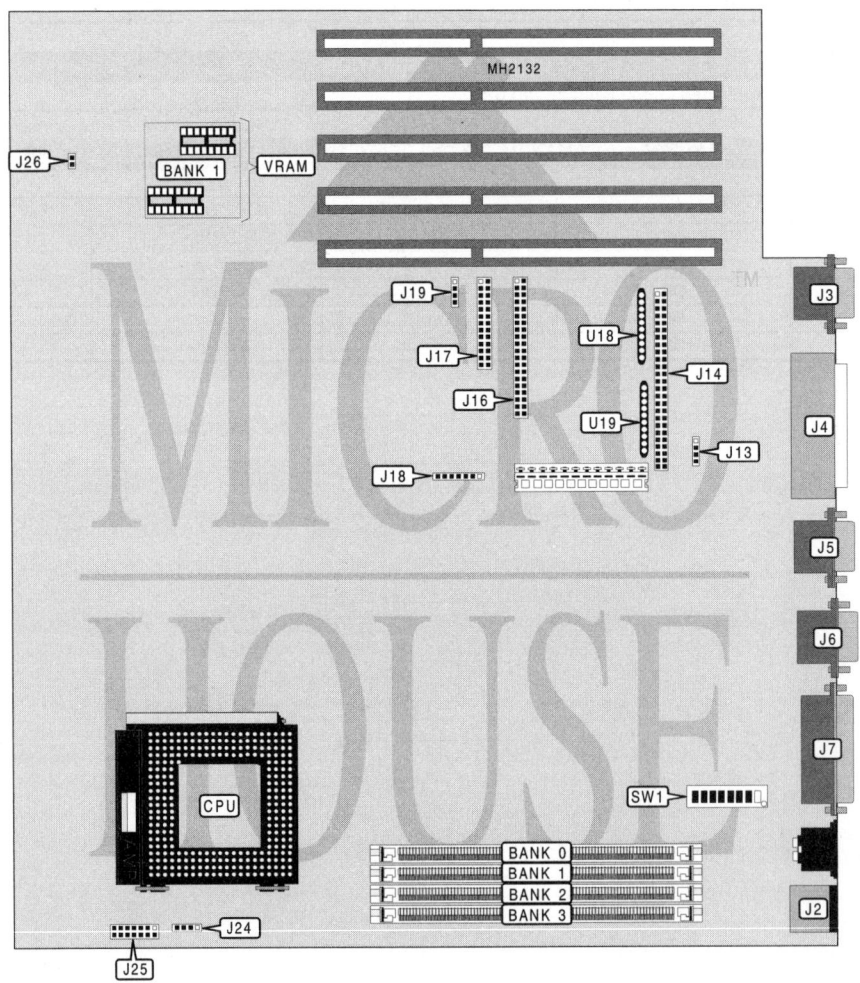

Continued on next page...

HEWLETT-PACKARD COMPANY
HP NETSERVER LE

. . . continued from previous page

CONNECTIONS			
Purpose	**Location**	**Purpose**	**Location**
PS/2 mouse port	J2	Floppy drive interface	J16
VGA port	J3	IDE interface	J17
SCSI connector (external)	J4	IDE interface LED	J19
Serial port 1	J5	Chassis fan power	J24
Serial port 2	J6	Control panel connector	J25
Parallel port	J7	Speaker	J26
External battery	J13	SCSI terminators	U18 & U19
SCSI connector (internal)	J14		
Note: J24 may not be present.			

USER CONFIGURABLE SETTINGS		
Function	**Jumper/Switch**	**Position**
⇨ Factory configured - do not alter	J18	pins 1 & 2 closed
⇨ Flash BIOS write protect enabled	SW1/1	Off
Flash BIOS write protect disabled	SW1/1	On
⇨ On board video disabled	SW1/2	On
On board video enabled	SW1/2	Off
⇨ Password enabled	SW1/3	Off
Password disabled	SW1/3	On
⇨ CMOS memory normal operation	SW1/4	Off
CMOS memory clear	SW1/4	On
⇨ BIOS write protect enabled	SW1/5	On
BIOS write protect disabled	SW1/5	Off
⇨ Factory configured - do not alter	SW1/8	On

DRAM CONFIGURATION				
Size	**Bank 0**	**Bank 1**	**Bank 2**	**Bank 3**
4MB	(1) 1M x 36	NONE	NONE	NONE
8MB	(1) 1M x 36	(1) 1M x 36	NONE	NONE
8MB	(1) 2M x 36	NONE	NONE	NONE
12MB	(1) 1M x 36	(1) 1M x 36	(1) 1M x 36	NONE
12MB	(1) 2M x 36	(1) 1M x 36	NONE	NONE
16MB	(1) 2M x 36	(1) 1M x 36	(1) 1M x 36	NONE
16MB	(1) 1M x 36	(1) 1M x 36	(1) 1M x 36	(1) 1M x 36
16MB	(1) 2M x 36	(1) 2M x 36	NONE	NONE
16MB	(1) 4M x 36	NONE	NONE	NONE
20MB	(1) 4M x 36	(1) 1M x 36	NONE	NONE
20MB	(1) 2M x 36	(1) 1M x 36	(1) 1M x 36	(1) 1M x 36
24MB	(1) 4M x 36	(1) 1M x 36	(1) 1M x 36	NONE
24MB	(1) 2M x 36	(1) 2M x 36	(1) 2M x 36	NONE
24MB	(1) 4M x 36	(1) 2M x 36	NONE	NONE
28MB	(1) 4M x 36	(1) 1M x 36	(1) 1M x 36	(1) 1M x 36
32MB	(1) 2M x 36	(1) 2M x 36	(1) 2M x 36	(1) 2M x 36
32MB	(1) 4M x 36	(1) 2M x 36	(1) 2M x 36	NONE

Continued on next page. . .

HEWLETT-PACKARD COMPANY
HP NETSERVER LE

. . . continued from previous page

DRAM CONFIGURATION (CON'T)				
Size	Bank 0	Bank 1	Bank 2	Bank 3
32MB	(1) 4M x 36	(1) 4M x 36	NONE	NONE
32MB	(1) 8M x 36	NONE	NONE	NONE
36MB	(1) 8M x 36	(1) 1M x 36	NONE	NONE
40MB	(1) 4M x 36	(1) 2M x 36	(1) 2M x 36	(1) 2M x 36
40MB	(1) 8M x 36	(1) 1M x 36	(1) 1M x 36	NONE
40MB	(1) 8M x 36	(1) 2M x 36	NONE	NONE
44MB	(1) 8M x 36	(1) 1M x 36	(1) 1M x 36	(1) 1M x 36
48MB	(1) 4M x 36	(1) 4M x 36	(1) 4M x 36	NONE
48MB	(1) 8M x 36	(1) 2M x 36	(1) 2M x 36	NONE
48MB	(1) 8M x 36	(1) 4M x 36	NONE	NONE
56MB	(1) 8M x 36	(1) 2M x 36	(1) 2M x 36	(1) 2M x 36
64MB	(1) 8M x 36	(1) 4M x 36	(1) 4M x 36	NONE
64MB	(1) 4M x 36	(1) 4M x 36	(1) 4M x 36	(1) 4M x 36
64MB	(1) 8M x 36	(1) 8M x 36	NONE	NONE
80MB	(1) 8M x 36	(1) 4M x 36	(1) 4M x 36	(1) 4M x 36
96MB	(1) 8M x 36	(1) 8M x 36	(1) 8M x 36	NONE
128MB	(1) 8M x 36	(1) 8M x 36	(1) 8M x 36	(1) 8M x 36

CPU TYPE CONFIGURATION		
Type	SW1/6	SW1/7
80487SX	Off	On
80486DX	On	Off

VIDEO MEMORY CONFIGURATION		
Size	Bank 0	Bank 1
256KB	(2) 256 x 4	NONE
512KB	(2) 256 x 4	(2) 256 x 4
Note: The location of Bank 0 is unidentified.		

HEWLETT-PACKARD COMPANY
HP NETSERVER LM

Processor	80486DX/80486DX2/Pentium (depends on CPU card installed)
Processor Speed	33/60/66(internal)/66/90MHz (depends on CPU card installed)
Chip Set	Hewlett Packard
Max. Onboard DRAM	384MB (256MB on external memory card)
Cache	None
BIOS	Phoenix
Dimensions	330mm x 218mm
I/O Options	32-bit external memory card, 32-bit CPU card, floppy drive interface, IDE interface, SCSI interface (2), parallel port, VGA feature connector, VGA port
NPU Options	None

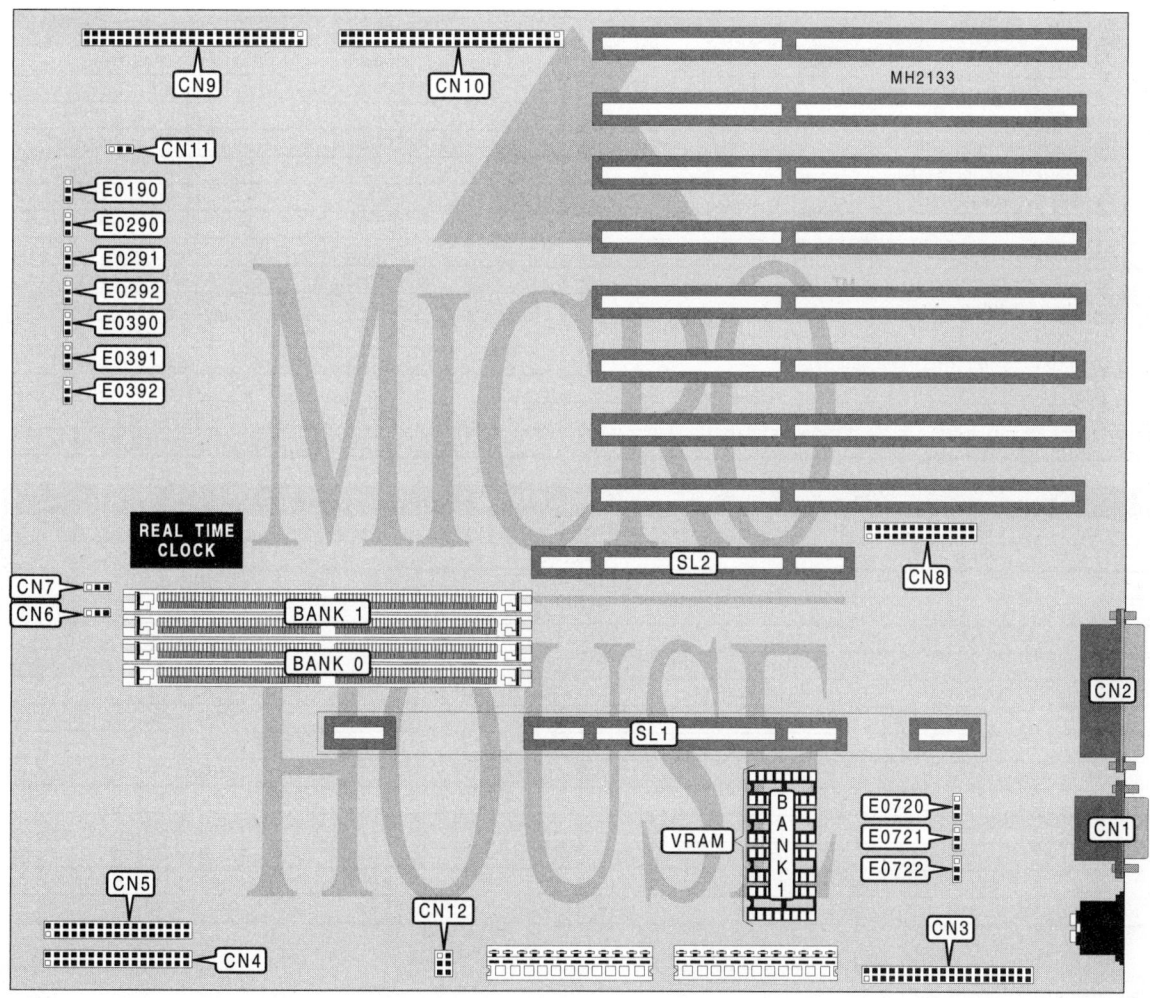

Continued on next page...

HEWLETT-PACKARD COMPANY
HP NETSERVER LM

...continued from previous page

CONNECTIONS			
Purpose	**Location**	**Purpose**	**Location**
VGA port	CN1	VGA feature connector	CN8
Parallel port	CN2	SCSI - 2 connector (channel B)	CN9
IDE interface	CN3	SCSI - 2 connector (channel A)	CN10
Control panel connector	CN4	IDE interface LED	CN11
Floppy drive interface	CN5	External battery	CN12
Chassis fan power	CN6	32-bit CPU card	SL1
IDE interface LED	CN7	32-bit external memory card	SL2

USER CONFIGURABLE SETTINGS		
Function	**Jumper**	**Position**
✧ Flash BIOS write protect enabled	E0190	pins 1 & 2 closed
Flash BIOS write protect disabled	E0190	pins 2 & 3 closed
✧ On board video enabled	E0290	pins 1 & 2 closed
On board video disabled	E0290	pins 2 & 3 closed
✧ Floppy drive write enabled	E0291	pins 2 & 3 closed
Floppy drive write disabled	E0291	pins 1 & 2 closed
✧ CMOS memory normal operation	E0292	pins 1 & 2 closed
CMOS memory clear	E0292	pins 2 & 3 closed
✧ Password enabled	E0390	pins 2 & 3 closed
Password disabled	E0390	pins 1 & 2 closed
✧ Flash BIOS write protect enabled	E0721	pins 1 & 2 closed
Flash BIOS write protect disabled	E0721	pins 2 & 3 closed
✧ I/O address select 46E8H	E0722	pins 1 & 2 closed
I/O address select 03C3H	E0722	pins 2 & 3 closed

DRAM CONFIGURATION		
Size	**Bank 0**	**Bank 1**
8MB	(2) 1M x 36	NONE
16MB	(2) 1M x 36	(2) 1M x 36
16MB	(2) 2M x 36	NONE
24MB	(2) 2M x 36	(2) 1M x 36
32MB	(2) 2M x 36	(2) 2M x 36
32MB	(2) 4M x 36	NONE
40MB	(2) 4M x 36	(2) 1M x 36
48MB	(2) 4M x 36	(2) 2M x 36
64MB	(2) 4M x 36	(2) 4M x 36
64MB	(2) 8M x 36	NONE
72MB	(2) 8M x 36	(2) 1M x 36
80MB	(2) 8M x 36	(2) 2M x 36
96MB	(2) 8M x 36	(2) 4M x 36
128MB	(2) 8M x 36	(2) 8M x 36

Continued on next page...

HEWLETT-PACKARD COMPANY
HP NETSERVER LM

. . . continued from previous page

DRAM JUMPER CONFIGURATION		
Size installed	E0391	E0392
1M x 36 or 2M x 36	pins 1 & 2 closed	pins 1 & 2 closed
4M x 36 or 8M x 36	pins 2 & 3 closed	pins 2 & 3 closed

VIDEO MEMORY CONFIGURATION		
Size	Bank 0	Bank 1
512KB	(4) 256K x 4	NONE
1MB	(4) 256K x 4	(4) 256K x 4

Note: The location of Bank 0 is unidentified.

VIDEO JUMPER CONFIGURATION	
Size	E0720
512KB	pins 1 & 2 closed
1MB	pins 2 & 3 closed

222 Motherboard Settings & Specifications

IBM CORPORATION
APTIVA 2134/2176 A-1

Processor	Pentium
Processor Speed	100/120/133/150/166/200MHz
Chip Set	Unidentified
Video Chip Set	None
Maximum Onboard Memory	128MB
Maximum Video Memory	None
Cache	256/512KB
BIOS	Unidentified
Dimensions	330mm x 218mm
I/O Options	Floppy drive interface, IDE interfaces (2), parallel port, PS/2 mouse port, serial ports (2), VESA video feature connector, VGA port, riser slot, cache slot, feature connector, VGA interface, power supply connectors (2)
NPU Options	None

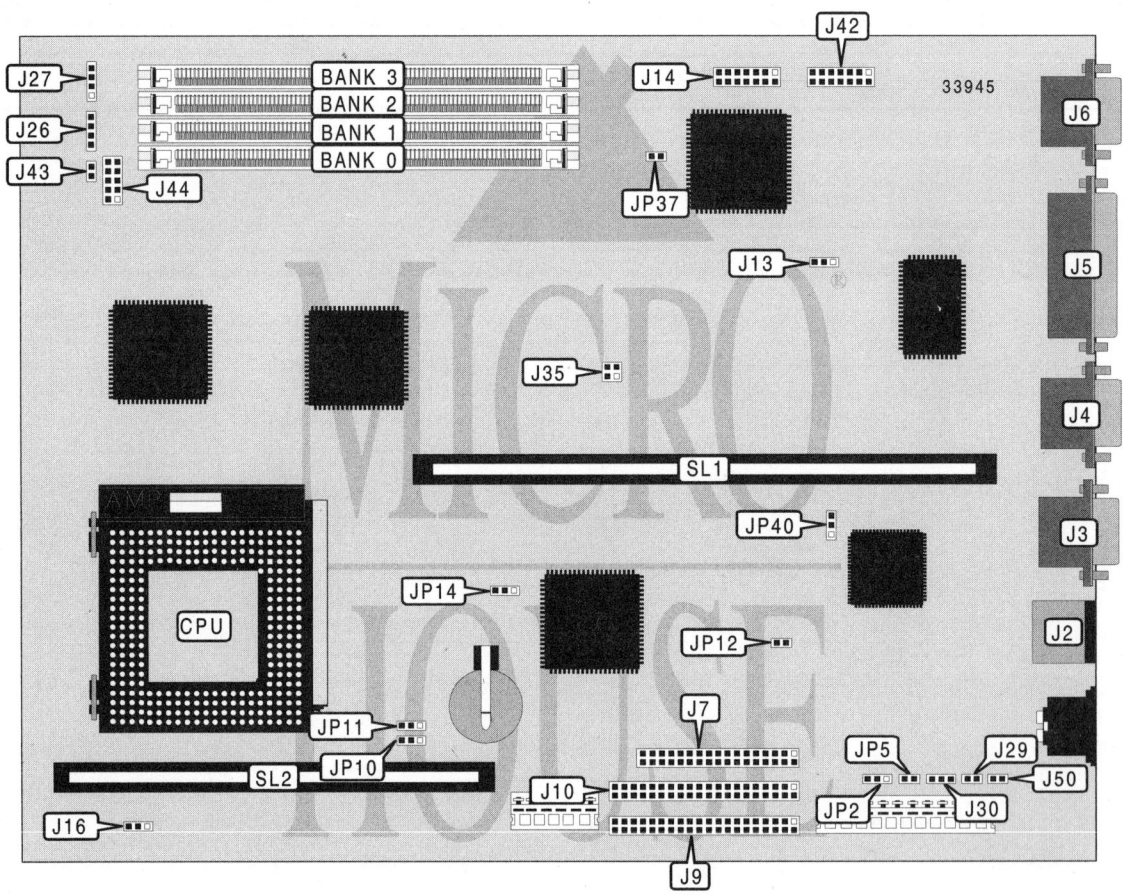

Continued on next page...

IBM CORPORATION
APTIVA 2134/2176 A-1

...continued from previous page

CONNECTIONS			
Purpose	**Location**	**Purpose**	**Location**
PS/2 mouse port	J2	Speaker	J27
Serial port 1	J3	Power supply connector	J29
Serial port 2	J4	Power supply connector	J30
Parallel port	J5	VGA interface	J42
VGA port	J6	Chassis fan power	J43
Floppy drive interface	J7	Feature connector	J44
IDE interface 1	J9	External speaker connector	J50
IDE interface 2	J10	Wake up on ring connector	JP5
VESA video feature connector	J14	Riser slot	SL1
LED connector	J26	Cache slot	SL2

USER CONFIGURABLE SETTINGS		
Function	**Label**	**Position**
Flash BIOS normal operation	J13	Pins 1 & 2 closed
Flash BIOS recovery mode	J13	Pins 2 & 3 closed
⇨ Smart energy system enabled	JP2	Pins 2 & 3 closed
Smart energy system disabled	JP2	Pins 1 & 2 closed
PS/2 mouse enabled	JP12	Pins 1 & 2 closed
PS/2 mouse disabled	JP12	Pins 2 & 3 closed
⇨ CMOS memory normal operation	JP14	Pins 1 & 2 closed
CMOS memory clear	JP14	Pins 2 & 3 closed
On board video enabled	JP37	Closed
On board video disabled	JP37	Open
PS/2 mouse & keyboard enabled	JP40	Pins 1 & 2 closed
PS/2 mouse & keyboard disabled	JP40	Pins 2 & 3 closed

DRAM CONFIGURATION				
Size	**Bank 0**	**Bank 1**	**Bank 2**	**Bank 3**
8MB	(1) 2M x 36	None	None	None
8MB	(1) 1M x 36	(1) 1M x 36	None	None
8MB	None	None	(1) 1M x 36	(1) 1M x 36
12MB	(1) 1M x 36	None	(1) 1M x 36	(1) 1M x 36
16MB	(1) 4M x 36	None	None	None
16MB	(1) 2M x 36	(1) 2M x 36	None	None
16MB	(1) 1M x 36	(1) 1M x 36	(1) 1M x 36	(1) 1M x 36
16MB	(1) 2M x 36	None	(1) 1M x 36	(1) 1M x 36
16MB	None	None	(1) 2M x 36	(1) 2M x 36
20MB	(1) 1M x 36	None	(1) 2M x 36	(1) 2M x 36
24MB	(1) 2M x 36	(1) 2M x 36	(1) 1M x 36	(1) 1M x 36
24MB	(1) 1M x 36	(1) 1M x 36	(1) 2M x 36	(1) 2M x 36
24MB	(1) 4M x 36	None	(1) 1M x 36	(1) 1M x 36
24MB	(1) 2M x 36	None	(1) 2M x 36	(1) 2M x 36

Continued on next page...

IBM CORPORATION
APTIVA 2134/2176 A-1

...continued from previous page

DRAM CONFIGURATION (CON'T)				
Size	**Bank 0**	**Bank 1**	**Bank 2**	**Bank 3**
32MB	(1) 8M x 36	None	None	None
32MB	(1) 4M x 36	(1) 4M x 36	None	None
32MB	(1) 2M x 36	(1) 2M x 36	(1) 2M x 36	(1) 2M x 36
32MB	(1) 4M x 36	None	(1) 2M x 36	(1) 2M x 36
32MB	None	None	(1) 4M x 36	(1) 4M x 36
36MB	(1) 1M x 36	None	(1) 4M x 36	(1) 4M x 36
40MB	(1) 4M x 36	(1) 4M x 36	(1) 1M x 36	(1) 1M x 36
40MB	(1) 1M x 36	(1) 1M x 36	(1) 4M x 36	(1) 4M x 36
40MB	(1) 8M x 36	None	(1) 1M x 36	(1) 1M x 36
40MB	(1) 2M x 36	None	(1) 4M x 36	(1) 4M x 36
48MB	(1) 4M x 36	(1) 4M x 36	(1) 2M x 36	(1) 2M x 36
48MB	(1) 2M x 36	(1) 2M x 36	(1) 4M x 36	(1) 4M x 36
48MB	(1) 8M x 36	None	(1) 2M x 36	(1) 2M x 36
48MB	(1) 4M x 36	None	(1) 4M x 36	(1) 4M x 36
64MB	(1) 8M x 36	(1) 8M x 36	None	None
64MB	(1) 4M x 36	(1) 4M x 36	(1) 4M x 36	(1) 4M x 36
64MB	(1) 8M x 36	None	(1) 4M x 36	(1) 4M x 36
64MB	None	None	(1) 8M x 36	(1) 8M x 36
68MB	(1) 1M x 36	None	(1) 8M x 36	(1) 8M x 36
72MB	(1) 8M x 36	(1) 8M x 36	(1) 1M x 36	(1) 1M x 36
72MB	(1) 1M x 36	(1) 1M x 36	(1) 8M x 36	(1) 8M x 36
72MB	(1) 2M x 36	None	(1) 8M x 36	(1) 8M x 36
80MB	(1) 8M x 36	(1) 8M x 36	(1) 2M x 36	(1) 2M x 36
80MB	(1) 2M x 36	(1) 2M x 36	(1) 8M x 36	(1) 8M x 36
80MB	(1) 4M x 36	None	(1) 8M x 36	(1) 8M x 36
96MB	(1) 8M x 36	(1) 8M x 36	(1) 4M x 36	(1) 4M x 36
96MB	(1) 4M x 36	(1) 4M x 36	(1) 8M x 36	(1) 8M x 36
96MB	(1) 8M x 36	None	(1) 8M x 36	(1) 8M x 36
128MB	(1) 8M x 36	(1) 8M x 36	(1) 8M x 36	(1) 8M x 36

CACHE CONFIGURATION	
Size	**SL1**
256KB	256KB module installed
512KB	512KB module installed

CACHE JUMPER CONFIGURATION	
Size	**J16**
256KB	Pins 2 & 3 closed
512KB	Pins 1 & 2 closed

Continued on next page...

IBM CORPORATION
APTIVA 2134/2176 A-1

...continued from previous page

CPU SPEED SELECTION	
CPU clock speed	**JP35**
50MHz	Pins 1 & 2 closed
55MHz	Open
60MHz	Pins 3 & 4 closed
66MHz	Pins 1 & 2, 3 & 4 closed

CPU MULTIPLIER SELECTION			
Multiplier	**Clock speed**	**JP10**	**JP11**
1/3	50MHz	Pins 2 & 3 closed	Pins 1 & 2 closed
2/5	60MHz	Pins 1 & 2 closed	Pins 1 & 2 closed
1/2	66MHz	Pins 1 & 2 closed	Pins 2 & 3 closed
2/3	60MHz	Pins 2 & 3 closed	Pins 2 & 3 closed

226 Motherboard Settings & Specifications

IBM CORPORATION
APTIVA 2136

Processor	CX M1/IBM/Pentium
Processor Speed	100/120/133/150/166/200MHz
Chip Set	Unidentified
Video Chip Set	Unidentified
Maximum Onboard Memory	128MB (EDO supported)
Maximum Video Memory	1MB
Cache	256/512KB
BIOS	Unidentified
Dimensions	330mm x 218mm
I/O Options	Floppy drive interface, green PC connector, IDE interfaces (2), parallel port, PS/2 mouse port, serial ports (2), VGA feature connector, VGA port, riser slot, fax/modem/voice connector, line in, CD-ROM audio in, audio in connector,
NPU Options	None

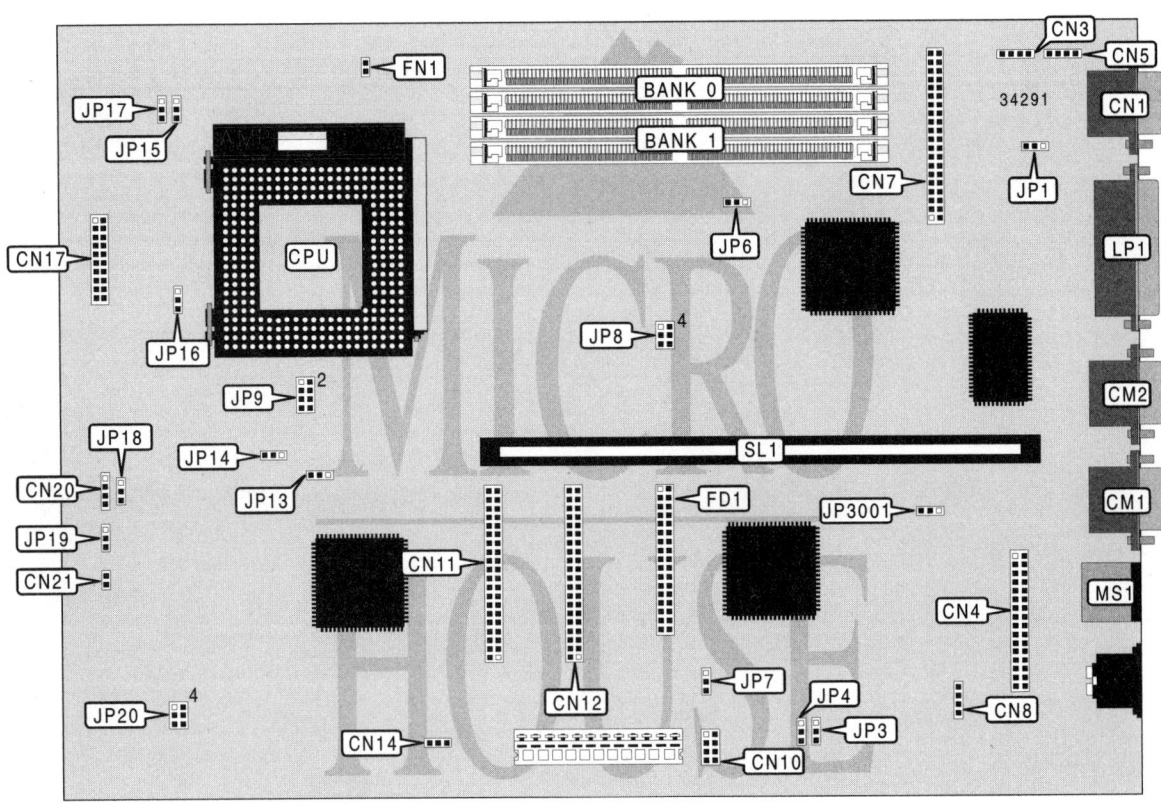

Continued on next page...

IBM CORPORATION
APTIVA 2136

...continued from previous page

CONNECTIONS			
Purpose	**Location**	**Purpose**	**Location**
Floppy drive interface	FD1	Software shutdown connector	CN14
Chassis fan power	FN1	Power LED & keylock	CN17/pins 3 - 5
VGA port	CN1	IDE interface LED	CN20
Fax/modem/voice connector	CN3	Power switch	CN21
Audio in connector	CN4	Serial port	CM1
Line in	CN5	Serial port	CM2
VGA feature connector	CN7	Green PC connector	JP19
CD-ROM audio in	CN8	Parallel port	LP1
Wavetable connector	CN10	PS/2 mouse port	MS1
IDE interface 1	CN11	Riser slot	SL1
IDE interface 2	CN12		

USER CONFIGURABLE SETTINGS		
Function	**Label**	**Position**
◊ On board video enabled	JP1	Pins 2 & 3 closed
On board video disabled	JP1	Pins 1 & 2 closed
◊ Factory configured - do not alter	JP3	Pins 1 & 2 closed
◊ Password enabled	JP4	Pins 1 & 2 closed
Password disabled	JP4	Pins 2 & 3 closed
◊ BIOS select flash BIOS	JP7	Pins 2 & 3 closed
BIOS select block ROM	JP7	Pins 1 & 2 closed
◊ LED select IDE & floppy LEDs	JP18	Pins 1 & 2 closed
LED select IDE LED only	JP18	Pins 2 & 3 closed
◊ Factory configured - Software shut down enabled	JP20	Pins 1 & 2, 4 & 5 closed
◊ Flash BIOS write protect disabled	JP3001	Pins 2 & 3 closed
Flash BIOS write protect enabled	JP3001	Pins 1 & 2 closed

DRAM CONFIGURATION		
Size	**Bank 0**	**Bank 1**
8MB	(2) 1M x 32	None
16MB	(2) 2M x 32	None
16MB	(2) 1M x 32	(2) 1M x 32
24MB	(2) 2M x 32	(2) 1M x 32
32MB	(2) 4M x 32	None
32MB	(2) 2M x 32	(2) 2M x 32
40MB	(2) 4M x 32	(2) 1M x 32
48MB	(2) 4M x 32	(2) 2M x 32
64MB	(2) 8M x 32	None
64MB	(2) 4M x 32	(2) 4M x 32
72MB	(2) 8M x 32	(2) 1M x 32
80MB	(2) 8M x 32	(2) 2M x 32
96MB	(2) 8M x 32	(2) 4M x 32
128MB	(2) 8M x 32	(2) 8M x 32
Note: Board accepts EDO memory. Banks are interchangeable.		

Continued on next page...

IBM CORPORATION
APTIVA 2136

. . . continued from previous page

CACHE CONFIGURATION

Size	Bank 0
256KB	(2) 32K x 32
512KB	(2) 64K x 32

Note: The location of the cache is unidentified.

CACHE JUMPER CONFIGURATION

Size	JP6
256KB	Pins 1 & 2 closed
512KB	Pins 2 & 3 closed

CACHE OPERATION CONFIGURATION

Type	JP16
⇨ Interleave burst	Pins 1 & 2 closed
Linear burst	Pins 2 & 3 closed

VIDEO MEMORY CONFIGURATION

Note: 1MB video memory is factory installed and is not configurable. The location is unidentified.

CPU SPEED SELECTION (CYRIX)

CPU speed	Clock speed	Multiplier	JP8	JP15	JP17
120MHz	50MHz	2x	1 & 4	1 & 2	2 & 3
150MHz	60MHz	2x	2 & 5	1 & 2	2 & 3
166MHz	66MHz	2x	3 & 6	1 & 2	2 & 3

Note: Pins designated should be in the closed position.

CPU SPEED SELECTION (IBM)

CPU speed	Clock speed	Multiplier	JP8	JP15	JP17
120MHz	50MHz	2x	1 & 4	1 & 2	2 & 3
150MHz	60MHz	2x	2 & 5	1 & 2	2 & 3
166MHz	66MHz	2x	3 & 6	1 & 2	2 & 3

Note: Pins designated should be in the closed position.

CPU SPEED SELECTION (INTEL)

CPU speed	Clock speed	Multiplier	JP8	JP15	JP17
100MHz	66MHz	1.5x	3 & 6	1 & 2	1 & 2
120MHz	60MHz	2x	2 & 5	1 & 2	2 & 3
133MHz	66MHz	2x	3 & 6	1 & 2	2 & 3
150MHz	60MHz	2.5x	2 & 5	2 & 3	2 & 3
166MHz	66MHz	2.5x	3 & 6	2 & 3	2 & 3
200MHz	66MHz	3x	3 & 6	2 & 3	1 & 2

Note: Pins designated should be in the closed position.

Continued on next page. . .

IBM CORPORATION
APTIVA 2136

. . . continued from previous page

CPU VOLTAGE SELECTION	
Type	**JP9**
Single	Pins 1 & 2, 3 & 4, 5 & 6, 7 & 8 closed
Dual	Open

CPU VOLTAGE SELECTION (SINGLE)	
Voltage	**JP14**
3.35v	Pins 2 & 3 closed
3.5v	Pins 1 & 2 closed

CPU VOLTAGE SELECTION (DUAL)			
Voltage	**V core**	**JP13**	**JP14**
3.35v	2.5v	Pins 2 & 3 closed	Pins 2 & 3 closed
3.35v	2.8v	Pins 1 & 2 closed	Pins 2 & 3 closed
3.5v	2.5v	Pins 2 & 3 closed	Pins 1 & 2 closed
3.5v	2.8v	Pins 1 & 2 closed	Pins 1 & 2 closed

230 Motherboard Settings & Specifications

IBM CORPORATION
APTIVA 2144, 2168 TYPE H-2, I-2

Processor	CX M1/Pentium
Processor Speed	75/90/100/120/133/150/166MHz
Chip Set	Unidentified
Video Chip Set	Unidentified
Maximum Onboard Memory	128MB (EDO supported)
Maximum Video Memory	2MB
Cache	256/512KB
BIOS	Unidentified
Dimensions	330mm x 218mm
I/O Options	Floppy drive interface, IDE interfaces (2), parallel port, PS/2 mouse port, ports (2), VESA feature connector, VGA port, VGA interface, riser slot, cache slots (2), VRM connector, modem wake up connector, power supply connectors (2)
NPU Options	None

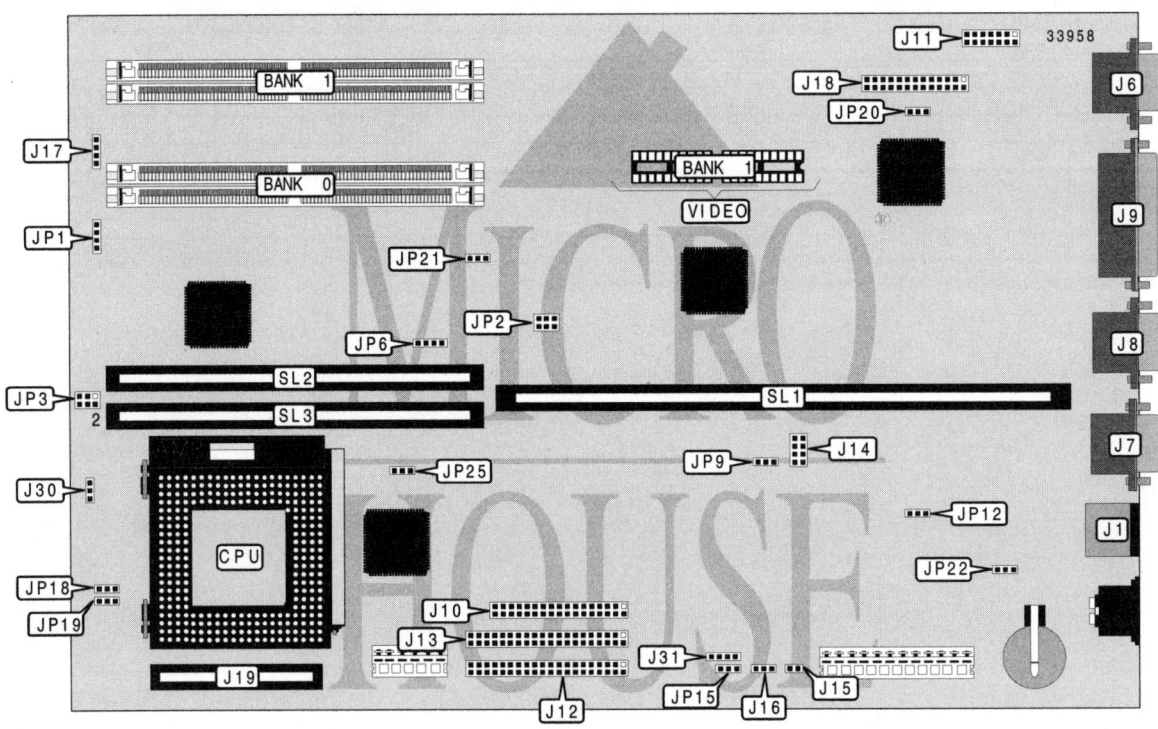

Continued on next page...

IBM CORPORATION
APTIVA 2144, 2168 TYPE H-2, I-2

...continued from previous page

CONNECTIONS			
Purpose	**Location**	**Purpose**	**Location**
PS/2 mouse port	J1	32-bit PCI slots	J16
VGA port	J6	Power LED	J17 pins 1 & 2
Serial port 1	J7	IDE interface LED	J17 pins 3 & 4
Serial port 2	J8	VESA feature connector	J18
Parallel port	J9	External VRM connector	J19
Floppy drive interface	J10	Chassis fan power	J30
VGA interface	J11	Modem wake up connector	J31
IDE interface 1	J12	Speaker	JP1
IDE interface 2	J13	Riser slot	SL1
VRM connector	J14	Cache slot 2	SL2
Power supply connector	J15	Cache slot 1	SL3

USER CONFIGURABLE SETTINGS		
Function	**Label**	**Position**
Flash BIOS normal operation	JP9	Pins 1 & 2 closed
Floppy drive write protect enabled	JP12	Pins 1 & 2 closed
Floppy drive write protect disabled	JP12	Open
Smart Energy System enabled	JP15	Pins 2 & 3 closed
Smart Energy System disabled	JP15	Pins 1 & 2 closed
† CMOS memory normal operation	JP22	Pins 1 & 2 closed
CMOS memory clear	JP22	Open

DRAM CONFIGURATION		
Size	**Bank 0**	**Bank 1**
8MB	(2) 1M x 36	None
16MB	(2) 2M x 36	None
16MB	(2) 1M x 36	(2) 1M x 36
24MB	(2) 2M x 36	(2) 1M x 36
32MB	(2) 4M x 36	None
32MB	(2) 2M x 36	(2) 2M x 36
40MB	(2) 4M x 36	(2) 1M x 36
48MB	(2) 4M x 36	(2) 2M x 36
64MB	(2) 8M x 36	None
64MB	(2) 4M x 36	(2) 4M x 36
72MB	(2) 8M x 36	(2) 1M x 36
80MB	(2) 8M x 36	(2) 2M x 36
96MB	(2) 8M x 36	(2) 4M x 36
128MB	(2) 8M x 36	(2) 8M x 36

Note: Board accepts EDO memory. Board also accepts x 32 SIMMs. Banks are interchangeable.

DRAM JUMPER CONFIGURATION	
Type	**JP20**
Normal DRAM	Pins 1 & 2 closed
EDO DRAM	Pins 2 & 3 closed

Continued on next page...

IBM CORPORATION
APTIVA 2144, 2168 TYPE H-2, I-2

...continued from previous page

CACHE CONFIGURATION		
Size	**SL1**	**SL2**
256KB	256KB module installed	Not installed
512KB	256KB module installed	256KB module installed

CACHE JUMPER CONFIGURATION	
Size	**JP6**
256KB	Pins 1 & 3, 2 & 4 closed
512KB	Pins 3 & 5, 4 & 6 closed

VIDEO MEMORY CONFIGURATION		
Size	**Bank 0**	**Bank 1**
1MB	1MB	None
2MB	1MB	(2) 256K x 16

Note: The location of bank 0 is unidentified.

CPU SPEED SELECTION					
CPU speed	**Clock speed**	**Multiplier**	**JP2**	**JP3**	**JP25**
75MHz	50MHz	1.5x	1 & 3, 2 & 4	1 & 3	1 & 2
90MHz	60MHz	1.5x	1 & 3, 4 & 6	1 & 3	1 & 2
100MHz	66MHz	1.5x	3 & 5, 4 & 6	1 & 3	1 & 2
120MHz	60MHz	2x	1 & 3, 4 & 6	1 & 3, 2 & 4	1 & 2
133MHz	66MHz	2x	3 & 5, 4 & 6	1 & 3, 2 & 4	1 & 2
150MHz	60MHz	2.5x	1 & 3, 4 & 6	1 & 3, 2 & 4	2 & 3
166MHz	66MHz	2.5x	3 & 5, 4 & 6	1 & 3, 2 & 4	2 & 3

Note: Pins designated should be in the closed position.

CPU TYPE SELECTION		
Type	**JP18**	**JP19**
Cyrix	Pins 2 & 3 closed	Pins 2 & 3 closed
Intel	Pins 1 & 2 closed	Pins 1 & 2 closed

CPU VOLTAGE SELECTION	
Voltage	**JP21**
3.3v	Pins 2 & 3 closed
5v	Pins 1 & 2 closed

IBM CORPORATION
APTIVA 2159

Processor	Pentium
Processor Speed	133/150/166/200MHz
Chip Set	Unidentified
Video Chip Set	Unidentified
Maximum Onboard Memory	128MB (EDO supported)
Maximum Video Memory	2MB
Cache	256/512KB
BIOS	Unidentified
Dimensions	330mm x 218mm
I/O Options	Floppy drive interface, IDE interfaces (2), parallel port, PS/2 mouse port, serial port, VESA feature connector, VGA port, VGA interface, riser slot, cache slot, VRM connector, USB connector, Media console connector, wake up on ring connector
NPU Options	None

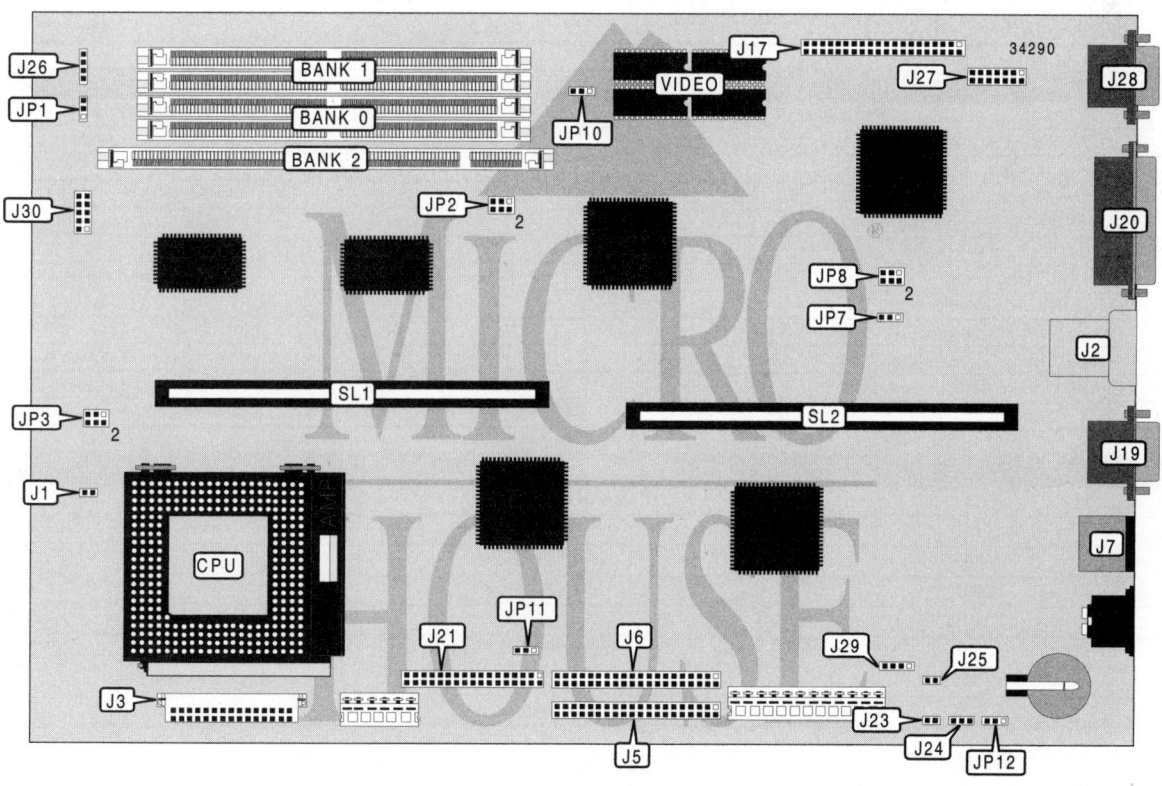

Continued on next page...

IBM CORPORATION
APTIVA 2159

. . . continued from previous page

CONNECTIONS			
Purpose	**Location**	**Purpose**	**Location**
Chassis fan power	J1	Soft off power supply	J23
USB connector	J2	Auxiliary 5v connector	J24
VRM connector	J3	Wake up on ring connector	J25
IDE interface 1	J5	IDE interface LED	J26
IDE interface 2	J6	VGA interface	J27
PS/2 mouse port	J7	VGA port	J28
VESA feature connector	J17	Speaker	J29
Serial port	J19	Media console connector	J30
Parallel port	J20	Cache slot	SL1
Floppy drive interface	J21	Riser slot	SL2

USER CONFIGURABLE SETTINGS		
Function	**Label**	**Position**
External speaker enabled	JP1	Pins 1 & 2 closed
External speaker disabled	JP1	Open
Flash BIOS write protect disabled	JP7	Pins 1 & 2 closed
Flash BIOS write protect enabled	JP7	Pins 2 & 3 closed
⇨ Factory configured - do not alter	JP8	Unidentified
On board video enabled	JP10	Pins 1 & 2 closed
On board video disabled	JP10	Pins 2 & 3 closed
Floppy drive write protect disabled	JP11	Pins 1 & 2 closed
Floppy drive write protect enabled	JP11	Pins 2 & 3 closed
⇨ CMOS memory normal operation	JP12	Pins 1 & 2 closed
CMOS memory clear	JP12	Pins 2 & 3 closed

DRAM CONFIGURATION		
Size	**Bank 0**	**Bank 1**
8MB	(2) 1M x 36	None
16MB	(2) 2M x 36	None
16MB	(2) 1M x 36	(2) 1M x 36
24MB	(2) 2M x 36	(2) 1M x 36
32MB	(2) 4M x 36	None
32MB	(2) 2M x 36	(2) 2M x 36
40MB	(2) 4M x 36	(2) 1M x 36
48MB	(2) 4M x 36	(2) 2M x 36
64MB	(2) 8M x 36	None
64MB	(2) 4M x 36	(2) 4M x 36
72MB	(2) 8M x 36	(2) 1M x 36
80MB	(2) 8M x 36	(2) 2M x 36
96MB	(2) 8M x 36	(2) 4M x 36
128MB	(2) 8M x 36	(2) 8M x 36

Note: Board accepts EDO memory. Board also accepts x 32 SIMMs. Banks are interchangeable.

Continued on next page. . .

IBM CORPORATION
APTIVA 2159

... continued from previous page

DIMM CONFIGURATION	
Size	Bank 0
8MB	(1) 1M x 64
16MB	(1) 2M x 64
32MB	(1) 4M x 64
64MB	(1) 8M x 64

CACHE CONFIGURATION	
Size	SL1
256KB	256KB module installed
512KB	512KB module installed

VIDEO MEMORY CONFIGURATION
Note: Bank 0 is factory installed with 2MB of video memory and is not configurable.

CPU SPEED SELECTION				
CPU speed	Clock speed	Multiplier	JP2	JP3
133MHz	66MHz	2x	1 & 3, 2 & 4	2 & 4, 3 & 5
150MHz	60MHz	2.5x	3 & 5, 4 & 6	3 & 5, 4 & 6
166MHz	66MHz	2.5x	1 & 3, 2 & 4	3 & 5, 4 & 6
200MHz	66MHz	3x	1 & 3, 2 & 4	1 & 3, 4 & 6
Note: Pins designated should be in the closed position.				

IBM CORPORATION
APTIVA 2168

Processor	80486SX/80486SX2/80487SX/80486DX/80486DX2/P24T
Processor Speed	25/33/50(internal)/66(internal)MHz
Chip Set	Unidentified
Video Chip Set	Unidentified
Maximum Onboard Memory	64MB
Maximum Video Memory	1MB
Cache	None
BIOS	Unidentified
Dimensions	254mm x 218mm
I/O Options	Floppy drive interface, IDE interfaces (2), parallel port, PS/2 mouse port, serial ports (2), VESA feature connector, VGA port, riser slot, wake up on ring connector
NPU Options	None

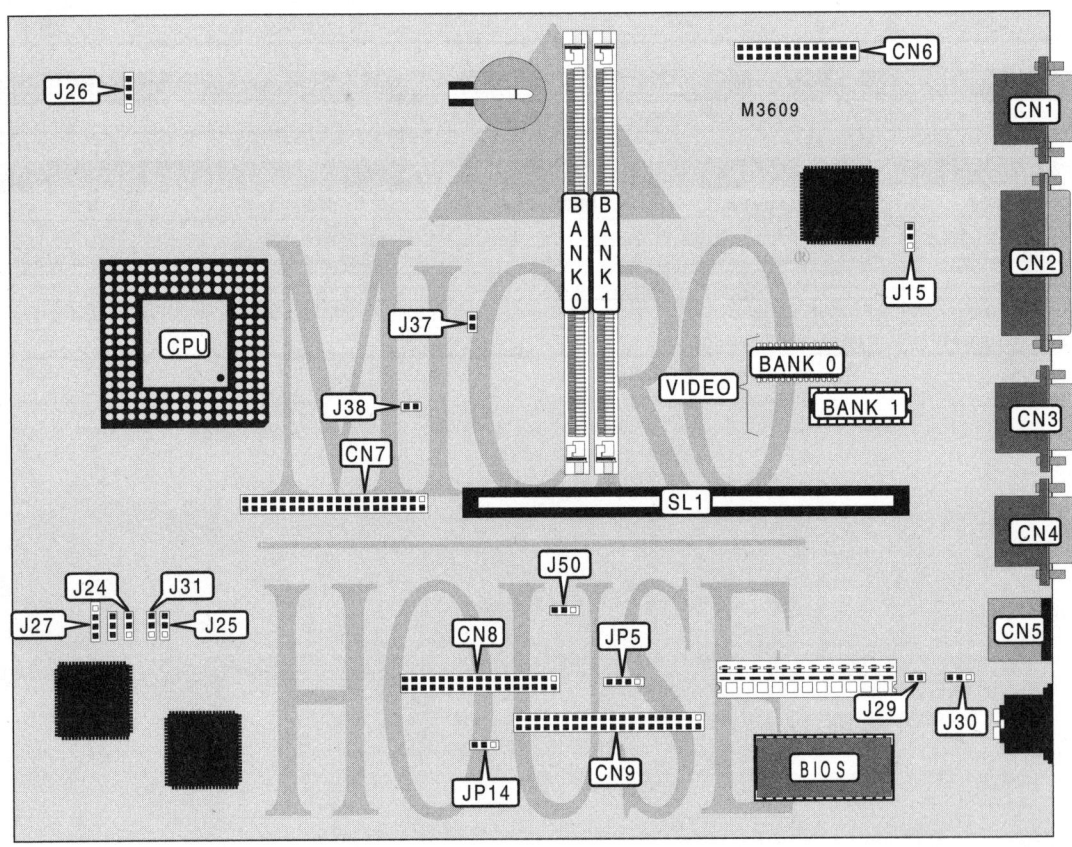

Continued on next page...

IBM CORPORATION
APTIVA 2168

. . . continued from previous page

CONNECTIONS			
Purpose	**Location**	**Purpose**	**Location**
VGA port	CN1	IDE interface 2	CN9
Parallel port	CN2	IDE interface LED	J26
Serial port	CN3	Speaker	J27
Serial port	CN4	Auxiliary power connector	J29
PS/2 mouse port	CN5	Auxiliary power connector	J30
VESA feature connector	CN6	Chassis fan power	J38
IDE interface 1	CN7	Wake up on ring connector	JP5
Floppy drive interface	CN8	Riser slot	SL1

USER CONFIGURABLE SETTINGS		
Function	**Label**	**Position**
On board video enabled	J15	Pins 1 & 2 closed
On board video disabled	J15	Pins 2 & 3 closed
Parity enabled	J50	Pins 1 & 2 closed
Parity disabled	J50	Pins 2 & 3 closed
Password normal operation	JP14	Pins 1 & 2 closed
Password clear	JP14	Pins 2 & 3 closed

DRAM CONFIGURATION		
Size	**Bank 0**	**Bank 1**
2MB	(1) 512K x 36	None
4MB	(1) 1M x 36	None
6MB	(1) 512K x 36	(1) 1M x 36
8MB	(1) 2M x 36	None
10MB	(1) 512K x 36	(1) 2M x 36
12MB	(1) 2M x 36	(1) 1M x 36
16MB	(1) 4M x 36	None
16MB	(1) 2M x 36	(1) 2M x 36
18MB	(1) 4M x 36	(1) 512K x 36
20MB	(1) 1M x 36	(1) 4M x 36
24MB	(1) 4M x 36	(1) 2M x 36
32MB	(1) 8M x 36	None
32MB	(1) 4M x 36	(1) 4M x 36
34MB	(1) 8M x 36	(1) 512K x 36
36MB	(1) 1M x 36	(1) 8M x 36
40MB	(1) 8M x 36	(1) 2M x 36
48MB	(1) 4M x 36	(1) 8M x 36
64MB	(1) 8M x 36	(1) 8M x 36
Note: Banks are interchangeable.		

Continued on next page. . .

IBM CORPORATION
APTIVA 2168

. . . continued from previous page

VIDEO MEMORY CONFIGURATION

Size	Bank 0	Bank 1
512KB	512KB	None
1MB	512KB	(1) 256K x 16

Note: 1MB video memory may be already factory installed. Bank 0 is factory installed and is not configurable.

CPU SPEED SELECTION

Speed	J37
25MHz	Closed
33MHz	Open
50iMHz	Closed
66iMHz	Open

CPU TYPE SELECTION

Processor installed	Processor upgrade	J24	J25	J31
80486SX	80486SX2	Pins 1 & 2 closed	Pins 2 & 3 closed	Pins 1 & 2 closed
80486SX	80487SX	Pins 2 & 3 closed	Pins 2 & 3 closed	Pins 1 & 2 closed
80486SX	80486DX	Pins 1 & 2 closed	Pins 2 & 3 closed	Pins 1 & 2 closed
80486SX	80486DX2	Pins 1 & 2 closed	Pins 2 & 3 closed	Pins 1 & 2 closed
80486SX	P24T	Pins 2 & 3 closed	Pins 2 & 3 closed	Pins 1 & 2 closed
80486SX2	P24T	Pins 2 & 3 closed	Pins 1 & 2 closed	Pins 2 & 3 closed
80486DX	80486SX2	Pins 2 & 3 closed	Pins 1 & 2 closed	Pins 2 & 3 closed
80486DX	80486DX2	Pins 1 & 2 closed	Pins 1 & 2 closed	Pins 2 & 3 closed
80486DX	P24T	Pins 1 & 2 closed	Pins 1 & 2 closed	Pins 2 & 3 closed
80486DX2	P24T	Pins 2 & 3 closed	Pins 1 & 2 closed	Pins 2 & 3 closed

IBM CORPORATION
APTIVA M30 (250-0441), APTIVA M31 (250-0441), APTIVA M40 (12-10609), APTIVA M41 (250-0442), APTIVA M50 (250-0440), APTIVA M53 (250-0443), APTIVA M71 (250-0444)

Processor	CX M1/Pentium
Processor Speed	75/100/133MHz
Chip Set	VLSI
Video Chip Set	Trident
Maximum Onboard Memory	128MB (EDO supported)
Maximum Video Memory	2MB
Cache	256/512KB
BIOS	Unidentified
Dimensions	330mm x 218mm
I/O Options	Floppy drive interface, IDE interfaces (2), parallel port, PS/2 mouse port, serial ports (2), VESA feature connector, VGA port, riser slot, cache slots (2), internal VGA connector, power switch connector, wake up on ring connector
NPU Options	None

Continued on next page...

IBM CORPORATION
APTIVA M30 (250-0441), APTIVA M31 (250-0441),
APTIVA M40 (12-10609), APTIVA M41 (250-0442),
APTIVA M50 (250-0440), APTIVA M53 (250-0443),
APTIVA M71 (250-0444)

...continued from previous page

CONNECTIONS

Purpose	Location	Purpose	Location
PS/2 mouse port	CN2	Internal VGA connector	J11
Serial port 2	CN3	Power switch connector	J16
Serial port 1	CN4	IDE interface LED	J17
Parallel port	CN5	VESA feature connector	J18
VGA port	CN6	Speaker	JP1
Floppy drive interface	CN7	Chassis fan power	JP2
IDE interface 2	CN8	Riser slot	SL1
IDE interface 1	CN9	Cache slots	SL2 & SL3
Wake up on ring connector	J1		

USER CONFIGURABLE SETTINGS

Function	Label	Position
✧ Factory configured - do not alter	JP2	Unidentified
✧ CMOS memory normal operation	JP12	Pins 1 & 2 closed
CMOS memory clear	JP12	Pins 2 & 3 closed
Floppy drive write enabled	JP22	Pins 1 & 2 closed
Floppy drive write disabled	JP22	Pins 2 & 3 closed

DRAM CONFIGURATION

Size	Bank 0	Bank 1
8MB	(2) 1M x 36	None
16MB	(2) 2M x 36	None
16MB	(2) 1M x 36	(2) 1M x 36
24MB	(2) 1M x 36	(2) 2M x 36
32MB	(2) 4M x 36	None
32MB	(2) 2M x 36	(2) 2M x 36
40MB	(2) 1M x 36	(2) 4M x 36
48MB	(2) 4M x 36	(2) 2M x 36
64MB	(2) 8M x 36	None
64MB	(2) 4M x 36	(2) 4M x 36
72MB	(2) 1M x 36	(2) 8M x 36
80MB	(2) 8M x 36	(2) 2M x 36
96MB	(2) 4M x 36	(2) 8M x 36
128MB	(2) 8M x 36	(2) 8M x 36

Note: Board accepts EDO memory. Board also accepts x 32 SIMMs. Banks are interchangeable.

Continued on next page...

IBM CORPORATION
APTIVA M30 (250-0441), APTIVA M31 (250-0441),
APTIVA M40 (12-10609), APTIVA M41 (250-0442),
APTIVA M50 (250-0440), APTIVA M53 (250-0443),
APTIVA M71 (250-0444)

...continued from previous page

CACHE CONFIGURATION			
Size	SL2	SL3	TAG
256KB	256KB module installed	Not installed	(1) 32K x 8
512KB	256KB module installed	256KB module installed	(1) 32K x 8

Note: The location of the TAG is unidentified.

CACHE JUMPER CONFIGURATION	
Size	JP6
None	Pins 1 & 3, 2 & 4 closed
256KB	Pins 1 & 3, 2 & 4 closed
512KB	Pins 3 & 5, 4 & 6 closed

VIDEO MEMORY CONFIGURATION		
Size	Bank 0	Bank 1
1MB	1MB	None
2MB	1MB	1MB

Note: The location of bank 0 is unidentified. The size of the memory chips are unidentified.

CPU SPEED SELECTION		
CPU	Speed	JP23
CX M1	3/1	Pins 4 & 6 closed
CX M1	2/1	Pins 2 & 4 closed
P54	3/2	Open
P54	2/1	Pins 2 & 4 closed
P54C	-	Pins 1 & 3 closed
P55C	-	Pins 3 & 5 closed
ASM M1	-	Open

CPU MULTIPLIER SELECTION	
Multiplier	JP25
2x	Pins 1 & 2 closed
2.5x	Pins 2 & 3 closed

CPU TYPE SELECTION	
Type	JP9
CX M1	Pins 2 & 3 closed
P54C	Pins 1 & 2 closed
P55C	N/A

CPU VOLTAGE SELECTION	
Voltage	JP21
3.3v	Pins 2 & 3 closed
5v	Pins 1 & 2 closed

IBM CORPORATION
EDUQUEST 9606 (MODELS 040/04X)

Processor	80486SLC
Processor Speed	25/50(internal)MHz
Chip Set	Unidentified
Video Chip Set	Unidentified
Maximum Onboard Memory	16MB
Maximum Video Memory	512KB
Cache	None
BIOS	Unidentified
Dimensions	254mm x 218mm
I/O Options	Floppy drive interface, IDE interface, parallel port, PS/2 mouse port, serial port, feature connector, monitor connector, riser slot
NPU Options	Unidentified

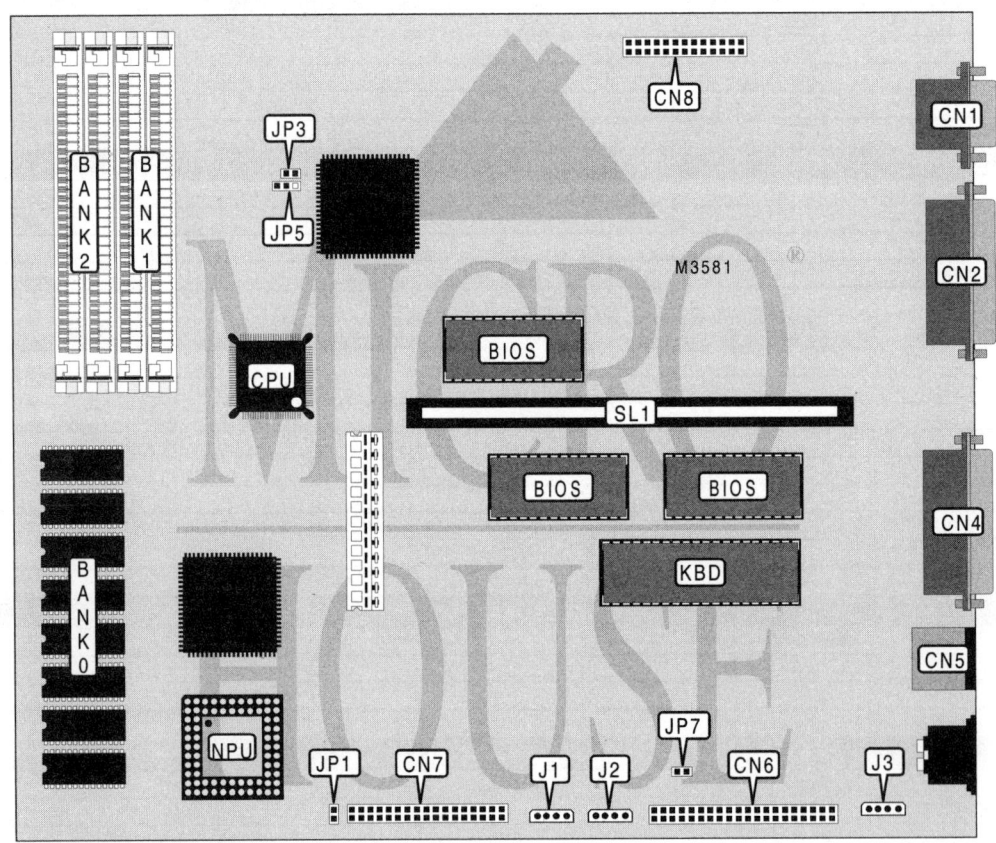

Continued on next page. . .

IBM CORPORATION
EDUQUEST 9606 (MODELS 040/04X)

...continued from previous page

CONNECTIONS

Purpose	Location	Purpose	Location
Monitor connector	CN1	Feature connector	CN8
Parallel port	CN2	Floppy drive power connector	J1
Serial port	CN4	Floppy drive power connector 5.25"	J2
PS/2 mouse port	CN5	IDE interface power connector	J3
IDE interface	CN6	Riser slot	SL1
Floppy drive interface	CN7		

USER CONFIGURABLE SETTINGS

Function	Label	Position
⇨ Factory configured - do not alter	JP1	Open
⇨ Feature connector not used with an Action Media card	JP3	Open
Feature connector uses adapter card and feature video connector	JP3	Closed
⇨ On board video enabled	JP5	Pins 1 & 2 closed
On board video disabled	JP5	Pins 2 & 3 closed
⇨ Password normal operation	JP7	Open
Password clear	JP7	Closed

DRAM CONFIGURATION (MODELS 040/04X)

Size	Bank 0	Bank 1	Bank 2
1MB	4MB	None	None
3MB	4MB	(2) 1M x 9	None
5MB	4MB	(2) 1M x 9	(2) 1M x 9
8MB	4MB	(2) 4M x 9	None
16MB	4MB	(2) 4M x 9	(2) 4M x 9

Note: Bank 0 is factory installed and is not configurable. When 16MB is installed, bank 0 is disabled.

VIDEO MEMORY CONFIGURATION

Note: Board is installed with 512KB memory. The location is unidentified.

IBM CORPORATION
INTELLISTATION (TYPE 6888)

Processor	Pentium II
Processor Speed	233/266MHz
Chip Set	Unidentified
Video Chip Set	Unidentified
Maximum Onboard Memory	Unidentified
Maximum Video Memory	1MB
Cache	256/512KB (located on Pentium II CPU)
BIOS	Unidentified
Dimensions	254mm x 218mm
I/O Options	Ethernet 10BaseT connector, floppy drive interface, IDE interfaces (2), parallel port, PS/2 mouse port, serial ports (2), VGA feature connector, VGA port, riser slot, IR connector, USB connectors (2), line out, line in, CD-ROM audio in, wavetable connector, telajack connector, wake on LAN connector, wake on modem connector
NPU Options	None

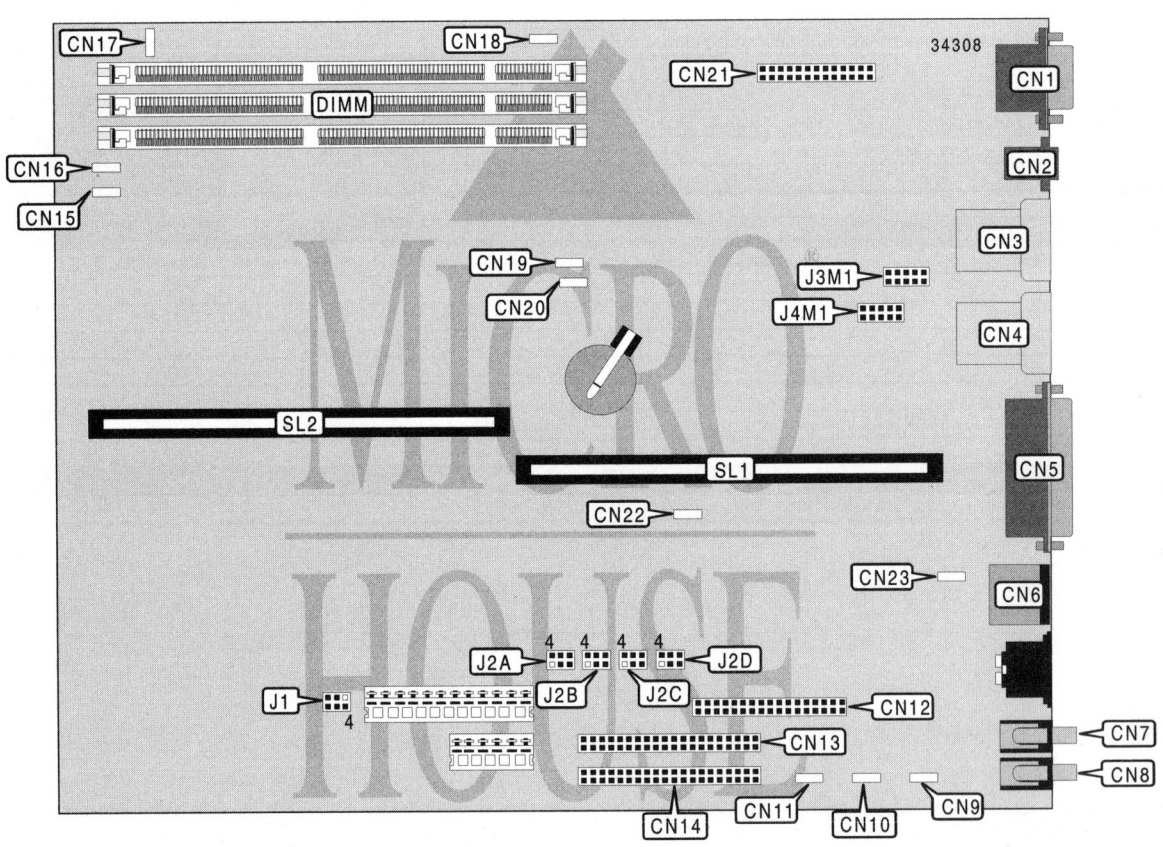

Continued on next page...

IBM CORPORATION
INTELLISTATION (TYPE 6888)

. . . continued from previous page

CONNECTIONS			
Purpose	**Location**	**Purpose**	**Location**
VGA port	CN1	Soft off power supply	CN15
Ethernet 10BaseT connector	CN2	Power LED/ IDE interface LED	CN16
USB connector 2	CN3	Chassis fan power	CN17
USB connector 1	CN4	SCSI interface LED	CN18
Parallel port	CN5	Wake on LAN connector	CN19
PS/2 mouse port	CN6	Wake on modem connector	CN20
Line in	CN7	VGA feature connector	CN21
Line out	CN8	Chassis security connector	CN22
Telajack connector	CN9	+5v auxiliary connector	CN23
CD-ROM audio in	CN10	IR connector	J3M1
Wavetable connector	CN11	Serial port 2	J4M1
Floppy drive interface	CN12	Riser slot	SL1
IDE interface 1	CN13	CPU Slot 1	SL2
IDE interface 2	CN14		

USER CONFIGURABLE SETTINGS		
Function	**Label**	**Position**
⇨ Flash BIOS normal operation	J1	Pins 5 & 6 closed
Flash BIOS recovery mode	J1	Pins 4 & 5 closed
Floppy drive write protect disabled	J2A	Pins 5 & 6 closed
Floppy drive write protect enabled	J2A	Pins 4 & 5 closed
⇨ CMOS memory normal operation	J2C	Pins 5 & 6 closed
CMOS memory clear	J2C	Pins 4 & 5 closed
⇨ Factory configured - do not alter	J2C	Pins 2 & 3 closed
Password normal operation	J2D	Pins 2 & 3 closed
Password clear	J2D	Pins 1 & 2 closed
Setup enabled	J2D	Pins 5 & 6 closed
Setup disabled	J2D	Pins 4 & 5 closed

DRAM CONFIGURATION
Note: The maximum memory and configuration is unidentified.

CACHE CONFIGURATION
Note: 256KB/512KB cache is located on the Pentium II CPU.

VIDEO MEMORY CONFIGURATION
Note: The size and location of video memory is unidentified.

CPU SPEED SELECTION		
Speed	**J2A**	**J2B**
233MHz	Pins 2 & 3 closed	Pins 2 & 3, 5 & 6 closed
266MHz	Pins 1 & 2 closed	Pins 1 & 2, 4 & 5 closed

IBM CORPORATION
INTELLISTATION (TYPE 6899)

Processor	Pentium Pro
Processor Speed	200MHz
Chip Set	Unidentified
Video Chip Set	None
Maximum Onboard Memory	1GB (EDO supported)
Maximum Video Memory	None
Cache	256/512KB (located on Pentium Pro CPU)
BIOS	Unidentified
Dimensions	330mm x 218mm
I/O Options	Floppy drive interface, IDE interfaces (2), parallel port, PS/2 mouse port, serial ports (2), riser slot, IR connector, VRM connector, USB connector, line in, line out, microphone in, wake on modem connectors (2), wake on LAN connector, CD-ROM audio in
NPU Options	None

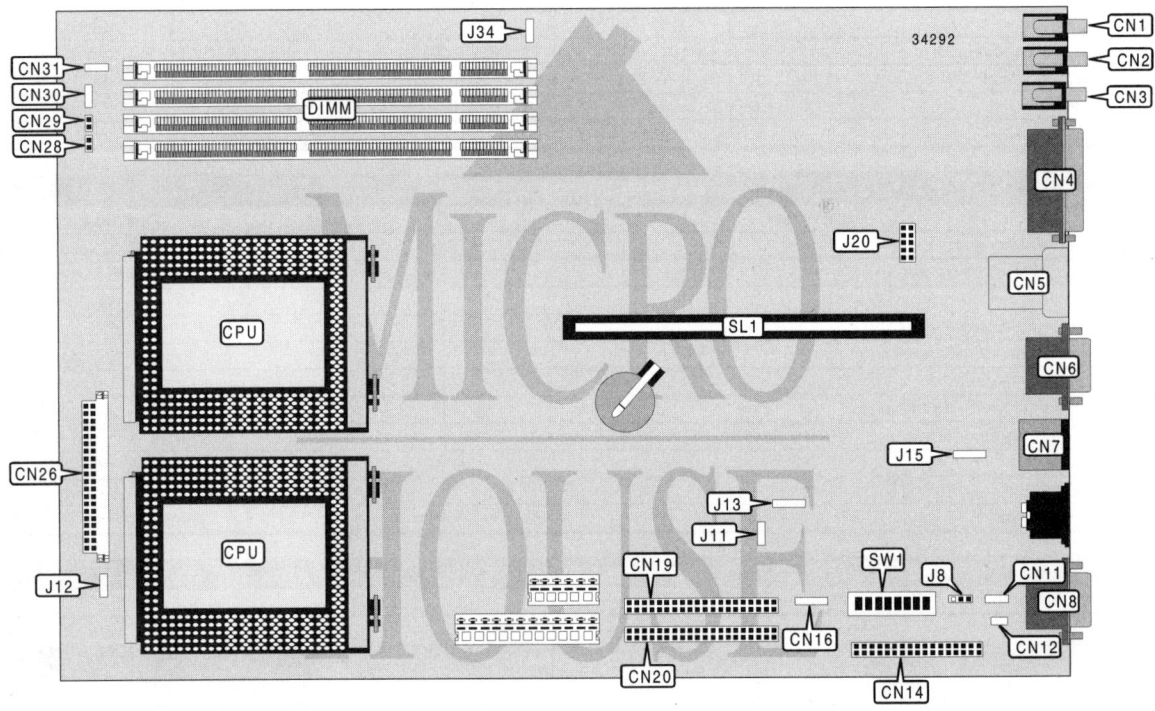

Continued on next page...

IBM CORPORATION
INTELLISTATION (TYPE 6899)

...continued from previous page

CONNECTIONS

Purpose	Location	Purpose	Location
Line out	CN1	IDE interface 2	CN20
Line in	CN2	VRM connector	CN26
Microphone in	CN3	Power LED	CN28
Parallel port	CN4	IDE interface LED	CN29
USB connector	CN5	Chassis fan power	CN30
Serial port 1	CN6	Speaker	CN31
PS/2 mouse port	CN7	Wake up on modem connector	J11
IR connector	CN8	Chassis fan power	J12
5v auxiliary connector	CN11	Wake up on modem connector	J13
Soft off power supply	CN12	Wake up on LAN connector	J15
Floppy drive interface	CN14	Serial port 2	J20
SCSI interface LED	CN16	CD-ROM audio in	J34
IDE interface 1	CN19	Riser slot	SL1

USER CONFIGURABLE SETTINGS

Function	Label	Position
✧ CMOS memory normal operation	J8	Pins 1 & 2 closed
CMOS memory clear	J8	Pins 2 & 3 closed
✧ Factory configured - do not alter	SW1/6	N/A
✧ Serial port 2 enabled	SW1/7	On
Serial port 2 disabled	SW1/7	Off
✧ Floppy drive write protect disabled	SW1/8	Off
Floppy drive write protect enabled	SW1/8	On

DIMM CONFIGURATION

Size	Bank 0	Bank 1	Bank 2	Bank 3
8MB	(1) 1M x 64	None	None	None
16MB	(1) 2M x 64	None	None	None
16MB	(1) 1M x 64	(1) 1M x 64	None	None
24MB	(1) 2M x 64	(1) 1M x 64	None	None
24MB	(1) 1M x 64	(1) 1M x 64	(1) 1M x 64	None
32MB	(1) 4M x 64	None	None	None
32MB	(1) 2M x 64	(1) 2M x 64	None	None
32MB	(1) 1M x 64	(1) 1M x 64	(1) 1M x 64	(1) 1M x 64
40MB	(1) 4M x 64	(1) 1M x 64	None	None
48MB	(1) 4M x 64	(1) 2M x 64	None	None
48MB	(1) 2M x 64	(1) 2M x 64	(1) 2M x 64	None
64MB	(1) 8M x 64	None	None	None
64MB	(1) 4M x 64	(1) 4M x 64	None	None
64MB	(1) 2M x 64	(1) 2M x 64	(1) 2M x 64	(1) 2M x 64
72MB	(1) 8M x 64	(1) 1M x 64	None	None
80MB	(1) 8M x 64	(1) 2M x 64	None	None

Continued on next page...

IBM CORPORATION
INTELLISTATION (TYPE 6899)

...continued from previous page

DIMM CONFIGURATION (CON'T)				
Size	**Bank 0**	**Bank 1**	**Bank 2**	**Bank 3**
96MB	(1) 8M x 64	(1) 4M x 64	None	None
96MB	(1) 4M x 64	(1) 4M x 64	(1) 4M x 64	None
128MB	(1) 8M x 64	(1) 8M x 64	None	None
128MB	(1) 4M x 64	(1) 4M x 64	(1) 4M x 64	(1) 4M x 64
128MB	(1) 16M x 64	None	None	None
192MB	(1) 8M x 64	(1) 8M x 64	(1) 8M x 64	None
256MB	(1) 8M x 64	(1) 8M x 64	(1) 8M x 64	(1) 8M x 64
256MB	(1) 16M x 64	(1) 16M x 64	None	None
256MB	(1) 32M x 64	None	None	None
384MB	(1) 16M x 64	(1) 16M x 64	(1) 16M x 64	None
512MB	(1) 16M x 64	(1) 16M x 64	(1) 16M x 64	(1) 16M x 64
512MB	(1) 32M x 64	(1) 32M x 64	None	None
768MB	(1) 32M x 64	(1) 32M x 64	(1) 32M x 64	None
1GB	(1) 32M x 64	(1) 32M x 64	(1) 32M x 64	(1) 32M x 64

Note: Board accepts EDO memory.

CACHE CONFIGURATION
Note: 256KB/512KB cache is located on the Pentium Pro CPU.

CPU SPEED SELECTION					
CPU speed	**SW1/1**	**SW1/2**	**SW1/3**	**SW1/4**	**SW1/5**
200MHz	On	Off	On	On	Off

IBM CORPORATION
INTELLISTATION Z PRO

Processor	Pentium Pro
Processor Speed	200MHz
Chip Set	Unidentified
Video Chip Set	None
Maximum Onboard Memory	1GB
Maximum Video Memory	None
Cache	256/512KB
BIOS	Unidentified
Dimensions	254mm x 218mm
I/O Options	Floppy drive interface, IDE interfaces (2), parallel port, PS/2 mouse port, serial ports (2), riser slot, IR connector, VRM connector, USB connector, audio connectors (3), CD-ROM audio in, wake on modem connectors (2), wake on LAN connector
NPU Options	None

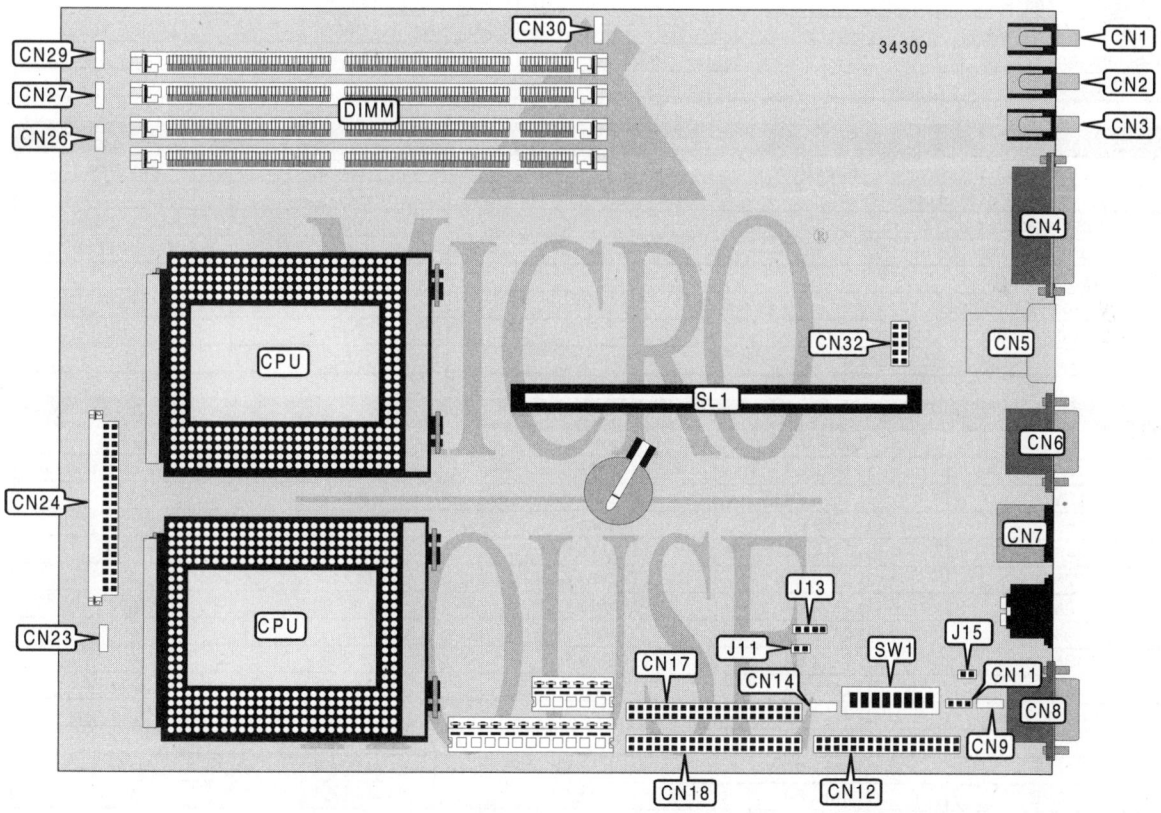

Continued on next page...

IBM CORPORATION
INTELLISTATION Z PRO

... continued from previous page

CONNECTIONS

Purpose	Location	Purpose	Location
Audio in	CN1	IDE interface 2	CN18
Audio in	CN2	Chassis fan power	CN23
Audio in	CN3	VRM connector	CN24
Parallel port	CN4	Power LED	CN26
USB connector	CN5	Front panel connector	CN27
Serial port 1	CN6	Speaker	CN29
PS/2 mouse port	CN7	CD-ROM audio in	CN30
IR connector	CN8	Serial port 2	CN32
+5V auxiliary connector	CN9	Wake on modem connector	J11
Floppy drive interface	CN12	Wake on modem connector	J13
SCSI interface LED	CN14	Wake on LAN connector	J15
IDE interface 1	CN17	Riser slot	SL1

USER CONFIGURABLE SETTINGS

Function	Label	Position
CMOS memory normal operation	CN11	Pins 1 & 2 closed
CMOS memory clear	CN11	Pins 2 & 3 closed
⇨ Factory configured - do not alter	SW1/6	Unidentified
Serial port 2 enabled	SW1/7	On
Serial port 2 disabled	SW1/7	Off
Floppy drive write protect disabled	SW1/8	Off
Floppy drive write protect enabled	SW1/8	On

DIMM CONFIGURATION

Size	Bank 0	Bank 1	Bank 2	Bank 3
8MB	(1) 1M x 64	None	None	None
16MB	(1) 1M x 64	(1) 1M x 64	None	None
16MB	(1) 2M x 64	None	None	None
24MB	(1) 1M x 64	(1) 1M x 64	(1) 1M x 64	None
32MB	(1) 1M x 64	(1) 1M x 64	(1) 1M x 64	(1) 1M x 64
32MB	(1) 2M x 64	(1) 2M x 64	None	None
32MB	(1) 4M x 64	None	None	None
48MB	(1) 2M x 64	(1) 2M x 64	(1) 2M x 64	None
64MB	(1) 2M x 64	(1) 2M x 64	(1) 2M x 64	(1) 2M x 64
64MB	(1) 4M x 64	(1) 4M x 64	None	None
64MB	(1) 8M x 64	None	None	None
96MB	(1) 4M x 64	(1) 4M x 64	(1) 4M x 64	None
128MB	(1) 4M x 64	(1) 4M x 64	(1) 4M x 64	(1) 4M x 64
128MB	(1) 8M x 64	(1) 8M x 64	None	None
128MB	(1) 16M x 64	None	None	None
192MB	(1) 8M x 64	(1) 8M x 64	(1) 8M x 64	None
256MB	(1) 8M x 64	(1) 8M x 64	(1) 8M x 64	(1) 8M x 64

Continued on next page...

IBM CORPORATION
INTELLISTATION Z PRO

...continued from previous page

\	\	DIMM CONFIGURATION (CON'T)			
Size	Bank 0	Bank 1	Bank 2	Bank 3	
256MB	(1) 16M x 64	(1) 16M x 64	None	None	
256MB	(1) 32M x 64	None	None	None	
384MB	(1) 16M x 64	(1) 16M x 64	(1) 16M x 64	None	
512MB	(1) 16M x 64	(1) 16M x 64	(1) 16M x 64	(1) 16M x 64	
512MB	(1) 32M x 64	(1) 32M x 64	None	None	
768MB	(1) 32M x 64	(1) 32M x 64	(1) 32M x 64	None	
1GB	(1) 32M x 64	(1) 32M x 64	(1) 32M x 64	(1) 32M x 64	

Note: The location of the banks is unidentified.

CACHE CONFIGURATION

Note: 256KB/512KB cache is located on the Pentium Pro CPU.

CPU SPEED SELECTION					
CPU speed	SW1/1	SW1/2	SW1/3	SW1/4	SW1/5
200MHz	On	Off	On	On	Off

IBM CORPORATION
OPAL 486SLC2 REV C

Processor	CX486SLC2
Processor Speed	50(internal)/66(internal)MHz
Chip Set	IBM
Max. Onboard DRAM	16MB
Cache	64/128KB
BIOS	AMI/MR
Dimensions	254mm x 218mm
I/O Options	32-bit VESA local bus slots (2)
NPU Options	80387SX

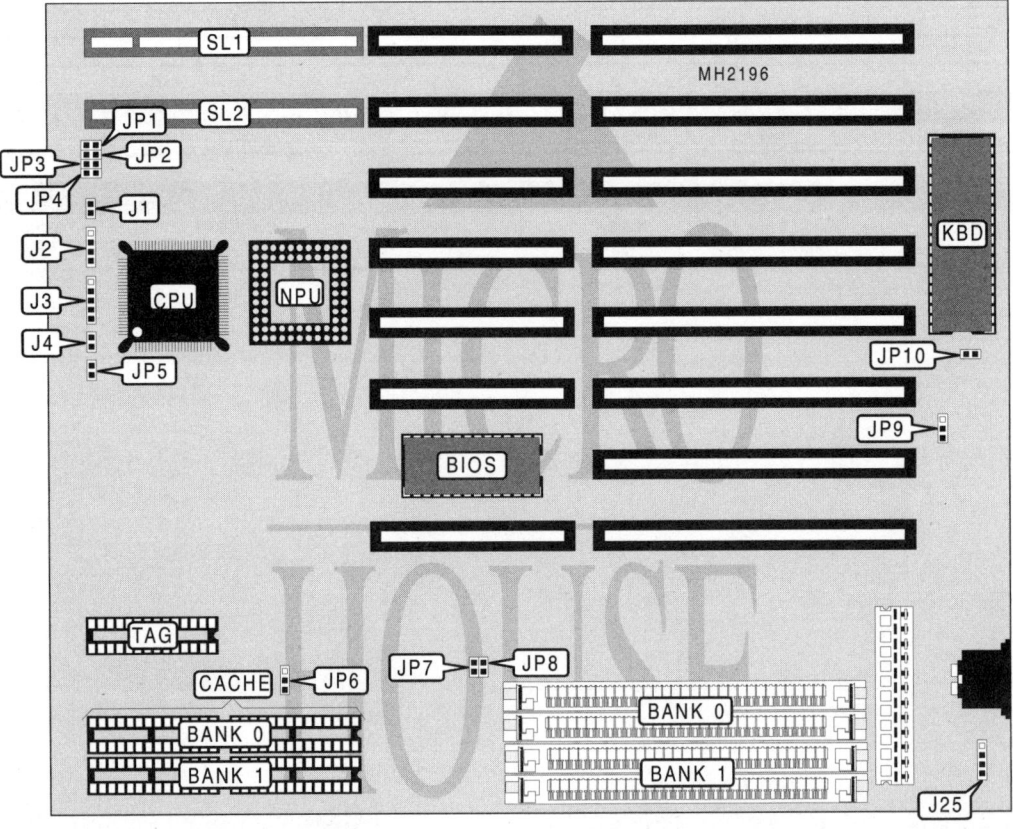

CONNECTIONS			
Purpose	**Location**	**Purpose**	**Location**
Reset switch	J1	Turbo switch	J4
Speaker	J2	External battery	J25
Power LED & keylock	J3	32-bit VESA local bus slots	SL1 & SL2

Continued on next page...

IBM CORPORATION
OPAL 486SLC2 REV C

...continued from previous page

USER CONFIGURABLE SETTINGS		
Function	**Jumper**	**Position**
⇨ CMOS memory normal operation	JP9	pins 2 & 3 closed
CMOS memory clear	JP9	pins 1 & 2 closed
⇨ Password enabled (MR BIOS only)	JP10	Closed
Password disabled (MR BIOS only)	JP10	Open

DRAM CONFIGURATION		
Size	**Bank 0**	**Bank 1**
512KB	(2) 256K x 9	NONE
1MB	(2) 256K x 9	(2) 256K x 9
2MB	(2) 1M x 9	NONE
4MB	(2) 1M x 9	(2) 1M x 9
8MB	(2) 4M x 9	NONE
10MB	(2) 1M x 9	(2) 4M x 9
16MB	(2) 4M x 9	(2) 4M x 9

CACHE CONFIGURATION			
Size	**Bank 0**	**Bank 1**	**TAG**
64KB	(2) 32K x 8	NONE	(1) 8K x 8
128KB	(2) 32K x 8	(2) 32K x 8	(1) 32K x 8

CACHE JUMPER CONFIGURATION	
Size	**JP6**
64KB	pins 2 & 3 closed
128KB	pins 1 & 2 closed

CPU SPEED CONFIGURATION		
Speed	**JP7**	**JP8**
50iMHz	Open	Closed
66iMHz	Closed	Open

BUS SPEED CONFIGURATION	
CPU speed	**JP5**
<=33MHz	Open
>33MHz	Closed

VESA ID CONFIGURATION				
ID	**JP1**	**JP2**	**JP3**	**JP4**
ID0	Open	Open	Open	Closed
ID1	Closed	Closed	Open	Closed
ID2	Closed	Open	Closed	Closed
ID3	Open	Closed	Closed	Closed

IBM CORPORATION
PC 330 P-60, PC 350 P-60

Processor	Pentium
Processor Speed	60/90MHz
Chip Set	Unidentified
Video Chip Set	Unidentified
Maximum Onboard Memory	128MB
Maximum Video Memory	Unidentified
Cache	256KB
BIOS	Unidentified
Dimensions	330mm x 218mm
I/O Options	Floppy drive interface, IDE interfaces (2), parallel port, PS/2 mouse port, serial ports (2), VGA port, riser slot
NPU Options	None

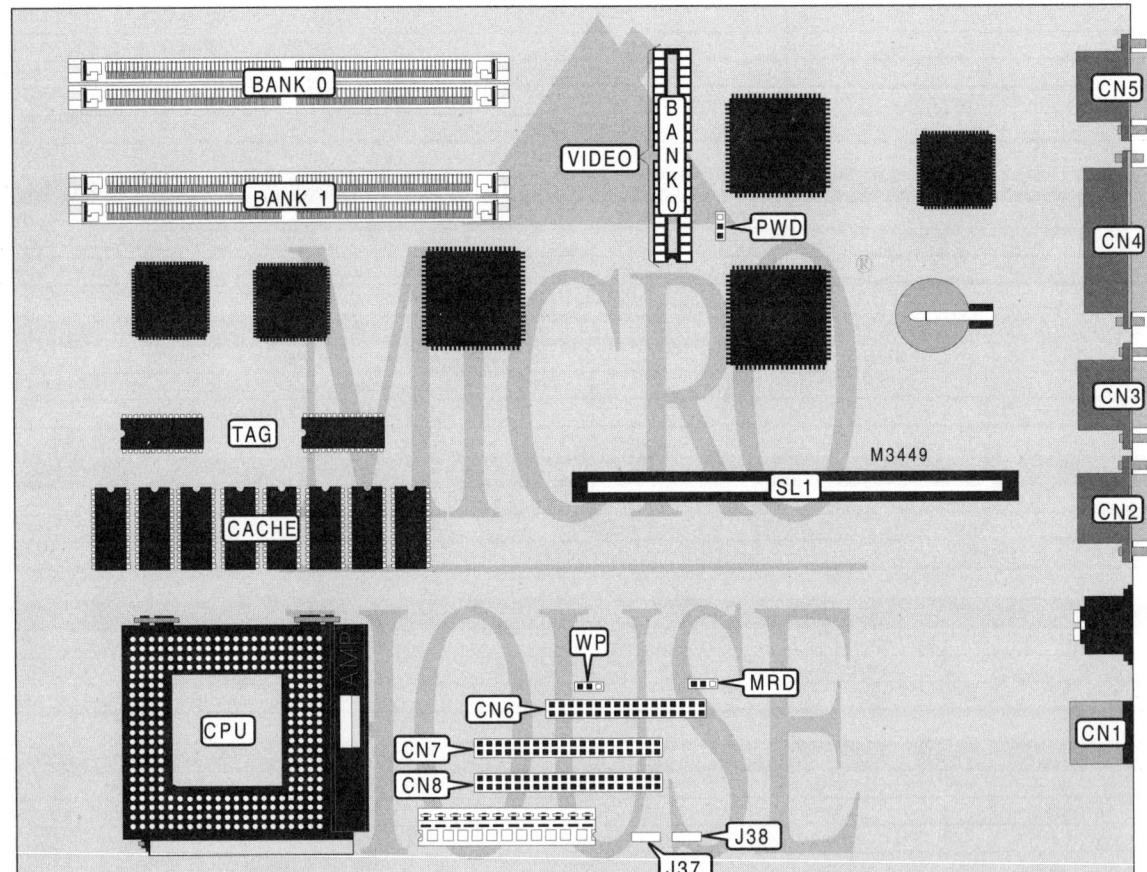

Continued on next page...

IBM CORPORATION
PC 330 P-60, PC 350 P-60

...continued from previous page

CONNECTIONS			
Purpose	**Location**	**Purpose**	**Location**
PS/2 mouse port	CN1	IDE interface	CN7
Serial port	CN2	IDE interface	CN8
Serial port	CN3	On/off switch connector	J37
Parallel port	CN4	On/off switch power supply connector	J38
VGA port	CN5	Riser slot	SL1
Floppy drive interface	CN6		

USER CONFIGURABLE SETTINGS		
Function	**Label**	**Position**
⇨ Modem answers on ring	MRD	Pins 2 & 3 closed
Modem does not answer on ring	MRD	Pins 1 & 2 closed
Password normal operation	PWD	Pins 1 & 2 closed
Password clear	PWD	Pins 2 & 3 closed
⇨ Floppy drive write protect disabled	WP	Pins 1 & 2 closed
Floppy drive write protect enabled	WP	Pins 2 & 3 closed

DRAM CONFIGURATION		
Size	**Bank 0**	**Bank 1**
8MB	(2) 1M x 36	None
16MB	(2) 2M x 36	None
16MB	(2) 1M x 36	(2) 1M x 36
24MB	(2) 2M x 36	(2) 1M x 36
24MB	(2) 1M x 36	(2) 2M x 36
32MB	(2) 4M x 36	None
32MB	(2) 2M x 36	(2) 2M x 36
40MB	(2) 4M x 36	(2) 1M x 36
40MB	(2) 1M x 36	(2) 4M x 36
48MB	(2) 4M x 36	(2) 2M x 36
48MB	(2) 2M x 36	(2) 4M x 36
64MB	(2) 8M x 36	None
64MB	(2) 4M x 36	(2) 4M x 36
72MB	(2) 8M x 36	(2) 1M x 36
72MB	(2) 1M x 36	(2) 8M x 36
80MB	(2) 8M x 36	(2) 2M x 36
80MB	(2) 2M x 36	(2) 8M x 36
96MB	(2) 8M x 36	(2) 4M x 36
96MB	(2) 4M x 36	(2) 8M x 36
128MB	(2) 8M x 36	(2) 8M x 36

CACHE CONFIGURATION
Note: 256KB cache is factory installed and is not configurable.

Continued on next page...

IBM CORPORATION
PC 330 P-60, PC 350 P-60

...continued from previous page

VIDEO MEMORY CONFIGURATION	
Size	**Bank 0**
1MB	(2) 256K x 16
Note: The maximum memory size is unidentified. This configuration is for an upgrade.	

IBM CORPORATION
PC 730/750 SERIES (TYPE 6877, 6887)

Processor	Pentium
Processor Speed	75/90/100/120/133/150/166MHz
Chip Set	Unidentified
Video Chip Set	None
Maximum Onboard Memory	128MB
Maximum Video Memory	None
Cache	256/512KB
BIOS	Unidentified
Dimensions	330mm x 218mm
I/O Options	Floppy drive interface, IDE interfaces (2), parallel port, PS/2 mouse port, serial ports (2), VESA pass through connector, VGA port, riser slot, cache slot, IR connector, VRM connector, DSP audio connector, external ring wake up connector, modem ring connector, LAN wake up connector, on/off switch connector, tamper connector
NPU Options	None

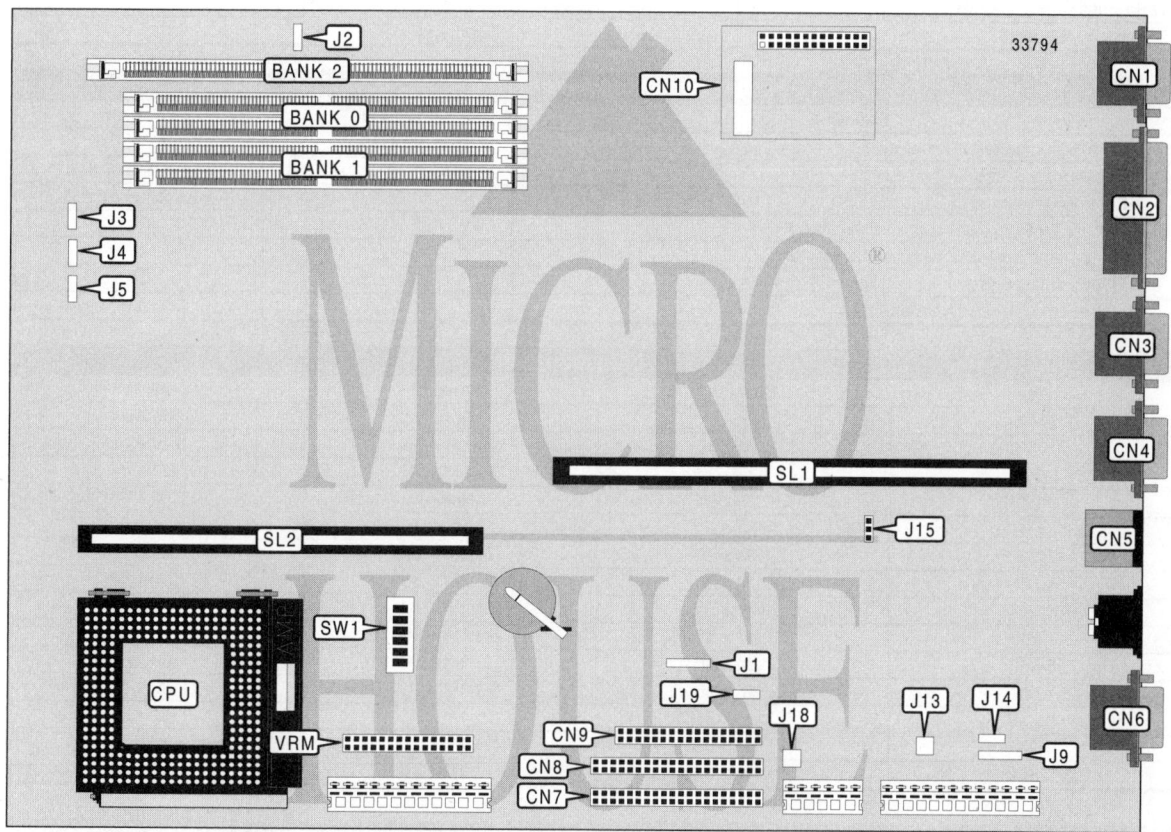

Continued on next page...

IBM CORPORATION
PC 730/750 SERIES (TYPE 6877, 6887)

...continued from previous page

CONNECTIONS

Purpose	Location	Purpose	Location
VGA port	CN1	Speaker	J3
Parallel port	CN2	IDE interface LED	J4
Serial port 2	CN3	Power LED	J5
Serial port 1	CN4	Modem ring connector	J9
PS/2 mouse port	CN5	External ring wake up connector	J13
IR connector	CN6	LAN wake up connector	J14
IDE interface 2	CN7	On/off switch connector	J18
IDE interface 1	CN8	Tamper connector	J19
Floppy drive interface	CN9	Riser slot	SL1
VESA pass through connector	CN10	Cache slot	SL2
DSP audio connector	J2	VRM connector	VRM

USER CONFIGURABLE SETTINGS

Function	Label	Position
✧ Factory configured - do not alter	J1	Unidentified
✧ Password enabled	J15	Pins 1 & 2 closed
Password disabled	J15	Pins 2 & 3 closed
✧ System administrator password enabled	SW1/5	On
System administrator password disabled	SW1/5	Off
✧ Floppy drive write protect disabled	SW1/6	Off
Floppy drive write protect enabled	SW1/6	On

DRAM CONFIGURATION

Size	Bank 0	Bank 1	Bank 2
16MB	None	None	(1) 2M x 64
16MB	(2) 1M x 36	(2) 1M x 36	None
24MB	None	(2) 1M x 36	(1) 2M x 64
24MB	(2) 1M x 36	None	(1) 2M x 64
32MB	None	None	(1) 4M x 64
32MB	(2) 2M x 36	(2) 2M x 36	None
40MB	(2) 1M x 36	(2) 2M x 36	(1) 2M x 64
40MB	None	(2) 1M x 36	(1) 4M x 64
48MB	(2) 1M x 36	(2) 1M x 36	(1) 4M x 64
64MB	(2) 2M x 36	(2) 2M x 36	(1) 4M x 64
72MB	(2) 1M x 36	(2) 4M x 36	(1) 4M x 64
80MB	(2) 2M x 36	(2) 4M x 36	(1) 4M x 64
96MB	(2) 4M x 36	(2) 4M x 36	(1) 4M x 64
128MB	(2) 4M x 36	(2) 8M x 36	(1) 4M x 64

CACHE CONFIGURATION

Size	SL1
256KB	256KB module installed
512KB	512KB module installed

Continued on next page...

IBM CORPORATION
PC 730/750 SERIES (TYPE 6877, 6887)

...continued from previous page

CPU SPEED SELECTION						
CPU speed	**Clock speed**	**Multiplier**	**SW1/1**	**SW1/2**	**SW1/3**	**SW1/4**
75MHz	50MHz	1.5x	Off	Off	On	On
90MHz	60MHz	1.5x	Off	Off	On	Off
100MHz	66MHz	1.5x	Off	Off	Off	On
120MHz	60MHz	2x	On	Off	On	Off
133MHz	66MHz	2x	On	Off	Off	On
150MHz	60MHz	2.5x	On	On	On	Off
166MHz	66MHz	2.5x	On	On	Off	On

IBM CORPORATION
SL-B, MT2133, MT2155, MT2168

Processor	80486SX/80487SX/0DP486/80486DX/80486DX2
Processor Speed	25/33/50(internal)/66(internal)MHz
Chip Set	Unidentified
Video Chip Set	Unidentified
Maximum Onboard Memory	64MB
Maximum Video Memory	1MB
Cache	128/256KB
BIOS	Unidentified
Dimensions	330mm x 218mm
I/O Options	32-bit VESA local bus slot, floppy drive interface, IDE interface, parallel port, PS/2 mouse port, serial ports (2), VESA feature connector, VGA port, riser slot
NPU Options	None

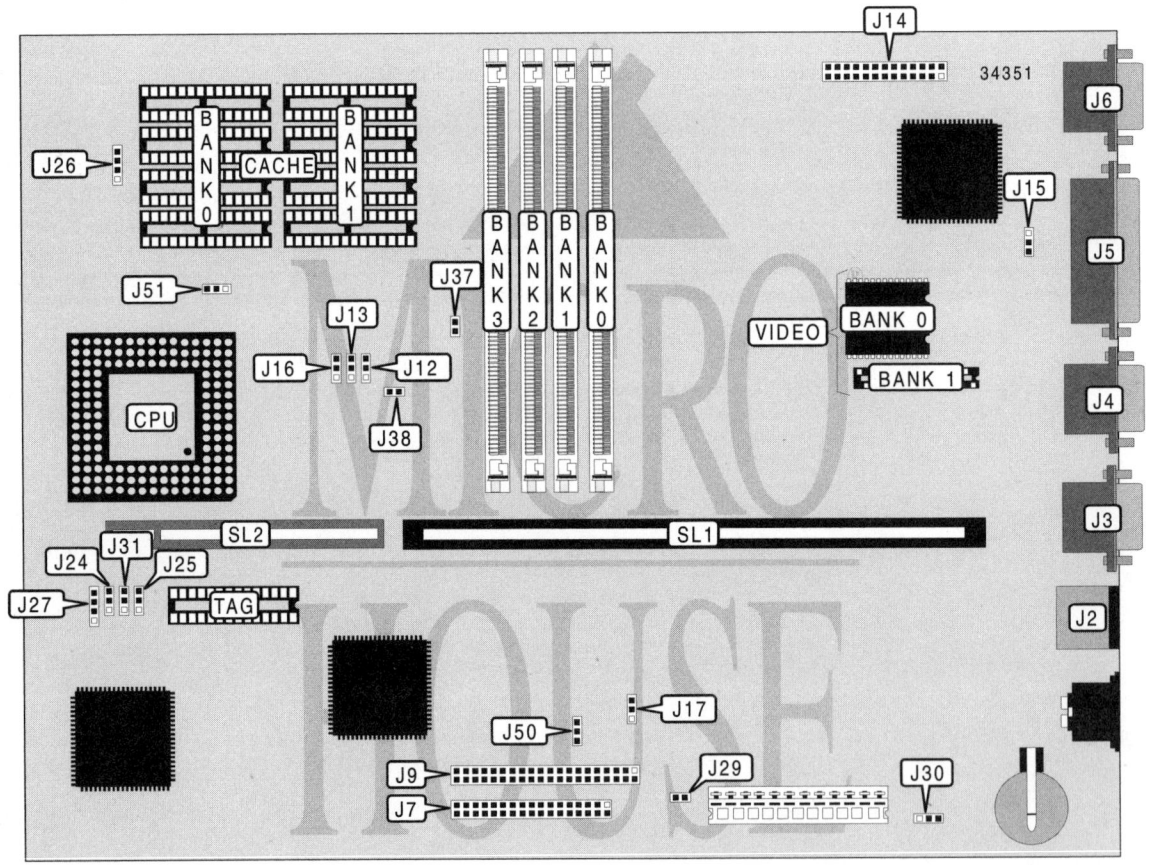

Continued on next page...

IBM CORPORATION
SL-B, MT2133, MT2155, MT2168

...continued from previous page

CONNECTIONS

Purpose	Location	Purpose	Location
PS/2 mouse port	J2	IDE interface LED	J26/pins 3 & 4
Serial port 1	J3	Speaker	J27
Serial port 2	J4	Soft off power supply	J29
Parallel port	J5	Soft off power supply	J30
VGA port	J6	Turbo switch	J37
Floppy drive interface	J7	Chassis fan power	J38
IDE interface	J9	Riser slot	SL1
VESA feature connector	J14	32-bit VESA local bus slot	SL2
Power LED	J26/pins 1 & 2		

USER CONFIGURABLE SETTINGS

Function	Label	Position
◊ On board video disabled	J15	Pins 1 & 2 closed
On board video enabled	J15	Pins 2 & 3 closed
◊ Factory configured - do not alter	J50	Unidentified

DRAM CONFIGURATION

Size	Bank 0	Bank 1	Bank 2	Bank 3
2MB	(1) 512K x 36	None	None	None
4MB	(1) 1M x 36	None	None	None
4MB	(1) 512K x 36	(1) 512K x 36	None	None
6MB	(1) 1M x 36	(1) 512K x 36	None	None
6MB	(1) 512K x 36	(1) 512K x 36	(1) 512K x 36	None
8MB	(1) 2M x 36	None	None	None
8MB	(1) 1M x 36	(1) 512K x 36	(1) 512K x 36	None
8MB	(1) 1M x 36	(1) 1M x 36	None	None
8MB	(1) 512K x 36	(1) 512K x 36	(1) 512K x 36	(1) 512K x 36
10MB	(1) 2M x 36	(1) 512K x 36	None	None
10MB	(1) 1M x 36	(1) 512K x 36	(1) 512K x 36	(1) 512K x 36
12MB	(1) 2M x 36	(1) 512K x 36	(1) 512K x 36	None
12MB	(1) 2M x 36	(1) 1M x 36	None	None
12MB	(1) 1M x 36	(1) 1M x 36	(1) 1M x 36	None
14MB	(1) 2M x 36	(1) 512K x 36	(1) 512K x 36	(1) 512K x 36
16MB	(1) 4M x 36	None	None	None
16MB	(1) 2M x 36	(1) 1M x 36	(1) 1M x 36	None
16MB	(1) 2M x 36	(1) 2M x 36	None	None
16MB	(1) 1M x 36	(1) 1M x 36	(1) 1M x 36	(1) 1M x 36
18MB	(1) 4M x 36	(1) 512K x 36	None	None
20MB	(1) 4M x 36	(1) 512K x 36	(1) 512K x 36	None
20MB	(1) 4M x 36	(1) 1M x 36	None	None
20MB	(1) 2M x 36	(1) 1M x 36	(1) 1M x 36	(1) 1M x 36
22MB	(1) 4M x 36	(1) 512K x 36	(1) 512K x 36	(1) 512K x 36

Continued on next page...

IBM CORPORATION
SL-B, MT2133, MT2155, MT2168

...continued from previous page

DRAM CONFIGURATION (CON'T)				
Size	**Bank 0**	**Bank 1**	**Bank 2**	**Bank 3**
24MB	(1) 4M x 36	(1) 1M x 36	(1) 1M x 36	None
24MB	(1) 4M x 36	(1) 2M x 36	None	None
24MB	(1) 2M x 36	(1) 2M x 36	(1) 2M x 36	None
28MB	(1) 4M x 36	(1) 1M x 36	(1) 1M x 36	(1) 1M x 36
32MB	(1) 4M x 36	(1) 2M x 36	(1) 2M x 36	None
32MB	(1) 4M x 36	(1) 4M x 36	None	None
32MB	(1) 2M x 36	(1) 2M x 36	(1) 2M x 36	(1) 2M x 36
36MB	(1) 1M x 36	(1) 4M x 36	(1) 4M x 36	None
40MB	(1) 4M x 36	(1) 2M x 36	(1) 2M x 36	(1) 2M x 36
40MB	(1) 2M x 36	(1) 8M x 36	None	None
48MB	(1) 4M x 36	(1) 4M x 36	(1) 4M x 36	None
56MB	(1) 2M x 36	(1) 4M x 36	(1) 4M x 36	(1) 4M x 36
64MB	(1) 4M x 36	(1) 4M x 36	(1) 4M x 36	(1) 4M x 36

CACHE CONFIGURATION			
Size	**Bank 0**	**Bank 1**	**TAG**
128KB	(4) 32K x 8	None	(1) 8K x 8
256KB	(4) 32K x 8	(4) 32K x 8	(1) 32K x 8

CACHE JUMPER CONFIGURATION					
Size	**J12**	**J13**	**J16**	**J17**	**J51**
128KB	2 & 3	1 & 2	2 & 3	1 & 2	1 & 2
256KB	1 & 2	2 & 3	1 & 2	2 & 3	2 & 3

Note: Pins designated should be in the closed position.

VIDEO MEMORY CONFIGURATION		
Size	**Bank 0**	**Bank 1**
512KB	512KB	None
1MB	512KB	512KB

Note: The size of the video memory chips is unidentified.

CPU TYPE SELECTION			
Type	**J24**	**J25**	**J31**
80486SX	Pins 2 & 3 closed	Pins 2 & 3 closed	Pins 1 & 2 closed
80487SX	Pins 1 & 2 closed	Pins 1 & 2 closed	Pins 2 & 3 closed
ODP486	Pins 1 & 2 closed	Pins 1 & 2 closed	Pins 2 & 3 closed
80486DX	Pins 2 & 3 closed	Pins 1 & 2 closed	Pins 2 & 3 closed
80486DX2	Pins 2 & 3 closed	Pins 1 & 2 closed	Pins 2 & 3 closed

IBM CORPORATION
VALUEPOINT 6472, 6482, 6484

Processor	80486SX/SL80486SX/80487SX/80486DX/SL80486DX/80486DX2/ SL80486DX2/80486DX4
Processor Speed	25/33/40/50/50(internal)/66(internal)/100(internal)MHz
Chip Set	Unidentified
Video Chip Set	Unidentified
Maximum Onboard Memory	128MB
Maximum Video Memory	2MB
Cache	128/256KB
BIOS	Unidentified
Dimensions	330mm x 218mm
I/O Options	Floppy drive interface, IDE interfaces (2), 32-bit VESA/PCI bus slot, parallel port, PS/2 mouse port, serial ports (2), VGA port, riser slot
NPU Options	None

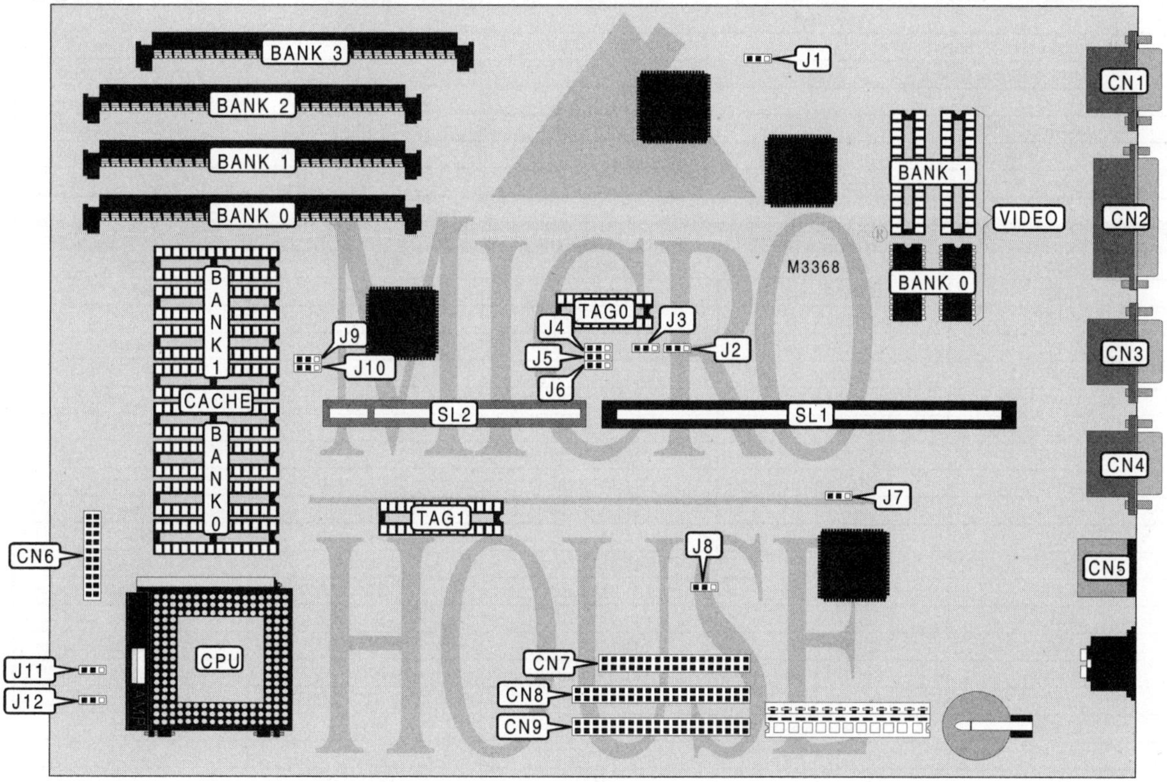

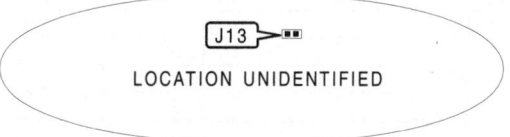

LOCATION UNIDENTIFIED

Continued on next page...

IBM CORPORATION
VALUEPOINT 6472, 6482, 6484

. . . continued from previous page

CONNECTIONS			
Purpose	**Location**	**Purpose**	**Location**
VGA port	CN1	Floppy drive interface	CN7
Parallel port	CN2	IDE interface	CN8
Serial port	CN3	IDE interface	CN9
Serial port	CN4	Riser slot	SL1
PS/2 mouse port	CN5	32-bit VESA/PCI bus slot	SL2
Front panel connector	CN6		

USER CONFIGURABLE SETTINGS		
Function	**Label**	**Position**
On board video enabled	J1	Pins 1 & 2 closed
On board video disabled	J1	Pins 2 & 3 closed
Mouse IRQ12 enabled	J7	Pins 1 & 2 closed
Mouse IRQ12 disabled	J7	Pins 2 & 3 closed
Floppy drive write protect enabled	J8	Pins 2 & 3 closed
Floppy drive write protect disabled	J8	Pins 1 & 2 closed

DRAM CONFIGURATION				
Size	**Bank 0**	**Bank 1**	**Bank 2**	**Bank 3**
4MB	(1) 1M x 36	None	None	None
8MB	(1) 1M x 36	(1) 1M x 36	None	None
8MB	(1) 2M x 36	None	None	None
12MB	(1) 1M x 36	(1) 1M x 36	(1) 1M x 36	None
12MB	(1) 1M x 36	(1) 2M x 36	None	None
16MB	(1) 4M x 36	None	None	None
16MB	(1) 1M x 36	(1) 1M x 36	(1) 2M x 36	None
16MB	(1) 1M x 36	(1) 1M x 36	(1) 1M x 36	(1) 1M x 36
16MB	(1) 2M x 36	(1) 2M x 36	None	None
20MB	(1) 1M x 36	(1) 2M x 36	(1) 2M x 36	None
20MB	(1) 1M x 36	(1) 4M x 36	None	None
24MB	(1) 2M x 36	(1) 2M x 36	(1) 2M x 36	None
24MB	(1) 1M x 36	(1) 1M x 36	(1) 2M x 36	(1) 2M x 36
24MB	(1) 1M x 36	(1) 1M x 36	(1) 4M x 36	None
28MB	(1) 1M x 36	(1) 2M x 36	(1) 2M x 36	(1) 2M x 36
28MB	(1) 1M x 36	(1) 1M x 36	(1) 4M x 36	(1) 1M x 36
32MB	(1) 4M x 36	(1) 4M x 36	None	None
32MB	(1) 8M x 36	None	None	None
32MB	(1) 2M x 36	(1) 2M x 36	(1) 4M x 36	None
32MB	(1) 2M x 36	(1) 2M x 36	(1) 2M x 36	(1) 2M x 36
36MB	(1) 1M x 36	(1) 4M x 36	(1) 4M x 36	None
40MB	(1) 1M x 36	(1) 1M x 36	(1) 8M x 36	None
40MB	(1) 1M x 36	(1) 1M x 36	(1) 4M x 36	(1) 4M x 36
48MB	(1) 4M x 36	(1) 4M x 36	(1) 4M x 36	None
48MB	(1) 2M x 36	(1) 2M x 36	(1) 8M x 36	None

Continued on next page. . .

IBM CORPORATION
VALUEPOINT 6472, 6482, 6484

...continued from previous page

DRAM CONFIGURATION (CON'T)				
Size	Bank 0	Bank 1	Bank 2	Bank 3
48MB	(1) 2M x 36	(1) 2M x 36	(1) 4M x 36	(1) 4M x 36
52MB	(1) 1M x 36	(1) 4M x 36	(1) 4M x 36	(1) 4M x 36
64MB	(1) 8M x 36	(1) 8M x 36	None	None
64MB	(1) 4M x 36	(1) 4M x 36	(1) 8M x 36	None
64MB	(1) 4M x 36	(1) 4M x 36	(1) 4M x 36	(1) 4M x 36
68MB	(1) 1M x 36	(1) 8M x 36	(1) 4M x 36	(1) 4M x 36
72MB	(1) 1M x 36	(1) 1M x 36	(1) 8M x 36	(1) 8M x 36
80MB	(1) 2M x 36	(1) 2M x 36	(1) 8M x 36	(1) 8M x 36
84MB	(1) 1M x 36	(1) 8M x 36	(1) 8M x 36	(1) 4M x 36
96MB	(1) 8M x 36	(1) 8M x 36	(1) 8M x 36	None
96MB	(1) 4M x 36	(1) 4M x 36	(1) 8M x 36	(1) 8M x 36
100MB	(1) 1M x 36	(1) 8M x 36	(1) 8M x 36	(1) 8M x 36
128MB	(1) 8M x 36	(1) 8M x 36	(1) 8M x 36	(1) 8M x 36

CACHE CONFIGURATION			
Size	Bank 0	Bank 1	TAG 0 & 1
128KB	(4) 32K x 8	None	Chips installed
256KB	(4) 32K x 8	(4) 32K x 8	Chips installed

Note: The TAG chip sizes are unidentified.

CACHE JUMPER CONFIGURATION		
Size	J9	J10
128KB	Pins 1 & 2 closed	Pins 1 & 2 closed
256KB	Pins 2 & 3 closed	Pins 2 & 3 closed

VIDEO MEMORY CONFIGURATION		
Size	Bank 0	Bank 1
1MB	(2) 512KB	None
2MB	(2) 512KB	(2) 256K x 16

Note: Bank 0 is factory installed and is not configurable.

CPU SPEED SELECTION		
Speed	J2	J3
25MHz	Pins 2 & 3 closed	Pins 1 & 2 closed
33MHz	Pins 2 & 3 closed	Pins 2 & 3 closed
40MHz	Pins 1 & 2 closed	Pins 1 & 2 closed
50MHz	Pins 1 & 2 closed	Pins 2 & 3 closed
50iMHz	Pins 2 & 3 closed	Pins 1 & 2 closed
66iMHz	Pins 2 & 3 closed	Pins 2 & 3 closed
100iMHz	Pins 1 & 2 closed	Pins 2 & 3 closed

Continued on next page...

IBM CORPORATION
VALUEPOINT 6472, 6482, 6484

...continued from previous page

CPU TYPE SELECTION	
Type	**J11**
80486SX	Pins 2 & 3 closed
80487SX	Pins 1 & 2 closed
80486SX2	Pins 1 & 2 closed
80486DX	Pins 1 & 2 closed
80486DX2	Pins 1 & 2 closed
80486DX4	Pins 1 & 2 closed

CPU TYPE SELECTION	
Type	**J12**
SL-enhanced	Pins 1 & 2 closed
Non SL-enhanced	Pins 2 & 3 closed

CPU VOLTAGE SELECTION	
Setting	**J13**
All CPU types	Closed
80486DX4 only	VRM installed

VESA/PCI SELECTION			
Setting	**J4**	**J5**	**J6**
VESA card used	Pins 2 & 3 closed	Pins 2 & 3 closed	Pins 2 & 3 closed
PCI card used	Pins 1 & 2 closed	Pins 1 & 2 closed	Pins 1 & 2 closed

IBM CORPORATION
VALUEPOINT P60/D

Processor	Pentium
Processor Speed	60/66MHz
Chip Set	Intel
Max. Onboard DRAM	128MB
Cache	256KB
BIOS	IBM
Dimensions	330mm x 218mm
I/O Options	32-bit riser card, floppy drive interface, IDE interface, parallel port, PS/2 mouse port, serial ports (2), VGA port
NPU Options	None

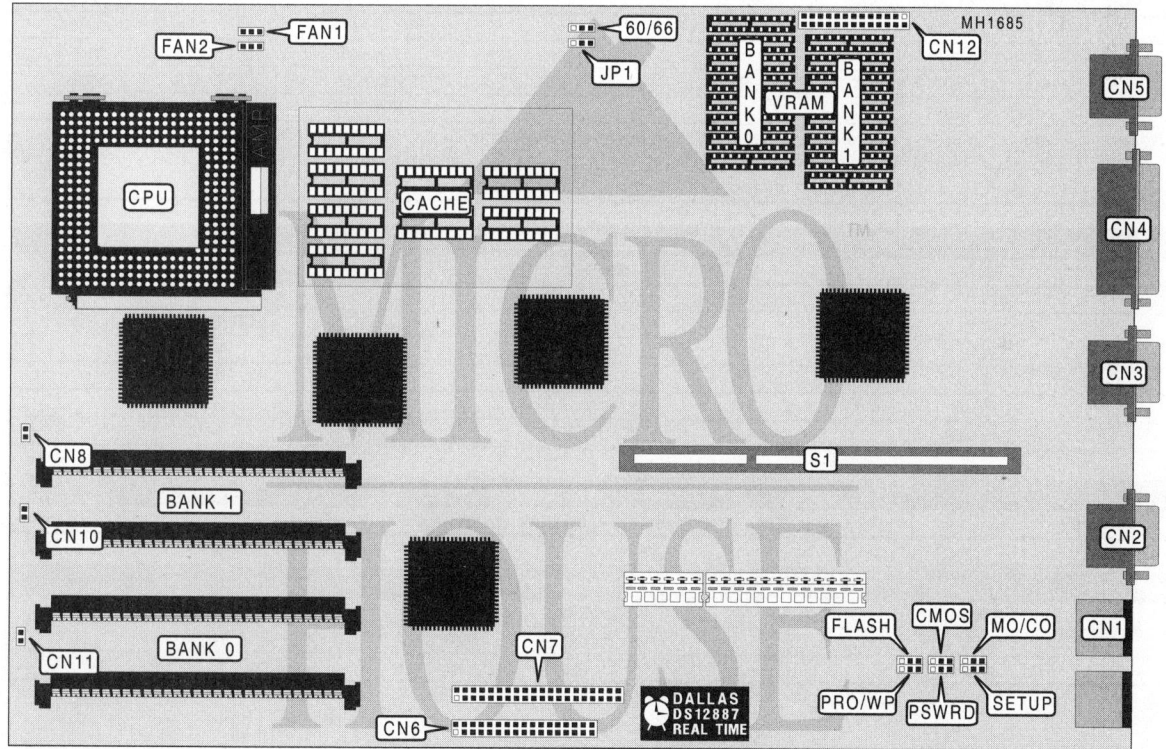

CONNECTIONS

Purpose	Location	Purpose	Location
PS/2 mouse port	CN1	IDE interface	CN7
Serial port 1	CN2	Speaker	CN8
Serial port 2	CN3	Power LED & keylock	CN10
Parallel port	CN4	IDE interface LED	CN11
VGA port	CN5	Video feature connector	CN12
Floppy drive interface	CN6	32-bit riser card	S1

Continued on next page . . .

IBM CORPORATION
VALUEPOINT P60/D

. . . continued from previous page

USER CONFIGURABLE SETTINGS		
Function	**Jumper**	**Position**
⇨ CPU speed select 60MHz	60/66	pins 1 & 2 closed
CPU speed select 66MHz	60/66	pins 2 & 3 closed
⇨ CMOS memory normal	CMOS	pins 1 & 2 closed
CMOS memory clear	CMOS	pins 2 & 3 closed
⇨ Flash BIOS write protect enabled	FLASH	pins 1 & 2 closed
Flash BIOS write protect disabled	FLASH	pins 2 & 3 closed
⇨ Monitor type select color	MO/CO	pins 2 & 3 closed
Monitor type select monochrome	MO/CO	pins 1 & 2 closed
⇨ Flash ROM select write protect enabled	PRO/WP	pins 2 & 3 closed
Flash ROM select programming	PRO/WP	pins 1 & 2 closed
⇨ Power-on password normal operation	PSWRD	pins 1 & 2 closed
Power-on password reset	PSWRD	pins 2 & 3 closed
Notes: To set a Power-On Password you must use the Configuration Utility that came with the system. If you lose power while updating the Flash-BIOS, move the Flash jumper to the recovery mode setting and use the flash update utility diskette that came with the system.		

DRAM CONFIGURATION		
Size	**Bank 0**	**Bank 1**
8MB	(2) 1M x 36	None
16MB	(2) 1M x 36	(2) 1M x 36
32MB	(2) 4M x 36	None
64MB	(2) 4M x 36	(2) 4M x 36
128MB	(2) 8M x 36	(2) 8M x 36
128MB	(2) 16M x 36	None

CACHE CONFIGURATION
The cache is permanently set to 256KB and is not user configurable.

VRAM CONFIGURATION		
Size	**Bank 0**	**Bank 1**
1MB	(8) 256K x 4	None
2MB	(8) 256K x 4	(8) 256K x 4

INTEL CORPORATION
ADVANCED/ATX

Processor	Pentium
Processor Speed	75/90/100/120/150/166MHz
Chip Set	Intel
Max. Onboard DRAM	128MB
Cache	256/512KB
BIOS	AMI
Dimensions	220mm x 305mm
I/O Options	Parallel port, serial ports (2), game port, VGA port, VGA feature connector, 32-bit PCI slots (4), floppy drive interface, IDE interfaces (2), IR connector, VRM connector
NPU Options	None

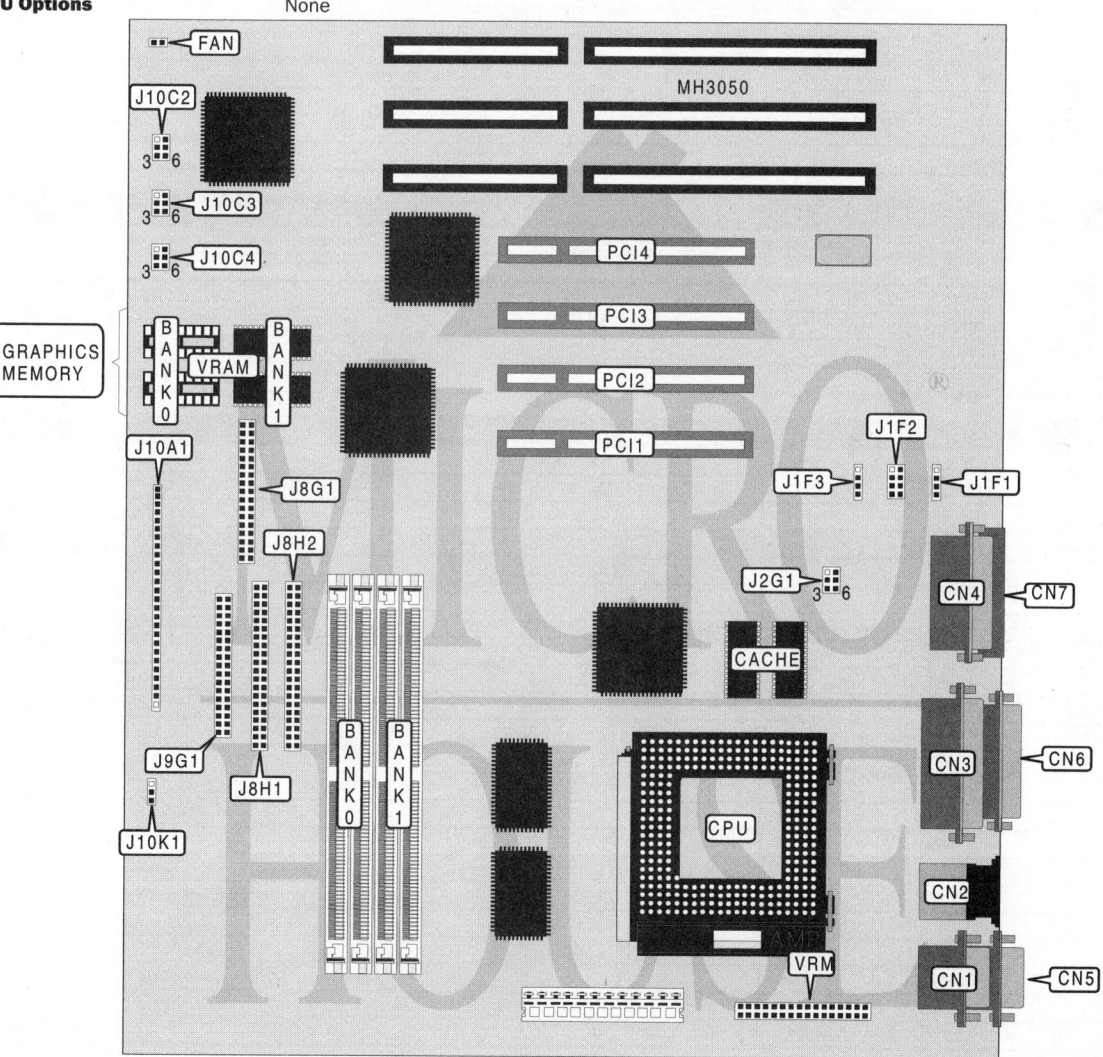

Continued on next page...

INTEL CORPORATION
ADVANCED/ATX

. . . continued from previous page

CONNECTIONS			
Purpose	**Location**	**Purpose**	**Location**
Serial port 1	CN1	IDE interface	J8H1
PS/2 mouse port	CN2	IDE interface	J8H2
Parallel port	CN3	Floppy drive interface	J9G1
Game port	CN4	Power LED	J10A1 (pins 1 & 2)
Serial port 2	CN5	Green PC connector	J10A1 (pins 3 & 4)
VGA port	CN6	IR connector	J10A1 (pins 6 - 10)
Audio port	CN7	IDE interface LED	J10A1 (pins 12 - 15)
Chassis fan power	FAN	Green PC LED	J10A1 (pins 17 - 19)
CD-ROM connector	J1F1	Reset switch	J10A1 (pins 21 & 22)
Wave table upgrade	J1F2	Speaker	J10A1 (pins 23 - 26)
Audio connector	J1F3	32-bit PCI slots	PCI1 - PCI4
Video feature connector	J8G1	Voltage regulator module	VRM

USER CONFIGURABLE SETTINGS		
Function	**Jumper**	**Position**
⇨ CMOS memory normal operation	J10C3	pins 2 & 3 closed
CMOS memory clear	J10C3	pins 1 & 2 closed
Password memory clear	J10C3	pins 4 & 5 closed
⇨ CMOS access enabled	J10C4	pins 5 & 6 closed
CMOS access disabled	J10C4	pins 4 & 5 closed

DRAM CONFIGURATION		
Size	**Bank 0**	**Bank 1**
8MB	(2) 1M x 32	NONE
16MB	(2) 1M x 32	(2) 1M x 32
16MB	(2) 2M x 32	NONE
24MB	(2) 1M x 32	(2) 2M x 32
24MB	(2) 2M x 32	(2) 1M x 32
32MB	(2) 2M x 32	(2) 2M x 32
32MB	(2) 4M x 32	NONE
40MB	(2) 1M x 32	(2) 4M x 32
40MB	(2) 4M x 32	(2) 1M x 32
48MB	(2) 2M x 32	(2) 4M x 32
48MB	(2) 4M x 32	(2) 2M x 32
64MB	(2) 4M x 32	(2) 4M x 32
64MB	(2) 8M x 32	NONE
72MB	(2) 1M x 32	(2) 8M x 32
72MB	(2) 8M x 32	(2) 1M x 32
80MB	(2) 2M x 32	(2) 8M x 32
80MB	(2) 8M x 32	(2) 2M x 32
96MB	(2) 4M x 32	(2) 8M x 32
96MB	(2) 8M x 32	(2) 4M x 32
128MB	(2) 8M x 32	(2) 8M x 32

Note: The exact location of Bank 0 and Bank 1 are unidentified.

Continued on next page. . .

INTEL CORPORATION
ADVANCED/ATX

...continued from previous page

CACHE CONFIGURATION	
Size	**Bank 0**
256KB	(2) 32k X 32

CPU SPEED CONFIGURATION		
Speed	**J2G1**	**J10C4**
75MHz	pins 1 & 2, 5 & 6 closed	pins 1 & 2 or 2 & 3 closed
90MHz	pins 1 & 2, 4 & 5 closed	pins 1 & 2 or 2 & 3 closed
100MHz	pins 2 & 3, 5 & 6 closed	pins 1 & 2 or 2 & 3 closed
120Mhz	pins 1 & 2, 4 & 5 closed	pins 1 & 2 or 2 & 3 closed
133Mhz	pins 2 & 3, 5 & 6 closed	pins 1 & 2 or 2 & 3 closed
150Mhz	pins 1 & 2, 4 & 5 closed	pins 1 & 2 or 2 & 3 closed
160Mhz	pins 2 & 3, 5 & 6 closed	pins 1 & 2 or 2 & 3 closed

CPU SPEED RATIO CONFIGURATION	
Setting	**J10C2**
1.5 x	pins 2 & 3, 4 & 5 closed
2 x	pins 1 & 2, 4 & 5 closed
2.5 x	pins 1 & 2, 5 & 6 closed

CPU VOLTAGE CONFIGURATION	
Voltage	**J10K1**
3.135 - 3.36v	pins 2 & 3 closed
3.46 - 3.63v	pins 1 & 2 closed

GRAPHIC MEMORY CONFIGURATION		
Size	**BANK 0**	**BANK 1**
1MB	(2) 256K x 16	NONE
2MB	(2) 256K x 16	(2) 256K x 16

272 Motherboard Settings & Specifications

INTEL CORPORATION
ADVANCED/ML

Processor	Pentium
Processor Speed	75/90/100/120/133/150/166MHz
Chip Set	Intel
Video Chip Set	None
Maximum Onboard Memory	128MB (EDO supported)
Maximum Video Memory	None
Cache	256/512KB
BIOS	Phoenix
Dimensions	304mm x 178mm
I/O Options	32-bit PCI slots (4), floppy drive interface, green PC connector, IDE interfaces (2), parallel port, PS/2 mouse port, serial ports (2), IR connector
NPU Options	None

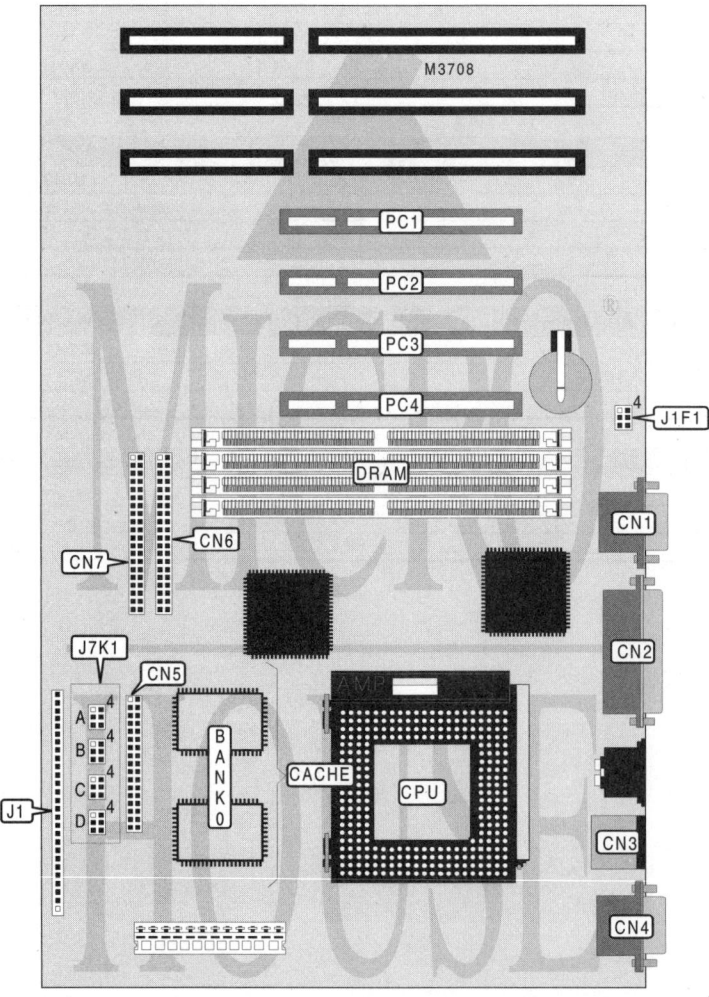

Continued on next page...

INTEL CORPORATION
ADVANCED/ML

. . . continued from previous page

CONNECTIONS			
Purpose	**Location**	**Purpose**	**Location**
Serial port 1	CN1	Reset switch	J1 pins 4 & 5
Parallel port	CN2	Power LED & keylock	J1 pins 6 - 10
PS/2 mouse port	CN3	IDE interface LED	J1 pins 11 - 14
Serial port 2	CN4	Green PC connector	J1 pins 15 - 19
Floppy drive interface	CN5	IR connector	J1 pins 20 - 25
IDE interface 1	CN6	Speaker	J1 pins 26 - 29
IDE interface 2	CN7	32-bit PCI slots	PC1 - PC4
Chassis fan power	J1 pins 1 - 3		

USER CONFIGURABLE SETTINGS		
Function	**Label**	**Position**
⇨ Flash BIOS normal operation	J1F1	Pins 1 & 2 closed
Flash BIOS recovery mode	J1F1	Pins 2 & 3 closed
⇨ Flash BIOS write protect enabled	J1F1	Pins 4 & 5 closed
Flash BIOS write protect disabled	J1F1	Pins 5 & 6 closed
⇨ Password normal operation	J7K1A	Pins 1 & 2 closed
Password clear	J7K1A	Pins 2 & 3 closed
⇨ CMOS memory normal operation	J7K1A	Pins 4 & 5 closed
CMOS memory clear	J7K1A	Pins 5 & 6 closed
⇨ Setup access enabled	J7K1B	Pins 1 & 2 closed
Setup access disabled	J7K1B	Pins 2 & 3 closed

DRAM CONFIGURATION		
Size	**Bank 0**	**Bank 1**
8MB	(2) 1M x 36	None
16MB	(2) 2M x 36	None
16MB	(2) 1M x 36	(2) 1M x 36
24MB	(2) 2M x 36	(2) 1M x 36
32MB	(2) 4M x 36	None
32MB	(2) 2M x 36	(2) 2M x 36
40MB	(2) 4M x 36	(2) 1M x 36
48MB	(2) 4M x 36	(2) 2M x 36
64MB	(2) 8M x 36	None
64MB	(2) 4M x 36	(2) 4M x 36
72MB	(2) 8M x 36	(2) 1M x 36
80MB	(2) 8M x 36	(2) 2M x 36
96MB	(2) 8M x 36	(2) 4M x 36
128MB	(2) 8M x 36	(2) 8M x 36
128MB	(2) 16M x 36	None

Note: Board accepts EDO memory. Board also accepts x 32 SIMMs. The location of banks 0 & 1 are unidentified.

Continued on next page...

INTEL CORPORATION
ADVANCED/ML

...continued from previous page

CACHE CONFIGURATION

Size	Bank 0
256KB	(2) 32K x 32
512KB	(2) 64K x 32

Note: Board comes from the factory with 256KB or 512KB cache installed.

CPU SPEED SELECTION

CPU speed	Clock speed	Multiplier	J7K1C	J7K1D
75MHz	50MHz	1.5x	2 & 3, 5 & 6	1 & 2, 4 & 5
90MHz	60MHz	1.5x	2 & 3, 4 & 5	1 & 2, 4 & 5
100MHz	66MHz	1.5x	1 & 2, 5 & 6	1 & 2, 4 & 5
120MHz	60MHz	2x	2 & 3, 4 & 5	2 & 3, 4 & 5
133MHz	66MHz	2x	1 & 2, 5 & 6	2 & 3, 4 & 5
150MHz	60MHz	2.5x	2 & 3, 4 & 5	2 & 3, 5 & 6
166MHz	66MHz	2.5x	1 & 2, 5 & 6	2 & 3, 5 & 6

Note: Pins designated should be in the closed position.

CPU TYPE SELECTION

Type	J7K1B
OVD	Pins 5 & 6 closed
◇ VRE	Pins 4 & 5 closed

INTEL CORPORATION
ADVANCED/MN (MORRISSON)

Processor   Pentium
Processor Speed   75/90/100/120MHz
Chip Set   Unidentified
Max. Onboard DRAM 128MB
Cache   256/512KB
BIOS   AMI
Dimensions   330mm x 218mm
I/O Options   PS/2 mouse port, parallel port, serial ports (2), VGA port, VGA feature connector, green PC connector, floppy drive interface, IDE interfaces (2)
NPU Options   None

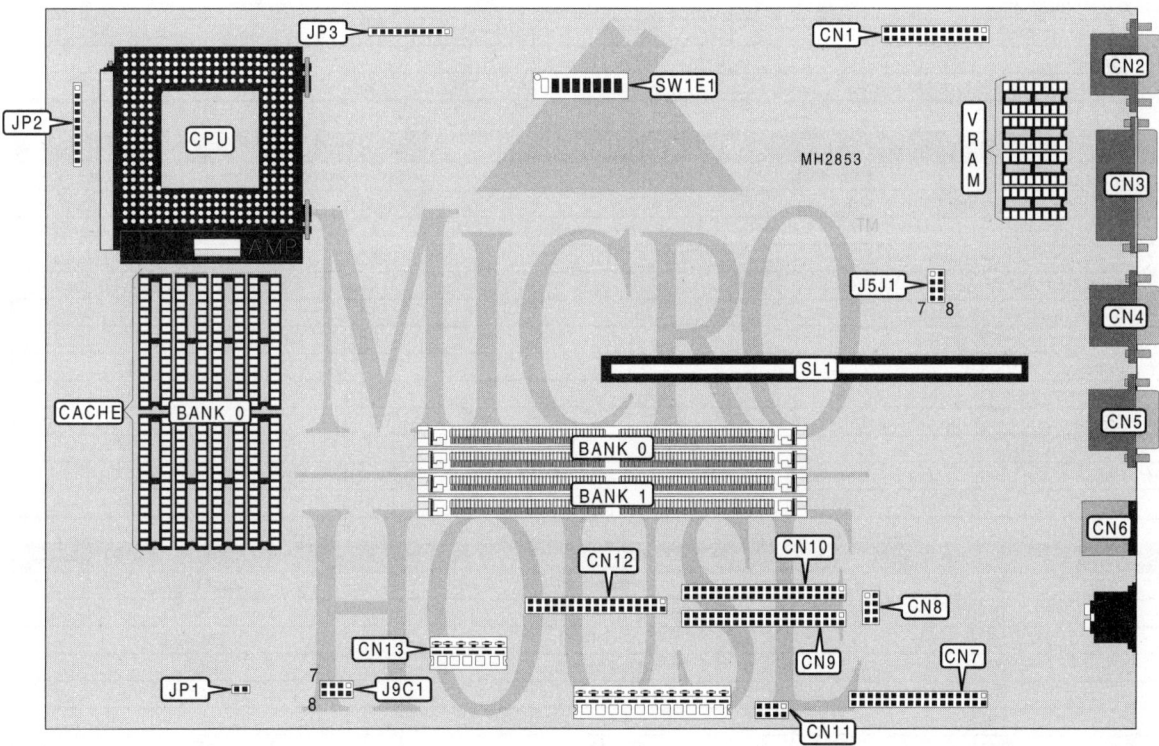

Continued on next page...

INTEL CORPORATION
ADVANCED/MN (MORRISSON)

...continued from previous page

CONNECTIONS			
Purpose	**Location**	**Purpose**	**Location**
VGA feature connector	CN1	IDE interface	CN10
VGA port	CN2	CD-ROM audio connector	CN11
Parallel port	CN3	Floppy drive interface	CN12
Serial port 1	CN4	Power supply remote connector	CN13
Serial port 2	CN5	Green PC connector	JP1
PS/2 mouse port	CN6	Front panel connector	JP2
Audio I/O connector	CN7	Front panel connector	JP3
Wave table connector	CN8	Riser Card	SL1
IDE interface	CN9		
Note: The actual sizes of jumpers CN7, CN8, CN10, JP2, JP3 are unidentified. They are shown for location purposes only.			

USER CONFIGURABLE SETTINGS			
Function		**Jumper/Switch**	**Position**
⇨	ISA clock speed select 1/6	J5J1	pins 5 & 7 open
	ISA clock speed select 1/8	J5J1	pins 5 & 7 closed
⇨	Recovery boot enabled	J5J1	pins 1 & 3 closed
	Recovery boot disabled	J5J1	pins 1 & 2 closed
⇨	CPU type select VR rated	J9C1	pins 1 & 3 closed
	CPU type select VRE rated	J9C1	pins 5 & 7 closed
⇨	Password normal operation	SW1E1/3	Off
	Password clear	SW1E1/3	On
⇨	CMOS memory normal operation	SW1E1/4	Off
	CMOS memory clear	SW1E1/4	On
⇨	CMOS setup utility access enabled	SW1E1/5	Off
	CMOS setup utility access disabled	SW1E1/5	On

DRAM CONFIGURATION		
Size	**Bank 0**	**Bank 1**
8MB	(2) 1M x 36	NONE
8MB	NONE	(2) 1M x 36
16MB	(2) 2M x 36	NONE
16MB	NONE	(2) 2M x 36
16MB	(2) 1M x 36	(2) 1M x 36
24MB	(2) 1M x 36	(2) 2M x 36
24MB	(2) 2M x 36	(2) 1M x 36
32MB	(2) 2M x 36	(2) 2M x 36
48MB	(2) 2M x 36	(2) 4M x 36
48MB	(2) 4M x 36	(2) 2M x 36
64MB	(2) 4M x 36	(2) 4M x 36
72MB	(2) 1M x 36	(2) 8M x 36
72MB	(2) 8M x 36	(2) 1M x 36
128MB	(2) 8M x 36	(2) 8M x 36

Continued on next page...

INTEL CORPORATION
ADVANCED/MN (MORRISSON)

... continued from previous page

CACHE CONFIGURATION	
Size	Bank 0
256KB	(8) 32K x 8
512KB	(8) 64K x 8

CACHE JUMPER CONFIGURATION		
Size	SW1E1/1	SW1E1/2
256KB	Off	Off
512KB	Off	On

CPU SPEED CONFIGURATION			
Speed	SW1E1/6	SW1E1/7	SW1E1/8
75MHz	Off	Off	Off
90MHz	Off	On	Off
100MHz	Off	Off	On
120MHz	On	On	Off

VRAM CONFIGURATION

VRAM is upgradable to 2MB, but the chip size is unidentified.

INTEL CORPORATION
AG430HX

Processor	Pentium
Processor Speed	75/90/100/120/133/150/166/200MHz
Chip Set	Intel
Video Chip Set	ATI
Maximum Onboard Memory	128MB (EDO supported)
Maximum Video Memory	2MB
Cache	256KB
BIOS	Intel
Dimensions	304mm x 243mm
I/O Options	32-bit PCI slots (4), floppy drive interface, green PC connector, IDE interfaces (2), parallel port, PS/2 mouse port, serial ports (2), VESA feature connector, VGA port, IR connector, USB connectors (2), soft off power supply, wavetable connectors (2), telephony connector, audio out connector, microphone in connector, audio in connector, MIDI/game port, CD-ROM connector
NPU Options	None

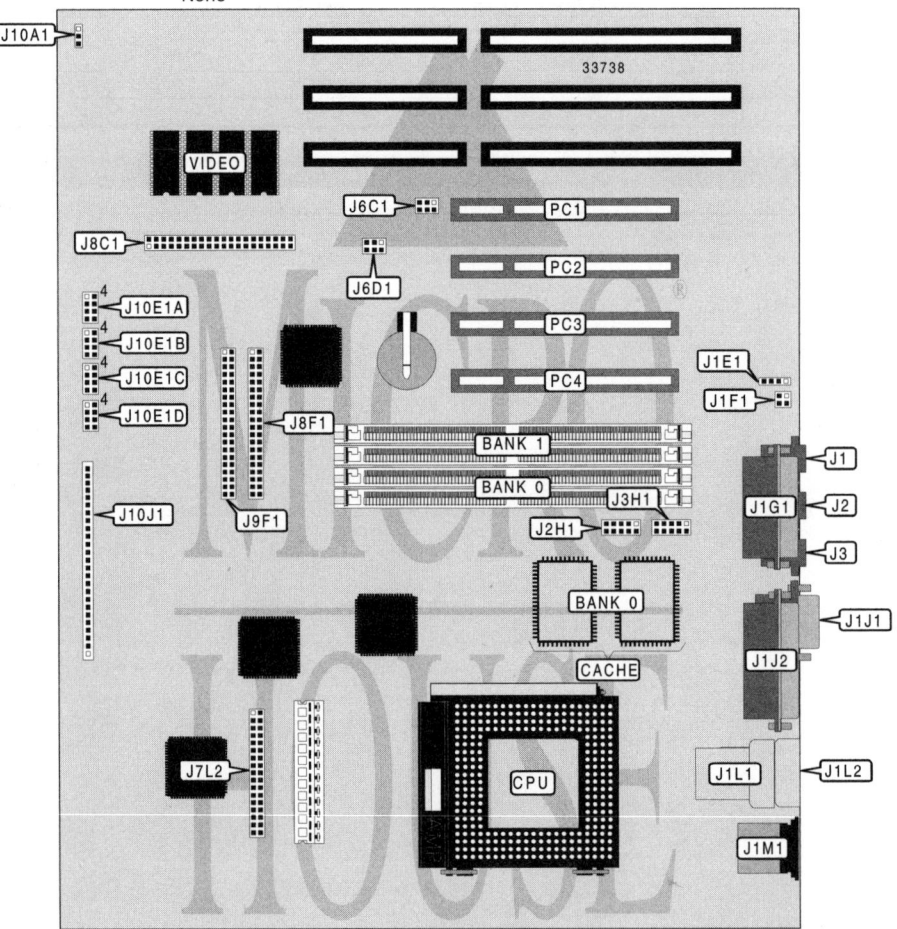

Continued on next page...

INTEL CORPORATION
AG430HX

...continued from previous page

CONNECTIONS			
Purpose	**Location**	**Purpose**	**Location**
Microphone in connector	J1	Wavetable connector	J6D1
Audio in connector	J2	Floppy drive interface	J7L2
Audio out connector	J3	VESA feature connector	J8C1
CD-ROM connector	J1E1	IDE interface 2	J8F1
Telephony connector	J1F1	IDE interface 1	J9F1
MIDI/game port	J1G1	Chassis fan power	J10A1
VGA port	J1J1	Front panel power switch	J10J1 pins 1 & 2
Parallel port	J1J2	Green PC connector	J10J1 pins 3 & 4
USB connector	J1L1	IR connector	J10J1 pins 6 - 11
USB connector	J1L2	IDE interface LED	J10J1 pins 13 - 16
PS/2 mouse port	J1M1	Green PC LED	J10J1 pins 18 - 21
Serial port 1	J2H1	Reset switch	J10J1 pins 22 & 23
Serial port 2	J3H1	Speaker	J10J1 pins 24 - 27
Wavetable connector	J6C1	32-bit PCI slots	PC1 - PC4

USER CONFIGURABLE SETTINGS		
Function	**Label**	**Position**
✧ Password enabled	J10E1A	Pins 1 & 2 closed
Password disabled	J10E1A	Pins 2 & 3 closed
✧ CMOS memory normal operation	J10E1A	Pins 4 & 5 closed
CMOS memory clear	J10E1A	Pins 5 & 6 closed
✧ Setup access enabled	J10E1B	Pins 1 & 2 closed
Setup access disabled	J10E1B	Pins 2 & 3 closed
✧ Flash BIOS normal operation	J10E1B	Pins 4 & 5 closed
Flash BIOS recovery mode	J10E1B	Pins 5 & 6 closed

DRAM CONFIGURATION		
Size	**Bank 0**	**Bank 1**
8MB	(2) 1M x 32	None
16MB	(2) 2M x 32	None
16MB	(2) 1M x 32	(2) 1M x 32
24MB	(2) 2M x 32	(2) 1M x 32
24MB	(2) 1M x 32	(2) 2M x 32
32MB	(2) 4M x 32	None
32MB	(2) 2M x 32	(2) 2M x 32
40MB	(2) 4M x 32	(2) 1M x 32
40MB	(2) 1M x 32	(2) 4M x 32
48MB	(2) 4M x 32	(2) 2M x 32
48MB	(2) 2M x 32	(2) 4M x 32
64MB	(2) 8M x 32	None
64MB	(2) 4M x 32	(2) 4M x 32
72MB	(2) 8M x 32	(2) 1M x 32

Continued on next page...

INTEL CORPORATION
AG430HX

...continued from previous page

DRAM CONFIGURATION (CON'T)		
Size	**Bank 0**	**Bank 1**
72MB	(2) 1M x 32	(2) 8M x 32
80MB	(2) 8M x 32	(2) 2M x 32
80MB	(2) 2M x 32	(2) 8M x 32
96MB	(2) 8M x 32	(2) 4M x 32
96MB	(2) 4M x 32	(2) 8M x 32
128MB	(2) 8M x 32	(2) 8M x 32

Note: Board accepts EDO memory. Board also accepts x 36 SIMMs. Banks are interchangeable.

CACHE CONFIGURATION
Note: 256KB cache is factory installed and is not configurable.

VIDEO MEMORY CONFIGURATION
Note: 2MB video memory is factory installed and is not configurable.

CPU SPEED SELECTION				
CPU speed	**Clock speed**	**Multiplier**	**J10E1C**	**J10E1D**
75MHz	50MHz	1.5x	2 & 3, 5 & 6	1 & 2, 4 & 5
90MHz	60MHz	1.5x	2 & 3, 4 & 5	1 & 2, 4 & 5
100MHz	66MHz	1.5x	1 & 2, 5 & 6	1 & 2, 4 & 5
120MHz	60MHz	2x	2 & 3, 4 & 5	2 & 3, 4 & 5
133MHz	66MHz	2x	1 & 2, 5 & 6	2 & 3, 4 & 5
150MHz	60MHz	2.5x	2 & 3, 4 & 5	2 & 3, 5 & 6
166MHz	66MHz	2.5x	1 & 2, 5 & 6	2 & 3, 5 & 6
200MHz	66MHz	3x	1 & 2, 5 & 6	1 & 2, 5 & 6

Note: Pins designated should be in the closed position.

INTEL CORPORATION
ALTSERVER/CS

Processor	Pentium
Processor Speed	75/90/100/120/133/166MHz
Chip Set	Intel
Maximum Onboard Memory	256MB
Cache	256/512KB
BIOS	AMI
Dimensions	330mm x 305mm
I/O Options	32-bit PCI slots (3), floppy drive interface, IDE interface, SCSI interfaces (2), parallel port, PS/2 mouse interface, serial ports (2), server monitor feature connector, VGA interface, cache slot
NPU Options	None

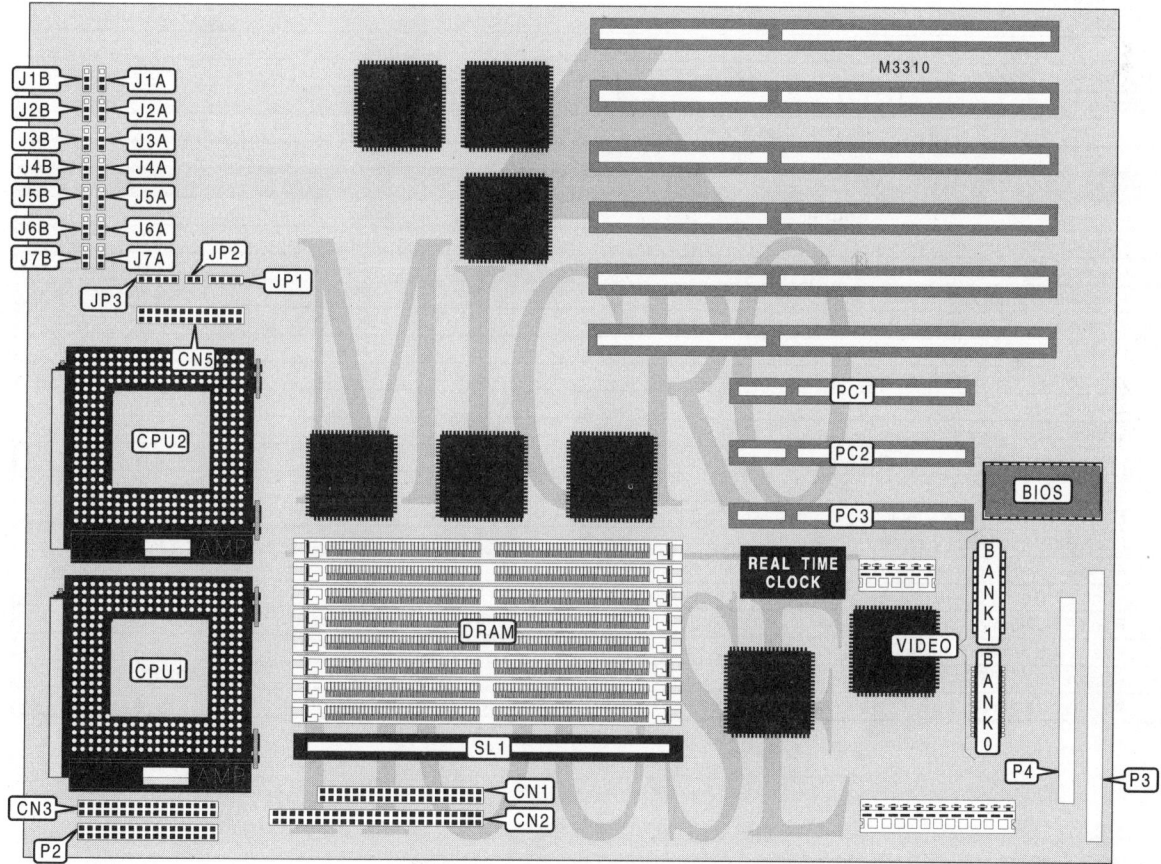

Continued on next page...

INTEL CORPORATION
ALTSERVER/CS

...continued from previous page

CONNECTIONS			
Function	**Label**	**Function**	**Label**
IDE interface	CN1	Serial port 1	P3 pins 7 - 14
SCSI interface	CN2	Serial port 2	P3 pins 15 - 22
Floppy drive interface	CN3	Wide SCSI interface	P3 pins 23 - 40
Server monitor feature connector	CN5	VGA interface	P3 pins 41 - 52
Speaker	JP1	Parallel port	P3 pins 53 - 72
Reset switch	JP2	Wide SCSI interface	P3 pins 98 - 113
Front panel connector	JP3	SCSI terminator	P4
Front panel connector	P2	Cache slot	SL1
PS/2 mouse interface	P3 pins 1 - 3	32-bit PCI slots	PC1 - PC3
Keyboard	P3 pins 4- 6		
Note: The location of pin 1 on all connectors is unidentified.			

USER CONFIGURABLE SETTINGS		
Setting	**Label**	**Position**
✧ CMOS memory normal operation	J1B	Pins 1 & 2 closed
CMOS memory clear	J1B	Pins 2 & 3 closed
✧ Password normal operation	J2B	Pins 1 & 2 closed
Password clear	J2B	Pins 2 & 3 closed
✧ Primary CPU installed in socket 1	J3B	Pins 1 & 2 closed
Primary CPU installed in socket 2	J3B	Pins 2 & 3 closed
✧ Monitor type select color	J4A	Pins 1 & 2 closed
Monitor type select monochrome	J4A	Pins 2 & 3 closed
✧ Factory configured - do not alter (disable and ground)	J4B	Pins 1 & 2 closed
Factory configured - do not alter (enable kick start)	J4B	Pins 2 & 3 closed
✧ Flash BIOS boot block enabled	J5A	Pins 1 & 2 closed
Flash BIOS boot block disabled	J5A	Pins 2 & 3 closed
✧ Flash BIOS write protect disabled	J6A	Pins 1 & 2 closed
Flash BIOS write protect enabled	J6A	Pins 2 & 3 closed
✧ Flash BIOS normal boot	J7A	Pins 1 & 2 closed
Flash BIOS recovery mode	J7A	Pins 2 & 3 closed
✧ Factory configured - do not alter (option high)	J7B	Pins 1 & 2 closed
Factory configured - do not alter (option low)	J7B	Pins 2 & 3 closed

Continued on next page...

INTEL CORPORATION
ALTSERVER/CS

. . . continued from previous page

	DRAM			
Size	Bank 0	Bank 1	Bank 2	Bank 3
8MB	(2) 1M x 36	None	None	None
16MB	(2) 2M x 36	None	None	None
16MB	(2) 1M x 36	(2) 1M x 36	None	None
24MB	(2) 2M x 36	(2) 1M x 36	None	None
24MB	(2) 1M x 36	(2) 1M x 36	(2) 1M x 36	None
24MB	(2) 1M x 36	(2) 2M x 36	None	None
32MB	(2) 4M x 36	None	None	None
32MB	(2) 2M x 36	(2) 1M x 36	(2) 1M x 36	None
32MB	(2) 2M x 36	(2) 2M x 36	None	None
32MB	(2) 1M x 36	(2) 1M x 36	(2) 1M x 36	(2) 1M x 36
40MB	(2) 4M x 36	(2) 1M x 36	None	None
40MB	(2) 2M x 36	(2) 1M x 36	(2) 1M x 36	(2) 1M x 36
40MB	(2) 1M x 36	(2) 2M x 36	(2) 2M x 36	None
40MB	(2) 1M x 36	(2) 4M x 36	None	None
48MB	(2) 4M x 36	(2) 1M x 36	(2) 1M x 36	None
48MB	(2) 4M x 36	(2) 2M x 36	None	None
48MB	(2) 2M x 36	(2) 2M x 36	(2) 2M x 36	None
48MB	(2) 2M x 36	(2) 4M x 36	None	None
56MB	(2) 4M x 36	(2) 1M x 36	(2) 1M x 36	(2) 1M x 36
56MB	(2) 1M x 36	(2) 2M x 36	(2) 2M x 36	(2) 2M x 36
64MB	(2) 8M x 36	None	None	None
64MB	(2) 4M x 36	(2) 2M x 36	(2) 2M x 36	None
64MB	(2) 4M x 36	(2) 4M x 36	None	None
64MB	(2) 2M x 36	(2) 2M x 36	(2) 2M x 36	(2) 2M x 36
72MB	(2) 8M x 36	(2) 1M x 36	None	None
72MB	(2) 1M x 36	(2) 4M x 36	(2) 4M x 36	None
72MB	(2) 1M x 36	(2) 8M x 36	None	None
80MB	(2) 8M x 36	(2) 1M x 36	(2) 1M x 36	None
80MB	(2) 8M x 36	(2) 2M x 36	None	None
80MB	(2) 4M x 36	(2) 2M x 36	(2) 2M x 36	(2) 2M x 36
80MB	(2) 2M x 36	(2) 4M x 36	(2) 4M x 36	None
80MB	(2) 2M x 36	(2) 8M x 36	None	None
88MB	(2) 8M x 36	(2) 1M x 36	(2) 1M x 36	(2) 1M x 36
96MB	(2) 8M x 36	(2) 2M x 36	(2) 2M x 36	None
96MB	(2) 8M x 36	(2) 4M x 36	None	None
96MB	(2) 4M x 36	(2) 4M x 36	(2) 4M x 36	None
96MB	(2) 4M x 36	(2) 8M x 36	None	None
104MB	(2) 1M x 36	(2) 4M x 36	(2) 4M x 36	(2) 4M x 36
112MB	(2) 8M x 36	(2) 2M x 36	(2) 2M x 36	(2) 2M x 36
112MB	(2) 2M x 36	(2) 4M x 36	(2) 4M x 36	(2) 4M x 36
128MB	(2) 8M x 36	(2) 4M x 36	(2) 4M x 36	None
128MB	(2) 8M x 36	(2) 8M x 36	None	None

Continued on next page. . .

INTEL CORPORATION
ALTSERVER/CS

...continued from previous page

		DRAM (CON'T)		
Size	Bank 0	Bank 1	Bank 2	Bank 3
128MB	(2) 4M x 36	(2) 4M x 36	(2) 4M x 36	(2) 4M x 36
136MB	(2) 1M x 36	(2) 8M x 36	(2) 8M x 36	None
144MB	(2) 2M x 36	(2) 8M x 36	(2) 8M x 36	None
160MB	(2) 8M x 36	(2) 4M x 36	(2) 4M x 36	(2) 4M x 36
160MB	(2) 4M x 36	(2) 8M x 36	(2) 8M x 36	None
192MB	(2) 8M x 36	(2) 8M x 36	(2) 8M x 36	None
200MB	(2) 1M x 36	(2) 8M x 36	(2) 8M x 36	(2) 8M x 36
208MB	(2) 2M x 36	(2) 8M x 36	(2) 8M x 36	(2) 8M x 36
224MB	(2) 4M x 36	(2) 8M x 36	(2) 8M x 36	(2) 8M x 36
256MB	(2) 8M x 36	(2) 8M x 36	(2) 8M x 36	(2) 8M x 36

Note: The orientation of the banks is unidentified.

CACHE SIZE	
Size	SL1
256KB	Installed
512KB	Installed

Note: Cache can either be asynchronous or burst synchronous.

		CPU SPEED		
Setting	J1A	J2A	J5B	J6B
75MHz	Pins 1 & 2 closed	Pins 1 & 2 closed	Pins 1 & 2 closed	Pins 2 & 3 closed
90MHz	Pins 1 & 2 closed	Pins 1 & 2 closed	Pins 1 & 2 closed	Pins 1 & 2 closed
100MHz	Pins 1 & 2 closed	Pins 1 & 2 closed	Pins 2 & 3 closed	Pins 2 & 3 closed
120MHz	Pins 1 & 2 closed	Pins 2 & 3 closed	Pins 1 & 2 closed	Pins 1 & 2 closed
133MHz	Pins 1 & 2 closed	Pins 2 & 3 closed	Pins 2 & 3 closed	Pins 2 & 3 closed
166MHz	Pins 2 & 3 closed	Pins 2 & 3 closed	Pins 2 & 3 closed	Pins 2 & 3 closed

CPU VOLTAGE	
Setting	J3A
STD/VRE CPU installed	Pins 1 & 2 closed
N/A	Pins 2 & 3 closed

VIDEO MEMORY		
Size	Bank 0	Bank 1
512KB	(1) 256K x 16	None
1MB	(1) 256K x 16	(1) 256K x 16

INTEL CORPORATION
CLASSIC R

Processor	80486SX/80486DX/80486DX2
Processor Speed	25/33/50(internal)/66(internal)MHz
Chip Set	VLSI
Max. Onboard DRAM	32MB
Cache	64/128/256KB
BIOS	Phoenix
Dimensions	330mm x 218mm
I/O Options	Floppy drive interface, IDE interface, parallel port, PS/2 mouse port, serial ports (2), VESA feature connector, VGA port, riser slot
NPU Options	None

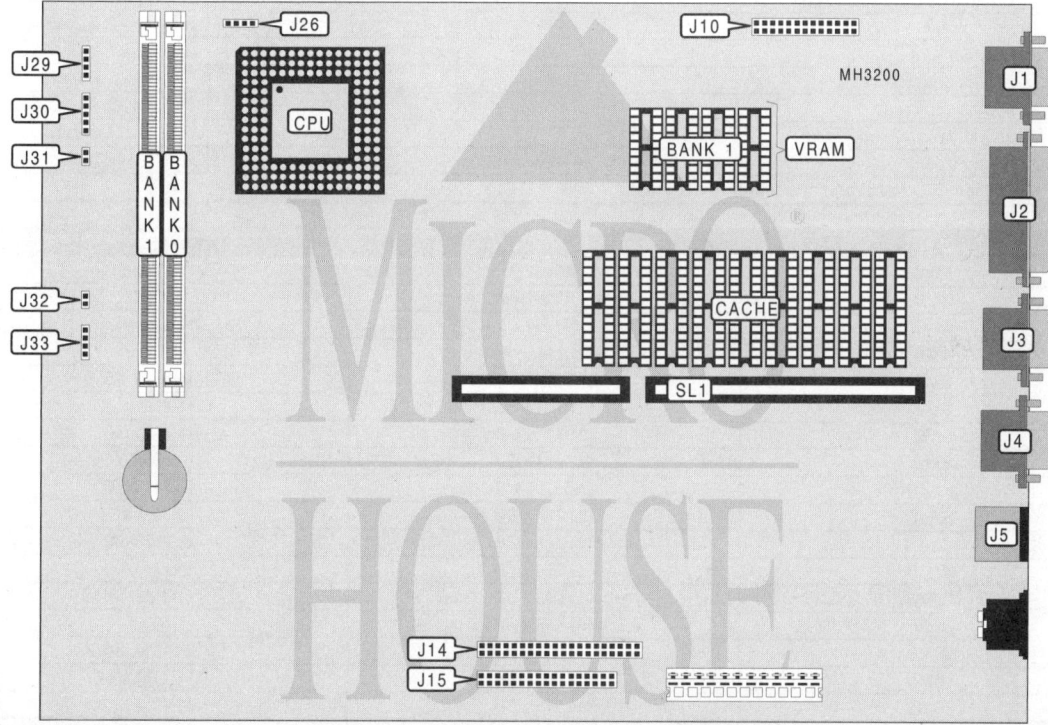

CONNECTIONS

Purpose	Location	Purpose	Location
VGA port	J1	Chassis fan power	J26
Parallel port	J2	IDE interface LED	J29
Serial port 2	J3	Power LED & keylock	J30
Serial port 1	J4	Reset switch	J31
PS/2 mouse port	J5	Chassis fan power	J32
VESA feature connector	J10	Speaker	J33
IDE interface	J14	Riser slot	SL1
Floppy drive interface	J15		

Continued on next page...

INTEL CORPORATION
CLASSIC R

...continued from previous page

USER CONFIGURABLE SETTINGS		
Function	**Jumper**	**Position**
◇ 12v to flash BIOS enabled	J12	pins 1 & 2 closed
12v to flash BIOS disabled	J12	pins 2 & 3 closed
◇ Flash BIOS recovery mode disabled	J13	pins 1 & 2 closed
Flash BIOS recovery mode enabled	J13	pins 2 & 3 closed
◇ On board video enabled	J16	pins 1 & 2 closed
On board video disabled	J16	pins 2 & 3 closed
◇ Floppy drive write protect enabled	J17	pins 2 & 3 closed
Floppy drive write protect disabled	J17	pins 1 & 2 closed
◇ Password enabled	J20	pins 2 & 3 closed
Password clear	J20	pins 1 & 2 closed
◇ CMOS access enabled	J21	pins 1 & 2 closed
CMOS access disabled	J21	pins 2 & 3 closed
◇ CMOS memory normal operation	J28	Closed
CMOS memory clear	J28	Open

Note: The location of the above jumpers are unidentified.

DRAM CONFIGURATION		
Size	**Bank 0**	**Bank 1**
2MB	(1) 512K x 36	NONE
4MB	(1) 512K x 36	(1) 512K x 36
4MB	(1) 1M x 36	NONE
6MB	(1) 512K x 36	(1) 1M x 36
6MB	(1) 1M x 36	(1) 512K x 36
8MB	(1) 1M x 36	(1) 1M x 36
8MB	(1) 2M x 36	NONE
10MB	(1) 512K x 36	(1) 2M x 36
10MB	(1) 2M x 36	(1) 512K x 36
12MB	(1) 1M x 36	(1) 2M x 36
12MB	(1) 2M x 36	(1) 1M x 36
16MB	(1) 2M x 36	(1) 2M x 36
16MB	(1) 4M x 36	NONE
18MB	(1) 512K x 36	(1) 4M x 36
18MB	(1) 4M x 36	(1) 512K x 36
20MB	(1) 1M x 36	(1) 4M x 36
20MB	(1) 4M x 36	(1) 1M x 36
24MB	(1) 2M x 36	(1) 4M x 36
24MB	(1) 4M x 36	(1) 2M x 36
32MB	(1) 4M x 36	(1) 4M x 36

CACHE CONFIGURATION			
Size	**Bank 0**	**Bank 1**	**TAG**
64KB	(4) 8K x 8	(4) 8K x 8	(1) 8K x 8
128KB	(4) 32K x 8	NONE	(1) 8K x 8
256KB	(4) 32K x 8	(4) 32K x 8	(1) 32K x 8

Note: The orientation of Banks 0 & 1 and TAG is unidentified.

Continued on next page...

INTEL CORPORATION
CLASSIC R

. . . continued from previous page

CACHE JUMPER CONFIGURATION				
Size	J11 pins 1 & 2	J11 pins 3 & 4	J11 pins 5 & 6	J11 pins 7 & 8
64KB	Open	Open	Open	Open
128KB	Closed	Open	Closed	Open
256KB	Closed	Closed	Open	Closed
Note: The location of J11 is unidentified.				

CPU TYPE CONFIGURATION				
Type	J22	J23	J24	J25
80486SX (PQFP)	pins 2 & 3 closed	pins 1 & 2 closed	pins 1 & 2 closed	pins 1 & 2 closed
80486SX (PGA)	pins 1 & 2 closed	pins 2 & 3 closed	pins 2 & 3 closed	pins 2 & 3 closed
80486DX	pins 2 & 3 closed	pins 1 & 2 closed	pins 1 & 2 closed	pins 1 & 2 closed
80486DX2	pins 2 & 3 closed	pins 1 & 2 closed	pins 1 & 2 closed	pins 1 & 2 closed
Note: The locations of J22, J23, J24 & J25 are unidentified. The location of the PQFP socket is unidentified.				

CPU SPEED CONFIGURATION		
Speed	J18	J19
25MHz	pins 1 & 2 closed	pins 1 & 2 closed
33MHz	pins 1 & 2 closed	pins 2 & 3 closed
50iMHz	pins 1 & 2 closed	pins 1 & 2 closed
66iMHz	pins 1 & 2 closed	pins 2 & 3 closed
Note: The locations of J18 & J19 are unidentified.		

VRAM CONFIGURATION		
Size	Bank 0	Bank 1
512KB	512KB	NONE
1MB	512KB	(4) 256K x 4
Note: Bank 0 is factory installed and is not configurable. The location is unidentified.		

INTEL CORPORATION
CU430HX

Processor	Pentium
Processor Speed	75/90/100/120/133/150/166/200MHz
Chip Set	Intel
Video Chip Set	ATI
Maximum Onboard Memory	192MB (EDO supported)
Maximum Video Memory	4MB
Cache	256/512KB
BIOS	Unidentified
Dimensions	300mm x 210mm
I/O Options	Floppy drive interface, green PC connector, IDE interfaces (2), parallel port, PS/2 mouse port, serial ports (3), VGA header connector, VGA port, riser slot, cache slot, IR connector, USB connector, LAN connector, microphone port, audio output port, CD audio connector, modem connector, wave table connector, MIDI/audio interface
NPU Options	None

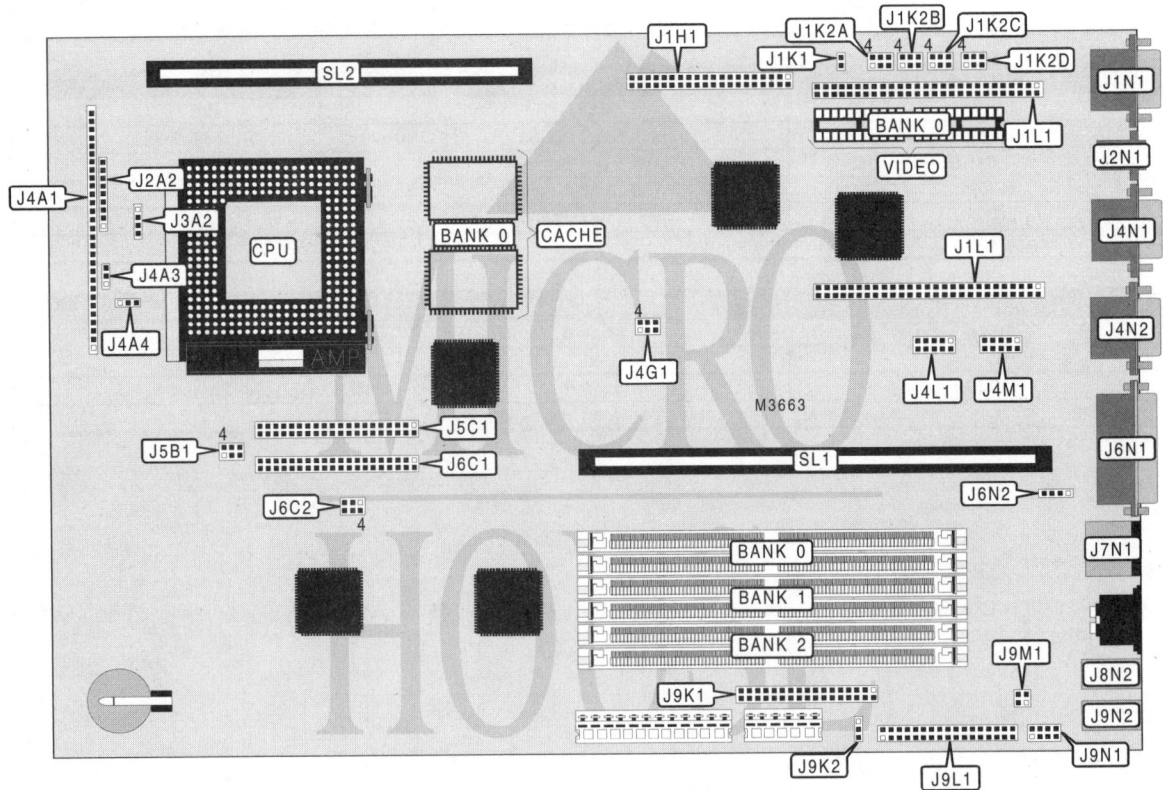

Continued on next page...

INTEL CORPORATION
CU430HX

...continued from previous page

CONNECTIONS			
Purpose	**Location**	**Purpose**	**Location**
Security connector	J1K1	Serial port 2	J4M1
VGA header connector	J1H1	USB connector	J4N1
VGA port	J1N1	Serial port 3	J4N2
Front panel connector	J2A2	IDE interface 1	J5C1
LAN connector	J2N1	IDE interface 2	J6C1
Power LED/IDE interface LED	J3A2	Parallel port	J6N1
Chassis fan power	J4A1 pins 1 - 3	CD audio connector	J6N2
Reset switch	J4A1 pins 4 & 5	PS/2 mouse port	J7N1
Power LED	J4A1 pins 7 - 10	Microphone port	J8N2
IDE interface LED	J4A1 pins 11 - 14	Floppy drive interface	J9K1
Power supply on connector	J4A1 pins 15 & 16	MIDI/audio interface	J9L1
Green PC connector	J4A1 pins 17 & 18	Modem connector	J9M1
IR connector	J4A1 pins 20 - 25	Wave table connector	J9N1
Speaker	J4A1 pins 26 - 29	Audio output port	J9N2
Keylock	J4A3	Riser slot	SL1
Chassis fan power	J4A4	Cache slot	SL2
Serial port 1	J4L1		

USER CONFIGURABLE SETTINGS		
Function	**Label**	**Position**
⇨ Password normal operation	J1K2A	Pins 1 & 2 closed
Password clear	J1K2A	Pins 2 & 3 closed
⇨ CMOS memory normal operation	J1K2A	Pins 4 & 5 closed
CMOS memory clear	J1K2A	Pins 5 & 6 closed
⇨ Setup access enabled	J1K2B	Pins 1 & 2 closed
Setup access disabled	J1K2B	Pins 2 & 3 closed
⇨ Factory configured - do not alter	J1K2B	Pins 5 & 6 closed
⇨ 2 PCI slots on riser card	J4G1	Pins 1 & 2, 4 & 5 closed
3 PCI slots on riser card	J4G1	Pins 2 & 3, 5 & 6 closed
⇨ Flash BIOS normal operation	J6C2	Pins 1 & 2 closed
Flash BIOS recovery mode	J6C2	Pins 2 & 3 closed

DRAM CONFIGURATION			
Size	**Bank 0**	**Bank 1**	**Bank 2**
16MB	(2) 1M x 36	(2) 1M x 36	None
16MB	(2) 2M x 36	None	None
24MB	(2) 2M x 36	(2) 1M x 36	None
24MB	(2) 1M x 36	(2) 1M x 36	(2) 1M x 36
32MB	(2) 4M x 36	None	None
32MB	(2) 2M x 36	(2) 2M x 36	None
40MB	(2) 4M x 36	(2) 1M x 36	None
48MB	(2) 4M x 36	(2) 2M x 36	None

Continued on next page...

INTEL CORPORATION
CU430HX

...continued from previous page

DRAM CONFIGURATION (CON'T)			
Size	Bank 0	Bank 1	Bank 2
48MB	(2) 4M x 36	(2) 1M x 36	(2) 1M x 36
64MB	(2) 8M x 36	None	None
64MB	(2) 4M x 36	(2) 4M x 36	None
80MB	(2) 8M x 36	(2) 2M x 36	None
80MB	(2) 8M x 36	(2) 1M x 36	(2) 1M x 36
88MB	(2) 8M x 36	(2) 2M x 36	(2) 1M x 36
96MB	(2) 8M x 36	(2) 4M x 36	None
96MB	(2) 4M x 36	(2) 4M x 36	(2) 4M x 36
96MB	(2) 8M x 36	(2) 2M x 36	(2) 2M x 36
104MB	(2) 8M x 36	(2) 4M x 36	(2) 1M x 36
112MB	(2) 8M x 36	(2) 4M x 36	(2) 2M x 36
128MB	(2) 8M x 36	(2) 4M x 36	(2) 4M x 36
128MB	(2) 8M x 36	(2) 8M x 36	None
136MB	(2) 8M x 36	(2) 8M x 36	(2) 1M x 36
144MB	(2) 8M x 36	(2) 8M x 36	(2) 2M x 36
160MB	(2) 16M x 36	(2) 4M x 36	None
192MB	(2) 8M x 36	(2) 8M x 36	(2) 8M x 36

Note: Board accepts EDO memory. Board also accepts x 32 SIMMs.

CACHE CONFIGURATION		
Size	Bank 0	SL1
256KB	(2) 32K x 32	None
512KB	(2) 32K x 32	256KB module installed

VIDEO MEMORY CONFIGURATION		
Size	Bank 0	J1L1
1MB	(2) 128K x 32	None
4MB	(2) 128K x 32	Module installed

Note: Module is inserted in both connectors labeled J1L1.

CPU SPEED SELECTION				
CPU speed	Clock speed	Multiplier	J1K2C	J1K2D
75MHz	50MHz	1.5x	2 & 3, 5 & 6	1 & 2, 4 & 5
90MHz	60MHz	1.5x	2 & 3, 4 & 5	1 & 2, 4 & 5
100MHz	66MHz	1.5x	1 & 2, 5 & 6	1 & 2, 4 & 5
120MHz	60MHz	2x	2 & 3, 4 & 5	2 & 3, 4 & 5
133MHz	66MHz	2x	1 & 2, 5 & 6	2 & 3, 4 & 5
150MHz	60MHz	2.5x	2 & 3, 4 & 5	2 & 3, 5 & 6
166MHz	66MHz	2.5x	1 & 2, 5 & 6	2 & 3, 5 & 6
200MHz	66MHz	3x	1 & 2, 5 & 6	1 & 2, 5 & 6

Note: Pins designated should be in the closed position.

Continued on next page...

INTEL CORPORATION
CU430HX

. . . continued from previous page

CPU TYPE SELECTION	
Type	**J6C2**
VR	Pins 4 & 5 closed
VRE	Pins 5 & 6 closed

VCC2 SELECTION	
Setting	**J5B1**
VCC2 not connected	Open
VCC2 connected (processors using MMX technology)	Pins 1 & 4, 2 & 5, 3 & 6 closed

INTEL CORPORATION
ENDEAVOUR

Processor	Pentium
Processor Speed	75/90/100/120MHz
Chip Set	Intel
Video Chip Set	Unidentified
Maximum Onboard Memory	128MB (EDO supported)
Maximum Video Memory	Unidentified
Cache	256/512KB
BIOS	AMI
Dimensions	330mm x 218mm
I/O Options	32-bit PCI slots (4), CD-ROM interface, floppy drive interface, green PC connector, IDE interfaces (2), parallel port, PS/2 mouse port, serial ports (2), cache slot, IR connector, audio connector, wave table connector, video connector
NPU Options	None

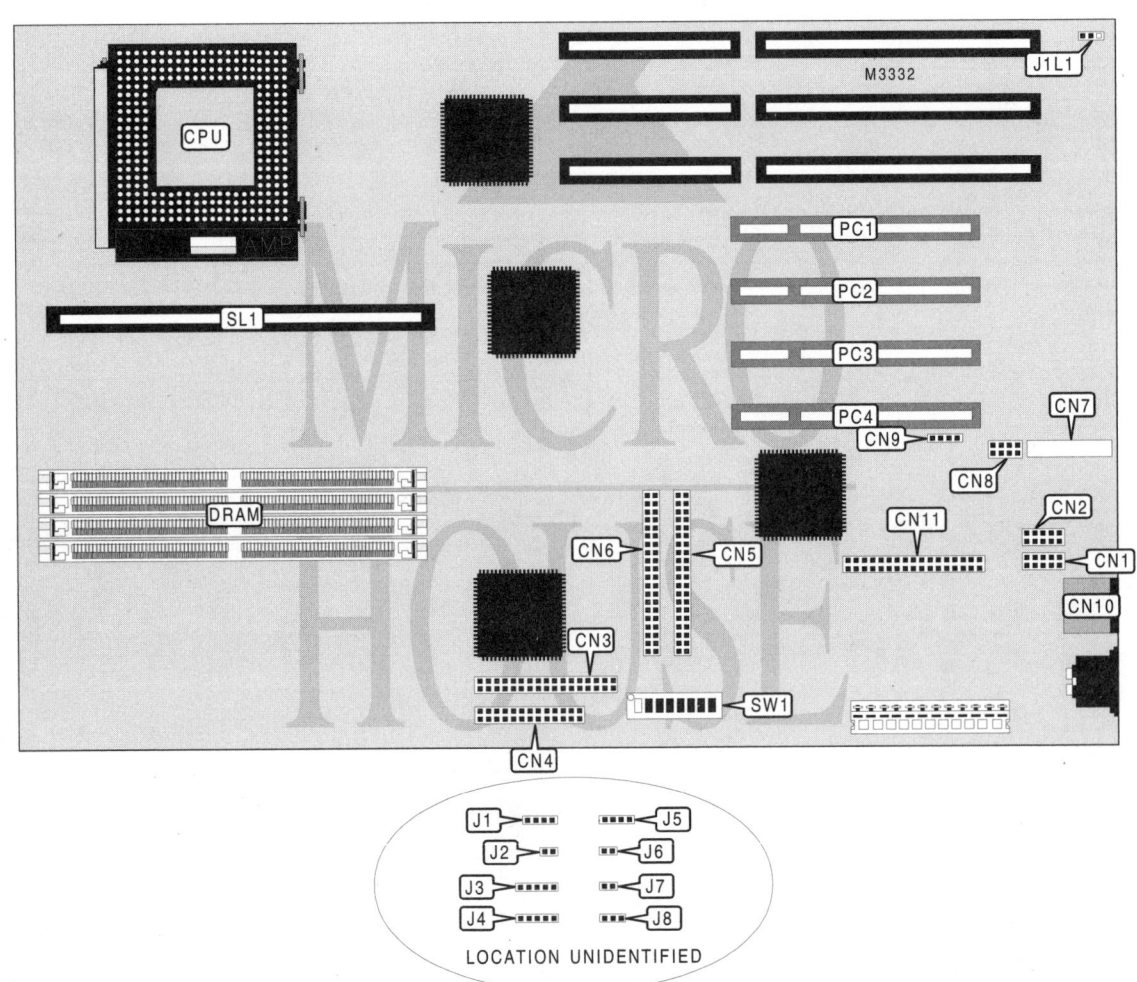

Continued on next page...

INTEL CORPORATION
ENDEAVOUR

. . . continued from previous page

CONNECTIONS				
Function	**Label**	**Function**	**Label**
Serial port	CN1	Speaker	J1
Serial port	CN2	Green PC connector	J2
Floppy drive interface	CN3	IR connector	J3
Parallel port	CN4	Power LED & keylock	J4
IDE interface	CN5	IDE interface LED	J5
IDE interface	CN6	Turbo LED	J6
Video connector (optional)	CN7	Reset switch	J7
Wave table connector	CN8	Chassis fan power	J8
CD-ROM interface	CN9	32-bit PCI slots	PC1 - PC4
PS/2 mouse port	CN10	Cache slot	SL1
Audio connector	CN11		

USER CONFIGURABLE SETTINGS		
Setting	**Label**	**Position**
◇ Flash BIOS normal operation	J1L1	Pins 1 & 2 closed
Flash BIOS recovery mode	J1L1	Pins 2 & 3 closed
◇ Adjusts ISA bus to CPU type installed	SW1/1	Off
◇ CPU type select non VRE compliant	SW1/2	Off
CPU type select VRE compliant	SW1/2	On
◇ Password normal operation	SW1/3	Off
Password clear	SW1/3	On
◇ CMOS memory normal operation	SW1/4	Off
CMOS memory clear	SW1/4	On
◇ Setup access enabled	SW1/5	Off
Setup access disabled	SW1/5	On
◇ Internal CPU bus clock select	SW1/6	Off

DRAM CONFIGURATION		
Size	**Bank 0**	**Bank 1**
8MB	None	(2) 1M x 36
8MB	(2) 1M x 36	None
16MB	None	(2) 2M x 36
16MB	(2) 2M x 36	None
16MB	(2) 1M x 36	(2) 1M x 36

Continued on next page. . .

INTEL CORPORATION
ENDEAVOUR

...continued from previous page

	DRAM CONFIGURATION (CON'T)	
Size	**Bank 0**	**Bank 1**
24MB	(2) 2M x 36	(2) 1M x 36
24MB	(2) 1M x 36	(2) 2M x 36
32MB	(2) 4M x 36	None
32MB	(2) 2M x 36	(2) 2M x 36
32MB	None	(2) 4M x 36
40MB	(2) 4M x 36	(2) 1M x 36
40MB	(2) 1M x 36	(2) 4M x 36
48MB	(2) 4M x 36	(2) 2M x 36
48MB	(2) 2M x 36	(2) 4M x 36
64MB	(2) 8M x 36	None
64MB	(2) 4M x 36	(2) 4M x 36
64MB	None	(2) 8M x 36
72MB	(2) 8M x 36	(2) 1M x 36
72MB	(2) 1M x 36	(2) 8M x 36
80MB	(2) 8M x 36	(2) 2M x 36
80MB	(2) 2M x 36	(2) 8M x 36
96MB	(2) 8M x 36	(2) 4M x 36
96MB	(2) 4M x 36	(2) 8M x 36
128MB	(2) 8M x 36	(2) 8M x 36

Note: Board accepts EDO memory. The orientation of the banks is unidentified.

CACHE CONFIGURATION	
Size	**SL1**
256KB	Installed
512KB	Installed

VIDEO MEMORY CONFIGURATION

Note: Depending on board version, video memory is installed. The maximum memory and chip types are unidentified.

	CPU SPEED SELECTION	
Speed	**SW1/7**	**SW1/8**
75MHz	On	Off
90MHz	Off	Off
100MHz	On	On
120MHz	Off	Off

MISCELLANEOUS TECHNICAL NOTE

The location of pin 1s on the connectors are unidentified.

INTEL CORPORATION
NX440LX

Processor	Pentium II
Processor Speed	233/266/300MHz
Chip Set	Intel
Video Chip Set	Cirrus Logic
Maximum Onboard Memory	384MB (EDO supported)
Maximum Video Memory	4MB
Cache	256/512KB (located on Pentium II CPU)
BIOS	Unidentified
Dimensions	254mm x 218mm
I/O Options	Parallel port, PS/2 mouse port, serial ports (2), VGA port, USB connector, LAN connector, line in, line out, microphone in, AGP slot, Yamaha wavetable connector, CD-ROM connector
NPU Options	None

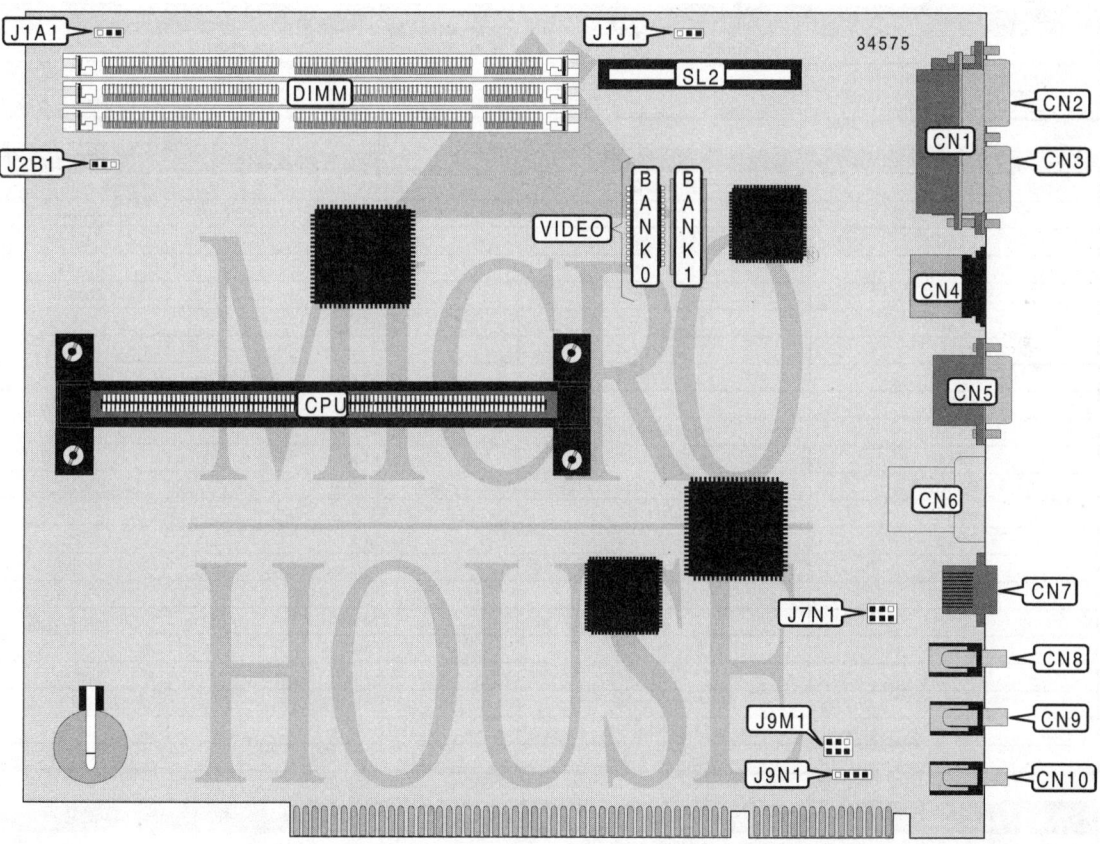

Continued on next page...

INTEL CORPORATION
NX440LX

...continued from previous page

CONNECTIONS

Purpose	Location	Purpose	Location
Parallel port	CN1	Microphone in	CN9
VGA port	CN2	Line in	CN10
Serial port 1	CN3	Chassis fan power	J2B1
PS/2 mouse port	CN4	Yamaha wavetable connector	J7N1
Serial port 2	CN5	Yamaha wavetable connector	J9M1
USB connector	CN6	CD-ROM connector	J9N1
LAN connector	CN7	AGP slot	SL2
Line out	CN8		

USER CONFIGURABLE SETTINGS

Function	Label	Position
On board video enabled	J1J1	Pins 1 & 2 closed
On board video disabled	J1J1	Pins 2 & 3 closed

DIMM CONFIGURATION

Size	Bank 0	Bank 1	Bank 2
8MB	(1) 1M x 64	None	None
16MB	(1) 2M x 64	None	None
16MB	(1) 1M x 64	(1) 1M x 64	None
24MB	(1) 2M x 64	(1) 1M x 64	None
24MB	(1) 1M x 64	(1) 1M x 64	(1) 1M x 64
32MB	(1) 4M x 64	None	None
32MB	(1) 2M x 64	(1) 2M x 64	None
40MB	(1) 4M x 64	(1) 1M x 64	None
48MB	(1) 4M x 64	(1) 2M x 64	None
48MB	(1) 2M x 64	(1) 2M x 64	(1) 2M x 64
64MB	(1) 8M x 64	None	None
64MB	(1) 4M x 64	(1) 4M x 64	None
72MB	(1) 8M x 64	(1) 1M x 64	None
80MB	(1) 8M x 64	(1) 2M x 64	None
96MB	(1) 8M x 64	(1) 4M x 64	None
96MB	(1) 4M x 64	(1) 4M x 64	(1) 4M x 64
128MB	(1) 8M x 64	(1) 8M x 64	None
128MB	(1) 16M x 64	None	None
192MB	(1) 8M x 64	(1) 8M x 64	(1) 8M x 64
256MB	(1) 16M x 64	(1) 16M x 64	None
384MB	(1) 16M x 64	(1) 16M x 64	(1) 16M x 64

CACHE CONFIGURATION

Note: 256KB/512KB cache is located on the Pentium II CPU.

Continued on next page...

INTEL CORPORATION
NX440LX

...continued from previous page

VIDEO MEMORY CONFIGURATION		
Size	Bank 0	Bank 1
2MB	2MB	None
4MB	2MB	2MB

Note: Board uses RAMBUS memory modules.

FLASH BIOS SELECTION	
Setting	J1A1
⇨ Normal operation	Pins 1 & 2 closed
Configuration mode	Pins 2 & 3 closed
Recovery mode	Open

MISCELLANEOUS TECHNICAL NOTE
Video port and memory are optional and may not be present.

INTEL CORPORATION
PD440FX

Processor	Pentium II
Processor Speed	233/266MHz
Chip Set	Intel
Video Chip Set	None
Maximum Onboard Memory	256MB (EDO supported)
Maximum Video Memory	None
Cache	256/512KB
BIOS	AMI/Intel
Dimensions	288mm x 237mm
I/O Options	32-bit PCI slots (4), CD-ROM audio interface, floppy drive interface, game/MIDI port, green PC connector, IDE interfaces (2), parallel port, PS/2 mouse port, serial ports (2), CPU slot, IR connector, USB connectors (2), ATX power connector, telephony connectors (2), line in connectors (2), line out connector, microphone connector, wavetable connector, Yamaha wave table connectors (2)
NPU Options	None

Continued on next page...

INTEL CORPORATION
PD440FX

...continued from previous page

CONNECTIONS			
Purpose	**Location**	**Purpose**	**Location**
ATX power connector	ATX	IDE interface LED	J6F1
Game/MIDI port	J1G1	Yamaha wavetable connector	J7C1
Microphone connector	J1G2	Yamaha wavetable connector	J7D1
Line in connector	J1G3	IDE interface 1	J8H1
Line out connector	J1G4	IDE interface 2	J8H2
Serial port 2	J1J1	Floppy drive interface	J8H3
Parallel port	J1J2	Chassis fan power	J9A1
Serial port 1	J1K1	Soft off power	J9D1 pins 1 & 2
USB connector 1	J1L1	Green PC connector	J9D1 pins 3 & 4
USB connector 2	J1L2	IR connector	J9D1 pins 6 - 11
PS/2 mouse port	J1M1	IDE interface LED	J9D1 pins 13 - 16
Telephony connector	J2F1	Green PC LED	J9D1 pins 18 - 20
Wavetable connector	J2F2	Reset switch	J9D1 pins 22 &23
Telephony connector	J2F3	Speaker	J9D1 pins 24 - 27
CD-ROM audio connector	J2F6	GP I/O connector	J10H1
Line in connector	J3F1	32-bit PCI slots	PC1 – PC4
Chassis fan power	J4F1	Slot 1 processor connector	SL1
Chassis security connector	J6C1		

USER CONFIGURABLE SETTINGS		
Function	**Label**	**Position**
⇨ Flash BIOS normal operation	J9C1A	Pins 5 & 6 closed
Flash BIOS recovery mode	J9C1A	Pins 4 & 5 closed
⇨ CMOS memory normal operation	J9C1C	Pins 5 & 6 closed
CMOS memory clear	J9C1C	Pins 4 & 5 closed
⇨ Password enabled	J9C1D	Pins 1 & 2 closed
Password disabled	J9C1D	Pins 2 & 3 closed
⇨ Flash BIOS write protect disabled	J9C1D	Pins 5 & 6 closed
Flash BIOS write protect enabled	J9C1D	Pins 4 & 5 closed

DRAM CONFIGURATION		
Size	**Bank 0**	**Bank 1**
8MB	(2) 1M x 36	None
16MB	(2) 2M x 36	None
16MB	(2) 1M x 36	(2) 1M x 36
24MB	(2) 2M x 36	(2) 1M x 36
32MB	(2) 4M x 36	None
32MB	(2) 2M x 36	(2) 2M x 36
40MB	(2) 4M x 36	(2) 1M x 36
48MB	(2) 4M x 36	(2) 2M x 36
64MB	(2) 8M x 36	None
64MB	(2) 4M x 36	(2) 4M x 36

Continued on next page...

INTEL CORPORATION
PD440FX

...continued from previous page

DRAM CONFIGURATION (CON'T)		
Size	**Bank 0**	**Bank 1**
72MB	(2) 8M x 36	(2) 1M x 36
80MB	(2) 8M x 36	(2) 2M x 36
96MB	(2) 8M x 36	(2) 4M x 36
128MB	(2) 8M x 36	(2) 8M x 36
128MB	(2) 16M x 36	None
136MB	(2) 16M x 36	(2) 1M x 36
144MB	(2) 16M x 36	(2) 2M x 36
160MB	(2) 16M x 36	(2) 4M x 36
192MB	(2) 16M x 36	(2) 8M x 36
256MB	(2) 16M x 36	(2) 16M x 36

Note: Board accepts EDO memory. Board also accepts x 32 SIMMs.

CACHE CONFIGURATION

Note: The location of the 256KB/512KB cache is unidentified.

CPU SPEED SELECTION					
CPU speed	**Clock speed**	**Multiplier**	**J9C1A**	**J9C1B**	**J9C1C**
233MHz	66MHz	3.5x	2 & 3	2 & 3, 5 & 6	2 & 3
266MHz	66MHz	4x	1 & 2	1 & 2, 4 & 5	2 & 3

Note: Pins designated should be in the closed position.

INTEL CORPORATION
PREMIERE/PCI II BABY-AT

Processor	Pentium
Processor Speed	75/90MHz
Chip Set	Intel
Max. Onboard DRAM	128MB
Cache	256KB
BIOS	AMI
Dimensions	330mm x 218mm
I/O Options	32-bit PCI bus slots (3), floppy drive interface, IDE interfaces (2), parallel port, serial ports (2)
NPU Options	None

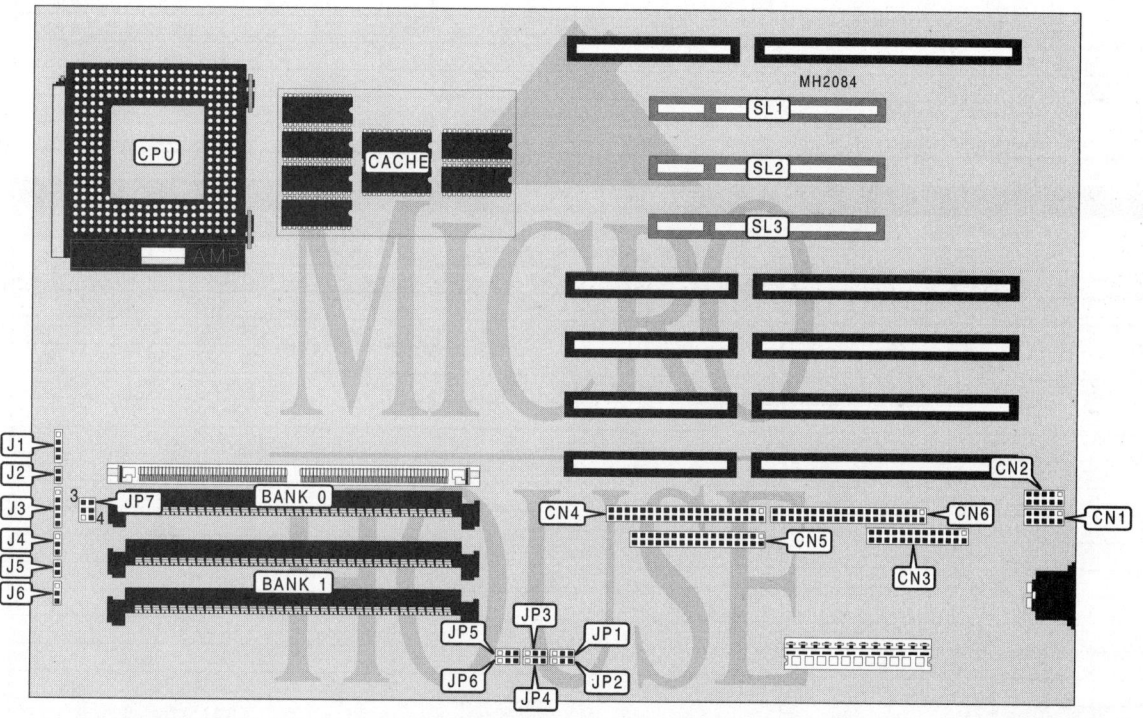

CONNECTIONS			
Purpose	Location	Purpose	Location
Speaker	J1	Serial port 2	CN2
Reset switch	J2	Parallel port	CN3
Power LED & keylock	J3	IDE interface (PCI bus)	CN4
IDE interface LED	J4	Floppy drive interface	CN5
Turbo LED	J5	IDE interface (ISA bus)	CN6
Turbo switch	J6	32-bit PCI bus slots	SL1 - SL3
Serial port 1	CN1		

Continued on next page . . .

INTEL CORPORATION
PREMIERE/PCI II BABY-AT

...continued from previous page.

USER CONFIGURABLE SETTINGS

Function	Jumper	Position
Monitor type select color	JP1	pins 2 & 3 closed
Monitor type select monochrome	JP1	pins 1 & 2 closed
Password disabled	JP2	pins 1 & 2 closed
Password enabled	JP2	pins 2 & 3 closed
BIOS setup enabled	JP3	pins 1 & 2 closed
BIOS setup disabled	JP3	pins 2 & 3 closed
Flash BIOS update enabled	JP4	pins 1 & 2 closed
Flash BIOS update disabled	JP4	pins 2 & 3 closed
CMOS memory normal operation	JP5	pins 1 & 2 closed
CMOS memory clear	JP5	pins 2 & 3 closed
Flash normal mode at boot	JP6	pins 2 & 3 closed
Flash recovery mode at boot	JP6	pins 1 & 2 closed

DRAM CONFIGURATION

Size	Bank 0	Bank 1
2MB	(2) 256K x 36	NONE
4MB	(2) 256K x 36	(2) 256K x 36
4MB	(2) 512K x 36	NONE
6MB	(2) 256K x 36	(2) 512K x 36
6MB	(2) 512K x 36	(2) 256K x 36
8MB	(2) 512K x 36	(2) 512K x 36
8MB	(2) 1M x 36	NONE
10MB	(2) 1M x 36	(2) 256K x 36
10MB	(2) 256K x 36	(2) 1M x 36
12MB	(2) 1M x 36	(2) 512K x 36
12MB	(2) 512K x 36	(2) 1M x 36
16MB	(2) 1M x 36	(2) 1M x 36
16MB	(2) 2M x 36	NONE
18MB	(2) 2M x 36	(2) 256K x 36
18MB	(2) 256K x 36	(2) 2M x 36
20MB	(2) 2M x 36	(2) 512K x 36
20MB	(2) 512K x 36	(2) 2M x 36
24MB	(2) 2M x 36	(2) 1M x 36
24MB	(2) 1M x 36	(2) 2M x 36
32MB	(2) 2M x 36	(2) 2M x 36
32MB	(2) 4M x 36	NONE
34MB	(2) 4M x 36	(2) 256K x 36
34MB	(2) 256K x 36	(2) 4M x 36
36MB	(2) 4M x 36	(2) 512K x 36
36MB	(2) 512K x 36	(2) 4M x 36
40MB	(2) 4M x 36	(2) 1M x 36
40MB	(2) 1M x 36	(2) 4M x 36
48MB	(2) 4M x 36	(2) 2M x 36

Continued on next page...

INTEL CORPORATION
PREMIERE/PCI II BABY-AT

. . . continued from previous page.

DRAM CONFIGURATION		
Size	**Bank 0**	**Bank 1**
48MB	(2) 2M x 36	(2) 4M x 36
64MB	(2) 4M x 36	(2) 4M x 36
64MB	(2) 8M x 36	NONE
66MB	(2) 8M x 36	(2) 256K x 36
66MB	(2) 256K x 36	(2) 8M x 36
68MB	(2) 8M x 36	(2) 512K x 36
68MB	(2) 512K x 36	(2) 8M x 36
72MB	(2) 8M x 36	(2) 1M x 36
72MB	(2) 1M x 36	(2) 8M x 36
80MB	(2) 8M x 36	(2) 2M x 36
80MB	(2) 2M x 36	(2) 8M x 36
96MB	(2) 8M x 36	(2) 4M x 36
96MB	(2) 4M x 36	(2) 8M x 36
128MB	(2) 8M x 36	(2) 8M x 36

CACHE CONFIGURATION	
Size	**Bank 0**
256KB	(8) 32K x 8
Note: Cache is factory installed at is not configurable.	

CPU SPEED CONFIGURATION	
Size	**JP7**
75MHz	pins 2 & 3 closed
◊ 90MHz	pins 1 & 2 closed

INTEL CORPORATION
RU430HX

Processor	Pentium
Processor Speed	75/90/100/120/133/150/166/180/200MHz
Chip Set	Intel
Video Chip Set	S3
Maximum Onboard Memory	128MB (EDO supported)
Maximum Video Memory	2MB
Cache	256/512KB
BIOS	AMI
Dimensions	229mm x 219mm
I/O Options	CD-ROM connector, floppy drive interface, green PC connector, IDE interfaces (2), parallel port, PS/2 mouse port, serial ports (2), VESA feature connector, VGA port, riser slot, IR connectors (2), serial port/USB connector, microphone in connector, line out connector, MIDI/audio input connector, wave table connector, telephony connector
NPU Options	None

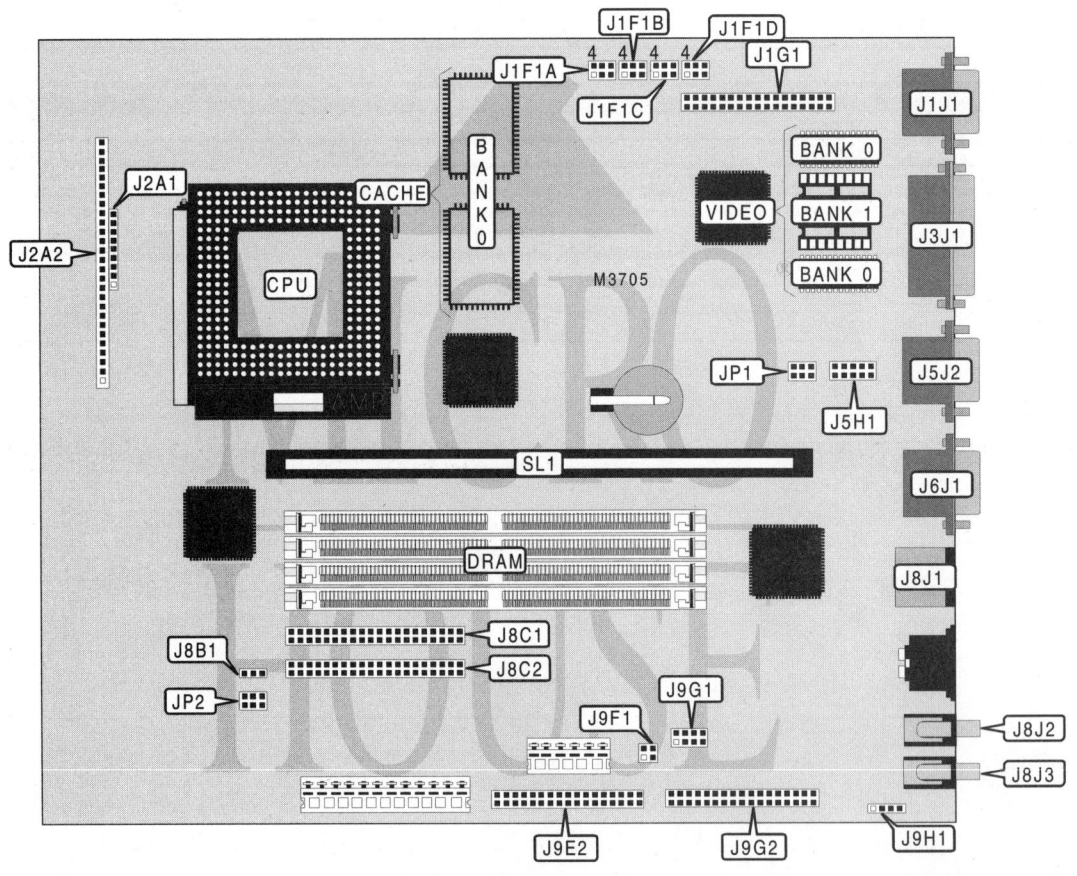

Continued on next page...

INTEL CORPORATION
RU430HX

...continued from previous page

CONNECTIONS			
Purpose	**Location**	**Purpose**	**Location**
VESA feature connector	J1G1	Serial port/USB connector	J5J2
VGA port	J1J1	Serial port 1	J6J1
IDE interface LED	J2A1 pins 1 & 2	Soft off connector	J8B1
Reset switch	J2A1 pins 3 & 4	IDE interface 2	J8C1
IR connector	J2A1 pins 6 - 9	IDE interface 1	J8C2
Chassis fan power	J2A2 pins 1 & 2	PS/2 mouse port	J8J1
Reset switch	J2A2 pins 4 & 5	Microphone in connector	J8J2
Power LED & keylock	J2A2 pins 7 - 10	Line out connector	J8J3
IDE interface LED	J2A2 pins 11 - 14	Floppy drive interface	J9E2
Soft on power connector	J2A2 pins 15 & 16	Telephony connector	J9F1
Green PC connector	J2A2 pins 17 & 18	Wave table connector	J9G1
IR connector	J2A2 pins 20 - 25	MIDI/audio input connector	J9G2
Speaker	J2A2 pins 26 - 29	CD-ROM connector	J9H1
Parallel port	J3J1	Riser slot	SL1
Serial port 2	J5H1		

USER CONFIGURABLE SETTINGS		
Function	**Label**	**Position**
⇨ Password normal operation	J1F1A	Pins 1 & 2 closed
Password clear	J1F1A	Pins 2 & 3 closed
⇨ CMOS memory normal operation	J1F1A	Pins 4 & 5 closed
CMOS memory clear	J1F1A	Pins 5 & 6 closed
⇨ Setup access enabled	J1F1B	Pins 1 & 2 closed
Setup access disabled	J1F1B	Pins 2 & 3 closed
⇨ Factory configured - do not alter	JP1	Unidentified
⇨ Factory configured - do not alter	JP2	Unidentified

DRAM CONFIGURATION		
Size	**Bank 0**	**Bank 1**
8MB	(2) 1M x 36	None
16MB	(2) 2M x 36	None
16MB	(2) 1M x 36	(2) 1M x 36
24MB	(2) 2M x 36	(2) 1M x 36
32MB	(2) 4M x 36	None
32MB	(2) 2M x 36	(2) 2M x 36
40MB	(2) 4M x 36	(2) 1M x 36
48MB	(2) 4M x 36	(2) 2M x 36

Continued on next page...

INTEL CORPORATION
RU430HX

...continued from previous page

DRAM CONFIGURATION (CON'T)		
Size	Bank 0	Bank 1
64MB	(2) 8M x 36	None
64MB	(2) 4M x 36	(2) 4M x 36
72MB	(2) 8M x 36	(2) 1M x 36
80MB	(2) 8M x 36	(2) 2M x 36
96MB	(2) 8M x 36	(2) 4M x 36
128MB	(2) 8M x 36	(2) 8M x 36

Note: Board accepts EDO memory. Board also accepts x 32 SIMMs. The location of banks 0 & 1 are unidentified.

CACHE CONFIGURATION	
Size	Bank 0
256KB	(2) 32K x 32
512KB	(2) 64K x 32

Note: Board will come factory installed with one of the two above cache sizes.

VIDEO MEMORY CONFIGURATION		
Size	Bank 0	Bank 1
1MB	1MB	None
2MB	1MB	(2) 256K x 16

Note: Bank 0 is factory installed and is not configurable.

CPU SPEED SELECTION				
CPU speed	Clock speed	Multiplier	J1F1C	J1F1D
75MHz	50MHz	1.5x	2 & 3, 5 & 6	1 & 2, 4 & 5
90MHz	60MHz	1.5x	2 & 3, 5 & 6	1 & 2, 4 & 5
100MHz	66MHz	1.5x	1 & 2, 5 & 6	1 & 2, 4 & 5
120MHz	60MHz	2x	2 & 3, 4 & 5	2 & 3, 4 & 5
133MHz	66MHz	2x	1 & 2, 5 & 6	2 & 3, 4 & 5
150MHz	60MHz	2.5x	2 & 3, 4 & 5	2 & 3, 5 & 6
166MHz	66MHz	2.5x	1 & 2, 5 & 6	2 & 3, 5 & 6
180MHz	60MHz	3x	2 & 3, 4 & 5	1 & 2, 5 & 6
200MHz	66MHz	3x	1 & 2, 5 & 6	1 & 2, 5 & 6

Note: Pins designated should be in the closed position.

CPU TYPE SELECTION	
Type	J1F1B
Standard or VR	Pins 4 & 5 closed
VRE	Pins 5 & 6 closed

INTEL CORPORATION
VS440FX

Processor	Pentium Pro
Processor Speed	150/166/180/200MHz
Chip Set	Intel
Video Chip Set	None
Maximum Onboard Memory	256MB (EDO supported)
Maximum Video Memory	None
Cache	256/512KB (located on Pentium Pro CPU)
BIOS	Intel
Dimensions	305mm x 244mm
I/O Options	32-bit PCI slots (4), CD-ROM interface, floppy drive interface, green PC connector, IDE interfaces (2), parallel port, PS/2 mouse port, serial ports (2), IR connector, wavetable connector, telephony connector, audio out connector, microphone in connector, audio in connector, MIDI/game port
NPU Options	None

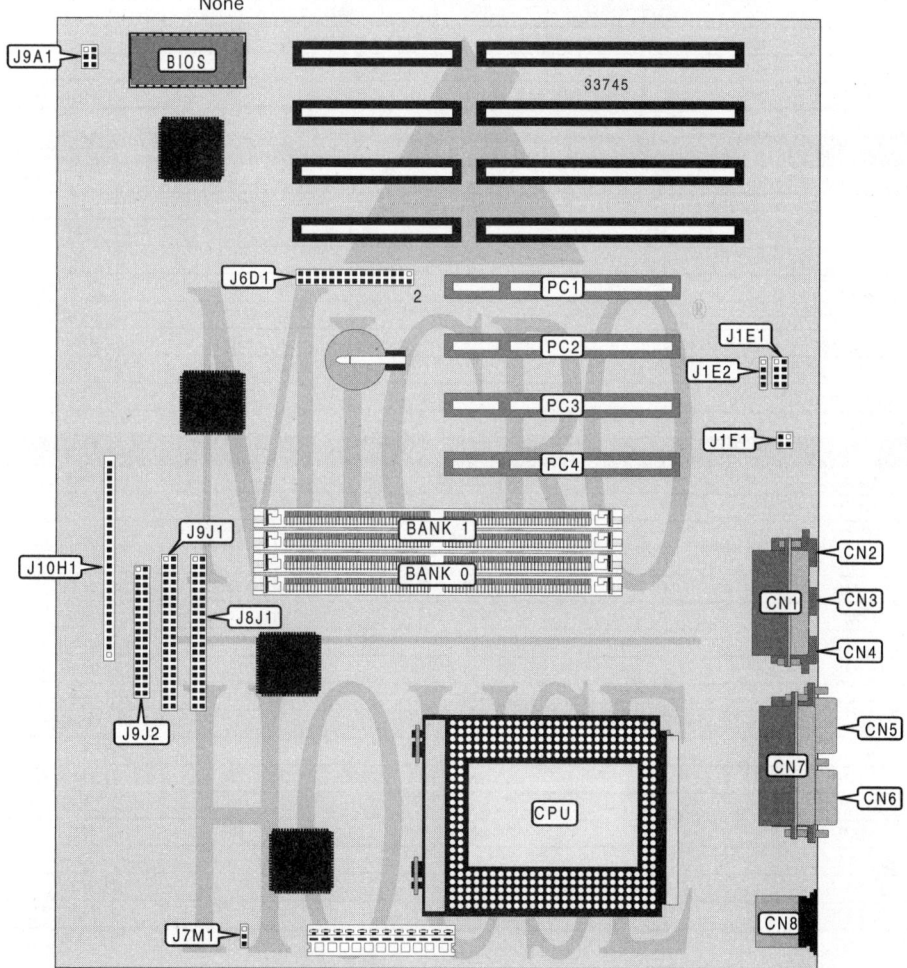

Continued on next page...

INTEL CORPORATION
VS440FX

...continued from previous page

CONNECTIONS

Purpose	Location	Purpose	Location
MIDI/game port	CN1	IDE interface 1	J8J1
Microphone in connector	CN2	Chassis fan power	J9A1
Audio in connector	CN3	IDE interface 2	J9J1
Audio out connector	CN4	Floppy drive interface	J9J2
Serial port 1	CN5	Front panel power switch	J10H1 pins 1 & 2
Serial port 2	CN6	Green PC connector	J10H1 pins 3 & 4
Parallel port	CN7	IR connector	J10H1 pins 6 - 11
PS/2 mouse port	CN8	IDE interface LED	J10H1 pins 13 - 16
Wavetable connector	J1E1	Power LED	J10H1 pins 18 - 20
CD-ROM connector	J1E2	Reset switch	J10H1 pins 22 - 23
Telephony connector	J1F1	Speaker	J10H1 pins 24 - 27
Chassis fan power	J7M1	32-bit PCI slots	PC1 - PC4

USER CONFIGURABLE SETTINGS

Function	Label	Position
⇨ CMOS memory normal operation	J6D1	Pins 20 & 22 closed
CMOS memory clear	J6D1	Pins 18 & 20 closed
⇨ Password enabled	J6D1	Pins 27 & 29 closed
Password disabled	J6D1	Pins 25 & 27 closed
⇨ Setup access enabled	J6D1	Pins 28 & 30 closed
Setup access disabled	J6D1	Pins 26 & 28 closed
⇨ Flash BIOS normal operation	J6D1	Pins 4 & 6 closed
Flash BIOS recovery mode	J6D1	Pins 2 & 4 closed

DRAM CONFIGURATION

Size	Bank 0	Bank 1
8MB	(2) 1M x 36	None
16MB	(2) 2M x 36	None
16MB	(2) 1M x 36	(2) 1M x 36
24MB	(2) 2M x 36	(2) 1M x 36
32MB	(2) 4M x 36	None
32MB	(2) 2M x 36	(2) 2M x 36
40MB	(2) 1M x 36	(2) 4M x 36
48MB	(2) 4M x 36	(2) 2M x 36
64MB	(2) 8M x 36	None
64MB	(2) 4M x 36	(2) 4M x 36
72MB	(2) 8M x 36	(2) 1M x 36
80MB	(2) 8M x 36	(2) 2M x 36
96MB	(2) 8M x 36	(2) 4M x 36
128MB	(2) 16M x 36	None
128MB	(2) 8M x 36	(2) 8M x 36
136MB	(2) 16M x 36	(2) 1M x 36

Continued on next page...

INTEL CORPORATION
VS440FX

. . . continued from previous page

	DRAM CONFIGURATION (CON'T)	
Size	**Bank 0**	**Bank 1**
144MB	(2) 16M x 36	(2) 2M x 36
160MB	(2) 16M x 36	(2) 4M x 36
192MB	(2) 16M x 36	(2) 8M x 36
256MB	(2) 16M x 36	(2) 16M x 36

Note: Board accepts EDO memory. Board also accepts x 32 SIMMs. Banks are interchangeable.

CACHE CONFIGURATION
Note: 256KB or 512KB cache is located on the Pentium Pro CPU.

	CPU SPEED SELECTION		
CPU speed	**Clock speed**	**Multiplier**	**J6D1**
150MHz	60MHz	2.5x	10 & 12, 11 & 13, 17 & 19
166MHz	66MHz	2.5x	10 & 12, 11 & 13, 19 & 21
180MHz	60MHz	3x	9 & 11, 12 & 14, 17 & 19
200MHz	66MHz	3x	9 & 11, 12 & 14, 19 & 21

Note: Pins designated should be in the closed position.

IPC CORPORATION, LTD.
IPC SE (MB586PCI#10), SEL (MB586PCI#10), VALUEMAGIC (MB586PCI#10)

Processor	Pentium
Processor Speed	60/66MHz
Chip Set	Intel
Max. Onboard DRAM	128MB
Cache	256KB
BIOS	Unidentified
Dimensions	330mm x 218mm
I/O Options	32-bit PCI slots (3), floppy drive interface, IDE interfaces (2), parallel port, serial ports (2)
NPU Options	None

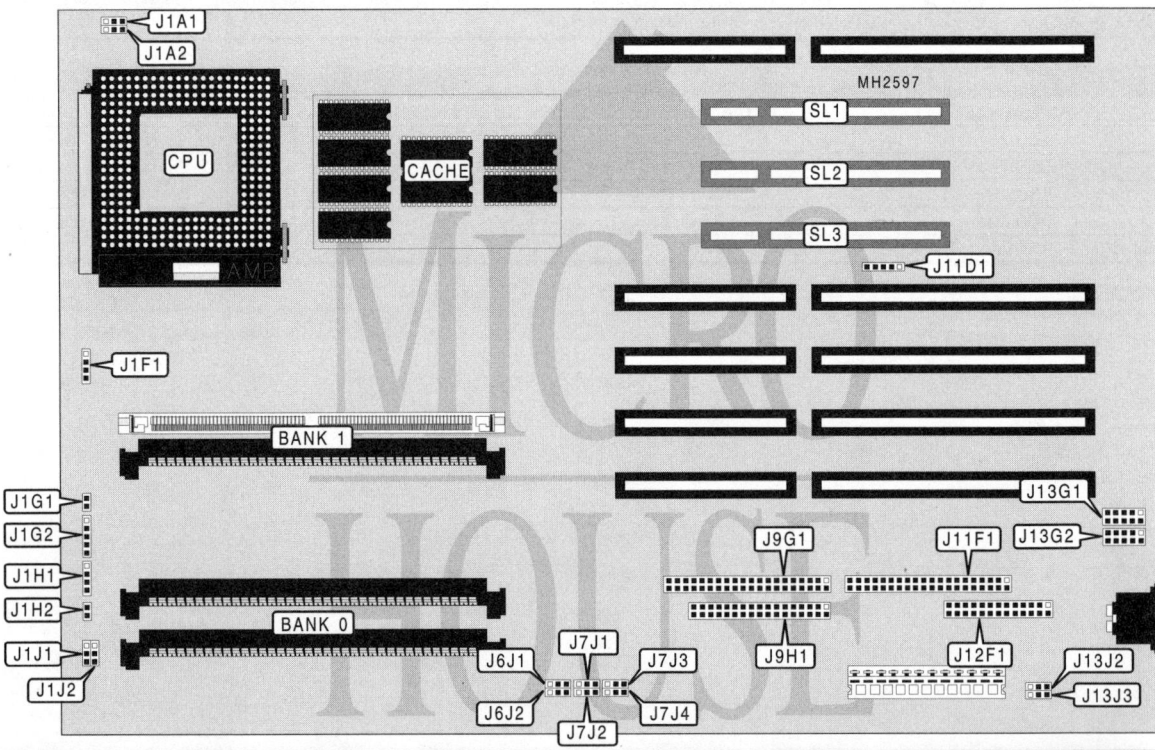

CONNECTIONS			
Purpose	**Location**	**Purpose**	**Location**
Chassis fan power (fast)	J1A1	IDE interface	J9G1
Chassis fan power (slow)	J1A2	Floppy drive interface	J9H1
Speaker	J1F1	Auxiliary power connector	J11D1
Power LED & keylock	J1G2	IDE interface	J11F1
Reset switch	J1G1	Parallel port	J12F1
IDE interface LED	J1H1	Serial port 1	J13G1
Turbo LED	J1H2	Serial port 2	J13G2
Turbo switch	J1J1	32-bit PCI slots	SL1 - SL3

Continued on next page...

IPC CORPORATION, LTD.
IPC SE (MB586PCI#10), SEL (MB586PCI#10), VALUEMAGIC (MB586PCI#10)

...continued from previous page

USER CONFIGURABLE SETTINGS

Function	Jumper	Position
⇨ CMOS memory normal operation	J6J1	pins 1 & 2 closed
CMOS memory clear	J6J1	pins 2 & 3 closed
⇨ Flash recovery select normal mode	J6J2	pins 2 & 3 closed
Flash recovery select recovery mode	J6J2	pins 1 & 2 closed
⇨ Setup entry enabled	J7J1	pins 1 & 2 closed
Setup entry disabled	J7J1	pins 2 & 3 closed
⇨ Flash BIOS write protect enabled	J7J2	pins 2 & 3 closed
Flash BIOS write protect disabled	J7J2	pins 1 & 2 closed
⇨ Monitor type select color	J7J3	pins 2 & 3 closed
Monitor type select monochrome	J7J3	pins 1 & 2 closed
⇨ Password enabled	J7J4	pins 1 & 2 closed
Password disabled	J7J4	pins 2 & 3 closed
⇨ Factory configured - do not alter	J13J3	Open

DRAM CONFIGURATION

Size	Bank 0	Bank 1
8MB	(2) 512K x 36	(2) 512K x 36
8MB	(2) 1M x 36	NONE
10MB	(2) 1M x 36	(2) 256K x 36
10MB	(2) 256K x 36	(2) 1M x 36
12MB	(2) 1M x 36	(2) 512K x 36
12MB	(2) 512K x 36	(2) 1M x 36
16MB	(2) 1M x 36	(2) 1M x 36
16MB	(2) 2M x 36	NONE
18MB	(2) 2M x 36	(2) 256K x 36
18MB	(2) 256K x 36	(2) 2M x 36
20MB	(2) 2M x 36	(2) 512K x 36
20MB	(2) 512K x 36	(2) 2M x 36
24MB	(2) 2M x 36	(2) 1M x 36
24MB	(2) 1M x 36	(2) 2M x 36
32MB	(2) 2M x 36	(2) 2M x 36
32MB	(2) 4M x 36	NONE
34MB	(2) 4M x 36	(2) 256K x 36
34MB	(2) 256K x 36	(2) 4M x 36
36MB	(2) 4M x 36	(2) 512K x 36
36MB	(2) 512K x 36	(2) 4M x 36
40MB	(2) 4M x 36	(2) 1M x 36
40MB	(2) 1M x 36	(2) 4M x 36
48MB	(2) 4M x 36	(2) 2M x 36

Continued on next page...

IPC CORPORATION, LTD.
IPC SE (MB586PCI#10), SEL (MB586PCI#10), VALUEMAGIC (MB586PCI#10)

...continued from previous page.

DRAM CONFIGURATION (CON'T)

Size	Bank 0	Bank 1
48MB	(2) 2M x 36	(2) 4M x 36
64MB	(2) 4M x 36	(2) 4M x 36
64MB	(2) 8M x 36	NONE
66MB	(2) 8M x 36	(2) 256K x 36
66MB	(2) 256K x 36	(2) 8M x 36
68MB	(2) 8M x 36	(2) 512K x 36
68MB	(2) 512K x 36	(2) 8M x 36
72MB	(2) 8M x 36	(2) 1M x 36
72MB	(2) 1M x 36	(2) 8M x 36
80MB	(2) 8M x 36	(2) 2M x 36
80MB	(2) 2M x 36	(2) 8M x 36
96MB	(2) 8M x 36	(2) 4M x 36
96MB	(2) 4M x 36	(2) 8M x 36
128MB	(2) 8M x 36	(2) 8M x 36

CACHE CONFIGURATION

Note: This board is factory installed with 256KB cache. It is not configurable.

CPU SPEED CONFIGURATION

Speed	J1J2
60MHz	pins 2 & 3 closed
66MHz	pins 1 & 2 closed

CPU VOLTAGE CONFIGURATION

Voltage	J13J2
5v (60MHz)	pins 1 & 2 closed
5.27v (66MHz)	pins 2 & 3 closed

MICRONICS COMPUTERS, INC.
M54LI (REV. 1B)

Processor	Pentium
Processor Speed	75/90/100/120/133MHz
Chip Set	SIS
Max. Onboard DRAM	128MB
Cache	256/512KB
BIOS	Phoenix
Dimensions	330mm x 218mm
I/O Options	PS/2 mouse interface, parallel port, serial ports (2), 32-bit PCI slots (3), floppy drive interface, IDE interfaces (2)
NPU Options	None

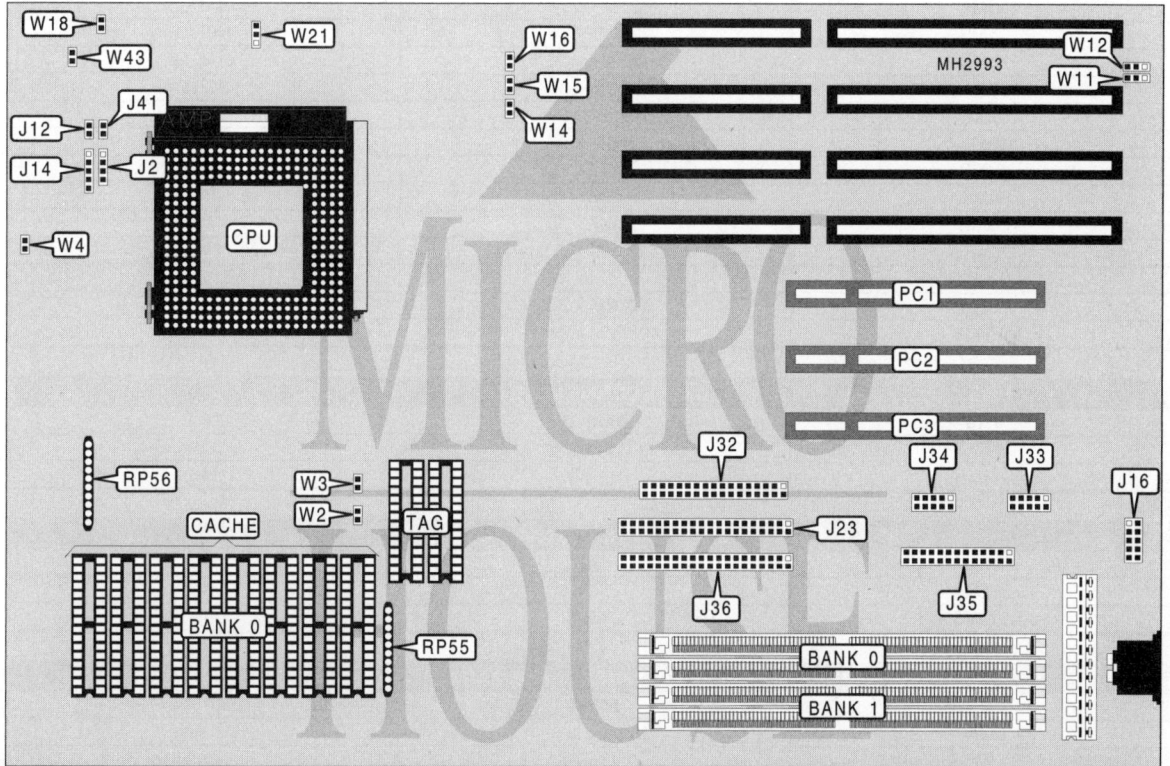

CONNECTIONS

Purpose	Location	Purpose	Location
Speaker	J2	Serial port 2	J34
Reset switch	J12	Parallel port	J35
Power LED & keylock	J14	IDE interface 1	J36
PS/2 mouse interface	J16	IDE interface LED	J41
IDE interface 2	J23	32-bit PCI slots	PC1 - PC3
Floppy drive interface	J32	Turbo LED	W43
Serial port 1	J33		

Continued on next page...

MICRONICS COMPUTERS, INC.
M54LI (REV. 1B)

...continued from previous page

USER CONFIGURABLE SETTINGS		
Function	**Jumper**	**Position**
⇨ CMOS memory normal operation	W18	Open
CMOS memory clear	W18	Closed
⇨ BIOS normal operation	W21	pins 1 & 2 closed
BIOS recovery mode	W21	pins 2 & 3 closed

DRAM CONFIGURATION		
Size	**Bank 0**	**Bank 1**
8MB	(2) 1M x 36	NONE
16MB	(2) 1M x 36	(2) 1M x 36
16MB	(2) 2M x 36	NONE
24MB	(2) 2M x 36	(2) 1M x 36
32MB	(2) 4M x 36	NONE
32MB	(2) 2M x 36	(2) 2M x 36
40MB	(2) 4M x 36	(2) 1M x 36
48MB	(2) 4M x 36	(2) 2M x 36
64MB	(2) 8M x 36	NONE
64MB	(2) 4M x 36	(2) 4M x 36
72MB	(2) 8M x 36	(2) 1M x 36
80MB	(2) 8M x 36	(2) 2M x 36
96MB	(2) 8M x 36	(2) 4M x 36
128MB	(2) 8M x 36	(2) 8M x 36

CACHE CONFIGURATION		
Size	**Bank 0**	**TAG**
256KB	(8) 32K x 8	(2) 32K x 8
512KB	(8) 64K x 8	(2) 32K x 8

CACHE JUMPER CONFIGURATION		
Size	**W2**	**W3**
256KB	Open	Open
512KB	Closed	Open

CACHE VOLTAGE CONFIGURATION		
Voltage	**RP55**	**RP56**
3.3v	Not installed	Installed
5v	Installed	Not installed

CPU SPEED CONFIGURATION				
Speed	**W4**	**W14**	**W15**	**W16**
75MHz	Open	Closed	Closed	Open
90MHz	Open	Closed	Open	Closed
100MHz	Open	Open	Closed	Open
120MHz	Closed	Closed	Open	Closed
133MHz	Closed	Open	Closed	Open

Continued on next page...

MICRONICS COMPUTERS, INC.
M54LI (REV. 1B)

...continued from previous page

DMA CONFIGURATION		
DMA	**W11**	**W12**
DMA 1	pins 1 & 2 closed	pins 1 & 2 closed
DMA 3	pins 2 & 3 closed	pins 2 & 3 closed

MICRONICS COMPUTERS, INC.
M54PI (DIABLO BOARD)

Processor	Pentium
Processor Speed	90/100MHz
Chip Set	Intel
Max. Onboard DRAM	192MB
Cache	512KB
BIOS	Phoenix
Dimensions	254mm x 218mm
I/O Options	32-bit PCI slots (3), floppy drive interface, IDE interface (2), parallel port, PS/2 mouse port, serial ports (2)
NPU Options	None

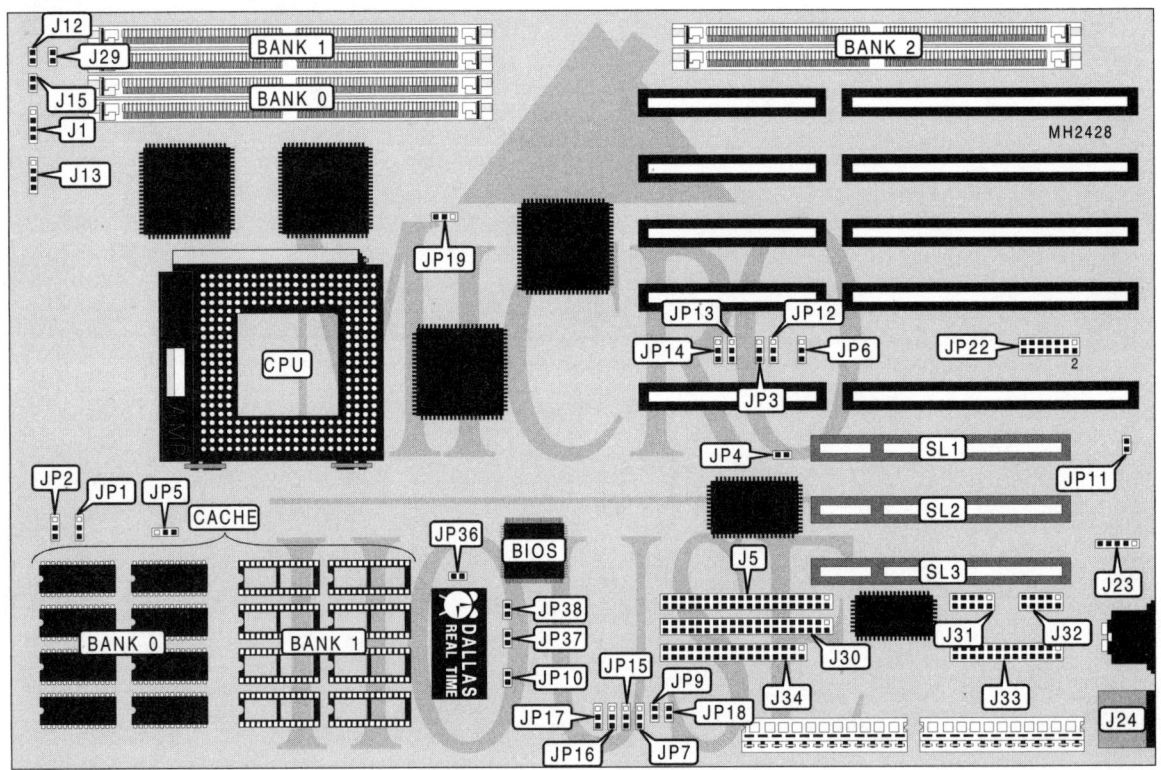

CONNECTIONS			
Purpose	**Location**	**Purpose**	**Location**
Speaker	J1	IDE interface LED	J29
PCI IDE interface	J5	ISA IDE interface	J30
Reset switch	J12	Serial port 1	J31
Power LED & keylock	J13	Serial port 2	J32
Turbo LED	J15	Parallel port	J33
External keyboard connector	J23	Floppy drive interface	J34
PS/2 mouse port	J24	32-bit PCI slots	SL1-SL3

Continued on next page...

MICRONICS COMPUTERS, INC.
M54PI (DIABLO BOARD)

...continued from previous page

USER CONFIGURABLE SETTINGS		
Function	**Jumper**	**Setting**
◇ Factory configured - do not alter	JP1	pins 1 & 2 closed
◇ Host bus frequency select 2/3	JP2	pins 1 & 2 closed
Host bus frequency select 1/2	JP2	pins 2 & 3 closed
◇ PCI IDE on IRQ14	JP3	pins 1 & 2 closed
PCI IDE on IRQ15	JP3	pins 2 & 3 closed
◇ PCI IDE interface enabled	JP4	Open
PCI IDE interface disabled	JP4	Closed
◇ Keyboard SMI using SIO-SMI	JP6	pins 1 & 2 closed
Keyboard SMI using IRQ10	JP6	pins 2 & 3 closed
◇ Normal BIOS mode	JP7	pins 1 & 2 closed
BIOS recovery mode	JP7	pins 2 & 3 closed
◇ Flash BIOS write protect enabled	JP9	Open
Flash BIOS write protect disabled	JP9	Closed
◇ Normal operation	JP10	Closed
Clear RTC	JP10	Open
◇ Monitor type select color	JP11	Closed
Monitor type select monochrome	JP11	Open
◇ ISA IDE on IRQ15	JP12	pins 2 & 3 closed
ISA IDE on IRQ14	JP12	pins 1 & 2 closed
◇ Parallel port on IRQ7	JP17	pins 1 & 2 closed
Parallel port on IRQ5	JP17	pins 2 & 3 closed
◇ Super I/O chip SMC665 enabled	JP18	Open
Super I/O chip SMC665 disabled	JP18	Closed
◇ Factory configured - do not alter	JP22	Open

DRAM CONFIGURATION			
Size	**Bank 0**	**Bank 1**	**Bank 2**
8MB	(2) 1MB x 36	NONE	NONE
16MB	(2) 1MB x 36	(2) 1MB x 36	NONE
16MB	(2) 2MB x 36	NONE	NONE
24MB	(2) 1MB x 36	(2) 1MB x 36	(2) 1MB x 36
24MB	(2) 1MB x 36	(2) 2MB x 36	NONE
32MB	(2) 2MB x 36	(2) 2MB x 36	NONE
32MB	(2) 1MB x 36	(2) 1MB x 36	(2) 2MB x 36
40MB	(2) 1MB x 36	(2) 2MB x 36	(2) 2MB x 36
40MB	(2) 1MB x 36	(2) 4MB x 36	NONE
48MB	(2) 2MB x 36	(2) 4MB x 36	NONE
48MB	(2) 1MB x 36	(2) 1MB x 36	(2) 4MB x 36
56MB	(2) 1MB x 36	(2) 2MB x 36	(2) 4MB x 36
64MB	(2) 4MB x 36	(2) 4MB x 36	NONE
64MB	(2) 8MB x 36	NONE	NONE
72MB	(2) 1MB x 36	(2) 4MB x 36	(2) 4MB x 36
72MB	(2) 1MB x 36	(2) 8MB x 36	NONE
80MB	(2) 2MB x 36	(2) 4MB x 36	(2) 4MB x 36

Continued on next page...

MICRONICS COMPUTERS, INC.
M54PI (DIABLO BOARD)

...continued from previous page

DRAM CONFIGURATION (CON'T)			
Size	Bank 0	Bank 1	Bank 2
80MB	(2) 2MB x 36	(2) 8MB x 36	NONE
80MB	(2) 1MB x 36	(2) 1MB x 36	(2) 8MB x 36
96MB	(2) 4MB x 36	(2) 4MB x 36	(2) 4MB x 36
96MB	(2) 4MB x 36	(2) 8MB x 36	NONE
96MB	(2) 2MB x 36	(2) 2MB x 36	(2) 8MB x 36
104MB	(2) 1MB x 36	(2) 4MB x 36	(2) 8MB x 36
112MB	(2) 2MB x 36	(2) 4MB x 36	(2) 8MB x 36
128MB	(2) 8MB x 36	(2) 8MB x 36	NONE
128MB	(2) 4MB x 36	(2) 4MB x 36	(2) 8MB x 36
136MB	(2) 1MB x 36	(2) 8MB x 36	(2) 8MB x 36
144MB	(2) 2MB x 36	(2) 8MB x 36	(2) 8MB x 36
160MB	(2) 4MB x 36	(2) 8MB x 36	(2) 8MB x 36
192MB	(2) 8MB x 36	(2) 8MB x 36	(2) 8MB x 36

CACHE CONFIGURATION		
Size	Bank 0	Bank 1
256KB	(8) 32K x 8	NONE
512KB	(8) 32K x 8	(8) 32K x 8

CACHE JUMPER CONFIGURATION		
Size	JP5	JP19
256KB	pins 2 & 3 closed	pins 1 & 2 closed
512KB	pins 1 & 2 closed	pins 2 & 3 closed

CPU SPEED CONFIGURATION			
Speed	JP36	JP37	JP38
90MHz	Closed	Open	Closed
100MHz	Open	Closed	Open

ISA IDE DME CHANNEL SELECTION		
Channel	JP13	JP14
6	pins 1 & 2 closed	pins 1 & 2 closed
7	pins 2 & 3 closed	pins 2 & 3 closed

ECP MODE PARALLEL PORT DMA SELECTION		
Channel	JP15	JP16
1	pins 1 & 2 closed	pins 1 & 2 closed
3	pins 2 & 3 closed	pins 2 & 3 closed

MICRONICS COMPUTERS, INC.
M 6 M E

Processor	Pentium Pro
Processor Speed	120/133/150/166/180/200MHz
Chip Set	Intel
Video Chip Set	Cirrus Logic
Maximum Onboard Memory	512MB (EDO supported)
Maximum Video Memory	2MB
Cache	256/512KB (located on Pentium Pro CPU)
BIOS	Phoenix
Dimensions	330mm x 218mm
I/O Options	32-bit PCI slots (3), floppy drive interface, IDE interface, SCSI interface, Ultra Wide SCSI interface, parallel port, PS/2 mouse port, serial ports (2), VESA feature connector, VGA interface, IR connector, VRM connectors (2), soft power standby/signal connector, soft power switch
NPU Options	None

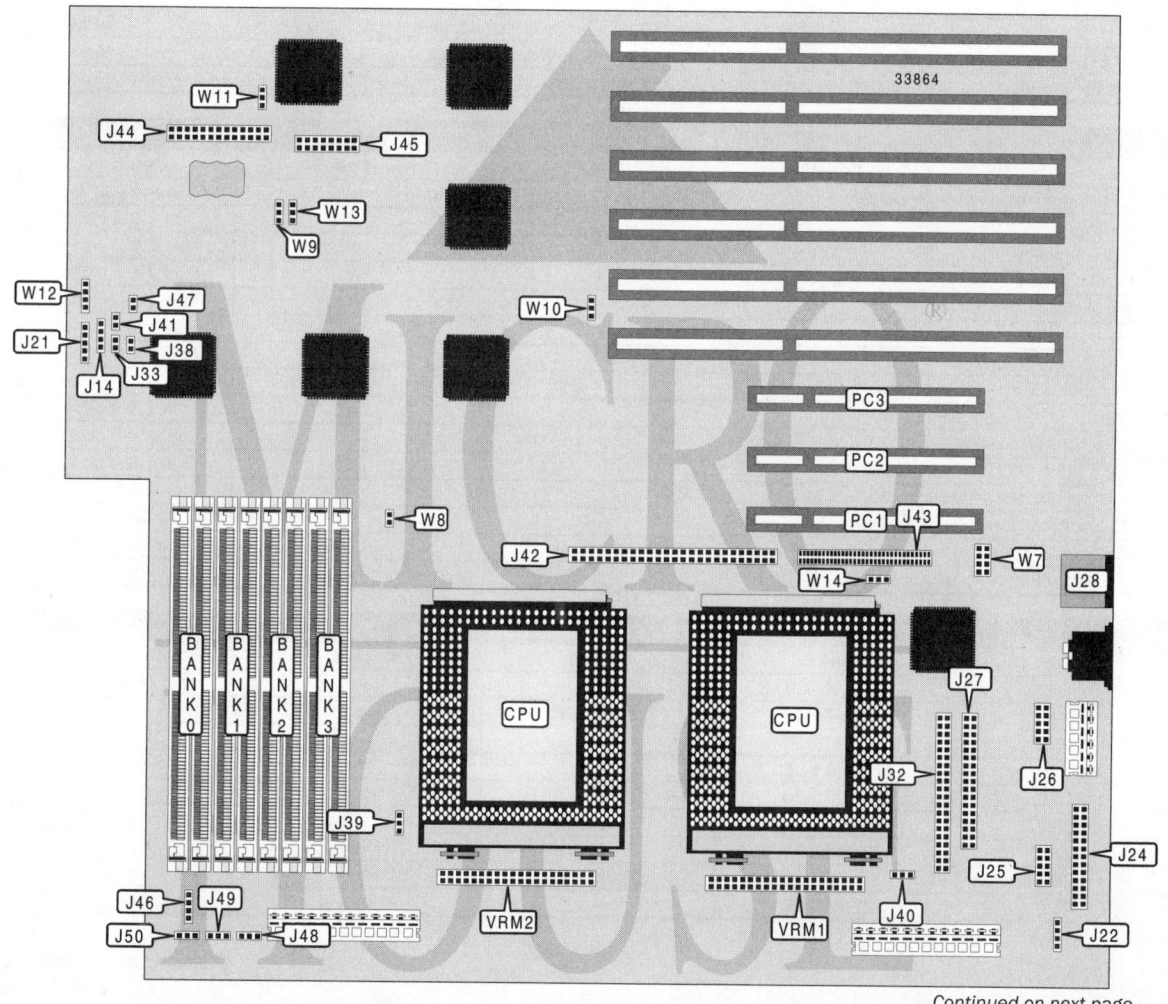

Continued on next page...

MICRONICS COMPUTERS, INC.
M6ME

...continued from previous page

CONNECTIONS

Purpose	Location	Purpose	Location
Speaker	J14	Chassis fan power	J40
Power LED & keylock	J21	Reset switch	J41
IR connector	J22	Fast SCSI interface	J42
Parallel port	J24	Ultra Wide SCSI interface	J43
Serial port 1	J25	VESA feature connector	J44
Serial port 2	J26	VGA interface	J45
Floppy drive interface	J27	Soft power standby/signal connector	J46
PS/2 mouse port	J28	Soft power switch	J47
IDE interface	J32	32-bit PCI slots	PC1 - PC3
IDE interface LED	J33	VRM connector 1	VRM1
Turbo LED	J38	VRM connector 2	VRM2
Chassis fan power	J39		

USER CONFIGURABLE SETTINGS

Function	Label	Position
♦ CMOS memory normal operation	W9	Pins 1 & 2 closed
CMOS memory clear	W9	Pins 2 & 3 closed
♦ SCSI enabled	W10	Pins 1 & 2 closed
SCSI disabled	W10	Pins 2 & 3 closed
♦ On board video enabled	W11	Pins 1 & 2 closed
On board video disabled	W11	Pins 2 & 3 closed
Soft power enabled	W12	Pins 1 & 2 closed
Soft power forced on (for power cycling)	W12	Pins 2 & 3 closed
♦ Real time clock normal operation	W13	Pins 1 & 2 closed
Real time clock clear	W13	Pins 2 & 3 closed
♦ Ultra Wide SCSI select auto select	W14	Pins 1 & 2 closed
Ultra Wide SCSI select Ultra Wide SCSI	W14	Pins 2 & 3 closed
♦ Factory configured - do not alter	J48	Unidentified
♦ Factory configured - do not alter	J49	Unidentified
♦ Factory configured - do not alter	J50	Unidentified

DRAM CONFIGURATION

Size	Bank 0	Bank 1	Bank 2	Bank 3
8MB	(2) 1M x 36	None	None	None
16MB	(2) 1M x 36	(2) 1M x 36	None	None
16MB	(2) 2M x 36	None	None	None
24MB	(2) 1M x 36	(2) 1M x 36	(2) 1M x 36	None
24MB	(2) 2M x 36	(2) 1M x 36	None	None
32MB	(2) 1M x 36	(2) 1M x 36	(2) 1M x 36	(2) 1M x 36
32MB	(2) 2M x 36	(2) 1M x 36	(2) 1M x 36	None
32MB	(2) 2M x 36	(2) 2M x 36	None	None
32MB	(2) 4M x 36	None	None	None

Continued on next page...

MICRONICS COMPUTERS, INC.
M 6 M E

. . . continued from previous page

Size	Bank 0	Bank 1	Bank 2	Bank 3
40MB	(2) 2M x 36	(2) 1M x 36	(2) 1M x 36	(2) 1M x 36
40MB	(2) 2M x 36	(2) 2M x 36	(2) 1M x 36	None
40MB	(2) 4M x 36	(2) 1M x 36	None	None
48MB	(2) 2M x 36	(2) 2M x 36	(2) 1M x 36	(2) 1M x 36
48MB	(2) 2M x 36	(2) 2M x 36	(2) 2M x 36	None
48MB	(2) 4M x 36	(2) 1M x 36	(2) 1M x 36	None
48MB	(2) 4M x 36	(2) 2M x 36	None	None
56MB	(2) 2M x 36	(2) 2M x 36	(2) 2M x 36	(2) 1M x 36
56MB	(2) 4M x 36	(2) 1M x 36	(2) 1M x 36	(2) 1M x 36
56MB	(2) 4M x 36	(2) 2M x 36	(2) 1M x 36	None
64MB	(2) 2M x 36	(2) 2M x 36	(2) 2M x 36	(2) 2M x 36
64MB	(2) 4M x 36	(2) 2M x 36	(2) 1M x 36	(2) 1M x 36
64MB	(2) 4M x 36	(2) 2M x 36	(2) 2M x 36	None
64MB	(2) 4M x 36	(2) 4M x 36	None	None
64MB	(2) 8M x 36	None	None	None
72MB	(2) 4M x 36	(2) 2M x 36	(2) 2M x 36	(2) 1M x 36
72MB	(2) 4M x 36	(2) 4M x 36	(2) 1M x 36	None
72MB	(2) 8M x 36	(2) 1M x 36	None	None
80MB	(2) 4M x 36	(2) 2M x 36	(2) 2M x 36	(2) 2M x 36
80MB	(2) 4M x 36	(2) 4M x 36	(2) 1M x 36	(2) 1M x 36
80MB	(2) 4M x 36	(2) 4M x 36	(2) 2M x 36	None
80MB	(2) 8M x 36	(2) 1M x 36	(2) 1M x 36	None
80MB	(2) 8M x 36	(2) 2M x 36	None	None
88MB	(2) 4M x 36	(2) 4M x 36	(2) 2M x 36	(2) 1M x 36
88MB	(2) 8M x 36	(2) 1M x 36	(2) 1M x 36	(2) 1M x 36
88MB	(2) 8M x 36	(2) 2M x 36	(2) 1M x 36	None
96MB	(2) 4M x 36	(2) 4M x 36	(2) 2M x 36	(2) 2M x 36
96MB	(2) 4M x 36	(2) 4M x 36	(2) 4M x 36	None
96MB	(2) 8M x 36	(2) 2M x 36	(2) 1M x 36	(2) 1M x 36
96MB	(2) 8M x 36	(2) 2M x 36	(2) 2M x 36	None
96MB	(2) 8M x 36	(2) 4M x 36	None	None
104MB	(2) 4M x 36	(2) 4M x 36	(2) 4M x 36	(2) 1M x 36
104MB	(2) 8M x 36	(2) 2M x 36	(2) 2M x 36	(2) 1M x 36
104MB	(2) 8M x 36	(2) 4M x 36	(2) 1M x 36	None
112MB	(2) 4M x 36	(2) 4M x 36	(2) 4M x 36	(2) 2M x 36
112MB	(2) 8M x 36	(2) 4M x 36	(2) 1M x 36	(2) 1M x 36
112MB	(2) 8M x 36	(2) 2M x 36	(2) 2M x 36	(2) 2M x 36
112MB	(2) 8M x 36	(2) 4M x 36	(2) 2M x 36	None
120MB	(2) 8M x 36	(2) 4M x 36	(2) 2M x 36	(2) 1M x 36
128MB	(2) 4M x 36	(2) 4M x 36	(2) 4M x 36	(2) 4M x 36
128MB	(2) 8M x 36	(2) 4M x 36	(2) 2M x 36	(2) 2M x 36
128MB	(2) 8M x 36	(2) 4M x 36	(2) 4M x 36	None

Continued on next page. . .

MICRONICS COMPUTERS, INC.
M 6 M E

. . . continued from previous page

\	DRAM CONFIGURATION (CON'T)			
Size	**Bank 0**	**Bank 1**	**Bank 2**	**Bank 3**
128MB	(2) 8M x 36	(2) 8M x 36	None	None
128MB	(2) 16M x 36	None	None	None
192MB	(2) 16M x 36	(2) 8M x 36	None	None
200MB	(2) 8M x 36	(2) 8M x 36	(2) 8M x 36	(2) 1M x 36
200MB	(2) 16M x 36	(2) 4M x 36	(2) 4M x 36	(2) 1M x 36
200MB	(2) 16M x 36	(2) 8M x 36	(2) 1M x 36	None
208MB	(2) 8M x 36	(2) 8M x 36	(2) 8M x 36	(2) 2M x 36
208MB	(2) 16M x 36	(2) 4M x 36	(2) 4M x 36	(2) 2M x 36
208MB	(2) 16M x 36	(2) 8M x 36	(2) 1M x 36	(2) 1M x 36
208MB	(2) 16M x 36	(2) 8M x 36	(2) 2M x 36	None
216MB	(2) 16M x 36	(2) 8M x 36	(2) 2M x 36	(2) 1M x 36
224MB	(2) 8M x 36	(2) 8M x 36	(2) 8M x 36	(2) 4M x 36
224MB	(2) 16M x 36	(2) 4M x 36	(2) 4M x 36	(2) 4M x 36
224MB	(2) 16M x 36	(2) 8M x 36	(2) 2M x 36	(2) 2M x 36
224MB	(2) 16M x 36	(2) 8M x 36	(2) 4M x 36	None
232MB	(2) 16M x 36	(2) 8M x 36	(2) 4M x 36	(2) 1M x 36
240MB	(2) 16M x 36	(2) 8M x 36	(2) 4M x 36	(2) 2M x 36
256MB	(2) 8M x 36	(2) 8M x 36	(2) 8M x 36	(2) 8M x 36
256MB	(2) 16M x 36	(2) 8M x 36	(2) 4M x 36	(2) 4M x 36
256MB	(2) 16M x 36	(2) 8M x 36	(2) 8M x 36	None
256MB	(2) 16M x 36	(2) 16M x 36	None	None
264MB	(2) 16M x 36	(2) 8M x 36	(2) 8M x 36	(2) 1M x 36
264MB	(2) 16M x 36	(2) 8M x 36	(2) 8M x 36	(2) 1M x 36
272MB	(2) 16M x 36	(2) 8M x 36	(2) 8M x 36	(2) 2M x 36
272MB	(2) 16M x 36	(2) 16M x 36	(2) 1M x 36	(2) 1M x 36
280MB	(2) 16M x 36	(2) 16M x 36	(2) 2M x 36	(2) 1M x 36
288MB	(2) 16M x 36	(2) 8M x 36	(2) 8M x 36	(2) 4M x 36
288MB	(2) 16M x 36	(2) 16M x 36	(2) 2M x 36	(2) 2M x 36
288MB	(2) 16M x 36	(2) 16M x 36	(2) 4M x 36	None
296MB	(2) 16M x 36	(2) 16M x 36	(2) 4M x 36	(2) 1M x 36
304MB	(2) 16M x 36	(2) 16M x 36	(2) 4M x 36	(2) 2M x 36
320MB	(2) 16M x 36	(2) 16M x 36	(2) 4M x 36	(2) 4M x 36
320MB	(2) 16M x 36	(2) 8M x 36	(2) 8M x 36	(2) 8M x 36
328MB	(2) 16M x 36	(2) 16M x 36	(2) 8M x 36	(2) 1M x 36
336MB	(2) 16M x 36	(2) 16M x 36	(2) 8M x 36	(2) 2M x 36
352MB	(2) 16M x 36	(2) 16M x 36	(2) 8M x 36	(2) 4M x 36
384MB	(2) 16M x 36	(2) 16M x 36	(2) 8M x 36	(2) 8M x 36
384MB	(2) 16M x 36	(2) 16M x 36	(2) 16M x 36	None
392MB	(2) 16M x 36	(2) 16M x 36	(2) 16M x 36	(2) 1M x 36
400MB	(2) 16M x 36	(2) 16M x 36	(2) 16M x 36	(2) 2M x 36
416MB	(2) 16M x 36	(2) 16M x 36	(2) 16M x 36	(2) 4M x 36
448MB	(2) 16M x 36	(2) 16M x 36	(2) 16M x 36	(2) 8M x 36
512MB	(2) 16M x 36	(2) 16M x 36	(2) 16M x 36	(2) 16M x 36
Note:	Board accepts EDO memory. Board also accepts x 32 SIMMs.			

Continued on next page. . .

MICRONICS COMPUTERS, INC.
M 6 M E

...continued from previous page

CACHE CONFIGURATION
Note: 256KB/512KB cache is located on the Pentium Pro CPU.

VIDEO MEMORY CONFIGURATION
Note: Board accepts 1MB/2MB video memory. The location and chip sizes are unidentified.

CPU SPEED SELECTION

CPU speed	Clock speed	Multiplier	W7	W8
120MHz	60MHz	2x	1 & 2, 3 & 4, 5 & 6, 7 & 8	Closed
133MHz	66MHz	2x	1 & 2, 3 & 4, 5 & 6, 7 & 8	Open
150MHz	60MHz	2.5x	1 & 2, 3 & 4, 5 & 6	Closed
166MHz	66MHz	2.5x	1 & 2, 3 & 4, 5 & 6	Open
180MHz	66MHz	3x	1 & 2, 3 & 4, 7 & 8	Closed
200MHz	66MHz	3x	1 & 2, 3 & 4, 7 & 8	Open

MICRONICS COMPUTERS, INC.
M 6 M I

Processor	Pentium Pro
Processor Speed	150/166/180/200MHz
Chip Set	Intel
Video Chip Set	None
Maximum Onboard Memory	384MB (EDO supported)
Maximum Video Memory	None
Cache	512KB (on Pentium Pro CPU)
BIOS	Phoenix
Dimensions	330mm x 218mm
I/O Options	32-bit PCI slots (4), bus mouse port, CD-ROM audio input connector, floppy drive interface, IDE interfaces (2), parallel port, PS/2 mouse port, serial ports (2), IR connector, VRM connector, USB connectors (2), microphone connector, audio line in connector, audio line out connector, external audio connector, wavetable connector, game/MIDI port
NPU Options	None

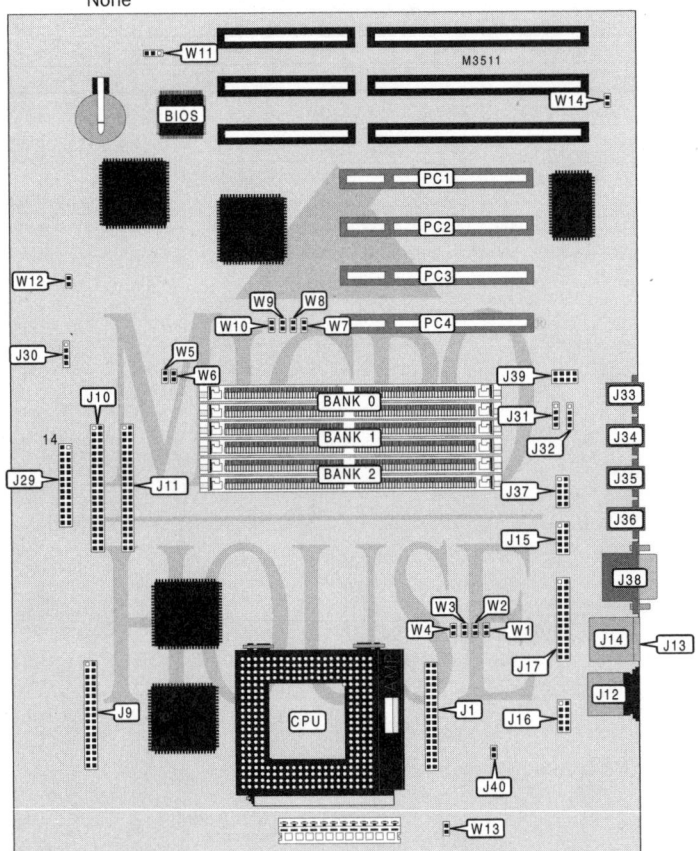

Continued on next page...

MICRONICS COMPUTERS, INC.
M 6 M I

...continued from previous page

CONNECTIONS

Purpose	Location	Purpose	Location
VRM connector	J1	IDE interface LED	J29 pins 23 & 24
Floppy drive interface	J9	Turbo LED	J29 pins 25 & 26
IDE interface 1	J10	IR connector	J30
IDE interface 2	J11	CD-ROM audio connector	J31
PS/2 mouse port	J12	Modem connector	J32
USB connector	J13	Microphone in connector	J33
USB connector	J14	Audio line in connector	J34
Serial port 2	J15	Audio line out connector	J35
Serial port 1	J16	Speaker out connector	J36
Parallel port	J17	External audio connector	J37
System power on/off connector	J29 pins 1 & 2	Game/MIDI port	J38
IR connector	J29 pins 6 - 10	Wavetable connector	J39
Reset switch	J29 pins 12 & 13	Chassis fan power	J40
Speaker	J29 pins 14 - 17	32-bit PCI slots	PC1 - PC4
Power LED & keylock	J29 pins 18 - 22		

USER CONFIGURABLE SETTINGS

Function	Label	Position
◇ CMOS memory normal operation	W11	Pins 1 & 2 closed
CMOS memory clear	W11	Pins 2 & 3 closed
◇ Factory configured - do not alter (AT bus clock select)	W12	Closed
◇ Factory configured - do not alter (system power supply enabled)	W13	Open
◇ Internal sound enabled	W14	Open
Internal sound disabled	W14	Closed

DRAM CONFIGURATION

Size	Bank 0	Bank 1	Bank 2
8MB	(2) 1M x 36	None	None
16MB	(2) 1M x 36	(2) 1M x 36	None
16MB	(2) 2M x 36	None	None
24MB	(2) 2M x 36	(2) 1M x 36	None
24MB	(2) 1M x 36	(2) 1M x 36	(2) 1M x 36
32MB	(2) 4M x 36	None	None
32MB	(2) 2M x 36	(2) 1M x 36	(2) 1M x 36
40MB	(2) 2M x 36	(2) 2M x 36	(2) 1M x 36
40MB	(2) 4M x 36	(2) 1M x 36	None
48MB	(2) 2M x 36	(2) 2M x 36	(2) 2M x 36
48MB	(2) 4M x 36	(2) 1M x 36	(2) 1M x 36
48MB	(2) 4M x 36	(2) 2M x 36	None
56MB	(2) 4M x 36	(2) 2M x 36	(2) 1M x 36
64MB	(2) 4M x 36	(2) 2M x 36	(2) 2M x 36
64MB	(2) 4M x 36	(2) 4M x 36	None

Continued on next page...

MICRONICS COMPUTERS, INC.
M 6 M I

...continued from previous page

DRAM CONFIGURATION (CON'T)			
Size	**Bank 0**	**Bank 1**	**Bank 2**
64MB	(2) 8M x 36	None	None
72MB	(2) 4M x 36	(2) 4M x 36	(2) 1M x 36
72MB	(2) 8M x 36	(2) 1M x 36	None
80MB	(2) 4M x 36	(2) 4M x 36	(2) 2M x 36
80MB	(2) 8M x 36	(2) 1M x 36	(2) 1M x 36
80MB	(2) 8M x 36	(2) 2M x 36	None
96MB	(2) 8M x 36	(2) 2M x 36	(2) 2M x 36
96MB	(2) 4M x 36	(2) 4M x 36	(2) 4M x 36
96MB	(2) 8M x 36	(2) 4M x 36	None
128MB	(2) 8M x 36	(2) 4M x 36	(2) 4M x 36
128MB	(2) 8M x 36	(2) 8M x 36	None
128MB	(2) 16M x 36	None	None
160MB	(2) 8M x 36	(2) 8M x 36	(2) 4M x 36
160MB	(2) 16M x 36	(2) 2M x 36	(2) 2M x 36
160MB	(2) 16M x 36	(2) 4M x 36	None
192MB	(2) 8M x 36	(2) 8M x 36	(2) 8M x 36
192MB	(2) 16M x 36	(2) 4M x 36	(2) 4M x 36
192MB	(2) 16M x 36	(2) 8M x 36	None
256MB	(2) 16M x 36	(2) 8M x 36	(2) 8M x 36
256MB	(2) 16M x 36	(2) 16M x 36	None
384MB	(2) 16M x 36	(2) 16M x 36	(2) 16M x 36

Note: Board accepts EDO memory. Board also accepts x 32 SIMMs.

CACHE CONFIGURATION
Note: 512KB cache is located on the Pentium Pro CPU.

CPU SPEED SELECTION						
Speed	**W5**	**W6**	**W7**	**W8**	**W9**	**W10**
150MHz	Closed	Open	Closed	Closed	Closed	Open
166MHz	Open	Closed	Closed	Closed	Closed	Open
180MHz	Closed	Open	Closed	Closed	Open	Closed
200MHz	Open	Closed	Closed	Closed	Open	Closed

CPU VOLTAGE SELECTION				
Voltage	**W1**	**W2**	**W3**	**W4**
VID enabled	Open	Open	Open	Open
Non VID 2.9v	Closed	Open	Open	Closed
Non VID 3.1v	Closed	Open	Closed	Closed
Non VID 3.3v	Closed	Closed	Open	Closed

MICRONICS COMPUTERS, INC.
M 6 P I

Processor	Pentium Pro
Processor Speed	150/166/180/200MHz
Chip Set	Unidentified
Video Chip Set	None
Maximum Onboard Memory	512MB
Maximum Video Memory	None
Cache	256KB (on Pentium Pro CPU)
BIOS	Phoenix
Dimensions	337mm x 216mm
I/O Options	32-bit PCI slots (3), floppy drive interface, IDE interfaces (2), parallel port, serial ports (2), IR connectors (2), VRM connector
NPU Options	None

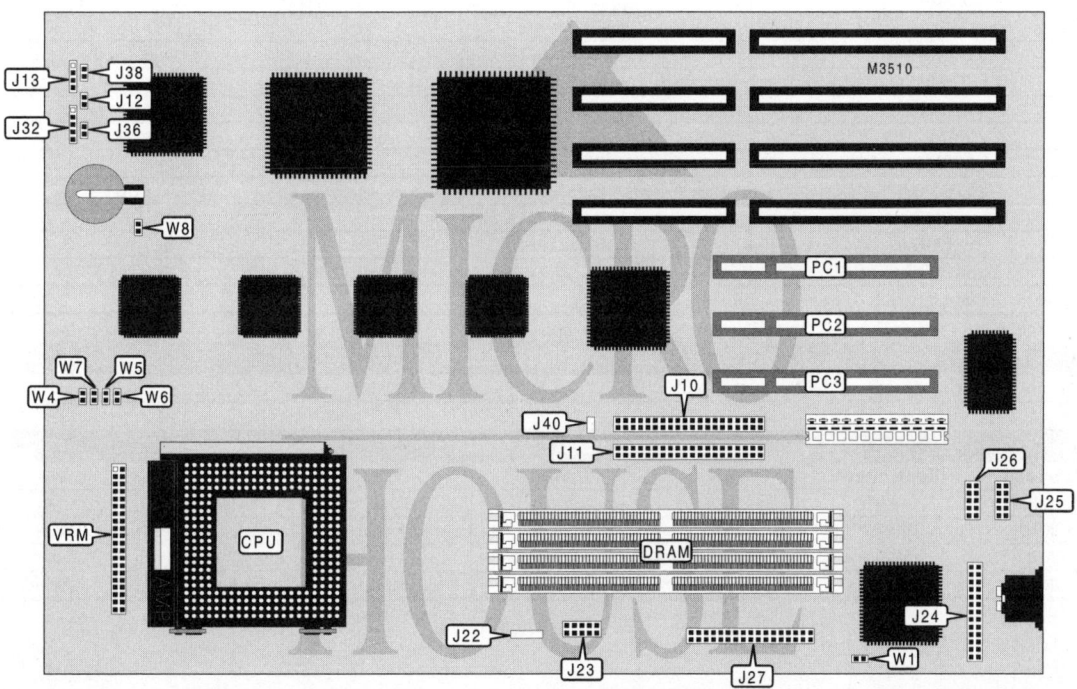

CONNECTIONS			
Purpose	Location	Purpose	Location
IDE interface 1	J10	Serial port 2	J26
IDE interface 2	J11	Floppy drive interface	J27
IDE interface LED	J12	Power LED & keylock	J32
Speaker	J13	Turbo LED	J36
IR connector	J22	Reset switch	J38
IR connector	J23	32-bit PCI slots	PC1 - PC3
Parallel port	J24	VRM connector	VRM
Serial port 1	J25		

Continued on next page...

MICRONICS COMPUTERS, INC.
M 6 P I

. . . continued from previous page

USER CONFIGURABLE SETTINGS		
Function	**Label**	**Position**
Jumper information unavailable	J40	Unidentified
⇨ CMOS memory normal operation	W1	Open
CMOS memory clear	W1	Closed

DRAM CONFIGURATION		
Size	**Bank 0**	**Bank 1**
8MB	(2) 1M x 36	None
16MB	(2) 2M x 36	None
16MB	(2) 1M x 36	(2) 1M x 36
32MB	(2) 4M x 36	None
32MB	(2) 2M x 36	(2) 2M x 36
64MB	(2) 8M x 36	None
64MB	(2) 4M x 36	(2) 4M x 36
128MB	(2) 16M x 36	None
128MB	(2) 8M x 36	(2) 8M x 36
256MB	(2) 16M x 36	(2) 16M x 36
256MB	(2) 32M x 36	None
512MB	(2) 32M x 36	(2) 32M x 36

Note: The location of banks 0 & 1 are unidentified.

CACHE CONFIGURATION
Note: 256KB cache is located on the Pentium Pro CPU.

CPU SPEED SELECTION						
CPU speed	**Clock speed**	**W4**	**W5**	**W6**	**W7**	**W8**
150MHz	60MHz	Closed	Closed	Closed	Open	Open
166MHz	66MHz	Closed	Closed	Closed	Open	Closed
180MHz	60MHz	Closed	Open	Closed	Closed	Open
200MHz	66MHz	Closed	Open	Closed	Closed	Closed

MICRONICS COMPUTERS, INC.
M7S-HI

Processor	AM K5/AM K6/Pentium
Processor Speed	75/90/100/120/133/150/166/200MHz
Chip Set	Intel
Video Chip Set	None
Maximum Onboard Memory	256MB (EDO supported)
Maximum Video Memory	None
Cache	256/512KB
BIOS	Phoenix
Dimensions	305mm x 244mm
I/O Options	32-bit PCI slots (4), CD-ROM audio in connector, floppy drive interface, game port, green PC connector, IDE interfaces (2), parallel port, PS/2 mouse port, serial ports (2), IR connector, VRM connector, USB connectors (2), ATX power connector, microphone in connector, line in connector, line out connector, telephony connector, wavetable connector
NPU Options	None

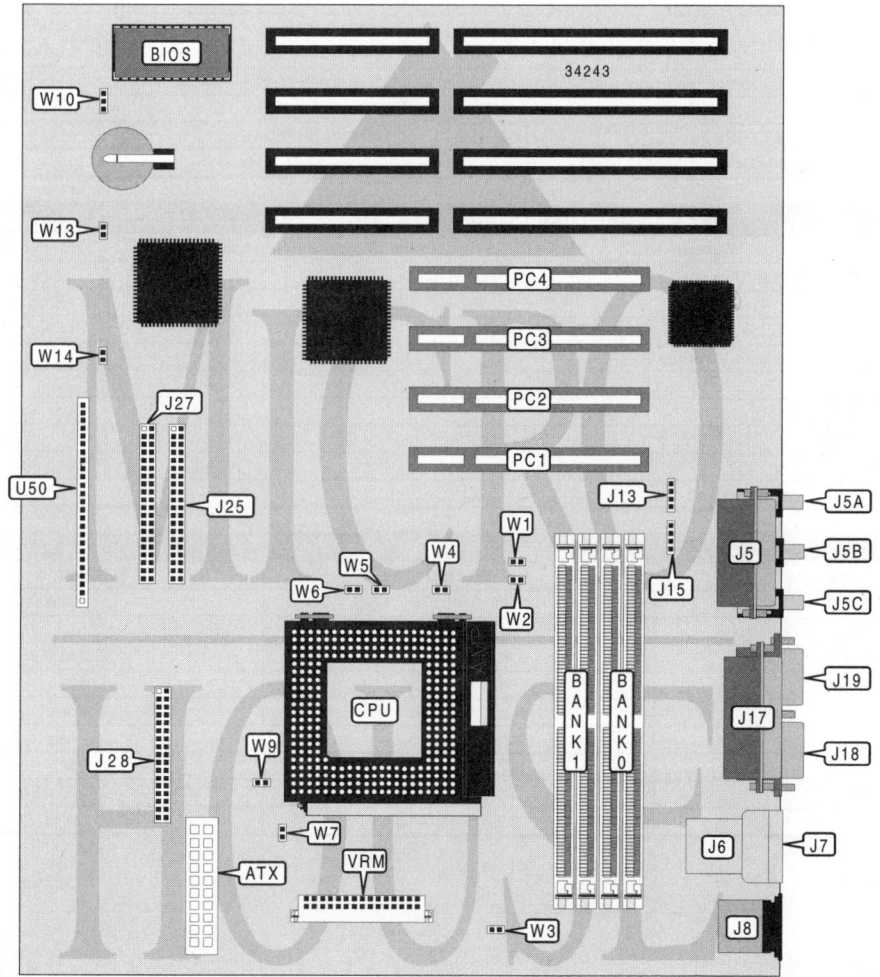

Continued on next page...

MICRONICS COMPUTERS, INC.
M7S-HI

...continued from previous page

CONNECTIONS

Purpose	Location	Purpose	Location
ATX power connector	ATX	IDE interface 2	J25
Game port	J5	IDE interface 1	J27
Microphone in connector	J5A	Floppy drive interface	J28
Line in connector	J5B	32-bit PCI slots	PC1 – PC4
Line out connector	J5C	Soft off power supply	U50/pins 1 & 2
USB connector 1	J6	Green PC connector	U50/pins 3 & 4
USB connector 2	J7	IR connector	U50/pins 6 - 11
PS/2 mouse port	J8	IDE interface LED	U50/pins 13 - 16
CD-ROM audio in connector	J13	Power LED	U50/pins 19 - 21
Wavetable connector	J14	Reset switch	U50/pins 22 & 23
Telephony connector	J15	Speaker	U50/pins 24 - 27
Parallel port	J17	VRM connector	VRM
Serial port 2	J18	Chassis fan power	W3
Serial port 1	J19	Chassis fan power	W9

Note: The location of J14 is unidentified.

USER CONFIGURABLE SETTINGS

Function	Label	Position
⇨ CMOS memory normal operation	W10	Pins 1 & 2 closed
CMOS memory clear	W10	Pins 2 & 3 closed
⇨ Cacheable DRAM range select normal	W12	Open
Cacheable DRAM range select extended	W12	Closed
⇨ AT bus clock select 1/4	W13	Closed
AT bus clock select 1/3	W13	Open
⇨ Soft off power enabled	W14	Open
Soft off power disabled	W14	Closed

Note: The location of J12 is unidentified.

DRAM CONFIGURATION

Size	Bank 0	Bank 1
8MB	(2) 1M x 36	None
16MB	(2) 2M x 36	None
16MB	(2) 1M x 36	(2) 1M x 36
24MB	(2) 2M x 36	(2) 1M x 36
32MB	(2) 4M x 36	None
32MB	(2) 2M x 36	(2) 2M x 36
40MB	(2) 4M x 36	(2) 1M x 36
48MB	(2) 4M x 36	(2) 2M x 36
64MB	(2) 8M x 36	None

Continued on next page...

MICRONICS COMPUTERS, INC.
M7S-HI

...continued from previous page

DRAM CONFIGURATION (CON'T)		
Size	**Bank 0**	**Bank 1**
64MB	(2) 4M x 36	(2) 4M x 36
72MB	(2) 8M x 36	(2) 1M x 36
80MB	(2) 8M x 36	(2) 2M x 36
96MB	(2) 8M x 36	(2) 4M x 36
128MB	(2) 8M x 36	(2) 8M x 36
128MB	(2) 16M x 36	None
136MB	(2) 16M x 36	(2) 1M x 36
144MB	(2) 16M x 36	(2) 2M x 36
160MB	(2) 16M x 36	(2) 4M x 36
192MB	(2) 16M x 36	(2) 8M x 36
256MB	(2) 16M x 36	(2) 16M x 36

Note: Board accepts EDO memory.

CACHE CONFIGURATION	
Size	**Bank 0**
256KB	(2) 32K x 32
512KB	(2) 64K x 32

Note: The location of bank 0 is unidentified.

CPU SPEED SELECTION (AMD)							
CPU speed	**Clock speed**	**Multiplier**	**W1**	**W2**	**W4**	**W5**	**W6**
75MHz	50MHz	1.5x	N/A	N/A	N/A	Open	Open
90MHz	60MHz	1.5x	Closed	Open	Closed	Open	Open
100MHz	66MHz	1.5x	Open	Closed	Open	Open	Open
120MHz	60MHz	2x	Closed	Open	Closed	Open	Closed
133MHz	66MHz	2x	Open	Closed	Open	Open	Closed
150MHz	60MHz	2.5x	Closed	Open	Closed	Closed	Closed
166MHz	66MHz	2.5x	Open	Closed	Open	Closed	Closed
200MHz	66MHz	3x	Open	Closed	Open	Closed	Open

Note: If an AM K6 processor is installed, a VRM module must be installed. The jumper settings for W1 – W3 with a 75MHZ processor are unidentified.

CPU SPEED SELECTION (INTEL)							
CPU speed	**Clock speed**	**Multiplier**	**W1**	**W2**	**W4**	**W5**	**W6**
90MHz	60MHz	1.5x	Closed	Open	Closed	Open	Open
100MHz	66MHz	1.5x	Open	Closed	Open	Open	Open
120MHz	60MHz	2x	Closed	Open	Closed	Open	Closed
133MHz	66MHz	2x	Open	Closed	Open	Open	Closed
150MHz	60MHz	2.5x	Closed	Open	Closed	Closed	Closed
166MHz	66MHz	2.5x	Open	Closed	Open	Closed	Closed
200MHz	66MHz	3x	Open	Closed	Open	Closed	Open

Note: If a MMX processor is installed, a VRM module must be installed.

Continued on next page...

MICRONICS COMPUTERS, INC.
M 7 S - H I

. . . continued from previous page

CPU TYPE SELECTION	
Type	W7
STD/VR	Open
⇨ VRE	Closed

MICRONICS COMPUTERS, INC.
STINGRAY

Processor	Pentium II
Processor Speed	233/266/300/333MHz
Chip Set	Intel
Video Chip Set	None
Maximum Onboard Memory	256MB (EDO supported)
Maximum Video Memory	None
Cache	256/512KB
BIOS	Award
Dimensions	305mm x 244mm
I/O Options	32-bit PCI slots (4), floppy drive interface, green PC connector, IDE interfaces (2), parallel port, PS/2 mouse port, serial ports (2), IR connector, USB connectors (2), ATX power connector, CPU slot 1
NPU Options	None

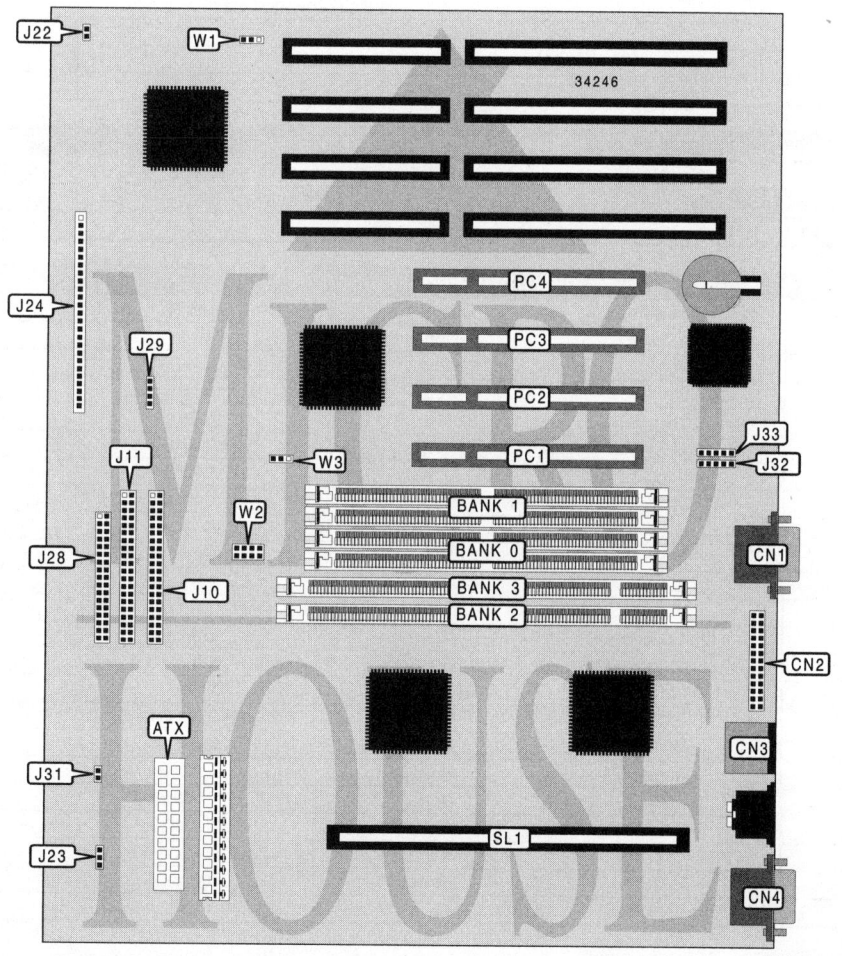

Continued on next page...

MICRONICS COMPUTERS, INC.
STINGRAY

. . . continued from previous page

CONNECTIONS

Purpose	Location	Purpose	Location
ATX power connector	ATX	IDE interface LED	J24/pins 13 - 16
Serial port 2	CN1	Power LED	J24/pins 18 - 20
Parallel port	CN2	Reset switch	J24/pins 22 & 23
PS/2 mouse port	CN3	Speaker	J24/pins 24 - 27
Serial port 1	CN4	Floppy drive interface	J28
IDE interface 1	J10	Keylock	J29
IDE interface 2	J11	Turbo LED	J31
Chassis fan power	J22	USB connector 1	J32
Chassis fan power	J23	USB connector 2	J33
IDE interface LED	J24/pins 1 & 2	32-bit PCI slots	PC1 – PC4
Green PC connector	J24/pins 3 & 4	CPU slot 1	SL1
IR connector	J24/pins 6 - 10		

USER CONFIGURABLE SETTINGS

Function	Label	Position
⇨ CMOS memory normal operation	W1	Pins 1 & 2 closed
CMOS memory clear	W1	Pins 2 & 3 closed

DIMM/DRAM CONFIGURATION

Size	Bank 0	Bank 1	Bank 2	Bank 3
8MB	(2) 1M x 36	None	None	None
8MB	None	None	(1) 1M x 64	None
16MB	(2) 2M x 36	None	None	None
16MB	(2) 1M x 36	(2) 1M x 36	None	None
16MB	(2) 1M x 36	None	(1) 1M x 64	None
16MB	None	None	(1) 2M x 64	None
16MB	None	None	(1) 1M x 64	(1) 1M x 64
16MB	(2) 1M x 36	None	(1) 1M x 64	None
24MB	(2) 2M x 36	(2) 1M x 36	None	None
24MB	(2) 2M x 36	None	(1) 1M x 64	None
24MB	None	None	(1) 2M x 64	(1) 1M x 64
24MB	(2) 1M x 36	None	(1) 1M x 64	(1) 1M x 64
32MB	(2) 4M x 36	None	None	None
32MB	(2) 2M x 36	(2) 2M x 36	None	None
32MB	(2) 2M x 36	None	(1) 2M x 64	None
32MB	None	None	(1) 4M x 64	None
32MB	None	None	(1) 2M x 64	(1) 2M x 64
32MB	(2) 2M x 36	None	(1) 2M x 64	None
40MB	(2) 4M x 36	(2) 1M x 36	None	None
40MB	(2) 4M x 36	None	(1) 1M x 64	None
40MB	None	None	(1) 1M x 64	(1) 4M x 64
48MB	(2) 4M x 36	(2) 2M x 36	None	None

Continued on next page. . .

MICRONICS COMPUTERS, INC.
STINGRAY

. . . continued from previous page

Size	Bank 0	Bank 1	Bank 2	Bank 3
\multicolumn{5}{c}{**DIMM/DRAM CONFIGURATION (CON'T)**}				
48MB	(2) 2M x 36	None	(1) 4M x 64	None
48MB	None	None	(1) 2M x 64	(1) 4M x 64
48MB	(2) 2M x 36	None	(1) 2M x 64	(1) 2M x 64
64MB	(2) 8M x 36	None	None	None
64MB	(2) 4M x 36	(2) 4M x 36	None	None
64MB	(2) 4M x 36	None	(1) 4M x 64	None
64MB	None	None	(1) 8M x 64	None
64MB	None	None	(1) 4M x 64	(1) 4M x 64
64MB	(2) 4M x 36	None	(1) 4M x 64	None
72MB	(2) 8M x 36	None	(1) 1M x 64	None
72MB	(2) 8M x 36	(2) 1M x 36	None	None
72MB	None	None	(1) 1M x 64	(1) 8M x 64
80MB	(2) 2M x 36	None	(1) 8M x 64	None
80MB	(2) 2M x 36	None	(1) 8M x 64	None
80MB	(2) 8M x 36	(2) 2M x 36	None	None
80MB	None	None	(1) 2M x 64	(1) 8M x 64
96MB	(2) 4M x 36	None	(1) 8M x 64	None
96MB	(2) 4M x 36	None	(1) 4M x 64	(1) 4M x 64
96MB	(2) 8M x 36	None	(1) 4M x 64	None
96MB	(2) 8M x 36	(2) 4M x 36	None	None
96MB	None	None	(1) 4M x 64	(1) 8M x 64
128MB	(2) 8M x 36	None	(1) 8M x 64	None
128MB	(2) 8M x 36	None	(1) 8M x 64	None
128MB	(2) 8M x 36	(2) 8M x 36	None	None
128MB	(2) 16M x 36	None	None	None
128MB	None	None	(1) 8M x 64	(1) 8M x 64
192MB	(2) 8M x 36	None	(1) 8M x 64	(1) 8M x 64
136MB	(2) 16M x 36	(2) 1M x 36	None	None
144MB	(2) 16M x 36	(2) 2M x 36	None	None
160MB	(2) 16M x 36	(2) 4M x 36	None	None
192MB	(2) 16M x 36	(2) 8M x 36	None	None
256MB	(2) 16M x 36	(2) 16M x 36	None	None
256MB	None	None	(1) 16M x 64	(1) 16M x 64

Note: Board accepts EDO memory. The table reflects only some of the possible configurations. Rules follow: 1) when only SIMM bank 0 is filled, DIMM bank 2 or DIMM banks 2 & 3 can be used, and 2) when SIMM banks 0 & 1 are both filled, only DIMM bank 3 can only be used.

Size	Bank 0
\multicolumn{2}{c}{**CACHE CONFIGURATION**}	
256KB	(2) 32K x 32
512KB	(2) 64K x 32

Note: The location of bank 0 is unidentified.

Continued on next page. . .

MICRONICS COMPUTERS, INC.
STINGRAY

. . . continued from previous page

CPU SPEED SELECTION				
CPU speed	**Clock speed**	**Multiplier**	**W2**	**W3**
233MHz	66MHz	3.5x	1 & 2, 7 & 8	1 & 2
266MHz	66MHz	4x	1 & 2, 3 & 4, 5 & 6	1 & 2
300MHz	66MHz	4.5x	1 & 2, 5 & 6	1 & 2
333MHz	66MHz	5x	1 & 2, 3 & 4	1 & 2
Note: Pins designated should be in the closed position.				

MICRONICS COMPUTERS, INC.
TWISTER AT

Processor	CX M1/AM K5/AM K6/Pentium
Processor Speed	75/90/100/120/133/150/166/180/200/233MHz
Chip Set	Intel
Video Chip Set	None
Maximum Onboard Memory	256MB (EDO supported)
Maximum Video Memory	None
Cache	256/512KB
BIOS	Award
Dimensions	330mm x 218mm
I/O Options	32-bit PCI slots (5), floppy drive interface, green PC connector, IDE interfaces (2), parallel port, PS/2 mouse interface, serial ports (2), IR connector, USB connectors (2)
NPU Options	None

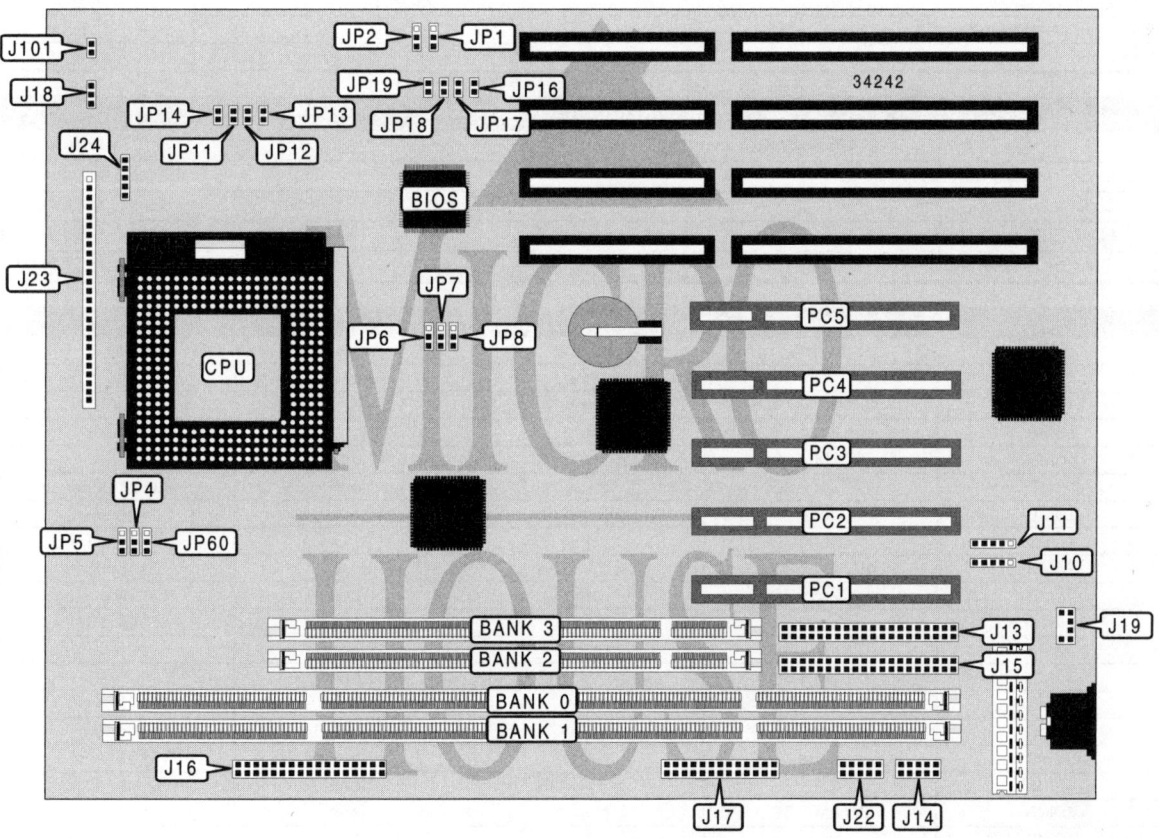

Continued on next page...

MICRONICS COMPUTERS, INC.
TWISTER AT

...continued from previous page

CONNECTIONS

Purpose	Location	Purpose	Location
USB connector 1	J10	Green PC connector	J23/pins 3 & 4
USB connector 2	J11	IR connector	J23/pins 6 - 10
IDE interface 2	J13	IDE interface LED	J23/pins 13 - 16
Serial port 2	J14	Power LED	J23/pins 18 - 20
IDE interface 1	J15	Reset switch	J23/pins 22 & 23
Floppy drive interface	J16	Speaker	J23/pins 24 - 27
Parallel port	J17	Power LED & keylock	J24
Chassis fan power	J18	SCSI interface LED	J101
PS/2 mouse interface	J19	32-bit PCI slots	PC1 – PC5
Serial port 1	J22		

USER CONFIGURABLE SETTINGS

Function	Label	Position
◊ CMOS memory normal operation	JP1	Pins 1 & 2 closed
CMOS memory clear	JP1	Pins 2 & 3 closed
Flash BIOS normal operation	JP2	Pins 2 & 3 closed
Flash BIOS reserved	JP2	Pins 1 & 2 closed

DIMM/DRAM CONFIGURATION

Size	Bank 0	Bank 1	Bank 2	Bank 3
8MB	(2) 1M x 36	None	None	None
8MB	None	None	(1) 1M x 64	None
16MB	(2) 2M x 36	None	None	None
16MB	(2) 1M x 36	(2) 1M x 36	None	None
16MB	(2) 1M x 36	None	None	(1) 1M x 64
16MB	None	None	(1) 2M x 64	None
16MB	None	None	(1) 1M x 64	(1) 1M x 64
24MB	(2) 2M x 36	(2) 1M x 36	None	None
24MB	(2) 2M x 36	None	None	(1) 1M x 64
24MB	None	None	(1) 2M x 64	(1) 1M x 64
32MB	(2) 4M x 36	None	None	None
32MB	(2) 2M x 36	(2) 2M x 36	None	None
32MB	(2) 2M x 36	None	None	(1) 2M x 64
32MB	None	None	(1) 4M x 64	None
32MB	None	None	(1) 2M x 64	(1) 2M x 64
40MB	(2) 4M x 36	(2) 1M x 36	None	None
40MB	(2) 4M x 36	None	None	(1) 1M x 64
40MB	None	None	(1) 1M x 64	(1) 4M x 64
48MB	(2) 4M x 36	(2) 2M x 36	None	None
48MB	(2) 2M x 36	None	None	(1) 4M x 64
48MB	None	None	(1) 2M x 64	(1) 4M x 64
64MB	(2) 8M x 36	None	None	None

Continued on next page...

MICRONICS COMPUTERS, INC.
TWISTER AT

...continued from previous page

DIMM/DRAM CONFIGURATION (CON'T)

Size	Bank 0	Bank 1	Bank 2	Bank 3
64MB	(2) 4M x 36	(2) 4M x 36	None	None
64MB	(2) 4M x 36	None	None	(1) 4M x 64
64MB	None	None	(1) 8M x 64	None
64MB	None	None	(1) 4M x 64	(1) 4M x 64
72MB	(2) 8M x 36	None	None	(1) 1M x 64
72MB	(2) 8M x 36	(2) 1M x 36	None	None
72MB	None	None	(1) 1M x 64	(1) 8M x 64
80MB	(2) 2M x 36	None	None	(1) 8M x 64
80MB	(2) 2M x 36	None	None	(1) 8M x 64
80MB	(2) 8M x 36	(2) 2M x 36	None	None
80MB	None	None	(1) 2M x 64	(1) 8M x 64
96MB	(2) 4M x 36	None	None	(1) 8M x 64
96MB	(2) 8M x 36	None	None	(1) 4M x 64
96MB	(2) 8M x 36	(2) 4M x 36	None	None
96MB	None	None	(1) 4M x 64	(1) 8M x 64
128MB	(2) 8M x 36	None	None	(1) 8M x 64
128MB	(2) 8M x 36	None	None	(1) 8M x 64
128MB	(2) 8M x 36	(2) 8M x 36	None	None
128MB	(2) 16M x 36	None	None	None
128MB	None	None	(1) 8M x 64	(1) 8M x 64
136MB	(2) 16M x 36	(2) 1M x 36	None	None
144MB	(2) 16M x 36	(2) 2M x 36	None	None
160MB	(2) 16M x 36	(2) 4M x 36	None	None
192MB	(2) 16M x 36	(2) 8M x 36	None	None
256MB	(2) 16M x 36	(2) 16M x 36	None	None
256MB	None	None	(1) 16M x 64	(1) 16M x 64

Note: Board accepts EDO memory. Banks 2 & 3 are interchangeable.

CACHE CONFIGURATION

Size	Bank 0
256KB	(2) 32K x 32
512KB	(2) 64K x 32

Note: The location of the cache is unidentified.

CPU SPEED SELECTION (CYRIX)

CPU speed	Clock speed	Multiplier	JP4	JP5	JP6	JP7	JP8	JP60
150MHz	50MHz	2x	1 & 2	1 & 2	2 & 3	2 & 3	1 & 2	Open
166MHz	60MHz	2x	1 & 2	1 & 2	2 & 3	1 & 2	2 & 3	Open

Note: Pins designated should be in the closed position.

Continued on next page...

MICRONICS COMPUTERS, INC.
TWISTER AT

. . . continued from previous page

CPU SPEED SELECTION (AMD)

CPU speed	Clock speed	Multiplier	JP4	JP5	JP6	JP7	JP8	JP60
75MHz	50MHz	1.5x	1 & 2	1 & 2	2 & 3	2 & 3	2 & 3	Open
90MHz	60MHz	1.5x	1 & 2	1 & 2	2 & 3	2 & 3	1 & 2	Open
100MHz	66MHz	1.5x	1 & 2	1 & 2	2 & 3	1 & 2	2 & 3	Open
120MHz	60MHz	1.5x	1 & 2	1 & 2	2 & 3	2 & 3	1 & 2	Open
133MHz	66MHz	2x	1 & 2	2 & 3	2 & 3	1 & 2	2 & 3	Open
166MHz	66MHz	2.5x	2 & 3	2 & 3	2 & 3	1 & 2	2 & 3	Open
200MHz	66MHz	3x	2 & 3	1 & 2	2 & 3	1 & 2	2 & 3	Open
233MHz	66MHz	3.5x	1 & 2	1 & 2	2 & 3	1 & 2	2 & 3	1 & 2

Note: Pins designated should be in the closed position.

CPU SPEED SELECTION (INTEL)

CPU speed	Clock speed	Multiplier	JP4	JP5	JP6	JP7	JP8	JP60
75MHz	50MHz	1.5x	1 & 2	1 & 2	2 & 3	2 & 3	2 & 3	Open
90MHz	60MHz	1.5x	1 & 2	1 & 2	2 & 3	2 & 3	1 & 2	Open
100MHz	66MHz	1.5x	1 & 2	1 & 2	2 & 3	1 & 2	2 & 3	Open
120MHz	60MHz	2x	1 & 2	2 & 3	2 & 3	2 & 3	1 & 2	Open
133MHz	66MHz	2x	1 & 2	2 & 3	2 & 3	1 & 2	2 & 3	Open
150MHz	60MHz	2.5x	2 & 3	2 & 3	2 & 3	2 & 3	1 & 2	Open
166MHz	66MHz	2.5x	2 & 3	2 & 3	2 & 3	1 & 2	2 & 3	Open
180MHz	60MHz	3x	2 & 3	1 & 2	2 & 3	2 & 3	1 & 2	Open
200MHz	66MHz	3x	2 & 3	1 & 2	2 & 3	1 & 2	2 & 3	Open
233MHz	66MHz	3.5x	1 & 2	1 & 2	2 & 3	1 & 2	2 & 3	Open

Note: Pins designated should be in the closed position.

CPU TYPE SELECTION

Type	JP11	JP12	JP13	JP14	JP16	JP17	JP18	JP19
CX6X86	Open	Closed	Open	Open	Open	Closed	Open	Open
CX6X86L	Open	Open	Open	Closed	Open	Closed	Open	Open
AM K5	Open	Open	Closed	Open	Open	Closed	Open	Open
AM K6	Open	Open	Open	Closed	Open	Closed	Open	Open
AM K6 233MHz	Closed	Open	Open	Open	Open	Closed	Open	Open
P54C	Open	Closed	Open	Open	Open	Closed	Open	Open
P54CS	Open	Closed	Open	Open	Open	Closed	Open	Open
P54CTB	Open	Closed	Open	Open	Open	Closed	Open	Open
P55C	Open	Open	Open	Closed	Open	Closed	Open	Open

MICRONICS COMPUTERS, INC.
W 6 - L I

Processor	Pentium Pro
Processor Speed	150/166/180/200MHz
Chip Set	Intel
Video Chip Set	None
Maximum Onboard Memory	512MB (EDO supported)
Maximum Video Memory	None
Cache	256/512KB (located on Pentium Pro CPU)
BIOS	Phoenix
Dimensions	330mm x 218mm
I/O Options	32-bit PCI slots (4), CD-ROM connector, floppy drive interface, game port, green PC connector, IDE interfaces (2), Fast SCSI interface, Ultra Wide SCSI interface, parallel port, PS/2 mouse port, serial ports (2), IR connectors (2), USB connectors (2), ATX power connector, microphone in connector, line out connector, line in connector, modem/telephony connector, wavetable connector, VRM connector
NPU Options	None

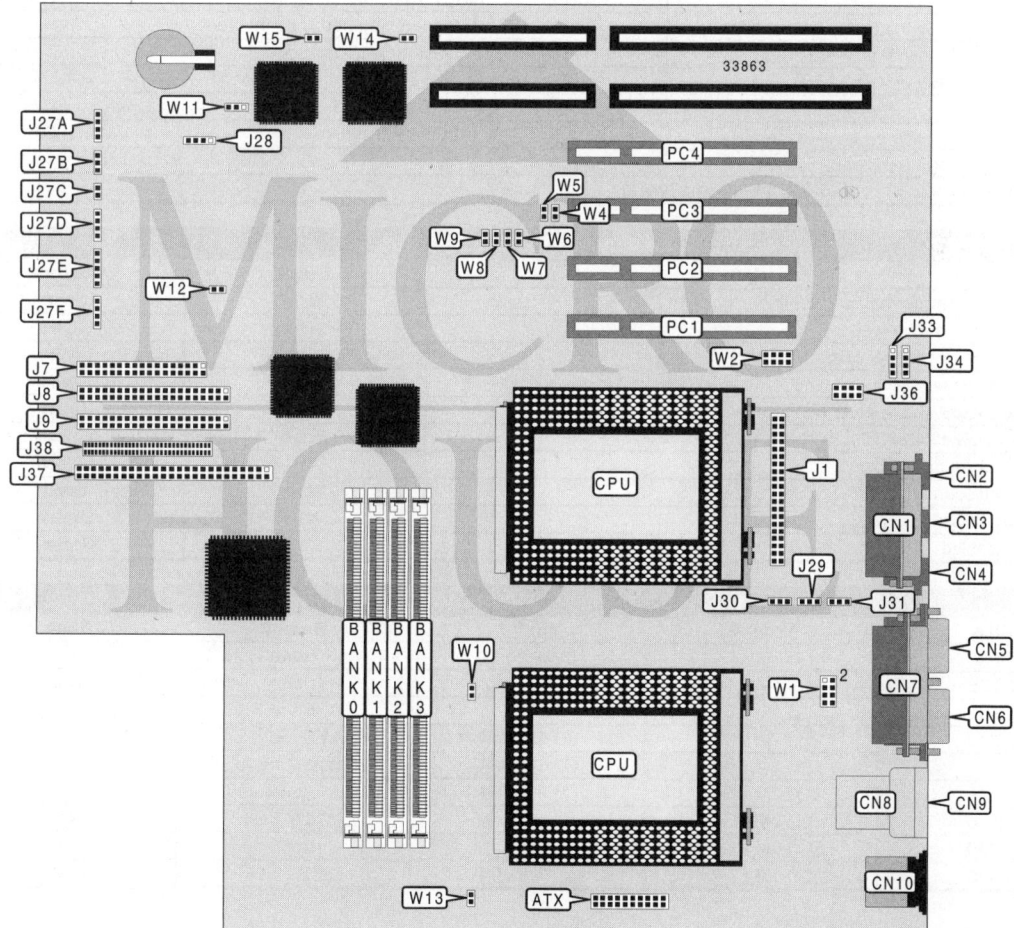

Continued on next page...

MICRONICS COMPUTERS, INC.
W6-LI

. . . continued from previous page

CONNECTIONS

Purpose	Location	Purpose	Location
ATX power connector	ATX	Reset switch	J27B
Game port	CN1	Power LED	J27C
Microphone in connector	CN2	IDE interface LED	J27D
Line in connector	CN3	IR connector	J27E
Line out connector	CN4	Green PC connector	J27F
Serial port 1	CN5	IR connector	J28
Serial port 2	CN6	CPU fan	J29
Parallel port	CN7	CPU fan	J30
USB connector 1	CN8	Chassis fan power	J31
USB connector 2	CN9	CD-ROM connector	J33
PS/2 mouse port	CN10	Modem/telephony connector	J34
VRM connector	J1	Wavetable connector	J36
Floppy drive interface	J7	Fast SCSI interface	J37
IDE interface 1	J8	Ultra Wide SCSI interface	J38
IDE interface 2	J9	32-bit PCI slots	PC1 - PC4
Speaker	J27A		
Note: Do not use both IR connectors at the same time.			

USER CONFIGURABLE SETTINGS

Function	Label	Position
⇨ Host Bus Agent normal operation	W10	Open
Host Bus Agent reserved	W10	Closed
⇨ CMOS memory normal operation	W11	Pins 1 & 2 closed
CMOS memory clear	W11	Pins 2 & 3 closed
⇨ System power supply enabled	W13	Open
System power supply disabled	W13	Closed
⇨ On board sound enabled	W14	Closed
On board sound disabled	W14	Open
⇨ SCSI enabled	W15	Closed
SCSI disabled	W15	Open

DIMM CONFIGURATION

Size	Bank 0	Bank 1	Bank 2	Bank 3
8MB	(1) 1M x 64	None	None	None
16MB	(1) 2M x 64	None	None	None
16MB	(1) 1M x 64	(1) 1M x 64	None	None
24MB	(1) 2M x 64	(1) 1M x 64	None	None
24MB	(1) 1M x 64	(1) 1M x 64	(1) 1M x 64	None
32MB	(1) 2M x 64	(1) 2M x 64	None	None
32MB	(1) 2M x 64	(1) 1M x 64	(1) 1M x 64	None
32MB	(1) 4M x 64	None	None	None
32MB	(1) 1M x 64	(1) 1M x 64	(1) 1M x 64	(1) 1M x 64

Continued on next page. . .

MICRONICS COMPUTERS, INC.
W6-LI

. . . continued from previous page

Size	Bank 0	Bank 1	Bank 2	Bank 3
\multicolumn{5}{c}{DIMM CONFIGURATION (CON'T)}
40MB	(1) 2M x 64	(1) 2M x 64	(1) 1M x 64	None
40MB	(1) 2M x 64	(1) 1M x 64	(1) 1M x 64	(1) 1M x 64
40MB	(1) 4M x 64	(1) 1M x 64	None	None
48MB	(1) 2M x 64	(1) 2M x 64	(1) 2M x 64	None
48MB	(1) 2M x 64	(1) 2M x 64	(1) 1M x 64	(1) 1M x 64
48MB	(1) 4M x 64	(1) 2M x 64	None	None
48MB	(1) 4M x 64	(1) 1M x 64	(1) 1M x 64	None
56MB	(1) 2M x 64	(1) 2M x 64	(1) 2M x 64	(1) 1M x 64
56MB	(1) 4M x 64	(1) 2M x 64	(1) 1M x 64	None
56MB	(1) 4M x 64	(1) 1M x 64	(1) 1M x 64	(1) 1M x 64
64MB	(1) 2M x 64	(1) 2M x 64	(1) 2M x 64	(1) 2M x 64
64MB	(1) 4M x 64	(1) 2M x 64	(1) 2M x 64	None
64MB	(1) 4M x 64	(1) 2M x 64	(1) 1M x 64	(1) 1M x 64
64MB	(1) 4M x 64	(1) 4M x 64	None	None
64MB	(1) 8M x 64	None	None	None
80MB	(1) 4M x 64	(1) 2M x 64	(1) 2M x 64	(1) 2M x 64
80MB	(1) 4M x 64	(1) 4M x 64	(1) 2M x 64	None
80MB	(1) 4M x 64	(1) 4M x 64	(1) 1M x 64	(1) 1M x 64
80MB	(1) 8M x 64	(1) 2M x 64	None	None
80MB	(1) 8M x 64	(1) 1M x 64	(1) 1M x 64	None
96MB	(1) 4M x 64	(1) 4M x 64	(1) 2M x 64	(1) 2M x 64
96MB	(1) 4M x 64	(1) 4M x 64	(1) 4M x 64	None
96MB	(1) 8M x 64	(1) 2M x 64	(1) 2M x 64	None
96MB	(1) 8M x 64	(1) 2M x 64	(1) 1M x 64	(1) 1M x 64
96MB	(1) 8M x 64	(1) 4M x 64	None	None
112MB	(1) 4M x 64	(1) 4M x 64	(1) 4M x 64	(1) 2M x 64
112MB	(1) 8M x 64	(1) 2M x 64	(1) 2M x 64	(1) 2M x 64
112MB	(1) 8M x 64	(1) 4M x 64	(1) 2M x 64	None
112MB	(1) 8M x 64	(1) 4M x 64	(1) 1M x 64	(1) 1M x 64
128MB	(1) 16M x 64	None	None	None
128MB	(1) 4M x 64	(1) 4M x 64	(1) 4M x 64	(1) 4M x 64
128MB	(1) 8M x 64	(1) 4M x 64	(1) 2M x 64	(1) 2M x 64
128MB	(1) 8M x 64	(1) 4M x 64	(1) 4M x 64	None
128MB	(1) 8M x 64	(1) 8M x 64	None	None
160MB	(1) 16M x 64	(1) 2M x 64	(1) 2M x 64	None
160MB	(1) 16M x 64	(1) 2M x 64	(1) 1M x 64	(1) 1M x 64
160MB	(1) 16M x 64	(1) 4M x 64	None	None
160MB	(1) 8M x 64	(1) 4M x 64	(1) 4M x 64	(1) 4M x 64
160MB	(1) 8M x 64	(1) 8M x 64	(1) 2M x 64	(1) 2M x 64
160MB	(1) 8M x 64	(1) 8M x 64	(1) 4M x 64	None
192MB	(1) 16M x 64	(1) 4M x 64	(1) 2M x 64	(1) 2M x 64

Continued on next page. . .

MICRONICS COMPUTERS, INC.

W6-LI

...continued from previous page

DIMM CONFIGURATION (CON'T)				
Size	Bank 0	Bank 1	Bank 2	Bank 3
192MB	(1) 16M x 64	(1) 4M x 64	(1) 4M x 64	None
192MB	(1) 16M x 64	(1) 8M x 64	None	None
192MB	(1) 8M x 64	(1) 8M x 64	(1) 4M x 64	(1) 4M x 64
192MB	(1) 8M x 64	(1) 8M x 64	(1) 8M x 64	None
224MB	(1) 16M x 64	(1) 4M x 64	(1) 4M x 64	(1) 4M x 64
224MB	(1) 16M x 64	(1) 8M x 64	(1) 2M x 64	(1) 2M x 64
224MB	(1) 16M x 64	(1) 8M x 64	(1) 4M x 64	None
224MB	(1) 8M x 64	(1) 8M x 64	(1) 8M x 64	(1) 4M x 64
256MB	(1) 16M x 64	(1) 16M x 64	None	None
256MB	(1) 16M x 64	(1) 8M x 64	(1) 4M x 64	(1) 4M x 64
256MB	(1) 16M x 64	(1) 8M x 64	(1) 8M x 64	None
256MB	(1) 8M x 64	(1) 8M x 64	(1) 8M x 64	(1) 8M x 64
288MB	(1) 16M x 64	(1) 16M x 64	(1) 2M x 64	(1) 2M x 64
288MB	(1) 16M x 64	(1) 16M x 64	(1) 4M x 64	None
288MB	(1) 16M x 64	(1) 8M x 64	(1) 8M x 64	(1) 4M x 64
320MB	(1) 16M x 64	(1) 16M x 64	(1) 4M x 64	(1) 4M x 64
320MB	(1) 16M x 64	(1) 16M x 64	(1) 8M x 64	None
320MB	(1) 16M x 64	(1) 8M x 64	(1) 8M x 64	(1) 8M x 64
384MB	(1) 16M x 64	(1) 16M x 64	(1) 16M x 64	None
384MB	(1) 16M x 64	(1) 16M x 64	(1) 8M x 64	(1) 8M x 64
448MB	(1) 16M x 64	(1) 16M x 64	(1) 16M x 64	(1) 8M x 64
512MB	(1) 16M x 64	(1) 16M x 64	(1) 16M x 64	(1) 16M x 64

Note: Board accepts EDO memory. x 72 DIMMs may also be used but not if x 64 DIMMs are installed.

CACHE CONFIGURATION

Note: 256KB/512KB cache is located on the Pentium Pro CPU.

CPU SPEED SELECTION

CPU speed	Clock speed	Multiplier	W4	W5	W6	W7
150MHz	60MHz	2.5x	Closed	Open	Closed	Closed
166MHz	66MHz	2.5x	Open	Closed	Closed	Closed
180MHz	60MHz	3x	Closed	Open	Closed	Closed
200MHz	66MHz	3x	Open	Closed	Closed	Closed

CPU SPEED SELECTION (CON'T)

CPU speed	Clock speed	Multiplier	W8	W9	W12
150MHz	60MHz	2.5x	Closed	Open	Closed
166MHz	66MHz	2.5x	Closed	Open	Closed
180MHz	60MHz	3x	Open	Closed	Closed
200MHz	66MHz	3x	Open	Closed	Closed

Continued on next page...

MICRONICS COMPUTERS, INC.
W6-LI

...continued from previous page

CPU VOLTAGE SELECTION		
Voltage	**W1**	**W2**
⇨VID enabled	Open	Open
2.9v	Pins 1 & 2, 7 & 8 closed	Pins 1 & 2, 7 & 8 closed
3.1v	Pins 1 & 2, 5 & 6, 7 & 8 closed	Pins 1 & 2, 5 & 6, 7 & 8 closed
3.3v	Pins 1 & 2, 3 & 4, 7 & 8 closed	Pins 1 & 2, 3 & 4, 7 & 8 closed

MICRO-STAR INTERNATIONAL CO., LTD.
MS-5144

Processor	CX M1/AM K5/Pentium
Processor Speed	90/100/120/133/150/166/200MHz
Chip Set	SIS
Video Chip Set	None
Maximum Onboard Memory	384MB (EDO supported)
Maximum Video Memory	None
Cache	256/512KB
BIOS	AMI/Award
Dimensions	250mm x 220mm
I/O Options	32-bit PCI slots (4), floppy drive interface, IDE interfaces (2), parallel port, PS/2 mouse port, serial ports (2), IR connector, USB connector
NPU Options	None

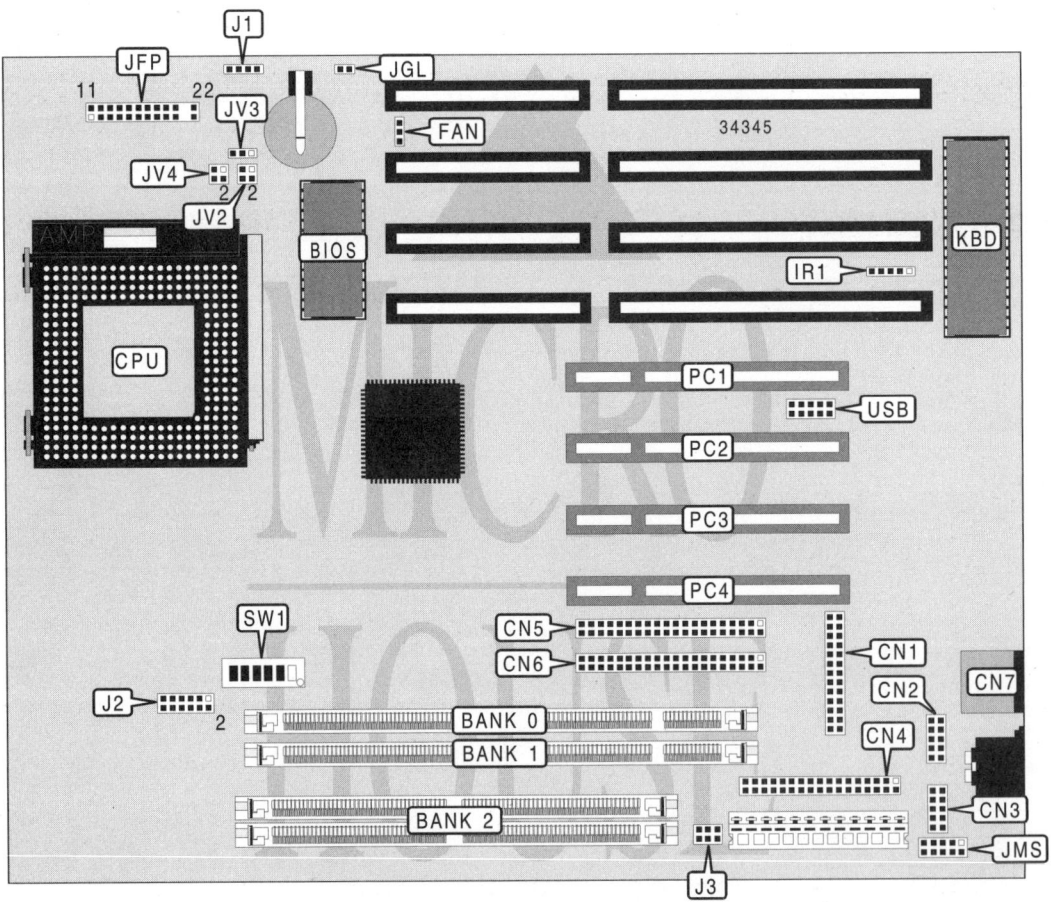

Continued on next page...

MICRO-STAR INTERNATIONAL CO., LTD.
MS-5144

. . . continued from previous page

CONNECTIONS			
Purpose	**Location**	**Purpose**	**Location**
Parallel port	CN1	Power LED & keylock	JFP/pins 1 - 5
Serial port 2	CN2	Speaker	JFP/pins 7 - 10
Serial port 1	CN3	Turbo LED	JFP/pins 12 & 13
Floppy drive interface	CN4	Reset switch	JFP/pins 19 & 20
IDE interface 2	CN5	IDE interface LED	JFP/pins 21 & 22
IDE interface 1	CN6	Green PC LED	JGL
PS/2 mouse port	CN7	PS/2 mouse interface	JMS
Chassis fan power	FAN	32-bit PCI slots	PC1 - PC4
IR connector	IR1	USB connector	USB

USER CONFIGURABLE SETTINGS		
Function	**Label**	**Position**
⇨ Factory configured - do not alter	J1	Unidentified
⇨ Factory configured - do not alter	J3	Unidentified

DIMM/DRAM CONFIGURATION			
Size	**Bank 0**	**Bank 1**	**Bank 2**
8MB	(1) 1M x 64	None	None
12MB	(1) 1M x 64	None	(2) 512K x 36
16MB	(1) 2M x 64	None	None
16MB	(1) 1M x 64	(1) 1M x 64	None
16MB	(1) 1M x 64	None	(2) 1M x 36
20MB	(1) 2M x 64	None	(2) 512K x 36
24MB	(1) 2M x 64	(1) 1M x 64	None
24MB	(1) 1M x 64	None	(2) 2M x 36
32MB	(1) 4M x 64	None	None
32MB	(1) 2M x 64	(1) 2M x 64	None
32MB	(1) 2M x 64	None	(2) 2M x 36
36MB	(1) 4M x 64	None	(2) 512K x 36
40MB	(1) 4M x 64	(1) 1M x 64	None
40MB	(1) 1M x 64	None	(2) 4M x 36
40MB	(1) 4M x 64	None	(2) 1M x 36
48MB	(1) 4M x 64	(1) 2M x 64	None
48MB	(1) 2M x 64	None	(2) 4M x 36
48MB	(1) 4M x 64	None	(2) 2M x 36
64MB	(1) 8M x 64	None	None
64MB	(1) 4M x 64	(1) 4M x 64	None
64MB	(1) 4M x 64	None	(2) 4M x 36
68MB	(1) 8M x 64	None	(2) 512K x 36
72MB	(1) 8M x 64	(1) 1M x 64	None
72MB	(1) 1M x 64	None	(2) 8M x 36
72MB	(1) 8M x 64	None	(2) 1M x 36

Continued on next page. . .

MICRO-STAR INTERNATIONAL CO., LTD.
MS-5144

...continued from previous page

	DIMM/DRAM CONFIGURATION (CON'T)		
Size	**Bank 0**	**Bank 1**	**Bank 2**
80MB	(1) 8M x 64	(1) 2M x 64	None
80MB	(1) 2M x 64	None	(2) 8M x 36
80MB	(1) 8M x 64	None	(2) 2M x 36
96MB	(1) 8M x 64	(1) 4M x 64	None
96MB	(1) 8M x 64	None	(2) 4M x 36
96MB	(1) 4M x 64	None	(2) 8M x 36
128MB	(1) 16M x 64	None	None
128MB	(1) 8M x 64	(1) 8M x 64	None
128MB	(1) 8M x 64	None	(2) 8M x 36
132MB	(1) 16M x 64	None	(2) 512K x 36
136MB	(1) 1M x 64	None	(2) 16M x 36
136MB	(1) 16M x 64	None	(2) 1M x 36
144MB	(1) 2M x 64	None	(2) 16M x 36
144MB	(1) 16M x 64	None	(2) 2M x 36
160MB	(1) 4M x 64	None	(2) 16M x 36
160MB	(1) 16M x 64	None	(2) 4M x 36
192MB	(1) 8M x 64	None	(2) 16M x 36
192MB	(1) 16M x 64	None	(2) 8M x 36
256MB	(1) 32M x 64	None	None
256MB	(1) 16M x 64	(1) 16M x 64	None
256MB	(1) 16M x 64	None	(2) 16M x 36
384MB	(1) 32M x 64	None	(2) 16M x 36

Note: Board accepts EDO memory. Banks 0 & 1 are interchangeable.

DIMM VOLTAGE CONFIGURATION	
Voltage	**J2**
3.3v	Pins 1 & 2, 3 & 4 closed
5v	Pins 9 & 10, 11 & 12 closed

CACHE CONFIGURATION
Note: The location and chip sizes are unidentified.

CPU SPEED SELECTION (CYRIX)								
CPU speed	**Clock speed**	**Multiplier**	**SW1/1**	**SW1/2**	**SW1/3**	**SW1/4**	**SW1/5**	**SW1/6**
150MHz	60MHz	2x	On	Off	On	Off	Off	On
166MHz	66MHz	2x	On	Off	Off	Off	Off	On
200MHz	66MHz	2x	On	Off	Off	On	Off	On

Continued on next page...

MICRO-STAR INTERNATIONAL CO., LTD.
MS-5144

...continued from previous page

CPU SPEED SELECTION (AMD)								
CPU speed	**Clock speed**	**Multiplier**	**SW1/1**	**SW1/2**	**SW1/3**	**SW1/4**	**SW1/5**	**SW1/6**
90MHz	60MHz	1.5x	Off	Off	On	Off	Off	Off
100MHz	66MHz	1.5x	Off	Off	Off	Off	Off	Off
120MHz	60MHz	1.5x	Off	Off	On	Off	Off	Off
133MHz	66MHz	1.5x	Off	Off	Off	Off	Off	Off
166MHz	66MHz	2.5x	On	On	Off	Off	Off	Off

CPU SPEED SELECTION (INTEL)								
CPU speed	**Clock speed**	**Multiplier**	**SW1/1**	**SW1/2**	**SW1/3**	**SW1/4**	**SW1/5**	**SW1/6**
90MHz	60MHz	1.5x	Off	Off	On	Off	Off	Off
100MHz	66MHz	1.5x	Off	Off	Off	Off	Off	Off
120MHz	60MHz	2x	On	Off	On	Off	Off	Off
133MHz	66MHz	2x	On	Off	Off	Off	Off	Off
150MHz	60MHz	2.5x	On	On	On	Off	Off	Off
166MHz	66MHz	2.5x	On	On	Off	Off	Off	Off
200MHz	66MHz	3x	Off	On	Off	Off	Off	Off

CPU VOLTAGE SELECTION (SINGLE)			
Voltage	**JV2**	**JV3**	**JV4**
3.38v	Open	Pins 2 & 3 closed	Open
3.52v	Pins 1 & 2 closed	Pins 2 & 3 closed	Open

CPU VOLTAGE SELECTION (DUAL)				
Voltage	**V core**	**JV2**	**JV3**	**JV4**
3.3v	2.8v	Pins 1 & 2, 3 & 4 closed	Pins 1 & 2 closed	Open

350 Motherboard Settings & Specifications

PACKARD BELL
PB450, LEGEND-CD 486SX

Processor	80486SX/SL80486SX/80486DX/SL80486DX/80486DX2/SL80486DX2/80486DX4/P24T
Processor Speed	25/33/50(internal)/66(internal)/75(internal)/100(internal)MHz
Chip Set	OPTI
Video Chip Set	Cirrus Logic
Maximum Onboard Memory	64MB
Maximum Video Memory	2MB
Cache	128/512KB
BIOS	Unidentified
Dimensions	254mm x 218mm
I/O Options	Floppy drive interface, IDE interfaces (2), parallel port, PS/2 mouse port, serial ports (2), VESA feature connector, VGA port, riser slot
NPU Options	None

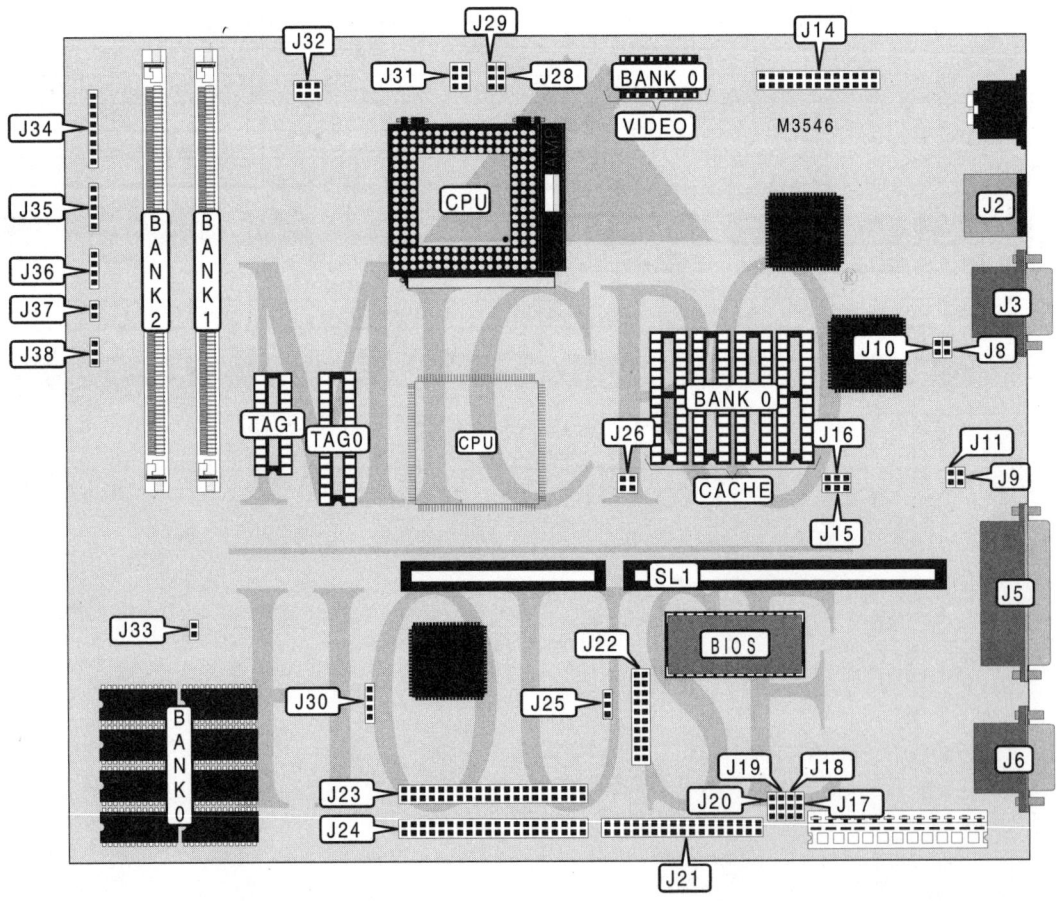

Continued on next page...

PACKARD BELL
PB450, LEGEND-CD 486SX

...continued from previous page

CONNECTIONS			
Purpose	**Location**	**Purpose**	**Location**
PS/2 mouse port	J2	IDE interface 1	J24
VGA port	J3	External battery	J30
Parallel port	J5	Front panel connector	J34
Serial port 1	J6	Power LED & keylock	J35
VESA feature connector	J14	Speaker	J36
Floppy drive interface	J21	Chassis fan power	J38
Serial port 2/modem connector	J22	Riser slot	SL1
IDE interface 2	J23		

USER CONFIGURABLE SETTINGS		
Function	**Label**	**Position**
⇨ Monitor type select color	J8	Closed
Monitor type select monochrome	J8	Open
⇨ Video IRQ9 disabled	J9	Open
Video IRQ9 enabled	J9	Closed
⇨ Factory configured - do not alter	J10	Unidentified
⇨ Factory configured - do not alter	J11	Unidentified
⇨ Flash BIOS normal operation	J17	Pins 2 & 3 closed
Flash BIOS boot block enabled	J17	Pins 1 & 2 closed
⇨ DRAM parity disabled	J18	Pins 2 & 3 closed
DRAM parity enabled	J18	Pins 1 & 2 closed
⇨ On board video enabled	J19	Pins 2 & 3 closed
On board video disabled	J19	Pins 1 & 2 closed
⇨ On board I/O enabled	J20	Pins 2 & 3 closed
On board I/O disabled	J20	Pins 1 & 2 closed
Battery type select internal	J30	Pins 3 & 4 closed
Battery type select external	J30	Closed
⇨ LDEV# bypass enabled	J33	Closed
LDEV# bypass disabled (PCI card present)	J33	Open
Speaker type select internal	J36	Pins 3 & 4 closed
Speaker type select external	J36	Closed
⇨ On board memory enabled	J37	Open
On board memory disabled	J37	Closed

Continued on next page...

PACKARD BELL
PB450, LEGEND-CD 486SX

. . . continued from previous page

DRAM CONFIGURATION			
Size	Bank 0	Bank 1	Bank 2
4MB	4MB	None	None
5MB	4MB	(1) 256K x 36	None
6MB	4MB	(1) 256K x 36	(1) 256K x 36
6MB	4MB	(1) 512K x 36	None
8MB	4MB	(1) 512K x 36	(1) 512K x 36
8MB	4MB	(1) 1M x 36	None
12MB	4MB	(1) 1M x 36	(1) 1M x 36
12MB	4MB	(1) 2M x 36	None
16MB	4MB	(1) 2M x 36	(1) 1M x 36
20MB	4MB	(1) 2M x 36	(1) 2M x 36
20MB	4MB	(1) 4M x 36	None
24MB	4MB	(1) 4M x 36	(1) 1M x 36
24MB	4MB	(1) 1M x 36	(1) 4M x 36
28MB	4MB	(1) 2M x 36	(1) 4M x 36
36MB	4MB	(1) 4M x 36	(1) 4M x 36
36MB	4MB	(1) 8M x 36	None
40MB	4MB	(1) 8M x 36	(1) 1M x 36
52MB	4MB	(1) 8M x 36	(1) 4M x 36
64MB	4MB	(1) 8M x 36	(1) 8M x 36

Note: If 64MB is installed, J37 must be closed.

CACHE CONFIGURATION			
Size	Bank 0	TAG0	TAG1
128KB	(4) 32K x 8	(1) 32K x 8	(1) 64K x 1
512KB	(4) 128K x 8	(1) 32K x 8	(1) 64K x 1

CACHE JUMPER CONFIGURATION	
Size	J26
128KB	Open
512KB	Pins 1 & 2, 3 & 4 closed

VIDEO MEMORY CONFIGURATION	
Size	Bank 0
2MB	(2) 256K x 16

CPU SPEED SELECTION	
Speed	J25
25MHz	Pins 1 & 2 closed
33MHz	Pins 2 & 3 closed
50iMHz	Pins 1 & 2 closed
66iMHz	Pins 2 & 3 closed
75iMHz	Pins 1 & 2 closed
100iMHz	Pins 2 & 3 closed

Continued on next page. . .

PACKARD BELL
PB450, LEGEND-CD 486SX

...continued from previous page

CPU TYPE SELECTION		
Type	**J28**	**J31**
80486SX	Pins 2 & 3 closed	Pins 5 & 6 closed
SL80486SX	Pins 1 & 2 closed	Pins 1 & 2, 3 & 4 closed
80486DX	Pins 2 & 3 closed	Pins 1 & 2, 3 & 4 closed
SL80486DX	Pins 1 & 2 closed	Pins 1 & 2, 3 & 4 closed
80486DX2	Pins 2 & 3 closed	Pins 1 & 2, 3 & 4 closed
SL80486DX2	Pins 1 & 2 closed	Pins 1 & 2, 3 & 4 closed
80486DX4	Pins 2 & 3 closed	Pins 1 & 2, 3 & 4 closed
P24T	Pins 1 & 2 closed	Pins 1 & 2, 3 & 4 closed

CPU MULTIPLIER SELECTION (80486DX4 ONLY)	
Multiplier	**J29**
2x	Pins 2 & 3 closed
3x	Open

CPU VOLTAGE SELECTION	
Voltage	**J32**
3.3v	Pins 1 & 3, 2 & 4 closed
5v	Pins 3 & 5, 4 & 5 closed

DMA CHANNEL SELECTION		
Channel	**J15**	**J16**
▷ 1	Pins 1 & 2 closed	Pins 1 & 2 closed
3	Pins 2 & 3 closed	Pins 2 & 3 closed

PACKARD BELL
PENTIUM 90MHZ

Processor Pentium
Processor Speed 90MHz
Chip Set Unidentified
Max. Onboard DRAM 72MB
Cache 256KB
BIOS Unidentified
Dimensions 330mm x 218mm
I/O Options Floppy drive interface, IDE interfaces (2), parallel port, PS/2 mouse port, serial ports (2), VGA feature connector, VGA port
NPU Options None

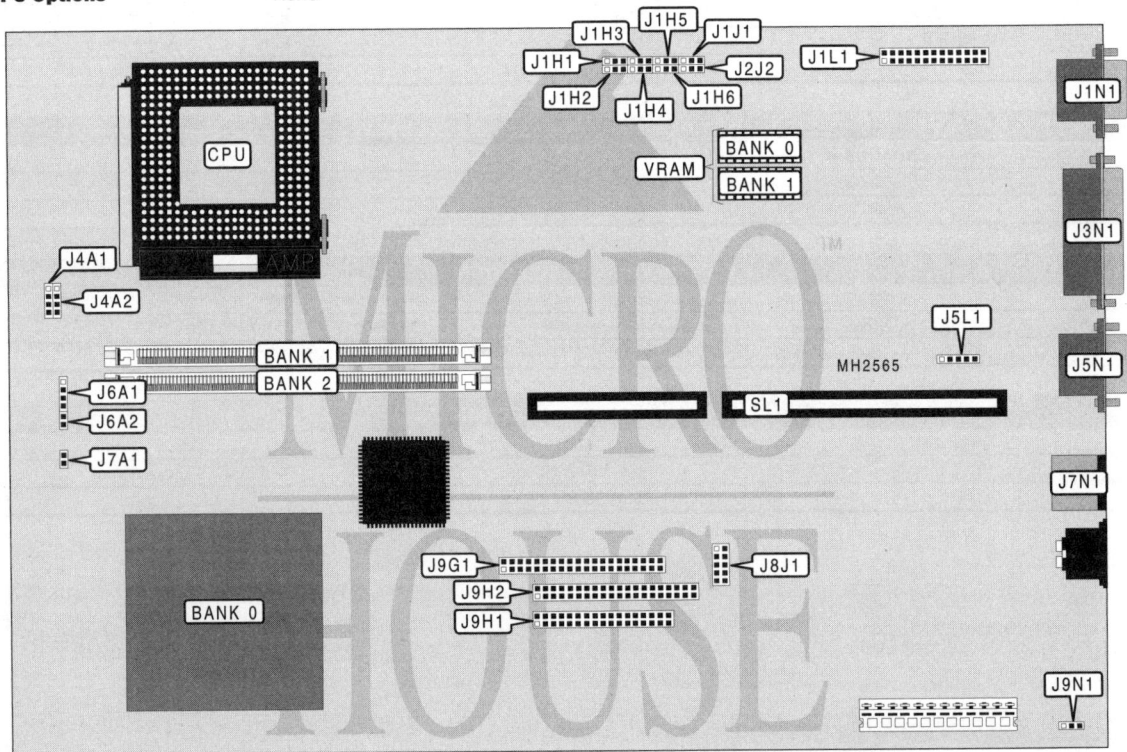

CONNECTIONS			
Purpose	Location	Purpose	Location
VESA feature connector	J1L1	Reset switch	J6A2
VGA port	J1N1	IDE interface LED	J7A1
Parallel port	J3N1	PS/2 mouse port	J7N1
Chassis fan power	J4A1	Serial port 1	J8J1
Chassis fan power	J4A2	Floppy drive interface	J9H1
3v power connector	J5L1	ISA IDE interface	J9H2
Serial port 2	J5N1	PCI IDE interface	J9G1
Speaker	J6A1	Riser Card	SL1

Continued on next page...

PACKARD BELL
PENTIUM 90MHZ

...continued from previous page

USER CONFIGURABLE SETTINGS

Function	Jumper	Position
✧ Recovery mode disabled	J1H1	pins 2 & 3 closed
Recovery mode enabled	J1H1	pins 1 & 2 closed
✧ BIOS setup entry enabled	J1H2	pins 1 & 2 closed
BIOS setup entry disabled	J1H2	pins 2 & 3 closed
✧ Setup entry enabled	J1H3	pins 1 & 2 closed
Setup entry disabled	J1H3	pins 2 & 3 closed
✧ Password disabled	J1H4	pins 2 & 3 closed
Password enabled	J1H4	pins 1 & 2 closed
✧ Monitor type select color	J1H5	pins 2 & 3 closed
Monitor type select monochrome	J1H5	pins 1 & 2 closed
✧ CMOS memory normal operation	J1H6	pins 1 & 2 closed
CMOS memory clear	J1H6	pins 2 & 3 closed
✧ Factory configured - do not alter	J5A2	N/A
✧ Factory configured - do not alter	J6A3	N/A
✧ CPU voltage select 3.3v	J9N1	pins 1 & 2 closed
CPU voltage select 5.0v	J9N1	pins 2 & 3 closed

Note: The location of jumpers J5A2 & J6A3 are unidentified.

DRAM CONFIGURATION

Size	Bank 0	Bank 1	Bank 2
8MB	8MB	NONE	NONE
10MB	8MB	(1) 256K x 36	(1) 256K x 36
12MB	8MB	(1) 512K x 36	(1) 512K x 36
16MB	8MB	(1) 1M x 36	(1) 1M x 36
24MB	8MB	(1) 2M x 36	(1) 2M x 36
40MB	8MB	(1) 4M x 36	(1) 4M x 36
72MB	8MB	(1) 8M x 36	(1) 8M x 36

Note: Bank 0 is factory installed and is not configurable.

CACHE CONFIGURATION

Note: This board has 256KB of cache factory installed. The location is unidentified.

CPU SPEED CONFIGURATION

Speed	J1J1	J1J2
90MHz	pins 2 & 3 closed	pins 2 & 3 closed

VIDEO MEMORY CONFIGURATION

Size	Bank 0	Bank 1
1MB	NONE	NONE
2MB	(1) 256K x 16	(1) 256K x 16

Note: This board has 1MB of VRAM factory installed. The location is unidentified.

SHUTTLE COMPUTER INTERNATIONAL, INC.
HOT-613 (SINGLE)

Processor	Pentium Pro
Processor Speed	180/200MHz
Chip Set	Intel
Video Chip Set	None
Maximum Onboard Memory	512MB (EDO supported)
Maximum Video Memory	None
Cache	256/512KB (located on Pentium Pro CPU)
BIOS	Award
Dimensions	305mm x 240mm
I/O Options	32-bit PCI slots (4), floppy drive interface, green PC connector, IDE interfaces (2), parallel port, PS/2 mouse port, serial ports (2), IR connector, USB connectors (2), ATX power connector
NPU Options	None

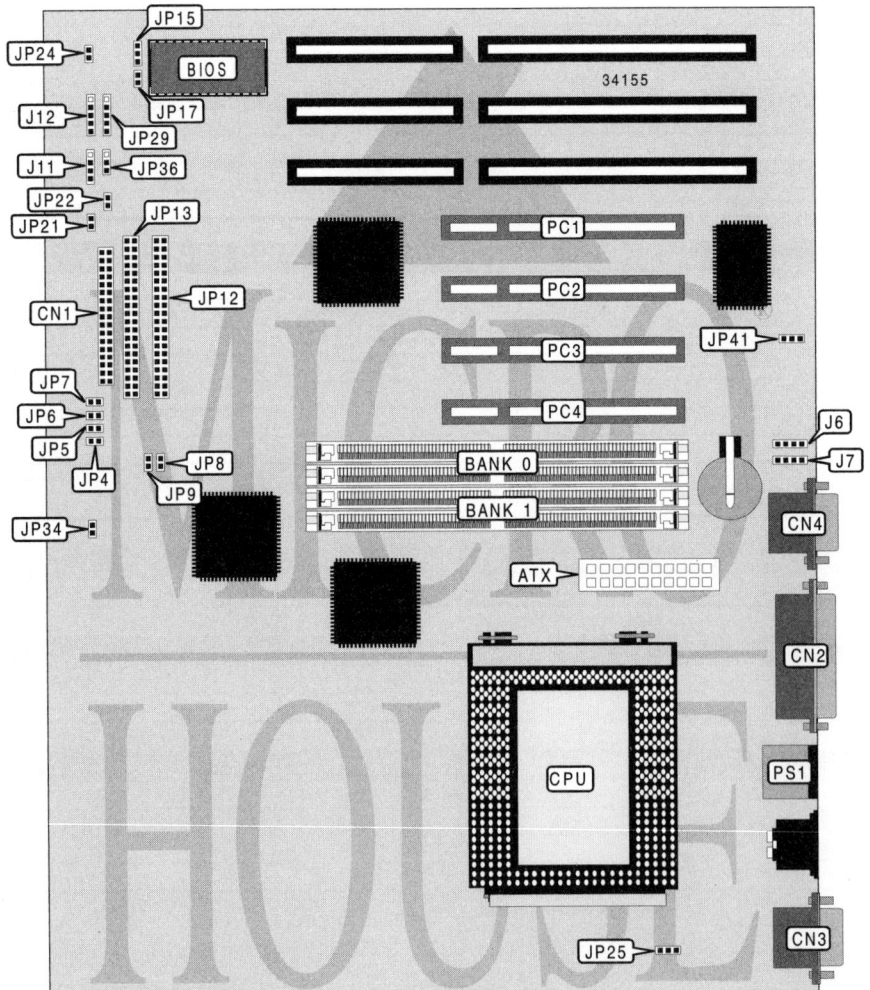

Continued on next page...

SHUTTLE COMPUTER INTERNATIONAL, INC.
HOT-613 (SINGLE)

...continued from previous page

CONNECTIONS			
Purpose	**Location**	**Purpose**	**Location**
ATX power connector	ATX	IDE interface 2	JP13
Floppy drive interface	CN1	IDE interface LED	JP21
Parallel port	CN2	Green PC connector	JP22
Serial port	CN3	Reset switch	JP24
Serial port	CN4	Chassis fan power	JP25
USB connector	J6	IR connector	JP29
USB connector	J7	Remote power on connector	JP34
Speaker	J11	Green PC LED	JP36
Power LED & keylock	J12	32-bit PCI slots	PC1 – PC4
IDE interface 1	JP12	PS/2 mouse port	PS1

USER CONFIGURABLE SETTINGS		
Function	**Label**	**Position**
Flash BIOS voltage select 12v	JP15	Pins 1 & 2 closed
Flash BIOS voltage select 5v	JP15	Pins 2 & 3 closed
⇨ Factory configured - do not alter	JP17	Unidentified
⇨ CMOS memory normal operation	JP41	Pins 2 & 3 closed
CMOS memory clear	JP41	Pins 1 & 2 closed

DRAM CONFIGURATION		
Size	**Bank 0**	**Bank 1**
8MB	(2) 1M x 36	None
16MB	(2) 2M x 36	None
16MB	(2) 1M x 36	(2) 1M x 36
24MB	(2) 2M x 36	(2) 1M x 36
32MB	(2) 4M x 36	None
32MB	(2) 2M x 36	(2) 2M x 36
40MB	(2) 4M x 36	(2) 1M x 36
48MB	(2) 4M x 36	(2) 2M x 36
64MB	(2) 8M x 36	None
64MB	(2) 4M x 36	(2) 4M x 36
80MB	(2) 8M x 36	(2) 2M x 36
96MB	(2) 8M x 36	(2) 4M x 36
128MB	(2) 8M x 36	(2) 8M x 36
128MB	(2) 16M x 36	None
160MB	(2) 16M x 36	(2) 4M x 36
192MB	(2) 16M x 36	(2) 8M x 36
256MB	(2) 16M x 36	(2) 16M x 36
256MB	(2) 32M x 36	None
320MB	(2) 32M x 36	(2) 8M x 36
384MB	(2) 32M x 36	(2) 16M x 36
512MB	(2) 32M x 36	(2) 32M x 36

Note: Board accepts EDO memory. Board also accepts x 32 SIMMs.

Continued on next page...

SHUTTLE COMPUTER INTERNATIONAL, INC.
HOT-613 (SINGLE)

...continued from previous page

CACHE CONFIGURATION
Note: 256KB/512KB cache is located on the Pentium Pro CPU.

CPU SPEED SELECTION

CPU speed	Clock speed	Multiplier	JP4	JP5	JP6	JP7	JP8	JP9
180MHz	60MHz	3x	Closed	Open	Closed	Closed	1 & 2	1 & 2
200MHz	66MHz	3x	Closed	Open	Closed	Closed	2 & 3	2 & 3

Note: Pins designated should be in the closed position.

SIEMENS NIXDORF INFORMATIONSSYSTEME AG
SYSTEM BOARD PCD-5H

Processor	Pentium
Processor Speed	60MHz
Chip Set	Unidentified
Video Chip Set	Unidentified
Maximum Onboard Memory	128MB
Maximum Video Memory	2MB
Cache	256KB
BIOS	AMI
Dimensions	330mm x 218mm
I/O Options	Floppy drive interface, IDE interface, parallel port, PS/2 mouse port, serial ports (2), VESA feature connector, VGA port, riser slot
NPU Options	None

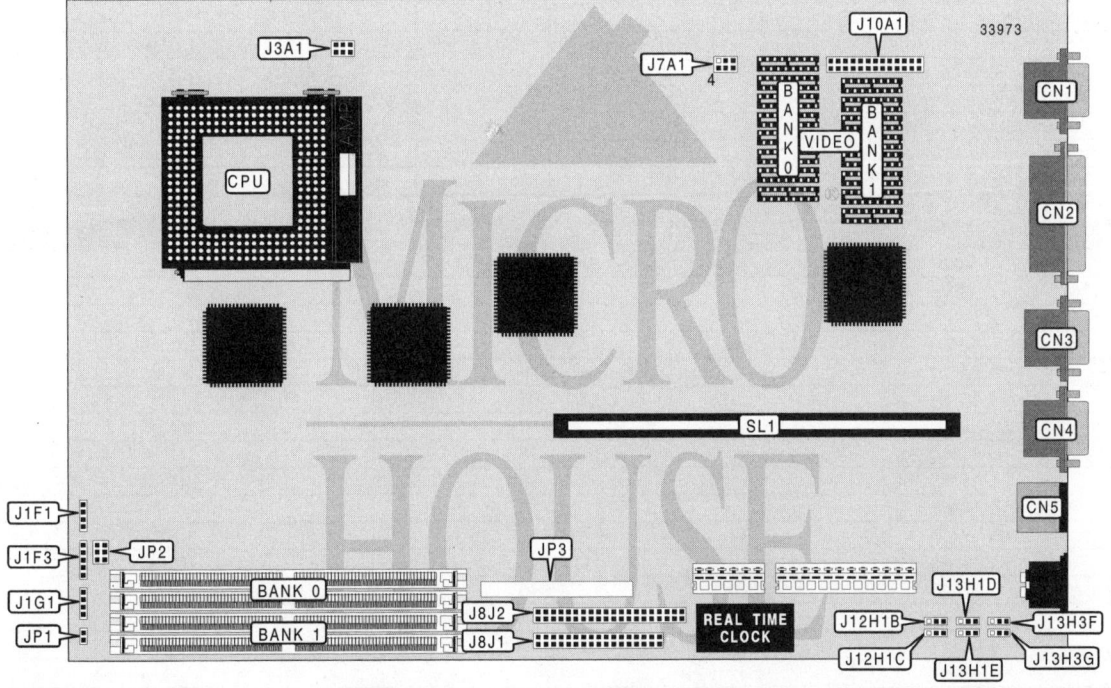

CONNECTIONS			
Purpose	**Location**	**Purpose**	**Location**
VGA port	CN1	IDE interface LED	J1G1
Parallel port	CN2	Chassis fan power	J3A1
Serial port 2	CN3	Floppy drive interface	J8J1
Serial port 1	CN4	IDE interface	J8J2
PS/2 mouse port	CN5	VESA feature connector	J10A1
Speaker	J1F1	Riser slot	SL1
Power LED	J1F3		

Continued on next page...

SIEMENS NIXDORF INFORMATIONSSYSTEME AG
SYSTEM BOARD PCD-5H

. . . continued from previous page

	USER CONFIGURABLE SETTINGS		
	Function	**Label**	**Position**
†	Factory configured - do not alter	JP1	Unidentified
†	Factory configured - do not alter	JP2	Unidentified
†	Factory configured - do not alter	JP3	Unidentified
†	Factory configured - do not alter	J7A1	Pins 5 & 6 closed
†	Flash BIOS normal operation	J12H1B	Pins 2 & 3 closed
	Flash BIOS recovery mode	J12H1B	Pins 1 & 2 closed
†	Flash BIOS write protect enabled	J12H1C	Pins 1 & 2 closed
	Flash BIOS write protect disabled	J12H1C	Pins 2 & 3 closed
†	CMOS memory normal operation	J13H1D	Pins 1 & 2 closed
	CMOS memory clear	J13H1D	Pins 2 & 3 closed
†	Factory configured - do not alter	J13H1E	Unidentified
†	Monitor type select color	J13H3F	Pins 2 & 3 closed
	Monitor type select monochrome	J13H3F	Pins 1 & 2 closed
†	Setup menu access enabled	J13H3G	Pins 1 & 2 closed
	Setup menu access disabled	J13H3G	Pins 2 & 3 closed

DRAM CONFIGURATION		
Size	**Bank 0**	**Bank 1**
8MB	(2) 1M x 36	None
16MB	(2) 2M x 36	None
16MB	(2) 1M x 36	(2) 1M x 36
24MB	(2) 2M x 36	(2) 1M x 36
32MB	(2) 4M x 36	None
32MB	(2) 2M x 36	(2) 2M x 36
40MB	(2) 4M x 36	(2) 1M x 36
48MB	(2) 4M x 36	(2) 2M x 36
64MB	(2) 8M x 36	None
64MB	(2) 4M x 36	(2) 4M x 36
72MB	(2) 8M x 36	(2) 1M x 36
80MB	(2) 8M x 36	(2) 2M x 36
96MB	(2) 8M x 36	(2) 4M x 36
128MB	(2) 8M x 36	(2) 8M x 36

CACHE CONFIGURATION
Note: 256KB cache is factory installed and is not configurable. The location is unidentified.

VIDEO MEMORY CONFIGURATION		
Size	**Bank 0**	**Bank 1**
1MB	1MB	None
2MB	1MB	1MB
Note: The size of the video memory chips is unidentified.		

SILICON STAR INTERNATIONAL, INC.
AN6

Processor	Pentium II/Pentium Pro
Processor Speed	150/166/180/200/233/266MHz
Chip Set	Intel
Video Chip Set	None
Maximum Onboard Memory	1GB (EDO supported)
Maximum Video Memory	None
Cache	256/512KB (located on CPU)
BIOS	Award
Dimensions	305mm x 245mm
I/O Options	32-bit PCI slots (4), floppy drive interface, green PC connector, IDE interfaces (2), parallel port, PS/2 mouse port, serial ports (2), IR connector, USB connectors (2), ATX power connector, CPU Slot 1
NPU Options	None

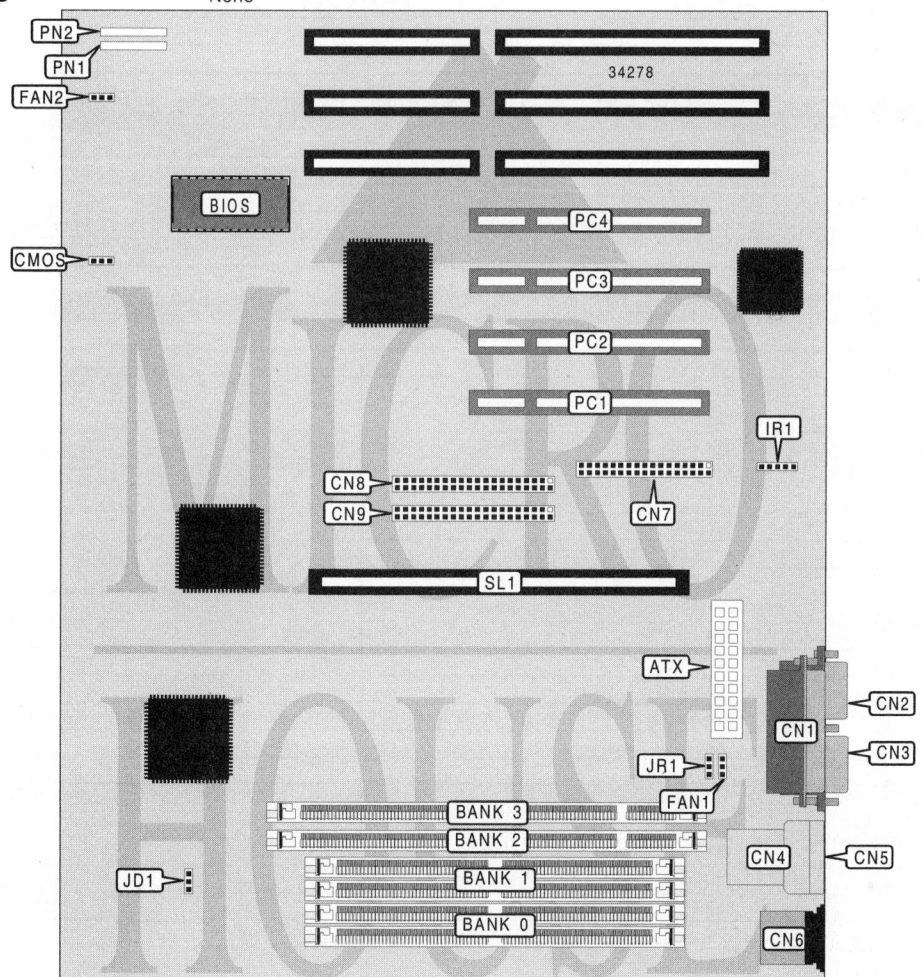

Continued on next page. . .

SILICON STAR INTERNATIONAL, INC.
AN6

...continued from previous page

CONNECTIONS			
Purpose	**Location**	**Purpose**	**Location**
ATX power connector	ATX	Chassis fan power	FAN1
Parallel port	CN1	Chassis fan power	FAN2
Serial port 2	CN2	IR connector	IR1
Serial port 1	CN3	32-bit PCI slots	PC1 – PC4
USB connector	CN4	Power LED & keylock	PN1/pins 1 - 5
USB connector	CN5	IDE interface LED	PN1/pins 7 & 8
PS/2 mouse port	CN6	Green PC connector	PN1/pins 13 & 14
Floppy drive interface	CN7	Reset switch	PN2/pins 1 & 2
IDE interface 2	CN8	Speaker	PN2/pins 4 - 7
IDE interface 1	CN9	CPU Slot 1	SL1

USER CONFIGURABLE SETTINGS		
Function	**Label**	**Position**
⇨ CMOS memory normal operation	CMOS	Pins 1 & 2 closed
CMOS memory clear	CMOS	Pins 2 & 3 closed
⇨ Power on select high active	JR1	Pins 2 & 3 closed
Power on select low active	JR1	Pins 1 & 2 closed

DIMM/DRAM CONFIGURATION				
Size	**Bank 0**	**Bank 1**	**Bank 2**	**Bank 3**
8MB	(2) 1M x 36	None	None	None
8MB	None	None	(1) 1M x 64	None
16MB	(2) 2M x 36	None	None	None
16MB	(2) 1M x 36	(2) 1M x 36	None	None
16MB	(2) 1M x 36	None	None	(1) 1M x 64
16MB	None	None	(1) 2M x 64	None
16MB	None	None	(1) 1M x 64	(1) 1M x 64
24MB	(2) 2M x 36	(2) 1M x 36	None	None
24MB	None	(2) 2M x 36	(1) 1M x 64	None
24MB	None	None	(1) 2M x 64	(1) 1M x 64
32MB	(2) 4M x 36	None	None	None
32MB	(2) 2M x 36	(2) 2M x 36	None	None
32MB	(2) 2M x 36	None	None	(1) 2M x 64
32MB	None	None	(1) 4M x 64	None
32MB	None	None	(1) 2M x 64	(1) 2M x 64
40MB	(2) 4M x 36	(2) 1M x 36	None	None
40MB	(2) 4M x 36	None	None	(1) 1M x 64
40MB	None	None	(1) 1M x 64	(1) 4M x 64
48MB	(2) 4M x 36	(2) 2M x 36	None	None
48MB	(2) 2M x 36	None	None	(1) 4M x 64
48MB	None	None	(1) 2M x 64	(1) 4M x 64
64MB	(2) 8M x 36	None	None	None

Continued on next page...

SILICON STAR INTERNATIONAL, INC.
AN6

...continued from previous page

DIMM/DRAM CONFIGURATION (CON'T)				
Size	**Bank 0**	**Bank 1**	**Bank 2**	**Bank 3**
64MB	(2) 4M x 36	(2) 4M x 36	None	None
64MB	(2) 4M x 36	None	None	(1) 4M x 64
64MB	None	None	(1) 8M x 64	None
64MB	None	None	(1) 4M x 64	(1) 4M x 64
72MB	(2) 8M x 36	None	None	(1) 1M x 64
72MB	(2) 8M x 36	(2) 1M x 36	None	None
72MB	None	None	(1) 1M x 64	(1) 8M x 64
80MB	None	(2) 2M x 36	(1) 8M x 64	None
80MB	(2) 2M x 36	None	None	(1) 8M x 64
80MB	(2) 8M x 36	(2) 2M x 36	None	None
80MB	None	None	(1) 2M x 64	(1) 8M x 64
96MB	(2) 4M x 36	None	None	(1) 8M x 64
96MB	None	(2) 8M x 36	(1) 4M x 64	None
96MB	(2) 8M x 36	(2) 4M x 36	None	None
96MB	None	None	(1) 4M x 64	(1) 8M x 64
128MB	(2) 8M x 36	None	None	(1) 8M x 64
128MB	(2) 8M x 36	None	None	(1) 8M x 64
128MB	(2) 8M x 36	(2) 8M x 36	None	None
128MB	(2) 16M x 36	None	None	None
128MB	None	None	(1) 8M x 64	(1) 8M x 64
136MB	(2) 16M x 36	(2) 1M x 36	None	None
144MB	(2) 16M x 36	(2) 2M x 36	None	None
160MB	(2) 16M x 36	(2) 4M x 36	None	None
192MB	(2) 16M x 36	(2) 8M x 36	None	None
256MB	(2) 32M x 36	None	None	None
256MB	(2) 16M x 36	(2) 16M x 36	None	None
256MB	None	None	(1) 16M x 64	(1) 16M x 64
264MB	(2) 32M x 36	(2) 1M x 36	None	None
272MB	(2) 32M x 36	(2) 2M x 36	None	None
288MB	(2) 32M x 36	(2) 4M x 36	None	None
320MB	(2) 32M x 36	(2) 8M x 36	None	None
384MB	(2) 32M x 36	(2) 16M x 36	None	None
384MB	(2) 16M x 36	(2) 16M x 36	(1) 16M x 64	None
512MB	(2) 32M x 36	(2) 32M x 36	None	None
512MB	(2) 16M x 36	(2) 16M x 36	(1) 16M x 64	(1) 16M x 64
520MB	(2) 32M x 36	(2) 32M x 36	(1) 1M x 64	None
528MB	(2) 32M x 36	(2) 32M x 36	(1) 2M x 64	None
768MB	(2) 32M x 36	(2) 32M x 36	(1) 32M x 64	None
1024MB	(2) 32M x 36	(2) 32M x 36	(1) 32M x 64	(1) 32M x 64

Note: Board accepts EDO memory. Board also accepts x 32 SIMMs.

DIMM VOLTAGE CONFIGURATION	
Voltage	**JD1**
⇨3.3V	Pins 2 & 3 closed
5v	Pins 1 & 2 closed

Continued on next page...

SILICON STAR INTERNATIONAL, INC.
AN6

. . . continued from previous page

CACHE CONFIGURATION
Note: 256KB/512KB cache is located on the CPU.

SOYO COMPUTER CO., LTD.
6 F B

Processor	Pentium Pro
Processor Speed	150/166/180/200MHz
Chip Set	Intel
Video Chip Set	None
Maximum Onboard Memory	512MB (EDO supported)
Maximum Video Memory	None
Cache	256/512KB (located on Pentium Pro CPU)
BIOS	Award
Dimensions	254mm x 218mm
I/O Options	32-bit PCI slots (5), floppy drive interface, green PC connector, IDE interfaces (2), parallel port, PS/2 mouse port, serial ports (2), IR connector, VRM connector, USB connector
NPU Options	None

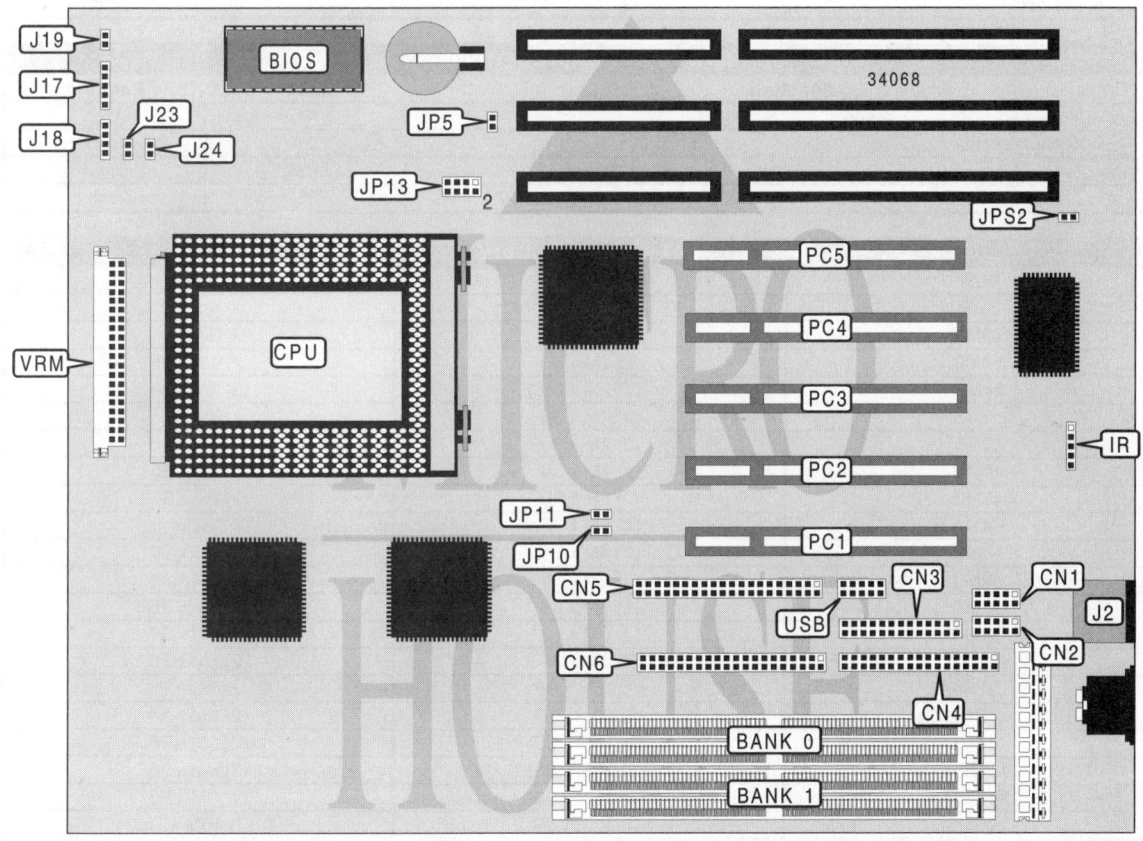

Continued on next page. . .

SOYO COMPUTER CO., LTD.
6 F B

. . . continued from previous page

\<CONNECTIONS\>			
Purpose	**Location**	**Purpose**	**Location**
Serial port 2	CN1	Power LED & keylock	J17
Serial port 1	CN2	Speaker	J18
Parallel port	CN3	Reset switch	J19
Floppy drive interface	CN4	Green PC connector	J23
IDE interface 1	CN5	IDE interface LED	J24
IDE interface 2	CN6	32-bit PCI slots	PC1 – PC5
IR connector	IR	USB connector	USB
PS/2 mouse port	J2	VRM connector	VRM

USER CONFIGURABLE SETTINGS		
Function	**Label**	**Position**
⇨ CMOS memory normal operation	JP5	Open
CMOS memory clear	JP5	Closed
⇨ PS/2 mouse disabled	JPS2	Open
PS/2 mouse enabled	JPS2	Closed

DRAM CONFIGURATION		
Size	**Bank 0**	**Bank 1**
8MB	(2) 1M x 36	None
16MB	(2) 2M x 36	None
16MB	(2) 1M x 36	(2) 1M x 36
24MB	(2) 2M x 36	(2) 1M x 36
32MB	(2) 4M x 36	None
32MB	(2) 2M x 36	(2) 2M x 36
40MB	(2) 4M x 36	(2) 1M x 36
48MB	(2) 4M x 36	(2) 2M x 36
64MB	(2) 8M x 36	None
64MB	(2) 4M x 36	(2) 4M x 36
72MB	(2) 8M x 36	(2) 1M x 36
80MB	(2) 8M x 36	(2) 2M x 36
96MB	(2) 8M x 36	(2) 4M x 36
128MB	(2) 8M x 36	(2) 8M x 36
128MB	(2) 16M x 36	None
136MB	(2) 16M x 36	(2) 1M x 36
144MB	(2) 16M x 36	(2) 2M x 36
160MB	(2) 16M x 36	(2) 4M x 36
192MB	(2) 16M x 36	(2) 8M x 36
256MB	(2) 16M x 36	(2) 16M x 36

Note: Board accepts EDO memory. Board also accepts x 32 SIMMs. Banks are interchangeable.

CACHE CONFIGURATION
Note: 256KB/512KB cache is located on the Pentium Pro CPU.

Continued on next page. . .

SOYO COMPUTER CO., LTD.
6 F B

...continued from previous page

CPU SPEED SELECTION					
CPU speed	**Clock speed**	**Multiplier**	**JP10**	**JP11**	**JP13**
150MHz	60MHz	2.5x	Closed	Open	3 & 4, 5 & 6, 7 & 8
166MHz	66MHz	2.5x	Open	Closed	3 & 4, 5 & 6, 7 & 8
180MHz	60MHz	3x	Closed	Open	1 & 2, 5 & 6, 7 & 8
200MHz	66MHz	3x	Open	Closed	1 & 2, 5 & 6, 7 & 8
Note: Pins designated should be in the closed position.					

SOYO COMPUTER CO., LTD.
SY-5TE2/E5/E0

Processor	CX M1/Pentium
Processor Speed	75/90/100/120/133/150/166/180/200MHz
Chip Set	Intel
Maximum Onboard Memory	128MB
Cache	256/512KB
BIOS	Award
Dimensions	330mm x 218mm
I/O Options	32-bit PCI slots (4), floppy drive interface, green PC connector, IDE interfaces (2), parallel port, PS/2 mouse port, serial ports (2), VRM connector, cache slot
NPU Options	None

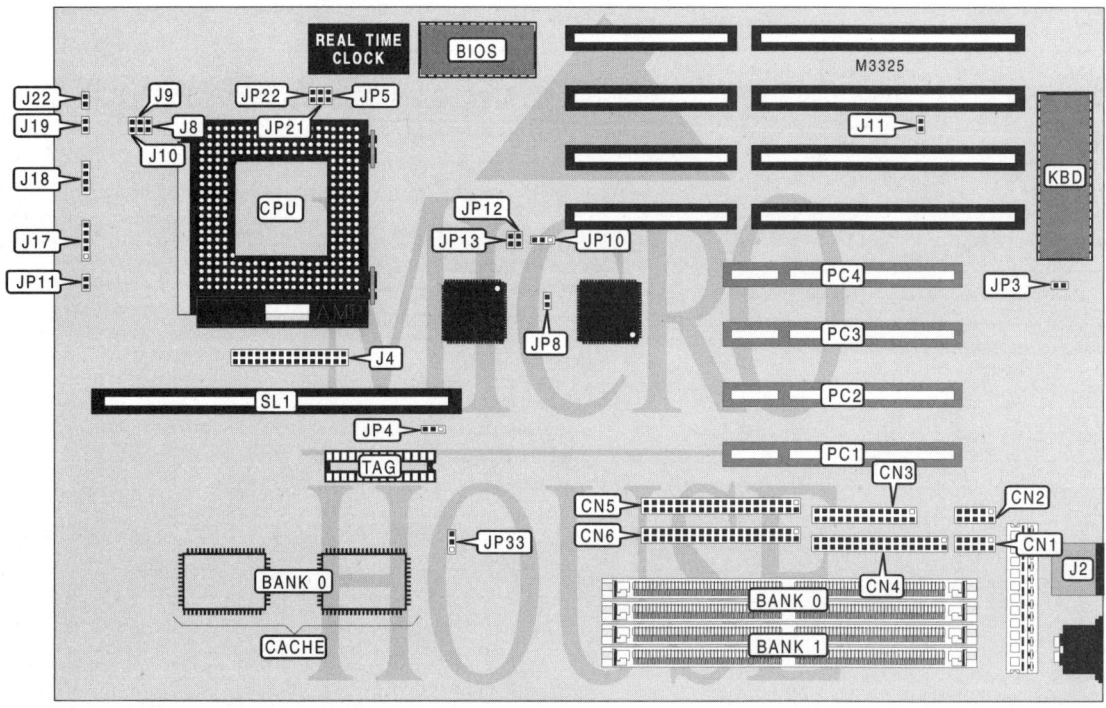

J5, JP9, JP17, JP24
JP2, JP14, JP18, JP25
JP6, JP15, JP19, JP26
JP7, JP16, JP23, JP30
LOCATION UNIDENTIFIED

Continued on next page...

SOYO COMPUTER CO., LTD.
SY-5TE2/E5/E0

. . . continued from previous page

CONNECTIONS			
Function	**Label**	**Function**	**Label**
Serial port 2	CN1	Power LED & keylock	J17
Serial port 1	CN2	Speaker	J18
Parallel port	CN3	Reset switch	J19
Floppy drive interface	CN4	Turbo LED	J22
IDE interface 2	CN5	Green PC connector	JP8
IDE interface 1	CN6	IDE interface LED	JP11
PS/2 mouse port	J2	32-bit PCI slots	PC1 - PC4
VRM connector	J4	Cache slot	SL1

USER CONFIGURABLE SETTINGS			
	Setting	**Label**	**Position**
✧	Factory configured - do not alter	J5	Unidentified
✧	PS/2 mouse disabled	J11	Open
	PS/2 mouse enabled	J11	Closed
✧	Factory configured - do not alter	JP2	Unidentified
✧	Monitor type select color	JP3	Closed
	Monitor type select monochrome	JP3	Open
✧	CMOS memory normal operation	JP5	Open
	CMOS memory clear	JP5	Closed
✧	Factory configured - do not alter	JP6	Pins 1 & 2 closed
✧	Factory configured - do not alter	JP7	Pins 1 & 2 closed
✧	Factory configured - do not alter	JP9	Unidentified
✧	AT bus clock speed select /4 (all CPUs except 75 & 120MHz)	JP10	Pins 2 & 3 closed
	AT bus clock speed select /3 (75 & 120MHz only)	JP10	Pins 1 & 2 closed
✧	Factory configured - do not alter	JP14	Pins 1 & 2 closed
✧	Factory configured - do not alter	JP15	Unidentified
✧	Factory configured - do not alter	JP16	Unidentified
✧	Factory configured - do not alter	JP17	Unidentified
✧	Factory configured - do not alter	JP18	Unidentified
✧	Factory configured - do not alter	JP19	Unidentified
✧	Factory configured - do not alter	JP23	Unidentified
✧	Factory configured - do not alter	JP24	Unidentified
✧	Factory configured - do not alter	JP25	Unidentified
✧	Factory configured - do not alter	JP26	Unidentified
✧	Factory configured - do not alter	JP30	Pins 1 & 2 closed

Continued on next page. . .

SOYO COMPUTER CO., LTD.
SY-5TE2/E5/E0

...continued from previous page

DRAM		
Size	Bank 0	Bank 1
4MB	(2) 512K x 36	None
4MB	(2) 256K x 36	(2) 256K x 36
6MB	(2) 512K x 36	(2) 256K x 36
6MB	(2) 256K x 36	(2) 512K x 36
8MB	(2) 1M x 36	None
8MB	(2) 512K x 36	(2) 512K x 36
10MB	(2) 1M x 36	(2) 256K x 36
10MB	(2) 256K x 36	(2) 1M x 36
12MB	(2) 1M x 36	(2) 512K x 36
12MB	(2) 512K x 36	(2) 1M x 36
16MB	(2) 2M x 36	None
16MB	(2) 1M x 36	(2) 1M x 36
18MB	(2) 2M x 36	(2) 256K x 36
18MB	(2) 256K x 36	(2) 2M x 36
20MB	(2) 2M x 36	(2) 512K x 36
20MB	(2) 512K x 36	(2) 2M x 36
24MB	(2) 2M x 36	(2) 1M x 36
24MB	(2) 1M x 36	(2) 2M x 36
32MB	(2) 4M x 36	None
32MB	(2) 2M x 36	(2) 2M x 36
34MB	(2) 4M x 36	(2) 256K x 36
34MB	(2) 256K x 36	(2) 4M x 36
36MB	(2) 4M x 36	(2) 512K x 36
36MB	(2) 512K x 36	(2) 4M x 36
40MB	(2) 4M x 36	(2) 1M x 36
40MB	(2) 1M x 36	(2) 4M x 36
48MB	(2) 4M x 36	(2) 2M x 36
48MB	(2) 2M x 36	(2) 4M x 36
64MB	(2) 8M x 36	None
64MB	(2) 4M x 36	(2) 4M x 36
66MB	(2) 8M x 36	(2) 256K x 36
66MB	(2) 256K x 36	(2) 8M x 36
68MB	(2) 8M x 36	(2) 512K x 36
68MB	(2) 512K x 36	(2) 8M x 36
72MB	(2) 8M x 36	(2) 1M x 36
72MB	(2) 1M x 36	(2) 8M x 36
80MB	(2) 8M x 36	(2) 2M x 36
80MB	(2) 2M x 36	(2) 8M x 36
96MB	(2) 8M x 36	(2) 4M x 36
96MB	(2) 4M x 36	(2) 8M x 36
128MB	(2) 16M x 36	None
128MB	(2) 8M x 36	(2) 8M x 36

Note: Board accepts EDO memory.

Continued on next page...

SOYO COMPUTER CO., LTD.
SY-5TE2/E5/E0

. . . continued from previous page

CACHE SIZE			
Size	Bank 0	TAG	SL1
256KB	(2) 32K x 32	(1) 16K x 8	Not installed
512KB	(2) 32K x 32	(1) 16K x 8	Installed

CACHE JUMPER		
Size	JP4	JP33
256KB	Pins 1 & 2 closed	Pins 1 & 2 closed
512KB	Pins 2 & 3 closed	Pins 2 & 3 closed

CPU SPEED					
External speed	Internal speed	JP12	JP13	JP21	JP22
75MHz	50MHz	Open	Open	Open	Open
90MHz	60MHz	Closed	Open	Open	Open
100MHz	66MHz	Closed	Closed	Open	Open
100MHz	50MHz	Open	Open	Closed	Open
120MHz	60MHz	Closed	Open	Closed	Open
133MHz	66MHz	Closed	Closed	Closed	Open
150MHz	60MHz	Closed	Open	Closed	Closed
166MHz	66MHz	Closed	Closed	Closed	Closed
180MHz	60MHz	Closed	Open	Open	Closed
200MHz	66MHz	Closed	Closed	Open	Closed

CPU VOLTAGE			
Setting	J8	J9	J10
3.3v	Closed	Open	Open
3.45v - 3.6v	Open	Closed	Open

SUPER MICRO
P6DLS, P6SLS

Processor	Pentium II
Processor Speed	200/233/266/300/333/366/400MHz
Chip Set	Intel
Video Chip Set	None
Maximum Onboard Memory	1GB (EDO supported)
Maximum Video Memory	None
Cache	256/512KB (located on Pentium II CPU)
BIOS	AMI
Dimensions	305mm x 244mm
I/O Options	32-bit PCI slots (4), floppy drive interface, IDE interfaces (2), Ultra Wide SCSI interface, Ultra SCSI interface, parallel port, PS/2 mouse port, serial ports (2), IR connector, USB connectors (2), ATX power connector, AGP slot
NPU Options	None

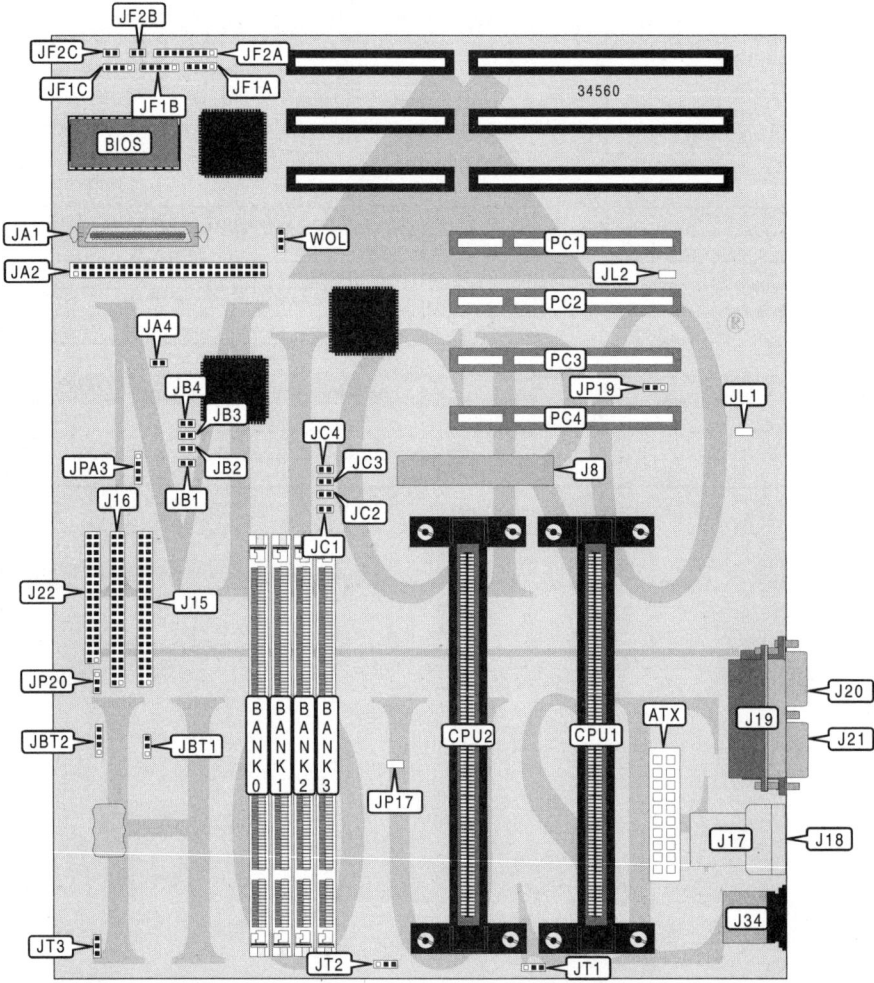

Continued on next page...

SUPER MICRO
P6DLS, P6SLS

. . . continued from previous page

CONNECTIONS			
Purpose	**Location**	**Purpose**	**Location**
ATX power connector	ATX	IDE interface LED	JF1A
AGP slot	J8	Power LED & keylock	JF1B
IDE interface 1	J15	Speaker	JF1C
IDE interface 2	J16	IR connector	JF2A
USB connector	J17	Soft off power supply	JF2B
USB connector	J18	Reset switch	JF2C
Parallel port	J19	Chassis intrusion connector	JL1
Serial port 1	J20	SCSI interface LED	JPA3
Serial port 2	J21	CPU fan	JT1
Floppy drive interface	J22	CPU fan	JT2
PS/2 mouse port	J34	Thermal control fan	JT3
Ultra Wide SCSI interface	JA1	32-bit PCI slots	PC1 – PC4
Ultra SCSI interface	JA2	Wake on LAN connector	WOL
External battery	JBT2		

USER CONFIGURABLE SETTINGS			
	Function	**Label**	**Position**
◇	Factory configured - do not alter	JA4	Unidentified
◇	CMOS memory normal operation	JBT1	Pins 1 & 2 closed
	CMOS memory clear	JBT1	Pins 2 & 3 closed
◇	Factory configured - do not alter	JC4	Open
◇	Factory configured - do not alter	JL2	Open
◇	Factory configured - do not alter	JP17	Pins 2 & 3 closed
◇	SMI select APIC SMI	JP19	Pins 1 & 2 closed
	SMI select PIIX4 SMI	JP19	Pins 2 & 3 closed
◇	Power on/off select save PD state	JP20	Pins 2 & 3 closed
	Power on/off select PIIX4	JP20	Pins 1 & 2 closed

DIMM CONFIGURATION				
Size	**Bank 0**	**Bank 1**	**Bank 2**	**Bank 3**
8MB	(1) 1M x 64	None	None	None
16MB	(1) 2M x 64	None	None	None
16MB	(1) 1M x 64	(1) 1M x 64	None	None
24MB	(1) 2M x 64	(1) 1M x 64	None	None
24MB	(1) 1M x 64	(1) 1M x 64	(1) 1M x 64	None
32MB	(1) 4M x 64	None	None	None
32MB	(1) 2M x 64	(1) 2M x 64	None	None
32MB	(1) 1M x 64	(1) 1M x 64	(1) 1M x 64	(1) 1M x 64
40MB	(1) 4M x 64	(1) 1M x 64	None	None
48MB	(1) 4M x 64	(1) 2M x 64	None	None

Continued on next page. . .

SUPER MICRO
P6DLS, P6SLS

...continued from previous page

\multicolumn{5}{c}{DIMM CONFIGURATION (CON'T)}

Size	Bank 0	Bank 1	Bank 2	Bank 3
48MB	(1) 2M x 64	(1) 2M x 64	(1) 2M x 64	None
64MB	(1) 8M x 64	None	None	None
64MB	(1) 4M x 64	(1) 4M x 64	None	None
64MB	(1) 2M x 64	(1) 2M x 64	(1) 2M x 64	(1) 2M x 64
72MB	(1) 8M x 64	(1) 1M x 64	None	None
80MB	(1) 8M x 64	(1) 2M x 64	None	None
96MB	(1) 8M x 64	(1) 4M x 64	None	None
96MB	(1) 4M x 64	(1) 4M x 64	(1) 4M x 64	None
128MB	(1) 8M x 64	(1) 8M x 64	None	None
128MB	(1) 4M x 64	(1) 4M x 64	(1) 4M x 64	(1) 4M x 64
128MB	(1) 16M x 64	None	None	None
256MB	(1) 8M x 64	(1) 8M x 64	(1) 8M x 64	(1) 8M x 64
256MB	(1) 16M x 64	(1) 16M x 64	None	None
384MB	(1) 16M x 64	(1) 16M x 64	(1) 16M x 64	None
1024MB	(1) 16M x 64	(1) 16M x 64	(1) 16M x 64	(1) 16M x 64

Note: Board accepts EDO memory.

CACHE CONFIGURATION

Note: 256KB/512KB cache is located on the Pentium II CPU.

CPU SPEED SELECTION

Speed	JB1	JB2	JB3	JB4	JC1	JC2	JC3
200MHz	Closed	Open	Closed	Closed	Open	Open	Open
233MHz	Open	Open	Closed	Closed	Open	Open	Open
266MHz	Closed	Closed	Open	Closed	Open	Open	Open
300MHz	Open	Closed	Open	Closed	Open	Open	Open
333MHz	Closed	Open	Open	Closed	Open	Open	Open
366MHz	Open	Open	Open	Closed	Open	Open	Open
400MHz	Closed	Closed	Closed	Open	Open	Open	Open

MISCELLANEOUS TECHNICAL NOTE

The CPU fan will automatically turn on when the CPU temperature exceeds the user defined temperature.

TYAN COMPUTER CORPORATION
S1662D (REV. 1.2)

Processor	Pentium Pro
Processor Speed	150/166/180/200MHz
Chip Set	Intel
Video Chip Set	None
Maximum Onboard Memory	1GB (EDO supported)
Maximum Video Memory	None
Cache	256/512KB (located on Pentium Pro CPU)
BIOS	AMI/Award
Dimensions	330mm x 218mm
I/O Options	32-bit PCI slots (5), floppy drive interface, IDE interfaces (2), parallel port, PS/2 mouse interface, serial ports (2), IR connectors (2), VRM connectors (2), USB connectors (2)
NPU Options	None

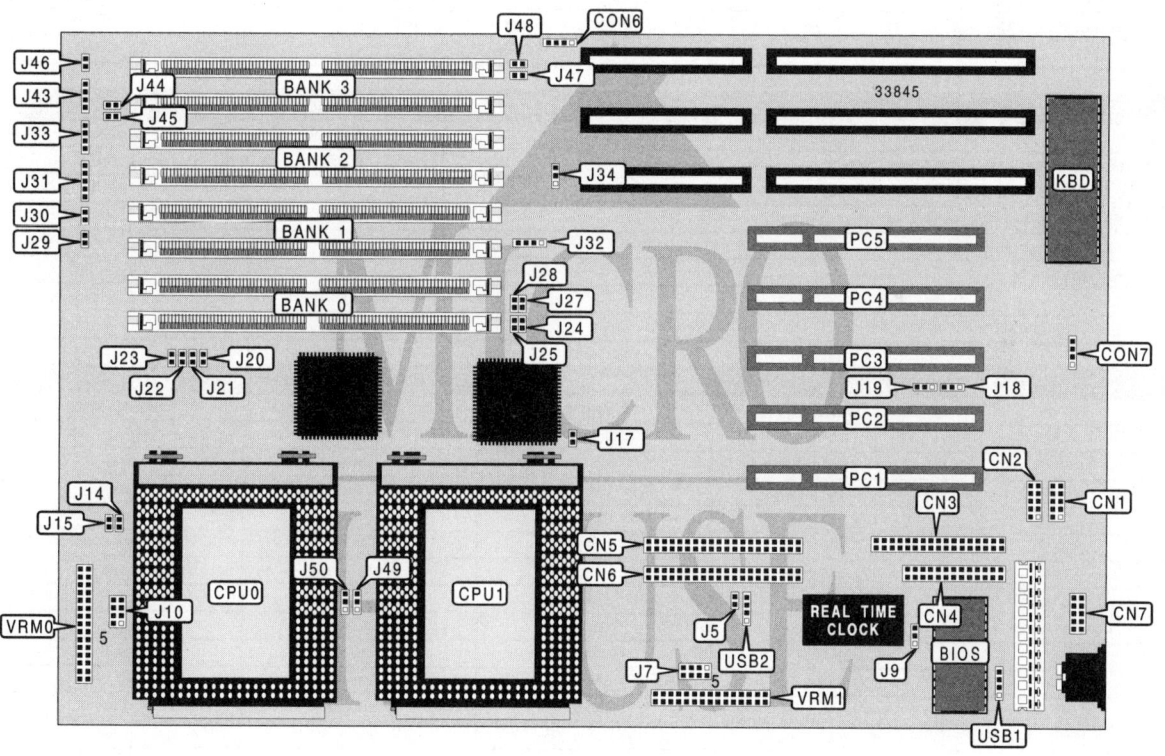

Continued on next page...

TYAN COMPUTER CORPORATION
S1662D (REV. 1.2)

...continued from previous page

CONNECTIONS

Purpose	Location	Purpose	Location
Serial port 2	CN1	Turbo switch	J30
Serial port 1	CN2	Power LED & keylock	J31
Floppy drive interface	CN3	Speaker	J33
Parallel port	CN4	IDE interface LED	J43
IDE interface 2	CN5	Reset switch	J46
IDE interface 1	CN6	32-bit PCI slots	PC1 - PC5
PS/2 mouse interface	CN7	USB connector	UBS1
IR connector	CON6	USB connector	USB2
IR connector	CON7	VRM connector	VRM0
Turbo LED	J29	VRM connector	VRM1

USER CONFIGURABLE SETTINGS

Function	Label	Position
✧ CMOS memory normal operation	J5	Open
CMOS memory clear	J5	Closed
✧ Flash BIOS voltage select 5v	J9	Pins 1 & 2 closed
Flash BIOS voltage select 12v	J9	Pins 2 & 3 closed
Factory configured - do not alter	J17	Unidentified
SMC I/O chip type select 665IR	J34	Pins 1 & 2 closed
SMC I/O chip type select 669IR	J34	Pins 2 & 3 closed

DRAM CONFIGURATION

Size	Bank 0	Bank 1	Bank 2	Bank 3
8MB	(2) 1M x 36	None	None	None
16MB	(2) 2M x 36	None	None	None
16MB	(2) 1M x 36	(2) 1M x 36	None	None
32MB	(2) 2M x 36	(2) 2M x 36	None	None
32MB	(2) 1M x 36	(2) 1M x 36	(2) 1M x 36	(2) 1M x 36
32MB	(2) 4M x 36	None	None	None
64MB	(2) 4M x 36	(2) 4M x 36	None	None
64MB	(2) 8M x 36	None	None	None
128MB	(2) 16M x 36	None	None	None
128MB	(2) 4M x 36	(2) 4M x 36	(2) 4M x 36	(2) 4M x 36
128MB	(2) 8M x 36	(2) 8M x 36	None	None
192MB	(2) 8M x 36	(2) 8M x 36	(2) 8M x 36	None
256MB	(2) 8M x 36	(2) 8M x 36	(2) 8M x 36	(2) 8M x 36
256MB	(2) 16M x 36	(2) 16M x 36	None	None
256MB	(2) 32M x 36	None	None	None
384MB	(2) 16M x 36	(2) 16M x 36	(2) 16M x 36	None
512MB	(2) 16M x 36	(2) 16M x 36	(2) 16M x 36	(2) 16M x 36

Continued on next page...

TYAN COMPUTER CORPORATION
S1662D (REV. 1.2)

...continued from previous page

		DRAM CONFIGURATION (CON'T)			
Size	Bank 0	Bank 1		Bank 2	Bank 3
512MB	(2) 32M x 36	(2) 32M x 36		None	None
640MB	(2) 32M x 36	(2) 16M x 36		(2) 16M x 36	(2) 16M x 36
768MB	(2) 32M x 36	(2) 32M x 36		(2) 32M x 36	None
768MB	(2) 32M x 36	(2) 32M x 36		(2) 16M x 36	(2) 16M x 36
832MB	(2) 32M x 36	(2) 32M x 36		(2) 32M x 36	(2) 8M x 36
896MB	(2) 32M x 36	(2) 32M x 36		(2) 32M x 36	(2) 16M x 36
1024MB	(2) 32M x 36	(2) 32M x 36		(2) 32M x 36	(2) 32M x 36
Note: Board accepts EDO memory. Board also accepts x 32 SIMMs.					

			DRAM VOLTAGE CONFIGURATION					
Voltage	J20	J21	J22	J23	J44	J45	J47	J48
3.3v	Closed	Closed	Closed	Closed	Open	Open	Open	Open
5v	Open	Open	Open	Open	Closed	Closed	Closed	Closed

CACHE CONFIGURATION
Note: 256KB/512KB cache is located on the Pentium Pro CPU.

			CPU SPEED SELECTION				
Speed	J14	J15	J24	J25	J27	J28	J32
150MHz	Open	Closed	Closed	Closed	Open	Closed	3 & 4
166MHz	Closed	Open	Closed	Closed	Open	Closed	1 & 2
180MHz	Open	Closed	Open	Closed	Closed	Closed	3 & 4
200MHz	Closed	Open	Open	Closed	Closed	Closed	1 & 2
Note: Pins designated should be in the closed position.							

	CPU TYPE SELECTION	
Type	J49	J50
CPU0 used as primary/dual/single CPU	Pins 1 & 2 closed	Pins 2 & 3 closed
CPU1 used as a single CPU system	Pins 2 & 3 closed	Pins 1 & 2 closed

Continued on next page...

TYAN COMPUTER CORPORATION
S1662D (REV. 1.2)

...continued from previous page

Voltage	J7	J10
CPU VOLTAGE SELECTION		
⇨ Auto select	Open	Open
2.1v	1 & 5	1 & 5
2.2v	2 & 6	2 & 6
2.3v	1 & 5, 2 & 6	1 & 5, 2 & 6
2.4v	3 & 7	3 & 7
2.5v	1 & 5, 3 & 7	1 & 5, 3 & 7
2.6v	2 & 6, 3 & 7	2 & 6, 3 & 7
2.7v	1 & 5, 2 & 6, 3 & 7	1 & 5, 2 & 6, 3 & 7
2.8v	4 & 8	4 & 8
2.9v	1 & 5, 4 & 8	1 & 5, 4 & 8
3.0v	2 & 6, 4 & 8	2 & 6, 4 & 8
3.1v	1 & 5, 2 & 6, 4 & 8	1 & 5, 2 & 6, 4 & 8
3.2v	3 & 7, 4 & 8	3 & 7, 4 & 8
3.3v	1 & 5, 3 & 7, 4 & 8	1 & 5, 3 & 7, 4 & 8
3.4v	2 & 6, 3 & 7, 4 & 8	2 & 6, 3 & 7, 4 & 8
3.5v	1 & 5, 2 & 6, 3 & 7, 4 & 8	1 & 5, 2 & 6, 3 & 7, 4 & 8

Note: Pins designated should be in the closed position.

Setting	J18	J19
SERIAL PORT SELECTION		
⇨ Used and COM 1 or 2	Pins 1 & 2 closed	Pins 1 & 2 closed
Used as IR connector	Pins 2 & 3 closed	Pins 2 & 3 closed

TYAN COMPUTER CORPORATION
S 1 6 7 2

Processor	Pentium Pro
Processor Speed	150/166/180/200MHz
Chip Set	Intel
Video Chip Set	None
Maximum Onboard Memory	768MB (EDO supported)
Maximum Video Memory	None
Cache	256/512KB (located on Pentium Pro CPU)
BIOS	AMI/Award
Dimensions	330mm x 218mm
I/O Options	32-bit PCI slots (4), floppy drive interface, IDE interfaces (2), parallel port, PS/2 mouse port, serial ports (2), IR connector, USB connectors (2), ATX power connector, soft on power supply
NPU Options	None

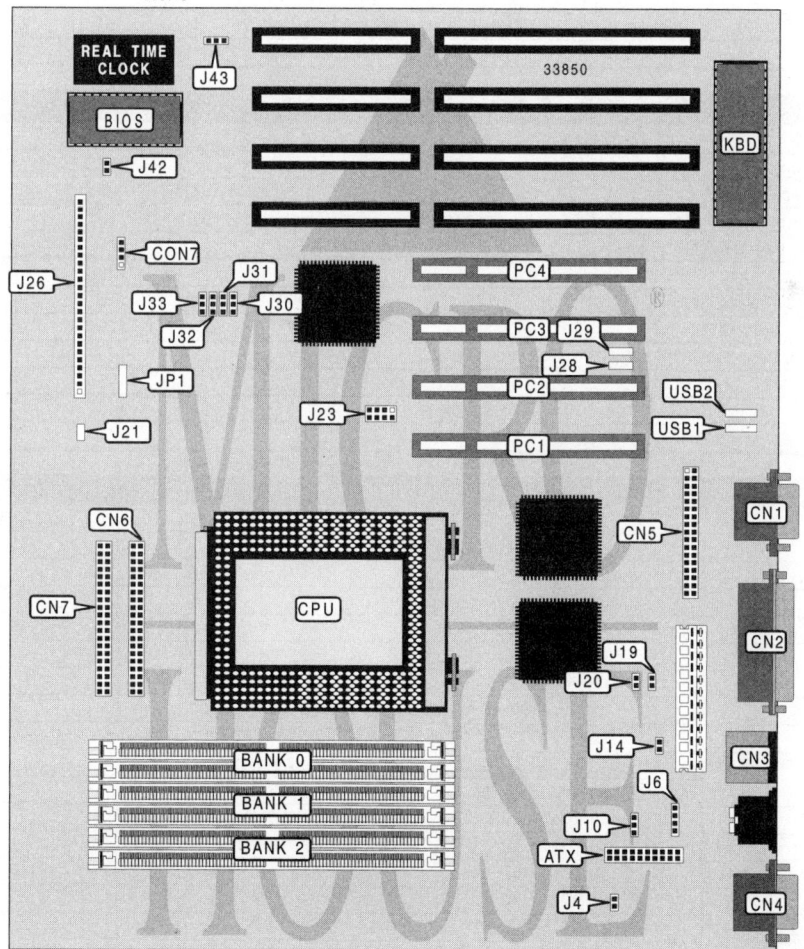

Continued on next page...

TYAN COMPUTER CORPORATION
S1672

...continued from previous page

CONNECTIONS			
Purpose	**Location**	**Purpose**	**Location**
ATX power connector	ATX	Soft on power supply	J26 pins 1 & 2
Serial port 1	CN1	IR connector	J26 pins 6 - 11
Parallel port	CN2	IDE interface LED	J26 pins 15 & 16
PS/2 mouse port	CN3	Power LED	J26 pins 18 & 20
Serial port 2	CN4	Reset switch	J26 pins 22 & 23
Floppy drive interface	CN5	Speaker	J26 pins 24 - 27
IDE interface 1	CN6	Keylock	JP1
IDE interface 2	CN7	32-bit PCI slots	PC1 - PC4
IR connector	CON7	USB connector	USB1
Chassis fan power	J14	USB connector	USB2

USER CONFIGURABLE SETTINGS		
Function	**Label**	**Position**
◇ Power supply select ATX	J4	Open
Power supply select AT	J4	Closed
SMC I/O chip type select 665IR	J10	Pins 1 & 2 closed
SMC I/O chip type select 669IR	J10	Pins 2 & 3 closed
◇ Factory configured - do not alter	J21	Unidentified
◇ Factory configured - do not alter	J28	Unidentified
◇ Factory configured - do not alter	J29	Unidentified
◇ CMOS memory normal operation	J42	Open
CMOS memory clear	J42	Closed
◇ Flash BIOS voltage select 5v	J43	Pins 1 & 2 closed
Flash BIOS voltage select 12v	J43	Pins 2 & 3 closed

DRAM CONFIGURATION			
Size	**Bank 0**	**Bank 1**	**Bank 2**
8MB	(2) 1M x 32	None	None
16MB	(2) 2M x 32	None	None
16MB	(2) 1M x 32	(2) 1M x 32	None
32MB	(2) 4M x 32	None	None
32MB	(2) 2M x 32	(2) 2M x 32	None
64MB	(2) 8M x 32	None	None
64MB	(2) 4M x 32	(2) 4M x 32	None
128MB	(2) 8M x 32	(2) 8M x 32	None
128MB	(2) 16M x 32	None	None
192MB	(2) 8M x 32	(2) 8M x 32	(2) 8M x 32
256MB	(2) 16M x 32	(2) 16M x 32	None
256MB	(2) 32M x 32	None	None
384MB	(2) 16M x 32	(2) 16M x 32	(2) 16M x 32
512MB	(2) 32M x 32	(2) 32M x 32	None
768MB	(2) 32M x 32	(2) 32M x 32	(2) 32M x 32

Note: Board accepts EDO memory.

Continued on next page...

TYAN COMPUTER CORPORATION
S 1 6 7 2

. . . continued from previous page

CACHE CONFIGURATION
Note: 256KB/512KB cache is located on the Pentium Pro CPU.

CPU SPEED SELECTION							
Speed	J6	J19	J20	J30	J31	J32	J33
150MHz	3 & 4	Closed	Open	Closed	Closed	Closed	Open
166MHz	1 & 2	Open	Closed	Closed	Closed	Closed	Open
180MHz	3 & 4	Closed	Open	Closed	Closed	Open	Closed
200MHz	1 & 2	Open	Closed	Closed	Closed	Open	Closed

CPU VOLTAGE SELECTION	
Voltage	J23
⇨ Auto select	Open
2.1v	1 & 5
2.2v	2 & 6
2.3v	1 & 5, 2 & 6
2.4v	3 & 7
2.5v	1 & 5, 3 & 7
2.6v	2 & 6, 3 & 7
2.7v	1 & 5, 2 & 6, 3 & 7
2.8v	4 & 8
2.9v	1 & 5, 4 & 8
3.0v	2 & 6, 4 & 8
3.1v	1 & 5, 2 & 6, 4 & 8
3.2v	3 & 7, 4 & 8
3.3v	1 & 5, 3 & 7, 4 & 8
3.4v	2 & 6, 3 & 7, 4 & 8
3.5v	1 & 5, 2 & 6, 3 & 7, 4 & 8
Note: Pins designated should be in the closed position.	

382 Motherboard Settings & Specifications

ZEOS INTERNATIONAL, LTD.
PANTERA 486

Processor	80486SX/80486DX/80486DX2/80486DX4/Pentium Overdrive
Processor Speed	25/33/50(internal)/66(internal)/75(internal)/100(internal)MHz
Chip Set	SMC
Max. Onboard DRAM	128MB
Cache	128/256KB (on external cache card)
BIOS	AMI
Dimensions	330mm x 218mm
I/O Options	32-bit PCI bus slots (3), floppy drive interface, IDE interface (2), parallel port, serial ports (2), SCSI interface, external cache card
NPU Options	None

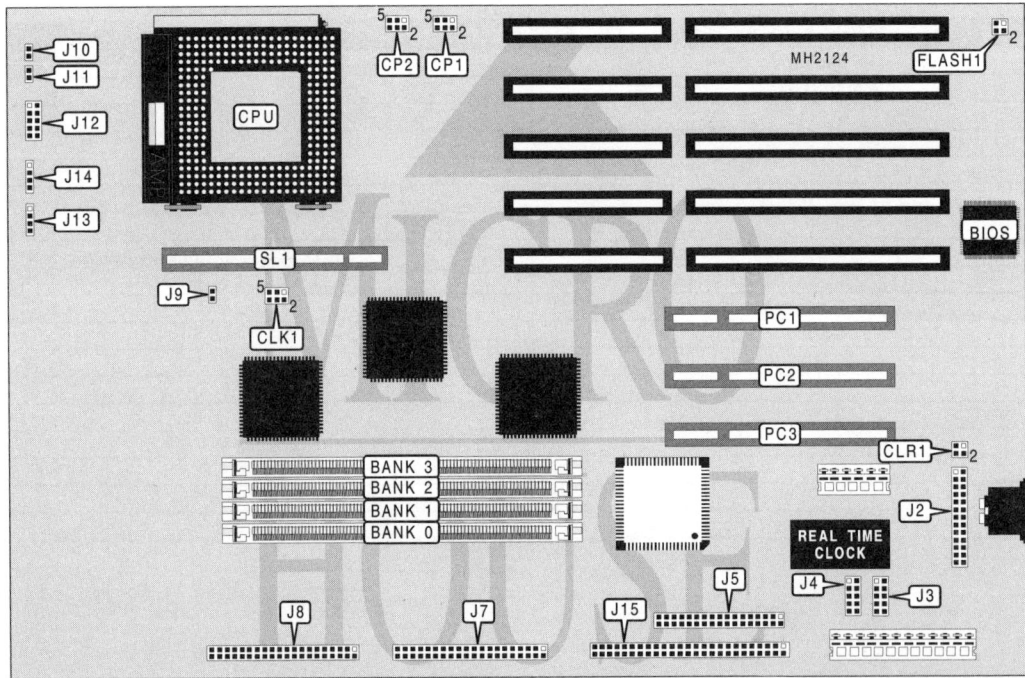

CONNECTIONS			
Purpose	**Location**	**Purpose**	**Location**
Parallel port	J2	Low power LED	J11
Serial port 2	J3	Power LED & keylock	J12
Serial port 1	J4	IDE interface LED	J13
Floppy drive interface	J5	Speaker	J14
IDE interface (secondary)	J7	SCSI connector	J15
IDE interface (primary)	J8	32-bit PCI bus slots	PC1 - PC3
Chassis fan power	J9	External cache card	SL1
Reset switch	J10		

Continued on next page...

ZEOS INTERNATIONAL, LTD.
PANTERA 486

...continued from previous page

USER CONFIGURABLE SETTINGS		
Function	**Jumper**	**Position**
⇨ CMOS memory normal operation	CLR1	pins 1 & 2 closed
CMOS memory clear	CLR1	pins 3 & 4 closed
⇨ Flash BIOS write protect enabled	FLASH1	pins 1 & 2 closed
Flash BIOS write protect disabled	FLASH1	pins 3 & 4 closed

DRAM CONFIGURATION				
Size	**Bank 0**	**Bank 1**	**Bank 2**	**Bank 3**
2MB	(1) 256K x 36	(1) 256K x 36	NONE	NONE
4MB	(1) 256K x 36	(1) 256K x 36	(1) 256K x 36	(1) 256K x 36
4MB	(1) 512K x 36	(1) 512K x 36	NONE	NONE
8MB	(1) 512K x 36	(1) 512K x 36	(1) 512K x 36	(1) 512K x 36
8MB	(1) 1M x 36	(1) 1M x 36	NONE	NONE
10MB	(1) 1M x 36	(1) 1M x 36	(1) 256K x 36	(1) 256K x 36
12MB	(1) 1M x 36	(1) 1M x 36	(1) 512K x 36	(1) 512K x 36
16MB	(1) 1M x 36	(1) 1M x 36	(1) 1M x 36	(1) 1M x 36
16MB	(1) 2M x 36	(1) 2M x 36	NONE	NONE
32MB	(1) 2M x 36	(1) 2M x 36	(1) 2M x 36	(1) 2M x 36
32MB	(1) 4M x 36	(1) 4M x 36	NONE	NONE
64MB	(1) 8M x 36	(1) 8M x 36	NONE	NONE
64MB	(1) 4M x 36	(1) 4M x 36	(1) 4M x 36	(1) 4M x 36
96MB	(1) 4M x 36	(1) 4M x 36	(1) 8M x 36	(1) 8M x 36
128MB	(1) 8M x 36	(1) 8M x 36	(1) 8M x 36	(1) 8M x 36

CPU TYPE CONFIGURATION	
Type	**CP1**
80486SX	pins 3 & 5, 4 & 6 closed
80486DX/DX2/DX4/Overdrive	pins 1 & 3, 2 & 4 closed

CPU SPEED CONFIGURATION	
Speed	**CLK1**
25MHz	pins 1 & 3, 4 & 6 closed
33MHz	pins 2 & 4, 3 & 5 closed
50iMHz	pins 1 & 3, 4 & 6 closed
66iMHz	pins 2 & 4, 3 & 5 closed
75iMHz	pins 1 & 3, 4 & 6 closed
100iMHz	pins 2 & 4, 3 & 5 closed

CPU VOLTAGE CONFIGURATION	
Voltage	**CP2**
3.3 volt	pins 1 & 3, 2 & 4 closed
5 volt	pins 3 & 5, 4 & 6 closed

ZEOS INTERNATIONAL, LTD.
PANTERA PENTIUM

Processor	Pentium
Processor Speed	75/90/100/120/133/150MHz
Chip Set	VLSI
Max. Onboard DRAM	384MB
Cache	256/512KB (on external cache card)
BIOS	Unidentified
Dimensions	330mm x 218mm
I/O Options	Parallel port, serial ports (2), Infrared COM port, 32-bit PCI slots (3), floppy drive interface, IDE interfaces (2), SCSI interface, 10-baseT connector, 10-base2 connector, Legacy connector, VRM connector, cache slot
NPU Options	None

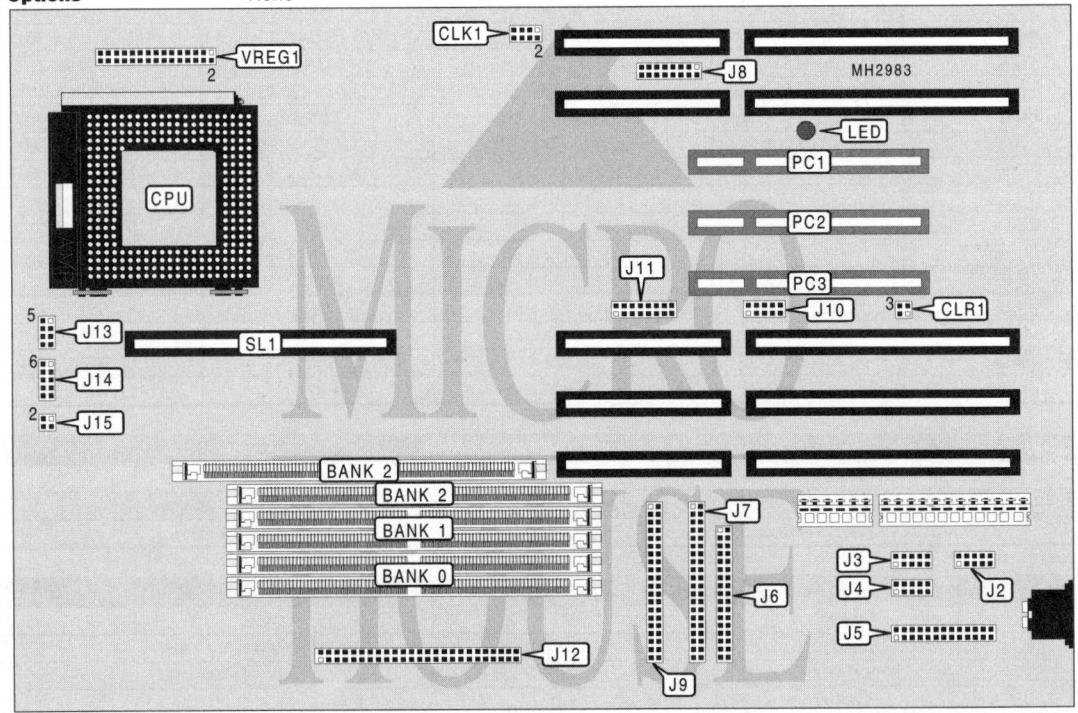

CONNECTIONS			
Purpose	**Location**	**Purpose**	**Location**
Serial port 1	J2	10-base2 connector	J11
IR COM connector	J3	SCSI connector	J12
Serial port 2	J4	IDE interface LED	J13 pins 1 & 2
Parallel port	J5	Speaker	J13 pins 5 - 9
Floppy drive interface	J6	Power LED & keylock	J14 pins 6 - 10
IDE interface 2	J7	Reset switch	J15 pins 2 & 4
Legacy connector	J8	32-bit PCI slots	PC1 - PC3
IDE interface 1	J9	External cache card	SL1
10-baseT connector	J10	VRM connector	VREG1

Continued on next page...

ZEOS INTERNATIONAL, LTD.
PANTERA PENTIUM

. . . . continued from previous page

USER CONFIGURABLE SETTINGS		
Function	**Jumper**	**Position**
◇ AMD LAN or LAN/SCSI chip not installed	CLK1	pins 7 & 8 open
AMD LAN or LAN/SCSI chip installed	CLK1	pins 7 & 8 closed
◇ Flash BIOS write protect enabled	CLR1	pins 1 & 2 closed
Flash BIOS write protect disabled	CLR1	pins 3 & 4 closed

DRAM CONFIGURATION			
Size	**Bank 0**	**Bank 1**	**Bank 2**
2MB	(2) 256K x 36	NONE	NONE
4MB	(2) 256K x 36	(2) 256K x 36	NONE
8MB	(2) 1M x 36	NONE	NONE
10MB	(2) 1M x 36	(2) 256K x 36	NONE
12MB	(2) 512K x 36	(2) 512K x 36	(2) 512K x 36
16MB	(2) 1M x 36	(2) 1M x 36	NONE
24MB	(2) 1M x 36	(2) 1M x 36	(2) 1M x 36
32MB	(2) 2M x 36	(2) 2M x 36	NONE
64MB	(2) 4M x 36	(2) 4M x 36	NONE
128MB	(2) 8M x 36	(2) 8M x 36	NONE
256MB	(2) 16M x 36	(2) 16M x 36	NONE
384MB	(2) 16M x 36	(2) 16M x 36	(2) 16M x 36

CACHE CONFIGURATION	
Size	**SL1**
256KB	256KB cache card installed
512KB	512KB cache card installed

CPU SPEED CONFIGURATION	
Speed	**CLK1**
75MHz	pins 5 & 6, 7 & 8 closed
90MHz	pins 7 & 8 closed
100MHz	pins 5 & 6 closed
120MHz	pins 1 & 2, 7 & 8 closed
133MHz	pins 1 & 2, 5 & 6 closed
150MHz	pins 1 & 2, 3 & 4, 7 & 8 closed

Note: The settings provided above apply to part numbers 010-0066-03, 010-0066-17, and 010-0066-18 only. Using these settings on boards with other part numbers may cause the system to lock up. See the following table for settings used by boards with other part numbers.

Continued on next page. . .

ZEOS INTERNATIONAL, LTD.
PANTERA PENTIUM

. . . continued from previous page

CPU SPEED CONFIGURATION	
Speed	**CLK1**
75MHz	pins 1 & 2, 5 & 6 closed
90MHz	pins 5 & 6 closed
100MHz (bus 66MHz)	pins 1 & 2 closed
100MHz (bus 50MHz)	pins 1 & 2, 3 & 4, 5 & 6 closed
120MHz	pins 3 & 4, 5 & 6 closed
133MHz	pins 1 & 2, 3 & 4 closed

DIAGNOSTIC LED		
LED	**Color**	**Function**
On	Red	Power good signal is enabled
Off	Red	Power good signal is disabled

Appendix A
Manufacturer Contact Information

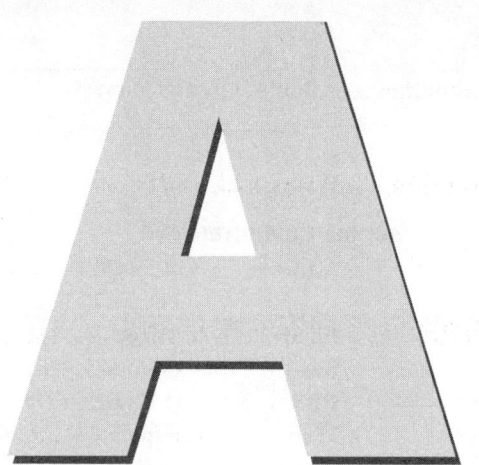

Appendix A lists contact information for most companies involved with motherboards and motherboard components as well as many major OEMs who build systems. In addition to mailing addresses and phone numbers for most companies, technical support numbers, fax numbers, fax-back services, BBSs, Web addresses, and e-mail addresses are provided where available.

A-TREND TECHNOLOGY CORPORATION

Address	46600 FREMONT BLVD.
	FREMONT, CA 94538
Phone	(510) 226-6290
Fax	(510) 226-6296
Toll Free	(800) 866-0188
Web	http://www.atrend.com
E-mail	atrend@ix.netcom.com

ABIT COMPUTER CORPORATION

Address	47889 FREMONT BLVD.
	FREMONT, CA 94538
Phone	(510) 623-0500
Fax	(510) 623-1092
Web	http://www.abit.com.tw

ACER, INC.

Address	2641 ORCHARD PARKWAY
	SAN JOSE, CA 95134
Phone	(408) 432-6200
Fax	(408) 922-2933
BBS	(408) 428-0140
Fax-Back	(800) 554-2494

Web   http://www.acer.com

ACHME COMPUTER, INC.
Address   4059 CLIPPER COURT
                FREMONT, CA 94538
Phone   (510) 623-8818
Fax   (510) 623-8585
BBS   (510) 623-7398
Web   http://www.achme.com
E-mail   support@achme.com

ACQUIRE COMPUTER SYSTEMS, INC.
Address   2631 DAVIDSON DR.
                FORT COLLINS, CO 80221
E-mail   webmaster@aquirecsi.com

ACQUTEK CORPORATION
Address   1549 SOUTH 1100 EAST, SUITE B
                SALT LAKE CITY, UT 84105
Phone   (801) 485-4594
Fax   (801) 485-4555
Web   http://www.acqu.com

ACTION INSTRUMENTS
Address   8601 AERO DRIVE
                SAN DIEGO, CA 92123
Phone   (619) 279-5726
Fax   (619) 279-2103
Web   http://www.actionio.com

ADAPTIVE SOLUTIONS, INC.
Address   1400 N.W. COMPTON DRIVE
                SUITE 340
                BEAVERTON, OR 97006
Phone   (503) 690-1236
Fax   (503) 690-1249
Toll Free   (800) 48-CNAPS
Web   http://www.asi.com

ADVANCED COMPUTER TECHNOLOGY, LTD.
Address   12/F, CHUANGS FINANCE CENTER
                81 85 LOCKHART ROAD
                WANCHAI,
                HONG KONG

ADVANCED INTEGRATION RESEARCH, INC.
Address	2188 DEL FRANCO STREET
	SAN JOSE, CA 95131
Phone	(408) 428-0800
Fax	(408) 428-0950
Toll Free	(800) 866-1945
BBS	(408) 428-1735
Web	http://www.airwebs.com
E-mail	air@ix.netcom.com

ADVANCED LOGIC RESEARCH, INC.
Address	9401 JERONIMO ROAD
	IRVINE, CA 92618
Fax	(714) 458-0532
Toll Free	(800) 257-1230
BBS	(714) 458-6834
Fax-Back	(714) 581-3332
Web	http://www.alr.com

ALARIS, INC.
Address	47338 FREMONT BLVD.
	FREMONT, CA 94538
Phone	(510) 770-5700
Fax	(510) 770-5769
Web	http://www.alaris.com

ALPHA MICROSYSTEMS
Address	2722 SOUTH FAIRVIEW STREET
	SANTA ANA, CA 92704
Phone	(714) 957-8705
Fax	(714) 957-8500
Toll Free	(888) 226-6398
Web	http://www.alphaconnect.com
E-mail	aconnect@alphamicro.com

AMDEK CORPORATION
Address	1901 ZANKER ROAD
	SAN JOSE, CA 95112

AMERICAN DIGICOM CORPORATION
Address	1233 MIDAS WAY
	SUNNYVALE, CA 94086
Phone	(408) 245-1580
Fax	(408) 245-1584
Web	http://www.digicomgroup.com

AMERICAN DIGITAL DATA ASSOCIATES
Address	418B CLOVERLEAF DRIVE
	BALDWIN PARK, CA 91706
Phone	(818) 369-2332
Fax	(818) 369-5109
Web	http://www.ads-intl.com

AMERICAN MEGATRENDS, INC.
Address	6145-F NORTHBELT PARKWAY
	NORCROSS, GA 30071
Phone	(770) 263-8181
Fax	(770) 246-8791
Toll Free	(800) 828-9264
BBS	(770) 246-8780
Fax-Back	(770) 246-8787
Web	http://www.megatrends.com

AMERICAN PREDATOR CORPORATION
Address	718 EAST EVELYN AVENUE
	SUNNYVALE, CA 94086
Phone	(408) 524-7900
Fax	(408) 524-7902
BBS	(408) 524-7908
Web	http://www.americanpredator.co

AMERICAN RESEARCH CORPORATION
Address	602 MONTEREY PASS ROAD
	MONTEREY PARK, CA 91754
Phone	(818) 284-1904
Fax	(818) 284-4213

AMPRO COMPUTERS, INC.
Address	990 ALMANOR AVENUE
	SUNNYVALE, CA 94086
Phone	(408) 522-2100
Toll Free	(800) 966-5200
Web	http://www.ampro.com

AMPTRON INTERNATIONAL, INC.
Address	1028 LAWSON STREET
	CITY OF INDUSTRY, CA 91748
Phone	(818) 912-5789
Fax	(818) 912-4725
Web	http://www.amptron.com
E-mail	amptron@deltanet.com

AMS, INC.
Address	12881 RAMONA BLVD.
	IRWINDALE, CA 91706
Phone	(818) 814-8851
Fax	(818) 814-0782
Toll Free	(800) 886-2671
Fax-Back	(800) 886-3536
Web	http://www.amstech.com

ANSEL COMMUNICATIONS, INC.
Address	8711 148TH AVENUE NORTHEAST
	REDMOND, WA 98052
Phone	(206) 869-4928
Fax	(206) 869-5015
Toll Free	(800) 341-7978
Web	http://www.ansel.com

ANTEC, INC.
Address	2859 BAYVIEW DRIVE
	FREMONT, CA 94538
Phone	(510) 770-1200
Fax	(510) 770-1288
Web	http://www.antec-inc.com
E-mail	antec@antec-inc.com

APRICOT COMPUTERS LIMITED
Address	3500 PARKSIDE
	BIRMINGHAM BUSINESS PARK
	BIRMINGHAM, B37 7YS
	UNITED KINGDOM
Phone	1217 177 171
Fax	1217 177 799
Web	http://www.apricot.co.uk

AQUARIUS SYSTEMS, INC.
Address	47381 BAYSIDE PARKWAY
	FREMONT, CA 94538
Phone	(510) 656-9800
Fax	(510) 656-9876

AREA ELECTRONICS SYSTEMS, INC.
Address	950 FEEANA STREET
	PLACENTIA, CA 92870
Phone	(714) 993-0300
Fax	(714) 993-0987

ARIMA COMPUTER CORPORATION
Address	6F, NO. 327, SUNG LUNG ROAD TAIPEI, TAIWAN, REP OF CHINA
Phone	2 749 5588
Fax	2 749 3399

ARNET CORPORATION
Address	618 GRASSMERE PARK DRIVE SUITE 6 NASHVILLE, TN 37211
Phone	(615) 834-8000
Fax	(615) 834-5399
Toll Free	(800) 366-8844
BBS	(615) 333-0423
Web	http://www.dgii.com

ARNOS INSTRUMENTS & COMPUTER SYSTEMS, INC.
Address	206 4585 CANADA WAY BURNABY, BC V5G 4L6 CANADA
Phone	(604) 298-9819
Web	http://www.aicom.com

ARTEK COMPUTER SYSTEMS, INC.
Address	47709 FREMONT BLVD. FREMONT, CA 94538
Phone	(510) 490-8402
Fax	(510) 490-8405

ASIA DATA, INC.
Address	B, 10F, NO. 525, CHUNG CHENG ROAD HSIN TIEN, TAIPEI, TAIWAN, REP OF CHINA
Phone	2 218 1799
Fax	2 218 1757

ASIA DIRECT CORPORATION
Address	11F, NO. 14, LANE 183, YUNG CHI ROAD TAIPEI, TAIWAN, REP OF CHINA
Phone	2 748 0102
Fax	2 748 0108

ASICOM, INC.
Address	46716 FREMONT BLVD.

	FREMONT, CA 94538
Phone	(510) 354-0900
Fax	(510) 354-0909
E-mail	asicom@aol.com

ASPEN SYSTEMS, INC.

Address	4026 YOUNGFIELD STREET
	WHEAT RIDGE, CO 80033-3862
Phone	(303) 431-4606
Fax	(303) 431-7196
Toll Free	(800) 992-9242
Web	http://www.aspsys.com
E-mail	aspen@aspsys.com

AST RESEARCH, INC.

Address	16215 ALTON PARKWAY
	IRVINE, CA 92618-3618
Phone	(714) 727-4141
Fax	(714) 727-9355
Fax-Back	(800) 926-1278
Web	http://www.ast.com

ASUS COMPUTER INTERNATIONAL

Address	721 CHARCOT AVENUE
	SAN JOSE, CA 95131
Phone	(408) 474-0567
Fax	(408) 474-0568
BBS	(408) 474-0555
Web	http://asustek.asus.com.tw

AT&T, INC.

Address	32 AVENUE OF THE AMERICAS
	NEW YORK, NY 10013
Phone	(212) 387-5400
Web	http://www.att.com

ATC/UNITRON COMPUTERS & COMPUTER PARTS

Address	PO BOX 2140
	5700 DA HELMOND,
	NETHERLANDS
Phone	492 528 899
Fax	492 55 42 45

ATEN RESEARCH, INC.

Address	340 THOR PLACE
	BREA, CA 92821

Phone	(714) 255-0566
Fax	(714) 255-0275
Web	http://www.aten.com

ATRONICS INTERNATIONAL, INC.
Address	44700-B INDUSTRIAL DRIVE
	FREMONT, CA 94538
Phone	(510) 656-8400
Fax	(510) 656-8560
BBS	(510) 226-2671
Web	http://www.atronics.com
E-mail	info@ati1.com

AURORA IMPEX CORPORATION
Address	3500 CHALLENGER STREET
	TORRANCE, CA 90503
Phone	(310) 327-0373
Fax	(310) 793-5658
Web	http://www.aurora.com.tw/img

AUSTIN COMPUTER SYSTEMS
Address	10300 METRIC BLVD.
	AUSTIN, TX 78758
Toll Free	(800) 624-8654
Web	http://www.goaustin.com

AUVA COMPUTER, INC.
Address	NO. 18, PEI YUAN RD. CHUNG LI IND., PARK
	TAOYUAN,
	TAIWAN, REP OF CHINA
Phone	3 452 8200
Fax	3 452 9155

AXIK COMPUTER, INC.
Address	540 WEDDELL DRIVE
	SUITE 5
	SUNNYVALE, CA 94089
Phone	(408) 255-8629
Fax	(408) 255-8660
Web	http://www.eumax.com

AXIOM TECHNOLOGY, INC.
Address	3857 SCHAEFER AVE.
	UNIT E
	CHINO, CA 91710-5458
Phone	(909) 464-1881

Fax	(909) 464-1882
Web	http://www.axiomtek.com
E-mail	yt@axiomtek.com

BADGER COMPUTERS
Address	10901 MALCOLM MCKINLEY DRIVE
	TAMPA, FL 33612
Phone	(813) 972-6486
Fax	(813) 972-6715
Toll Free	(800) 3-badger

BCM ADVANCED RESEARCH, INC.
Address	1 HUGHES
	IRVINE, CA 92718
Phone	(714) 470-1888
Fax	(714) 470-0883
Web	http://www.bcmcom.com

BEC COMPUTER ENTERPRISE
Address	425 PRIVET ROAD
	HORSHAM, PA 19044
Fax	(215) 672-5945
Toll Free	(800) 453-7630

BEK-TRONIC TECHNOLOGY, INC.
Address	2570 CORPORATE PLACE
	SUITE E-108
	MONTEREY PARK, CA 91754
Phone	(213) 266-8633
Fax	(213) 266-8073
Web	http://www.bek-tronic.com

BETHEL ELECTRONICS INTERNATIONAL, INC.
Address	YOUNGJIN B/D
	#16-18 HANGANGRO 3GA, YONGSAN-GU
	SEOUL, REP OF KOREA
Phone	2 704 5670
Fax	2 704 1839

BIOSTAR MICROTECH INTERNATIONAL CORPORATION
Address	4044 CLIPPER COURT
	FREMONT, CA 94538
Phone	(510) 226-6678
Fax	(510) 226-6188
Web	http://www.biostar-usa.com

BJMT TECHNOLOGY CORPORATION
Address	16666 JOHNSON DRIVE CITY OF INDUSTRY, CA 91745
Phone	(818) 369-5998
Fax	(818) 369-9658
Web	http://www.bjmt.com
E-mail	bjmt@address.net

BUFFALO PRODUCTS, INC.
Address	2805 19TH STREET SE SALEM, OR 97302
Phone	(503) 585-3414
Fax	(503) 585-4505
Toll Free	(800) 345-2356
Web	http://www.buffinc.com

CAF TECHNOLOGY, INC.
Address	1315 JOHNSON DRIVE CITY OF INDUSTRY, CA 91745
Phone	(818) 369-3690
Fax	(818) 369-3692

CALIFORNIA GRAPHICS & PERIPHERALS, INC.
Address	VIA PACUVIO 4 80121 NAPOLI, ITALY
Phone	81 661285
Fax	81 662839
Web	http://www.calgraph.com
E-mail	sales@mail.calgraph.com

CARDINAL TECHNOLOGIES, INC.
Address	1827 FREEDOM ROAD LANCASTER, PA 17601
Phone	(717) 293-3000
Fax	(717) 293-3055
BBS	(717) 293-3074
Fax-Back	(717) 399-2308
Web	http://www.cardtech.com
E-mail	prodinfo@cardtech.com

CHAINTECH COMPUTER COMPANY, LTD.
Address	12880 LAKELAND ROAD SANTA FE SPRINGS, CA 90670
Phone	(310) 906-1698

Fax	(310) 906-1699
Web	http://www.chaintech.com.tw

CHICONY, INC.

Address	53 PARKER
	IRVINE, CA 92718
Phone	(714) 380-0928
Fax	(714) 380-9204
Web	http://www.chicony.com

CMS ENHANCEMENTS, INC.

Address	THREE IMPERIAL PROMENADE
	SANTA ANA, CA 92707
Phone	(714) 437-0099
Fax	(714) 513-2465
Toll Free	(800) 555-1671
Fax-Back	(714) 445-5327
Web	http://www.cmsenh.com

COMMODORE BUSINESS MACHINES, INC.

Address	POSTFACH 13
	2150 NIEUW-VENNEP,
	NETHERLANDS

COMPAQ COMPUTER CORPORATION

Address	20555 STATE HIGHWAY 249
	PO BOX 692000
	HOUSTON, TX 77269-2000
Phone	(713) 370-0670
Fax	(713) 374-1740
Toll Free	(800) 345-1518
BBS	(713) 378-1418
Fax-Back	(800) 345-1518
Web	http://www.compaq.com

COMPULINK RESEARCH, INC.

Address	3949 COMMERCE PARKWAY
	MIRAMAR, FL 33025
Phone	(954) 450-7061
Fax	(954) 450-7062
Toll Free	(800) 611-1555
Web	http://www.clrusa.com

COMPUTREND SYSTEMS, INC.

Address	1306-1310 JOHN REED COURT
	CITY OF INDUSTRY, CA 91745

Phone	(818) 330-1011
Fax	(818) 369-6803
Toll Free	(800) 677-6477
BBS	(818) 330-9749
Web	http://www.premiopc.com

CONCORD OFFICE AUTOMATION INDUSTRIAL (HK), LTD.

Address	RM. 14-15, 7/F., VANTA INDUSTRIAL CENTRE
	21-33 TAI LIN PAI ROAD
	KWAI CHUNG, NT,
	HONG KONG
Phone	4 853 133
Fax	4 853 200
Web	http://www.concord.com.hk

CORE INTERNATIONAL, INC.

Address	6500 EAST ROGERS CIRCLE
	BOCA RATON, FL 33487
Phone	(561) 997-6033
Fax	(561) 997-6202
BBS	(561) 241-2929

CSS LABORATORIES, INC.

Address	1641 MCGAW AVENUE
	IRVINE, CA 92714
Phone	(714) 852-8161
Fax	(714) 852-0410
BBS	(714) 852-9231
Web	http://www.csslabs.com

CT CONTINENTAL CORPORATION

Address	2F, NO. 106, LANE 103, SEC. 2 NEI HU ROAD
	TAIPEI,
	TAIWAN, REP OF CHINA
Phone	2 627 0001
Fax	2 799 7691
E-mail	ctcoteam@ms2.hinet.net

CYBLE TECHNOLOGY, INC.

Address	5 FLOOR, LANE 327, 13 CHUNG SHAN ROAD, SECTION 2
	TAIPEI,
	TAIWAN, REP OF CHINA
Phone	2 248 5381

DASH COMPUTER, INC.

Address	470A LAKESIDE DRIVE

SUNNYVALE, CA 94086
- **Phone** (408) 773-1488
- **Fax** (408) 773-1580

DATAEXPERT CORPORATION
- **Address** 1178 SONORA COURT
  SUNNYVALE, CA 94086
- **Phone** (408) 737-8880
- **Fax** (408) 737-8390
- **Toll Free** (800) 328-2397
- **Web** http://www.dataexpert.com

DATAVAN INTERNATIONAL CORPORATION
- **Address** 4F, #120-12, CHUNG SHANG ROAD, SEC. 3
  CHUNG HO CITY
  TAIPEI,
  TAIWAN, REP OF CHINA
- **Phone** 2 222 8283
- **Fax** 2 222 7530
- **Web** http://www.datavan.com.tw
- **E-mail** datavan@tpts1.seed.net.tw

DAYTON MICRO
- **Address** 16057 KAPLAN AVENUE
  INDUSTRY, CA 91784
- **Phone** (818) 968-5358
- **Fax** (818) 968-9458
- **Web** http://www.daytonmicro.com

DD & TT ENTERPRISE USA CO.
- **Address** 5680 RICKENBACKER ROAD
  BELL, CA 90201
- **Phone** (213) 780-0099
- **Fax** (213) 780-0419

DECISION COMPUTER INTERNATIONAL CO., LTD.
- **Address** 4F, NO. 31-3, ALLEY 4, LANE 36
  MING-SHEN E. ROAD, SEC. 5
  TAIPEI,
  TAIWAN, REP OF CHINA
- **Phone** 2 766 5753
- **Fax** 2 766 5702
- **Web** http://www.decision.com.tw
- **E-mail** decision@c2.hinet.net

DELL COMPUTER CORPORATION

Address	2214 W BREAKER LANE
	SUITE D
	AUSTIN, TX 78758
Phone	(512) 338-4400
Fax	(512) 728-3653
Toll Free	(800) 624-9897
BBS	(512) 728-8528
Fax-Back	(800) 950-1329
Web	http://www.dell.com

DENSITRON CORPORATION

Address	10430 PIONEER BLVD.
	SUITE 2
	SANTA FE SPRINGS, CA 90670
Phone	(310) 941-5000
Fax	(310) 941-5757
Web	http://www.densitron.com
E-mail	sales@densitron.com

DESTINY COMPUTERS, INC.

Address	3480 INVESTMENT BLVD.
	HAYWARD, CA 94545
Phone	(510) 783-2727
Fax	(510) 783-3003
Web	http://www.destinycomp.com

DIAMOND FLOWER, INC.

Address	135 MAIN AVENUE
	SACRAMENTO, CA 95838
Phone	(916) 568-1234
Fax	(916) 568-1233
Toll Free	(800) 808-4334
BBS	(908) 390-4820
Web	http://www.dfiusa.com
E-mail	info@dfiusa.com

DIAMOND MULTIMEDIA SYSTEMS, INC.

Address	2880 JUNCTION AVENUE
	SAN JOSE, CA 95134
Phone	(408) 325-7000
Fax	(408) 325-7070
Fax-Back	option 6 at main
Web	http://www.diamondmm.com

DIGITAL EQUIPMENT CORPORATION
Address	111 POWDERMILL ROAD
	MAYNARD, MA 01754
Phone	(508) 493-2211
Fax	(508) 493-8780
Toll Free	(800) DIGITAL
BBS	(508) 264-7227
Fax-Back	(800) 344-4825
Web	http://www.digital.com

DIVERSIFIED TECHNOLOGY
Address	112 E. STATE STREET
	RIGDELAND, MS 39158-0748
Phone	(601) 856-4121
Fax	(601) 856-2888
Toll Free	(800) 443-2667

DTK COMPUTER, INC.
Address	18645 EAST GALE AVENUE
	SUITE 233
	CITY OF INDUSTRY, CA 91748
Phone	(626) 810-8880
Fax	(626) 810-5233
Toll Free	(800) 289-2385
BBS	(626) 854-0797
Fax-Back	(800) 806-1385
Web	http://www.dtkcomputer.com

DUNNET INTERNATIONAL TRADING COMPANY BV
Address	KIPSTRAAT 16
	3011 RT ROTTERDAM,
	NETHERLANDS
Phone	10 400 8100
Fax	10 412 0597

DYNA MICRO, INC.
Address	48434 MILMONT DRIVE
	FREMONT, CA 94538
Phone	(510) 438-6530
Fax	(510) 353-2020
Toll Free	(800) 787-8580
Web	http://www.addonics.com

EDOM INTERNATIONAL CORPORATION
Address	48834 KATO ROAD SUITE 107A

	FREEMONT, CA 94538
Phone	(510) 659-8482
Fax	(510) 659-8484
Web	http://www.edom.com

EFA CORPORATION

Address	3040 OAKMEAD VILLAGE DRIVE
	SANTA CLARA, CA 95051
Phone	(408) 987-5400
Fax	(408) 987-5415
Toll Free	(800) 800-3321
BBS	(408) 987-5418
Fax-Back	(408) 987-5435
Web	http://www.efacorp.com

ELISA TECHNOLOGY, INC.

Address	4368 ENTERPRISE STREET
	FREMONT, CA 94538
Phone	(510) 651-5817
Fax	(510) 651-4834

ELITEGROUP COMPUTER SYSTEMS, INC.

Address	45401 RESEARCH AVENUE
	FREMONT, CA 94539
Phone	(510) 226-7333
Fax	(510) 226-7350
Toll Free	(800) 829-8890
Web	http://www.ecsusa.com

EMPAC INTERNATIONAL

Address	47490 SEABRIDGE DRIVE
	FREMONT, CA 94538
Phone	(510) 683-8800
Fax	(510) 683-8662
Web	http://www.empac.com

EPSON, INC.

Address	20770 MADRONA AVENUE
	TORRANCE, CA 90503
Phone	(310) 782-0770
Fax	(310) 782-5220
Web	http://www.epson.com

ETC COMPUTER, INC.

Address	2917 BAYVIEW DRIVE
	FREMONT, CA 94538

Phone	(510) 226-6250
Fax	(510) 226-6252

ETEQ MICROSYSTEMS, INC.

Address	1900 MCCARTHY BLVD. SUITE 110 MILPITAS, CA 95035
Phone	(408) 432-8147
Fax	(408) 432-8146
Web	http://www.eteq.com

EURONE (HK) CO., LTD.

Address	18751 RAILROAD STREET CITY OF INDUSTRY, CA 91748
Phone	(818) 935-0260
Fax	(818) 935-0270

EVEREX SYSTEMS, INC.

Address	5020 BRANDIN COURT FREMONT, CA 94538
Phone	(510) 498-1111
Fax	(510) 683-2186
Toll Free	(800) 821-0806
BBS	(510) 226-9694
Fax-Back	(510) 683-2800
Web	http://www.everex.com

EVERGREEN SYSTEMS, INC.

Address	120 LANDING COURT NOVATO, CA 94945
Phone	(415) 897-8888
Fax	(415) 897-6158
Toll Free	(800) EVERSYS
BBS	(415) 898-9398
Web	http://www.eversys.com

FAIR FRIEND ENTERPRISE COMPANY, LTD.

Address	NO. 186, YUNG CHI ROAD TAIPEI, TAIWAN, REP OF CHINA
Phone	2 763 9696
Fax	2 768 0637

FAMOUS TECHNOLOGY CO., LTD.

Address	UNIT 203, 266-268, CHEUNG SHAWAN ROAD SHAMSHUIPO

	HOWLOON, HONG KONG
Phone	2 361 1663
Fax	2 725 1981
Web	http://www.magic-pro.com.hk

FIRST INTERNATIONAL COMPUTER, INC.

Address	980A MISSION COURT FREMONT, CA 94539
Phone	(510) 252-7777
Fax	(510) 252-8888
Toll Free	(800) 342-2636
BBS	(510) 252-7750
Fax-Back	(510) 252-8844
Web	http://www.fica.com
E-mail	sales@fica.com

FLASH TECH, INC.

Address	1300 JOHN REED COURT SUITE A CITY OF INDUSTRY, CA 91745
Phone	(818) 855-0700
Fax	(818) 855-0705
Web	http://www.flashtechinc.com
E-mail	flash@microsharp.net

FLYTECH GROUP INTERNATIONAL

Address	3008 SCOTT BLVD. SANTA CLARA, CA 95054
Phone	(408) 727-7373
Fax	(408) 727-7375
Web	http://www.flytech.com.tw

FONG KAI INDUSTRIAL CO.

Address	1461 EXCHANGE DRIVE RICHARDSON, TX 75081
Phone	(214) 644-1584
Fax	(214) 644-5343
Web	http://www.fkusa.com

FORCOM TECHNOLOGY CORPORATION

Address	3578 E. ENTERPRISE DRIVE ANAHEIM, CA 92807
Phone	(714) 666-8868
Fax	(714) 666-8838
Web	http://www.forcomtech.com

FOREX COMPUTER CORPORATION
Address	1-2F, NO. 637-1, CHUNG HSIN ROAD, SEC. 5
	SAN CHUNG
	TAIPEI HSIEN,
	TAIWAN, REP OF CHINA
Phone	2 999 3889
Fax	2 999 3952

FORTRESS SYSTEMS INTERNATIONAL
Address	4030 YANCEY ROAD
	CHARLOTTE, NC 28217
Phone	(704) 525-4495
Fax	(704) 525-4497
Toll Free	(800) 437-3920
Web	http://www.fsiinc.com

FREE COMPUTER TECHNOLOGY, INC.
Address	101 HAMMOND AVENUE
	FREMONT, CA 94539
Phone	(510) 226-2777
Fax	(510) 226-2778
Web	http://www.freetech.com

FRONTIER INDUSTRIAL, INC.
Address	121 BRENT CIRCLE
	WALNUT, CA 91789
Phone	(909) 594-7420

GATEWAY 2000
Address	610 GATEWAY DRIVE
	NORTH SIOUX CITY, SD 57049
Fax	(605) 232-2023
Toll Free	(800) 523-2000
Fax-Back	(800) 846-4526
Web	http://www.gateway.com

GCH SYSTEMS, INC.
Address	777 E. MIDDLEFIELD ROAD
	MOUNTAIN VIEW, CA 94043
Phone	(415) 968-3400
Fax	(415) 964-9747
Web	http://www.award.com

GEMLIGHT COMPUTER LTD.
Address	703-706, 7/F HEWLETT CENTRE
	54 HOI YUEN ROAD, KWUN TONG

	KOWLOON,
	HONG KONG
Phone	2 344 1638
Fax	2 790 9390
BBS	2357 5447
Web	http://www.gemlight.com.hk

GENESYS ATE, INC.

Address	1289 HAMMERWOOD AVENUE
	SUNNYVALE, CA 94089
Phone	(408) 541-1800
Fax	(408) 541-1700
Web	http://www.genetech.com

GENOA SYSTEMS CORPORATION

Address	6850 SANTA THERESA BLVD.
	SAN JOSE, CA 95119
Phone	(408) 362-2929
Fax	(408) 362-2998
BBS	(408) 362-2999
Web	http://www.genoasys.com

GESPAC

Address	50 WEST HOOVER AVE.
	MESA, AZ 85210
Phone	(602) 962-5559
Fax	(602) 962-5750
Web	http://www.gespac.com
E-mail	info@gespac.com

GIGA-BYTE TECHNOLOGY CO., LTD.

Address	18325 VALLEY BLVD.
	SUITE E
	LA PUENTE, CA 91748
Phone	(818) 854-9338
Fax	(818) 854-9339
BBS	(818) 369-3985
Web	http://www.giga-byte.com
E-mail	gigabyte@tpts1.seed.net.tw

GMX, INC.

Address	3223 ARNOLD LANE
	NORTHBROOK, IL 60062
Phone	(708) 559-0909
Fax	(708) 559-0942

GOLDSTAR ELECTRONICS INTERNATIONAL, INC.
Address	1000 SYLVAN AVENUE
	ENGLEWOOD CLIFFS, NJ 07632
Phone	(201) 816-2000
Fax	(201) 816-0636
Toll Free	(800) 243-0000

GVC TECHNOLOGIES, INC.
Address	400 COMMONS WAY
	ROCKWAY, NJ 07866
Phone	(201) 579-3630
Fax	(201) 579-2702
Web	http://www.gvc.com

HAUPPAUGE COMPUTER WORKS, INC.
Address	91 CABOT COURT
	HAUPPAUGE, NY 11788
Phone	(516) 434-1600
Fax	(516) 434-3198
Toll Free	(800) 443-6284
BBS	(516) 434-8454
Fax-Back	(516) 434-3198
Web	http://www.hauppauge.com
E-mail	sales@hauppauge.com

HERTZ COMPUTERS
Address	75 VARICK STREET
	NEW YORK, NY 10013
Phone	(212) 634-4000
Fax	(212) 634-4286
Toll Free	(888) 222-7280
Web	http://www.hertztec.com

HEWLETT-PACKARD COMPANY
Address	3000 HANNOVER STREET
	PALO ALTO, CA 94304
Phone	(800) 752-0900
Fax	(415) 857-5518
Toll Free	(800) 637-7740
BBS	(408) 553-3500
Fax-Back	(800) 231-9300
Web	http://www.hp.com

HOKKINS SYSTEMATION, INC.
Address	131 EAST BROKAW ROAD

	SAN JOSE, CA 95112
Phone	(408) 436-8303
Fax	(408) 436-3021
Toll Free	(800) 526-2328
BBS	(408) 436-1820
Web	http://www.hokkins.com
E-mail	hsi@hokkins.com

HORNET TECHNOLOGY CORPORATION

Address	4 FLOOR, #116, SHIN MING ROAD
	TAIPEI,
	TAIWAN, REP OF CHINA
Phone	2 791 4301
Fax	2 791 4310

HYUNDAI ELECTRONICS, INC.

Address	3101 N FIRST STREET
	SAN JOSE, CA 95134
Phone	(408) 232-8000
Fax	(408) 232-8123
Web	http://www.hea.com

I-BUS

Address	9174 SKY PARK COURT
	SAN DIEGO, CA 92123
Fax	(619) 268-7863
Toll Free	(800) 382-4229
Web	http://www.ibus.com
E-mail	info@ibus.com

IBM CORPORATION

Toll Free	(800) 772-2227
BBS	(919) 517-0001
Web	http://www.ibm.com

ICL

Address	WILLSTAETTER STRASSE 13
	40549 DUESSELDORF,
	GERMANY
BBS	346 560 748
Web	http://www.icl.com

INDUSTRIAL COMPUTER SOURCE

Address	9950 BARNES CANYON ROAD
	SAN DIEGO, CA 92121-2720
Phone	(619) 677-0877

Fax	(619) 677-0615
Toll Free	(800) 523-2320
Fax-Back	(800) 677-7329
Web	http://www.indcompsrc.com
E-mail	sales@indcompsrc.com

INFOMATIC POWER SYSTEMS CORPORATION (IPX)

Address	9945 SOUTH PIONEER BLVD.
	SANTA FE SPRINGS, CA 90670
Phone	(562) 948-2217
Fax	(562) 948-5264
Web	http://www.infomatic.com

INSIDE TECHNOLOGY A/S

Address	8 PRESTIGE CIRCLE
	SUITE 116
	ALLEN, TX 75002
Phone	(972) 390-8593
Fax	(972) 390-8609
Web	http://www.inside-usa.com
E-mail	inside@inside-usa.com

INTEL CORPORATION

Address	P.O. BOX 58119
	SANTA CLARA, CA 95052-8119
Phone	(408) 765-8080
Fax-Back	(800) 525-3019
Web	http://www.intel.com

INTELLIGENT COMPUTER PERIPHERALS

Address	4857 W. VAN BUREN
	PHOENIX, AZ 85043
Phone	(602) 353-0303
Fax	(602) 353-0051
Web	http://www.icp-vortex.com
E-mail	info@vortex.de

INTELLIGENT DATA SYSTEM

Address	BETHEL ASSEMBLY HALL, 32A-1
	YANGIAE-2DONG, SEOCHO-GU
	SEOUL,
	KOREA, REP OF
Phone	82 2 3460 132
Fax	82 2 529 1077
E-mail	bluesky@hanmesoft.co.kr

INTERLOGIC INDUSTRIES
Address	85 MARCUS DRIVE
	MELVILLE, NY 11747
Phone	(516) 420-8111
Fax	(516) 420-8007

INTERNATIONAL INSTRUMENTATION, INC.
Address	2282 TOWNSGATE ROAD
	WESTLAKE VILLAGE, CA 91361
Phone	(805) 495-7673
Fax	(805) 379-0701

IPC CORPORATION, LTD.
Address	10300 METRIC BLVD.
	AUSTIN, TX 78758
Phone	(512) 339-3500
Fax	(512) 339-7959
Web	http://austin.austin.com.sg/ip

ITT CORPORATION
Address	1300 AVENUE OF THE AMERICAS
	NEW YORK, NY 10019-5490
Phone	(212) 258-1000
Web	http://www.itt.com

J&J TECHNOLOGY, INC.
Address	4F, NO. 3, ALLEY 59, LANE 42, MING CHUAN ROAD
	HSIN TIEN
	TAIPEI,
	TAIWAN, REP OF CHINA
Phone	2 916 1630
Fax	2 917 6757
Web	http://www.jjtech.com
E-mail	jjtech@transend.com.tw

J-BOND COMPUTER SYSTEMS CORPORATION
Address	93 WEST MONTAGUE EXPRESSWAY
	MILPITAS, CA 95035
Phone	(408) 946-9622
Fax	(408) 946-2898
Web	http://www.jbond.com

J-MARK COMPUTER CORPORATION
Address	13111 BROOKS DRIVE
	SUITE A
	BALDWIN PARK, CA 91706

Phone	(818) 814-9472
Fax	(818) 960-5937
Web	http://www.j-mark.com
E-mail	j-mark@j-mark.com

JAMECO ELECTRONIC COMPONENTS

Address	1355 SHOREWAY ROAD BELMONT, CA 94002
Phone	(415) 592-8097
Fax	(415) 592-2503
Toll Free	(800) 831-4242
BBS	(415) 637-9025
Web	http://www.jameco.com
E-mail	tech@jameco.com

JAMICON CORPORATION

Address	1210 JOHN REED COURT CITY OF INDUSTRY, CA 91745
Phone	(626) 333-9168
Fax	(626) 330-8243
Web	http://www.jamicon.com
E-mail	jamicon@jamicon.com

JATON CORPORATION

Address	556 SOUTH MILPITAS BLVD. MILPITAS, CA 95035
Phone	(408) 942-9888
Fax	(408) 942-6699
BBS	(408) 263-8529
Web	http://www.jaton.com

JC INFORMATION SYSTEMS CORPORATION

Address	4487 TECHNOLOGY DRIVE FREMONT, CA 94538
Phone	(510) 659-8440
Fax	(510) 659-8449
Web	http://www.jcis.com
E-mail	info@jcis.com

JETPRO INFOTECH COMPANY, LTD.

Address	6 FLOOR, #43, PAO TSING STREET TAIPEI, TAIWAN, REP OF CHINA
Phone	2 753 3020
Fax	2 767 3847

JPN CORPORATION

Address	48006 FREMONT BLVD. FREMONT, CA 94538
Phone	(510) 770-3990
Fax	(510) 770-3994
BBS	(510) 226-0632

JUKO LABORATORIES, LTD.

Address	UNIT B8, 6/F, BLK. B, HOPETITE IND. CENTRE 3-5 WANG TAI ROAD KOWLOON BAY, HONG KONG
Phone	2 953 0300
Fax	2 953 0363

KINGSTON TECHNOLOGY CORPORATION

Address	17600 NEWHOPE STREET FOUNTAIN VALLEY, CA 92708
Phone	(714) 435-2600
Fax	(714) 438-2699
Toll Free	(800) 435-2620
BBS	(714) 435-2636
Fax-Back	(714) 435-2677
Web	http://www.kingston.com

KOUWELL ELECTRONIC CORPORATION

Address	7F, NO. 99, NAN KANG ROAD, SEC. 3 TAIPEI, TAIWAN, REP OF CHINA
Phone	2 783 1166
Fax	2 783 5500
Web	http://www.kouwell.com.tw

L & K MICRO SUPPLY, INC.

Address	711 CHARCOT AVENUE SAN JOSE, CA 95131
Phone	(408) 954-0640
Fax	(408) 954-0646
Web	http://www.lk-micro.com

LASER COMPUTER, INC.

Address	ENERGIEWEG 32 2382 NK ZOETERWOUDE, BELGIUM
Phone	71 410 801

LEADING EDGE PRODUCTS, INC.
Address	14 BRENT DRIVE
	HUDSON, MA 01749
Phone	(508) 562-3322
Fax	(508) 568-3618

LION COMPUTERS, INC.
Address	1001 S. LAWSON STREET
	CITY OF INDUSTRY, CA 91748
Phone	(818) 935-0200
Fax	(818) 935-0202
Web	http://www.likom.com.my

LONGBAR DEVELOPMENT LIMITED
Address	UNIT 15, 7/F, VANTA INDUSTRIAL CENTRE
	21-23 TAI LIN PAI ROAD,
	KWAI CHUNG, N.T.,
	HONG KONG
Phone	2 485 1178
Fax	2 485 1323
Web	http://www.longbar.com
E-mail	longbar@asiansources.com

M TECHNOLOGY, INC.
Address	1931 HARTOG DRIVE
	SAN JOSE, CA 95131
Phone	(408) 441-8818
Fax	(408) 441-8878
Web	http://www.mtiusa.com

MAGITRONICS
Address	10 HUB DRIVE
	MELVILLE, NJ 11747
Web	http://www.magitronic.com

MAGNAVOX
Address	1 PHILLIPS DRIVE
	KNOXVILLE, TN 37914
Phone	(615) 475-8869
Toll Free	(800) 851-8885
Web	http://www.magnavox.com

MAGUS DATA TECHNOLOGY, INC.
Address	3980 FOURTEENTH AVE., NO. 1-3
	MARKHAM, ONTARIO, L3R 0B1
	CANADA

Phone	(905) 513-0823
Fax	(905) 513-0822
BBS	(905) 513-6771

MAXTECH CORPORATION

Address	400 COMMONS WAY ROCKAWAY, NJ 07866
Phone	(201) 586-3008
Fax	(201) 586-3308
Web	http://www.maxcorp.com

MECER CORPORATION

Address	3217 WHIPPLE ROAD UNION CITY, CA 94587
Phone	(510) 475-5730
Fax	(510) 475-0982
Web	http://www.posiflexusa.com

MEGATEL COMPUTER CORPORATION

Address	125 WENDELL AVENUE WESTON, ONTARIO, M9N 3K9 CANADA
Phone	(416) 245-2953
Fax	(416) 245-6505
Web	http://www.megatel.ca

MEMOREX TELEX CORPORATION

Address	545 E. JOHN CARPENTER FREEWAY SUITE 200 IRVING, TX 75062
Phone	(972) 444-3500
Toll Free	(800) 980-6767

MICRO COMPUTER SYSTEMS CORPORATION

Address	23-25, WISMA MCS, JALAN JEJAKA 7 TAMAN MALURI CHE KUALA LUMPUR, MALAYSIA

MICRO EQUIPMENT CORPORATION

Address	2900 JONES MILL ROAD NORCROSS, GA 30071
Phone	(770) 447-1726
Fax	(770) 449-6103
Toll Free	(800) 226-8088
Web	http://www.mecworld.com

MICRO EXPRESS, INC.
Address	1811 KAISER NORTH BLVD.
	IRVINE, CA 92714
Phone	(714) 852-1400
Fax	(714) 852-1225
Toll Free	(800) 989-9900
Web	http://www.microexpress.net

MICRO WISE, INC.
Address	48057 FREMONT BLVD.
	FREMONT, CA 94538
Phone	(510) 656-9881
Fax	(510) 656-1996
Web	http://www.wiseland.com

MICRO-STAR INTERNATIONAL CO., LTD.
Address	4059 CLIPPER COURT
	FREMONT, CA 94538
Phone	(510) 623-8818
Fax	(510) 623-8585
Web	http://www.achme.com

MICROMATION TECHNOLOGY, INC.
Address	1350-5 LINCOLN AVENUE
	HOLBROOK, NY 11741
Phone	(516) 588-4159
Fax	(516) 588-0132

MICROMODULE SYSTEMS, INC.
Address	10500-A RIDGEVIEW COURT
	CUPERTINO, CA 95014
Phone	(408) 864-7437
Fax	(408) 864-6174
Toll Free	(888) 4MCM-MMS
Web	http://www.mms.com
E-mail	moreinfo@mms.com

MICRONICS COMPUTERS, INC.
Address	221 WARREN AVENUE
	FREMONT, CA 94539
Phone	(510) 651-2300
Fax	(510) 651-6982
Toll Free	(800) 577-0977
BBS	(510) 651-6837
Fax-Back	(510) 661-3199

Web http://www.micronics.com

MICROWAY, INC.
Address P.O. BOX 79
KINGSTON, MA 02364
Phone (508) 746-7341
Fax (508) 746-4678
Web http://www.microway.com

MINTA TECHNOLOGIES, CO.
Address 1901 ZANKER ROAD
SAN JOSE, CA 95112
Fax (408) 922-5729
Toll Free (800) 722-6335
Web http://www.minta.com

MITAC INTERNATIONAL CORPORATION
Address 3797 SPINNAKER COURT
FREMONT, CA 94538
Phone (510) 656-3333
Fax (510) 440-3777
Toll Free (800) 7561888
Web http://www.mitac.com.tw

MITSUBISHI ELECTRONICS
Address 5665 PLAZA DRIVE
CYPRESS, CA 90630
Phone (800) 843-2515
Fax (714) 236-6425
BBS (714) 236-6286
Fax-Back (714) 236-6453
Web http://www.mitsubishi-display.

MNC INTERNATIONAL, INC.
Address 2817 ANTHONY LANE SOUTH
MINNEAPOLIS, MN 55418-3254
Phone (612) 788-1099
Fax (612) 788-9365

MODULAR CIRCUIT TECHNOLOGY
Web http://www.jdr.com

MONOLITHIC SYSTEMS, INC. (COLORADO MSI)
Address 8150 S. ACKRON STREET
UNIT 402
ENGLEWOOD, CO 80112

Phone	(303) 790-0180
Fax	(303) 790-0182

MOTOROLA, INC.
Address	9442 CAPITAL OF TEXAS HIGHWAY N SUITE 320 AUSTIN, TX 78759
Phone	(512) 345-7655
Fax	(512) 891-8807

MPL
Address	TAEFERNSTRASSE 20, CH-5403 DAETWIL SWITZERLAND
Phone	56 493 3080
Fax	56 493 3020
Web	http://www.mpl.ch
E-mail	info@mpl.ch

MULTI MICRO SYSTEMS, INC.
Address	2124 ZANKER ROAD SAN JOSE, CA 95131
Phone	(408) 437-1555
Web	http://www.multimicrosys.com

MULTI-TECH SYSTEMS, INC.
Address	2205 WOODALE DRIVE MOUNDS VIEW, MN 55112
Phone	(612) 785-3500
Fax	(612) 785-9874
Toll Free	(800) 328-9717
BBS	(612) 785-3702
Fax-Back	(612) 717-5888
Web	http://www.multitech.com

MULTIBEST INDUSTRIAL & MANUFACTURING, INC.
Address	560 DENISON STREET UNIT 2 MARKHAM, ONTARIO, L3R 2M8 CANADA
Phone	(905) 889-0968

MYLEX CORPORATION
Address	34551 ARDENWOOD BLVD. FREMONT, CA 94555-3607
Phone	(510) 796-6100
Fax	(510) 745-7653

Toll Free	(800) 776-9539	
BBS	(510) 793-3491	
Web	http://www.mylex.com	

NCR CORPORATION

Address	1700 SOUTH PATTERSON BLVD. DAYTON, OH 45479
Phone	(513) 445-5000
Toll Free	(800) 225-5627
Web	http://www.ncr.com

NEC TECHNOLOGIES, INC.

Address	8 CORPORATE CENTER DRIVE MELVILLE, NY 11747
Phone	(516) 753-7000
Fax	(516) 753-7434
Toll Free	(800) 338-7549
Web	http://www.nec.com

NETPOWER

Address	545 OAKMEAD PARKWAY SUNNYVALE, CA 94086
Phone	(408) 522-9999
Fax	(408) 720-8558
Toll Free	(800) 801-0900
Web	http://www.netpower.com

NEWTON NET TECHNOLOGY, INC.

Address	6FLOOR, #30, HSIN YANG STREET TAIPEI, TAIWAN, REP OF CHINA
Phone	2 361 0691
Fax	2 371 0083

NEXGEN

Address	P.O. BOX 3453 SUNNYVALE, CA 94088-3453
Phone	(408) 435-0202
Fax	(408) 435-0262
Web	http://www.amd.com

NIAGARA SMD TECHNOLOGY, INC.

Address	136 SKYWAY AVENUE ETOBICOKE, ON M9W 4Y9 CANADA
Phone	(416) 675-2366

Fax	(416) 675-4242
Web	http://www.niagaratech.com

NORTHGATE COMPUTER SYSTEMS, INC.
Address	6840 HAVENHURST AVENUE
	VAN NUIS, CA 91406
Toll Free	(800) 446-5037
Web	http://www.northgate.net

NOVACOR, INC.
Address	1590 OAKLAND ROAD
	SUITE B-208
	SAN JOSE, CA 95131
Phone	(408) 441-6500
Fax	(408) 441-6811
Toll Free	(800) 486-6682
Web	http://www.nova.com

OCEAN INFORMATION SYSTEMS, INC.
Address	688 ARROW GRAND CIRLCE
	COVINA, CA 91722
Phone	(818) 339-8888
Fax	(818) 859-7668
Toll Free	(818) 339-8888
BBS	(818) 859-7639
Web	http://www.ocean-usa.com
E-mail	Webmaster@ocean-usa.com

OLIVETTI
Address	22425 E. APPLEWAY AVENUE
	LIBERTY LAKE, WA 99019-9534
Phone	(509) 927-5600
Fax	(509) 927-5774
Toll Free	(800) 255-4319
Web	http://www.olivetti.com

ORCHID TECHNOLOGY
Address	221 WARREN AVENUE
	FREMONT, CA 94539
Phone	(510) 683-0300
Fax	(510) 490-9312
BBS	(510) 683-0555
Web	http://www.orchid.com

PACKARD BELL
Address	5701 LINDERO CANYON ROAD

	BUILDING 3
	WEST LAKE VILLIAGE, CA 91362
Phone	(818) 865-1555
Fax	(818) 865-0379
Toll Free	(800) 733-4411
BBS	(801) 250-1600
Web	http://www.packardbell.com
E-mail	support@packardbell.com

PC & C RESEARCH CORPORATION

Address	5251 VERDUGO WAY #J
	CAMARILLO, CA 93012
Phone	(805) 484-1685
Fax	(805) 987-8088
Toll Free	(800) 843-1239

PC BRAND

Toll Free	(800) 541-8324
Web	http://sierrainc.com/pcbrand.h

PC WARE INTERNATIONAL, INC.

Address	4372 10TH STREET
	LONG ISLAND CITY, NY 11101
Phone	(718) 706-7770
Fax	(718) 706-7864
Toll Free	(800) 572-9273
Web	http://pcware.com

PEACOCK AG

Address	GRAF-ZEPPELIN-STRASSE 14
	33181 WUNNENBERG,
	GERMANY
Phone	295 7790
Fax	295 779 9291
Web	http://www.peacock.de
E-mail	info@peacock.de

PHILIPS CONSUMER ELECTRONICS, CO.

Address	601 MILNER AVENUE
	SCARBOROUGH, ON M1B 1M8
	CANADA
Phone	(416) 754-6245
Toll Free	(800) 387-0564
Web	http://www.philips.com

PINE TECHNOLOGY
Address	777 NEW DURHAM ROAD
	EDISON, NJ 08817
Phone	(908) 321-3700
Fax	(908) 321-3636
Web	http://www.pinegroup.com

PIONEX TECHNOLOGIES, INC.
Address	3 RIVERVIEW DRIVE
	SOMERSET, NJ 08873
Phone	(908) 356-9299
Fax	(908) 563-2661
Toll Free	(800) 313-1995
BBS	(908) 563-9150
Web	http://www.pionex.com
E-mail	pnxtech@pionex.com

POLOTEC, INC.
Address	2374 WALSH AVENUE
	SANTA CLARA, CA 95051
Phone	(408) 986-8417
Fax	(408) 986-8721
Web	http://www.polotec.com

POSITIVE CORPORATION
Phone	(414) 638-1851

POWERTECH ELECTRONICS, INC.
Address	5101 COMMERCE DRIVE
	BALDWIN PARK, CA 91706
Phone	(818) 337-6860
Fax	(818) 960-1690

PRECISION AMERICA, INC.
Address	262 OLD NEW BRUNSWICK ROAD
	PISCATAWAY, NJ 08854
Phone	(908) 981-1155
Fax	(908) 981-1559
Web	http://www.pai4pc.com

PROGEN TECHNOLOGY, INC.
Address	15501 REDHILL AVENUE
	TUSTIN, CA 92780
Phone	(714) 566-9200
Fax	(714) 566-9201
Toll Free	(800) PROGENT

BBS	(714) 549-9564
Web	http://www.progen.com
E-mail	progen@ix.netcom.com

PROLINK COMPUTER, INC.

Address	15336 EAST VALLEY BLVD. CITY OF INDUSTRY, CA 91746
Phone	(818) 369-3833
Fax	(818) 369-4883
Web	http://www.prolink-usa.com

PURETEK INDUSTRIAL CO., LTD.

Address	44110 OLD WARM SPRINGS BLVD FREMONT, CA 94538
Phone	(510) 656-8083
Fax	(510) 656-8085
Web	http://www.puretek.com

QDI COMPUTER, INC.

Address	11552 EAST WASHINGTON BLVD., UNIT D WHITTIER, CA 90606
Phone	(310) 908-1029
Fax	(310) 908-1033
Web	http://www.qdigrp.com

QDI COMPUTER, INC.

Address	1795A CIRTLAND COURT ADDISON, IL 60101
Phone	(708) 261-0018
Fax-Back	(708) 261-0016

QUICK TECHNOLOGY, INC.

Address	1542 EDINGER AVENUE, #B TUSTIN, CA 92680
Phone	(714) 258-4500
Fax	(714) 258-4508
Toll Free	(800) 950-8999
Web	http://www.iwillusa.com

QUICKPATH SYSTEMS, INC.

Address	46723 FREMONT BLVD. FREMONT, CA 94538
Phone	(510) 440-7288
Fax	(510) 440-7289
Toll Free	(800) 995-8828
BBS	(510) 440-7284

Web	http://www.quickpath.com
E-mail	qpinfo@quickpath.com

RADISYS CORPORATION
Address	5445 NE DAWSON CREEK DRIVE
	HILLSBORO, OR 97124
Phone	(503) 615-1100
Fax	(503) 615-1150
Toll Free	(800) 950-0044
Web	http://www.radisys.com

RECTRON ELECTRONIC ENTERPRISES, INC.
Address	1315 JOHN REED COURT
	INDUSTRY, CA 91745
Phone	(818) 333-3802
Fax	(818) 330-6296
Toll Free	(800) 883-7334

RELIALOGIC CORPORATION PRIVATE, LTD.
Address	48006 FREMONT BLVD.
	FREMONT, CA 94538
Phone	(510) 770-3990
Fax	(510) 770-3994
Toll Free	(800) 998-3966
BBS	(510) 226-0632
Web	http://www.paradisemmp.com
E-mail	rlogic@aol.com

REPLY CORPORATION
Address	4435 FORTRAN DRIVE
	SAN JOSE, CA 95134
Phone	(408) 942-4804
Fax	(408) 942-4897
Toll Free	(800) 955-5295
Web	http://www.reply.com

ROBOTECH, INC.
Address	43 EAST 7200 SOUTH
	MIDVALE, UT 84047
Phone	(801) 565-0645
Fax	(801) 565-0680
Toll Free	(800) 533-0633
BBS	(801) 565-0645
Fax-Back	(801) 553-0633-157
Web	http://www.robotechusa.com

S3, INC.
Address	PO BOX 58058
	SANTA CLARA, CA 95052-8058
Phone	(408) 980-5400
Web	http://www.s3.com

SAMSUNG ELECTRONICS, INC.
Address	105 CHALLENGER BLVD.
	RIDGEFIELD PARK, NJ 07660
Phone	(201) 229-7000
Fax	(201) 229-4110
Toll Free	(800) 446-0262
BBS	(201) 691-6238
Fax-Back	(201) 229-4053
Web	http://www.sosimple.com

SANYO ELECTRIC CO., LTD.
Address	52 7 25, EDOBOR, NISHI KU OSAKA,
	550 OSAKA,
	JAPAN
Phone	64 432 949
Fax	64 432 849
Web	http://www.sanyo.co.jp

SCI SYSTEMS, INC.
Address	8600 SOUTH MEMORIAL PARKWAY
	P.O. BOX 1000
	HUNTSVILLE, AL 35807
Phone	(205) 882-4569
Fax	(205) 882-4652
Web	http://www.asp-vme.com
E-mail	VMEbus@scismail.sci.com

SEANIX TECHNOLOGY, INC.
Address	6651 ELMBRIDGE WAY
	SUITE 150
	RICHMOND, B. V7C 4N1
	CANADA
Phone	(604) 273-3692
Fax	(604) 273-0768
Toll Free	(800) 663-5656
BBS	(604) 278-7418
Web	http://www.seanix.com

SEE-THRU DATA SYSTEMS, LTD.
Address	8TH FLOOR, ABERDEEN IND. BUILDING,234 ABERDEEN MAI
	ABERDEEN,
	HONG KONG
Phone	2 873 3883
Fax	2 873 3088
Web	http://www.seethru.com

SHUTTLE COMPUTER INTERNATIONAL, INC.
Address	1161 CADILLAC COURT
	MILPITAS, CA 95035-3055
Phone	(408) 945-1480
Fax	(408) 945-1481
BBS	(408) 956-5712
Web	http://www.shuttlela.com

SIEMENS NIXDORF INFORMATIONSSYSTEME AG
Address	DYBENDALSVAENGET 3
	2630 TASTRUP,
	DENMARK
Phone	44 774 600
Fax	44 774 610

SIIG, INC.
Address	6078 STEWART AVENUE
	FREMONT, CA 94538
Phone	(510) 657-8688
Fax	(510) 657-5962
BBS	(510) 353-7532
Web	http://www.siig.com

SILICON STAR INTERNATIONAL, INC.
Address	3F-7, NO. 79, SEC. 1, HSIN TAI WU ROAD
	HSI-CHI
	TAIPEI HSIEN,
	TAIWAN, REP OF CHINA
Phone	2 698 1888
Fax	2 698 1811
Web	http://www.abit.com.tw

SILICON VALLEY TECHNOLOGY
Address	1435 MCCANDLESS DRIVE
	MILPITAS, CA 95035
Phone	(408) 934-8444
Fax	(408) 934-8459

Web	http://www.mediavis.com

SIMA TECHNOLOGY CO., LTD.
Address	2F, NO. 294, DI HWA ST., SEC. 1 TAIPEI, TAIWAN, REP OF CHINA
Phone	2 557 8881
Fax	2 557 8880

SKYWELL TECHNOLOGY CORPORATION, LTD.
Address	7F, NO. 47, SEC. 2, CHENG TEH ROAD TAIPEI, TAIWAN, REP OF CHINA
Phone	2 559 9250
Fax	2 559 0349
Web	http://www.skywell.com.tw
E-mail	service@mail.skywell.com.tw

SMART D&M TECHNOLOGY CO., LTD.
Address	4FL., NO. 209 CHUNG YANG ROAD NAN KANG DISTRICT TAIPEI, TAIWAN, REP OF CHINA
Phone	2 651 4750
Fax	2 651 0428

SOLECTEK COMPUTER SUPPLY, INC.
Address	6370 NANCY RIDGE DRIVE SUITE 109 SAN DIEGO, CA 92121-3212
Phone	(619) 450-1220
Fax	(619) 457-2681
Toll Free	(800) 437-1518
Web	http://www.solectek.com

SOLTEK COMPUTER, INC.
Address	7F., #306-3 TA-TUNG RD., SEC. 1 HSI-CHIH TAIPEI HSIEN, TAIWAN, REP OF CHINA
Phone	2 698 2560
Fax	2 698 2561
Web	http://www.soltek.com.tw

SOYO COMPUTER CO., LTD.
Address	1209 JOHN REED COURT

	CITY OF INDUSTRY, CA 91745
Phone	(818) 330-1712
Fax	(818) 968-4161
Web	http://www.soyo.de

SPRING CIRCLE COMPUTER, INC.

Address	METAALWEG 25 6551 AC
	WEURT,
	NETHERLANDS
Phone	24 350 0640
Fax	24 350 0429

SPRINT MANUFACTURING CORPORATION

Address	12160 MORA DRIVE
	SANTA FE SPRINGS, CA 90670
Phone	(310) 941-2118

SPRITE, INC.

Address	1120 STEWART COURT
	SUITE G
	SUNNYVALE, CA 94086
Phone	(408) 773-8888
Fax	(408) 733-9999

SUK JUNG ELECTRONIC CO., LTD.

Address	YONGSAN-KU, 6F., SEOBUK B/D, 6-1
	SHINKEYE-DONG
	SEOUL,
	KOREA, REP OF
Phone	2 704 7211
Fax	2 704 7214

SUPER MICRO

Address	2178 PARAGON DRIVE
	SAN JOSE, CA 95131
Phone	(408) 451-1118
Fax	(408) 451-1110
BBS	(408) 451-1114
Web	http://www.supermicro.com
E-mail	supermicro_computer@msn.com

TAKEN CORPORATION

Address	5F, NO. 30, LANE 80, NAN KANG ROAD, SEC. 3
	TAIPEI,
	TAIWAN, REP OF CHINA
Phone	2 788 6071

Fax	2 788 6073
Web	http://www.taken.com.tw

TANDON CORPORATION
Phone	(414) 638-1851
Fax	(414) 638-1852
Web	http://www.sierrainc.com

TANDY/RADIO SHACK
Address	1500 ONE TANDY CENTER FORT WORTH, TX 76102
Phone	(817) 390-3011
Toll Free	(800) THE-SHACK
Fax-Back	(800) 323-6586
Web	http://www.tandy.com

TECHMEDIA COMPUTER SYSTEMS CORPORATION
Address	7345 ORANGEWOOD AVENUE GARDEN GROVE, CA 92841
Phone	(714) 379-6677
Fax	(714) 379-6688
Toll Free	(800) 379-0077
Web	http://www.techmedia.net

TECHNOLAND, INC.
Address	1050 STEWART DR. SUNNYVALE, CA 94086
Phone	(408) 992-0888
Fax	(408) 992-0808
Toll Free	(800) 292-4500
Web	http://www.technoland.com
E-mail	info@technoland.com

TEKNOR INDUSTRIAL COMPUTERS, INC.
Address	7900 GLADES ROAD BOCA RATON, FL 33434
Phone	(561) 883-6191
Fax	(561) 883-6690
Toll Free	(800) 387-4222
Web	http://www.teknor.com
E-mail	support@teknor.com

TEKRAM TECHNOLOGY CO., LTD.
Address	11500 METRIC BLVD. SUITE 190 AUSTIN, TX 78758

Phone	(512) 833-6550
Fax	(512) 833-7276
BBS	(512) 833-7985
Web	http://www.tekram.com
E-mail	sales@tekram.com.tw

TELEVIDEO SYSTEMS, INC.

Address	2345 HARRIS WAY SAN JOSE, CA 95131
Phone	(408) 954-8333
Fax	(408) 954-0622
Toll Free	(800) 835-3228
BBS	(408) 954-8231
Web	http://www.televideoinc.com

TEXAS INSTRUMENTS

Address	12201 SOUTHWEST FREEWAY STAFFORD, TX 77477
Phone	(713) 274-3388
Toll Free	(800) TI-TEXAS
Web	http://www.ti.com
E-mail	odin@msg.ti.com

TMC RESEARCH CORPORATION

Address	631 SOUTH MILPITAS BLVD. MILPITAS, CA 95035
Phone	(408) 262-0888
Fax	(408) 262-1082
BBS	(408) 946-6932
Web	http://www.mycomp-tmc.com

TOP MICROSYSTEMS, INC.

Address	3320 VICTOR COURT SANTA CLARA, CA 95054
Phone	(408) 980-9813
Fax	(408) 980-8626
Toll Free	(800) 827-8721

TORONTO MICROELECTRONICS, INC.

Address	5149 BRADCO BLVD. MISSISSAUGA, ON L4W 2A6 CANADA
Phone	(905) 625-3203
Fax	(905) 625-3717
Web	http://www.tme-inc.com

E-mail	sales@tme-inc.com

TOSHIBA
Address	9740 IRVINE BLVD. PO BOX 19724 IRVINE, CA 92713
Phone	(714) 455-0407
Fax	(714) 583-3140
Toll Free	(800) 999-4273
BBS	(714) 837-8864
Fax-Back	(714) 455-0407
Web	http://www.toshiba.com

TRENTON TECHNOLOGY, INC.
Address	2350 CENTENNIAL DRIVE GAINESVILLE, GA 30504
Phone	(770) 287-3100
Fax	(770) 287-3150
Toll Free	(800) 875-6031
Web	http://www.trentonprocessors.com
E-mail	sales@trentonprocessors.com

TROGON NOTEBOOK COMPUTER
Address	2531 NINA STREET PASADENA, CA 91107
Phone	(818) 792-0568
Fax	(818) 568-1515
Web	http://www.trogoncomputer.com

TULIP COMPUTERS
Address	HAMBAKENWETERING 2 5231 DC'S-HERTOGENBS, NETHERLANDS
Phone	73 640 5333
Fax	73 642 1915
Web	http://www.tulip.nl

TWINHEAD INTERNATIONAL CORPORATION
Address	1537 CENTER POINT DRIVE MILPITAS, CA 95035
Phone	(408) 945-0808
Fax	(408) 945-1080
Toll Free	(800) 545-8946
BBS	(408) 945-8334
Web	http://www.twinhead.com

TYAN COMPUTER CORPORATION
- **Address**: 1753 S MAIN STREET, MILPITAS, CA 95035
- **Phone**: (408) 956-8000
- **Fax**: (408) 956-8044
- **BBS**: (408) 956-8171
- **Web**: http://www.tyan.com

UNIVERSAL SCIENTIFIC INDUSTRIES CO., LTD.
- **Address**: 4107 SPICEWOOD SPRINGS ROAD, SUITE 206, AUSTIN, TX 78759
- **Phone**: (512) 502-8706
- **Fax**: (512) 502-8707

VISION TECHNOLOGIES
- **Address**: 770 SYCAMORE, NO. J450, VISTA, CA 92083
- **Phone**: (619) 603-0604
- **Fax**: (619) 603-9143
- **Toll Free**: (800) 808-4746

VISIONEX
- **Address**: 711 CHARCOT AVENUE, SAN JOSE, CA 95131
- **Phone**: (408) 954-0640
- **Fax**: (408) 954-0646

VTECH INDUSTRIES, INC.
- **Address**: 800 CHURCH STREET, LAKE ZURICH, IL 60047
- **Phone**: (708) 215-9806
- **Web**: http://www.vtechinc.com

WESTERN DIGITAL CORPORATION
- **Address**: 8105 IRVINE CENTER DRIVE, IRVINE, CA 92718
- **Phone**: (714) 932-5000
- **Fax**: (714) 932-6294
- **Toll Free**: (800) 832-4778
- **BBS**: (714) 753-1234
- **Fax-Back**: (714) 932-4300
- **Web**: http://www.wdc.com

WIN LAN ENTERPRISE CO., LTD.
- **Address**: 34, MINTSU ROAD

	TAMSHUI TOWN
	TAIPEI HSIEN,
	TAIWAN, REP OF CHINA
Phone	2 808 6278
Fax	2 809 3955
E-mail	winlan38@ms4.hinet.net

WINCAL TECHNOLOGY CORPORATION

Address	10012 NORWALK BLVD,
	SUITE 140
	SANTA FE SPRINGS, CA 90670
Phone	(310) 903-1440
Fax	(310) 903-1439

WISEWARE COMPUTER, INC.

Phone	(818) 333-8088

WYSE TECHNOLOGY, INC.

Address	3471 NORTH FIRST STREET
	SAN JOSE, CA 95134-1803
Phone	(408) 473-1200
Fax	(408) 473-2788
Toll Free	(800) 438-9973
BBS	(408) 922-4400
Fax-Back	(800) 800-9973
Web	http://www.wyse.com

XINETRON, INC.

Address	3022 SCOTT BLVD.
	SANTA CLARA, CA 95054
Phone	(408) 727-5509
Fax	(408) 727-6499
Toll Free	(800) 345-4415
Web	http://www.xinetron.com

YOUNG MICRO SYSTEMS, INC.

Web	http://www.youngmicro.com

YOUTH KEEP ENTERPRISES, LTD.

Address	P. O. BOX 67 265
	TAIPEI,
	TAIWAN, REP OF CHINA
Phone	2 505 6350

ZENITH DATA SYSTEMS

Address	LINKE WIENZEILE 192

	1150 WIEN,
	AUSTRIA
Phone	1 853 641 1211
Fax	1 853 641 3317
Web	http://www.zds-europe.com

ZEOS INTERNATIONAL, LTD.

Address	900 EAST KARCHER ROAD
	NAMPA, ID 83687
Fax	(208) 893-3424
Toll Free	(800) 438-3343
Fax-Back	(800) 845-2341
Web	http://www.micron.com
E-mail	support@zeos.com

ZETA INDUSTRIAL CO., LTD.

Address	11 FLOOR, #140, SECTION 2, ROOSEVELT ROAD
	TAIPEI,
	TAIWAN, REP OF CHINA
Phone	2 367 5480
Fax	2 367 1536

ZF MICROSYSTEMS, INC.

Address	1052 ELWELL COURT
	PALO ALTO, CA 94303
Phone	(415) 965-3800
Fax	(415) 965-4050
Web	http://www.zfmicro.com

ZIDA TECHNOLOGIES, LTD.

Address	UNIT 2 & 4, 10 FL, BLK A, 10/F., GOODVIEW IND. CEN
	FIN FAT STREET, TMTL 213, TUEN MUN
	NEW TERRITORIES,
	HONG KONG
Phone	2 453 3000
Fax	2 456 0717
Web	http://www.zida.com
E-mail	zidasale@zida.com

Manufacturer Index

Abit Computer
 Corporation
  contact information, 387
  motherboard settings,
   51-53
Acer, Inc., 387
Achme Computer,
 Inc., 388
Acquire Computer
 Systems, Inc., 388
Acqutek Corporation, 388
Action Instruments, 388
Adaptive Solutions,
 Inc., 388
Advanced Computer
 Technology, Ltd., 388
Advanced Integration
 Research, Inc.
  contact information, 389
  motherboard settings,
   54-59
Advanced Logic
 Research, Inc., 389
Alaris, Inc., 389
Alpha Microsystems, 389
Amdek Corporation, 389
American Digicom
 Corporation, 389
American Digital Data
 Associates, 390
American Megatrends,
 Inc.
  contact information, 390
  motherboard settings,
   60-90
American Predator
 Corporation, 390

American Research
 Corporation, 390
Ampro Computers,
 Inc., 390
Amptron International,
 Inc., 390
AMS, Inc., 391
Ansel Communications,
 Inc., 391
Antec, Inc., 391
Apricot Computers
 Limited, 391
Aquarius Systems,
 Inc., 391
Area Electronics Systems,
 Inc., 391
Arima Computer
 Corporation, 392
Arnet Corporation, 392
Arnos Instruments &
 Computer Systems,
 Inc., 392
Artek Computer Systems,
 Inc., 392
Asia Data, Inc., 392
Asia Direct Corporation,
 392
Asicom, 392
Aspen Systems, Inc., 393
AST Research, Inc.
  contact information, 393
  motherboard settings,
   91-98
Asus Computer
 International, 393
  motherboard settings,
   99-119

AT&T, Inc., 393
ATC/Unitron Computers
 & Computer Parts, 393
Aten Research, Inc., 393
A-Trend Technology
 Corporation, 387
Atronics International,
 Inc., 394
Aurora Impex
 Corporation, 394
Austin Computer
 Systems, 394
Auva Computer, Inc., 394
Axik Computer, Inc., 394
Badger Computers, 395
BCM Advanced
 Research, Inc., 395
BEC Computer
 Enterprise, 395
BEK-Tronic Technology,
 Inc., 395
Bethel Electronics
 International, Inc., 395
Biostar Microtech
 International
 Corporation, 395
BJMT Technology
 Corporation, 396
Buffalo Products,
 Inc., 396
CAF Technology, Inc.,
 396
California Graphics &
 Peripherals, Inc., 396
Cardinal Technologies,
 Inc., 396

Chaintech Computer Company, Ltd., 396
Chicony, Inc., 397
CMS Enhancements, Inc., 397
Commodore Business Machines, Inc., 397
Compaq Computer Corporation
    contact information, 397
    motherboard settings, 120-138
Compulink Research, Inc., 397
Computrend Systems, Inc., 397
Concord Office Automation Industrial (HK), Ltd., 398
Core International, Inc., 398
CSS Laboratories, Inc., 398
CT Continental Corporation, 398
Cyble Technology, Inc., 398
Dash Computer, Inc., 398
Dataexpert Corporation, 399
Datavan International Corporation, 399
Dayton Micro, 399
DD & TT Enterprise USA Co., 399
Decision Computer International Co., Ltd., 399
Dell Computer Corporation
    contact information, 400
    motherboard settings, 139-176
Densitron Corporation, 400
Destiny Computers, Inc., 400
Diamond Flower, Inc., 400

Diamond Multimedia Systems, Inc., 400
Digital Equipment Corporation
    contact information, 401
    motherboard settings, 177-191
Diversified Technology, 401
DTK Computer, Inc., 401
Dunnet International Trading Company BV, 401
Dyna Micro, Inc., 401
EDOM International Corporation, 401
EFA Corporation, 402
Elisa Technology, Inc., 402
Elitegroup Computer Systems, Inc., 402
EMPAC International, 402
Epson, Inc., 402
ETC Computer, Inc., 402
ETEQ Microsystems, Inc., 403
Eurone (HK) Co., Ltd., 403
Everex Systems, Inc., 403
Evergreen Systems, Inc., 403
Fair Friend Enterprise Company, Ltd., 403
Famous Technology Co., Ltd., 403
First International Computer, Inc.
    contact information, 404
    motherboard settings, 192-195
Flash Tech, Inc., 404
Flytech Group International, 404
Fong Kai Industrial Co., 404
Forcom Technology Corporation, 404

Forex Computer Corporation, 405
Fortress Systems International, 405
Free Computer Technology, Inc., 405
Frontier Industrial, Inc., 405
Gateway 2000, 405
GCH Systems, Inc., 405
Gemlight Computer Ltd., 405
Gemlight Computer, Ltd., 196-198
Genesys ATE, Inc., 406
Genoa Systems Corporation, 406
GESPAC, 406
Giga-Byte Technology Co., Ltd., 406
Giga-Byte Technology Co., Ltd., 199-215
GMX, Inc., 406
Goldstar Electronics International, Inc., 407
GVC Technologies, Inc., 407
Hauppauge Computer Works, Inc., 407
Hertz Computers, 407
Hewlett-Packard Company, 407
    motherboard settings, 216-221
Hokkins Systemation, Inc., 407
Hornet Technology Corporation, 408
Hyundai Electronics, Inc., 408
IBM Corporation
    contact information, 408
    motherboard settings, 222-268
I-Bus, 408
ICL, 408
Industrial Computer Source, 408

Infomatic Power Systems Corporation (IPX), 409
Inside Technology A/S, 409
Intel Corporation
   contact information, 409
   motherboard settings, 269-309
Intelligent Computer Peripherals, 409
Intelligent Data System, 409
Interlogic Industries, 410
International Instrumentation, Inc., 410
IPC Corporation, Ltd.
   contact information, 410
   motherboard settings, 310-312
IPX (Infomatic Power Systems Corporation), 409
ITT Corporation, 410
J&J Technology, Inc., 410
Jameco Electronic Components, 411
Jamicon Corporation, 411
Jaton Corporation, 411
J-Bond Computer Systems Corporation, 410
JC Information Systems Corporation, 411
Jetpro Infotech Company, Ltd., 411
J-Mark Computer Corporation, 410
JPN Corporation, 412
Juko Laboratories, Ltd., 412
Kingston Technology Corporation, 412
Kouwell Electronic Corporation, 412

L & K Micro Supply, Inc., 412
Laser Computer, Inc., 412
Leading Edge Products, Inc., 413
Lion Computers, Inc., 413
Longvar Development Limited, 413
M Technology, Inc., 413
Magitronics, 413
Magnavox, 413
Magus Data Technology, Inc., 413
Maxtech Corporation, 414
Mecer Corporation, 414
Megatel Computer Corporation, 414
Memorex Telex Corporation, 414
Micro Computer Systems Corporation, 414
Micro Equipment Corporation, 414
Micro Express, Inc., 415
Micro Wise, Inc., 415
Micromation Technology, Inc., 415
Micromodule Systems, Inc., 415
Micronics Computers, Inc.
   contact information, 415
   motherboard settings, 313-345
Micro-Star International Co., Ltd.
   contact information, 415
   motherboard settings, 346-349
Microway, Inc., 416
Minta Technologies, Co., 416
Mitac International Corporation, 416
Mitsubishi Electronics, 416

MNC International, Inc., 416
Modular Circuit Technology, 416
Monolithic Systems, Inc., 416
Motorola, Inc., 417
MPL, 417
Multi Micro Systems, Inc., 417
Multibest Industrial & Manufacturing, Inc., 417
Multi-Tech Systems, Inc., 417
Mylex Corporation, 417
NCR Corporation, 418
NEC Technologies, Inc., 418
Netpower, 418
Newton Net Technology, Inc., 418
Nexgen, 418
Niagara SMD Technology, Inc., 418
Northgate Computer Systems, Inc., 419
Novacor, Inc., 419
Ocean Information Systems, Inc., 419
Olivetti, 419
Orchid Technology, 419
Packard Bell
   contact information, 419
   motherboard settings, 350-355
PC & C Research Corporation, 420
PC Brand, 420
PC Ware International, Inc., 420
Peacock AG, 420
Philips Consumer Electronics, Co., 420
Pine Technology, 421
Pionex Technologies, Inc., 421
Polotec, Inc., 421
Positive Corporation, 421

Powertech Electronics, Inc., 421
Precision America, Inc., 421
Progen Technology, Inc., 421
Prolink Computer, Inc., 422
Puretek Industrial Co., Ltd., 422
QDI Computer, Inc., 422
Quick Technology, Inc., 422
Quickpath Systems, Inc., 422
Radisys Corporation, 423
Realialogic Corporation Private, Ltd., 423
Rectron Electronic Enterprises, Inc., 423
Reply Corporation, 423
Robotech, Inc., 423
S3, Inc., 424
Samsung Electronics, Inc., 424
Sanyo Electric Co., Ltd., 424
SCI Systems, Inc., 424
Seanix Technology, Inc., 424
See-Thru Data Systems, Ltd., 425
Shuttle Computer International, Inc., 356-358, 425
Siemens Nixdorf Informations systeme AG
   contact information, 425
   motherboard settings, 359-360
SIIG, Inc., 425
Silicon Star International, Inc.
   contact information, 425
   motherboard settings, 361-364

Silicon Valley Technology, 425
Sima Technology Co., Ltd., 426
Skywell Technology Corporation, Ltd., 426
Smart D&M Technology Co., Ltd., 426
Solectek Computer Supply, Inc., 426
Soltek Computer, Inc., 426
Soyo Computer Co., Ltd.
   contact information, 426
   motherboard settings, 365-371
Spring Circle Computer, Inc., 427
Sprint Manufacturing Corporation, 427
Sprite, Inc., 427
Suk Jung Electronic Co., Ltd., 427
Super Micro, 372-374, 427
Taken Corporation, 427
Tandon Corporation, 428
Tandy/Radio Shack, 428
Techmedia Computer Systems Corporation, 428
Technoland, Inc., 428
Teknor Industrial Computers, Inc., 428
Tekram Technology Co., Ltd., 428
Televideo Systems, Inc., 429
Texas Instruments, 429
TMC Research Corporation, 429
Top Microsystems, Inc., 429
Toronto Microelectronics, Inc., 429
Toshiba, 430

Trenton Technology, Inc., 430
Trogon Notebook Computer, 430
Tulip Computers, 430
Twinhead International Corporation, 430
Tyan Computer Corporation
   contact information, 431
   motherboard settings, 375-381
Universal Scientific Industries Co., Ltd., 431
Vision Technologies, 431
Visionex, 431
Vtech Industries, Inc., 431
Western digital Corporation, 431
Win Lan Enterprise Co., Ltd., 431
Wincal Technology Corporation, 432
Wiseware Computer, Inc., 432
Wyse Technology, Inc., 432
Xinetron, Inc., 432
Young Micro Systems, Inc., 432
Youth Keep Enterprises, Ltd., 432
Zenith Data Systems, 432
Zeos International, Ltd., 382-386, 433
Zeta Industrial Co., Ltd., 433
ZF Microsystems, Inc., 433
Zida Technologies, Ltd., 433
Zxiom Technology, Inc., 394

Index

Symbols

6FB motherboard (Soyo Computer Co., Ltd.), 365-367

A

Advanced/ATX motherboard (Intel Corporation), 269-271
Advanced/ML motherboard (Intel Corporation), 272-274
Advanced/MN (Morrisson) motherboard (Intel Corporation), 275-277
AG430HX motherboard (Intel Corporation), 278-280
Altserver/CS motherboard (Intel Corporation), 281-284
AMI BIOS, 6-9
  strings, 7-9
AN6 motherboard (Silicon Star International, Inc.), 361-364
Apollo III motherboard (American Megatrends, Inc.), 60-62
Aptiva motherboards
  2134/2176 A-1 motherboard (IBM Corporation), 222-225
  2136 motherboard (IBM Corporation), 226-229
  2144/2168 type H-2/I-2 motherboard (IBM Corporation), 230-232
  2159 motherboard (IBM Corporation), 233-235
  2168 motherboard (IBM Corporation), 236-238
  M30/M31/M40/M41/M50/M53/M71 motherboard (IBM Corporation), 239-241
ATX form factor, 15-17
Award BIOS, 9-10

B

Baby-AT form factor, 13-14
backplane systems, 12-13
BIOS, 3-10
  AMI, 6-9
  Award, 9-0
  OEMs, 6
  Phoenix, 10
Burst-EDO DRAM, 24
bus types (motherboards), 3

C

cache memory, 2
Celebris GL (ver. 2) motherboard (Digital Equipment Corporation), 177-181
chipsets, 4-5
Classic R motherboard (Intel Corporation), 285-291
CMOS RAM addresses, 43-47
CU430HX motherboard (Intel Corporation), 288

D

DECPC LPV/LPV+ motherboard (Digital Equipment Corporation), 182-184
DECPC LPX motherboard (Digital Equipment Corporation), 185-187
Deskpro motherboards
  4000/6000 (Pentium Pro), 120-121
  5120/5133/5150/5166, 122-123
Dimension XPS HXXX motherboard (Dell Computer Corporation), 139-141

Dimension XPS ProXXX motherboard (Dell Computer Corporation), 142-143
DIMM (dual in-line memory module), 24-29
documentation, 5
DRAM, 20-21
    Burst EDO, 24
    FPM (fast page mode), 22-23

E

EDO (Extended Data Out) RAM, 23-24
Eduquest 9606 (models 040/04X) motherboard (IBM Corporation), 242-243
Endeavour motherboard (Intel Corporation), 292-294
Extended Data Out (EDO) RAM, 23-24

F

fast page mode DRAM, 22-23
form factors, 3, 12-20
    ATX, 15-17
    Baby-AT, 13-14
    backplane systems, 12-13
    full-size AT, 13
    NLX, 17-20
FPM (fast page mode) DRAM, 22-23
full-size AT form factor, 13

G

GA-586AM motherboard (Giga-Byte Technology Co., Ltd.), 199-202
GA-586IS motherboard (Giga-Byte Technology Co., Ltd.), 203-205
GA-686DX motherboard (Giga-Byte Technology Co., Ltd.), 206-208
GA-686FX motherboard (Giga-Byte Technology Co., Ltd.), 209-212
GA-686NX motherboard (Giga-Byte Technology Co., Ltd.), 213-215
GMB-PIAK (ver. 1.01) motherboard (Gemlight Computer, Ltd.), 196-198
Goliath Quad motherboard (American Megatrends, Inc.), 63-68

H

Hot-613 motherboard (Shuttle Computer International, Inc.), 356-358
HP Netserver LE motherboard (Hewlett-Packard Company), 216-218
HP Netserver LM motherboard (Hewlett-Packard Company), 219-221

I

Intellistation (type 6888) motherboard (IBM Corporation), 244-245
Intellistation (type 6899) motherboard (IBM Corporation), 246-248
Intellistation Z Pro motherboard (IBM Corporation), 249-251
interface connectors, 39-42, 49
IPC SE (MB586PCI#10) motherboard (IPC Corporation, Ltd.), 310-312

J-K

jumpers
    default settings, 49
    undocumented, 50

KN-6000 motherboard (First International Computer, Inc.), 192-195
KN97-X motherboard (Asus Computer International), 99-102

L-M

labeling, 50
Legend-CD 486SX motherboard (Packard Bell), 350-353

M54LI (REV. 1B) motherboard (Micronics Computers, Inc.), 313-315
M54PI (Diablo Board) motherboard (Micronics Computers, Inc.), 316-318
M6ME motherboard (Micronics Computers, Inc.), 319-323
M6MI motherboard (Micronics Computers, Inc.), 324-326
M6PI motherboard (Micronics Computers, Inc.), 327-328

motherboards **441**

M7S-HI motherboard (Micronics Computers, Inc.), 329-332
main boards, *see* motherboards
Manhattan G Pentium motherboard (AST Research, Inc.), 91-93
Manhattan V Pentium motherboard (AST Research, Inc.), 94-98
Megapro motherboard (American Megatrends, Inc.), 69-73
Megarum motherboard (American Megatrends, Inc.), 74-77
memory, 20-30
  banks, 29-30
  Burst-EDO DRAM, 24
  cache, 2
  DIMM, 24-29
  DRAM, 20-21
  EDO RAM, 23-24
  FPM DRAM, 22-23
  SDRAM, 24
  SIMM, 3, 24-29
    30-pin, 27-28
    72-pin, 28
    capacities, 26-27
    converters, 28
    speeds, 21-22
Merlin PCI motherboard (American Megatrends, Inc.), 78-80
motherboards
  6FB (Soyo Computer Co., Ltd.), 365-367
  Advanced/ATX (Intel Corporation), 269-271
  Advanced/ML (Intel Corporation), 272-274
  Advanced/MN (Morrisson) (Intel Corporation), 275-277
  AG430HX (Intel Corporation), 278-280
  Altserver/CS (Intel Corporation), 281-284
  AN6 (Silicon Star International, Inc.), 361-364
  Apollo III (American Megatrends, Inc.), 60-62
  Aptiva 2134/2176 A-1 (IBM Corporation), 222-225
  Aptiva 2136 (IBM Corporation), 226-229
  Aptiva 2144/2168 type H-2/ I-2 (IBM Corporation), 230-232
  Aptiva 2159 (IBM Corporation), 233-235
  Aptiva 2168 (IBM Corporation), 236-238
  Aptiva M30/M31/M40/M41/M50/M53/M71 (IBM Corporation), 239-241
  BIOS, 3-10
    AMI, 6-9
    Award, 9-10
    OEMs, 6
    Phoenix, 10
  built-in interfaces, 3-4
  bus types, 3
  Celebris GL (ver. 2) (Digital Equipment Corporation), 177-181
  chipsets, 4-5
  Classic R (Intel Corporation), 285-291
  CMOS RAM addresses, 43-47
  CU430HX (Intel Corporation), 288
  DECPC LPV/LPV+ (Digital Equipment Corporation), 182-184
  DECPC LPX (Digital Equipment Corporation), 185-187
  Deskpro 4000/6000 (Pentium Pro) (Compaq Computer Corporation), 120-121
  Deskpro 5120/5133/5150/5166 (Compaq Computer Corporation), 122-123
  Dimension XPS HXXX (Dell Computer Corporation), 139-141
  Dimension XPS ProXXX (Dell Computer Corporation), 142-143
  documentation, 5
  Eduquest 9606 (models 040/04X), IBM Corporation, 242-243
  element naming conventions, 50
  Endeavour (Intel Corporation), 292-294
  form factors, 3, 12-20
    ATX, 15-17
    Baby-AT, 13-14
    backplane systems, 12-13
    full-size AT, 13
    NLX, 17-20
  GA-586AM (Giga-Byte Technology Co., Ltd.), 199-202
  GA-586IS (Giga-Byte Technology Co., Ltd.), 203-205
  GA-686DX (Giga-Byte Technology Co., Ltd.), 206-208
  GA-686FX (Giga-Byte Technology Co., Ltd.), 209-212
  GA-686NX (Giga-Byte Technology Co., Ltd.), 213-215
  GMB-P6IAK (ver. 1.01) (Gemlight Computer, Ltd.), 196-198
  Goliath Quad (American Megatrends, Inc.), 63-68

Hot-613 (Shuttle Computer International, Inc.), 356-358
HP Netserver LE (Hewlett-Packard Company), 216-218
HP Netserver LM (Hewlett-Packard Company), 219-221
Intellistation (type 6888) (IBM Corporation), 244-245
Intellistation (type 6899) (IBM Corporation), 246-248
Intellistation Z Pro (IBM Corporation), 249-251
interface connections, 49
interface onncectors, 39-42
IPC SE (MB586PCI#10), IPC Corporation, Ltd., 310-312
jumpers
   default settings, 49
   undocumented, 50
KN-6000 (First International Computer, Inc.), 192-195
KN97-X (Asus Computer International), 99-102
Legend-CD 486SX (Packard Bell), 350-353
M54LI (REV. 1B), Micronics Computers, Inc., 313-315
M54PI (Diablo Board), Micronics Computers, Inc., 316-318
M6ME (Micronics Computers, Inc.), 319-323

M6MI (Micronics Computers, Inc.), 324-326
M6PI (Micronics Computers, Inc.), 327-328
M7S-HI (Micronics Computers, Inc.), 329-332
Manhattan G Pentium (AST Research, Inc.), 91-93
Manhattan V Pentium (AST Research, Inc.), 94-98
Megapro (American Megatrends, Inc.), 69-73
Megarum (American Megatrends, Inc.), 74-77
memory, 20-30
   banks, 29-30
   Burst-EDO DRAM, 24
   cache, 2
   DIMM, 24-29
   DRAM, 20-21
   EDO RAM, 23-24
   FPM DRAM, 22-23
   SDRAM, 24
   SIMM, 3, 24-29
   speeds, 21-22
Merlin PCI (American Megatrends, Inc.), 78-80
MS-5144 (Micro-Star International Co., Ltd.), 346-349
NX440LX (Intel Corporation), 295-297
Opal 486SLC2 Rev C (IBM Corporation), 252-253
Optiplex DGX (Dell Computer Corporation), 147-151
Optiplex GM/GM+ (Dell Computer Corporation), 152-154

Optiplex GS (Dell Computer Corporation), 155-157
Optiplex GS+ (Dell Computer Corporation), 158-160
Optiplex GX Pro (Dell Computer Corporation), 161-163
Optiplex GXI (Dell Computer Corporation), 164-166
Optiplex GXL/GXM (Dell Computer Corporation), 144-146
Optiplex XL (Dell Computer Corporation), 167-169
Optiplex XM (Dell Computer Corporation), 167-169
Optiplex XMT (Dell Computer Corporation), 167-169
P/I-P65UP5 (Asus Computer International), 103-109
P/I-P6RP4 (Asus Computer International), 110-113
P/I-XP6NP5 (Asus Computer International), 114-116
P6DLS (Super Micro), 372-374
P6KDI (Advanced Integration Research, Inc.), 54-56
P6KPI (Advanced Integration Research, Inc.), 57-59
P6SLS (Super Micro), 372, 373, 374
Pantera 486 (Zeos International, Ltd.), 382-383

Pantera Pentium (Zeos International, Ltd.), 384-386
PB450 (Packard Bell), 350-353
PC 330 P-60/PC 350 P-60 (IBM Corporation), 254-256
PC 730 /750 series (type 6877, 6887) (IBM Corporation), 257-259
PCI/I-P54TP4 (Asus Computer International), 117-119
PD440FX (Intel Corporation), 298-300
Pegasus (American Megatrends, Inc.), 81-84
Pentium 90MHZ (Packard Bell), 354-355
PnP, 4
power management, 4
Poweredge 4100/6100 (Dell Computer Corporation), 170-173
Poweredge EL (Dell Computer Corporation), 167-169
Poweredge Webserver (Dell Computer Corporation), 167-169
Poweredge XE 51XX-2 (ver. 1) (Dell Computer Corporation), 174-176
PP6 (Rev. 0.2) (Abit Computer Corporation), 51-53
Premiere/PCI II Baby-AT (Intel Corporation), 301-303
Presario 7100 Series (Pentium System) (Compaq Computer Corporation), 124-126
Presario 9200/9600 (Compaq Computer Corporation), 127-128
Presario CDS 774/972/974/982/992 (Compaq Computer Corporation), 129-132
Presario CDTV 978 (Compaq Computer Corporation), 129-132
Presario Series (Compaq Computer Corporation), 133-134
Prioris MX 6200 (Digital Equipment Corporation), 188-191
processor sockets, 2
processors, 2, 30-39
  memory addressing limits, 31-32
  sockets, 35-39
  specifications, 30-31
  speed ratings, 32-35
Proliant 5000R (Compaq Computer Corporation), 135-136
Prolinea 5120/5133/5150/5166 (Compaq Computer Corporation), 137-138
replacement, 1
RU430HX (Intel Corporation), 304-306
S1662D (REV. 1.2), Tyan Computer Corporation, 375-378
S1672 (Tyan Computer Corporation), 379-381
SEL (MB586PCI#10), IPC Corporation, Ltd., 310-312
selection criteria, 1-5
SL-B/ MT2133/ MT2155/ MT2168 (IBM Corporation), 260-261
SL-B/ MT2133/ MT2155/MT2168 (IBM Corporation), 262
speed, 2, 11
Stingray (Micronics Computers, Inc.), 333-336
SY-5TE2/E5/EO (Soyo Computer Co., Ltd.), 368-371
System Board PCD-5H (Siemens Nixdorf Informationssysteme AG), 359-360
Titan II PCI (American Megatrends, Inc.), 85-90
Twister AT (Micronics Computers, Inc.), 337-340
Valuemagic (MB586PCI#10), IPC Corporation, Ltd., 310-312
Valuepoint 6472/6482/6484 (IBM Corporation), 263-266
Valuepoint P60/D (IBM Corporation), 267-268
Venturis GL (ver. 2) (Digital Equipment Corporation), 177-181
VS440FX (Intel Corporation), 307-309
W6-LI (Micronics Computers, Inc.), 341-345

MS-5144 motherboard (Micro-Star International Co., Ltd.), 346-349

N-O

NLX form factor, 17-20
NX440LX motherboard (Intel Corporation), 295-297

Opal 486SLC2 Rev C motherboard (IBM Corporation), 252-253

444 OPTIPLEX motherboards (Dell Computer Corporation)

OPTIPLEX
  motherboards (Dell Computer Corporation)
    GDX, 147-151
    GM/GM+, 152-154
    GS, 155-157
    GS+, 158-160
    GX Pro, 161-163
    GXI, 164-166
    GXL/GXM, 144-146
    XL, 167-169
    XM, 167-169
    XMT, 167-169

P

P/I-P65UP5 motherboard (Asus Computer International), 103-109
P/I-P6RP4 motherboard (Asus Computer International), 110-113
P/I-XP6NP5 motherboard (Asus Computer International), 114-116
P6DLS motherboard (Super Micro), 372-374
P6KDI motherboard (Advanced Integration Research, Inc.), 54-56
P6KPI motherboard (Advanced Integration Research, Inc.), 57-59
P6SLS motherboard (Super Micro), 372-374
Pantera 486 motherboard (Zeos International, Ltd.), 382-383
Pantera Pentium motherboard (Zeos International, Ltd.), 384-386
PB450 motherboard (Packard Bell), 350-353
PC 330 P-60/PC 350 P-60 motherboard (IBM Corporation), 254-256
PC 730/750 SERIES (TYPE 6877, 6887) motherboard (IBM Corporation), 257-259
PCI/I-P54TP4 motherboard (Asus Computer International), 117-119
PD440FX motherboard (Intel Corporation), 298-300
Pegasus motherboard (American Megatrends, Inc.), 81-84
Pentium 90MHZ motherboard (Packard Bell), 354-355
Phoenix BIOS, 10
PnP, 4
power management (motherboards), 4
Poweredge 4100/6100 motherboard (Dell Computer Corporation), 170-173
Poweredge EL motherboard (Dell Computer Corporation), 167-169
Poweredge Webserver motherboard (Dell Computer Corporation), 167-169
Poweredge XE 51XX-2 (ver.1) motherboard (Dell Computer Corporation), 174-176
PP6 (Rev. 0.2) motherboard (Abit Computer Corporation), 51-53
Premiere/PCI II Baby-AT motherboard (Intel Corporation), 301-303
Presario motherboards (Compaq Computer Corporation)
    7100 Series, 124-126
    9200/9600, 127-128
CDS 774/972/974/982/992, 129-132
CDTV 978, 129-132
Series, 133-134
Prioris MX 6200 motherboard (Digital Equipment Corporation), 188-191
processors, 2, 30-39
    memory addressing limits, 31-32
    sockets, 2, 35-39
    specifications, 30-31
    speed ratings, 32-35
Proliant 5000R motherboard (Compaq Computer Corporation), 135-136
PROLINEA 5120/5133/5150/5166 motherboard (Compaq Computer Corporation), 137-138

R

RAM EDO (Extended Data Out), 23-24
replacement motherboards, 1
ROM BIOS, 5-10
RU430HX motherboard (Intel Corporation), 304-306

S

S1662D (REV. 1.2) motherboard (Tyan Computer Corporation), 375-378
S1672 motherboard (Tyan Computer Corporation), 379-381
SDRAM (Synchronous DRAM), 24

SEL (MB586PCI#10) motherboard (IPC Corporation, Ltd.), 310-312
SIMM (single in-line memory module), 3, 24-29
    30-pin, 27-28
    72-pin, 28
    converters, 28
SL-B/MT2133/MT2155/MT2168 motherboard (IBM Corporation), 260-262
sockets, 35-39
Stingray motherboard (Micronics Computers, Inc.), 333-336
SY-5TE2/E5/EO motherboard (Soyo Computer Co., Ltd.), 368-371
Synchronous DRAM (SDRAM), 24
System Board PCD-5H motherboard (Siemens Nixdorf Informations systeme AG), 359-360

T

Titan II PCI motherboard (American Megatrends, Inc.), 85-90
Twister AT motherboard (Micronics Computers, Inc.), 337-340

U-V

Valuemagic (MB586PCI#10) motherboard, 310-312
Valuepoint 6472/6482/6484 motherboard (IBM Corporation), 263-266
Valuepoint P60/D motherboard (IBM Corporation), 267-268
Venturis GL (ver. 2) motherboard (Digital Equipment Corporation), 177-181
VS440FX motherboard (Intel Corporation), 307-309

W-Z

W6-LI motherboard (Micronics Computers, Inc.), 341-345

Order Your Copy of the Best Selling PC Repair and Upgrade Book Ever!

UPGRADING AND REPAIRING PCs
Eighth Edition

Scott Mueller is president of Mueller Technical Research, an international PC research and corporate training firm. Scott has trained over 10,000 PC professionals and enthusiasts in his seminars for Fortune 500 companies, the U.S. and foreign governments, and major PC hardware and software vendors throughout North and South America, Europe, and Australia

Push your PC's performance to the limit

- Know the differences between: Pentium II, Pentium MMX, Pentium Pro, and earlier CPUs and choose the best CPU for your needs
- Understand compatibility and feature sets of processor upgrade sockets, motherboards, and chipsets
- Use Universal Serial Bus ports and devices to simplify peripheral installation, configuration, and improve performance
- Squeeze the most performance, life, and reliability out of your hard drives
- Prevent memory headaches: pick the right speed and type of SIMMs and DIMMs, run more programs at once, and work with bigger files
- Integrate hot new hardware including 3D graphics accelerators, fast SDRAM memory, Zoomed Video and Cardbus PC Cards for your notebook, and NLX motherboards with support for Single Edge Contact processors and Accelerated Graphics Ports

ISBN: 0-7897-1295-4
Price: $49.99 USA/ $70.95 CAN

- ■ Super Value - all of the information from Scott's $1,300 3-day seminars in this handy reference
- ■ Upgrade and troubleshoot your entire PC - video, audio, and network cards; drives, processors, memory, and motherboards
- ■ Evaluate system components so you can choose the best hardware
- ■ Find hardware and software vendors in the massive appendix of vendor contact information

Look for the new Tenth Anniversary Edition of this best-seller coming in September 1998!

201 W. 103rd Street, Indianapolis, Indiana
1-800-428-5331 - Orders   1-800-835-3202 - FAX   1-800-858-7674 - Customer Service

UPGRADING AND REPAIRING NETWORKS

The Authoritative Guide to Expanding and Maintaining Your Network's Capabilities

Far more than just a "repair" manual, Que's *Upgrading and Repairing Networks* is the most comprehensive network support reference available! Learn about the inner workings of your network, how to install hardware, and troubleshoot problems. Gain in-depth knowledge of major network operating systems such as Netware 4.1, UNIX, and Windows NT. Learn about backup technology, linking to mainframes, and SMNP from the experts. Special sections include coverage on adding network services and upgrade options, Internet, remote access, and virus protection with troubleshooting tips to help you identify and solve problems. It's all the information you need to maintain or enhance your network.

- In-depth coverage of the major network operating systems
- Learn to configure 32-bit Windows client software for maximum network efficiency
- Get backup and disaster planning strategies from the experts
- Discover practical ways to protect your network from viruses
- Add printers, CD-ROMs, modems, and wireless components to your network
- Establish secure access to the Internet for your network
- Install hubs, routers, repeaters, and bridges
- Learn how to locate and repair common network problems within servers, workstations, network links and peripherals

ISBN: 0-7897-0181-2
Price: $59.99 USA / $81.95 CAN

201 W. 103rd Street, Indianapolis, Indiana
1-800-428-5331 - Orders   1-800-835-3202 - FAX   1-800-858-7674 - Customer Service

Order These New Books from Que's Scott Mueller Library Today!

UPGRADING AND REPAIRING PCs
Quick Reference
Second Edition

Scott Mueller's *Upgrading and Repairing PCs Quick Reference, Second Edition* is the condensed version of the greatest-selling computer repair and upgrade book ever. As a perfect companion to sit next to your toolbox while working, this reference contains all of the necessary information that you need - at arm's reach.

ISBN: 0-7897-1669-0
Price: $19.99 USA / $28.95 CAN

This edition provides you with accurate tables and settings for repairing hardware and the convenience of scale for portability. Use the vendor reference that includes the top 100 vendors with their address, phone numbers, and URLs. Get the critical information you need for memory, IRQ, and BIOS tables, drive controller specifications, processor models and specifications, configurations, settings and more. *Upgrading and Repairing PCs Quick Reference Second Edition* is the fastest way to get started working on PCs.

201 W. 103rd Street, Indianapolis, Indiana
1-800-428-5331 - Orders   1-800-835-3202 - FAX   1-800-858-7674 - Customer Service

Order These New Books from Que's Scott Mueller Library Today!

Computer Dictionary
Data Communications, PC Hardware, and Internet Terms

The *Computer Dictionary* offers more than simple descriptions. By giving detailed explanations that can span as much as several pages to exhaustively define the term, this reference gives the most detailed definitions you'll need. In addition, you can find cross-references for each term - pointing towards another entry where related technology is explained.

- Locate information on a technology's competition
- Use the expert advice to avoid mentioned problems and pitfalls within a technology
- Take advantage of charts, tables, drawings, diagrams, and a cross-referenced index to increase your understanding of terms and acronyms

ISBN: 0-7897-1670-4
Price: $19.99 USA / $28.95 CAN

201 W. 103rd Street, Indianapolis, Indiana
1-800-428-5331 - Orders   1-800-835-3202 - FAX   1-800-858-7674 - Customer Service

SAVE $200

Special Offer for Purchasers of the
Micro House PC Hardware Library

With the purchase of the complete 3 book set of the *Micro House PC Hardware Library*, you are eligible to purchase any of the following *Support on Site* modules from Micro House with a special discount of $200 U.S. off of the regular prices listed below. To get this offer, call Micro House at (800) 926-8299 or (303) 443-3388 and mention ad code: MCP.

Support On Site for Hardware	Reg. $995 U.S.
Support On Site for Applications	Reg. $1295 U.S.
Support On Site for Networks	Reg. $1495 U.S.

This is a limited time offer and is subject to change or cancellation without prior notice.

YOU'VE TRIED THE BEST...

ImageCast LE

Now that you've checked out ImageCast LE on your book bonus CD-ROM, you're taking advantage of TCP/IP multicasting technology to clone hard drives across your network. It's a powerful solution for Windows 95, Windows 3.X and DOS rollouts.

...NOW TRY THE REST!

ImageCast Deluxe

IF YOU NEED TO CLONE MORE PCs THAN IMAGECAST LE ALLOWS, OR YOU NEED TO SUPPORT WINDOWS NT, WINDOWS 98, NETWARE OR UNIX OSes ON CLONED DRIVES, GET OUR UPGRADE TO IMAGECAST DELUXE.

- Increased multicasting capability – from 10 PCs to thousands
- Full Microsoft Windows NT 4 and 5 support, including SID changing utility
- Microsoft Windows 98 support for new OS rollouts
- Post-imaging configuration/personalization features
- DHCP support
- Various licensing options: corporate, technician, system integrator, etc.
- Free between-version Deluxe updates – new features are free
- Free technical support
- Full product manual*
- Free SupportSource technical support database of NIC cards on CD-ROM*
- Free Network Technical Guide 500-page book on CD-ROM*

THE LEADER IN FAST DRIVE CLONING WITH MULTICASTING

* Available with physical product delivery. Not available on online downloads. Online version includes electronic manual.

Call us: 800-926-8299   303-443-3388
Visit us: www.imagecast.com

Just another day at the office.

You're putting out fires every day. With most hardware problems, there's no time to look for the manual, hunt down an obscure document on the Internet or hang on hold for hours. You need to fix the problem right now.

Turn to Support On Site™ for Hardware from Micro House International. It's the central source for all the information you need to put out those hardware support fires. All in one place—manuals, diagrams, tech notes, specs and news—even jump to the Web for a tightly focused search. All instantly accessible with a powerful new technical support environment called SupportSource ™. Get Support On Site for Hardware, and face tomorrow's inferno with confidence.

MULTI VENDOR DATA FOR HARDWARE SUPPORT

ZIFF-DAVIS HARDWARE KNOWLEDGEBASE

INCLUDES MICRO HOUSE TECHNICAL LIBRARY

CALL NOW OR GET ONLINE
Sample thousands of Support On Site for Hardware documents with our free demo.

Now you're fireproof.

SUBSCRIPTIONS BEGIN UNDER $70/MONTH

CONSTANTLY UPDATED

ENDORSED BY NOVELL®, DIGITAL® & OTHERS

 ZIFF-DAVIS SUPPORT PUBLISHING

 MICROHOUSE®

SUPPORTSOURCE
©1998 Micro House International, Inc.

1.800.926.8299   1.303.443.3388
www.supportsource.com